The Labour Party

The Labour Party

A Centenary History

Edited by

Brian Brivati
Reader in History
Kingston University

and

Richard Heffernan
Lecturer in Politics
Open University

Foreword by Tony Blair

Preface by Michael Foot

First published in Great Britain 2000 by
MACMILLAN PRESS LTD
Houndmills, Basingstoke, Hampshire RG21 6XS and London
Companies and representatives throughout the world

A catalogue record for this book is available from the British Library.

ISBN 0-333-74649-X hardcover
ISBN 0-333-74650-3 paperback

First published in the United States of America 2000 by
ST. MARTIN'S PRESS, LLC,
Scholarly and Reference Division,
175 Fifth Avenue, New York, N.Y. 10010

ISBN 0-312-23458-9

Library of Congress Cataloging-in-Publication Data
The Labour Party : a centenary history / [edited by] Brian Brivati and Richard
Heffernan.
p.   cm.
Includes bibliographical references and index.
ISBN 0-312-23458-9
1. Labour Party (Great Britain)—History. I. Brivati, Brian. II. Heffernan, Richard.

JN1129.L32 L245   2000
324.24107—dc21
                                                                00-027833

This book is printed on paper suitable for recycling and made from fully managed and sustained
forest sources.

10   9   8   7   6   5   4   3   2   1
09   08   07   06   05   04   03   02   01   00

Printed and bound in Great Britain by
Antony Rowe Ltd, Chippenham, Wiltshire

This volume is dedicated to the memory of
Jill Craigie
a socialist and feminist inspiration.

Contents

Notes on Contributors	ix
Preface	xi
Michael Foot	
Foreword	xvii
Tony Blair	
Acknowledgements	xxii

Part I: Labour's First Century

Introduction	1
Brian Brivati and Richard Heffernan	
Out of the bowels of the Movement: The Trade Unions and the Origins of the Labour Party 1900–18	8
Robert Taylor	
Labour In and Out of Government, 1923–1935	50
Keith Laybourn	
The Attlee Years, 1935–1955	68
Kevin Jefferys	
The Age of Wilson 1955–1979	87
Lewis Baston	
The Wilderness Years, 1979–1994	112
Eric Shaw	
From Old to New Labour, 1994–2000	143
Martin J Smith	

Part II: Centenary Reflections

In Defence of New Labour	163
Denis Healey	
The Legacy of the SDP	166
David Owen	
A Tory View of 1964–70	170
John Biffen	
The Challenge of Co-operation	172
Calum MacDonald	
The Global Future	176
Clare Short	
Reinterpreting Labour's History of Failure	178
Austin Mitchell	
An End of Century Report Card	183
Angela Eagle	

Part III: Themes in Labour's First Century

Trade Union Freedom and the Labour Party: Arthur Deakin, Frank Cousins and the Transport and General Workers Union 1945–1964   187
Robert Taylor

Norms and Blocks:
Trade Unions and the Labour Party since 1964   220
Steve Ludlam

Leaders and Followers: The Politics of the Parliamentary Labour Party   246
Richard Heffernan

Crimes and Misdemeanours: Managing Dissent in the Twentieth and Twenty-First Century Labour Party   268
Tim Bale

Labour's Constitution and Public Ownership: From 'Old' Clause Four to 'New' Clause Four   292
Tudor Jones

A 'miracle of politics': the rise of Labour, 1900–45   322
Andrew Chadwick

'The future Labour offered':
industrial modernisation projects in the British Labour Party from Gaitskell to Blair   346
Brian Brivati

Labour's international policy: A story of conflict and contention   363
Dan Keohane

Beyond Euro-Scepticism? Labour and the European Union since 1945   383
Richard Heffernan

Questions of Gender: Labour and Women   402
Christine Collette

Labour and Welfare Politics   422
Nick Ellison

Labour Local Government 1900–1999   449
Lewis Baston

Labour's literary dominance   485
Brian Brivati

Index   503

Notes on Contributors

Tim Bale, Lecturer in Politics, Victoria University of Wellington

Lewis Baston, Senior Research Fellow at the Centre for the Understanding of Society and Politics, Kingston University

Lord Biffen, former Conservative Cabinet Minister

Rt Hon Tony Blair MP, Prime Minister and leader of the Labour Party.

Brian Brivati, Reader in Modern British History, Kingston University.

Andrew Chadwick, Lecturer in Politics and Research Fellow of the Centre for Social and Economic Research, The University of the West of England.

Christine Collette, Lecturer in Politics, Edge Hill College

Angela Eagle, Labour MP for Wallasey

Nick Ellison, Lecturer in Sociology and Social Policy, University of Durham

Rt Hon Michael Foot, leader of the Labour Party 1980–83

Rt Hon Lord Healey, deputy leader of the Labour Party, 1980–83

Richard Heffernan, Lecturer in Politics, Open University

Kevin Jefferys, Reader in History, University of Plymouth

Tudor Jones, Senior Lecturer in Politics at Coventry University

Dan Keohane, Lecturer in International Relations, Keele University

Keith Laybourn, Professor of History, University of Huddersfield

Steve Ludlam, Lecturer in Politics, University of Sheffield

Calum MacDonald, Labour MP for Western Isles

Austin Mitchell, Labour MP for Grimsby

Rt Hon Lord Owen CH, leader of the SDP 1983–90

Eric Shaw, Senior Lecturer in Politics, University of Stirling

Rt Hon Clare Short MP, Secretary of State for International Development

Martin J. Smith, Professor of Politics, University of Sheffield

Robert Taylor, Employment Editor, *Financial Times*

Preface

Rt Hon Michael Foot

How much can new Labour learn from the old? Not much, according to some of the new leaders, except what pitfalls or renewed follies to avoid. Latter-day wisdom, the proper interpretation of present-day opportunities, has given our party the chance to shape the future for decades ahead. But others may still object: true reading of history has been our best guide hitherto. We shall cast aside this advice at our peril: our most unforgivable failure at such a moment would be to set our sights too low.

Labour's Museum of Labour History – like the hundred-year-old Labour Party itself – has had what the sports-writers used to call a chequered career – when the beloved home team has formed the habit of conceding valuable home points to unscrupulous visitors: sometimes we have faced the future with a glorious confidence as in 1945 and now, but sometimes confronting the possibility of absolute extinction. These lapses were not always proof of a serious moral or political failure. Sometimes the bravest choices were taken by leaders or groups of their steadfast followers at the moments of supreme anguish. New departures for Labour were frequently sought before the present system of testing opinion was so skilfully devised by the present leaders or their spin-doctors.

My own first encounters with the directors of the Museum of Labour History happened at a period when the history of the party itself looked a good deal brighter than its prospects. We were in the middle of one of those constantly recurring epochs when the Labour Party, according to the pundits, had made itself unelectable. Throughout the century, these periods have been much more frequent than latter-day experts have been willing to acknowledge, and maybe, in the depths of these moments of dejection which did seem unbreakable, the leaders or the led would take refuge in romantic reconstructions offering no sure escape from existing perils. However, Oscar Wilde once insisted, in his essay on the future of socialism, that a map which did not include Utopia was not worth having.

The Museum itself was operating then in a most suitable, indeed a uniquely appropriate environment, the Limehouse Town Hall, which had been controlled for generations by Labour councils who naturally offered it sustained support. Especially this was so in the pre-1914 period when one of the leaders of that council was the lion-hearted George Lansbury. He had launched his campaigns there on behalf of the poorest members of the community, and a few other causes hardly less commendable, such as the rights of women and the claims of subject peoples against British imperialism. For me and those of us of a slightly earlier generation, Lansbury had a special appeal: he led the modern revolt against the iniquities of a the old poor law, both before 1914 and again in the 1930s when the same kind of bureaucratic persecutions were even less excusably applied. Thus, thanks to the initiative of the first Labour councils, thanks to Lansbury, Limehouse had a resonance throughout the whole Labour movement. All the more were we aggrieved when an ill-named Liberal caucus took temporary control of the Poplar Council, and informed us that there would be no more financial favours for the occupants of Limehouse Town Hall. These modern Liberals looked much more like the stony-faced Whig lords and ladies who had imposed the old poor law rather than those who had joined campaigns to protect the victims. We had an expert witness who could keep us informed on all these desperate developments. Among the Museum's own directors, still alive and kicking, was Albert Jacobs. Most especially sadly for him, whose democratic socialism was so intimately associated with London's East End, we had to look elsewhere if the Museum was to survive.

Today the Museum is much more securely, even abundantly and prestigiously established in Manchester. None of these terms individually selected would suggest an adequate indication of the work which has had to be done since the transfer from London. All of them together give but the palest hint of the glory of the present spectacle. The banners and the posters and the artifacts offer a series of instructions all on their own, many of which might have been lost forever after the Limehouse fiasco. Side by side with them are the archives of the Labour Party, covering the whole hundred years of its history, still preserved in the loving, scholarly care of Stephen Byrd, who originally served the Labour Party in the same work at Walworth Road and who willingly transferred his skills and dedication to Manchester. The idea that these two traditions or schools in all their various manifestations must be combined under the same roof and authority occurred to Graham Stringer, leader of the Labour Party in Manchester at that time. Not merely did he offer financial support from his own council and enable others in the surrounding areas to do the same; he had the vision for the future of what could be achieved with arrival of the archives. He had another eager accomplice in all these endeavours in John Monks of the TUC, not yet the General Secretary, but already our foremost ally in that greater body.

At their side throughout the whole endeavour was the chairman of the trustees, the indispensable Jack Jones, and soon after our departure from Limehouse and even before we had started on the work in Manchester, we had our special stroke of luck: an application for the post of director from a genius in the field. Everyone who has ever had any dealings with Nick Mansfield would recognise this claim. He has put his own individual stamp on the whole enterprise, inspired his staff working for the Museum, and even trained a successor of almost equal quality to assist him: Catherine Rew. She undertakes the director's duties while he himself conducts a temporary transfer to Manchester University. Every fresh association has added to the potential greatness of the Museum. Thanks to Nick Mansfield especially, but also to all our other associations with Manchester, we can face the future without dishonouring our past.

Sometimes also the move to Manchester has helped to emphasise the deeper sources of Labour's inspiration, the larger world-wide aims of the Labour movement as a whole. Not that the exhibits at Limehouse were ever merely parochial in any derogatory sense of the word. The exhibit which always took pride of place there and which retains that same pre-eminence in Manchester, was the actual desk which belonged to Thomas Paine when he wrote the Rights of Man, before being hustled out of the country by the Tory totalitarians of that period. Clio Rickman, one of Paine's closest London collaborators, vouched for the authenticity of the desk, and the elaborate connection which now takes such an honourable place in Labour's history and Labour's Museum.

The socialism of the 1890s and the early 1900s appealed to a whole variety of tastes and traditions: the sheer richness of it should make us pause in wonder. So much came as a direct English legacy and yet it was truly and properly woven into an international fabric. No other political creed of the age could claim such richness or command such widespread intellectual contributions: scientists who saw their socialism as the essential fulfilment of the Darwinian discoveries; artists or the prophets of the world of art, like William Morris, who believed that no civilised society could be imagined without the artists' gift; men

and women of passion and compassion who could not sit quiet
amid the human misery they saw all around them; bureaucratic
centralisers who believed with an equal ardour that only the
power of the state could alleviate such chronic ills; students of
Karl Marx who thought they could foretell, and help to shape the
revolution which would bring these prizes within the grasp of
those who suffered such hardships and insults; men and women
who argued that they could use their new-found strength in the
trade unions, a revival of the old Guilds, to win immediate gains;
women's leaders fighting for elementary rights who saw Labour
leaders as their truest allies; men and women of every brand and
breed who inherited a peculiar English tradition of dissent, the
sons and daughters of the Chartists, the Radicals, the Levellers
who would always watch with a healthy scepticism any
established authority. All these helped to make the Labour
movement of Edwardian times, or to speak more exactly, the
Labour Party, founded at the Farringdon Hall in February 1900.
They could not yet sing together their favourite song, William
Blake's 'Jerusalem'; the tune had not yet been composed. They did
sing their very own 'England Arise', and they did it with a
genuine, full-throated fervour.

The forthcoming celebrations of the founding of the Labour
Party in February of next year will be able to renew that fervour
especially in the light of the historic victory of 1 May 1997. Tony
Blair has often declared with no dissent from any of his Labour
supporters, that he seeks not merely a five-year period of Labour
Government, but an even more substantial victory enabling our
party to undertake even greater tasks in the century ahead. Some
of us may recall how many of our previous leaders with the same
honest purpose have made the same claim. Leader Attlee and
several members of his Cabinet expressed that hope after 1945,
and Harold Wilson renewed the appeal in the 1960s. Today the
just hope looks more likely to be fulfilled than ever before. If it is
so, we must also proclaim still more assuredly that our
Government will not be seeking to stay in office just for its own
sake. Long Parliaments are not necessarily good things in
themselves: indeed, they may be tempted to become lazy or addled
or corrupt. Disputes about the pace of the socialist advance have
often been the most significant. The Fabians were not always
correct in their calculations – often, especially in their
international politics, it needed the imagination of an H. G. Wells
to life the argument to its proper level.

Some of the supposed deep-seated disputes between new
Labour and old may be resolved in facing these new challenges. A

Labour movement which turned its back on the deepening gulf between rich and poor, just at the moment when it seemed to be becoming even more severe, would not be worthy of the name. Even more urgently, the Labour movement cannot turn its back on the international solutions which alone can solve national clashes. The threat of world-wide nuclear destruction is not yet banished. Labour was elected in 1997 with commitments binding us to make fresh exertions to achieve the aim. The pledge of seeking a non-nuclear world was repeated in our Strategic Defence Review of 1997 and was repeated again by George Robertson, NATO's newly appointed Commander-in-Chief. It is not yet NATO's policy, but it is ours.

Sometimes, looking back indeed, defeats have been as honourable as victories, and have prepared the ground for more long-lasting victories later on. We can look back and judge our leaders or those who followed them more magnanimously. Keir Hardie's, Labour's first leader, fought battles for work or maintenance that prepared the way for the policies of the 1930s; his opposition to an imperialist war indeed helped to prepare the way for a better peace. His opposition to the Liberal chieftains of his day derived partly from their rejection of women's rights. The Keir Hardie who understood the claims of Indian freedom handed down his tradition to Harold Laski and indeed to the Attlee Government which accepted the demand for Indian independence. Ramsay MacDonald's Labour Party of the 1920s fought a losing battle for a better peace. All the more tragic was his own desertion of the party he had helped to build in 1931. But amid that seemingly fatal humiliation other leaders and the rank-and-file stepped forward to stop the rot: at their head, bravest of all, the George Lansbury of Limehouse noted above. He was a Christian pacifist of the deepest dye and Hitler's age was no time for pacifists. But the Lansbury of the 1930s led the party away from the shattering consequences of the 1931 disaster, the worst in our history. Almost as catastrophic in the collapse of the Labour vote was 1983, the nearest point since the 1920s when the Liberal vote overtook ours. It looked like another 1931, but the party under Neil Kinnock held fast and staged a recovery to outdo Lansbury's. By any just reckoning, he should have secured the victory of 1992 and the national recovery might have started five years earlier.

Needless to add in such a preview as this, we owe a special debt to the historians or the biographers or the political philosophers who have bestowed on our party the combined qualities of writing and political insight. Our rivals may take these combinations for granted, the Liberals with their Morleys and Trevelyans, the Tory leaders who often take the precaution of writing the history themselves. Our Labour Party did not always recognise this requirement, although we always had at our disposal a range of talent, approaching occasionally to the point of literary genius, to choose from. I recall how in the 1920s and the 1930s a series of writers inspired the movement: G. D. H. Cole, R. H. Tawney, Harold Laski, Noel Brailsford. Together the historical works of these fully engaged political activists rediscovered the true history of our country: Tawney with his exposure of where the worship of money had originated, Cole's *William Cobbett*, Brailsford's *Levellers*, Laski who played the chief role in linking our socialist aims with the world-wide campaign against imperialism.

In more recent times, in the period of Labour's defeat, the modern academic historians have helped to restore Labour's reputation to its proper place: Peter Hennessy's *Never Again*, Ben Pimlott's *Hugh Dalton* and *Harold Wilson*, Philip Williams' *Gaitskell*, Brian Brivati's *Hugh Gaitskell*, Kenneth Harris' *Attlee*. Looking back a little further we may acknowledge how much we owe to the reassessment of Caroline Benn's *Keir Hardie*, or David Marquand's *Ramsay MacDonald*. Manchester University has published an excellent series of 'Lives on the Left', with Jonathan Scheer's volume doing justice to George Lansbury. And covering the whole century and especially placing the 1945 Labour achievement in its proper context, Ken Morgan's work starting with his *Keir Hardie* and concluding with his *James Callaghan*.

Some of these, all of them in one sense, were the pupils of Alan Taylor. He concluded his 1945 history with the evidence of how the men and women of the Labour movement had sustained the cause of human rights and human freedom in the darkest days. Halfway through the century when, against all the odds, the most just of all wars had been won, the British people faced the future. They did not sing 'Land of Hope and Glory' or even 'England Arise', but, claimed Taylor, England had arisen, the England of the Labour movement. And in the years to come, if we are faithful to our best traditions, we can celebrate even greater victories.

Foreword

Rt Hon Tony Blair MP, Prime Minister

I feel immensely privileged to be leader of the Labour Party in its centenary year. Like the country, we take our history seriously, and this book provides a good opportunity to reflect on what we have learnt from the past, and should carry forward to the future.

I think Keir Hardie may be ruefully stroking his beard as he looks down on Britain today. The country has made astonishing material progress in the last 100 years. Many times richer, our horizons have been transformed, whether in health, education or travel. Yet could he believe that a minimum wage would have been in operation for less than a year of the whole 20th century? While astounded at what has changed, I believe he would be profoundly depressed at what has not changed: so many children still born into poverty, seven million adults who cannot read and write properly, nearly one in five households with no one working.

It is these daily realities for so many of our fellow citizens that have provided the animating force behind the existence of the Labour Party throughout the century. The Labour Party was founded out of practical interests rather than ideology. These interests came to be expressed in simple but enduring values – social justice, responsibility, democracy, tolerance – which have bound the party together throughout the century. And the values have ensured our major role in the great progressive movements of the last century, from the crusade for universal suffrage in Britain to the battle against apartheid in South Africa. But it is the realities of daily life that have been the basis of our most successful reforms.

I have no hesitation in describing the 1945 Labour Government as the greatest peacetime administration this century. Its achievements were marvellous, its leadership remarkable, its legacy comprehensive and radical. Attlee, Morrison, Bevin and Bevan are giants whose reputation has not been diminished by time. They formed a Government which shaped the agenda for a generation. They engineered the transition from war to peace without the mass unemployment which had disfigured our country after the Great War. They set about re-housing those who had lost their homes. They launched a crusade to tackle poverty from birth to death, setting up a universal system of national insurance. Above all, they created the National Health Service, the greatest achievement so far of Labour in Government in Britain, and still recognised around the world as a monumental feat of social reform. Internationally, too, the Attlee Government played a key role in creating some of the institutions which have helped bring peace and prosperity to Europe, and in starting an unstoppable trend towards decolonisation.

Nor should we underplay the achievements, in circumstances which were often difficult, of the Labour Governments which followed Attlee. The 1964 Labour administration expanded higher education, created the Open University, and increased opportunity by carrying forward the attack on class barriers and prejudice which had largely lain dormant since Labour lost power in 1951. In the 1970s, the Labour Government, tackling the consequences of a world financial crisis without the benefit of North Sea Oil, continued this social crusade with pioneering legislation on women's rights and race relations. But what these Governments could not do, except temporarily, was recreate the combination of policy advance and popular mobilisation which made the Government of 1945 so remarkable and enabled it to achieve so much. They were unable to give expression to a national sense of purpose and renewal whose support went well beyond our party's traditional base and whose principles were adopted by the opposition.

From the time I first joined, I realised that it was the deep roots of its members in British communities that have given our party life. It's because the party was built from the bottom up that it has survived so strongly while others have withered. In the dark days of the 1980s when we were out of power nationally, and the chances of regaining it seemed slim, Michael Foot held the party together at a national level, but locally tens of thousands of party members were working away on councils, in voluntary groups and the community putting our values into action.

But any honest assessment of Labour's first 100 years also contains a puzzle. Why has a popular progressive party, formed out of communities up and down the country, in a nation where reform is so necessary, spent the great majority of the last century out of power? The Conservative century has been punctuated by defining bursts of radicalism, but Keir Hardie would surely be disappointed at the relative lack of success of his party.

It is why, while celebrating our party's achievements, we must also look back and see the last 100 years as a time of missed opportunity and unfulfilled promise. Downing Street is steeped in history but too little of it is Labour history. As I walk up the staircase from my office, it gives me pride to see the pictures of the Labour Prime Ministers on the walls but I can't help reflecting on how few of them there are. And Britain is poorer, in every sense, as a result.

We can point to bad luck, bad timing and bad policies to explain our failure to dominate the last fifty years as seemed certain in 1945. But we must also accept that we failed as a party to keep the trust of the people. This was not because of our values, which remain those of the overwhelming decent majority of the people of this country, but because the ideology built on them became fossilised and out of date.

We failed, too, because the party structures designed to ensure we continued to reflect the people's real needs and ambitions in a world changing faster than ever before became instead obstacles to this aim. It meant a party formed by working families out of their desire for self-improvement and reform was seen as an obstacle to their progress.

And I think there is another reason that, over the course of the last century, has been significant. There are two strands of the British progressive tradition. On the one hand, the dominant socialist commitment to collective action in the pursuit of social justice; and on the other the liberal commitment to individual freedom in a market economy. Both have their place – for example since 1997 we have enacted the New Deal while at the same time introducing the Human Rights Act. The differences can be exaggerated, but the two strands have never been properly synthesised: this is an important dimension of the debate about the Third Way.

For those of us born after the War, our perspective is obviously dominated by the search for the partnership of radicalism, credibility and competence that characterised the 1945 government. After the 1970s and early 1980s, first Neil Kinnock and then John Smith, supported by tens of thousands of party members across the country, bravely began the process of change and renewal. They modernised both the ideology and the organisation to ensure we again spoke for working families, again addressed their fears and hopes through policies which could deliver their desire for a better life. It showed we were not afraid to renew ourselves and as such were ready to renew the country.

The result is that our party starts its second century once again in Government. It is worth remembering that after 1992 commentators argued that there never would be a Labour government again. And it's a Government, too, which remains true to the party's enduring values while adding significant new dimensions of programmatic reform.

Our aim is nothing less than to build a new and lasting consensus for our vision of a better Britain. Our policies now address the new realities of the modern world – the understanding that human capital now shapes the success of national economies, that how Government spends its money is as important as how much it spends, that the foundation of a modern welfare state must be full employment, that political reform is an essential partner of social and economic change, that Europe must be the centrepiece of our foreign policy, and that new issues like environmental protection must be grafted onto our analysis and prescription for the country.

In our first term of government, we have made education, training and skills our number one priority, ensured extra investment in public services is tied to improvements in the delivery of those services, given people who can work the chance to do so and invested heavily in support for families with children. Constitutional reform has been significant, progress in Northern Ireland substantial, and new purpose and impetus given to our role in the EU. But perhaps our greatest achievement so far has been to demonstrate that enterprise and fairness can be the twin driving forces of a Labour Government, indeed that they must go hand in hand if we are to build the kind of Britain the country wants. It is an important breakthrough. For decades, people's hearts have told them to vote Labour. They rightly associated us, the creators of the National Health Service, with compassion. But it was their heads which told them to vote Conservative. They did not believe we could deliver the economic prosperity and increased opportunity they want for themselves and their families.

Since 1997, we have shown that a Labour Government can run the economy competently, and begun to establish a new collective memory of what a Labour Government can do. Employment is up, inflation is low, the public finances are back on track. But we have also demonstrated that economic dynamism and social decency, head and heart, can be successfully combined.

However, I am very clear that this first term of government can only be the start: it is about laying the foundations for a sustained period of economic and social reform. While we have stopped the Conservative rot, and made good some of the outstanding weaknesses we inherited, there is a great deal more to do.

20th century politics was in many ways unrecognisable from government of the 19th century. Similarly, the 21st century is also going to see enormous change. The positions, the priorities, the labels – all will be different. And the question for the Labour Party is whether it simply has to adapt to change, or whether by anticipating the demands of the future, it can actually help shape it.

Across Europe, in fact wider, social democratic and socialist governments are making themselves the agents of reform. And what strikes each and every Prime Minister is that government must show itself as flexible, innovative and strategic as the fast-changing world outside. The challenge in front of us is nothing less than to modernise and renew our countries for a different world. But it is a challenge which our party's founders would recognise. If the rise of the knowledge economy is to hasten wider opportunity not social polarisation, progressive parties must be develop the right strategies; if the consciousness of younger people about the importance of the environment is to be matched by politicians, we must be in the lead; if the partial revolution in women's life chances is to be completed, and its implications managed, we need to be thinking in radical ways; if democratic governance is to be deepened at international and local level, it is up to us.

I am determined we will fulfil these ambitions. We need to learn lessons from both our successes and failures if we are to continue to fulfil this party's historic goals in the new century. I hope this book may help us in this task.

Acknowledgements

Many thanks are due to contributors to the book for their promptness in meeting deadlines and tolerating late requests to revisit their chapters in production and proof. In addition, we would like to thank the Centre for the Understanding of Society and Politics (CUSP) at Kingston University for supporting this project and the Rt Hon Michael Foot for contributing a foreword and the Rt Hon Tony Blair MP a preface. The research work for chaprter 5, 14, 19 and 20 was supported by a Leverhulme Trust-funded project on the history of Labour and Modernisation based at CUSP. Richard Heffernan found the Department of Political Science at the University of California, Los Angeles a very agreeable place in which to spend the year this volume was in preparation. And in particular, we would like to place on record our appreciation to Virginia Preston who managed the manuscript proofs with exemplary skill and patience; our thanks to her.

Brian Brivati
Richard Heffernan
London, December 1999

Part I
Labour's First Century

Introduction

Brian Brivati and Richard Heffernan

It is now one hundred years since the founding Conference of the Labour Representation Committee was held in the Memorial Hall in Farringdon Street, London, on Tuesday and Wednesday the 27th and 28th February 1900. On that occasion, the first resolution adopted read as follows:

That this conference is in favour of working-class opinion being represented in the House of Commons by men sympathetic with the aims and demands of the Labour movements, and whose candidatures are promoted by one or other of the organised movements represented by the constitution which this conference is about to frame.

Here, the intention expressed by the TUC meeting in Plymouth in September 1899 to establish a new political party to advance labour interests became reality at the dawn of the new century. At this founding conference the assembled representatives, overwhelmingly from the Trade Unions, set their party on a course expressed in Resolution 2:

That this conference is in favour of establishing a distinct Labour Group in Parliament, who shall have their own Whips, and agree upon their policy, which must embrace a readiness to co-operate with any party which for the time being may be engaged in promoting legislation in the direct interest of labour, and be equally ready to associate themselves with any party in opposing measures having an opposite tendency; and further, members of the Labour Group shall not oppose any candidature is being promoted in terms of Resolution 1.

The purpose of political parties in established democracies is to gain and hold power by winning elections. These two resolutions reflect the extent to which the Labour Party was founded to represent the working class and to win seats for the representatives of that class, especially those who formed trade unions. For many, the second resolution also suggests that the Labour Party set out to achieve that objective by a policy of the rational pursuit of maximum power. At that time this meant an alliance or some other form of cooperation with the Liberal Party. Yet, a lasting alliance with the Liberal Party was never a serious Labour option even at the time of the Gladstone–MacDonald Pact. The party's preference being to secure its independent existence by a willingness to cooperate only in the short term for its own instrumentalist purposes. Tony Blair has recently endorsed Roy Jenkins' lament that it is an artificial division between Labour and Liberals that has hamstrung centre-left politics throughout the twentieth century, so allowing the Conservative Party to dominate electoral politics. But despite the use Labour has made of Liberals such as Keynes and Beveridge, the party has prided itself on its independence from vested interests other than organised labour: indeed, the party was called into existence to serve the needs of the Labour movement. Its link with that movement has been a defining issue in the on-going debate about the nature of the party's existence.

If it were like other political parties, left or right of centre, then the notion of a volume of essays which are drawn back again and again to the relationship between an entity called 'the party' and a separate entity called 'the movement', would be deeply counter intuitive. That it does not appear so (and anyone with even a passing acquaintance with the Labour Party of the last 100 years knows that it is not so), provides the clearest indication of the simple truth that these essays emphasise: the Labour Party is different. This volume reflects on the nature of that difference and illuminates the distinctive character the Labour Party has taken in its first 100 years. The following essays seek to place the historical Labour Party in both a narrative and a thematic context. Contributors include historians, sociologists, political scientists and both current and retired members of the Parliamentary Labour Party and the Conservative Party. The book is motivated by the cheerful assumption that a contemporary political party can best be understood by detailed and informed reference to its historical past. Naturally, the subject area covered in a history of this kind cannot be inclusive and this volume makes no such claims. Its subject matter probably demonstrates the subjective choice of both the editors and the contributors. And it is a collection of opinions as diverse and contradictory as the history of the Labour Party demands.

Over the course of that history, the changing politics of Labour's own 'broad, progressive coalition' have been fashioned by the party's ideological outlook and its political objectives. That outlook and those objectives have reflected the changing fashions of contemporary politics as much as they have echoed the genetic code the party has acquired at its birth. Labour, both in historical and contemporary perspective, is a product of the various political, economic, social and culture environments in which it is located, and in which it has been located. All political parties find they are constrained by institutional, electoral, social, cultural and economic environments (at both a national and international level), and their historical experiences are often a set of narrative in which they try to successfully or unsuccessfully negotiate, circumvent or even successfully or unsuccessfully ignore them. Labour has been both an office seeking and a policy seeking party, willing to secure office in order to pursue reform; and willing to forgo office for the purity of a policy position. Obviously, the most avowedly policy seeking political party is obliged to recognise the importance of successful office seeking, if not in the short term, then certainly in the long term. The ability to secure office (at least sometimes) is a raison d'etre of any party that wishes to continue in existence.

The two constant themes in Labour's first century have been firstly, that its modus operandi is to use Parliament to pursue political influence; to this end the party utilises the existing constitution as the means of its advance, prioritising the election of Members of Parliament, and secondly, that Labour has been a broad church, its membership embracing both radical and moderate opinion stretching across the left-right socialist perspective. The existing state, parliamentary politics, and the ever present commitment to what Fabians described as the 'inevitability of gradualism', have been ever present throughout the party's history. And, thanks in no small part to the institutional setting of the two-party system copperfastened by the plurality electoral system, all major British political parties have to an enormous extent been 'coalitions of interests', groupings stretching across a political left-right spectrum. Of course, with the brief (and unusual) exceptions of the leadership tenures of George Lansbury and Michael Foot, Labour's leadership has long been the reliable redoubt of the centre-right of the party.

Yet other than its institutional character and its favoured modus operandi, one recurrent question raised in studies of the party's past and present: is what is Labour for? It is argued that Labour was created to represent certain values rather than certain policies. These values, of social justice, of fairness and what Hugh Gaitskell called, support for the bottom dog, are what really matters. But it is actually rather difficult to argue that it was ideas rather than interests that inspired the creation of the Labour Party. Those early debates which led to the first meeting of the Labour Representation Committee were about whether or not parliamentary representation, separate from the New Liberal wing of the Old Gladstonian Liberal Party, would further the sectional interests of organised labour. The argument was not won by an appeal to values but by an appeal to interest group politics. It was only after the party was founded and finally called the Labour Party, after 1906, indeed only once its federal constitution was drawn up in 1918 and significant policy programmes were developed in 1918, 1927, 1935 and 1945 and after, were the values which informed its purpose fully worked out.

Armed with its ideological outlook and its set of political objectives Labour has had to acknowledge the need to both simultaneously work with and seek to change the grain of British politics in whatever contemporary form it has taken. British politics in the twentieth century have been characterised by a duality of collectivism and individualism, a movement of both of trend and cycle illustrated by the rise and decline of public doctrines expressed as ideological politics. In a grand historical sweep the period since 1800 may be categorised as the age of Adam Smith, the age of Maynard Keynes and the age of Frederich Hayek. The gradual, if hesitant, post-1880 rise of a more collectivist politics was typified by the rise of Labour. Reform minded Conservatism aside, Labour has been the political movement which articulated (and occasionally enacted as policy) social democratic aspirations in the 1940s, 1950s, 1960s and 1970s, a reformist agenda informed by statist welfare politics, state planning and Keynesian economics.

Thus the question 'what was the Labour Party for' could be answered in the period 1918–1970 with considerable confidence and mutual understanding across the political spectrum. The Labour Party was for the promotion of a set of policies that would extend and protect the interests of organised labour, by extension the broader working class and if possible the country as a whole. The programme to fulfil that purpose was hesitantly fleshed out and in policy terms was fashioned in 1931–40 and during Labour's participation in the Wartime Coalition of 1940–45; in the event, it was more or less implemented by the Attlee government 1945–51. Historians who argue that 1945 did not represent a triumph of socialist enthusiasm miss the point. The society that the Labour Party was founded to create was created between 1945–51. Its historic mission fulfilled in its first ever majority government, it fought a long rearguard action in defence of the Attlee settlement. In turn the kind of society and economy created by the long boom and the Attlee reforms influenced and informed the development of the values that the Labour Party came to represent.

Full employment was the ideological glue bonding the sectional interests to the eternal values. In full employment Labour could keep its key client group strong and society healthy. Core values could be expressed as policy. That it was organised labour, in the winter of discontent, that destroyed the old Labour Party as a governing force is the supreme irony of Labour's first century. It took just over a decade from the foundation of the Party for its leading figures to forge a coherent expression of the Party's values and purposes. The result was the 1918 constitution. It took a similar period after the 1983 election for the leadership to realise that the electoral life of the old Labour Party was over. After the death of John Smith, who was by no means certain of victory in a general election against John Major, the party began to reinvent itself in all the areas that had seemed unthinkable before 1994: clause IV, the power of conference, the union link, the engagement with the market economy and so on. Perhaps at that point a new political should have been created but the old and the new struggled, and continue to struggle, within the same entity.

Political parties should exist for purposes beyond the mere survival of their brand identity. If they do not, then the legitimacy of politics itself is undermined. Reformist left of centre parties need purpose even more than right of centre parties because they must, at some level, appeal to people to put their own interests below those of others. You might argue that left of centre parties can go through periods in which they do not have a clear purpose. That way they survive and continue to occupy political space until they have a renewal of ideological energy. But this argument leads to what we may call the Hattersley Headache.

Roy Hattersley, Labour's deputy leader in 1983–92, resolutely set his face against any suggestion that he should defect from Labour in 1980–82 and join in the setting up of the Social Democratic Party. As fiercely loyal to Labour as he was opposed to its then left-wing stance, Hattersley argued with his social democratic friends that they should remain in the Labour Party. He told them that eventually the Labour Party would return to its senses and that the battle had to be won from within. Yet, twenty odd years on, his contemporary headache comes from the fact that by the time Labour moderated its appeal, the social democratic politics he believed in had disappeared from Labour's agenda. Incomes policies, progressive taxation, ever increasingly levels of public expenditure, the universalist welfare state, the public sector in profit generating industries, and an egalitarian education system had ceased to be elements of the centre ground of British politics. They were history and may now appear as mystifying and exotic to the current generation of students as temperance, the capital levy and imperial preference.

Today, faced with a choice between managing, focusing, restricting, or constricting the market for a social purpose or empowering, freeing and liberalising the market in an economic interest, Labour's policy (and its core instinct) was always to favour the first course of action. This, as an old Gaitskellite revisionist such as Roy Hattersley can attest, is no longer the case.

A political party is multidimensional. It can alter drastically in a number of ways but remain the same thing. The social and political furniture of political parties is constantly rearranged and modelled in the hunt for electoral success. The essence of democratic socialist politics could survive alteration in individual aspects or in a combination of aspects but not in all aspects simultaneously. Yet, in the 1990s the underlying assumptions of the Labour Party's ideology were transformed way beyond the dictates of the changed conditions the UK faced, its ethos was altered consciously to exclude its traditional members and styles of discourse, its formal structures were brought into line with the long standing informal reality of the exercise of internal power. All aspects of its existence have either been altered or are in the process of being altered. The new political party, or rather, the new historical entity that is New Labour, is, with one bound released from its history. The new party is freed from the weight of expectations that history brings: who expects real social and economic change from New Labour? The new party is liberated from the welter of contradictions that history had created. New Labour need apologise to no one for embracing the market economy. But the most important liberation is from class based politics and the representation of interests rather than ideas or values. The next logical step is to break the trade union link, though aside from finance this is already irrelevant to the new party.

New Labour is a party governed only by ideas; primarily an idea of itself as the force for modernisation, in particular, institutional modernisation. This identity is most clearly expressed in the constitutional reform programme, indeed institutional modernisation is the most coherent and broadly supported element in the much discussed Third Way, in the idea of New Labour. Commemorating Labour's centenary therefore provokes two awkward and on-going questions: Firstly, what is it that makes a political party what it is, rather than something else? Secondly, should we ask ourselves weather the journey that began in the Farringdon Road has now finally reached an end. Has the expiry date of that political project long passed? Yet, if we are singing 'The Labour Party is dead' should we also sing, 'Long live the New Labour Party'? If New Labour is a new political party, then what is it for? Indeed, if it is a new party, what, if anything, happened to the old political party? These and other questions, the answers to which illuminate where the Labour Party has come from and where it is going, are the subject of the diverse but related essays in this volume.

Out of the Bowels of the Movement: The Trade Unions and the Origins of the Labour Party 1900–18

Robert Taylor

'It was not Keir Hardie who formed this party. It grew out of the bowels of the Trades Union Congress.' Ernest Bevin, TGWU general secretary to the 1935 Labour Party conference.[1]

The brutal realism displayed by the most powerful British trade union leader of the inter-war years may have upset the sensitivities of many rank and file members of the Labour Party during the 1930s but Bevin's words expressed a harsh and abiding truth. Without the initiative and sustained financial and political support derived from the trade unions there would have been no Labour Party at all. And yet too often in labour history the vital role played by the trade unions in the party's formation and early development has been ignored, underplayed, derided or merely taken for granted when compared to the intellectual contributions made by the Independent Labour Party, the Fabian Society and even the Social Democratic Federation.[2] However, as Egon Wertheimer, London correspondent of *Vorwarts* the German Social Democratic newspaper, explained in his 1928 classic account of the Labour Party, its 'fluctuations in strength and organisation have always been dependent upon the fluctuations in trade union membership and to all intents and purposes on that alone'.[3]

It was the 'collective allegiance' of the trade unions to the party that from the beginning provided Labour with its distinctive character. The block votes of trade union members overwhelmingly dominated its policy-making annual conference, providing a substantial check on the power and aspirations of more left-wing trades councils and socialist societies which themselves usually consisted mainly of trade union activists. After 1918 the trade unions acted as a cautious counter-weight to the aspirations of constituency party delegates. Labour's National Executive Committee was under the majority control of the trade unions' own elected representatives from the beginning. Between 1918 and 1937 the block votes of the trade unions were even directly responsible for the election of the executive's constituency section although not for the actual nomination of those eligible to stand. Inside the parliamentary Labour party, which established its autonomy after its formation in 1906, trade union sponsored Labour MPs constituted its majority, at least until 1929. 'The Labour members are a lot of ordinary workmen who neither know nor care about anything but the interests of their respective trade unions and a comfortable life for themselves', grumbled Beatrice Webb, recording the remarks of the Fabian, William Stephen Sanders, on 12 February 1912.[4] Even at the 1918 general election as many as 50 out of the 57 victorious Labour candidates were sponsored by the trade unions, half of them coming from the all-powerful Miners' Federation which dominated many parliamentary constituencies on the coalfields of south Wales, Durham and Northumberland. The trade union-sponsored MPs were to remain for the most part – a loyal, self-effacing, inarticulate and moderating ballast on which the parliamentary leadership could depend for usually unquestioning support. On only two significant occasions did they threaten to disrupt the party. The first time was during the August 1931 crisis when they were set to oppose planned Labour austerity measures to protect sterling, which involved a cut in the unemployment insurance fund and unemployment benefit. The precipitated defection of most of Labour's senior leadership into a national government resolved the issue but it was the formidable intervention of the Trades Union Congress that proved to be decisive. The second time the trade union connection provoked a crisis inside the parliamentary party was during the first half of 1969 when Prime Minister Harold Wilson tried to modernise the trade unions through the use of legislation designed to curb unofficial strikes. At the end of turbulent events that seemed at moments to threaten the government's existence, Wilson backed down before the massed ranks of the TUC general council and their trade union-sponsored allies among Labour MPs.

Trade union finances were always crucial for the funding of Labour's national machine and constituency parties. With the lack of a large mass individual membership or business allies, Labour's necessary and only dominant paymasters were the trade unions until almost the end of the century when the arrival of New Labour's corporate friends, eager to fill the party's coffers, lessened the need to depend on them.[5] Moreover, trade union officials and activists at national and local level made up the bulk of the party's rank and file. No substantial and vibrant Labour activism in the constituencies was evident until the late 1930s. It was overwhelmingly the contribution made by the trade unions to Labour that enable it to become a credible national political party, capable of contesting elections and forming governments. Perhaps just as important for the party, the trade unions were primarily responsible for Labour's ethos as well as its ideology and policy programmes. 'As a popular institution, the Labour party was nothing without the unions' explained Ross McKibbin in his seminal study of its early years. 'The Labour party is bound to the unions not just by cash and card votes but by personalities and doctrines, common experience and sentiment – and mutual advantage', Martin Harrison observed in his analysis of the party-union link in the 1950s.[7]

The important role the trade unions played in Labour's formative years has often been viewed more as a source of chronic weakness for the party than one of its strengths. On the left, the party's ideology of Labourism, stemming almost entirely from its trade union origins, was often criticised as a defensive and incoherent reflection of the severe limitations and lack of theoretical rigour allegedly displayed by the British working class during the early decades of the century. In the writings of Marxist scholars, notably by Ralph Miliband, John Saville, David Coates and Tom Nairn the trade unions were portrayed as a formidable, defensive barrier to Labour's Socialist advance, supposedly holding back the masses from commitment to a militant socialism, less inhibited by the inevitable constraints imposed on the opportunities for political action by reformist parliamentary politics and industrial relations voluntarism.[8]

But hostility to the trade union contribution to the party's history has also grown more recently among New Labour modernisers.[9] To them, Labourism is a sectionalist, introspective ideology derived from a divisive class-based politics that they claim fatally weakened the centre-left to the long-term electoral advantage of the Conservatives. The trade unions' historic role in the Labour Party is often viewed by modernisers as hostile to economic and industrial change. In pursuit of their sectionalist interests it has been claimed, they undermined the country's radical political forces contained with success before 1914 within an inclusive and progressive alliance dominated by the Liberals.

Neither the views of the Marxists nor the New Labour modernisers stand up to serious analysis and yet both have provided substance to misconceptions that continue to distort the party's early history. Labour's centennial year is therefore an appropriate moment to reassess the role the trade unions played in the party's formation and early development. As Lewis Minkin wrote in his important study of Labour and the trade unions:

It is easy to understand why the Labour Party should be so often and so easily characterised as an instrument of the trade unions. Its family history, its resources and its producer obligations, all weighed in the same direction to a degree which was highly unusual on the European left.[10]

It is true Labour's trade union connection brought the party difficulties in achieving long-term success in winning general elections and governing the country effectively. Recent attempts have been made to suggest the party was broadly similar in its ideology, outlook and ethos to the pre-1914 German Social Democrats and the French Socialists in the era of Jean Jaures.[11] But what is most striking about the Labour Party during its formative years is the extent to which it differed significantly from its mainland European Socialist counterparts. Wertheimer wrote that:

On the continent the various Socialist parties have for the most part been built up along the lines of individual membership and owe their main strength to their small local groups. The Labour Party on the other hand is predominantly a federal organisation. On the continent it is at least theoretically possible that the trade unions could be crushed without inflicting vital injury to the political movement but in Great Britain the relationship is so close that neither can receive the slightest blow without its effect being felt by the other.[12]

David Marquand has concurred with that fundamental insight.

In a sense not true of its counterparts on the mainland of Europe, Labour has been a trade union party, created, financed and in the last analysis controlled by a highly decentralised trade union movement, which was already in existence before it came into being. Above all its ethos – the symbols, rituals, shared memories and unwritten understandings which have shaped the life of the party and given it its unmistakable style – has been saturated with the ethos of trade unionism.[13]

In other western European countries – such as Germany, Sweden and France – Social Democratic parties were formed before the emergence of nationally-based trade union federations. The opposite was the case in Britain. In 1900 the Trades Union Congress (TUC) was already 32 years old and had, through its respectable and assiduous Parliamentary Committee, become an influential pressure group, pursuing its lobbying activities on governments as an organised sectionalist interest.[14] The lack of a separate political party based on working class representation, let alone any commitment to Socialism, did not look like an impediment to the furtherance of limited trade union objectives, at least until the late 1890s. After all, from the 1870s a small number of trade union-funded Lib-Lab MPs had existed in the

House of Commons to champion specific working class or trade union demands. They enjoyed limited success in alliance with radical allies in the Liberal party like Sir Charles Dilke and A J Mundella. In the period between the Third Reform Act of 1884 and the end of the nineteenth century, trade union parliamentary political activity was concerned primarily with the functional representation of the labour interest. The Socialist challenge to the existing political system was confined to the margins, even after the formation of the socialist but pragmatic Independent Labour Party in 1893.

Although the apparent integration of the trade union establishment into the fabric of the country's political and industrial system should not be exaggerated, the state was not seen by most trade union leaders as an ever-present threat to their freedom to bargain with willing employers. On the contrary, a growing network of influence had been developed from the 1860s, particularly by the craft trade unions across a range of industrial sectors. This resulted from the slow but uneven spread of voluntarism, that system of negotiated collective bargaining where the state's limited role was to offer means of conciliation when mutually agreed by both sides of industry. In pre-1914 Britain – for all its undoubted heightened sense of class consciousness – trade union activists belonged to a rich diversity of voluntary and autonomous associations such as friendly societies, mutual aid bodies, charitable organisations, co-operatives and the like. The tendency to appeal to sturdy working class self-reliance was not, however, universal. Millions of unskilled low-paid workers and their families continued to enjoy no such access to financial means such as savings to guarantee to them security as well as respectability. But the existence of such civil associations does not suggest working class organisations like trade unions were regarded either by governments or employers as a dangerous threat to their power or authority.

Another important difference existed between centre-left pre-1914 British politics and those of the European continent that is often overlooked. No other European country possessed a broad-based centre-left mass party like the Liberals, able to appeal to a substantial section of the working class not through a detailed programme of reform but the propagation of a shared set of moral values which blended political and economic freedom. Of course – as we shall see – the Liberal party found it increasingly difficult to accommodate the force of an emerging self-confident trade union movement within its ranks. But Liberalism's ethical appeal to many respectable, prudent and thrifty working class male voters up to the outbreak of the Great War should not be neglected. Nor can the tenacity of working class Conservatism be ignored either. Through Disraeli, Lord Randolph Churchill and F E Smith, Tory Democracy was much more than a populist slogan. Among many trade unionists, especially in the Lancashire cotton industry and southern English towns, the Conservative cause attracted significant electoral working class support. The extent and tenacity of working-class Conservatism remains an overlooked subject for serious research. It is, however, a sobering fact that the 6,000 strong branch of the Conservatives' Primrose League in Bolton in 1900 was larger than the entire national membership of the Independent Labour Party.[15]

In fact, trade union conversion to the idea of forming an autonomous Labour Party to contest parliamentary and other elections was not the teleological consequence of social and political change. Nor perhaps even more important should it be assumed any widespread trade union willingness existed to encourage Labour's effective evolution as a party committed to democratic Socialism. Enthusiasts used to look back nostalgically from the high water-mark of Labour's political dominance immediately after its 1945 election triumph and wrote of the party's 'onward march'. In doing so they produced a distorted Whig version of Labour history.[16] Labour's 'magnificent journey' was portrayed as an inexorable and even effortless ascent to the New Jerusalem, temporarily halted by the 1931 debacle. Nothing could be further from the truth. Labour's evolution during its formative years owed far less to underlying social and economic forces in a class-divided society or even to the extension of the parliamentary franchise to all adult males over 18 and women over 28 with property under the 1918 Reform Act, and much more to what the liberal historian H A L Fisher once called the 'contingent and unforeseen'.[17] Central to Labour's political success were the changing attitudes within Britain's trade unions as they moved from a belief in pressure group politics and producer interest representation to a broad commitment to a political party genuinely committed to the pursuit of power. Such a transition had hardly begun to take place among the rank and file in the trade unions before 1914, let alone the wider working classes, even if their leaders and activists might be more advanced in their thinking. The uneven pace of trade union commitment to Labour Party politics reflected different industrial experiences, structural diversity in local job markets, community traditions and the varying attractions of Socialism as a unifying ideology. It also reflected the tenacity or weakness of Liberalism at local level to counter a trend towards labour representation.

Indeed, in its uncertain early years the Labour Party exposed its own fragilities and limitations with which it struggled for most of the century – thanks mainly to the position of the trade unions. Historians continue to debate whether the party was on the brink either of terminal decline or a significant electoral advance on the eve of the Great War. What could not have been predicted in August 1914 was that within four years the Labour Party appeared to have replaced the Liberals as the main centre-left force in British politics. Such a political breakthrough looked most improbable before the outbreak of military conflict. Labour's electoral position in the summer of 1914 remained tentative, insecure and difficult. Nothing really important separated Labour from most of the governing Liberal party. On political issue after issue between 1900 and 1914 the two centre-left forces were in practical agreement whatever theoretical differences may have existed between them. Indeed, Labour was not explicitly committed during that period to any agreed form of democratic Socialism nor even a recognisable programme of political and social reform. In the progressive alliance the Liberals were still very much the dominant partner.

But on the other hand, it is also clear that Labour's organic links with the trade unions were already beginning to provide the party with a federal structure that would guarantee its political independence whatever common opinions the party might continue to share with the Liberals. It was this 'open and honourable' organisation, forged between the trade unions and leading pragmatic Socialists mainly from the Independent Labour Party like Keir Hardie, Ramsay MacDonald and Philip Snowden that ensured the new party established an apparently institutional permanence before 1914. There was no doubting the truth of Hardie's wise observation made back in 1897 that 'no labour movement can ever hope to succeed in this country without the co-operation of the trade unions. Some of us have held the opinion from the beginning that it was possible to make trade unionism and ILPism interchangeable terms for electoral purposes'.[18]

The loosely organised coalition of trade unions and socialists formed in 1900 survived an uncertain childhood. It did so only because the trade unions continued to believe in the need for a separate Labour Party to articulate their limited and defensive political agenda in parliament. In 1914 it was certainly clear the party still had a long way to go in convincing many rank and file trade union members they ought to abandon their existing political loyalties in favour of Labour in a first-past-the-post parliamentary electoral system where only an estimated 60 per cent of the male working class enjoyed the right to vote at any one time. The evidence suggests a substantial minority of trade unionists who themselves only accounted for 23 per cent of the entire workforce in 1913 were less than enthusiastic about bank-rolling a political party to represent their collective interests from their own union subscriptions. The one-off compulsory political fund ballots, held by trade unions affiliated to the Labour Party under the terms of the 1913 Trade Union Act that sought to undo the consequences of the Osborne judgement, revealed as many as 40 per cent of the rank and file in the largest nine trade unions were opposed to any specific financial support for independent working class parliamentary representation. In addition, the overwhelming majority of trade union members displayed their indifference over the issue by failing to participate in the ballots at all. Trade union resistance to Labour as a separate political party was especially evident on coalfields like those of Nottinghamshire and Derbyshire where Liberalism remained strong and among many workers in the spinning sector of the Lancashire textile industry. As British trade unionism at that time was dominated by the citadels of coal and cotton, such a substantial and potentially hostile or indifferent attitude by large numbers of organised workers revealed the severe limitations imposed on the political ambitions of the pre-1914 trade union movement.

However, perhaps a more salient fact about the political fund ballots was that a majority of trade union members who participated in them at least expressed their clear approval for the creation of separate political trade union funds. Members in only nine out of 101 trade unions balloted between late 1913 and mid-April 1916 actually voted against the creation of separate funds for political purposes. As a result, Labour's financial base and consequently its organisational independence was firmly established by the time of the Great War. Despite doubts and divisions over tactics and strategy displayed by what was seen by many as an often inept and uncertain parliamentary leadership and chairman Ramsay MacDonald's apparent hankering for a permanent electoral entente with the Liberals in the spring of 1914, it was clear that the Labour Party had come to stay. But at that time it could hardly yet be described as a credible alternative government. The political commitment of the trade unions – despite the upsurge in industrial conflict and interest in syndicalism in 1912/1913 and above all the sharp growth in membership density from 14.6 per cent to 23.1 per cent between 1910 and 1913 – ensured that Labour would not disappear easily into the embrace of a revived Liberal party identified with a new political programme.

In 1900, however, even such a modest outcome within 14 years had looked most implausible. Indeed, the inaugural conference held to form the Labour Representation Committee was almost completely ignored by the outside world. This should have come as no surprise. Previous attempts made both in the 1860s through the Labour Representation League and again in the 1880s with the creation of the Labour Electoral Association, to establish a political organisation that would provide independent representation for the organised working class interest in Parliament, failed to make much progress. This was partly due to inertia and indifference, especially displayed among many craft-based trade unions. So why should the decision taken by a less than decisive majority of trade unions at the TUC's 1899 Plymouth Congress enjoy any more hope of proving a success?

It is true a growing number of national trade union officials by the 1890s had concluded that the working class they represented needed a more direct, effective and influential voice in parliament. The annual reports of the TUC's Parliamentary Committee during the period chronicle an increasing anger and frustration inside the TUC over its inability to influence government ministers to heed and implement organised labour's public policy agenda. From the demand for old age pensions to the provision of free school meals for the children of the poor, from the introduction of an eight-hour working day for the miners to measures to combat unemployment through a commitment to 'the right to work', the trade unions believed they were not being heard with enough effect by the political establishment. Their delegations went cap in hand to lobby cabinet ministers but they usually left dissatisfied. The TUC's efforts to use private member's Bills as a way of advancing their causes were also being frustrated as parliamentary time for such procedures was restricted and tighter party discipline made it harder to mobilise support.

As the TUC Parliamentary Committee explained in its 1899 annual report to Congress:

With the present mode of procedure of the House of Commons it is almost impossible to get any useful Bill through the House unless the government allow it to pass by withdrawing its opposition, and in their opinion, if any remedy is to be affected it must be done by the working classes at the polls.[19]

Certainly the TUC could look for some assistance to the small group of trade union funded Lib-Lab MPs. Stalwarts like Thomas Burt, Alexander MacDonald, Henry Broadhurst, Charles Fenwick, Ben Pickard and George Howell spoke up often with common sense and passion on trade union and working class issues at Westminster.[20] But during the 1890s in a decade when trade union membership increased from three-quarters of a million to just over two million, the Lib-Labs had only been able to increase their parliamentary representation from eight to eleven MPs. With no state payment of wages to MPs before 1911, working class aspirants keen to represent labour interests in the House of Commons had to depend on the willingness of middle-class Liberal associations to nominate and finance them and such support was usually unforthcoming to the obvious irritation of the Liberal party's national leadership.

There was no mood of complacency inside the TUC in the face of such setbacks. The voices of organised labour – no matter how rational and practical they might be on the issues that concerned them – believed they were making insufficient impact on government in proportion to their growing numerical strength. Moreover, many trade union leaders were concerned about the future legitimacy of their own organisations. They came to suspect a growing number of employers were intent on organising a concerted offensive against them through the formation of powerful national strike-breaking associations, stimulated in part by developments in the United States where trusts and monopolies were starting to confront trade unions in an aggressive manner. Such trade union anxieties over hostile employer attitudes were linked to a number of anti-union court judgements, which appeared to threaten the 1870s industrial relations legal settlement that was supposed to have guaranteed organised labour immunity from the ravages of the common law and assertion of absolute property rights.[21]

However, in 1899 trade union pressure for independent working class parliamentary representation was still confined mainly either to the smaller trade unions who were trying to organise unskilled manual workers or those in artisan trades that feared the consequences of technological change on their existing workplace organisations. Many of those trade unions were led or influenced by Socialists from the Independent Labour Party, the Fabian Society and the Social Democratic Federation. Such a development, however, did not really pose a serious danger to the intellectual domination of Lib-Labism inside the TUC. Nonetheless, the resolution moved by the Amalgamated Society of Railway Servants – based on a motion coming from its Doncaster branch – at the 1899 Plymouth Trades Union Congress turned out to be a seminal moment in the history of the Labour Movement.

Its inoffensive but convoluted language sought to maximise as much support from TUC delegates as possible. The resolution declared:

That this Congress, having regard to its decisions in former years, and with a view to securing a better representation of the interests of labour in the House of Commons, hereby instructs the parliamentary committee to invite the co-operation of all the co-operative, socialistic, trade union and other working organisations to jointly co-operate on lines mutually agreed upon, in convening a special congress of representatives from such of the above-named organisations as may be willing to take part to devise ways and means for securing the return of an increased number of labour members to the next Parliament.[22]

James Holmes from the Amalgamated Society of Railway Servants, in his speech proposing the motion, said if the TUC intended to put its principles into effect it must be 'free of all political parties.' He was seconded by Jimmy Sexton from the National Union of Dock Labourers who argued the motion was designed to bring an end to 'the present state of chaos and difficulty' and 'avoid the present disgraceful confusion', where trade union men opposed each other on separate political platforms. Ben Tillett, general secretary of the Dock, Wharf, Riverside and General Labourer's union said the TUC had 'not taken up an intelligent political attitude since its formation' and he contrasted the more favourable situation in France and Germany where workers had more definite programmes. Pete Curran, organiser of the National Union of Gasworkers and General Labourers, was also enthusiastic, arguing the proposed new body would 'create free organisations and lead to the formulation of a definite programme'. Outright opposition in the TUC debate to the proposal for independent labour representation was limited and unpersuasive. Thomas Ashton of the Amalgamated Association of Operative Cotton Spinners tried unsuccessfully to put an end to the debate by calling for next business. He argued in the face of vocal dissent from some delegates the ASRS proposition was of 'an impracticable character'. Ashton went on to suggest:

If this proposal was passed not one trade unionist out of ten thousand would take notice of it. Therefore why should the time of Congress be wasted? If their society was to interfere in politics, it would go down immediately; but by keeping clear of politics it would become a strong organisation.

However, the motion was carried – amidst scenes of great jubilation – by 546,000 votes to 434,000 against but an estimated third of the TUC delegates had abstained. Both the Miners' Federation and the cotton unions may have disliked the motion but they failed to mobilise effectively to stop its passage. Perhaps they assumed the proposed new body would prove to be as unsuccessful as previous attempts to form a parliamentary force designed to represent organised labour's wider interests. Certainly the preparation for the conference to form the planned Labour Representation Committee suggested more moderate union leaders intended to keep a close eye on its development. As many as four out of the five appointed trade union members on the 11-strong preparatory committee for the inaugural conference were Lib-Labs and prominent members of the TUC Parliamentary Committee not Socialists. These were Sam Woods, MP, president of the Lancashire and Cheshire miners and secretary of the TUC Parliamentary Committee; W C Steadman MP and general secretary of the Barge Builders union; C W Bowerman general secretary of the London Society of Compositors and Treasurer of the TUC and Richard Bell, general secretary of the Amalgamated Railway Servants. Only Will Thorne, general secretary of the Gasworkers and General Labourers union, could remotely be described as a full-blooded Socialist. However, the other six members of the conference preparatory committee did represent Socialist organisations with two each from the Independent Labour Party (Keir Hardie and Ramsay MacDonald), the Fabian Society (E R Pease and George Bernard Shaw) and the Marxist Social Democratic Foundation (Harry Quelch and R H Taylor).

The tentative, cautious and defensive nature of the trade union initiative for parliamentary representation, was apparent from the proceedings of the LRC's resulting inaugural conference. Only 129 delegates representing 62 trade unions with a combined membership of 568,177 bothered to attend the gathering. Together they made up well under half of the total 1899 trade union with a combined membership of 1,200,000 affiliated to the TUC. Two of the largest trade unions which sent delegates – the Amalgamated Society of Engineers and the Lancashire and Cheshire Miners' Federation – did not even immediately affiliate to the LRC they had helped to create. The Railway Servants and the Boot and Shoe Operatives were the only other trade unions of any substantial size that attended the Memorial Hall gathering but at least they agreed to affiliate to the LRC immediately after its formation. The Co-operative Movement refused a request to become involved.

The debate among the overwhelmingly trade union delegates at the Memorial Hall meeting on what the LRC should stand for was not particularly conclusive either. No success was achieved in an attempt, initiated by the Social Democratic Federation, to commit the new body to Socialism as its ultimate objective. The SDF decided to disaffiliate from the LRC by the end of 1901 in disgust at what its leaders saw as the body's excessive moderation. The defeat of the Socialists in 1900 reflected an astute recognition by Keir Hardie and his Independent Labour Party colleagues of what was politically possible from the new body without endangering potential trade union support which was seen by them as vital for the LRC's parliamentary success. It was Hardie who moved the crucial amendment declaring the LRC's intention was to create in the House of Commons 'a Labour party, having its own policy, its own whips and acting in all that concerned the welfare of the workers in a manner free and unhampered by entanglements with other parties'.[23] It would be up to each of the affiliated bodies who constituted the LRC's federal structure to determine how their candidates should be selected only on the condition that if elected they would agree to form a single, distinctive Labour parliamentary group and act in accordance with its collective decisions. Trade union leaders were vocal in expressing their strong support for Hardie's limited objectives for the new body. These included men like Ben Tillett, William Davis, general secretary of the National Society of Amalgamated Brassworkers, Pete Curran and George Wardle of the Railway Servants. However, it was also evident from the beginning, that the trade unions were sensitive to the charge that they intended to exercise a potentially dominant role over the LRC's activities if they chose to do so. Initially, the intention had been to provide as many as 12 of the 17 places on the LRC's executive committee to trade union representatives giving them overwhelming numerical superiority. Ben Cooper of the Cigar Makers proposed this, arguing he did not think the non-union bodies at the conference could complain if they only made up a third of the committee's representation. But Joseph Burgess of the ILP, seconded by Hardie, pressed successfully for the formation of a smaller 13-strong executive committee made up of only seven representatives from the trade unions, with two each from the ILP and the Social Democratic Federation and one from the Fabian Society. Burgess's motion was carried, if only narrowly by 44 votes to 38 against but more comfortably when the trade union card vote was counted by 331,000 to 161,000. However, as the ILP'S Philip Snowden noted in his memoirs: 'The large representation of the Socialist bodies was an unexpected act of generosity on the part of the trade unions who had a membership of over half a million represented at the conference compared with only 23,000 membership of the three Socialist societies.'[24] Moreover, attempts by some trade unions to insist the LRC's executive members drawn from their organisations should be selected directly by the TUC Parliamentary Committee alone was roundly defeated.

George Barnes, left-wing general secretary of the Amalgamated Society of Engineers, who attended the inaugural conference took a prosaic view of the LRC's purpose. As he reflected in his autobiography: 'Perfectionist propaganda and bewildering programmes should be resolutely tabooed. He will best contribute to the working of Labour who leaves his isms on the doorsteps when entering the pending conference.' In Barnes's view, labour representation was about 'practical participation in the life of the nation and not a sundry of abstract theories on the one hand or the furtherance of sectional trade union views on the other.'[25]

It was that cautious realism and suspicion of Socialist ideology which is so striking about the views and attitudes of many of the national trade union officials who attended the LRC's early conferences, a number of whom were elected as Labour members of Parliament in 1906. The seven trade union officials on the first executive committee were hardly first-rung leaders. It was implicit that the LRC had a particular political role to play but that it should not use it in any way to usurp the functions performed by either the TUC or the recently formed General Federation of Trade Unions. As Gareth Steadman-Jones has argued the 'founding moment of the Labour Party was not revolution abroad or political upheaval at home but a defensive solution to the employer's counter-offensive of the 1890s. The LRC was the generalisation of the structural role of the trade unions into the form of a political party'.[26]

The trade unions were not anxious to exercise a direct or day to day control over the new body they were mainly responsible for creating. They offered no nominee for the post of the LRC's unpaid secretary, although Sam Woods was approached but refused to accept it. Eventually the 33-year-old Ramsay MacDonald from the ILP was appointed to the position. Nor did the TUC or its affiliate trade unions offer the organisation any premises for its administrative needs. In its early years the LRC was run from a back room in MacDonald's flat at 3 Lincoln's Inn Fields in London, not moving to 28 Victoria Street nearer to Parliament until March 1904 when MacDonald first began to receive an annual salary. The TUC and many trade unions took an arms-length view of the new organisation's development. They might not wish it to become an unruly body outside their control and many remained suspicious of the intentions of the Socialists but on the other hand they were keen to protect the LRC's independence and opposed any suggestion it should become a mouthpiece of purely sectional interests by bringing it more directly under either TUC or affiliate union control. These contradictory tensions revealed the uncertainties harboured by many trade union leaders about the LRC's purpose.

The hesitant and circumscribed attitude towards the LRC's early development, even among those trade unions who were counted among its founding fathers, reflected their deep ambivalence over its long-term future. 'The Labour Party was tied to the unions but they would guarantee it neither continuous support nor obvious direction', noted Ross McKibbin.[27] Clearly the LRC was not formed in 1900 because most trade unions were intent on the rejection of Lib-Labism and the creation of a separate Socialist party. Nor were they even prepared at that stage to suggest they had created a new conventional political party at all. As David Marquand wrote: 'For the most part, the trade unions represented at the conference saw it as a way of defending their interests, not as a way of changing society'.[28] In fact, it is almost impossible to categorise trade union leaders in the 1900s neatly under self-contained labels such as Lib-Lab or Socialist, let alone Fabian, Marxist or ILP member. Many could be described at different or even the same time as eclectic believers in a wide range of often contradictory political positions within an ill-defined progressivism. Most trade union activists certainly found no difficulty in subscribing to the basic tenets of Liberalism, whether defined as traditional, radical or New. They believed overwhelming in the virtues of Free Trade, especially after the spring of 1903 when Joseph Chamberlain challenged the economic orthodoxy of the time by launching his tariff reform campaign. 'The free trade fiscal system had before 1914, an ideological value for the working class beyond any conceivable socialist doctrine', noted McKibbin.[29] They also supported the introduction of democratic self-government within the United Kingdom, beginning with Home Rule for Ireland. They sought an extension in the parliamentary suffrage to cover all adults, including women. Some even wanted the introduction of proportional representation in elections. Many believed in temperance and were often strong enthusiasts for banning or at least controlling the perceived excesses of the liquor trade. Most were practising Nonconformists who demanded a non-denominational education system. They were all believers in liberal internationalism, in favour of open diplomacy, arbitration of disputes between states and curbs on the arms trade. They were united – with radical Liberals – in opposition to the Boer War and hostile to the import of Chinese workers into South Africa after the end of that conflict.

It is true some of the trade union leaders held a suspicious, if not downright hostile view of what the state's role ought to be in economic and social policy-making. Many were keen to reinforce not weaken local institutions and uphold voluntary collective agreements with employers. A number of trade union leaders (with those from the Miners' Federation after its affiliation to the party in 1909 in the vanguard alongside the Railway Servants) began to campaign for the public ownership of industry. Many also favoured an activist state to alleviate the evils of unemployment through the creation of tax-funded public works programmes. Trade unions also supported political action in tackling poverty through such measures as a national minimum wage. The idea of a wider National Minimum, a safety net cast over the social abyss to help the poor, was strongly favoured. Growing interest was also displayed among some trade union leaders in forms of industrial rationalisation, designed to improve corporate efficiency. But trade unions were not unequivocal champions before 1914 of a centralised welfare state based on notions of social citizenship. They remained uncertain of government entanglements and keen to protect their own friendly society and mutual aid functions; many of them had built these up for their members since the mid-nineteenth century. Trade union dislike of the 1911 National Insurance Act was indicative of this negative attitude towards state intrusion over the behaviour of the worker citizen.[30]

But what really brought at least a semblance of unity to the LRC in its early days was its firm commitment to protect the independence of trade unions from the threats of employers, the courts and the state. This took the form of seeking the restoration of the negative freedoms enshrined in their legal immunities from civil actions in industrial disputes. Trade union leaders emphasised the need for self-reliance, 'free' collective bargaining, and support for the voluntarist tradition of industrial relations unhampered by state-enforced legal regulation. Their behaviour was consistent with their belief in a laissez-faire political economy as they sought to ensure their industrial activities remained untrammelled by wider political and social objectives. Trade unions were determined as far as they could to uphold an implicit if ill-defined division of responsibility between their Labour Party and themselves. This delicate balancing act required sensitivity, understanding and tolerance. On the one hand, the trade unions were prepared to accept and support the autonomous character of the parliamentary Labour party after 1906 although they were also keen to ensure no conflicts on aims and values should emerge between the party's political leadership and themselves. On the other hand, they insisted on preserving their independence in developing industrial relations strategies in relation to the state and employers.

In fact, most trade union leaders at that stage regarded the Labour Party as essentially a pressure group in the House of Commons, lobbying the Liberal government to introduce measures of relevance to their interests. They did not differ substantially in their fundamental political beliefs from most Liberals, particularly those on the party's radical wing. The so-called New Liberalism of David Lloyd George and Winston Churchill, dominant in the emergence of a progressive social policy between 1908 and 1911 was much more reformist and interventionist than anything envisaged by the trade unions and the Labour Party. Its MPs after 1906 tended to concentrate their limited energies (most continued to earn their living as trade union officials) on championing social and industrial issues of direct interest to the working classes. In the first session of the new Liberal Parliament they were unexpectedly successful in ensuring the passage of the Trade Disputes Act which gave trade unions a range of protective legal immunities which had been beyond their wildest dreams in reversing the Taff Vale judgement. The Workmen's Compensation Act passed in 1906 also owed much to Labour Party and TUC pressure. On the 'right to work' agenda the party's MPs adopted a clearly distinctive position, reflecting organised labour interests. Their overwhelmingly optimistic, rational but often sentimental view of politics was widely shared across the organisational divide that was supposed increasingly to separate the Liberals from the Labour Party. As Biagini and Reid concluded:

The central demands of progressive popular politics remained largely those of radical liberalism well into the twentieth century: for open government and the rule of law, for freedom from intervention both at home and abroad and for individual liberty and community-centred democracy.[31]

A strong continuity of tradition and practice therefore existed between Lib-Labism and Labourism. The two forces were bound together by a common understanding and commitment to the radical values of respectable 'free-born Englishmen' which often dated back to the Chartists and beyond, including the need to nurture self-respect and a sense of moral responsibility. This ethical outlook was often more pronounced inside the trade unions than it was among many middle-class Socialists. As Alastair Reid's essay on the life of Robert Knight, general secretary of the Boilermakers Society from 1871 to 1898, illustrates, the so-called Old Unionism he believed in was neither defensive nor anomalous.[32] The trade union generation, so crucial to the formation of the Labour Party was not divided by policy or principle, from those who had worshipped at the feet of Mr Gladstone. Indeed, the Grand Old Man in his later years used to favour the selection of labour candidates in working-class constituencies. As he told the 1891 conference of the National Liberal Federation in Newcastle: 'There ought to be a great effor of the Liberal party to extend the labour representation in Parliament ... An addition of numeral force to that representation is not only desirable but in the highest degree urgent'.[33] In Alistair Reid's words, the emerging Labour Party should be seen not as 'an entirely new departure in working-class politics nor as the demise of socialism in the deadly embrace of "labourist" Old Unionism but rather as a dynamic recomposition of popular radicalism in adaptation to a new political environment.'[34] John Belchem has persuasively argued that the trade union converts to Socialism were 'not seeking to subvert but to extend and complete the radical project'. 'They hoped to construct a broad labour alliance which would harness the moral fervour of Lib-Labism and the funds and resources of its collective associations, the necessary foundation for independent labour representation. In this practical and ethical formulation, socialism offered a revitalised language for united radical advance'.[35] The broad inclusivity of pre-Great War working class politics was symbolised by the 1914 parliamentary celebrations in honour of Sir Thomas Burt, father of the House of Commons and Lib-Lab MP for the mining constituency of Morpeth in Northumberland since 1874 This was an occasion when Socialists and Labour men of all shades of opinion gathered to pay common homage to a man who had done so much to champion working class interests. Clearly there was enough room on the centre-left before the Great

War to accommodate a diversity of trade union and Labour leaders from different generations and ideologies.

The Labour Party before 1914 was hardly regarded as a subversive threat to the constitution, let alone a danger to the existing social and economic system. But then under strong trade union influence it never really saw itself playing such a hostile role. Indeed, the mobilisation of the trade unions behind the party's respectable parliamentary strategy reflected a deep and implicit understanding about the respective roles of Labour's industrial and political wings in a division of their joint responsibilities. As Alan Fox noted in his perceptive analysis of the emerging Labour alliance:

The continued freedom of the unions to pursue a measure of joint regulation with employers and to employ in the process a diversity of industrial and political weapons and sanctions owed much to the determination of the unions themselves. But that determination was bringing success because it was exerted within a relatively favourable social context which generations of working-class activists, inside and outside the unions, had played a part in creating. The whole inheritance of constitutionality, rule of law and political freedom, profoundly flawed though it was by class privilege, prejudice and gross inequalities of power, provided footholds and leverages for organised groups among the working class, provided they showed no intention of using them to overturn the social system.[36]

However, it is also true such mutual harmony at Westminster among trade union sponsored-Labour MPs was not always so apparent at local government level or on other elected representative institutions such as School Boards where the Liberals and the emerging Labour Party often found themselves engaged in bitter conflict with each other for competitive advantage. A diversity of recent regional and local political studies point to the dangers of generalisation over the complex and multi-layered relations that existed between the two parties within the progressive alliance. Labour's trade union connection was vital -from the start – in making the difference to the party's chances of success or failure in contrasting areas of the country. In industrial towns such as Bradford, Leicester and Preston as well as in Wales, Labour's pre-1914 advances were derived mostly from the dominant pressure exercised by a vibrant, home-grown trade unionism.[37] But the vital role of trade unionism in the development of local Labour politics was less evident in much of London (outside the East End and Battersea), the north-east of England, Scotland, the west midlands and parts of industrial Lancashire.[38] The party's grass-roots strength tended to parallel the level of trade union density. It is true there were some exceptions like Colne Valley where the ultra-left Victor Grayson won a sensational by-election victory in 1908 without overt trade union support. For the most part, however, the Labour Party found it hardest to advance where trade unionism was weakest on the ground.

Many Socialists in the early Labour Party may have disliked what they regarded as the limited advance of trade unions in embracing their ideology. But for the most part they accepted they could progress only at the pace of the slowest. The Labour Party's initial development therefore depended very much on the readiness of the trade unions to affiliate and this was determined by unexpected outside events which vindicated the case for independent labour representation but did not pose a direct challenge to a widespread and strongly held trade union belief in the politics of popular radicalism. This was apparent from the first upsurge in support for the LRC. At the new body's first annual conference in 1901 in Manchester, Philip Snowden remembered a prevailing 'feeling of despondency'. 'It looked as if this new effort was going to share the fate of previous attempts to secure the direct representation of Labour', he wrote.[39] Only 32 trade unions attended that meeting, representing a mere 339,577 members, a less impressive turn-out than had occurred at the Memorial Hall founding conference. The LRC's performance in the 1900 general election had been unimpressive. It ran 15 candidates but only two were elected – Keir Hardie who first won Merthyr Tydfil in 1895 and Richard Bell with tacit Liberal support in Derby.

But the early demise of the LRC was saved shortly afterwards by the controversial judgement made by the Law Lords in July 1901 against the Amalgmated Society of Railway Servants in the Taff Vale company case. This important decision and the lack of urgency displayed by the Unionist government in dealing with its consequences shocked the trade union movement and seemed to provide the necessary stimulus for a surge in trade union affiliations that guaranteed the LRC's long-term future. Their Lordships ruled that a trade union could be sued for damages caused by its members in a trade dispute. The Taff Vale judgement seemed to open the way for employers to launch a legal assault on existing trade union freedoms. The TUC and its affiliates believed the law needed to be amended as a matter of urgency to ensure trade unions received proper legal protection against such a possible threat. This meant applying pressure on the established political parties and the existence of the LRC provided them with a useful institutional means of ensuring this was possible. The resulting increase in trade union affiliations to the LRC reflected a collective fear among organised trade union activists about what might happen to their freedom to operate unchallenged if Taff Vale was not reversed quickly. Between early 1901 and early 1903 the new body's affiliated trade union membership rose from 376,000 to 861,000. Such a dramatic increase was due primarily to the affiliation of some textile unions along with the Amalgamated Society of Engineers. The LRC seized the opportunity of Taff Vale to launch a direct appeal to the trade unions to unite behind its activities and combat 'a well organised movement to prejudice public opinion against the industrial effects of trade unionism'. 'Menaced on every hand in workshop, court of law and press, trade unionism has no refuge except the ballot box and labour representation', explained the LRC's 1902 report.[40]

Just as important for the organisation's hopes of permanency, however, was the decision made by the party's delegates at its Newcastle 1903 conference to establish a compulsory parliamentary fund of 4p a year per member for the financing of LRC candidates at the next general election and paying them an annual salary of £200 for maintenance if elected. Affiliated union payments increased as a result from 10s per thousand members to nearly £5. 'Hitherto Labour war chests have been left in the possession of the unions which filled them and were only used for candidates connected with those unions', wrote MacDonald. 'Now we are to have a trade union levy paid into a common fund and Labour candidates – not necessarily trade unionists – run from that fund. If the committee responsible for drafting the scheme has enough statesmanship in it to steer clear of the difficulties, the next election will be unique in the annals of Labour'.[41] Delegates also agreed the LRC should not identify itself with or promote the interests of any other political party and instead should develop its own policies. As Pete Curran reasoned they needed to create a party that 'could stand politically on its own legs'.[42] If this was not the case, he reasoned, why should they not find redemption through an existing political party? The LRC's independence from the TUC was made even clearer in the following year when the conference agreed unanimously to make payment by affiliates into the parliamentary fund for candidates a compulsory condition of membership. Henderson told the delegates that the LRC wanted to 'get away from mere trade representation' and instead favoured 'Labour representation with a proper sense of the term'[43] which meant that the LRC must be responsible for the raising of all its own finances.

The relationship of the LRC to the TUC was a issue of bewildering contention. The TUC Parliamentary Committee continued to pursue its own political lobbying role at Westminster. In 1904 the TUC general purposes committee sprung a surprise on that year's Congress by ruling resolutions submitted over the LRC's constitution did not fall within its jurisdiction and this was accepted by delegates. In the following year under the so-called Caxton Hall agreement the TUC agreed to endorse all LRC selected candidates at the next general election. An early proposal that a National Labour Institute should be formed to cover the LRC, the TUC and the GFTU came to nothing but a Joint Board was established between them in November 1905 in an attempt to try and ensure greater cohesion and unity on common policy. In practice, there was to remain a good deal of overlap between the various bodies that made up the Labour movement. However, Henderson insisted in 1904 that while the TUC ought to 'create and develop public opinion so far as the great industrial questions were concerned, it was for the Labour Party to seek to give legislative expression to the needs of Congress on the floor of the House of Commons'.[44] Four years later he told Congress that the party and the TUC would become as 'mother and daughter, almost equal in size and retain confidence in each other for the legislative and administrative work of the Labour Party would be to give effect to the resolutions of Congress'.[45] But this view was by no means acceptable to the TUC. A discussion by the TUC Parliamentary Committee in 1908 on where to draw a demarcation line of responsibility between the Labour Party and the TUC to prevent over-lapping failed to reach a conclusive answer. The TUC argued that the Parliamentary Committee enjoyed much greater freedom and influence over government departments unlike the party that was generally in opposition to every government. As David Shackleton told the 1908 Congress: 'Our feeling is that if there is not that distinctive trade union element we shall always be in the position of fighting the government of the day; and we are desirous of being able to continue our negotiations with any government, apart from the fight that goes on in the country between the three parties'.[46] It is noticeable that the TUC Parliamentary Committee was not really eclipsed as an effective force by the new party until after Shackleton's departure from political life in 1910 when he was appointed as special labour adviser to the radical Winston Churchill at the Home Office. But the tortuous discussion over the trade union role in the new party was not the most important issue that was to decide its future. Much more significant for

Labour's survival was the secret agreement signed at the time of the 1903 TUC Congress between MacDonald as LRC secretary and Herbert Gladstone, the Liberal Chief Whip. It was this pact – not publicly revealed until the opening of the Herbert Gladstone archives in the 1950s – that was to provide LRC-approved labour candidates with a clear run against sitting Unionists in up to 32 of the 50 parliamentary constituencies which they contested in the 1906 general election. The seats were mainly confined to areas of industrial south Lancashire where the Liberals enjoyed limited support among working class male voters, often susceptible in the past to the electoral appeal of Conservatism.

But there was no question of the LRC embracing Socialism. The attempt by Socialists to commit the new body to an ideological stance against the evils of capitalism was narrowly defeated at the 1903 conference. A motion from West Ham trades council called on the LRC to make its ultimate objective 'the overthrow' by the workers of 'the present competitive system of capitalism and the institution of a system of public ownership of all the means of production, distribution and exchange'.[47] However, this was voted down albeit by a narrow margin of 4,000 votes with 295,000 votes against and 291,000 in favour. Repeated attempts before 1914 to turn Labour into a Socialist party by adopting such a position on collective ownership failed, mainly because ILP leaders like Hardie and MacDonald feared correctly that such a move would alienate the trade unions. It might then in turn lead to their disaffiliation from the LRC in protest and push Labour onto the political fringe. As Bruce Glasier, the ILP romantic, told the 1907 party conference the ILP and the Fabians had joined 'fairly and frankly recognising that the trade unions as such were not pledged to socialism.' 'They did not want to pledge a single member before they had convictions', he added. 'The trade unions had been honourable and absolutely fair with them and they ought to be the same in return. When the trade unions became Socialists they would declare it themselves'.[48] Hardie threw his formidable support behind that argument. 'It would be a serious tactical error for the conference to attempt to impose socialism on an unprepared people. It was the business of those who were socialists to carry on their propaganda until the time came when the trade unions would themselves see that socialism was as essential to them as trade unionism'. Hardie may have been content to debate publicly the virtues of socialism but he did not support resolutions that threatened Labour's trade union membership by trying to make such an ideological commitment a condition for belonging to the party. Such attitudes from ILP leaders reflected the realities of the time. Pete Curran may have been a Socialist but he also recognised that any attempt to force his ideology onto the rest of the party would undermine its electoral credibility. As he explained to the 1907 conference: 'The trade unionists who make up the bulk of the movement and contribute to its funds will not pledge themselves to this class consciousness. They had got them out of the old rut of political neutrality into the position of political independence'. Any attempt to make such a commitment to Socialism a sine-qua-non of Labour membership would 'clear them out of the movement'. He accused those pressing such a demand of indulging in 'a back-handed attempt to create dissension'.

But while the ILP leaders were keen not to identify the LRC with Socialism for pragmatic reasons, many trade union activists also agreed with MacDonald and Hardie that the LRC needed to become much more than a purely trade union pressure group. The attempt by the Lib-Labs in the trade unions in 1903–1904 to limit the LRC's role failed. However, at the same time it was also recognised the organisation needed to utilise the energy of the Socialists without undermining the tactical need for an affinity of interest with a Liberal Party, whose own political fortunes began to revive after 1904. In a series of parliamentary by-election victories – most notably at Clitheroe in 1902 where David Shackleton, then general secretary of the Darwin Weavers' Association, was returned unopposed and in 1903 in Barnard Castle where Arthur Henderson of the Ironfounders union was elected in a three-cornered contest as well as Woolwich which returned Will Crooks of the Coopers union – the LRC demonstrated it was able to make effective political headway in favourable circumstances. But few even in the LRC predicted the parliamentary breakthrough achieved by the new body at the 1906 general election. Most of the 29 LRC-backed MPs elected to the Commons were national trade union leaders or officials and all were from the working class. It is true the overall result was much more a triumph for a resurgent Liberalism after eleven years in the political wilderness but the LRC's leaders believed their new organisation was rightly an important part of that achievement.[49] With their arrival at Westminster the Labour contingent agreed to transform the LRC into the Labour Party but this did not mean the new MPs were ready to embrace Socialism. This was evident from the closely fought contest for the chairmanship of the newly formed parliamentary party that revealed the underlying strength of the trade unions. Keir Hardie found a formidable opponent for that key position from David

Shackleton. The two men tied by 14 to 14 on a first ballot after a show of hands failed to settle the matter and it was only MacDonald's reluctant decision to vote for Hardie that carried the day for the ILP leader by one vote on a second ballot. Shackleton was an important figure in Labour's evolution. At the end of 1906 the TUC showed their appreciation of his political talents by throwing a dinner in his honour for his key role in the campaign to repeal the Taff Vale judgement through the passage of the Trade Disputes Act. In his speech to the assembled gathering Shackleton claimed victory stemmed from Labour MPs having 'acted honourably, fairly and peaceably in the interests of the class they represented'.[50] However, he was also effusive in his praise for the role played by leading Liberals in bringing the matter to a satisfactory conclusion. In his quiet, under-stated way Shackleton reflected that pragmatic and respectable strain in the new party that stemmed directly from its trade union roots and was a clear counterweight to the Socialists.

However, the euphoria of 1906 was soon to disappear inside the Labour Party. In the years leading up to the Great War the parliamentary party experienced considerable difficulties in maintaining its distinctive independence from the Liberals in the House of Commons while outside in the country it failed to extend its electoral reach beyond a limited core vote in specific localities. G D H Cole believed 'Labour's political fortunes in 1914 were on the ebb and the hopes aroused by the advent of the party in 1906 had suffered a sad reverse.'[51] The vast majority of trade union-sponsored Labour MPs continued to pin their faith in Liberalism. As Beatrice Webb noted in her diary in February 1914 on the annual party conference, MacDonald in 'his old-fashioned radicalism – in his friendliness to Lloyd George – represents the views and aspirations of the bulk of trade unionists'.[52] But Labour MPs owed their parliamentary seats to the willingness of local Liberal associations not to challenge them directly with their own candidates thereby splitting the non-Conservative vote. The two general elections held in 1910 exposed the Labour Party's difficulties in making any advance beyond their gains of four years earlier. In any contest against both a Liberal and Unionist candidate Labour did particularly badly. As Neil Blewett argued: 'Labour's incursions into new territory in January 1910 were almost uniformly disastrous'.[53] The election result 12 months later was no better, with 27 of the 42 Labour MPs being elected in straight fights with Conservatives in the absence of Liberal opposition, while three were unopposed. In addition, eleven were elected in two-member parliamentary seats in which only one Labour candidate was put forward alongside a Liberal.

However, Labour's disappointing performance in the two 1910 general elections was compensated for by the affiliation of the Miners' Federation to the party after its second rank and file ballot on the issue in 1908. Its conversion to Labour affiliation was of enormous significance for the party's long-term future. With an estimated membership of over 600,000 the Federation was by far the largest trade union in the country, accounting for as many as a quarter of all trade union members. Indeed, they were six times as large as the next biggest union. Moreover, before 1908 the Federation had always been the most energetic champion of Lib-Labism. Initially, the Federation's leadership was somewhat dismissive of the LRC's creation. Ben Pickard, the federation's president, advised other trades to follow the example of the miners and select parliamentary constituencies and suitable candidates to represent their sectional interests in parliament and doubted the wisdom of establishing a political body that sought to speak for the trade union movement as a whole. His views appeared to reflect those of the rank and file. In 1906 the Federation's members voted decisively against affiliation to the Labour Party not through a vote by an executive committee of activists or delegate conference as was the case in other unions but through the use of a democratic rank and file ballot. Clearly the federation's decision to affiliate to Labour two years later in 1908 was not due to sudden fears about the union's future security after the House of Lord's Taff Vale judgement. What therefore explains its crucial change of attitude?

Dr Roy Gregory in his history of the miners at that time described the conversion of the coalfields to the cause of Labour affiliation as being 'swifter and more far-reaching than anything before or since'.[54] However, the discussions within the Federation prior to the 1908 ballot do not suggest this involved a great matter of principle. It seems to have been much more a tactical question of timing. As Enoch Edwards, Federation president told the union's 1906 conference: 'All were agreed there can only be in this country one Labour party. It must be clear to everybody, we might not get it today or tomorrow but we have a high regard for the solidarity of that Federation than to injure for a moment its usefulness. The question like all others will ripen and solve itself if we only take of ourselves and do not destroy the hopefulness that is all around'.[55] In arguing the case in support of affiliation, Stephen Walsh, the Miners MP assured delegates at its 1907 conference that if it joined the Labour Party the Federation would bring a 'greater and better balance' to its counsels and did not 'necessarily mean' there would be any 'antagonism to any other party nor potentially mean socialism'.[56] However, the Federation's entry into the Labour Party did not automatically mean rank and file miners were willing to switch their political allegiances in accordance with the views of union activists. In parliamentary by-elections between 1910 and the outbreak of the Great War in August 1914 the Labour Party suffered clear losses in a number of predominantly mining constituencies – Hanley, Chesterfield and north-east Derbyshire.

Dr James Hinton even believes that by the end of the period 'the alliance of socialists with trade union leaders in the Labour Party may have been on the point of collapse.'[57] Such an observation may seem exaggerated but it was probable the progressive alliance would have lost the next general election, coming in 1915. The mood in the Labour Party at its spring 1914 annual conference was hardly one of optimism about its immediate future. As Arthur Henderson told the assembled delegates:

The present condition of affairs in the industrial and political Labour movement demands a closer unity than has hitherto been achieved. Repeated attempts in past years have proved fruitless and it is a remarkable that national organisations which are constantly using their efforts to reconcile and unify the interests of sectional trade unions are not more fully alive to the immense possibilities that lie in the path of a consolidated industrial and political movement such as the needs of Labour so insistently demand.[58]

Beatrice Webb held out little hope in the ability of Labour MPs to improve matters. In her diary for 12 February 1914 she wrote with a few exceptions – MacDonald, Hardie, Snowden and Henderson – they were a 'lot of ordinary workmen who neither know nor care about anything but the interests of their respective trade unions and a comfortable life for themselves'.[59] Her acidic private comments were undoubtedly laced with social snobbery but they reflected a genuine problem. Up until the Great War the Labour Party was not a credible challenge to the existing political establishment.

But the traumatic experience of the military conflict over the next four years transformed Labour's electoral fortunes. This happened for a variety of unrelated reasons. The unexpected downfall of Asquith and consequent split in the Liberal party after the creation of the Lloyd George coalition government in December 1916 undoubtedly strengthened Labour's political position.[60] But a concentration on high politics does not provide an adequate explanation of Labour's rise during the later period of the war. First and foremost, it was the dramatic growth in trade union strength and influence under the exigencies of war that enhanced the party's prospects. The formation of the War Emergency Workers National Committee in August 1914 – made up of TUC, GFTU and Labour Party representatives – provided an organisational unity for the movement in developing a successful strategy both to protect and promote organised labour's economic interests and develop a wider political agenda.[61] The trade unions – though mostly not jingoistic – were overwhelmingly supportive of the national war effort, reflecting the stoical and determined patriotic mood of their own rank and file and the wider working classes. The trade unions not only supported Britain's entry into the war despite the opposition of Labour Party leaders like MacDonald and Snowden but they also welcomed Labour's subsequent entry into Asquith's coalition government in April 1915. This came with Henderson's appointment as the party's representative in the cabinet, nominally as President of the Board of Education but in fact organised labour's voice in government. The trade unions also demonstrated their own self-restraint and loyalty in the cause of victory by signing the so-called Treasury agreement in the spring of 1915, which promised a suspension of restrictive employment practices such as demarcation between skills until the end of hostilities and acceptance of state control of the munitions industry. It is true divisions emerged in the Labour Movement over the introduction of military conscription, which pitted the demands of the state with a trade union belief in the defence of basic individual rights. But what was remarkable about the Home Front during the war was the way in which the trade unions and the Labour Party were able to stick together despite severe internal pressures and tensions. MacDonald's opposition to the war was complex and did not lead to his ostracism from his colleagues. Moreover, the trade union leaders never took their support for the war as far as a complete break with its critics inside the Labour movement.

In fact, the strategic position of the trade unions as industrial organisations was enormously strengthened by the demands of war placed upon them by the state. As Hugh Clegg pointed out 'the work of the parliamentary Labour party was reduced as a consequence of the new channels opened up for the unions to deal directly with government departments and members of the cabinet, especially after Henderson entered the government in May 1915 as the voice of labour'.[62] During the war years the trade union leaders were brought into the government's policy-making process in a way that had never happened or even been contemplated before. As a result they acquired experience, self-confidence and responsibility. Trade unions were no longer treated by politicians and civil servants as objects of barely-concealed contempt or condescension. The war also strengthened the position of those who believed in the virtues of collectivism. From its beginning, the War Emergency Workers' National Committee favoured increasing state intervention over economic and industrial policy to improve the war effort and ensure social cohesion. On controversial issues such as rent levels and the need for food controls to combat war profiteering and the introduction of military conscription, the committee articulated organised labour's views. It also did so after 1916 with its call for the introduction of a redistributive approach to equality of sacrifice with the 'conscription of riches', which demanded the better-off should make proportionate sacrifices for the achievement of victory.

It was the same committee, dominated by trade union representatives, that drew upon the services of the Fabian Sidney Webb, giving him a remit to draw up a credible Labour reconstruction plan for the post-war world. Despite their readiness to use his talents, Webb remained unimpressed by the trade union leaders he had to deal with. 'The trade union leaders are hopeless', he wrote to his wife Beatrice. 'I spent two hours [on his *Labour After The War* document] struggling with their complacent stupidity and apathy'.[63] But whatever his personal prejudices against them, Webb was trusted by union leaders and he was able to articulate their often inchoate aspirations, at least to their satisfaction.

At first sight, the impact of the war appeared to restrengthen the Labour Party as the representative voice of the organised working class. In 1918 it looked more than ever to be the party of the trade unions. They dominated its organisation both inside and outside parliament to a greater extent than they had done so during its first eighteen years. Max Beer in his study of British Socialism described the Labour Party of 1918 as being nothing more than 'an extended parliamentary committee of the TUC' and its annual conferences as 'little else than second and by no means improved editions of the trades union congresses'.[64] Such trade union domination of the party at the end of the war was understandable, not least because of the power and influence they had acquired in their relations with the state. Moreover, a dramatic upsurge had taken place in the number of workers belonging to trade unions. Admittedly the expansion in trade union membership really began in 1911 but it accelerated during the war. In 1914 trade union density was 24.7 per cent of the employed workforce; by 1918 it had climbed to 38 per cent.

But despite this remarkable development, most – though not all – trade union leaders wanted Labour to become more than simply a party of the growing trade unions. This was clear from the internal party discussions held during 1917 and early 1918 that led to the approval of the party's new constitution and the publication of its first general programme – *Labour and the New Social Order*. For the first time, Labour provided itself with a distinctive national identity in order to become a credible alternative to the mainstream political parties. Its internal reform was basically an attempt to transcend the intricacies of Labour's trade union connection without abandoning the relationship altogether. Trade union leaders as much as Labour's political leaders agreed the party needed as far as possible to expand its electoral appeal beyond the ranks of the organised working class if it wanted to grow into a serious political force in pursuit of parliamentary power. The impact of the Great War certainly widened the breadth of Labour's political appeal and the party's idealistic aspirations began to break out of the limitations imposed by a trade union driven agenda as it sought to take electoral advantage of the inner-party conflict which convulsed the Liberals after the downfall of Asquith. At the same time, Labour's leadership recognised the party's progress still depended both on reassuring and strengthening its relations with the trade unions. The genuine dilemma facing the party in 1918 was fully recognised by Henderson. He was worried that the trade unions might abandon Labour if the party leadership tried to push through a modernisation strategy that went too far in diminishing their influence inside the party's organisation. Henderson believed Labour needed to cultivate the trade unions and recognise they would continue to exercise a legitimate interest in its affairs, not merely because their funding and personnel remained so vital to the party's electoral activities. As he explained in January 1918 to a Fabian Society meeting: 'The Labour Party was not designed to be a national party. It was founded as the LRC for the purpose of increasing labour representation in Parliament on group lines. A national party cannot consist of a federation of organisations. It must be based on the electorate'.[65]

If the Labour Party was to make a successful national appeal among the new working class male voters enfranchised in 1918 it needed to run candidates in as many parliamentary constituencies as possible. On the other hand, Henderson accepted the Labour Party could not transform itself overnight into a nation-wide political organisation with a substantial individual mass membership. 'We must not swamp the old machinery because it is the only means of securing the money needed to be a political party', Henderson warned. 'We must therefore graft the new constituency system onto the old federation.'[66] As he explained in an article in the *Daily Herald*:

The big unions have their share of power in the Labour Party but no more than their share. It must not be forgotten that their support is absolutely necessary to the party's existence. They are the bankers of the movement. But we also recognise the party derives much of its influence from the men and women with energy, enthusiasm and ideas who compose the political side of the movement'.[67]

Henderson was, however, concerned that the larger trade unions might reject the proposed new party constitution and insist that Labour should become much more of a trade union dominated party under their direct control. Beatrice Webb wrote in her diary from the Nottingham conference on 21 January 1918 that the cotton unions under the influence of Tom Shaw, a pro-war Socialist, wanted 'the Labour Party to remain a close preserve of the officials of the great unions, acting as a select group in the House, making terms with either of the principal parties and securing places for leading trade union officials either as ministers or as permanent officials'.[68] Henderson was right to be anxious about such an outcome and he went out of his way to mollify trade union worries. In a powerfully argued speech to the January 1918 conference he told delegates he could 'imagine no greater mistake than to attempt to create a new organisation based solely on individual membership'. 'The idea might be worth aiming at ', he conceded but he 'hoped they would not lose their sense of proportion while aiming at the ideal'. Henderson warned such an outcome was 'practically impossible'. 'Imagine the executive saying to the trade unions upon whom the party had depended they had no further use for them'.[69] On the other hand, Labour needed to become a genuinely people's party and not remain a trade union party. It had therefore somehow to strike a balance between the needs of its affiliate trade unions and the demands of the new mass electorate. This was never going to be easy. In his book – The *Aims of Labour* – Henderson emphasised: 'We are casting the net wide because we realise that real political democracy cannot be organised on the basis of class interest.'[70] He favoured the creation of an individual mass membership because it was not possible to relate directly with the voters through associational representation. 'The weakness of the old constitution was that it placed the centre of gravity in the national society and not in the constituency organisation', he conceded. 'It did not enable the individual voter to get into touch with the party (except in one or two isolated cases like Woolwich or Barnard Castle) except through the trade union, the socialist society or the co-operative society'.[71] However, Henderson did not go so far as MacDonald who personally disliked the trade union dominance of the party's new national structure. In his book – *Socialism After the War* – MacDonald emphasised that: 'The political movement of Socialism ought to retain its connection with the trade union movement but ought not to allow itself to be swallowed up so that the Labour political movement is dominated by trade union officials who, solely by virtue of their position within their union, find themselves in places of political authority.'[72]

It was always a matter of degree. In fact, little real enthusiasm could be found among most union leaders for the creation of a new purely trade union-based party to replace Labour. The dominant trade union view was perhaps exemplified by William Purdy of the Shipwrights who stressed in his speech as chairman to the 1918 Labour conference that a national political party could not be 'built up on a purely industrial or craft basis'. 'The hope of the working classes of the future' lay in a 'strong industrial organisation backed up by a strong political party', he told delegates.[73] 'Our aim is not to serve sectional interests alone or to set class against class'. It is worth remembering that Purdy's remarks were made to a conference where 615 of the 852 delegates were from affiliated trade unions and they accounted for 2,497,000 out of the 2,726,000 votes represented there. His vision was of Labour as a national and not a purely class-based party. However, on the eve of the January 1918 conference Henderson feared the proposed constitution would be rejected by the trade unions because they believed the creation of constituency organisations based on individual membership would weaken their power and influence and strengthen the position of the ILP and what some saw as middle-class Socialist infiltration. As Beatrice Webb noted: 'Henderson wants to make the best of both worlds. By the new constitution he aims at combining the mass vote and financial support of the big batallions incorporated in the national unions with the initiative and enthusiasm of the brainworking individual members of the local Labour parties'.[74] In the event, the constitution was not thrown out but it was referred back for amendment by 1,337,000 votes to 1,318,000 against under pressure, mainly from the Miners' Federation and the Textile Workers. In the month interval before the conference reconvened. a number of changes were made to the draft constitution to appease trade union concerns. The number of trade union seats on the national executive were increased from 11 to 13 and it was made clear that the parliamentary party was to be involved in drawing up the election manifesto. As a result, the constitution was passed by a comfortable majority at the recall conference.

The vital connection between the party and the trade unions was in fact reinforced by Labour's explicit commitment to common ownership, enshrined in the new constitution. Clause IV was to gain later notoriety, viewed by many as an electoral liability as it was pickled into dogma and became wrongly synonymous with state-owned nationalisation. The offending words committed Labour

to secure for the producers by hand and by brain the full fruits of their industry and the most equitable distribution thereof that may be possible, upon the basis of the common ownership of the means of production and the best obtainable system of popular administration and control of each industry and service.[75]

Surprisingly in 1918, this aroused little controversy inside the party. Indeed, those carefully worded but vague sentences reflected what had become almost a trade union conventional wisdom. It was not just the experience of collectivism during wartime that had reassured union leaders about the sense of such a commitment. Revolutionary events in Russia during 1917 also helped to radicalise many of Labour's rank and file, although many trade union leaders regarded the commitment to common ownership as a moderate socialist alternative to extra-parliamentary action.

However, the party's more distinctive position in British politics was better articulated in 1918 by the publication of its first substantive programme – *Labour and The New Social Order*. This often eloquent and wide-ranging document, mainly written by Sidney Webb but with the approval of Henderson and MacDonald, was much more than a manifesto for the next general election. It evoked an ambitious and idealistic social vision, promising the creation of a better society through democratic parliamentary political action. Out of the horrors of military conflict, humanity would build a new society by peaceful means of cooperation. The elegiac tone of the opening paragraphs of the document evoke a deep sense of loss. But they were complemented by a sweeping and radical denunication of the economic system which was blamed for the catastrophe of the Great War.

What this war is consuming is not merely the security, the homes, the livelihood and the lives of millions of innocent families, and an enormous proportion of all the accumulated wealth of the world but also the very basis of the peculiar social order in which it has arisen. The individualist system of capitalist production, based on the private ownership and competitive administration of land and capital, which has in the past couple of centuries become the dominant form, with its reckless 'profiteering' and wage slavery; with its glorification of the unhampered struggle for the means of life and its hypocritical pretence of the 'survival of the fittest'; with the monstrous inequality of circumstances which it produces and the degradation and brutalisation, both moral and spiritual, resulting therefrom, may, we hope, indeed have received a death-blow. With it must go the political system and ideas in which it naturally found expression. We of the Labour Party, whether in opposition or in due course called upon to form an administration will certainly lend no hand to its revival. On the contrary, we shall do our utmost to see that it is buried with the millions whom it has done to death.[76]

The document went on to proclaim that the party's objective was to build 'a new social order based not on fighting but on fraternity – not on the competitive struggle for the means of bare life but on the deliberately planned co-operation in production and distribution for the benefit of all who participate by hand or by brain'. Labour's aim was to replace capitalism through the 'socialisation of industry so as to secure the elimination of every kind of inefficiency and waste' as well as 'the application both of more honest determination to produce the very best and of more science and intelligence to every branch of the nation's work'. Those laudable aspirations were to be expressed through the 'four pillars' of the House of Labour. These were 'the universal endorsement of a national minimum; the democratic control of industry; the revolution of national finance and the use of surplus wealth for the common good.

However, even with commitments to a new party organisation, constitution and utopian programme, Labour's future by no means looked secure. 'Unless the two old parties have completely lost their cunning, it is difficult to imagine that such a crazy piece of machinery as the existing Labour Party will play a big part in the reconstruction of the UK and the British Empire after the war', Beatrice Webb confessed in her diary on 20 March 1918.[77] The December 1918 general election result hardly looked like a triumph for the Labour Party. It won only 57 parliamentary seats, with 50 of them occupied by mainly pro-war candidates financially sponsored by the trade unions. Nearly half of the parliamentary party (25) were Miners' Federation-backed MPs. Labour's main leaders – MacDonald, Snowden and Henderson – were all defeated. Although Labour contested 361 parliamentary constituencies and polled 20.8 per cent of the total vote, hardly more than one in ten eligible votes were cast for Labour on a low turnout of 58.9 per cent. However, the self-destructive divisions of the Liberals, the refusal of Ireland's Sinn Fein to take its seats in the House of Commons and the vagaries of the electoral system all helped to make the Labour Party the largest grouping on the opposition benches.

The outlook for the party in the immediate aftermath of the Great War was not as bleak as the electoral statistics might suggest. Labour was now a national political party – thanks mainly to the self-confident and burgeoning trade unions. It is true in 1918 as Dr Gordon Philips has explained: 'Labour had not become the kind of popular crusade which, in different ways, Chartism and Liberalism had once been. It did not mobilise the working class in large demonstrations and enthusiastic audiences. It failed to establish an effective party press. It tried but failed to form the kind of cultural offshoots which had helped the growth of the German Social Democrats. Its principal raison d'etre in short became electoral success.'[78]

In fact, it was Labour's ubiquitous trade union connection that was more crucial than ever after the 1918 reforms. The party was able to claim that it provided the collective expression of working class consciousness through its organic relationship with trade unionism. Labour was pragmatic, undoctrinaire, flexible, and sentimental because of the strength of its trade union links. They helped to root the party in the realities of industrial politics. Inevitably as a result, Labour looked more like the party of producer interests. It is true that after 1918 the party was committed to the creation of a Socialist Commonwealth. It was this idealistic objective that provided the doctrinal unity required to keep the political and industrial wings of the Labour movement together. Labour's trade union connection was never under any serious threat after 1918. However, the party-trade union relationship always proved to be difficult, complex and occasionally tempestuous. In this sense, it resembled a marriage but one where divorce never looked a credible option. It is true that taking the twentieth century as a whole, the Labour Party did not enjoy great political success. Whether this was due in any part to its trade union connection is a debatable issue. Certainly Labour's links with the trade unions emphasised the sectional needs of the organised working class. But Labour could only succeed in becoming a people's party if it governed in the wider national interest as defined by its leaders. However, without the trade unions, Labour was nothing. They gave the party its financial support, their loyalty, their personnel, above all they provided a distinctive identity based on a defensive but also principled class solidarity. Between 1900 and 1918 Labour came of age – thanks to the trade unions. They saved it from political irrelevance. By eventually embracing democratic Socialism they gave the party an ideology. In 1918 this may have sounded utopian but it captured much of the popular national mood of the time. After the horrors of the Great War, the Labour Party claimed to identify and articulate the idealistic and radical spirit of hope and idealism among millions of people in bereavement who yearned for the creation of a world free from fear, exploitation and conflict. The eloquent language of *Labour and the New Social Order* appealed to many in the younger generation. As the radical American journalist Mary Heaton Vorse wrote in November 1918:

Wherever you went, whether in the London Workers' Committee or in the Federation of Women Workers, this talk of a new England was forever with you. You could not for a moment get out of earshot of this demand. Talk flowed up and down England. It swept into the homes of working people, through the shop committees and the workers' committees, from the Guild Socialists, to the trade unions and to the Women's Co-operative Guild, over to the study classes of the Welsh miners. There was everywhere a ferment, everywhere a demand for a new world.[79]

Labour's replacement of the Liberals as the main centre-left party in British politics was by no means inevitable, even after the 1918 general election. But the creation of the Labour Party should not be regarded as a strategic mistake committed by the trade unions that by dividing the country's progressive forces paved the way to the twentieth century domination of the Conservatives. The conversion of the trade unions to the establishment of a distinctive political party to represent the interests of the working classes in Parliament and their later endorsement of democratic Socialism as Labour's cause should not be seen as the result of a series of dogmatic lurches in the wrong direction but a tactical strategy of pragmatism, a prudent and limited response to external events. The Labour Party by 1918 was more than a trade union lobby group or an electoral machine. The emerging party was the product of a heightened trade union consciousness, made starker by the spectacular growth of organised labour between 1914 and 1918. Labour was both a pressure group representing a sectional interest but also growing into a credible party capable of forming a government for the nation as a whole. In 1918 under the influence of Henderson rather than MacDonald in alliance with senior trade union leaders, the party found itself very much in an uneasy transition between those two potentially conflicting purposes.

In fact, in the years ahead Labour was never really able easily to reconcile the underlying tensions between the movement's parliamentary and industrial purposes. While the trade unions created Labour and ensured it enjoyed a long life, they were also instrumental in limiting its ability to transform itself into an effective democratic Socialist party with a mass individual membership of the kind that MacDonald wanted. The intrinsic difficulties of holding the party-union connection together was to trouble Labour for the rest of the century. The seeds of incipient conflict over the function and purpose of structure were apparent in the party's birth in 1900. Bevin's crude imagery of bowel movements merely drew attention to the fundamental, underlying tensions that have always run through the Labour movement. The trade union link imposed severe limits to the electoral reach of the party and often paralysed its efforts to govern in the wider national interest. On the other hand, without that vital connection, Labour would never have transformed itself into a potential party of government. This was always to be the fundamental dilemma facing Labour leaders: how to nurture the party's core vote in the ranks of the organised working class but also how to win electoral support among the rest of the working class and above all among the burgeoning non-union white-collar salariat. From Ramsay MacDonald to Tony Blair, that particular problem has remained familiar. No amount of selective amnesia, however, can wipe away the dominant role played by the trade unions in making the party what it became during the twentieth century.

Appendix I: Trade Union Affliations to the LRC 1900–1905

1900: 66 trade unions attended the inaugural conference representing 568,177 members. They included:

Amalg Society of Engineers	85,000
Amalg Society of Railway Servants	54,000
Gas Workers and General Labourers	48,038
Boot and Shoe Operatives	31,000
Miners Federation (Lancs and Cheshire)	29,000
Spinners Operatives	18,151
Friendly Society of Ironfounders	17,887

Associated Shipwrights	15,583
Typographical Association	15,000
Dock Labourers	12,000

At the LRC's first annual conference held in Manchester on 1 February 1901 the Engineers were not present because they had decided not to affiliate. Nor were the Lancashire and Cheshire Miners. This meant the largest unions were the Railway Servants, the Gasworkers and General Labourers, followed by the Boot and Shoe Operatives. The picture looked no better in 1902 with 455,450 affiliate union members in 65 unions out of a total affiliated membership excluding trades councils of 469,311.

It was the 1903 Newcastle conference which witnessed the affiliated union breakthrough in the aftermath of the House of Lords's Taff Vale decision. The main unions which then affiliated to the LRC were:

Association of Lancashire Textile Workers	103,000
Amalgamated Society of Engineers	84,000
Amalgmated Society of Carpenters and Joiners	62,000
Boilermakers and Iron and Steel Ship Builders	49,000

Source: LRD Annual Conference Reports 1900-1903.

Appendix II: Main Trade Union Votes on Political Funds, 1914- May 5 1917

Trade Union	In Favour	Against
Miners' Federation	261,643	194,800
National Union of Railwaymen	102,270	34,953
Amalg Weavers' Association	98,158	75,893
Amalg Society of Engineers	20,586	12,740
National Union of General Workers	27,802	4,339
National Amalg Union of Labour	18,214	7,470
Boot and Shoe Operatives	6,085	1,935
Co-op Employees*	11,130	11,967
Railway Clerks' Association	5,496	1,340
Amalg Society of Carpenters and Joiners	13,336	11,738

* A second political fund ballot was held that reversed the first by 13,754 votes in favour and 5,854 against.

Source: Chief Registrar of Friendly Societies Annual Report for 1915, Part C Trade Unions HMSO 1917.

Notes

The main published sources on the party-trade union connection used in this essay are H Clegg, A Fox and A F Thompson, Volume One, Oxford 1964; H Clegg, Volume Two, Oxford 1985, of the *History of British Trade Unionism*; *A History of the Labour Party from 1914* by G D H Cole, London 1948; *Labour and Socialism: A History of the British Labour Movement 1867-1974* by J Hinton, Brighton 1983;R Price, *Labour In British Society*, London 1986; and A Thorpe, *A History of the British Labour Party*, Macmillan 1997. However, the most stimulating book on the subject still remains *Modern British Politics* by Samuel Beer, London 1965.

1 Labour Party Conference Report 1935, p 180.

2 No history of the Labour party-trade union connection from 1900 to 2000 exists. Nor is there any detailed account of the conversion of the trade unions to the cause of Labour affiliation. Lewis Minkin's impressive and important study, *The Contentious Alliance*, Edinburgh 1991 is concerned primarily with the period of the 1980s. Martin Harrison's *Trade Unions and The Labour Party*, London 1960 is excellent for its time but it is a contemporary rather than an historical account. R McKibbin, *The Evolution of The Labour Party 1910-1924*, Oxford 1974 is indispensable. However,there are *also Trade Unions in British Politics* edited by C Cook and B Pimlott, second edtion London 1991; H M Drucker, *Doctrine and Ethos in the Labour Party*, London 1979; H Pelling, *The Origins of the Labour Party*, Oxford 1965, pgs 192-215; F Bealey and H Pelling, *Labour and Politics 1900-1906*, London 1958; P P Poirier, *Advent of the Labour Party*, London 1958. C Wrigley's essay in *The First Labour Party 1906-1914* edited by K D Brown, London 1985.

3 E Wertheimer, Portrait of the Labour Party, London 1928 p 3.

4 B Webb, Diary, Volume Three 1905-1924, edited by N and J MacKenzie, London 1984, p 196.

5 The best recent account of trade union funding of the Labour party can be found in M Pinto-Duschinsky, British Political Finance 1830-1980, Washington 1981.

6 R McKibbin, *The Evolution of the Labour Party 1910-1924*, Oxford 1974 p 246.

7 M Harrison, *Trade Unions and The Labour Party since 1945*, London 1960 pgs 340-341.

8 R Miliband, *Parliamentary Socialism*, 1964 paperback edition; D Coates, *The Labour Party and The Struggle for Socialism*, Cambridge 1975; T Nairn, *The Nature of the Labour Party in Towards Socialism*, edited by P Anderson and R Blackburn London 1965; and J Saville, *The Labour Movement in Britain*, London 1988.

9 P Gould, *The Unfinished Revolution*, London 1998; R Liddle and P Mandelson, *The Blair Revolution*, London 1996; T Blair, 'Let Us Face The Future – 1945 Anniversary Lecture', Fabian Society 1999. The Prime Minister's erroneous knowledge of the birth of the party he leads could be seen in his 1999 party conference speech when he said:

'Born in separation from other progressive forces in British politics, out of the visceral need to represent the interests of an exploited workforce, our base, our appeal, our ideology was too narrow.'

10 L Minkin, *The Contentious Alliance*, Edinburgh 1991, p 11.

11 S Berger, *The British Labour Party and the German Social Democrats 1900-1931*, Oxford 1994 and J N Horne, *Labour At War; France and Britain 1914-1918*, Oxford 1991.

12 Wertheimer ibid. p 1.

13 D Marquand, *The Progressive Dilemma*, London 1991, p 17.

14 R Martin, *The TUC: Growth of a Pressure Group 1868-1976*, Oxford 1980 p18-97. Also see B Roberts, *The Trades Union Congress 1868-1921*, London 1958.

15 M Pugh, *The Tories and the People 1880-1935*, Oxford 1985 p 2.

16 F Williams, *Magnificent Journey*, London 1948.

17 H A Fisher, *The History of Europe*, London 1938 p 1.

18 F Reid, *Keir Hardie*, London 1975, p 37. Also see K Morgan, *Keir Hardie*, London 1975.

19 TUC Annual Report 1899 p 31.

20 H Clegg, A Fox, and A F Thompson, *A History of British Trade Unions Vol One 1889-1910*, Oxford 1964 p 285.

21 See J Saville, 'The Trade Disputes Act of 1906', *Historical Studies in Industrial Relations*, No 1 March 1996.

22 TUC Annual Report 1899 pgs 64-65.

23 LRC conference report 1900 p 12.

24 P Snowden, *An Autobiography*, London 1934, p 92.

25 G Barnes, *From Workshop to War Cabinet*, London 1920, p 59.

26 G Steadman-Jones, *Languages of Class*, Cambridge 1983, p 238.

27 R McKibbin, *Why Was There No Marxism in Britain?*, *Ideologies of Class: Social Relations in Britain 1880 -1950*, Oxford 1990, p 38.

28 D Marquand, *Ramsay MacDonald*, London 1974, p71.

29 R McKibbin, ibid., p 31.

30 P Thane, 'The Working Class and State Welfare', *Historical Journal*, 27, 4 1984 and also see J Harris, *Society and the State in Twentieth Century Britain*, The Cambridge Social History of Britain 1750-1950 Volume 3 edited by F M L Thompson, Cambridge 1990 and H Pelling, 'The Working Class and the Origins of the Welfare State' in his volume, *Popular Politics and Society in Late Victorian Britain*, London second edition 1979.

31 E Biagini and A Reid (eds) *Currents of Radicalism*, Cambridge 1991, p 5. Also see A W Humphrey. *A History of Labour Representation*, London, 1912.

32 Ibid. p 214-243.

33 National Liberal Federation annual meeting proceedings, October 1891, p.106.

34 A Reid, p 243.

35 J Belchem, *Popular Radicalism in Nineteenth Century Britain*, London 1996, pp 149-150.

36 A Fox, *History and Heritage: The Social Origins of the British Indus-trial Relations System*, London 1985, p 230.

37 The most impressive study of Labour's early grassroots can be found in D Tanner, *Political Change and the Labour Party 1900-1918*, Cambridge 1990. But also see M Savage, *The Dynamics of Working-Class Politics: The Labour Movement in Preston 1880-1940*, Cambridge 1987; J Lawrence, *Speaking for The People; Party, Language and Popular Politics in England 1867-1914*, Cambridge 1998; K Laybourn, 'The Bradford ILP and Trade Unionism c 1890 – 1914' in *The Centennial History of the Independent Labour Party*, Halifax 1992; K O Morgan, 'The New Liberalism and the Challenge of the Labour Party: The Welsh Experience 1885-1929', *Welsh History Review*, 6, 1973.

38 See in particular P Thompson, *Socialists, Liberals and Labour, The Struggle for London 1885-1914*, London 1967 and P F Clarke, *Lanca-shire and the New Liberalism*, Cambridge 1971.

39 P Snowden Vol One ibid. p 94.

40 LRC Annual Report 1902 p 12.

41 D Marquand p 75.

42 LRC Conference Report 1903 p 27.

43 LRC Conference report 1904 p 52.

44 TUC Congress Report 1904 p 91.

45 TUC Congress Report 1908 p 161.

46 Ibid. p 121.

47 LRC Conference Report 1903 p 36.

48 Labour Party Conference Report 1907 p 52.

49 A K Russell, *Liberal Landslide: The General Election of 1906*, Newton Abbot 1973.

50 TUC Congress Report 1906 p 17.

51 G D H Cole, *A History of The Labour Party Since 1914*, London, p 3.

52 B Webb, *Diaries*, p 170.

53 N Blewett, *The Peers, The Parties and the People*, London 1972 p 32.

54 R Gregory, *The Miners and British Politics 1906-1914*, Oxford 1968, p vii. Also see H Beynon and T Austin, *Masters and Servants: Class and Patronage in The Making of a Labour Organisation*, London 1994; R Page Arnot, *The Miners: A History of the Miners' Federation of Great Britain 1889-1910*, London 1949; A Taylor, '"Trailed on the tail of a comet": The Yorkshire Miners and the ILP 1885-1908' in *Centennial History of the Independent Labour Party*, Halifax 1992.

55 Miners Federation annual conference report 1906, p13.

56 Ibid report 1907 p 52.

57 J Hinton, *Labour and Socialism: A History of the British Labour Movement 1918-1979*, London 1988.

58 Labour Party Conference Report 1914 p 16.

59 B Webb, *Diary*, Volume 3, 1905-1924, London 1984, p 196.

60 J Turner, *British Politics and The Great War: Coalition and Conflict 1915-1918*, New Haven 1992.

61 R Harrison, 'The War Emergency Workers' National Committee 1914-1920' in A Briggs and J Saville (eds), *Essays in Labour History 1886-1923,* London 1971.

62 H Clegg, *A History of British Trade Unions since 1889*, Vol 11 1911-1933, Oxford, 1985 p 225.

63 B Webb, *Diaries 1912–1924*, ed M. Cole, London 1952, p.89.

64 M Beer, *A History of British Socialism*, London 1940 edition, p 395.

65 *Fabian News* February 1918 p 6.

66 Labour Party Conference Report 1918 p 34.

67 quoted in S Berger p 24.

68 B Webb, *Diary*, Vol 3 p 294.

69 Labour party annual conference report January 1918 p 99.

70 A Henderson, *The Aims of Labour*, London 1917, p 61.

71 Ibid p88.

72 R MacDonald, *Socialism After The War*, London 1917, p 40.

73 Labour party conference report June 1918 p 25.

74 B Webb, *Diary*, Vol 3 p 294.

75 J Winter, *Socialism and The Challenge of War*, London 1974 p 260.

76 *Labour and The New Social Order*, Labour Party 1918 p1-2.

77 B Webb, *Diary*, Vol 3 p 304.

78 G Philips, *The Rise of the Labour Party 1893-1931*, London 1992 p 33.

79 quoted by D T Rodgers, *Atlantic Crossings: Social Politics in a Progressive Age*, Cambridge Mass, 1998 p 294.

Labour in and out of Government, 1923–35

Keith Laybourn

I

On 6 December 1923 the Labour Party returned 191 MPs to Parliament, an electoral achievement which permitted it to form the first, minority, Labour Government towards the end of January 1924. Twelve years later, in November 1935, Labour had recovered its parliamentary position, winning 154 seats after the financial and political debacle of 1931 had seen the end of the second Labour government and reduced its parliamentary representation to 52 MPs. The years between 1923 and 1935 were thus momentous ones for the Labour Party, producing both political highs and lows and shaping Labour's future. Yet, regardless of the roller-coaster of Labour's political ride, the one thing that is certain about this period is that Labour had clearly emerged as the second party of British politics seeing off the challenge of the Liberal Party.

Four major debates have been associated with Labour's development in these years. The first focuses upon the issue of whether or not the Labour Party had replaced the Liberal Party as the progressive party of British politics. Although much of this debate has focused upon the years between 1900 and 1918, the final events of this changeover of political power occurred in the early 1920s. Yet was this changeover of political power the result of Labour's growing working-class support, following its capture of trade-union support, an accident of war resulting from the political split in the Liberal Party between David Lloyd George and H. H. Asquith, in 1916, or the product of the political events of 1918 to 1924?[1] Secondly, there is the related debate, much more directly relevant to this essay, that Labour's political power was fragile and could have been swept away by other political parties if they had only known.[2] This suggests that Labour's political rise was still in the balance in the 1920s. Thirdly, there is the question of why Ramsay MacDonald abandoned the second Labour Government in 1931 to form a National Government? In this case the myths of grand design and pre-arrangement have been challenged, and largely destroyed, by David Marquand's biography of MacDonald, published more than 20 years ago, which began a spate of research demythologising the events of 1931.[3] Fourthly, and less contentiously, there has been the examination of Labour's speedy recovery from the political disasters of 1931, which John Stevenson and Chris Cook suggest was based upon the fact that Labour's political power base had barely been damaged and that the almost two million voters who switched from Labour to the National Government candidates were won back by 1935. Nevertheless, Labour also became involved in planning its future socialist policies.[4]

In examining these debates this essay maintains that Labour had already asserted its political superiority over the Liberal Party by the end of the First World War, with its winning of the trade union vote which was ultimately to prove crucial in the securing of political power. Further, it is clear that Labour benefited from this working-class support to the extent that it did not have to rely on its increasingly effective organisation for political success. The Labour Party's political development was, of course, set back by the defection of Ramsay MacDonald to the newly-formed National Government in August 1931, but that was a political setback which did not blunt the party's political organisation and served to encourage the reassessment of Labour's policies. Despite its fluctuating political fortunes, the Labour Party had emerged as a party of government in this period and was still politically powerful in 1935.

The most dramatic development of the interwar years was the replacement of the Liberal Party by the Labour Party as the second party in British politics. In 1918 the Liberal Party, though divided, was still the second largest parliamentary party in Britain. However, in 1922, and again in 1923, it was dramatically overtaken by the Labour Party, although it did stage a minor recovery in 1929. In contrast, the Labour Party's growth appeared almost inexorable. Without examining the intense debates, and sub-debates in detail, touched upon in another essay, it is clear that there had been a considerable change in progressive politics in Britain. Whilst Henry Pelling, Ross McKibbin, and many others, have stressed that emergence of trade-union support for the Labour Party ensured that it captured the working-class vote, more recent contributors, such as P. F. Clarke, Michael Bentley and Duncan Tanner, have maintained either that Labour came through to replace the Liberal Party because of its split in 1916, or that even then there was still a prospect that the Liberal Party could maintain its control of the progressive vote.[5] In fact the debate has moved on with more recent contributors, such as Bill Lancaster, stressing the need to examine communities and regions in more detail.[6] For the inter-war years, however, the question is how far had the degeneration of the Liberal Party gone and how deep-rooted was Labour's trade-union and working-class support. In 1918 the Liberals, divided between the supporters of Asquith and the supporters of Lloyd George, returned more MPs than the burgeoning Labour Party. In this respect it is the second debate, promoted by the work of Christopher Howard that has more direct relevance to the years 1923 to 1935.

Howard has questioned the effectiveness of Labour's organisation in the 1920s: 'The image of a vibrant expanding new party was an illusion. Labour was fortunate that its opponents were deceived'.[7] Yet Labour leaders would not have agreed with this assessment, even though the title of Howard's article, 'Expectation born to death' is drawn from MacDonald's 1921 comment, that 'the Labour party knocks the heart out of me and expectations are like babies born to death'.[8]

Exactly why the Labour Party grew so rapidly in the decade after the First World War has been a matter of considerable debate between those advocating the long-term growth of working-class support for the Labour Party and those stressing the division of the Liberal Party during the First World War. Almost unwittingly, Howard accepts the first of these argument when he notes that 'Widespread electoral support bore little resemblance to restricted party membership, however, and disappointments were common'.[9] If Howard's assumption of the weakness of Labour's political organisation is correct, such a gap could only be explained by class voting which took no note of party organisation and activity. But the issue is confused by the fact that he also asserts that both the Liberals and Conservatives would have been more successful had they seen through the illusion and perceived the real weakness of the Labour Party's organisation. Howard does not appear to have made his mind up whether it was class politics or the illusion of a rapidly organising Labour Party that accounts for Labour's electoral successes in the 1920s. He does not even consider the difficulties the Liberal Party faced when its support was being squeezed both from the left and the right.

Nevertheless, the crux of his argument is that Labour's national and constituency activity failed to sustain much active support. The Labour leadership recognised this to be partly true, acknowledging that Labour failed to win the rural areas, that its national and local newspapers were always in a precarious financial position, and even the urban and industrial strongholds lacked faith when the Labour governments were unable to deliver the improved society it offered. Even in Aberavon, MacDonald's own constituency between 1922 and 1929, it was noted in 1926 that

with unemployment rising and short-time working now widespread, rank-and-file criticism of the leadership was growing. The future was no longer assured, and at the next election 'JRM will have to work very hard otherwise the seat is lost'.

Howard also adds that

MacDonald was no doubt relieved to leave all this behind and move to the safer and cheaper seat of Seaham Harbour in 1928. MacDonald may well have said that Aberavon finally asked too much of him, but it might be as well to ask whether the leadership expected too much of the local parties. Despite the heady success of the immediate post-war period, ... and the nostalgic testimony of many who battled through the period, the picture gained from local party records does not suggest that this was the golden age of working-class politics.[10]

A rather different picture is provided by Ross McKibbin and Bernard Barker,[11] who both argue that the Labour Party was making a determined effort to improve both its national and local organisation and that, by and large, succeeded in so doing. But which view is correct? To what extent was the Labour Party well organised and effective throughout the 1920s?

It is clear that the Labour Party made great advances after the First World War. The National Executive Committee reorganised its activities, appointing four standing sub-committees organisation and elections; policy and programme; literature, research and publicity, and finance and general purposes. Egerton Wake became the party's national agent and vigorously pursued the move to give the movement direction. A star speaker system was introduced, permitting leading party figures to tour the country, and most constituencies had a local Labour Party, compared with about a quarter at the beginning the First World War. Local newspapers were produced to supplement the *Daily Herald*. There were deficiencies but these developments were a vast improvement on what had previously existed.

The impact of this improved organisation is to be seen in the growth of the individual membership which the Labour Party's 1918 Constitution permitted. The Huddersfield Labour Party had 500 to 600 individual members in the late 1920s, the six Leeds constituency parties had between 1,500 and 2,000 members from most of the 1920s and the indications are that the Bradford Labour Party had far in excess of the Leeds figure.[12] Yet it was the ubiquitous trade union movement which provided ten or more members to every local Labour Party individual member.

By 1918 the Labour Party was shaped, even if it was not totally dominated, by the trade unions. In 1900 the Labour Representation Committee Executive included seven trade unionists and five socialists. In 1902 it had nine trade unionists, one representative of the trades councils and three socialists (two ILP and one Fabian). The Labour Party Constitution of 1918 allowed for the election of 13 of the 23 members of the new National Executive Committee and allowed trade unions to vote in the election of the rest. Throughout the 1920s, and particularly after 1926, the Joint Council of Labour, which brought together the Parliamentary Labour Party (PLP), the TUC and the Labour Party, became increasingly important in making the decisions for the 'constitutional' Labour movement. In 1934 it was renamed the National Council of Labour and the TUC was the most important force on this body, in the shape of Ernest Bevin (from 1932) and Walter Citrine.

If the Labour Party had become the party of the working class it had done so through the agency of the trade union movement and the price it had to pay was the restriction of its policies to a pale version of Clause Four, introduced gradually and selectively. Using the large block vote of the Transport and General Workers, and other unions, Ernest Bevin was able to dominate the Labour Party annual conferences throughout the 1930s on issues such as the threat of fascism. Indeed, Bevin remarked that the Labour Party 'grew out of the bowels of the TUC'.[13] This is not to say that the Labour Party did not have the opportunity to do something to extend its economic and social policy, for this often operated in a different sphere from trade unionism, although Bevin and the TUC Economic Planning Committee (1932) were part of the process.[14]

The relationship between the Labour Party and the trade unions was complex and not without major difficulties. Lewis Minkin, in his monumental work, has suggested that whilst the Labour Party and the trade unions are often seen as working closely together they often developed distinct policies and strategies, and operated in different spheres, which sometimes led to a contentious relationship. He argues that the metaphor that the Labour Party was the 'offspring of the TUC' is misleading because there has often been a disparity in the policies adopted by both organisations.[15] Nevertheless, he maintains that the two bodies built up a common set of attitudes and rules between 1900 and 1948 – based upon loyalty and anti-communism – and that these operated effectively in a type of 'golden age' between 1948 and 1959 before becoming subject to increased strains and changes in recent times. For the inter-war years, then, there were difficulties as the ground rules were being built up and it is not surprising that there should some sharp disagreements in their relationships. The Labour Party's 1918 Constitution provided the potential for conflict between the broad socialist goals and the narrower base of trade union objectives. The use of the Emergency Powers Act by the 1924 Labour Government to deal with industrial disputes also created tensions with the trade unions. The reluctance of the Labour Government of 1929–31 to abolish the Trades Dispute and Trade Union Act of 1927, which made sympathetic strike action illegal and restricted the flow of trade union funds to the Labour Party, provided yet another source of conflict. The fact is that the Labour Government was dependent upon Liberal Party support to continue in office and the Liberals were opposed to the withdrawal of the 1927 Act. The deflationary policies of the Labour governments of 1924 and 1929-1931, their failure to tackle the issue of unemployment and willingness to reduce unemployment benefits in 1931 also added to the strains of this relationship.

The different spheres of influence and responsibilities between the Labour Party and the trade unions have been recognised by many contemporaries. W. J. Brown, of the Civil Service Clerical Association, reflecting upon the 1924 Labour Government, expressed the view that there was a general assumption that the Labour Cabinet would apply the policy of the TUC in industrial matters but that the reality was that

there would be a permanent difference in point of view between Government on the one hand and the Trade Union on the other: and that difference in point of view did not arise from any wickedness on the part of the political side, or on the part of the industrial side, but arose from the fact that the Trade Unions had different functions to follow than the functions of Government.[16]

Walter Citrine, General Secretary of the TUC, wrote that the trade unions did not dominate the Labour Party and suggested that the Labour Party and the trade unions 'work together and consult from time to time when any matter of policy is in question'.[17] Trade union leaders did not seem to expect too much of the Labour Party in government and in June 1931 the Transport and General Workers' Union admitted that 'the results of the work of Government can rarely be seen in its own lifetime'.[18]

The closeness of the trade unions and the Labour party clearly challenges the views of Howard, as do other factors. Most obviously the tendency of Liberal and Conservative parties to form 'anti-socialist' or 'citizens' alliances at local elections is a reflection of the fact that Labour was making a serious challenge to these parties at the local level.[19] By 1923, the message was clear; Labour was the party of the working class. It had built upon its pre-war and wartime roots and was not the fragile party that Howard suggests.

II

The organisational development of the Labour Party was also improved by the successful creation of a women's section to the Labour Party, although this did bring its own very specific problems. Like all political parties, Labour had to address women's issues when the 1918 Franchise Act had given the vote to all women over the age of 30, and especially once the age limit was reduced to 21 in 1928. It took its first step when the Women's Labour League, formed in 1906, which fused with the Labour Party in 1918, formed the basis of the women's section of the Labour Party and by 1922 more than 100,000 women had joined the 650 women's sections of local Labour parties. There were also about 35,000 women in the Women's Co-operative Guild which acted with the Labour Party although it was an independent body.[20] These developments raised serious gender issues since the presence of these women's organisations began to challenge the Labour Party's commitment to the 'equality of the sexes', for women now helped to define the political agenda. Marion Phillips, of the Women's Labour League, who became the Chief Women's Officer within the Labour Party, emphasised the need for the women's section to integrate with Labour Party politics whereas Margaret Llewellyn Davies, of the Women's Co-operative Guild, suggested that the Labour Party was offering the women very little. As a consequence the Labour Party was faced with some division and debate over the needs for specific policies for women in the 1920s.

The most obvious points of conflict were to be associated with the female demands for both birth control and family allowances. On the issue of birth control, there were many women within the Labour Party who saw it as the way to release themselves from a cycle of poverty and from constant ill health. The issue emerged strongly in May 1924 when a women's deputation went to John Wheatley, Minister of Health in the first Labour Government, asking him to lift the ban that made it illegal for local health

authorities to distribute birth control information.[21] Marion
Phillips, however, felt that birth control should not become a
political issue to divide Labour and there was the fear that the
Catholic members within the Labour Party would be upset by the
dissemination of information on birth control.[22] This was a view
with which the National Executive Committee of the Labour
Party agreed and it reported at the Labour Party's Liverpool
conference, 1925

That the subject of birth control is in its nature not one which should be
made a political party issue, but should remain another upon which
members of the party should be free to hold and promote their individual
convictions.[23]

Similar debates developed in connection with the demand for
family allowances, which many trade union leaders, such as
Ernest Bevin, objected to. Marion Phillips argued that such a
provision would 'increase the irresponsibility of fatherhood' and
opposed the supportive fulsome report of the Women's Co-
operative Guild.[24]

There was little evidence throughout the 1920s that the
Labour Party had taken women's issues on board in the
gradualist socialist programmes it offered. There was even less
evidence of such commitments in the 1930s. With the collapse of
the second Labour government Labour's main purpose was the
maintenance of unity in order to recover political power and
gender issues became less important that they had been in the
1920s. In the final analysis the Labour Party found itself
incapable of fully integrating gender issues within its social
democratic structure once planning, the survival of the party, and
the rejection of communist attempts to affiliate with the party
became more important than women's issues. Nevertheless, the
women's section became an important section of the party and its
organisational growth gave the Labour Party resilience.

III

The results of Labour's increasing electoral support and
organisational improvements came with the formation of the first
Labour government on 22 January 1924. This minority
government, led by James Ramsay MacDonald, was dependent
upon Liberal support. MacDonald's government only survived
because the Liberal Party felt that it was too risky, in its own
interests, to bring it down. Indeed the Liberal Party saved it by
voting against a motion to reduce the Minister of Labour's salary
in May 1924. Nevertheless, MacDonald was not prepared to come
to terms with the Liberal Party. Indeed he informed a packed

House of Commons in his first speech as Prime Minister, in February 1924, that 'Coalitions are detestable, are dishonest'. Although his government was in a minority, it would 'bring before this House proposal to deal with great national and international problems, and we are not afraid of what fate we may meet in the process'.[25]

The first Labour administration achieved very little, other than the introduction of John Wheatley's Housing Act which encouraged local authorities to build houses for rent to the working classes. Indeed, it alienated both trade unionists, over the use of the Emergency Powers Act against strikes and socialists with regard to the moderation of the rest of its policies. Its attempt to reveal itself as a responsible government combined with its dependence upon Liberal support, and its gradual approach meant that it was almost unable to further socialism either in or outside Britain. MacDonald's administration had nine members who were or had been associated with the Union of Democratic Control (UDC) but it did nothing to change the Treaty of Versailles, which the UDC saw as the cause of political instability in Europe, and supported the Dawes Plan, an American scheme for helping the Germans to pay their reparations. Its only significant international achievements was that it established diplomatic relations with Soviet Russia and offered the prospect of trade with Russia as a part solution to unemployment in Britain.

The first Labour government lasted almost ten months before being ousted in the furore over the Campbell case, when J. R. Campbell, assistant editor of the *Workers' Weekly*, was arrested and charged with incitement to mutiny by the Attorney General and then released because he was only the sub-editor of the paper. The resulting debate and vote of no confidence in the House of Commons led to MacDonald's resignation and the government's defeat in an election which saw the publication of the infamous and potentially damaging Zinoviev Letter, which suggested that the Communist Party was using the Labour Party to achieve its own revolutionary objectives.

Out of office for four and a half years, the Labour Party rather drifted under MacDonald's leadership. There were certainly tensions between the leading figures and various suggestions that J. R. Clynes, the vice-chairman of the Parliamentary Labour Party, or Philip Snowden should take over. There was also some frustration at MacDonald's comparative inaction during the General Strike of 1926, although the chairman and the Chief Whip of the Parliamentary Labour Party were invited to all the

General Council meetings with the Miners' Executive in order to co-ordinate industrial and parliamentary activity.[26] This increasing frustration with MacDonald was exhibited in a letter from Snowden attached to the MacDonald diaries. Having suggested that some tensions between them should be ended he wrote that:

you must excuse me from writing quite so plainly. I am expressing the feeling of all my colleagues who have talked to me on the subject. We are feeling that somehow – it is difficult to explain – we cannot get inside you. You seem to be protected by some impenetrable barrier. I called it aloofness in my last letter. It was not so in the old days of the NAC [of the ILP].[27]

IV

The second Labour government, also a minority one, offered little more to the furtherance of British socialism than the first. It came into power in May 1929 at a time when the economy was improving and unemployment falling but was set back by the Wall Street Crash of November 1929 and the disastrous economic impact it had upon world trade. Faced with rising unemployment, increasing expenditure and financial imbalances, MacDonald's government was forced to accept the recommendations of the all-party Sir George May Committee examination of the national finances in 1931 of the need to introduce massive public expenditure cuts. It was the government's attempt to balance the budget that raised the prospect of the ten (initially 20) per cent cut in unemployment benefits, which divided the Labour Cabinet on the 23 and 24 August 1931, and paved the way for the formation of MacDonald's' National Government. The very fact that the Labour Cabinet discussed a cut in unemployment benefit questioned Labour's commitment to a decent standard of living for those who could not be guaranteed work, something the Labour Party had stressed since the 'Right to Work' campaign of 1908. It also demonstrated that the second Labour Government and Philip Snowden, its Chancellor of the Exchequer, in particular, were slaves to the Treasury dogma of balancing the budget.

The collapse of the second Labour government has, of course, produced its own debates. From the 1930s it was typical to argue that MacDonald had betrayed the second Labour government and carried out his 'long-thought-out plan'. L. MacNeill Weir captured the spirit of accusations levelled against MacDonald, maintaining that he was never a socialist, was an opportunist, that he schemed to ditch the Labour government and that he was guilty of betrayal. Indeed, Weir wrote that

The members of the Labour Cabinet naturally assumed on that Saturday night, 23 August (1931) that Mr. Baldwin would be asked to form a government. But it is significant that MacDonald had something quite different in view. Without a word of consultation with his Cabinet colleagues, without even informing them of his intention to set up a National Government with himself as Prime Minister he proceeded to carry out his long-thought-out plan.[28]

This view has been challenged by David Marquand and other writers. Marquand insists that there is little to suggest that MacDonald schemed to ditch the second Labour government and that MacDonald's only fault is that he held on to his nineteenth-century principles too long. MacDonald's almost religious acceptance that the gold standard and free trade, plus his belief in the primacy of the state over party, ensured that he lacked the 'ability and willingness to jettison cherished assumptions in the face of changing realities'.[29]

The evidence suggests that Marquand is correct. MacDonald was as good a socialist as any of the early Labour leaders, writing for the Socialist Library, and was committed to the gradual extension of state powers over industry. He was an opportunist, but gave up his chairmanship of the Parliamentary Labour Party in 1914 in order to oppose the First World War. There is no specific evidence to suggest that MacDonald schemed to bring about the end of the second Labour Government, only innuendo and speculation. Indeed, Malcolm MacDonald, Ramsay's son, records that his father had telephoned him at lunchtime on 22 August to the effect that 'He feels pretty certain that he will resign either tonight or tomorrow, and there is compelling evidence that he was contemplating a political career in Labour's back benches.'[30] Partial as this source is, it is also obvious that, given the economic circumstances, it would have been difficult for MacDonald to have arranged the type of political scheming contemplated by his critics.[31] It was the need to cut expenditure in the drive to balance the budget and secure financial loans from abroad to keep Britain on a gold standard and within the free trade system, that forced the Cabinet to agree, by 11 to nine votes, to reduce unemployment benefits by 10 per cent. It was clear that the Cabinet was fairly evenly divided and this seems to have prompted MacDonald to take the resignations of his Cabinet to King George V. It was only a confluence of other events – including the support of the opposition leaders for a national

Government headed by MacDonald and the appeal of the King – that led MacDonald to form the National Government.

MacDonald's action led to the condemnation of the Labour Party and the trade unions. Indeed, when the financial crisis did occur the issue was not the future of socialism but one of a conflict between the second Labour government, committed to operating the gold standard and free trade and thus faced with reducing government expenditure and unemployment benefits, and a TUC which felt that any such action would be a betrayal of the interests of the working classes. This was evident on 20 August 1931 when a deputation from the General Council of the TUC, along with a deputation from the Labour Party Executive, met with members of the Labour Cabinet, including Snowden and MacDonald. There was certainly no meeting of minds between MacDonald and Snowden, on the one hand, and Bevin, Citrine, Hayday and Pugh, on the other. Citrine denied that the economic situation was desperate because 'There are enormous resources in this country',[32] but it was clear that neither the Labour Cabinet nor the TUC were going to come to an accommodation. The Labour Cabinet split soon afterwards and paved the way for the formation of a National Government. Labour was even less enamoured of MacDonald when his National Government abandoned the gold standard in September 1931, an action which had it been taken in August might have reduced the need for some expenditure cuts and allowed the second Labour government to continue.

The general election of October 1931 saw the Labour Party reduced to 52 MPs from the 289 won in 1929 and the National Government secured 556 seats, a parliamentary majority of 497. Why this occurred and what it meant for Labour Party politics has been open to question. It would appear that Labour lost just under two million votes, down from about 8.4 million in 1929 to 6.65 million in 1931. This might well have been the result of the financial events surrounding the collapse of the Labour government impacting upon the election results, although John Stevenson and Chris Cook suggest that the result had more to do with Labour frustrating its supporters and performing badly in parliamentary by-elections in 1930 and 1931. But above all they argue 'The simple reason why Labour had lost four out of five seats it was defending was that its opponents were united.'[33] Indeed, there were 449 straight fights against Labour in 1931 compared with only 99 in 1929.

Labour reacted well to this defeat. Its organisation remained strong, and local parties recovered and in November 1932 made good some of the municipal losses incurred in November 1931. It also began to revitalise the party with a 'Million New Member Campaign' in 1932, which increased individual membership by 100,000 within a year. In January 1933 Labour set up a Central By-Election Insurance Fund to help needy constituencies put forward candidates. But perhaps more important than such improvements in organisation was the decision to develop and re-examine its socialist policies.

V

Until 1931 it seemed that the state was to be the Labour Party's vehicle for achieving socialism and the Webbs embroidered this with the idea of a 'Social Parliament' which would administer the major industries and services through many tiers of committees. Those who challenged this commitment to statist socialism were ignored. Indeed, at the 1920 Labour Party conference resolutions were carried demanding the more effective publicising of the Labour Party's plans for the nationalisation of land, gas, water, electricity and banking and for the creation of workers' committees, district councils and national boards to this effect.[34] The 1922 Labour Party conference placed a commitment to the nationalisation of land, mines and 'other essential public services' in the party's election programme.[35] The Independent Labour Party attempted to drive Labour toward more radical proposals in its *Socialism in Our Time* campaign of 1926 and 1927 but the party would not be pushed. Instead it responded with its own programme, *Labour and the Nation* (1928), which accepted some of the demands of *Socialism in Our Time*, including public ownership, although not of the Bank of England and the joint stock banks. Instead it adopted a 'step by step' approach and stated that the Labour Party would 'without haste, but without rest, with careful preparation, with the use of the best technical knowledge and managerial skills, and with due compensation to the persons affected' socialise the basic industries. Of the ideology of the party it spoke of 'tentative doctrineless socialism' brought about 'by experimental methods, without violence or disturbances'.[36] *Labour and the Nation* was accepted by the party conference in 1928.[37]

By 1931, then, the Labour Party had identified a number of industries it wished to nationalise, with due compensation and in the fullness of time. Yet the events of 1931 led to the questioning of the 'inevitability of gradualness' and to the realisation that Labour lacked a policy on many important domestic issues. At that juncture it appeared that there had to be a more detailed commitment to public ownership and that some alternative socialist strategy had to be developed in the place of the discredited policies of Labour's departed leaders. Indeed, Labour's 1931 general election manifesto, *Labour's Call to Action: The Nation's Opportunity*, revealed a modest leftward drift, blaming the crisis on capitalist breakdown and advocating public ownership and planning as the solution to Britain's economic problems.

R. H. Tawney and Stafford Cripps also began to consider the need for a more speedy transition to socialism on the grounds that slow change was unlikely to undermine the capitalist base from which it would emerge.[38] Yet the problem faced was that of reconciling their schemes with the demands of a far more cautious trade union movement dominated by Bevin, who particular, wanted a programme of practical policies which could easily be applied to reduce the high level of unemployment. Indeed, Bevin had produced his *My Plan for 2,000,000 Workless* in 1932 which advocated a variety of schemes including the reduction of retirement age, the raising of the school leaving age and the creation of employment through major building schemes. His focus was extremely narrow and social rather than socialist and one is reminded of Minkin's suggestion that there were, in the 1920s, some obvious differences between the trade union leaders and the Labour Party. The trade unions stressed the democratic right to decide about wages and conditions of employment whilst the Labour Party claimed and operated a system of parliamentary privilege.[39] This may explain why the trade union-domination of the Labour Party in the 1930s did not inhibit the social planning that was evident within intellectual socialist groups. In the end the moderate and right-wing socialists in the Labour Party prevailed and developed their policies under the guise of planning.

Labour's notions of social planning were conducted mainly by the New Fabian Research Bureau (1931), the TUC Economic Committee (1932) and a new policy committee of the NEC, with four sub-committees created for the purpose in 1931. The most important of these NEC sub-committees was Finance and Trade, chaired by Hugh Dalton, who virtually wrote Labour's economic and financial policy in the 1930s. None the less, few of these policies would have had influence without the support of the National Council of Labour and here the support of Ernest Bevin and Walter Citrine, who dominated this body, was vital. Thus, there was never likely to be a commitment to full-scale re-organisation since that would require a complete change in the relations between the state and the economy which Bevin was not prepared to contemplate in the short term.

A commitment to nationalising the joint stock banks was agreed at the Labour Party conference of 1932, and promoted by the Labour left.[40] Yet such radicalism was not to last as, over the next few years, Labour restricted itself to a policy of nationalising the Bank of England and became increasingly attracted to the policies of J. M. Keynes, who suggested that economic policies could achieve full employment through indirect controls.

Hugh Dalton was the powerhouse behind Labour's new moderate, but planned, socialist policies. Essentially Fabian in outlook, he dismissed the various alternatives put forward and argued that 'Labour needed better policies and better people'.[41] At first, he joined Cole's New Fabian Research Bureau (NFRB) as a member of its directing body, visiting the Soviet Union with a group of New Fabians in the summer of 1932. He returned convinced that the First and Second Five Year Plans of the Soviet Union indicated that planning could work and that Britain required something similar, though not under a communist regime. From then onwards, planning socialism became Dalton's main objective. He wanted to redistribute the resources of Britain in order to tackle the horrendous problem of unemployment and he took this commitment into the NEC's eight-man Policy Committee where he emerged as chairman of the Finance and Trade sub-committee. Here he developed the idea that planning was to be free from market pressures, have the ability to overcome official resistance and should call upon experts. According to his Labour Party document *Socialism and the Condition of the People* (1933), there ought to be 'a well-planned rush'.[42] When this was debated at the 1933 conference it was accepted that there was a need to nationalise joint-stock banks, the steel industry and other vital industries. Nevertheless, there was a mixed economy element in Dalton's proposals.

Dalton's influence was further evident in Labour's new policy document, *For Socialism and Peace,* accepted by the party conference in 1934, which made specific commitments to planning and nationalisation whilst not specifying which industries would be subject to public ownership. This was a very contentious document which was criticised for being rather general, but it had gained widespread support at the 1934 conference for it was 'based on a concordat between political moderates and their trade union counterparts'.[43]

The policies outlined in *For Socialism and Peace* were more closely examined by Dalton in his *Practical Socialism for Britain*

(1935), which emphasised that planning under capitalism was possible and maintained that it could speed up the transition to socialism. It played down the importance of Keynesian expansionism but acknowledged the importance of a National Investment Board to control and direct the level of long-term investment. The emphasis was, however, to be placed upon the nationalisation of basic industries.[44]

These schemes were played down further during the November 1935 general election but shortly afterwards the TUC presented specific plans for the socialisation of the cotton industry to the 1935 Labour Party conference. These and other proposals were eventually distilled into *Labour's Immediate Programme*, adopted at the party conference in 1937, which removed the commitment to nationalise joint stock banks but committed Labour to a limited programme of nationalisation. Thus over almost 20 years the Labour Party had moved from an unspecified commitment to public ownership to offering a modest programme of nationalisation and state intervention which was to provide a blueprint for the post-war Attlee governments.

VI

Between 1923 and 1935 the Labour Party had clearly established its political supremacy in British progressive politics, turning its working class, women's, and trade-union vote into parliamentary success. It had become a party of government that withstood the defection of Ramsay MacDonald, one of its formative leaders, who left the party apparently driven on by his sense of national duty rather than some compulsion to ditch and betray Labour. In the 1930s the party sedulously developed both its statist view of socialism and its organisation. At the general election of 1935 it recovered almost all the votes it had lost in 1931. Indeed, at the 1935 party conference Jennie Adamson, only the second women to act as Chairman, reflected that 'Labour now constitutes a formidable opposition in the House of Commons.'[45] Indeed, if the events of 1931 were a baptism of fire for the Labour Party, it clearly rose like a phoenix from the ashes because of its effective organisational structure and the strong sense of class consciousness which led its working-class supporters to vote for it. During the 1920s and 1930s the Labour Party truly became the party of the working class and progressive interests in British politics, and firmly established itself as the second party of government.

Notes

1 Keith Laybourn, 'The Rise of the Labour Party and the Decline of Liberalism: The State of the Debate', *History*, Vol. 80 No 259 June 1995 pp. 207–26.

2 Christopher Howard, 'Expectations born to death: local Labour Party expansion in the 1920s', in J. Winter, ed., *The Working Class in Modern British History: Essays in Honour of Henry Pelling*, Cambridge, Cambridge University Press 1983.

3 David Marquand, *Ramsay MacDonald*, London, Jonathan Cape 1977.

4 John Stevenson and Chris Cook, *The Slump*, London, Jonathan Cape 1977, pp. 114–26, 245–64.

5 Henry Pelling, *The Origins of the Labour Party*, London, Macmillan 1954; Ross McKibbin, *The Evolution of the Labour Party 1910–1924* : Oxford, Oxford University Press 1974; P. F. Clarke, *Lancashire and the New Liberalism*, Cambridge, Cambridge University Press 1971; M. Bentley, *The Climax of Liberal Politics: British Liberalism in Theory and Practice 1868–1918*, London, Edward Arnold 1987; D. Tanner, *Political Change and the Labour Party*, Cambridge, Cambridge University Press 1991.

6 Bill Lancaster, *Radicalism, Co-operation and Socialism: Leicester working-class politics 1860–1906*, Leicester: Leicester University Press 1987.

7 Howard, 'Expectations born to death', p. 81.

8 *Ibid.,* p. 65.

9 *Ibid.,* p. 78.

10 *Ibid.,* p. 74.

11 McKibbin, *Evolution of the Labour Party*; Bernard Barker, 'Anatomy of Reform: The Social and Political Leadership of the Labour Leadership of Yorkshire', *International Review of Social History*, Vol 18 1973 pp. 1–27.

12 Drawn from the minutes of the central Labour parties of Bradford, Halifax and Leeds for the 1920s. Also see Jack Reynolds and Keith Laybourn, *Labour Heartland: A History of the Labour Party in West Yorkshire during the Inter War Years 1918–1939*, Bradford: Bradford University Press 1987, p. 42.

13 *Labour Party Conference Report, 1935*, London, Labour Party 1935, p. 179.

14 A. Booth, *British Economic Policy 1931–1949: Was there a Keynesian Revolution*, London, Harvester Wheatsheaf 1989; S. Glynn and A. Booth, *The Road to Full Employment* , London, Allen & Unwin 1987.

15 Lewis Minkin, *The Contentious Alliance: Trade Unions and the Labour Party*, Edinburgh: Edinburgh University Press 1991, p. 1.

16 TUC, *Congress Report, 1925*, London, TUC , pp. 363–4.

17 W. M. Citrine, *The Trade Unions in the General Election*, London, TUC 1931, p. 5.

18 TGWU *Record*, June 1931, p. 327 quoted in R. Shackleton, 'Trade Unions and the Slump' in Ben Pimlott and Chris Cook, eds., *Trade Unions in British Politics* :London, Longman 1982, p. 123.

19 Reynolds and Laybourn, *Labour Heartland*, pp. 58–61, 158–161.

20 Pamela Graves, *Labour Women: Women in British Working-Class Politics 1918–1932*, Cambridge, Cambridge University Press 1994, p.1.

21 *Ibid.*, p. 85.

22 Marion Phillips, 'Birth Control – A Plea for Careful Consideration', *Labour Women,* March 1924, p. 34; Graves, *Labour Women*, p. 86.

23 *Labour Party Conference Report 1925*, London, Labour Party 1925, p.44.

24 Graves, *Labour Women*, p. 99.

25 David Marquand, 1924–1932, in David Butler, *Coalitions in British Politics*, London, Macmillan 1978, p. 52; Marquand, *MacDonald*, pp.311–12.

26 *Labour Party Annual Conference Report, 1926*, London, Labour Party 1926, p. 192.

27 PRO, 30/69 item 173, MacDonald Diaries, 1910–1937.

28 L. MacNeill Weir, *The Tragedy of Ramsay MacDonald.*, London, Secker & Warburg 1938, p. 383.

29 Marquand, *MacDonald*, p. 795.

30 *Ibid.*, p. 631.

31 Keith Laybourn. *The Rise of Labour*, London, Edward Arnold 1998, pp. 76–83.

32 TUC, General Council, Minutes, 20–21 August 1931.

33 Stevenson and Cook, *The Slump* , p. 107.

34 *Labour Party Conference Report, 1920*, London, Labour Party 1920, pp. 181–3.

35 *Labour Party Conference Report, 1922*, London, Labour Party 1922, pp. 222–3

36 *Labour and the Nation* , London, Labour Party 1928, p. 6.

37 *Labour Party Conference Report, 1928*, London, Labour Party 1928, pp. 200–3, 212–15.

38 R. H. Tawney, *The Choice before the Labour Party*, London, Socialist League 1933; Sir S. Cripps, *Problems of a Socialist Government*, London, Gollancz 1933.

39 Minkin, *Contentious Alliance*, pp. 30–4.

40 Ben Pimlott, *Labour and the Left in the 1930s*, Cambridge, Cambridge University Press 1977.

41 Ben Pimlott, *Hugh Dalton* , London, Macmillan, 1985, p. 206.

42 *Ibid.*, p. 213.

43 David Howell, *British Social Democracy*, London, Croom Helm 1976, p. 72.

44 *Ibid.*, p. 217–8.

45 *Labour Party Annual Conference Report, 1935*, London, Labour Party 1935, p. 158.

The Attlee years, 1935–55

Kevin Jefferys

'Labour comes of age', proclaimed Kingsley Martin in the *New Statesman* shortly after the party's stunning election victory in the summer of 1945.[1] This chapter sets out to explore how far the party did mature and 'come of age' during the two decades in which it was presided over by Clement Attlee - at first sight one of Labour's most unlikely and unassuming leaders. As Prime Minister for six years after the war, Attlee has attracted several biographers, though no one has yet produced a volume aimed at examining the 'Attlee years'.[2] The 20-year period between 1935 and 1955 has instead been investigated primarily in the context of Labour's longer-term history. Within this broader setting, the battle-lines have been well marked out. On the one hand, there is what Ben Pimlott calls the 'we wuz robbed' school of party history, which includes writers such as Ralph Miliband, David Coates, James Hinton and John Saville. What these observers have in common is a dislike of Labour gradualism, regarding this as a betrayal of the radical potential for fundamental change in British society.[3] To set against this perspective, several historians give a higher priority to Labour's achievements, especially those of Attlee's 1945–51 administrations. In several sympathetic though not uncritical accounts, it has been conceded that Labour faced on-going problems despite its successes in office, but that such problems were not directly the result of any betrayal of socialism, however defined.[4]

These distinctive approaches to the writing of Labour history emerge at various points in what follows. Inevitably, an overview of the Attlee years cannot do justice to all aspects of the party's history over a 20-year period. The reader seeking a detailed analysis of the role of the trade unions, for example, or the development of Labour's international policy, will need to look elsewhere in the collection. There are three main areas of concern here. Firstly, the different stages in the party's evolution after 1935 will be outlined. Secondly, attention is focused on a series of questions which help us to understand the Attlee era as a whole. How and why did Labour's electoral fortunes change across two decades? What did the party want to achieve? How successful was it in implementing its aims? And what are we to make of the enigmatic figure whose tenure of leadership stretched from the 'depression' of the 1930s through the 'austerity' of the 1940s and into the 'affluence' of the 1950s? The third concern of the chapter is historiographical. As well as venturing onto the main battleground among Labour historians, as identified above, an attempt will be made to assess related controversies such as the concern with the nature and extent of 'consensus' during and after the war. This final objective, aiming to direct readers to a range of historical debates, is difficult in relation to Attlee's early years as leader. Labour historians, it has been noted, too frequently either ignore the 1930s or gear their accounts to the 'romance saga of the how the road towards the great leap forward in 1945 was taken'.[5] The starting point here is to emphasise just how weak the party was throughout the 1930s, facing as it did the massed ranks of the National government.

Labour in opposition, 1935–40

Attlee became leader at a time when Labour had not recovered from the débâcle of 1931. The economic crisis had cruelly highlighted the limitations of the formative Labour movement, both in terms of a lack of imaginative leadership and a failure to devise coherent, sustainable policies. After the break-up of Ramsay MacDonald's second administration the party was reduced at the 1931 election to a rump of less than 50 MPs led by the veteran left-winger George Lansbury. It seemed for a time that Labour might be reduced to the status of a pressure group rather than a serious opposition. The newly-formed Socialist League attracted much rank-and-file support with its advocacy of direct attacks on the capitalist system, fuelled by mass unemployment peaking at nearly three million. But the challenge from the left was gradually contained. Key trade union leaders, notably the powerful head of the Transport Workers' Union, Ernest Bevin, had little sympathy with the Socialist League. Equally important, what remained of the Parliamentary Labour Party (PLP) came increasingly under the control of centrist figures such as Arthur Greenwood and Clem Attlee, MP for Limehouse, who took over from Lansbury shortly before the election called by Prime Minister Stanley Baldwin in the autumn of 1935.

The 1935 election demonstrated that a crushing defeat at the polls could not be rapidly reversed – a lesson to be repeated in the 1980s. Labour regained ground in industrial constituencies and pushed up its share of the total vote, but made no serious inroads into the ascendancy of the Tory-dominated National government. The shadows of 1931 continued to loom large. The number of Labour MPs rose to over 150, well short of the 287 returned in

1929, and Baldwin was re-elected with a majority that looked impregnable. Labour was left with virtually no representation in rural Britain. The party held none of the twelve seats in the 'second city' of Birmingham, and could boast only two MPs in the south of England outside London below the Severn-Wash 'line'.[6] There was at least the compensation of the return of more experienced parliamentarians, including five members of the 1931 Cabinet, though this hardly produced an abundance of talent. Having taken over the leadership in the first instance only for the duration of the election, Major Attlee triumphed in a PLP ballot over Greenwood and London County Council chief Herbert Morrison, whose disappointment was such that he refused to accept the consolation prize of the deputy leadership. Many colleagues regarded Attlee as being everything MacDonald was not: hard-working, straight and loyal to majority party opinion. But his taciturn manner led others to underrate and question his ability; Hugh Dalton lamented on hearing news of the leadership contest that a 'mouse shall lead them'.[7]

Attlee did preside over a gradual redefinition of policy in the second half of the 1930s. The former academic and economist Dalton spearheaded a move towards a form of democratic socialism which combined demand management with physical control economic planning. The result was *Labour's Immediate Programme* of 1937, a wide-ranging policy-document which advocated a combination of state intervention to tackle unemployment and proposals for social reform that went well beyond the government orthodoxy of the day. Although many of the ideas were familiar, what was novel was Labour spelling out its programme in such detail, rather than simply providing a wish-list of desirable policies. This domestic rethink – foreshadowing much of Labour's policy in office after 1945 – was also accompanied by a new realism in foreign policy. With Hitler in power in Germany, the party gradually abandoned its traditional neo-pacifism and became increasingly hostile to the appeasement of the fascist dictators pursued by the Prime Minister after 1937, Neville Chamberlain.

Personal antipathy towards Chamberlain led Labour leaders to decline his half-hearted offer for the party to join him in government once war had been declared in September 1939, but there was little doubt that Labour was supportive of the fight against Nazism.[8]

Attlee was not the feeble stop-gap that some imagined, but his critics were right to fear that he would struggle to make an impression as a national leader. The average swing against the government in by-elections after 1935 was lower than it had been in the early 1930s, and Labour continued to make only modest gains in local elections. In what would later be called 'middle England', the opposition was considered to be the party of the unemployed and the blue-collar trade unionist. The widespread assumption that Labour was heading for another general election defeat helps to explain why Attlee was so preoccupied by internal party matters. In early 1939 he had to devote much time to countering the movement in favour of a broad popular front to oppose the government, a controversy which led to the expulsion of left-wingers Cripps and Bevan. And in the summer, with war on the horizon, the leader faced fresh challenges from those seeking to promote the leadership claims of Greenwood and Morrison. Critics such as Dalton found that the 'poor little Rabbit' was tenacious in surviving, but to what effect remained unclear. At best the 1930s had produced only a limited revival. The party's organisation had remained intact and indeed individual membership and trade union affiliations were rising. But electorally Labour remained as remote from power as it had been since 1931.

Nor was it obvious that the outbreak of war would produce a rapid change of fortune. Labour's adherence to an electoral truce, which outlawed by-election contests between the major parties for the duration of the war, was intended to demonstrate responsibility while leaving the party free to criticise ministers. But local party workers resented the truce as a brake upon their activities, and for several months Chamberlain continued to have little regard for Labour concerns, especially as the war remained 'phoney'. But in the spring of 1940 British military failings in Scandinavia provoked a sudden storm of criticism, even amongst many hitherto loyal Tory MPs. Historians are divided over the importance of Labour's role in the downfall of Chamberlain following the celebrated Norway debate of May 1940. On the one hand, party leaders took the critical step of choosing to divide the House, a move which could have back-fired by rallying Tory waverers behind the government. On the other hand, the key players were Conservative MPs who either voted against the Prime Minister or abstained, and Labour played little part in ensuring that it was Churchill who came to the fore when after much pressure (like 'trying to get a limpet off a corpse', said one critic) Chamberlain finally resigned.[9] The decision to join with Churchill in forming a new cross-party coalition was nevertheless a vital one. The majority of ministerial posts remained in Conservative hands, but Labour was rewarded with a share of power that had seemed unimagineable only months earlier. Although it could not be known at the time, May 1940 was to be the moment that opened up a new phase in the party's history - one that was to culminate in Labour's first-ever majority government.

Labour and the wartime coalition, 1940–45

Five years on from the formation of the coalition, Churchill confidently expected to reap the benefit of eventual victory over Nazi Germany. As cross-party co-operation came to an end, he looked forward to being returned at the head of a new Conservative administration, just as Lloyd George had been returned as 'the man who won the war' in 1918. Labour leaders believed in private that the best they could hope for was to limit the scale of Churchill's victory. Attlee's profile had been raised by ministerial experience, but not dramatically. Few pundits expected he could outpoll the nation's charismatic war leader, who was amongst those who gave credence to cruel jibes about the Labour leader. 'An empty taxi drew up', it was once joked, 'and Attlee got out'. In spite of this, Labour won with a landslide. In July 1945 the party secured almost half the popular vote, winning 393 seats compared with 210 for the Tories. The scale of Labour's victory was breathtaking in view of the party's malaise in the 1930s. The most striking successes came in areas that were hitherto largely Labour-free zones. Every constituency in Birmingham was captured and the party claimed 143 seats south of the Severn-Wash 'line' including the likes of Winchester, Wycombe and Great Yarmouth. Hence it was not Churchill but Attlee – looking 'very surprised indeed', according to the King – who went to Buckingham Palace to accept the royal invitation to form a new government.

The explanation for this remarkable turnaround lies in the history of the coalition. Wartime politics witnessed a pronounced swing to the left in public opinion, though this was masked at the time by the suspension of normal political activity and by Churchill's popularity as war leader. The movement of public opinion appeared to begin – after the humiliating evacuation of British forces from Dunkirk – as a reaction against the so-called 'guilty men'. Conservative leaders such as Chamberlain were blamed for leaving the nation in a parlous state, facing imminent invasion in the summer of 1940. By participating in the coalition, Labour leaders restored lost credibility and were later able to present themselves to the electorate as patriotic; efforts to whip up a 'red scare' based on Labour unreliability were to misfire badly in 1945. Equally important was the egalitarian ethic which followed on from the mobilisation of the civilian population and from the intense physical dangers of life in the Blitz. If the Great War had been fought for King and Country, then the conflict against Hitler came to be regarded as a 'people's war'. The degree of social levelling which resulted can easily be exaggerated, though the trend towards egalitarianism was a powerful one. In Paul Addison's vivid description, this was a time when Colonel Blimp – the reactionary cartoon character who represented the 'old gang' – found himself pursued through a land of Penguin specials by abrasive meritocrats, progressive churchmen and J. B. Priestley.[10] But government surveys early in the war found a marked absence of thinking along conventional party lines, making it difficult to speak of a decisive Labour breakthrough. Sensing a leftward swing which the party could not exploit, many activists made life difficult for their leaders by agitating against the continuance of the electoral truce.

Some accounts present the swing to the left as a two-stage process, with the Tory decline only deepening to the point where it became irreversible from late 1942 onwards. After the 'turn of the tide', when the defeat of Hitler could at last be seriously contemplated, Labour benefited from a sudden awakening of interest in welfare reform. Indicators of public feeling such as by-election results showed a marked anti-Conservative trend, exacerbated by Churchill's cool response to the Beveridge Report of December 1942. Sir William Beveridge's blueprint for a brighter future was immensely popular with the public, coming at just the moment when it was possible to see some light at the end of the wartime tunnel. Tory MPs agreed with the Prime Minister in seeing Beveridge as a 'sinister old man who wanted to give away a great deal of other people's money'. Labour backbenchers, by contrast, wanted to see immediate action, and voted *en bloc* against the cautious position of the Cabinet.[11] By concentrating so exclusively on the war effort, Churchill misjudged the desire of the British people to see a new beginning – a theme made central in Labour's propaganda at the end of the war. Attlee also fought a more measured campaign than the Prime Minister in 1945, responding with dignity to Churchill's tasteless claim that the introduction of socialism in Britain would require 'some form of Gestapo'. Although local Labour parties had been disrupted by the war, many were in a better shape than their moribund Tory counterparts, and Labour had the advantage of a membership that had risen by the end of the war to its highest-ever level of of 487,000.[12]

Labour was therefore in the right place at the right time in 1945. Attlee's party, it seemed, offered both immediate redress for a war-weary population and a long-term commitment to a reconstructed, 'welfare state'. In the words of David Howell: "'bread and butter plus a dream". That was the secret of 1945'.[13] Recent studies emphasise, however, that it would be wrong to exaggerate the extent to which the war genuinely radicalised opinion in a socialist direction. There is a danger of assuming too readily that in 1945 voters knew exactly what they wanted, and that what they wanted 'was contained between the covers of *Let Us Face the Future*', Labour's manifesto at the election.[14] It was more a case that the electorate was cynical after the Beveridge episode and disengaged from the political process. Public feeling as recorded by organisations such as Mass Observation was said to vary between anger and despondency at Churchill's 'betrayal' over Beveridge, believing that 'homes fit for heroes' would fail to materialise as they had after the First World War. By this reckoning, 1945 should primarily be explained in the terms of protest voting against the lack of Tory direction on domestic policy.[15] Certainly historians ignore at their peril the close connection between the 1945 result and the issue of 'reconstruction', which has also been the fore in studies of the coalition.

Traditionally, historians have followed Paul Addison's lead in arguing that the war created a new 'middle ground' upon which all parties would henceforth compete for power. Such an outcome was accepted but deplored by Correlli Barnett, who has been described as 'a thuggish younger brother' to Addison, replacing the idea of a benevolent consensus with one of 'foggy wrong-headedness'.[16] According to Barnett, Britain failed to give priority to much-needed industrial regeneration because too much time was spent thinking about how to create a New Jerusalem as evangelised by wartime 'do-gooders' such as Beveridge.[17] Without doubt, the atmosphere of a 'people's war' generated immense pressure for the creation of a brave new world, but several studies have argued that this did not imply the creation of a new consensus. Unity on external policy, it has been claimed, was not matched by genuine co-operation in domestic politics. The coalition was essentially a marriage of convenience; a shot-gun union that produced little in the way of domestic bliss. The coalition's reconstruction programme never proceeded very far because of intractable ideological differences between the parties. Mainstream Tory opinion, anticipating election victory and seeing no urgent need for fundamental change, continued to have grave doubts about the cost and need for extended social services. Reconstruction promised more than it delivered. By mid-1944 only the education bill was close to completion, and after the D-Day landings – which raised expectations of an early end to the war – the problem of securing agreement between the two wings of the coalition became ever more acute.[18]

This last line of thinking stresses two conclusions about wartime politics. One is that Labour's victory in 1945 had much to do with the inability of the Conservatives to ride with the tide of reconstruction, something for which Churchill had a large share of responsibility. The other is that the welfare state and mixed economy should not be regarded as the inevitable products of the war, which had made reform possible but not unavoidable. Labour did not simply appropriate consensus or become a hostage to it; the party retained a distinctive ideology and its leaders regarded the coalition primarily as 'a means of wresting acceptable social and economic reforms from the Conservatives after nine years in the political wilderness'.[19] Much of Labour's programme, including its commitment to a programme of nationalisation, became more acceptable during the war years when the public became accustomed to planning the economy. At the same time, partnership in Churchill's coalition allowed leaders such as Attlee, Bevin and Morrison to demonstrate their leadership capabilities. This schooling in the realities of high office, combined with the sharpening of policy and the scale of the victory at the polls in 1945, enabled Attlee to come to power in circumstances very different from those that attended the MacDonald administrations of the 1920s. At the end of the war Labour had not simply swept to power; for the first time in its history, the party was ready to use it.

Labour in government, 1945–51

Much more has been written about 1945-51 than about other aspects of the Attlee years. Before assessing the conflicting interpretations, however, we might first briefly outline the major stages in the history of the Attlee governments.[20] The new Prime Minister was to need all his hitherto concealed self-belief and toughness to remain at the helm for six gruelling years. Britain had lost a quarter of its national wealth in defeating Hitler and without urgent efforts to recover lost export markets, the government faced a 'financial Dunkirk'. Fortified by the negotiation of a controversial American loan, ministers forged ahead with an extensive reform programme. The pace of change in the early days was encouraged by the flamboyant Chancellor of the Exchequer, Dalton, whose economic policy was designed to favour ordinary working-class families who were still suffering from the privations associated with war. Food subsidies were retained in order to keep down living costs; progressive rates of taxation were kept in place; and regional development was pursued vigorously, so helping to avoid any return to high unemployment in pre-war industrial blackspots. Under the watchful guidance of Morrison, Labour's organisational supremo, several major industries were taken into public ownership. In later years the development of a mixed economy was to falter, but in the aftermath of war nationalisation provided a popular means of seeking to redeem industries such as coal mining that had been inefficient and unprofitable in private hands.

Concern about 'our people' – the working classes – also underpinned the rapid introduction of welfare reform. The 1946 National Insurance Act, building upon the Beveridge Report, provided for the first time a comprehensive safety net by bringing together benefits to insure against sickness, unemployment and old age. In housing, Labour faced the task of fitting a population enlarged by a million into properties reduced in number by 700,000 owing to bomb damage. After a slow start, nearly one million new homes were built. 80 per cent were council properties, a clear reversal of Tory priorities in the 1930s. But the jewel in Labour's welfare crown was the National Health Service (NHS), which introduced free access to a range of hospital and general practitioner services. The Conservatives voted against the 1946 NHS Act, though their hardline opposition softened as the popularity of free medical services became apparent, especially among working-class women previously unable to insure themselves against ill-health. Labour charges that the Tories would dismantle the welfare state were soon being denied. In the words of one Tory MP, 'No one shoots Santa Claus'.[21]

The government's honeymoon period came to an abrupt halt in 1947. In February ministers struggled to cope with the 'winter crisis': as fuel shortages were compounded by the coldest weather in living memory. As much of industry ground to a temporary halt, the Minister of Fuel and Power, Manny Shinwell, came under attack. 'Shiver with Shinwell' became a potent Tory slogan. In the summer fresh turmoil was created when it became clear that the American loan came with strings attached. The so-called 'convertibility clause' intensified Britain's balance-of-payments problem in trading with the affluent USA and brought sterling under enormous pressure on the foreign exchanges. Dalton as Chancellor was forced into a rapid tightening of economic policy -

a humiliation from which his reputation never recovered. In November, after controversy over the delivery of his emergency budget, Dalton resigned. In the wake of these recurrent economic difficulties, ministers were faced with a gradual erosion of public confidence. By the autumn the Conservatives were ahead in the opinion polls for the first time since 1945, and Attlee had to stave off fresh attempts by colleagues to unseat him. In domestic politics, 1947 marked an important point of transition from the confidence of the early months in power to a less buoyant phase in which ministers spoke of 'consolidating' advances already made.

The period between 1948 and the general election in 1950 became indelibly associated in the public mind with drabness and petty restrictions. This 'age of austerity' was closely identified with the persona of Dalton's successor at the Treasury, Sir Stafford Cripps, a vegetarian teetotaller noted for cold baths at four in the morning and a prodigious work rate that included three hours at his desk before breakfast. Hoping for similar self-discipline from the nation, Cripps continued with a wartime-style 'fair-shares' policy of food rationing. This was in spite of growing resentment among middle-class families over ever-lengthening queues to obtain food of dubious quality, such as the infamous South African fish snoek, which tasted so unappetising that the whole bulk consignment had to be sold off for reprocessing as cat food. Under Cripps, Labour's domestic policy became more pragmatic. Welfare expenditure was tightened, talk of 'socialist planning' was downplayed and sterling was devalued in order to make British exports more competitive overseas, above all in American markets. Churchill depicted devaluation as a national humiliation, and the opposition recovered further ground by claiming that scarcities in the shops were entirely the product of government mismanagement. This proved a telling theme at the general election in February 1950, which saw a swing against Labour of 2.9 per cent (compared with 12 per cent against the Conservatives in 1945), so leaving Labour in office but as Dalton said 'without authority or power'. Whereas many working-class areas remained loyal to Labour, the party fared badly in middle-class districts in southern England, where austerity remained a prime cause of voter disaffection. Attlee remained in Downing Street, but this time – unlike 1945 – there were no joyous celebrations in the streets.

For several months, the reconstituted government looked capable of confounding those who felt Labour could not survive another full term. But in the summer of 1950 the outbreak of the Korean war proved divisive and contentious. Many Labour MPs felt that the decision to send British troops to combat Communist forces in North Korea smacked of subservience to American wishes. More seriously, the decision to further increase an already large defence budget precipitated the first major split in party ranks since before the war. Nye Bevan as architect of the NHS refused to accept the case made by Hugh Gaitskell – Chancellor after Cripps resigned on medical grounds – that rearmament required spending cutbacks on the home front. Bevan's resignation over the principle of a free health service symbolised an emerging division over future strategy that was to bedevil Labour for years to come. 'The End is Nye' claimed Tory propagandists, and this turned out to be the case for Attlee when a further small swing was sufficient to bring the Tories back to power at the election of 1951. Churchill, having spent six fairly leisurely years recuperating from his wartime exploits, could finally leave behind the humiliation of defeat in 1945.

How then have commentators summed up the legacy of the post-war Labour governments? Among the majority of historians, Labour has received a fair trial. The counsel for the defence has been conducted by distinguished writers such as Kenneth Morgan, Henry Pelling, Alec Cairncross and Peter Hennessy. The Attlee government, so the argument runs, constituted Labour's finest hour. This was a period that went some towards satisfying wartime demands for a New Jerusalem: the economy recovered from the ravages of war while avoiding a return to mass unemployment, and ministers remained resolute in their determination to fulfil the Beveridge promise of social protection from 'the cradle to the grave'.[22] Other historians have been less impressed. For left-wing critics, the immediate post-years were marked by a further betrayal of socialist idealism and by wasted opportunities. Instead of using public backing to introduce wholesale socialist change, Labour opted for cautious reformism – failing for example to redistribute wealth significantly or to attack centres of power and privilege such as the House of Lords and the public schools. In a collection of fifteen essays edited by Jim Fyrth, the case for the prosecution receives its most extended treatment. John Saville's introduction sets the tone for the volume, claiming that the government 'disillusioned its own militants' by undertaking such modest reform, so providing a 'springboard for the rich to take off into the profiteers' paradise of the 1950s'.[23]

From an alternative but equally critical perspective, Correlli Barnett has attacked the government for introducing too much rather than too little socialism. In his concern to explain Britain's post-war 'industrial decline', Barnett continues his attack on evangelists of a 'Brave New World' who were allowed to prevail over those aware of the 'Cruel Real World' of lost exports and vanished overseas investment. The folly of giving priority to welfare reform over economic regeneration was compounded by Attlee's government, with the result that Britain missed a unique chance to remake itself industrially while her rivals were crippled by defeat and military occupation. In this line of thinking, the newly-imposed 'burden' of a welfare state was certain to be unsustainable in the longer term.[24] This forceful critique was taken up by Conservative politicians seeking to 'roll back the frontiers of the state' in the 1980s, though it finds little support among academic observers. Economic historians point out that Labour was remarkably successful at boosting industrial production, manufacturing output and the volume of exports (the latter up by 73.1 per cent between 1945 and 1951). Barnett's work has also been criticised for failing to take account of the political context of the period. The priority given to social needs was hardly surprising given the nation's verdict in 1945. Voters promised jam tomorrow were insistent that 'never again' should there a return to the misery associated with the 1930s. If there was a failure to modernise infrastructure, this was not surprising: the swift rise of European competition in the 1950s was not something that could be predicted in advance. Nor was there anything incompatible in aiming for both economic regeneration and social reform, as did other western European nations. Far from imposing crippling costs, the British version of the welfare state consumed quite limited resources: it was an 'austerity product' of an age of austerity.[25]

Critics of the government, whether of the left or right, have also been taken to task for failing to acknowledge the 'fair-shares' ethos left by the searing experience of war. Recent studies have been keen to stress that Labour ministers hoped to turn people into better citizens; values such as duty and responsibility were frequently extolled, and the needs of the community were always to come before the wishes of the individual. There was, in other words, a desire for moral as well as economic change, an unusual combination of what has been called 'hope and public purpose'. Indeed one cause of Labour's demise in 1950-51 has been identified as the party's mistaken view that voters fully shared its ethical vision. Measures to sustain a wartime sense of community, instead of turning people into active citizens, foundered in the face of apathy. Drinking and gambling remained more popular than loftier pursuits, as they always had been. But the effort had been made. 'There were many more responsible than the Labour

Party', conclude the authors of *England Arise*, for ensuring that the high ambitions of the war years were never fully realised.[26]

Several critiques of Attlee's record arguably use inappropriate yardsticks against which to measure the record of the government. Criticism has often been unduly influenced, in the view of this writer, by later developments in politics and society. Britain's 'industrial disease', for example, only became a matter of widespread concern from the 1960s onwards. Correlli Barnett's talk of decline finds little echo in the debates of the late 1940s, when the nation collectively took pride in having survived and recovered from war. One detailed study of Labour's regional policy criticises the government for failing to create the basis for self-sustaining industrial expansion, but is forced to acknowledge that the approach was successful in maintaining full unemployment and was put in abeyance by later Conservative governments in the more favourable economic conditions of the 1950s.[27] Further ahead still, Labour governments under Wilson and Callaghan proved to be disappointingly moderate in the eyes of party activists, and left-wing critics have read back from this a similar willingness on the part of Attlee's ministers to oppose radical solutions. But at the time, in the aftermath of war, few Labour MPs or party workers had clear ideas about what 'more socialism' might amount to in practice. For most of the movement, from the leadership down to the rank-and-file, there was shared pride in what were considered to be notable achievements. While a plurality of versions of 'socialism' continued as in the past, the majority regarded the party's time in government as successful and distinctive; the notion of a new consensus embracing those who voted against the introduction of the NHS was not familiar to the Labour activist of the late 1940s.[28]

Two underlying causes of this shared sense of pride stand out. One was that any successes were hard earned, achieved not only against the backcloth of grave economic problems but also in the face of stern opposition from hostile newspapers and a revitalised Tory opposition. Secondly Labour stalwarts remembered what came before. When judged against pre-1945 standards, Britain for the majority of its citizens had become a more tolerable place in which to live. It was, in the words of Peter Hennessy, a 'kinder, gentler and a far, far better place' than before the war.[29] Austerity, the inevitable by-product of war, grated among the middle-classes especially. But in 1951, while the Tories won more seats, Labour secured the highest-ever number of total votes, based on massive support in industrial strongholds. For the working classes who made up the bulk of the population, job security was of a sort unknown in the 1930s, fresh opportunities were opening up for the young in education, and pensions approximated as never before to a living income. Affordable, decent housing came within the reach of thousands of lower income families, and the NHS treated millions of patients in its early years of operation. One woman recalled how, on the evening before the health service was formally launched in July 1948, she was delivered of a baby shortly before midnight. The next morning she received a bill from the doctor; had the baby been born 15 minutes later, there would have been no charge. This was what Attlee meant when he spoke of having achieved a 'revolution without tears'.

Labour returns to opposition, 1951–55

Perhaps the most disappointing feature of the 1945 government was its aftermath. In spite of the pride felt in what had been achieved, Labour in opposition was soon prone to in-fighting. In March 1952 57 MPs defied the leadership by refusing to back an official amendment to the defence estimates, thereby marking the first major public act of defiance by the 'Bevanites'. Increasing support for the Bevanites in the constituencies set alarm bells ringing on the Labour centre-right. The dispute over defence convinced Attlee to stay on as leader, despite already being in his late sixties. He was re-elected unopposed; the party that for so long regarded him as a transient figure had ironically decided 'he could stay as long as he liked'.[30] Attlee calculated that if he stood down there would be nothing to prevent the succession of his arch-rival Morrison, whose inflexible dislike of the Bevanites he felt he would make matters worse. In the event, divisions multiplied despite Attlee's efforts at conciliation, with one senior figure describing the 1952 annual conference at Morecambe as 'one of the most unpleasant' in the party's history: 'The town was ugly, the hotels forbidding, the weather bad, and the Conference, at its worst, hideous.'[31] The bitterest moment came when it emerged that two of the party's old guard, Morrison and Dalton, had been knocked off the National Executive Committee by Bevanite pretenders Richard Crossman and Harold Wilson. 'More hatred, and more love of hatred, in our Party than I ever remember', Dalton wrote in his diary.[32]

This feuding reflected in part a battle for the leadership. With Attlee likely to retire at some stage soon, there was much manoeuvring for the succession. Bevan made much of the ideological clash over 'party purpose' between 'fundamentalists' wanting more nationalisation and 'revisionists' who favoured a less traditional agenda. But most disputes in the early 1950s were on foreign policy issues. Neither side had formulated a coherent programme to apply to domestic politics, and they shared more common ground than was apparent, particularly over the achievements of 1945–51. What this left in essence were differences of style and emphasis, compounded by a hardening of personal loyalties. The whole dispute reminded Douglas Jay of what one ancient writer called: '"stasis": faction for faction's sake in which the protagonists know which side they are on, but usually cannot remember why it all started'.[33] After the Morecambe conference, Attlee sought to get a grip by carrying a resolution banning all unofficial groupings inside the party. Thereafter, Bevanism at Westminster was confined to a small number of Nye Bevan's associates meeting informally. Bevan, having secured what he felt were concessions at Morecambe, also saw the need to mend fences. His willingness to stand again for shadow cabinet elections signalled a desire to re-enter the party mainstream, and opened up a period of 'armed truce' in Labour ranks. But this broke down in 1954 as it became more obvious that Churchill's government, benefiting from a surge of economic growth that finally ended 1940s austerity, was likely to secure re-election. Bevan resigned from the opposition front bench and found himself on the verge of expulsion after a bitterly resented attack on Attlee's defence policy in 1955.

The omens were not good going into the general election of May 1955 called by Churchill's successor, Anthony Eden. Eden increased the Conservative majority by over 40 seats and it was agreed by newspaper pundits that a combination of rising living standards and Labour disunity made the outcome a formality. The apathy of Labour activists was widely noted. The party organisation, later described by Harold Wilson as a 'rusty penny-farthing', was attacked at the time by the *Daily Mirror* as 'pathetically inferior', while the leadership was called 'too old, too tired, too weak'.[34] Attlee would clearly not stay long following this defeat, though when the PLP met for the first time in the new parliament, he suggested continuing for a short period. To his critics, this was confirmation of his determination to thwart the ambitions of Morrison. Certainly the prospects for the emerging favourite for the succession, Hugh Gaitskell, were enhanced when in the months after the election Hugh Dalton launched 'Operation Avalanche' – an attempt to dislodge ageing members of the shadow Cabinet. By urging others showing 'signs of senility' to follow his lead in retiring, Dalton helped to encourage the view that Morrison's age made him an unsuitable adversary for Eden.

With Bevan's record of rebellion counting against him, Gaitskell was in a strong position when Attlee finally went in December 1955. Gaitskell polled over twice as many PLP votes in the ensuing ballot as Bevan, with Morrison trailing badly in third place. After twenty years at the helm, the Attlee years were over.

Conclusion

Many Labour historians have regarded the early 1950s as the start of a period of protracted decline in the party's fortunes. For left-wing critics, such as John Saville, the 13 'wasted years' in the wilderness after 1951 confirmed that party leaders had suffered for their moderation; they had 'slowly but inexorably fragmented the diffuse radical consciousness' of the 1940s.[35] Others regard a relatively inflexible response to social change as the key to Labour's problems. One of the few detailed local studies of the party highlights its narrow social base in the 1950s and its inward-looking culture, which posed great difficulties in coming to terms with new-found consumer affluence and the emergence of youth groups.[36] Both main schools of thought arguably exaggerate the scale of defeat in 1955 and the extent to which the election should be seen as part of a process of inexorable decline. Labour still commanded the loyalty of over 12 million voters (46.4 per cent of the total), a figure that compares favourably with 8 million at Attlee's first election back in 1935. With both major parties recording lower total votes than in 1951 on a reduced turnout, senior Tories were concerned that they were not making much headway among traditional Labour voters who abstained rather than backing Eden. H. G. Nicholas, author of an earlier Nuffield election study, pointed out that far from heralding irreversible Labour decline, the 1955 result continued the post-war pattern of 'evenly divided' contests. The only real difference, he concluded, was that voters preferred to declare their colours by 'staying at home rather than by marking their ballot papers'.[37]

In a similar vein too much should not be made of Attlee's shortcomings in his final years as leader. In opposition after 1951 (as before 1939), Attlee had proved a far from inspiring figure. He may have hoped for unity but he had no strategy for achieving it, failing to respond to an increasingly confident Tory government and producing no coherent programme of policy revision. Instead the party became mired ever deeper in squabbling, and it was a measure of how far things had been allowed to drift that such an eminent figure as Bevan should be on the verge of expulsion shortly before the 1955 election. By insisting on remaining as leader until he was over seventy, Attlee damaged both his own reputation and the party's prospects.[38] And yet for many in the Labour movement he remained a revered figure. His achievements as Prime Minister had given him an enduring appeal. Indeed it was considered a testimony to the success of his brand of state collectivism that Churchill's administration made no frontal assault on the reforms introduced by the 1945 government. Proud of its record in maintaining full employment and introducing an extensive programme of welfare reform, the party even after the 1955 defeat remained confident that the forward march towards socialism would soon be resumed. To return to the imagery used by Kingsley Martin at the outset of this chapter, the party had endured many growing pains and found that maturing from adolescence into adulthood did not bring all the answers; indeed it threw up a host of new and unforeseen difficulties. But the transition had been worthwhile and real; Labour under Attlee had 'come of age'.

Notes

1 *New Statesman*, 4 August 1945.
2 See especially Kenneth Harris, *Attlee*, London: Weidenfeld and Nicolson 1982 and Robert Pearce, *Attlee*, Harlow: Addison Wesley Longman 1997.
3 For example, Ralph Miliband, *Parliamentary Socialism*, London: Allen & Unwin 1961; David Coates, *The Labour Party and the Struggle for Socialism*, Cambridge: Cambridge University Press 1975; James Hinton, *Labour and Socialism. A History of the British Labour Movement 1867-1974*, Brighton: Wheatsheaf Books 1983.
4 For example, Kevin Jefferys, *The Labour Party since 1945*, London and Basingstoke: Macmillan 1993; Steven Fielding, *Labour: Decline and Renewal*, Manchester: Manchester University Press, 1994; Andrew Thorpe, *A History of the British Labour Party*, London and Basingstoke: Macmillan 1997.
5 Nick Smart, *National Government 1931-40*, London and Basingstoke: Macmillan forthcoming. I am grateful to Dr Smart for allowing me to see an advance copy of this work.
6 Thorpe, *History of Labour*, p. 88.
7 Ben Pimlott (ed), *The Political Diaries of Hugh Dalton 1918-40, 1945-60*, London: Cape 1986, p. 196 – entry for 26 November 1935.
8 See Ben Pimlott, *Labour and the Left in the 1930s*, London: Allen & Unwin 1977.
9 For a review of the debate, see Kevin Jefferys, 'May 1940: The Downfall of Neville Chamberlain', *Parliamentary History*, Vol 10 Pt 2 1991 pp. 363-78.
10 Paul Addison, *The Road to 1945. British Politics and the Second World War*, London: Cape 1975, pp. 127-33.
11 Kevin Jefferys, *The Churchill Coalition and Wartime Politics 1940-45*, Manchester: Manchester University Press 1991, pp. 114–22.

12 Thorpe, *History of Labour*, p. 106.

13 David Howell, *British Social Democracry. A Study in Development and Decay*, London: Croom Helm 1976, p. 132.

14 Tony Mason and Peter Thompson, 'Reflections on a Revolution? The political mood in wartime Britain', in Nick Tiratsoo (ed), *The Attlee Years*, London: Pinter 1991, p. 55.

15 Steven Fielding, 'What did "the people" want?: the meaning of the 1945 general election', *The Historical Journal*, Vol 35 No 3 1992, pp. 623-39.

16 Addison, *Road to 1945*; Stephen Brooke, *Labour's War. The Labour Party during the Second World War*, Oxford: Oxford University Press 1992, p. 6.

17 Correlli Barnett, *The Audit of War: The Illusion and Reality of Britain as a Great Nation*, London: Macmillan 1986.

18 Jefferys, *Churchill Coalition*, esp. chapters 5 and 7.

19 Brooke, *Labour's War*, p. 10.

20 The following section is based on Kevin Jefferys, 'Rebuilding Postwar Britain: Conflicting Views of the Attlee Governments 1945–51', *New Perspective*, Vol 3 No 3 1998, pp. 31-4. I am grateful to *New Perspective* for allowing me to reproduce parts of the article.

21 Richard Law MP, cited in Harriet Jones, The Conservative Party and the Welfare State 1942-55, London University PhD 1992, p. 392.

22 Kenneth O. Morgan, *Labour in Power 1945-51*, Oxford: Oxford University Press 1984; Henry Pelling, *The Labour Governments 1945–51*, London and Basingstoke: Macmillan 1984; Alec Cairncross, *Years of Recovery: British Economic Policy 1945–51*, London: Methuen 1985; Peter Hennessy, *Never Again. Britain 1945–1951*, London: Cape 1992.

23 John Saville, Introduction, in Jim Fyrth (ed), *Labour's High Noon. The Government and the Economy 1945-51*, London: Lawrence & Wishart 1993, p. xxxvii.

24 Correlli Barnett, *The Lost Victory. British Dreams, British Realities 1945-1950*, London and Basingstoke: Macmillan 1995.

25 David Edgerton, 'The Prophet Militant and Industrial: the Peculiarities of Correlli Barnett', *Twentieth Century British History*, Vol 2 1991, pp. 360-79; Jose Harris, 'Enterprise and the Welfare State: a Comparative Perspective', in Alan O'Day and Terry Gourvish (eds), *Britain since 1945*, London and Basingstoke: Macmillan 1991; Jim Tomlinson, *Democratic Socialism and Economic Policy. The Attlee Years 1945–51*, Cambridge: Cambridge University Press 1997, p. 261.

26 Steven Fielding, Peter Thompson and Nick Tiratsoo, *'England Arise!' The Labour Party and Popular Politics in 1940s Britain*, Manchester: Manchester University Press 1995, p. 218.

27 Jim Tomlinson, 'Inventing "Decline": the Falling Behind of the British Economy in the Postwar Years', *Economic History Review*, Vol 49 No 4 1996, pp. 734–60; Peter Scott, British Regional Policy 1945-51: A Lost Opportunity, *Twentieth Century British History*, Vol 8 No 3 1997, pp. 358-82.

28 Martin Francis, *Ideas and Policies under Labour, 1945-1951. Building a New Britain*, Manchester: Manchester University Press 1997, pp. 225-31.

29 Hennessy, *Never Again*, p. 454.

30 Pearce, *Attlee*, p. 176.

31 Douglas Jay, *Change and Fortune: A Political Record*, London: Hutchinson 1980, p. 223.

32 Pimlott (ed), *Dalton Diary*, 24-8 October 1952, p. 601.

33 Jay, *Change and Fortune*, p. 221.

34 *Daily Mirror*, 28 May 1955, cited in Kevin Jefferys, *Retreat from New Jerusalem: British Politics 1951-64*, London and Basingstoke: Macmillan 1997, p. 39.

35 John Saville, *The Labour Movement in Britain: A Commentary*, London: Faber 1988, p. 133.

36 Nick Tiratsoo, *Reconstruction, Affluence and Labour Politics: Coventry 1945-60*, London: Routledge 1990.

37 *The Observer*, 29 May 1955, cited in Jefferys, *Retreat*, p. 40.

38 Thorpe, *History of Labour*, pp. 139–42; Pearce, *Attlee*, pp. 188–9.

The Age of Wilson 1955–79

Lewis Baston

After a third election defeat in 1959, in which some doubted whether Labour could ever win again, Labour won four out of the five next elections. For a time it seemed that Labour had indeed become *a*, if not *the*, natural party of government. The Heath government of 1970–74 was unable to establish a firm grip on power and the opposition the Tories put up in 1964–70 and 1974–79 was unimpressive. Labour had arrived as a power in the land, rather than a temporary tenant of Downing Street called in to effect occasional reforms.

It says much about the Labour Party, and about perceptions of British history, that 1964–79 is mostly seen as an unproductive and ignominious period in the party's history. The spleen of Wilson and Callaghan's critics at the time and since is amazing to behold. Ken Coates in 1971 could describe Labour's recovery in the opinion polls in the run up to the 1970 election thus:

It even appeared for a moment that all the conscienceless equivocations and apostasies of the Wilson years had produced a climate morally null enough to renew itself.[1]

Francis Cripps and Frances Morrell – two advisers to a Cabinet Minister – wrote in 1979, in a volume flatly entitled *What Went Wrong*, that:

The choices the Parliamentary leadership made during the recurrent crises of 1974–79 showed that their primary political purpose was to protect the power of banking and multinational management and the international arrangements which supported them. If unemployment was the price they were prepared to pay it... Labour Ministers systematically implemented the free market strategy.[2]

The left wing analysis of 1964–79 resounds with the language of betrayal, treachery, bad faith and incompetence. Gregory Elliott could describe the Wilson government's record in 1993 as:

Burking democratic reform of conservative institutions, jettisoning economic expansion, scapegoating its own supporters, sponsoring a foreign policy of unrelievedly reactionary tenor, reneging upon virtually every commitment, Labour spurned friends and emboldened enemies.[3]

To New Labour 1964–79 is also a land that time forgot. According to Philip Gould:

Wilson failed to modernise Labour, which put the genuine modernisation of Britain beyond his reach. His failure to resolve the competing claims of left and right, and to move beyond both to a new modernising solution, made civil war in the Labour Party inevitable... [The Callaghan government] struggled to stay on a pragmatic course, while impotent in the face of global economic forces and domestic union power.[4]

For Gould the period between 1960 and 1985 is the lost generation of Labour politics, where the party drifted loose from its moorings with ordinary people, and ended up in a stagnant backwater.

Right wing versions portray the period as one of decay and degeneracy, in which a hapless government ceded its responsibilities to trade unions and presided over the disintegration of society and the decline of the British economy:

No theory of government was ever given a fairer test or a more prolonged experiment than democratic socialism received in Britain. Yet it was a miserable failure in every respect. Far from reversing the slow relative decline of Britain vis-à-vis its main industrial competitors, it accelerated it. We fell further behind them, until by 1979 we were widely dismissed as 'the sick man of Europe'.[5]

None of these verdicts is fair. There are several ways of assessing the performance of Labour in power. A once fashionable analysis is in terms of 'socialism' – did the achievements of the government match up to a benchmark of supposed 'socialist' practice? This can serve one of two ideological aims: to indict the leaders of the party for betrayal of Labour's true philosophy[6] or to point out that the Labour Party is not a fit vehicle for socialism at all.[7] To draw attention to and condemn the lack of 'socialism' in 1964–70 and 1974–79 is a rather banal observation.

Another critique contrasts the modest achievements of Labour government with the extravagant promises made in party manifestos; the 1964 election in particular aroused hope and energy and belief in a 'New Britain'[8] that went extremely sour when it turned out that the Wilson government was politics as usual – or worse.[9] The ideological journey of *Our Friends in the North*'s Nicky Hutchinson, from naïve enthusiasm for Wilson and T. Dan Smith to nihilist bitterness, is a sketch of the disillusioned hope of 1964.[10] The 'breach of promise' critique is substantial but perhaps too dominant in contemporary consciousness. Few governments can have broken promises as spectacularly as Thatcher's, which started with the prayer of St. Francis of Assisi in 1979 and claimed an economic miracle in 1987. Heath's promises of an end to lame ducks and price rises came to nothing. Wilson, it must be conceded, did not deliver the transformation he promised, but in this he is in good company.[11]

The two related concepts of consensus[12] and decline[13] underlie much writing on post-war history. The concept of a postwar consensus in the 1945–64 period masks a number of subtleties, which have recently become an area of attention for contemporary historians. The 1960s and 1970s pose an even more complicated problem. The 1970s are generally described in terms of the breakdown of consensus, paving the way for the rejection of the post-war consensus by the Thatcher governments. The Labour Party in 1973 and the Conservatives after 1979 adopted approaches that were self-consciously opposed to the usual way of doing things that had prevailed since 1945. Labour in 1964 and the Conservatives in 1970 presented rather more moderate policies in a way that suggested that radical change was about to happen.

There was never consensus in the sense of willing agreement on policy accompanied by an absence of party conflict; but there was a framework of policy within which governments operated in practice. The four Keynesian criteria of economic management – full employment, balance of payments equilibrium, low inflation and growth – were universally regarded as desirable and there was faith in the government's ability to ensure at least the first three through budgetary methods.

Despite an unprecedented increase in national well-being in 1945–73 British policymakers and citizens looked enviously at the economic miracles of West Germany, the US and even France and Italy. It had become a commonplace in the early 1960s that Britain was in decline; that her economy was not growing as fast as it should, that we were slipping behind our competitors, and that the failure of productivity to expand in line with world trends was at the root of the matter.

Decline was generally perceived as being a long-term phenomenon; Andrew Gamble observed in 1981 that 'Britain has now been in decline for a hundred years'[14] and Tony Benn when Minister of Technology argued that 'The fundamental economic problems of this country go back a hundred years or more'.[15] Britain was widely perceived as living beyond its means, through excessive pay claims, an oversized government sector, or in delusions of imperial grandeur.[16] While the great resources accumulated by Britain had been able to cushion decline from 1880 until the 1950s, the idea that Britain had to be transformed in some way to improve its performance took hold in the early 1960s. Gamble identifies three broad responses to the problem of decline: modernisation as promised by the mainstream political leadership of Wilson and Heath from the 1960s onwards, and solutions that emerged from the radical left and right during the 1970s.

Both Wilson in 1964–70 and Heath in 1970–74 stressed the theme of economic, social and institutional modernisation within the framework of the mixed economy[17] arguing for co-operation between the 'two sides of industry'. Incomes policy was a divisive question, although the lines of combat crosscut party division. Many in the Labour Party were distrustful because of its infringement of free collective bargaining, while many Conservatives regarded it as an unacceptable limitation of the free market. Others, such as Tony Crosland and Reggie Maudling, argued consistently for it, while most accepted it reluctantly as a price to pay to maintain full employment and low inflation simultaneously.[18]

The failure of the British economy to achieve higher growth, and the morbid symptoms of high inflation and mass unemployment that had appeared by 1974, led to the language of crisis replacing the language of decline. Britain had failed simultaneously on all four Keynesian measures – mass unemployment, rapid inflation, massive balance of payments deficit and negative growth – and industrial conflict was endemic. The successive 'failure' of Wilson and Heath's governments had led to a crisis of confidence in the political system. Labour won the October 1974 election on the smallest base of popular support a British majority government has ever had[19] – 39.2 per cent of those voting, and only 28.6 per cent of the electorate. Labour's electoral collapse in 1974 was, however, eclipsed by the slump in support for the Conservatives. The Liberal Party and Scottish and Welsh Nationalists prospered. A shooting war had already broken out in Northern Ireland. It became commonplace to ask whether Britain had become ungovernable and a series of doom-laden tracts predicted economic disaster or the imminent demise of British democracy.[20]

By 1978 the urgent crisis was over, but there were still well-recognised problems of long term performance. Britain's economy had recovered from the crisis, although unemployment was significantly higher than in 1945–73 and there was a realisation that long-term problems could not be ignored. Consensus politics was under challenge from left and right, but still had considerable vitality and their demise owed much to contingent, accidental factors rather than deeper forces. Broadly speaking, the Wilson government 1964–70 attempted to deal with the problems of *decline*, and failed; the Wilson-Callaghan government 1974–79 wrestled with the problems of *crisis*, and succeeded.

This chapter concentrates on the core of government policy – the economy, industry and industrial relations – plus the state of the Labour Party in the 1964–79 period. There was much more to Labour's record than this – there were important developments in social reform, the welfare state, territorial politics, Europe, foreign and colonial affairs and central administration; but it is beyond the scope of an essay of this kind to cover the waterfront. Its basic argument is that social democracy and consensus were more vital, and more viable, in the late 1970s than is usually asserted.

Economy and industry

Assessing the growth performance of a government is always problematic, and this is particularly true for the Labour governments elected in 1964 and 1974. The preceding years, 1964 and 1973, were the two best years in terms of growth that Britain has had since the war, at 5 per cent and 7 per cent respectively. Both were the result of unsustainable economic booms that had to be followed by periods of retrenchment. Elections take place at different points on the economic cycle. There are also lags – policy decisions in one year affect economic performance in the future rather than immediately.

The record of 1964–70 did fail to live up to expectations, although in itself it was not disastrous.[21] GDP growth in the 1964–68 economic cycle was 2.6 per cent, a little lower than previous post-war cycles but vastly more than pre-war or post-1973 performance. The disappointment was partly of Labour's own making. The party had gone into the 1964 election more or less obliged to promise faster growth than the Conservatives, and had claimed to have the scientific and planning techniques to deliver it. The result was the National Plan of 1965, which was predicated on growth of 3.8 per cent per annum.

The principles of Labour's economic programme were sound. The party aimed to provide a stable and predictable framework for business in the short and medium term, and to improve the supply side performance of the economy in the long term through investment, technological modernisation, education and training. Planning, prices and incomes control and a stable sterling parity would provide the first. Tax incentives, expanding education, the Ministry of Technology and its offshoots such as the Industrial Reorganisation Corporation, the Department of Economic Affairs and Regional Planning Councils, and measures such as Selective Employment Tax and the run-down of the coal industry, would provide the latter.[22] Planning and technology were the distinctive elements of Labour's 1964 appeal, but the rest of the Labour

programme was very similar to the left-wing Conservatism of
Reginald Maudling, Chancellor in 1962–64. [23]

The key economic issue at the time was the sterling exchange
rate. It has been argued that the Labour government missed
opportunities to transform the prospects by failing to devalue –
either as soon as it came to power in October 1964, or in 1965 or
the spring and summer of 1966.[24] The Wilson government ruled
out devaluation on taking power in October 1964 and adopted
expedients such as an import surcharge or deflating demand to
maintain sterling. The sterling constraint kept forcing
adjustments to policy for the next three years, the worst crunch
coming in July 1966. This crisis was resolved by deflationary
measures and public spending 'cuts'[25] which rendered the growth
projections in the National Plan totally impossible. This revealed
the similarity of Labour's economic management to the derided
'stop go' of the pre-Maudling Conservatives. A succession of
austere sounding policies, including 'total freeze' and 'severe
restraint' were proclaimed, in the same sort of way as had
Conservative Chancellors when the Tories were in office. To
Robert Bacon and Walter Eltis, bemoaning the state of Britain in
1976, the government's response to the July 1966 crisis was:

the decisive turning point after which the structure of the United
Kingdom economy deteriorated almost without interruption.[26]

After 1967, the pretence at having anything other than the
traditional Keynesian tools of economic management was
abandoned. Devaluation was accompanied by a harsh budget but
produced a balance of payments surplus in 1970. However, the
austerity of 1966–68 produced pessimistic assumptions about
growth, and depressed levels of investment, and made it more
difficult for potential investors to believe subsequent government
claims about the future of the economy.

If the medium-term policy failed because it was inconsistent,
the long-term policy never had much of a chance to succeed. Its
benefits were not apparent by 1970, but then they would have
been unlikely to appear so quickly anyway. Much of it was
scrapped after 1970. But, perhaps surprisingly, the productivity
gains promised from the white heat of technology did appear;
productivity increased much faster in the 1960s (4.2 per cent per
annum) than in the 1950s (2.2 per cent per annum).[27]

The Labour government handed over a relatively healthy
economy in June 1970. The main worry was that inflation was
heading upwards, thanks to an unusual sort of pre-election boom.
The government's budget had been cautious – and was later
criticised for being too cautious to be electorally successful – but

the lifting of restrictions on incomes led to a series of generous settlements in industry. The government's revenues and the balance of payments were in surplus, giving scope for expansionary policies aimed at once again increasing industrial investment. However, a series of destabilising shocks to the world economy took place between 1970 and 1974. The Bretton Woods system of currency alignment collapsed and the pound 'floated', buffeted by massive quantities of money sloshing around the world markets. The steady growth of world trade after 1945 had produced an increasingly interdependent international economy, in which imports and international investment played an ever more important part and speculative flows of money had become too large for governments to control. Commodity prices increased sharply in 1972–73, followed by the OPEC crisis in which oil prices quadrupled. This was coupled with the Heath government's policies of deregulating credit, cutting direct taxation and stimulating a massive boom.[28]

The economic upheaval of the early 1970s had produced a new set of constraints and opportunities for policy, replacing the comparatively clear objectives of full employment and a stable currency that had governed in 1945–70. The new situation was only dimly understood. Unemployment was high by post-war standards and inflation was taking off. The oil price rises were at once inflationary, by raising the price of a basic commodity, and deflationary, by sucking a large amount of purchasing power out of the economy. The exchange rate hung perilously on short-term money parked in London as a result of the oil crisis, which might take fright at any unsettling developments in Britain. 'Confidence' in sterling, an element in every past crisis, was more important than ever, and was running low after repeated balance of payments crises and spins around the stop-go cycle.[29]

Macroeconomic performance in Britain in the 1970s was undoubtedly unimpressive. During the 1973–79 economic cycle GDP growth per capita was 1.5 per cent per annum, which is the lowest of any post-war cycle. UK growth was lower than in other European countries, although countries with faster growth decelerated more than Britain so that the gap was less than in the long boom of 1950–73.[30] 1973–79 was a period of adjustment, a steep learning curve, during which errors were undoubtedly made – principally in 1973–75.[31] Economic and political conditions were so unstable it is unsurprising that investment and productivity fared poorly, in contrast to the late 1960s when both had fared relatively well.

Having taken office as a minority government in March, the imminence of another general election weighed heavily on the minds of Labour ministers in 1974 and decisions were taken with an extremely short time horizon in mind. There was an urgent need to win the support of the trade unions. Pensions and food subsidies were increased immediately and it was hoped the unions would moderate their wage demands. Although the 1974 budget was intended to be slightly deflationary the forecasts were so far adrift that its impact was at once expansionary and too severe on corporate profits. The government's economic policies in 1974–75 were badly out of step with the requirements of the situation.[32] Other countries were more successful by imposing restrictive policies in 1974 and squashing inflation, before expanding their economies after 1976.

By summer 1975 the unions had failed to deliver voluntary wage restraint as their part of the 'Social Contract' and wage settlements had risen to a ludicrous degree: 30 per cent was not unusual, and many agreements had shorter terms than one year. Britain was starting to acquire a hyper-inflationary economy. The government's efforts were geared more to the old concept of 'price rises' than accelerating inflation, relying as they did on food subsidies and price controls. More symptoms of instability were appearing; there were four 'budgets' in the thirteen months starting in March 1974 and forward projections of economic indicators, including those over which the government nominally had control such as public spending, increasingly lost all credibility.

The government's strategy shifted to what may naïvely be called the right after the European referendum of June 1975. Tony Benn was moved from the Department of Industry to Energy to reassure industry and the City and the leading trade union figures had become alarmed at the rate of inflation, and now agreed to impose a £6 a week limit on pay rises within the framework of the Social Contract. Cash limits and stricter management of public spending were introduced across Whitehall in 1975 and 1976 and enabled a fall of unprecedented size in real public spending in 1976 and 1977. By December 1975 the balance of payments on current account was improving from the shocking level of 1974, while inflation was heading down but unemployment was rising.

The apparent nadir of the government's economic fortunes, and management of the economy, was the IMF crisis of 1976.[33] The conventional wisdom about the turning points of British politics points to the IMF crisis as the end of the post-war

Keynesian social-democratic consensus and the beginning of a Thatcherite counter-revolution. A favourite text is part of Callaghan's speech to the chaotic 1976 Labour conference:

We used to think that you could spend your way out of a recession and increase employment by cutting taxes and boosting government spending. I tell you in all candour that that option no longer exists, and that insofar as it ever did exist, it only worked on each occasion since the war by injecting a bigger dose of inflation into the economy, followed by a higher level of unemployment as the next step.[34]

Another point of reference is the Cabinet meetings in November in which, like characters in a Greek drama, Cabinet ministers spoke up for great ideas like socialism (Benn), social democracy (Crosland), pragmatism (Callaghan) and global capitalism (Healey). The February 1977 death of Crosland, a universally recognised romantic lead as well as intellectual pioneer of Keynesian social democracy, adds to the retrospective view of 1976 as the end of an era. This view reeks of hindsight. There were important changes in 1975–76, it is true: the rising trend of public expenditure was halted and even temporarily reversed, the defeat of inflation assumed primary importance and full employment receded, and the government adopted monetary targets to this end, but of itself 1976 is not a historical turning point.

As Callaghan points out in his memoirs, his conference speech has been misrepresented ever since:

The passage … does not say that governments should never increase public expenditure or reduce taxation as methods of boosting employment. My argument was that in the circumstances of 1976 these measures were not appropriate, nor were they an alternative to facing up to the long-term changes that were required in our economy or society.[35]

Callaghan believed that demand management alone was not, in anything other than the short term, an effective way of guarding full employment; this was something Healey's policies had acknowledged for at least a year.[36] Ideologically, Callaghan repudiated this cruder form of Keynesianism, but in policy terms what was abandoned in 1975–76 was the irresponsible reflation and inflation of 1973–75, not 'full employment'. To the left, this had been abandoned earlier – unemployment stood at 1.15 million[37] at the end of 1975, having been 515,000 in May 1974, rising to 1.61 million in summer 1978 before falling sharply until Labour lost power. Rather than abandon full employment as an objective, Labour's 1979 manifesto explicitly refers to it.

The idea that Labour adopted 'monetarism' is also a red herring. Monetary targets, used pragmatically, are not incompatible with social justice or a large public sector. Applied for internal government purposes since 1973, their public adoption in summer 1976 was but one aspect of a range of anti-inflationary techniques, surely appropriate given the inflationary conditions, and not a lodestar of policy as it was in 1979–81 under Margaret Thatcher. If monetary targets were as important as all that, their abandonment in 1986 would have somehow marked another seismic shift in policy.[38]

The end of a rising trend in public spending is important, as is the fact that the axe fell heaviest on capital spending.[39] But a rising trend by definition cannot go on forever; it is perfectly consistent to be in favour of increasing public spending when it is 38 per cent of GDP and calling a halt at 46 per cent for fear that any more would impair the functioning of the economy. More urgently, this increasing expenditure could not be satisfactorily financed. The government had reached the acceptable limits of direct taxation. Although the standard rate was lower than it had been in the 1960s, the incidence of income tax had broadened greatly. Higher rates were excessive and raising indirect tax, at least in the short term, risked fuelling inflation by undermining the government–trade union incomes policy. In addition, borrowing money, increasing the Public Sector Borrowing Requirement, was not possible. The government was at the limit of its ability to borrow as the IMF crisis proved.

The IMF crisis looks superfluous in retrospect. Denis Healey is perhaps a little blasé in attributing the whole affair to misguided forecasts, but the actual cuts demanded were not significantly more severe than any domestically generated package. Market confidence was restored so quickly what Healey called 'Sod Off Day' came early and by 1979 the problem was the overvaluation of sterling.[40]

Figures released in early 1976 suggesting that the government spending accounted for around 60 per cent of GDP, relied on double counting and were eventually disproved, although not before they had caused a great deal of damage.[41] In reality the size and growth of the British state was not excessive. The state's share of GDP had expanded from 34 per cent in 1964 to 38 per cent in 1970, from 39 per cent in 1972 to 46 per cent in 1976. It then fell to 43 per cent in 1978. The 4 per cent increase in 1972–78 was the smallest of the principal European economies, and by 1978 the state's share of GDP was less than West Germany (48 per cent), France (45 per cent) and Italy (46 per cent). However, UK spending was financed to a greater extent than other countries through borrowing: 5 per cent of GDP in 1976 compared to a 3.2 per cent G7 average.[42]

Robust economic growth resumed in 1977 and reached 3 per cent in 1978; unemployment turned down and inflation sank back into single figures in 1978 under the impact of a successful incomes policy, before rising again as the second oil crisis and the collapse of the incomes policy worked their way through. By 1978 it was no longer ridiculous to talk of Britain as a stable and prosperous place, led by a kindly and popular Prime Minister[43] and a governemnt developing an important role in the world and Europe, having cast aside imperial pretensions – and proving a model of sorts in the way it was dealing with deindustrialisation. A contemporary observer of Labour Britain, the *Washington Post* correspondent Bernard Nossiter, wrote in his 1978 book *Britain: A Future that Works*:

By almost any indicator – statistical, political or the observation of unclouded eyes – Britain is a solid, healthy society, bursting with creative vigor. Its lacklustre performance in what Blake called 'these dark, Satanic mills' is less a symptom of sickness than of health. It is a country more at peace with itself than its own daily papers reflect.[44]

Even the pessimists Bacon and Eltis had recovered some cheer by the time of the second edition of their book in 1978:

The present strategy of export-led growth stands a good chance of success, but if it fails, Britain will still have the opportunity to adopt a new strategy based on the use of oil revenues to finance re-industriali-sation.[45]

In his 1997 biography of Callaghan Kenneth Morgan boldly titles a chapter 'A Successful Government' and points out that there was a sizeable stretch of quiet competence between the IMF crisis at the end of 1976 and the wretched early months of 1979 and the Winter of Discontent, a period which appeared to be the most thriving one that Britain had known since the heyday of Harold Macmillan in the later 1950s.[46]

The Labour government appeared, in its weary way, to have resolved the crisis. Philip Ziegler said of Wilson that 'he served the state pretty well'[47] and the same can be said even more definitely of Callaghan. Calm followed the upheavals of the crisis of the mid 1970s more rapidly and more completely – for a time – than is usually recalled.

The Labour government's prospective economic strategy in 1979 was an oil-fuelled version of the white heat of technology promised in 1964. Callaghan, in his famous 1976 speech, defended current and future government borrowing on the grounds that it was to be for investment rather than consumption. Labour stressed in its 1979 manifesto that:

The Labour Government will pursue policies which give a high priority to the return to full employment. This must go hand-in-hand with keeping down inflation. We therefore aim at a rate of growth of 3 per cent or more. Our North Sea oil gives us an advantage in securing full employment and a rise in living standards. The new technologies also hold out the prospect of faster growth and a better quality of life for all.[48]

This is a long way from the supposed 'abandonment of full employment'. It is, of course, impossible to say whether such a strategy might have paid off had Labour won in 1979; but one vital step had been taken. North Sea Oil was not necessarily a bonanza for Britain. The cost of oil to the rest of the economy took two huge leaps in 1973–74 and 1979, which was redistributed from the non-oil economy to the oil producers. North Sea oil could only serve the needs of the UK for industrial development if it was redistributed to useful areas through taxation. A policy was devised more or less from scratch when Labour arrived in power in 1974, producing Petroleum Revenue Tax. PRT produced £59 billion at 1992/3 prices, which had been intended to fund productive investment.[49]

Labour intended to steer the economy in the medium term by tripartite annual discussions between government, employers and unions based on what the German Social Democrats called *Modell Deutschland* – which was the most successful approach to riding out the 1974 crisis, and one which worked with the grain of British practice as it had developed. The details of this British version were, admittedly, very sketchy in 1979, and it is far from certain that the initiative would have meant any more than the Social Contract or the National Plan. But Labour – and some Conservatives[50] – were proposing a widened, and more business-friendly, system of consensus, rather than its abolition. The weakest link in the programme, and the main reason why it was never given a try, was the state of industrial relations in Britain.

Industrial relations

A dominant theme of politics in 1964–79 was industrial relations. The trade unions were at the intersection of macroeconomic policy, supply side reform and internal Labour Party politics. It was neither a particularly comfortable position for the unions, nor for governments of either party.[51] The British trade unions saw their role primarily as representing the interests of their members on pay, conditions and employment levels vis-à-vis employers, but they had assumed great responsibilities in economic policy.

Public support for trade unionism was slowly ebbing, even as trade union membership rose, in 1964–79. Only 12 per cent polled in 1964 said that trade unions were in general a 'bad thing', a proportion that grew to 24 per cent in 1970 and 31 per cent in summer 1978.[52] The reasons were not difficult to determine; they seemed, and were, a privileged sectional interest whose positive achievements (wage restraint) were almost as painful as their disruption of society (strikes). The Labour Party, by contrast, romanticised the trade union movement to a ridiculous degree and grew to depend on its leaders to implement economic policy. The structure of the Labour Party itself proved an obstacle to a thorough reform of industrial relations because of the trade union block votes that dominated conference and the NEC. Despite this, Labour was usually preferred in polls when questions were asked about which party had the best policy on strikes or industrial relations – by a margin of 33 per cent in September 1974, 9 per cent in August 1978 and even in April 1979 by 1 per cent.[53]

Legal judgements in the early 1960s, most notably *Rookes v Barnard* in 1964, and the modernisation agenda that had dominated the language of politics in that period could hardly have avoided the state of industrial relations. The Conservatives from 1965 were drawing up proposals to recast trade union law. The Labour government established the Donovan Commission in 1965 with a brief to review trade unions and employer organisations. Donovan reported in 1968 at a time when the situation had deteriorated to such an extent that the report's measured academic prose no longer seemed equal to the problem.

A worldwide crisis in industrial relations began in 1968. Long years of prosperity and low unemployment had generated aspirations among workers across the world. Strikes multiplied not just in Britain but also in the US, France, and most spectacularly Italy. In France and Italy strikes were bought off by government concessions on a range of issues including hours, holiday time and wages. As Donovan noted, the British system was more complicated in that the union movement was becoming less and less centralised. Trade union leaders were also bound into the government through the incomes policy and the politics of the Labour Party rather than led by left wing opponents of the governing party. Militancy in Britain took the form of a surge in unofficial industrial action, often bought off at plant level rather than national settlements.

The tragedy of the Labour government was its self-awareness. Wilson had been conscious of the link between the national modernisation Labour promised and the 'forces of conservatism' (to use a later phrase) within the Labour movement:

It is not enough to reject the organised conservatism of the Tory party. We cannot afford to perpetuate any form of dinosaur-type thinking in our own party.[54]

Barbara Castle produced a White Paper, *In Place of Strife*, which went well beyond the Donovan proposals and proposed statutory 'penal clauses', which aroused anger in the trade unions and disunity in the Cabinet. Callaghan extraordinarily voted against the government's policy in the NEC, which would have been a sacking offence in any normal circumstances. Reluctantly, Wilson and Castle backed off in June 1969.[55]

The Castle proposals, whose approach influenced the Heath government, were intended to 'encourage a more equitable, ordered and efficient system.' This entailed making trade unions more responsible, centralised organisations.[56] In rejecting *In Place of Strife* and retreating from anything more than the 'Solomon Binding' accord Labour did immense damage to its status as a party of government. It had resiled from measures that it had previously described as essential for national economic prosperity because it was strongly under the influence of the trade unions. The open divisions produced by *In Place of Strife* were a warning to the next Labour government that it attempted to reform industrial relations at its peril. It was precisely the wrong lesson. The mishandling of what had been correctly perceived as an issue of growing urgency and importance was perhaps the worst specific decision of the 1964–70 Wilson governments.

Industrial relations in 1969–70 confirmed the serious nature of the problem. Nearly 11 million days were lost in industrial disputes in 1970, the worst year since 1926. Labour's programme in 1970 was weak, but legislation was promised to 'overhaul negotiating and disputes procedures' as part of a charter for industrial relations. In the event, the Heath government attempted an all-encompassing legal transformation of industrial relations through the 1971 Industrial Relations Act. In the teeth of Labour and trade union opposition the Act rapidly proved a failure, pushing the Labour leadership and the unions back together.

Labour replaced the Industrial Relations Act with a 'Social Contract' with the trade unions which Wilson had made a central plank of Labour's appeal in 1974. In exchange for a favourable legal environment, and various state-delivered rights for workers, the unions would respect the needs of the national economy over strikes and wage claims without the cumbersome apparatus of an incomes policy. The Labour government moved quickly to end the miners' strike on the NUM's terms, and restored the legal position to the pre-1971 situation – but kept the aspects of the 1971 Act that the unions liked. The new phenomenon of secondary picketing, which worried many trade unionists and the general public, was virtually unregulated. Further legislation followed in 1976 in which the legal immunities that had permitted trade union activity since 1906 were widened. Despite promises since 1969, internal reform from the trade unions was absent. Individual rights at work were extended through the Employment Protection Act and the Sex Discrimination Act of 1975, the bulk of which survived the Conservative governments of 1979–97.

The failure of the Social Contract was evident by summer 1975 and a more traditional and effective incomes policy was agreed with the TUC which remained in force in various guises until the end of 1978. The effectiveness of the policies put into action in 1976–77 encouraged the policy error of a 5 per cent wages threshold imposed in late 1978. By that stage wage restraint had been taken further than ever before, and the crisis had receded to the extent that trade unionists felt willing once more to act assertively. Ford car workers and then lorry drivers broke the pay policy, and were followed by an apparently random outbreak of damaging strikes in the public sector by low paid workers in the Winter of Discontent of January and February 1979, who although miserably off had mostly been *beneficiaries* of the pay policy. Some of these strikes were conducted with a meanness of spirit that destroyed the romantic images of trade unionism that had sustained the 'Labour movement'. Even Tony Benn had to concede that people were behaving 'irrationally'; Callaghan found the intimidation associated with the disputes deeply depressing. Industrial conditions had become more Hobbes than Rousseau: a squalid war of all against all rather than a social contract. Central government was badly dislocated and reactive during the crisis.[57]

The 'Concordat'[58] of 14 February 1979 offered more than the Social Contract had for the government. The TUC and the government agreed an inflation target of 5 per cent by 1982, and the unions agreed a series of reforms of industrial dispute procedures including restrictions on secondary picketing and a strong recommendation for ballots before taking industrial action.[59]

However, as with the wider economic programme Labour offered, the Concordat approach was never given a sustained try. It was capable of several interpretations, but so was the Conservative policy offered in 1979, which was also aimed at giving 'responsible trade unionism' one last try, but mutated into a repudiation of this basic approach after 1982.[60]

The Internal Opposition

By the late 1970s the Labour Party was an unsteady rock on which to build a government or a coherent political approach. The trade unions, the party organisation and the parliamentary leadership had become detached and often antagonistic during 1964–79. The strains were apparent from the late 1960s. Elections within the big unions had been won by left-wing candidates who were distrustful of Labour's economic policy and outraged by *In Place of Strife*. In turn this affected voting at conference and in the NEC.

For the wider electorate, the disillusion of the hopes of 1964 and 1966 cast a long shadow over the Labour Party as Labour became unpopular on a scale, and for a duration, that was unprecedented and not surpassed until the 1992–97 Conservative government. Labour's share of the *total* electorate fell from 34 per cent in 1964 (36.3 per cent in 1966) to 31 per cent in 1970 and continued to decline gently in the next three elections before slumping in 1983. Even in 1997 Labour's vote had only recovered to 1970 levels. Labour's share of the *votes cast* was to tumble between 1970 and 1974.[61]

	1964	1966	1970	1974f	1974o	1979
Labour share of vote	44.1	48.0	43.1	37.2	39.2	36.9
Conservative share of vote	43.4	41.9	46.4	37.9	35.8	43.9
Labour share of electorate	34.0	36.4	31.0	29.3	28.6	28.1
Conservative share of electorate	33.4	31.7	33.4	29.9	26.1	33.3

The loss of the 1970 election reflected badly on Wilson and the party leadership. The campaign itself had been presidential in style, and lacking even in lip service to socialist pieties. The fall in the Labour vote allowed the left to argue that the government had failed by neglecting its core supporters, and that a shift to the left was the answer. Former ministers such as Tony Benn and (at that time) Reg Prentice embraced this analysis. The left carried nearly everything before it in policymaking in opposition, with only the pledge to nationalise 25 leading companies sticking in Wilson's throat.[62] The party performed an undignified U-turn on Europe, with which a large minority of the parliamentary party violently disagreed. The only issue that united all the parts of the party was obscurantist opposition to Heath's flawed Industrial Relations Act 1971. For much of the 1970 Parliament, Labour was an embarrassingly poor opposition to the troubled Heath government, and was widely seen as unprincipled, extreme or both. Labour only led strongly in the polls in summer 1971, and its support fell badly during 1973–74. The tactical brilliance of the February 1974 campaign, and – even more – the ineptitude of the Conservative effort, covered over the failings of Labour's performance in the longer term. The result was that Labour, at a time of acute crisis, took power in a condition aptly described by Treasury Minister Edmund Dell:

There is no comparable example of such intellectual and political incoherence in a party coming into office in the twentieth century history of the United Kingdom.[63]

The February 1974 manifesto was the most left wing manifesto since 1945. Its implementation in the calmer circumstances of the 1960s would have been difficult, but the failure to effect a fundamental and irreversible shift of resources from the better off to the worse off was hardly surprising in the economic circumstances of the 1907s. Michael Barratt Brown, one of the architects of the Alternative Economic Strategy (AES), conceded it was 'a commitment that few societies have ever achieved' and 'an almost impossible prescription' if redistribution had to take place without significant growth.[64] But the 1974 manifesto still served as a charge sheet by which the left of the party could indict the parliamentary leadership.

The divisions between the party and the parliamentary leadership were most apparent at the 1976 conference. Conference voted overwhelmingly for the radical *Labour's Programme 1976* and the Alternative Economic Strategy, and also endorsed the nationalisation of the clearing banks. Meanwhile Healey battled with a currency crisis and Callaghan delivered

Peter Jay's homily on the futility of demand management. Tony Benn recorded in his diary:

The Party expressed, with total clarity and almost unanimity, its desire for a more socialist policy; at the same time it ratified the relations with the trade union movement which it wants to develop; [even as] it decided it would support the Government.[65]

Labour was far from ideologically bankrup in the 1970s, but there were two inconsistent tendencies within the party. The Labour leadership accepted Britain's place in the international economy and thought that the limits of the acceptable size of the state were being reached. The Labour Party tended to believe that the undoubted crisis in capitalism paved the way for Britain's insulation from the world economy and a large expansion in state ownership and industrial democracy in Britain. These very different perspectives were to inform the party divisions which were to erupt after 1979. The interpretation of the AES as a radical variant of Keynesianism was no longer viable after 1974 because of its implications. [66]

Benn did not take the victory of the Labour left as historically inevitable, considering that Callaghan might use an election victory to defeat the left:

There is going to be a tremendous battle over the manifesto because Jim will want to make a deal with the Liberals and a watered-down manifesto the basis of our appeal to the country. If he does that and wins, then we have the basis of a Labour Government which will have abandoned entirely the argument for reform. Revisionism will have won. If we try that and are defeated it will open the way for the party to go left.[67]

Benn probably underestimated the strength of the left's position; the overwhelming defeats for the social democrats at the 1976 conference were a sign that the party had effectively gone left already. Whether, in the longer term, a Labour government could survive on such a slender base of support – even sympathy – in the party is debatable; but perhaps Benn was right to think that an election victory would have given what he called revisionism a new lease of life.

Conclusion: 1979

Labour won 36.9 per cent of the vote in 1979, only 2.3 points down on October and a minuscule 0.2 per cent down on February 1974. The Conservatives' victory was won on the same share of the vote that Labour had lost with in 1959. Considering that the Labour government had presided over the first fall in living standards since the war, industrial chaos was fresh in the electorate's memory,[68] and that the party was almost laughably disunited, to lose such a small share of the vote was remarkable. The full consequences of the party's turn to the left were not to become apparent until 1983, and even by 1992 Labour had not recovered the support Callaghan had obtained in 1979. The 1979 election saw a startlingly large swing to the Conservatives among the skilled working class in the south of England and the Midlands, but a low swing in the north of England and Scotland and among the professional and managerial class.[69]

In his biography of James Callaghan Kenneth Morgan makes a strong case for the Callaghan government as an ancestor of new Labour in its relative conservatism on social issues and its prudent economic policy. Labour in power had shown itself capable of developing a new agenda – consumer power, the environment, social equality, educational standards – which prefigured later thinking. There was awareness of some future trends. The Downing Street Policy Unit had worked in 1975–76 on a plan to sell council houses to tenants[70] but unfortunately did not proceed with it. Top rate tax cuts were being discussed as a possible future policy, if not for immediate introduction.[71] The Concordat approach to the economy and industrial relations was an underpinning of Australian Labour rule in the 1980s, although the British unions' fragmented structure needed urgent repair for the strategy to work. There were also severe problems with management in the nationalised industries and the public sector proper, which were becoming increasingly apparent.

Consensus represented a diminished portion of the political spectrum in 1979 but was not dead. Margaret Thatcher 'never had any illusion that if [the Conservatives] lost or even if we failed to win an overall majority I would be given another chance.'[72] There was no plausible successor to Thatcher who shared her fundamental critique of post-war Britain. The popular groundswell generated by the Winter of Discontent was ebbing by the time of the 1979 election. The 1979 Conservative manifesto was less radical than that of 1970 in important respects. The government radicalised while in office. The Thatcherite project was enabled by the implausibility of the Labour Party, free at last of its moorings to the old parliamentary leadership, the failures of Thatcher's opponents in the Conservative Party, and the division of the anti-Thatcher vote. Ironically, the continued hold that consensus thinking along the lines developing under the Callaghan government exercised over the electorate was shown by the instant appeal of the SDP when it defected from Labour in 1981.

The estrangement of party and government in the 1960s and 1970s was a baneful influence. The party's repudiation of the social democratic market economy in 1973 led to a long hike in the wilderness – in the opposite direction to the way Britain and Europe were evolving – until the Policy Review process in the late 1980s returned the party to the real world. The hope that electoral victory for social democracy in 1978 or 1979 would teach the same lesson that failure in 1983 and 1987 taught came to nothing. Paradoxically, the party created the conditions in which the right seized the opportunity to establish its ascendancy.

The Labour government of 1974–79 rode out a severe economic crisis and fast learnt the lessons of the post-1973 world. Its achievements are as underrated as the Winter of Discontent is overrated. The inevitable exhaustion of the social democracy exemplified by the Callaghan government is too easily assumed.

Notes

The author would like to thank Brian Brivati for his comments on an earlier draft.

1 Ken Coates *The Crisis of British Socialism*, Nottingham: Spokesman, 1971, p240.

2 Francis Cripps and Frances Morrell 'The Abandonment of Full Employment' in Ken Coates, ed, *What Went Wrong*, Nottingham: Spokesman, 1979, p95-102.

3 Gregory Elliott *Labourism and the English Genius*, London: Verso, 1993, p80.

4 Philip Gould *The Unfinished Revolution*, London: Little, Brown 1998, p35–36.

5 Margaret Thatcher *The Downing Street Years*, London: Harper-Collins, 1993, p7.

6 Much of the inquest in 1979–81 was dominated by this sort of analysis.

7 See Paul Foot *The Politics of Harold Wilson*, Harmondsworth: Penguin, 1968. The broad history of this position is outlined in Ralph Miliband *Parliamentary Socialism*, London: Merlin, 1973 edition).

8 Austin Mitchell and David Weinir *Last Time: Labour's Lessons from the Sixties*, London: Bellew, 1997, draws parallels with the mood of 1997.

9 The other consistently unpopular government of the post war period, that of John Major in 1992–97, had also broken promises – in its case on tax, which had been a central feature of its 1992 campaign. Perhaps the centrality of tax in 1992 and planning and modernisation in 1964 added to the electorate's disillusion and sense of having been defrauded.

10 Peter Flannery's BBC TV drama series *Our Friends in the North* was broadcast in 1996.

11 Peter Hennessy and Anthony Seldon (eds), *Ruling Performance*, Oxford, Blackwell, 1987, discuss government records 1945–87 in a broader context.

12 A considerable literature on consensus exists. See Paul Addison *The Road to 1945*, London: Jonathan Cape, 1975), Ben Pimlott 'The Myth of Consensus' in L.M. Smith, ed, *The Making of Britain: Echoes of Greatness*, London: Macmillan, 1988), Dennis Kavanagh and Peter Morris *Consensus Politics from Attlee to Major*, Oxford: Blackwell, 1994); Anthony Seldon 'Consensus: a Debate too Long?' in F.F. Ridley and Michael Rush *British Government and Politics since 1945*, Oxford: Oxford University Press, 1995, Harriet Jones and Michael Kandiah, eds, *The Myth of Consensus*, London: Macmillan, 1996.

13 Andrew Gamble *Britain in Decline*, London: Macmillan, 1981 and 1994, is a key text on the idea of British decline; see also David Reynolds *Britannia Overruled* Longman, 1991; *Jim Tomlinson* 'Inventing Decline: the falling behind of the British economy in the post war years', *Economic History Review* XLIX, 4, 1996, p731–757.

14 Gamble, 1994, p1.

15 Tony Benn *Out of the Wilderness Diaries 1963-67*, London: Arrow 1988, p553. In November 1966 Benn argued that after 1850 Britain celebrated 'empire' rather than 'engineering' and gradually dissipated her productive energies.

16 Roger Bacon and Walter Eltis *Britain's Economic Problem: Too Few Producers*, London: Macmillan, 1976.

17 Incidentally, the Conservative acceptance of steel nationalisation in 1970 – compared with 1951 – runs counter to the prevailing view that the parties' stance on this matter was diverging.

18 Michael Stewart *The Jekyll and Hyde Years*, London: Dent, 1977.

19 The Conservative government of 1922 was elected with 38.2 per cent of the vote, but 42 out of the 345 Conservative seats were uncontested, and some 'National Liberals' stood with Tory support. Allowing for these factors, Tory support was well over 40 per cent in 1922.

20 Robert Moss *The Collapse of British Democracy*, London: Maurice Temple Smith, 1975, is the most bizarre example, written by an *Economist* writer who occasionally advised Margaret Thatcher. In an Anglia TV series in early 1976 former Labour minister Lord Chalfont thought *It Could Happen Here* – 'It' being a communist takeover.

21 Nicholas Woodward 'Labour's economic performance 1964–70' p72-101 in *The Wilson Governments* R. Coopey, S. Fielding, N. Tiratsoo, eds, London: Pinter, 1993, is the most calm and balanced treatment of Wilson's economic record. See also Stewart, 1977.

22 Richard Coopey 'Industrial Policy in the White Heat of the Scientific Revolution' in Coopey, Woodward and Tiratsoo, eds, 1993.

23 Maudling had hoped that a strong economic boom, not subject to the usual 'stop' phase would create a virtuous cycle by which higher demand would call forth higher industrial investment and Britain could be raised to a faster plane of economic growth. To dampen the

inflationary effects early in the boom he aimed to win the goodwill and restraint of the trade unions over wages, and free up competition in the private sector through reforms such as the abolition of Resale Price Maintenance. The Maudling-Wilson policies were opposed by City interests as represented by Lord Cromer, Governor of the Bank of England 1961-66.

24 The historical argument on devaluation has not been concluded and probably never will. Clive Ponting *Breach of Promise*, London: Hamish Hamilton, 1989, regards failure to devalue in 1964–65 as a major error prompted by Anglo-American commitments; also Harold Wilson *The Labour Government 1964–70*, London: Weidenfeld and Nicolson, 1971, Ben Pimlott Harold Wilson, London: HarperCollins, 1992, and Philip Ziegler *Wilson: The Authorised Life*, London: Weidenfeld and Nicolson, 1993. Some of the reflections of those involved are collected in Mitchell and Weinir, 1997. After an economically productive devaluation in Britain in 1992 the devaluers appear to have the upper hand.

25 'Cuts' in the 1960s usually involved the reduction of planned increases in expenditure rather than reducing allocations in real terms.

26 Robert Bacon and Walter Eltis, *Britain's Economic Problem: Too Few Producers*, London: Macmillan, 1978 edition, p51.

27 Bacon and Eltis, *op. cit.* p35. Productivity growth in 1955–65 averaged 3 per cent; the first Wilson government undoubtedly succeeded in using technology to improve Britain's basic competitive position. But economic outcomes were such that the productivity gain was taken in higher unemployment rather than higher output.

28 Michael Artis and David Cobham *Labour's Economic Policies 1974–79*, Manchester: Manchester University Press, 1991. Richard Coopey and Nicholas Woodward, eds, *Britain in the 1970s*, London: UCL Press, 1996, discusses the economic record of the Heath and Labour governments.

29 Burk and Cairncross, *op. cit.*, p165–167.

30 According to OECD statistics cited in Nicholas Crafts 'Economic growth in the 1970s' in Coopey and Woodward, 1996, p83. Britain's growth rate was 15th out of 15 European comparators in 1950–73, 11th out of 15 in 1973–79.

31 None so crass as crude monetarism proved in 1979–81.

32 The story of 1974–76 is told from within the Treasury by Edmund Dell in *A Hard Pounding: Politics and Economic Crisis 1974–76*, Oxford: Oxford University Press, 1991, Joel Barnett *Inside the Treasury*, London: André Deutsch, 1982, and Denis Healey *The Time of My Life*, London: Michael Joseph, 1989. There was nothing that could be straightforwardly described as a 'Treasury view' on how to deal with the crisis. More anecdotal versions from different points of view seep through the pages of Tony Benn *Against the Tide: Diaries 1973–76*, London: Hutchinson, 1989, and Susan Crosland *Tony Crosland*, London: Jonathan Cape, 1982.

33 On the IMF, as well as ministerial memoirs and general histories, see Kathleen Burk and Alec Cairncross, *Goodbye Great Britain*, New Haven: Yale University Press, 1992.

34 A large extract from the speech is reproduced in James Callaghan *Time and Chance*, London: Collins 1987, p.425–427.

35 Callaghan, *op. cit.*, p.427.

36 The 1975 Budget had raised taxes in the middle of a recession, for instance.

37 On the contemporary definition. Using the claimant count total, unemployment did not reach 1 million until the first quarter of 1976; it peaked in the last quarter of 1977 at 1.2 million and then fell to 1.1 million in early 1979, *Economic Trends Annual Supplement* London: ONS, 1997 edition. These figures hardly betoken an 'abandonment of full employment' which took place in 1976.

38 Healey, 1989, p381–83, 490–92. Edmund Dell in his discussion of Healey in *The Chancellors*, London: HarperCollins, 1996, p.415 hardly mentions monetarism. Like Healey, he draws a distinction between an ideological belief in monetarism and the common sense observation that a sudden flood of monetary expansion as happened in 1971–73 can result in the classic problem of 'too much money chasing too few goods'.

39 Maurice Mullard *The Politics of Public Expenditure*, London: Routledge, 1993.

40 A more instructive episode is perhaps the 'gilts strike' of 1978, in which an electioneering budget was trimmed back by the power of the financial markets to refuse to fund the government's borrowing.

41 Leo Pliatzky *Getting and Spending*, Oxford: Blackwell, 1982.

42 Burk and Cairncross, *op. cit.*, p223–224.

43 According to Gallup Callaghan's approval rating never fell below 50 per cent between October 1977 and the end of 1978; 1978 was the first such year since 1960,and the only one until 1998. Approval of the government's record in general was running relatively high as well. David Butler and Gareth Butler *British Political Facts 1900-94*, London: Macmillan, 1995, contains long series of opinion poll data.

44 Bernard Nossiter *Britain: A Future that Works*, Boston: Houghton Mifflin, 1978, p105.

45 Bacon and Eltis, *op. cit.*, p.137.

46 Kenneth Morgan *Callaghan: A Life*, Oxford: Oxford University Press, 1997, p.557.

47 Anthony Seldon 'Anatomising Wilson: Philip Ziegler' *Contemporary Record* Vol 7 No 2, Autumn 1993, p.338–59.

48 *The Labour Way is the Better Way* Labour Party manifesto, May 1979.

49 Edmund Dell 'The Origins of Petroleum Revenue Tax' in *Contemporary Record* Vol 7 No 2, Autumn 1993, p.215–252.

50 The 1979 Conservative manifesto said that 'There should also be more open and informed discussion about the Government's economic objectives, as happens, for example, in Germany and other

countries, so that there is wider understanding of the consequences of unrealistic bargaining and industrial action.'

51 Robert Taylor, *The Trade Union Question in British Politics*, Oxford: Blackwell, 1993, an excellent overview of the post-war period, points out that the central problems were starting to become apparent at the end of the Attlee government; also Lewis Minkin *The Contentious Alliance*, Edinburgh, Edinburgh University Press, 1991.

52 In January 1979 this peaked at 44 per cent, level with those considering unions a good thing, but returned to the normal level of 29 per cent in summer 1979. Gallup data cited by Taylor, 1993, p371.

53 David Butler and Dennis Kavanagh *The British General Election of 1979*, London: Macmillan, 1980, p131.

54 Speech to 1966 Labour Party conference, as quoted in Tudor Jones *Remaking the Labour Party*, London: Routledge, 1996, p82.

55 As well as the general histories of industrial relations and the diaries and memoirs of the Wilson government, see Peter Jenkins *The Battle of Downing Street*, London: Charles Knight, 1970.

56 Robert Taylor 'Industrial Relations' in Anthony Seldon and David Marquand *The Ideas that Shaped Post War Britain*, London: Harper-Collins, 1996.

57 The events of the Winter of Discontent 1978–79 are still remembered as myth for the most part. The visual impact of Philip Whitehead's *The Writing on the Wall* TV series for Channel 4 is considerable, but nobody has yet analysed the period in the detail that Burk and Cairncross did for the IMF crisis.

58 The government tried to avoid calling it this, because a Concordat is strictly speaking an agreement between a spiritual and a temporal power. Which was which in 1979 is an interesting question.

59 On the Concordat see Taylor, *op. cit.*, p.259. The 5 per cent inflation target would have been extremely difficult to achieve, given the oil price rise and the Clegg Commission awards which settled the public sector strikes, which the government could do nothing about. As it turned out, inflation in 1982 was 8.6 per cent. Other options within the Concordat included the possibility of no-strike agreements in essential services, something that legal reform in 1980–93 did not produce.

60 Jim Prior *A Balance of Power*, London: Hamish Hamilton, 1986, demonstrates clearly the continuities of approach during the first phase of the Thatcher government.

61 Data from F.W.S. *Craig British Electoral Facts 1832–1987*, Aldershot: Dartmouth, 1989.

62 Michael Hatfield *The House the Left Built*, London: Gollancz, 1978; Mark Wickham-Jones *Economic Strategy and the Labour Party*, London: Macmillan, 1996. The revival of nationalisation contrasted with its near-burial as a Labour theme in the 1960s and did not convince the party leadership. Healey's caustic comment that the left were proposing to nationalise Marks and Spencer to make it as efficient as the Co-op reflected the realisation on the right that

ownership was not just irrelevant as Crosland suggested, but that state ownership posed particular problems of management for which the left did not have workable answers.

63 Dell, *A Hard Pounding*, p12.

64 Michael Barratt Brown, 'The Growth and Distribution of Income and Wealth', p34–73 in Coates (ed), 1979, p.59. Barratt Brown draws the lesson from this that the entire capitalist system needed to be replaced by socialism.

65 Tony Benn, *Against the Tide: Diaries 1973–76*, London: Hutchinson, 1989, pp.616–617.

66 Wickham-Jones, *op. cit.*, attempts a partial rehabilitation of the Alternative Economic Strategy.

67 Tony Benn *Conflicts of Interest: Diaries 1977–80*, London: Hutchinson, 1990, p78. Benn wrote this in March 1977 when an early election was an alternative to the Lib-Lab pact.

68 There was a sharp shift in party support and political attitudes in response to the strikes; a Labour lead of 5 per cent in November 1978 changed to a 20 per cent Conservative lead in February 1979. The damage done was not fully healed by May. Even another month would have helped. Callaghan's eloquent comment to Bernard Donoughue about a 'sea change' reflected his own despondency, rather than necessarily suggesting that Thatcher's victory was truly inevitable.

69 Michael Steed's appendix in Butler and Kavanagh, 1980, shows that for the first time constituency swings were bimodally distributed in 1979.

70 Joe Haines *The Politics of Power*, London: Jonathan Cape, 1977.

71 Barnett, 1982, p.140.

72 Margaret Thatcher, *The Path to Power*, London: HarperCollins, 1995, p.439.

The Wilderness Years 1979–1994

Eric Shaw

When Labour was vanquished by Mrs Thatcher in the election of 1979 not even the most pessimistic would have believed that the party would have to wander disconsolately for eighteen bleak years in the political wilderness and suffer three more crushing defeats before finally reaching the promised land in May 1997. Or that the party that arrived would be dramatically transformed from the one that departed. It has become received wisdom in the media that the transition to 'New Labour' really commenced with Tony Blair's election to the leadership in June 1994. In reality, without the nine-year leadership of Neil Kinnock it is impossible to envisage the emergence of a Blairite Labour Party: in virtually every respect the party's metamorphosis began under him. The first major theme of this chapter is to explore the process by which this occurred.

Labour loss of office provoked an outbreak of recrimination of a scale without precedent. Between 1979 and 1981 Labour was overwhelmed by a grass-roots insurgency which led to fundamental changes in the programme and rules of the party. Denver echoed a common sentiment when he concluded that the constitutional reforms of the early 1980s had 'decisively shifted power in the party away from the PLP to the constituency activists and the trade unions'.[1] As Labour's centenary beckons, 'elite domination' prevails to an unprecedented degree. Again, the vital changes took place under Kinnock and the second principal theme of this chapter is to explore how and why.

But first the liniments of Labour's crisis which began in 1979 and culminated in its worst election defeat in its history in 1983 must be traced.

The Crisis Years 1979–83

The crisis was over both policy and power. It expressed a formidable left-wing backlash rooted in disenchantment at the record of the outgoing Callaghan government – relentless cutbacks in public services, stagnant and falling wages for many workers, the rise in unemployment to a post-war high and the 'Winter of Discontent' for which responsibility was firmly nailed on ministers. All this was compounded – in the eyes of many activists – by the Government's persistent and, sometimes, contemptuous disregard of conference, the voice of the party. What was to be done?

Whilst the wider party lacked the means to enforce its policies upon a recalcitrant Labour Government it had control over its own rules – its constitution. Constitutions prescribe the way 'in which power is distributed and organised with regard to the authoritative making and implementing of decisions – the roles and their relations through which authority is distributed and exercised.'[2] Constitutionally, Labour was a highly pluralist party in which power was dispersed amongst a range of institutions – conference, the National Executive Committee (NEC), the Shadow Cabinet and the unions. But for much of Labour's history a pattern of integrated elite control prevailed. The crucial factor was the existence of a pattern of concurrent majorities: virtually all key institutions (the NEC, the Shadow Cabinet, the PLP, the major unions, conference) were controlled by the right and willing to defer to the Leader and his colleagues. The structure of integrated elite control was substantially weakened in the 1970s by the rise of left-wing unionism which removed the leadership's majority in both conference and the NEC. Notwithstanding, the parliamentary leadership was still protected from rank and file pressure by the effective autonomy of the Parliamentary Labour Party (PLP). For this reason, the left concentrated on securing rule-changes that would render the PLP more accountable to the constituencies. Spearheaded by the activist-based pressure group the Campaign for Labour Party Democracy three major reforms were espoused: the mandatory reselection of MPs (which would require all MPs to undergo a selection process before each election rather then being automatically readopted); the extension of the franchise for electing the leader, at the time confined to the Parliamentary Labour Party; and the transfer of the right to frame the manifesto from the joint control of the Shadow Cabinet (or Cabinet) and the NEC to sole control by the latter.

The leadership failed to prevent conference from approving two of the three constitutional reforms (NEC control over the manifesto was narrowly rejected. But Callaghan resigned before new leadership election procedures were installed in the hope that, with the franchise still precariously in the PLP's hands, Dennis Healey would succeed him. On the first ballot Healey secured 112 votes, Foot 83, John Silkin 38 and Shore 32. The latter two withdrew, urging their supporters to switch to Foot. On the second count Foot triumphed by 139 to 129 votes with his rival agreeing to stay on as his deputy. What may well have tipped the balance against Healey, rather ominously, was the decision by at least five and possibly six intending defectors on the right to vote for the veteran left-winger because they wanted to saddle the party with the man they calculated was least fitted for the post.[3] Once an unrepentant rebel, Foot had for a decade performed the role of conciliator: he saw his mission as leader as above all to maintain party unity. But even his emollient gifts proved inadequate to the task. Shortly after his election, in January 1981, the Wembley conference took place to determine the precise means for selecting future leaders. The majority view was this should take the form of an electoral college but there was no agreement over the relative proportion of the three constituents, MPs, trade unions and constituency Labour parties (CLPs). The PLP insisted that they should hold 50 per cent, an option Foot too favoured and it seemed within his grasp. Already the tide had turned against the left within the unions as the second largest, the Amalgamated Union of Engineering Workers, had fallen under right-wing control. Nor was there a majority for the left's preferred option, an equal three-way split amongst MPs, CLPs and the unions. But the AUEW behaved with extraordinary ineptitude: on the grounds that it was bound by its National Committee not to vote for *any* option which gave MPs less than an absolute majority, i.e. 50 per cent plus one, it abstained on the crucial vote. Another right-wing union, USDAW (the shop workers union) idiosyncratically chose a formula which gave 40 per cent to the unions and 30 per cent each to the PLP and the constituencies. CLPD organisers spotted that this was the only formula likely to muster a majority and adroitly persuaded all left-wing unions to vote for it.

The advance of the left convinced influential figures on the right that Labour was slipping irrevocable to the left. Former Cabinet members David Owen, Shirley Williams and Bill Rodgers began organising a breakaway and to recruit sympathisers.[4] Whatever lingering doubts they had were resolved by the outcome of the Wembley conference and the three former ministers, together with another former senior Labour politician, Roy Jenkins, established a new party, the Social Democratic Party. Later joined by almost two dozen Labour MP's this was the worst split in the party for half a century and the electoral consequences were to prove calamitous.

Almost immediately Labour was plunged into another bout of infighting when Tony Benn, the foremost figure on the left, announced (with minimal consultation) that he would challenge Healey for the deputy leadership. A protracted, bitter and extremely rancorous campaign spread over six months then ensued. The cost was immense as it fixed in the public mind for years to come an image of Labour as a strife-ridden party. John Silkin entered the fray with support from the Tribune Group as an alternative candidate of the left but he was eliminated after the first round. The Transport and General Workers Union (TGWU) held a consultative ballot which opted for Healey, but the union decided to back Silkin at the first round and at the second flung its considerable weight behind Benn! Healey won only by the narrowest of margins – by 50.4 per cent to 49.6 per cent – after the decisive intervention by 37 mainly left-wing MPs, including one of Foot's main lieutenants, Neil Kinnock, who deliberately abstained to block Benn.

In addition to its constitutional advances, the left was able to secure the adoption of many of its favoured policies. Its triumphs seemed impressive but in reality it had fatally overstretched itself. The circumstances of 1979–83 were highly propitious not because of any fundamental alteration in the balance of forces within the party but because a concatenation of short-time and fortuitous circumstances provided a unique window of opportunity. The standing of the right was damaged by the defection of some of its ablest and most energetic leaders to form the SDP and by the questioning of the loyalty of those who had remained. Victory on the crucial constitutional issues was obtained – very narrowly – by a mixture, of chance, good luck, tactical dexterity and the disunity and extraordinary incompetence of the right. All this masked the fact that the left's power base was a slim one, rooted primarily in the constituency grass-roots and amongst middle-level lay and full-time officials in the unions with perilously little support outside the party. Without exception, the press was hostile, often virulently so. There were very few in any position of influence within the major institutions of society – such as academia, broadcasting and the civil service – who had much sympathy for the Bennite programme, in striking contrast to their enthusiasm for the SDP.

Indeed, Benn's bid for the deputy leadership sowed the seeds of left-wing decline. Many influential left-wing union leaders regarded it as unnecessary and very divisive, and blamed the Bennite left for Labour's collapse in the opinion polls. Finally, the Benn's near miss provoked a backlash: right-wing and centrist unions began to operate in a much more organised and effective fashion and, as early as 1981 and 1982, they secured the removal of seven left-wingers from the NEC (an unprecedented turnover of members) and Benn and his allies were ejected from the chairs of key sub-committees.[5]

In January 1982, at a meeting in Bishop's Stortford it seemed that a modus vivendi had been reached but within months Foot found himself confronted with another crisis, this time sparked by external events. In April military forces dispatched by the Argentinean military government swiftly overran the disputed British-owned Falklands islands. How was Labour to respond? In an emergency debate a belligerent Foot denounced the invasion by 'a brutal military dictatorship' and backed the government's decision to send a task force to repossess the islands. But there was a significant minority in the party opposed to the venture and, as military hostilities began to move closer Foot's initial fervour began to cool as he oscillated between supporting the government's position and urging restraint to allow time for a negotiated solution. This unfortunately contrasted with the grim and determined Mrs Thatcher who gambled all on a quick military victory. The total success of the Task Force transformed the Government's position. Previously it had been limping well behind in the polls but the 'Falklands Factor' gave it a firm lead which it was never to lose. Conversely, Labour, squeezed by the new SDP–Liberal Alliance as well as by the Tories, slumped ever further behind and its prospects began to look dismal.

They were not improved by the imbroglio over Militant. Since the mid-1970s this group, an 'entryist' Trotskyist organisation seeking to infiltrate the party had been growing in influence, though it was never more than a minor force (except in Liverpool).[6] The right clamoured for disciplinary action but the left-controlled NEC was unwilling to move. Foot initially concurred but by the end of 1981 with the pressure from the PLP becoming difficult to contain he changed his mind. In December the NEC narrowly agreed to hold an enquiry into Militant. Conducted by the party's General Secretary, Ron Hayward, and its National Agent, David Hughes, the main finding of the report was that Militant was an entryist organisation, with its own organisation and disciplinary system and was thereby in breach of the constitution. It was endorsed by the NEC and conference but action against Militant leaders was soon bogged down in legal dispute. Though a handful of expulsions took place the NEC was outmanoeuvred by the Trotskyist group. The problem continued to fester and it took four more years before it was resolved.[7]

Other internal party controversies continued to divert the party when in the spring of 1983, still cresting on a wave of popularity, Mrs Thatcher called the election. The (so-called) Clause 5 meeting held to agree the manifesto for the 1983 election was the shortest ever. This, on the surface, seems odd, for the frontbench found itself faced with policies in which it found little merit and from whose formulation it had been largely excluded. The manifesto was a radical one: it proposed reflation of the economy to cut the swelling jobless queues to below one million within five years of taking office, a substantial increases in public expenditure, the imposition of exchange and import controls, a new partnership with the unions, ambitious schemes for economic planning and industrial democracy, extended public ownership and a major expansion of the public services. (*New Hope for Britain*, Labour Manifesto 1983). Despite the fact that it controlled the Shadow Cabinet, had growing support on the NEC, and had in the chair of key Home Policy Committee, the tough and wily right-winger John Golding, the anticipated resistance from the right did not materialise. Instead, Golding proposed that the draft manifesto be adopted without amendment. Why? He calculated that if the party was destined to capsize in the elections, it should do so with left-wing colours flying conspicuously on its masthead – to demonstrate for all time that the party could never win on a left-wing manifesto.

In the preceding year election preparations had been neglected, hence no effective campaign machinery existed at Head Office. The campaign itself was a disaster: far from cutting into the Tories' massive lead the Labour vote shrank even further. It was disorganised, ramshackle and uncoordinated with no obvious strategy or central messages.[8] Foot was obviously ill-at ease with television and ridiculed in a ferocious media assault which totally destroyed his credibility. Butler and Kavanagh concluded that 'it is difficult to think of any campaign fought by a major party since the war that was more inept than Labour's in 1983.'[9]

Even then the sheer dimensions of the defeat came as a shock. Only 209 chastened MPs survived, and at 27.6 per cent the party's vote was a mere 2 per cent more than the Liberal-SDP Alliance and its worst performance (in terms of votes per candidates) since 1900.[10] A whole range of factors contributed to this outcome including social structural changes, changing patterns of housing tenure; a battery of unpopular policies; the turbulence within the party, coupled with a leader, Michael Foot, regarded with incredulity by most of the electorate, a totally incompetent and amateurish campaign; and the emergence of a third force, the Liberal–SDP Alliance, rendered, by the accession of former Labour Cabinet ministers, a credible alternative governing formation.[11] The losses even within the party's natural constituency were so considerable that Crewe concluded that while 'the Labour vote remains largely working class...the working class has ceased to be largely Labour.'[12]

The Kinnock Years

Regaining Control of the Party

Shortly after the election Foot announced his resignation as leader. Four contestants entered the race for the succession, Neil Kinnock, the right-wing Roy Hattersley, the centrist Peter Shore and the left-wing Eric Heffer. (Tony Benn had lost his seat). This was the first election for the leadership to be decided not by the votes of the PLP – in which case Hattersley would almost certainly have won – but by the new electoral college. The balance of forces in the wider party benefited Kinnock. Though Hattersley could rely on support from two powerful unions, the GMB and the AEU, the majority of unions preferred a leader from the centre-left. Further, Kinnock was confidant of securing the bulk of the constituency vote. The fact that he was the obvious front-runner probably induced wavering MPs who in other circumstances would have backed a right-winger to opt for the victor. Kinnock's personal popularity, the belief that he had mastered the arts of modern communication and the fact that Hattersley was seen as a more divisive figure combined to accord him an easy victory. He won in all three sections of the electoral college, with no less than 71 per cent of the total vote. Hattersley, anticipating this, had concentrated his efforts on the deputy leadership with – in what was dubbed the 'dream ticket' – the active support of Kinnock. Hattersley crushed his main opponent, and standard-bearer of the left, Michael Meacher with surprising ease, by 67 per cent to 28 per cent.[13]

Kinnock's first concern was to re-establish the authority of the leadership and transform a divided party into a disciplined and cohesive force: only then would major policy departures become feasible. Attaining these objectives was to be no easy task. The new leader faced a range of pressures with limited resources: his base within the party was broad but shallow. He lacked a majority in the NEC and presided over a Shadow Cabinet most of whose members had not voted for him and regarded him with some scepticism. Further, as Kinnock later recalled, there was no 'instrument for inaugurating and pursuing change on the scale and in the direction that was needed. There was no tradition of the Parliamentary Labour Party or the Shadow Cabinet instituting and processing change and neither was there any means available for doing that.'[14] The new leader was determined to diminish the role of the NEC and to equip the Shadow Cabinet and his own private office with a policy-innovating capacity. With the NEC in the immediate aftermath of the 1983 electoral disaster in a more tractable mood, agreement was reached at the end of the year to overhaul policy-making procedures. The extensive network of study groups and policy sub-committees orbiting around the NEC with their large number of co-opted advisors – in which left-inclined pressure group representatives and academics had often figured prominently – was wound up. It was replaced by a much more tightly organised system of joint Shadow Cabinet – NEC committees, in appearance a partnership but in practice weighted in favour of the frontbench and the leader.

In the next few years developments decisively tilted the balance of policy-making rights in favour of the frontbench. The considerable additional resources that were being made available to the party including the state-provided 'Short Money' and additional sums furnished by the unions, were used to finance secretarial and research resources for the frontbench and to pay for a greatly expanded Leader's Office whilst the research establishment of the party's own Headquarters was steadily run down. For the first time in the party's history, a sizable policy advisory arm controlled by the leadership emerged. In consequence, as Minkin noted, it could now 'develop more of its own independent policy initiatives ... with union acquiescence, the PLP leadership became *the* source of virtually all major initiatives.'[15] Conversely, the NEC's own policy committees lost their ability to initiate and develop policy, though its approval for major departures in contentious areas (like defence) still had to be negotiated. However, the creation of sub-committees, the recruitment of outside advisors and the input of ideas and policy options were all now subject to filtering by the leadership. Combined with shifts in the pattern of political alignments within the party (which we examine below) these institutional changes meant that by 1986 responsibility for policy determination had largely passed to the leader and senior Shadow Cabinet colleagues.[16]

The accepted view holds that whilst presentation and packaging had dramatically improved in the years up to 1987, the 'product' – policy – was due to internal resistance scarcely unaltered.[17] This is misleading. Significant policy modifications did take place, though unevenly, depending on the balance of forces. If, for instance, an issue was a matter of high priority for the unions, then their co-operation was required to alter existing policy. A notable instance was industrial relations law. The 1983

Manifesto had called for the repeal of all Tory industrial relations legislation but the consistent message of opinion research was that it was very popular. This created a dilemma for Labour's leadership. The outcome after protracted negotiations was a compromise – which fell short of what the leadership ideally would have wanted – in which the commitment to repeal was retained but was coupled with a pledge that the unions would be legally obliged to hold ballots over strikes and for union executive elections, measures which were on simple democratic grounds, the most awkward to challenge.[18]

Another difficult area was pay. Hattersley, the Shadow Chancellor between 1983 and 1987, saw the need to develop a convincing anti-inflationary stance[19] and favoured a voluntary incomes policy but the majority of unions adamantly insisted upon the return to free collective bargaining. As a result, the statement *A New Partnership. A New Britain* agreed in 1985 by the TUC–Labour Party Liaison Committee was a rather anodyne document.[20] On this matter, Labour in 1987 remained a party in search of a policy.

On most other issues Kinnock could rely on a solid support the majority of trade unions.[21] Thus the elaborate schemes for planning and industrial democracy were discarded with state intervention viewed as a corrective to the market rather than as an alternative mechanism.[22] The thorny problem of how to respond to the Conservatives' privatisation programme was not so easily resolved. Initially, the policy, first adumbrated in 1982, that Labour would return to the public sector all privatised industries, and would pay compensation only on the principle of 'no speculative gain' was reaffirmed.[23] But since then British Telecom had been privatised and British Gas was next in line with the almost certain prospect of a massive increase in the number of share-holders. In these circumstances Labour's policy, as it stood, seemed a certain vote-loser yet feelings ran high in the party, especially within the public sector unions. A report was compiled under the joint chairmanship of John Smith from the right and David Blunkett from the left which remained committed to reversing privatisation though on the basis of full compensation.[24]

Thus incremental policy-changes did take place but internal constraints prevented really sweeping innovations. Assembling majorities at conference often involved patient and complex bargaining and the leadership often expended considerable efforts on consensus-building. Right-wing unions like the Engineers usually saw eye to eye with the party leadership but the consent in matters which really concerned them of large left of centre ones – the TGWU, NUPE (National Union of Public Employees) and MSF (Manufacturing, Science and Finance) – had to be organised. Kinnock later recalled that 'to have changed all policies simultaneously [in that period] would have fractured the party.'[25] He felt that he could not risk being repudiated on a major issue: the publicity would be highly adverse and the morale of his opponents boosted.[26]

Equally, the approval of the NEC for really contentious items could, in this period, never be guaranteed and meetings were – in Blunkett's words, 'often traumatic ... dramas ... with Kinnock employing persuasion, cajoling, bullying and arm-twisting to get his way.'[27] Such protracted discussions were time-consuming and tiring which meant that many decisions were inevitably negotiated compromises.

The Miners Strike, 1984–5

Further, progress was seriously disrupted by the impact of external events. The leadership was unable to curb the inflow of disruptive issues which time and again divided and distracted the energies of the party, a result of its vulnerability to implacable external pressures. By far the most compelling was the year-long miners' strike, the most momentous industrial conflict in the years of Conservative Government whose eventual outcome was the virtual disappearance of the coal industry and the disintegration of most mining communities. Reflecting on the strike after his resignation, Kinnock held it responsible for stealing a year 'out of the job we should have doing, renovating policy.'[28] It was an issue which for historical reasons ignited particularly deep passions within the party and an unprecedented number of members were involved in activities designed to support the strikers. The party and most union leaders were solidly behind the miners (at least verbally) and few on the right were prepared to publicly criticise them, whatever privately they might have thought.

From the start Kinnock did not share this enthusiasm. Born into a miner's family, representing a miners' constituency, he felt emotionally torn for he was convinced that industrial disputes were electorally damaging and that militant trade union leaders like Scargill frightened the voters. He had no doubt that a disastrous mistake had been made in not holding a ballot, which was required by union rules and successfully invoked in the two miners' strikes of the early 1970s. Whilst cautiously espousing the miners cause he was reluctant to debate the matter in Parliament, speak at miners' rallies or appear on picket lines.

His balancing act was difficult to sustain. On the one hand, the 1984 conference, disregarding his objections, passed several resolutions condemning the behaviour of the police during the strike and calling for total solidarity with the National Union of Miners (NUM).[29] On the other, he was under constant and unremitting pressure from the media the Government and indeed senior Labour frontbenchers, such as Gerald Kaufman and Roy Hattersley to condemn Scargill's refusal to organise a ballot and to repudiate violence on the picket line.[30] But he was anxious that not only would this provoke the anger of the rank and file but would make him a scapegoat for what he reckoned would be the strike's inevitable failure. Kinnock's handling of the situation was thus chastised from all quarters. His short-lived popularity of 1983 was dissipated, never really to return. His equivocal stance was condemned by most of the press as evidence of his weak, indecisive leadership. Later, he came to regret his failure to condemn the conduct of the strike more forcefully and was resolved in future to take a more robust line in managing the party.

The Soft Left

In fact, the chief casualty of the strike's collapse was to be the left. The strike was

a watershed. The NUM's ultimate defeat led to a loss of confidence at all levels of the labour movement. It left the base of the Labour Party increasingly reliant on the leadership to win elections for it.[31]

Large numbers of people at all levels and in all sections of the movement lost faith in extra-parliamentary mobilisation and mass industrial action and the bitterness of recrimination accelerated the fragmentation of the early 1980s Bennite coalition. The strike provoked the first public break within its ranks when a call by Dennis Skinner and Benn for 'all-out industrial action' to aid the miners provoked a furious row between Skinner and Tom Sawyer, Deputy General Secretary of NUPE, the second largest left-wing union.[32] But it was over an internal party matter that the old Bennite alliance finally fell apart.

After Foot's abortive drive against Militant the right and centre were itching for tougher measures and by the mid-1980s hostility was growing in sections of the left as well. Kinnock decided to use the issue as a platform to impress his authority on the party. He had been biding his time for a suitable opportunity and this occurred when, in a major tactical miscalculation, the Militant leadership in Liverpool issued redundancy notices to the council workforce. Kinnock seized the opportunity and at the 1985 conference launched a devastating attack which was enthusiastically received by delegates. This gave him the green light. The following year the NEC sent an enquiry team to Liverpool which uncovered unsavoury methods used by Militant to hold on to power. As a result, the soft left reversed its earlier opposition to disciplinary action and combined with the right on the NEC to push through expulsions of leading Tendency members and reorganisations of local parties it controlled. But hopes that the Trotskyist group would be easily demolished were soon dashed and once more the party was bogged down in a long struggle, though this finally concluded with its virtual eradication as an organised presence within the party. Coverage by the right-wing press throughout 1986 made little attempt to distinguish between Militant and the left in general, and the effect of the extensive publicity was, ironically, to reinforce the widespread impression that Labour was teeming with extremists.

In the NEC a soft left current emerged around Blunkett, Sawyer and Meacher (all formerly prominent Bennites) with many senior figures in left wing unions like NUPE, the TGWU and the NUR broadly sympathetic. For a time it became a significant factor in the internal politics of the party. As long as the right lacked the strength to reassert itself, and as long as the hard left continued to pose a threat to the leadership, soft leftists were in a position of strategic strength. This Kinnock appreciated and he patiently worked to win over leading soft leftists to construct a coalition solid enough to afford him a firm basis of support in all key party arenas. However, coalition requires compromise and concessions had to be made, notably the maintenance of the non-nuclear defence policy which was reaffirmed by an overwhelming majority at the 1984 conference. The right-wing majority in the Shadow Cabinet was profoundly unhappy with this but Kinnock was convinced that it formed the only basis around which the party could conceivably unite.[33]

The 1987 Election

The sheer scale of the electoral collapse of 1983 imparted a powerful impetus to the professionalisation of the party's campaigning and communications. In early 1986, Peter Mandelson, who had been appointed Director of Campaigns and Communications the previous year, presided over the formation of the 'Shadow Communications Agency', a group of advisors drawn mainly from the advertising world who were prepared to work for the party on a voluntary or expenses-only basis. Its role was be 'to draft strategy, conduct and interpret research, produce advertising and campaigning themes, and provide other communications support as necessary'.[34] The new approach to campaigning and communications that emerged involved the methodical application of modern, commercially-derived, techniques such as quantitative and (especially) qualitative opinion research, marketing and advertising, image management, and the projection of key messages through the mass media.[35] Several impressive campaigns were mounted but in the autumn of 1986 the Conservatives and their tabloid allies hit back with their highly effective 'loony left' offensive. This arraigned left-wing Labour councils in London with a host of accusations, mostly distortions or complete fabrications (though the occasional accurate one lent a whiff of credibility), reaching a crescendo during the by-election for the safe Labour seat of Greenwich (where the local party had selected a member of the hard left as candidate) – which was disastrously lost to the SDP. The effect on Labour of this high-volume campaign was devastating and is standing in the polls plummeted.

At this point, the election was called. Many within the party feared it might be relegated to third place but a meticulously planned campaign strategy swung into action with a drive and panache that caught virtually all observers by surprise. Within days, it was widely acclaimed for its adroit and effective deployment of modern techniques. But the campaign then stumbled. The first major upset was over defence. In response to a question speculating about war between a non-nuclear Britain and nuclear armed forces Kinnock rather carelessly spoke about making 'any occupation totally untenable.'[36] His words were taken out of context, twisted and remorselessly exploited. In what was widely seen as the most effective advert of the campaign, in the final days a full page picture appeared in the press of a soldier with his hands in the air and the simple caption 'Labour's policy on arms.' The fact that the party was pledged to use the savings accruing from relinquishing militarily unusable nuclear weapons to beef-up the country's conventional forces was totally ignored. What mattered was the image – that Labour was feeble and unpatriotic and could not be relied upon to stand up for Great Britain. The second upset was over tax. Treasury ministers claimed that Labour's pledges would cost £35 billion entailing the levying of massively heavier taxation. Although a gross exaggeration, Labour's response appeared unprepared and the charge was widely believed.

With high hopes raised by the excitement, vigour and professionalism of the campaign, the outcome was, in the party's own words, a 'devastatingly disappointing result'.[37] In comparison to the result achieved after the disorganised and inept 1983 campaign, its total vote had crept up only slightly and the Tory majority was hardly dented. Its share of the vote rose a mere 3.2 per cent to 30.8 per cent and it added 20 seats to reach a total of 229 – its second worst result since 1945.The one objective that was fully achieved was the winning of the battle of the opposition, as the gap between Labour and the Alliance widened from 2 points to 8. Nevertheless, Crewe concluded once more that it had 'come to represent a declining segment of the working class ... while failing to attract the affluent and expanding working class of the new estates and new service economy of the South. It was ... a regional class party.'[38]

The Policy Review

A second electoral massive defeat in 1987 shuck the party's self-confidence engendering a climate conducive to change. But in what direction? Much depended upon the analysis of why Labour had fared so disastrously. This was not a question of simply accommodating to 'reality'. Making sense of a complex and uncertain world involves the application of some framework of understanding, of conceptions of how events fit into meaningful and explicable patterns for 'people act not on the basis of objective reality but on the basis of *perceived reality* and of assumed cause-and-effect relationships operating in the world they perceive'.[39] To explain the direction which programmatic transformation took we need to explore how Kinnock and other influentials defined the situation they confronted and the inferences they drew.

It is here that the advertising executives and pollsters gathered in the Shadow Communications Agency played a decisive role. Through the regularly use focus groups, they monitored, analysed and interpreted the views of target voters and drew recommendations about Labour's appropriate response. The first major piece of research was conducted in late 1985 and described by the party's chief pollster, Philip Gould, as 'without a doubt ... the most important of any presented during the entire period I worked with the Labour Party. [ie from 1985 to the present]' A further major survey of public opinion called *Labour and Britain in the 1990s* appeared after the 1987 election: its influence was to be (according to Gould) 'enormous'.[40]

The two documents displayed – in Gould's words – 'the apparently unbridgeable gap between what Labour had become and what the British electorate now wanted'.[41] Sociological trends were gnawing away at Labour's traditional working class which was contracting, fragmenting and losing its political cohesion. People increasingly defined themselves less in terms of lifestyle and consumption patterns, not socio-economic status. They rejected collectivism as the doctrine of the weak, felt that the bulk of the unemployed were jobless through their own fault or choice and waxed enthusiastic about tax cuts, 'business, enterprise, achievement and individualism.' Labour was seen as the champion of the poor, the unemployed, 'minorities' and the failures in life but quite out of touch with the values and aspirations of the majority of the population. It was associated with positions 'that were beyond what ordinary, decent voters considered reasonable and sensible.' Seen as full of 'loonies,' extremists, 'reds', and militant trade unionists, the prospect of its return to power aroused fear and trepidation. There was ' a general sense that Labour's 'not for me', both because it had changed and because 'I've left that behind.' Voters were especially angered by Labour's perceived commitment to raise taxes steeply and squander the receipts on welfare 'scroungers.' The general conclusion was that Labour was thoroughly untrustworthy and incapable of running the country efficiently.

Such, the Agency asserted, was the picture that focus groups, time and again (indeed until 1994) painted. Their prescription was that the party must sharply disassociate itself from the poor, 'minorities',[42] high taxation, large-scale welfare spending and the unions so that the portrait lost credibility, and adopt policies which both reflected far more completely the aspirations and concerns of ordinary voters and (above all) would reassure and win back the trust of the electorate.[43]

The accuracy of the SCA's insights into electoral behaviour, the soundness of its methods and the validity of its conclusions were never systematically challenged, although its influence was often resented on the soft left. Their diagnosis and recommendations were highly influential in shaping the way Kinnock and others within the inner circle construed the outside world and Labour's position within it.[44] To a considerable degree, it set the parameters of policy choice. The extent of its impact upon varied according to the pattern of alignments within the party. Until the Cabinet reshuffle of autumn 1989, soft leftists remained in positions of considerable importance and, as we shall see, policies were adopted which the Agency (as well as the leadership) regarded as electorally unwise. As the influence of the soft left dwindled so did that of the SCA professionals grow. They developed very close links with the group of mainly young MPs who gathered around Kinnock (such as Gordon Brown, Tony Blair and Mandelson) – the modernisers of the new right. But as long as more progressive right-wingers like Smith and Hattersley remained as top rank frontbenchers, the Agency's diagnoses and prescriptions could not form a ruling strategic creed: this had to await Blair's assumption of the leadership. Thus in early 1992 the Shadow Chancellor, John Smith, refused to accept the Agency's urgent advice (backed strongly by Kinnock) that his tax plans be shelved.

Notwithstanding *Labour and Britain in the 1990s* was to permeate the so-called Policy Review, the comprehensive reappraisal of policy which the party undertook in the wake of the 1987 defeat.[45] There were two phases to the Review. The first culminated in the presentation to the 1989 conference of the second[46] report, *Meet the Challenge, Make the Change*. It included several substantial policy departures, but not the more ruthless expunging of existing policy that the leadership wanted. In the second phase the whole process was brought under much tighter leadership control. Kinnock and his inner circle used the third and forth reports, *Looking to the Future* (1990) and *Opportunity Britain* (1991) – from which the 1992 Manifesto was largely drawn – to place their stamp more emphatically on the party's programme.[47]

In most accounts, the real significance of the Policy Review has bee seen as the formal acceptance of the market as the best mechanisms for organising economic life. This – the argument runs – constituted an ideological transformation, the final vanquishing of the left and Labour's long-overdue adoption of continental social democracy.[48] This interpretation misses the real significance of the debates which took place within the party over the Policy Review. Firstly, the hard left – which with one or two exceptions, took little interest – was hardly engaged at all: the real contest was between the soft left and the right. Secondly, Labour governments had always accepted that the market should operate as the main coordinator of economic activity. In practical (if not rhetorical) terms central question had always been the form and extent of market management not the market itself. We shall return to this point below.

There were three major shifts in policy between the two phases of the Policy Review over labour law, defence and economic policy. In each case the mode of understanding the world, to which the inner leadership adhered, and the consequences for Labour they derived from this, drove policy choice.

Kinnock was determined to abrogate the existing policy of repealing most Tory industrial relations legislation both on the grounds that it lent credibility to the accusation that the party was in the pocket of the unions and conflicted with (what he believed should be) the party's economic priorities.[49] However, Michael Meacher, the Employment spokesman, wanted to restore to the unions greater freedom to engage in industrial action. Initially Meacher's view – backed by left-wing unions though not by the TUC – triumphed, to the fury of Kinnock.[50] In a frontbench reshuffle in October 1989 he was replaced by an ambitious young Kinnock protege (and right-wing moderniser) Tony Blair who worked closely with sympathetic TUC officials to secure acceptance of a package which committed the party to retaining most of the Conservative legislation on the statute book. This time union leaders, however reluctantly, were prepared to fall into line. The steep contraction in their industrial power, the drastic fall in membership, a much harsher legal framework and the steady dismantling of collective bargaining arrangements increasingly predisposed them to place an overriding priority on Labour's victory at the polls.[51]

One matter upon which all sections of the left felt deeply was the commitment to renounce the possession and use of nuclear weapons. Kinnock himself had been a passionate unilateralist though (he claimed) he had decided as early as 1986 that the policy was both electorally and politically unsustainable.[52] But it took him two years and a series of politically embarrassing twists and turns before he succeeded in inducing the party to abandon it. The profound changes in the international scene (the rise of Gorbachev, the disintegration of Communist regimes and the end of the cold war) were all used to justify the leader's argument but the crucial reason was electoral.

The scale of the task was demonstrated by the reaffirmation of the non-nuclear policy by a large majority at the 1987 conference.[53] When Kinnock hinted at a reversal of policy, a leading soft left ally, David Blunkett, warned of 'an unnecessary and devastating split in the party'. and in 1988 conference again reaffirmed unilateralism.[54] But Kinnock had now resolved that the non-nuclear policy must be scrapped. Opposition was softened up by a series of stratagems, including packing of the defence Policy Review group with an anti-unilateralist majority, careful wooing of doubters within the unions and on the NEC and, not least, the release of Shadow Agency research demonstrating the scale and intensity of public attachment to nuclear weapons. At the NEC meeting called in May 1989 to discuss a report compiled by Gerald Kaufman, Kinnock fervently and unequivocally repudiated unilateralism, implying he would resign if Labour stood by it. Opposition disintegrated and Kinnock's line was endorsed by conference.[54] The total renunciation of what was for many on the soft left virtually an article of faith – which would have precipitated an outburst of outrage within the party only a couple of years previously – was digested, albeit unhappily, with remarkably little public protest. This was largely due to what one experienced commentator called the 'profound, genuine and largely spontaneous change of mood in the grassroots,' engendered by the conviction 'that nothing, not even the most cherished items of dogma, must be allowed to stand in the way of beating Mrs Thatcher'.[55] In Henri of Navarre's celebrated formula, 'Paris is worth a mass'.

The final, and most crucial issue over which the party changed direction was the management of the economy. Bryan Gould, the Industry spokesman, was a staunch Keynesian and an unsparing critic of the City. He believed that Labour should run the economy 'in terms of demand management, public spending and fiscal policy, in the interests of those who live and work in the real economy rather than those who live off manipulating assets in the money economy.'[56] The inner leadership (including John Smith, the Shadow Chancellor) disagreed, believing that the Keynesian-welfare mix was no longer feasible. This was partly because of the major changes wrought by the Conservatives since 1979. The abolition of exchange controls, privatisation and deregulation, the dismantling of labour protection 'created a new conventional wisdom, a cultural ... and institutional transformation'[57] which it would have been very difficult to reverse. But most significant of all, in the framework which the inner leadership applied to make sense of the world, was the globalisation of the international economy, that is exponential growth in the scale and mobility of global short-term capital transfers in an increasingly deregulated financial regime. The swelling power of international financial markets and the relentless march to an ever-more integrated world economy had drastically narrowed the margin of manoeuvre of the nation-state. Thus John Smith warned that the UK inhabited an interdependent and highly unstable world 'where capital movements in Tokyo, New York and London can subvert the economic policies of nation states'.[58] Fiscal prudence and monetary rigour were essential for the penalty for forfeiting the confidence of the financial markets – as the French socialists painfully discovered in the 1980s – was likely to be a flight of capital, a rapidly depreciating currency and rampant inflation. The prospect itself of the victory of a Labour party pledged to boost welfare spending, a more progressive tax regime and redistribution could, it was feared, precipitate capital flight, thereby frightening the voters. Hence it was vital to reassure the markets that Labour would pursue 'sound', 'prudent' and 'market friendly' policies. For this reason Smith and the Shadow Chief Secretary, Margaret Beckett, engaged in the so-called 'prawn cocktail offensive' in a sustained (but not very successful) effort to woo the City.

Gould and his allies were not prepared to accept this analysis. Differences over macro-economic policy finally came to a head over the vexed question of membership of the European Community's Exchange Rate Mechanism (ERM). Gould condemned the ERM, as a straight-jacket which would force Britain into deflationary polices and undermine any attempt to expand employment and growth. Initially, as Convenor of the policy review group on the economy, Gould triumphed and UK membership of the ERM was made contingent on a set of tough conditions. In line with their shift to economic orthodoxy, Kinnock, Eatwell and Smith were eager proponents of ERM membership. It would, they believed, reassure the money markets of the party's fiscal rectitude, afford protection against speculation, and furnish with they hoped would be perceived as a feasible and electorally convincing counter-inflation strategy. The logic of commitment to the ERM at the existing parity, Larry Elliott pointed out, rendered Labour's macro-economic strategy 'virtually indistinguishable from Mr Major's. The ERM will mean low inflation but it also guarantees unemployment of 2.5 million or above for the foreseeable future.'[59] Smith acknowledged this. A fixed exchange rate regime would, he explained, depress inflationary expectations by denying employers the option of a competitive devaluation if they succumbed to pay claims too easily. If they conceded inflationary demands, they would price themselves out of markets with the result – as Smith pointed out – 'there would be unemployment, wouldn't there?'[60] In short, unemployment would be used as a means of curbing inflationary pressures.

The issue was resolved when, in the Shadow Cabinet reshuffle of October 1989 Gould was moved to the Environment portfolio with his place as Shadow Industry Secretary taken by the right-wing moderniser, Gordon Brown, another rapidly rising young Kinnock protege. All the conditions previously set for entry to the

ERM were scrapped and, indeed, the Government was urged to join as soon as possible which (to Mrs Thatcher's great regret) it did in October 1990. By the time the 1992 manifesto was drafted Labour was firmly pledged to maintaining ERM membership at the existing (clearly over-valued) parity. As the National Institute of Economic and Social Research concluded after a detailed study of Labour's policies, 'the economic policy differences between the two major parties are narrower now than they have been for about twenty years.'[61] When Britain was eventually forced out of the ERM in the humiliation of Black Wednesday in September 1992 there was little Labour could do but hope that its own support would be overlooked (which it was.)

The Marginalisation of the Soft Left

'Ultimately the reason we were able to get the policy reviews through without more blood on the floor,' Kinnock recalled, 'was because of the shift that took place, the alliance that developed between the traditional right and those who were certainly part of the soft left.'[62] Almost invariably when disagreements arose the soft left would swing behind the leadership, usually obtaining minimal or cosmetic concessions.[63] Why did it fail to arrest the drift to the rights? One relevant factors we have already surveyed: the strategic parameters were set by the Shadow Agency, inspiring a logic difficult to resist. However, internal party considerations also played a significant role.

The first was the inability of the soft left to operate in a concerted fashion. As Bryan Gould recalled, we lacked the 'unity of purpose to make ourselves effective as a counterweight to the right' largely because of a reluctance on the part of members to lay aside personal ambitions.[64] The frequent use of the electoral mechanism had a divisive effect as, behind the scenes, an incessant competitive scramble amongst prominent soft leftists for places on the NEC and the Shadow Cabinet aggravated jealousies and resentments.

Secondly, soft left politicians lacked an institutional mechanism to facilitate co-operation. For a quarter of a century the Tribune Group had operated as the main organised focus of the left and, after the formation of the Campaign Group in 1982, of the soft left specifically. However, by the second half of the 1980s it was transmuting into a vehicle of career promotion. One of its principal functions had been arranging a slate – in competition with the right – for the annual Shadow Cabinet elections. Its very success tempted the pure careerist to enrol whilst Kinnock actively encouraged loyalists to join. By the late

1980s Tribune MPs composed over half the PLP but many of the younger new entrants were politically hardly distinguishable from the right. One new MP exclaimed on appearing at his first Tribune meeting: 'I couldn't believe it – there were people like Gordon Brown, Tony Blair and Nick Brown, calling themselves "left"!. They're the new right.'[65]

Thirdly, there there was a constant procession of members of the soft left to the right. One example was Tom Sawyer who had progressed from being from being a leading Bennite in the early 1980s, to become a prominent soft leftist and to end by 1987 as 'the loyal link to and from the Leader's Office'.[66] The leader's command of patronage meant that this trail became a well-trodden one. Fourthly, less agreeable methods were applied to those who persisted in stepping out of line. The most commonly employed was to seek to discredit them by anonymous off-the-record briefings, orchestrated by Mandelson. As part of the professionalisation of communications, Labour's press officers had established close working relations with a number of political journalists. The access this gave them was used not only to project the party's message to the outside world but also as a weapon in intra-party struggles. Items by friendly and pliable journalists (especially on papers widely read within the party, such as the *Guardian* and the *Independent*) would appear portraying chosen victims in an unflattering light. Thus in the summer and autumn of 1989 stories began to circulate about Meacher's 'poor judgment' and 'unsuitability' as a frontbench employment spokesman. Similarly the phrase 'a Gould gaffe' began making a mysteriously frequent appearance in the press.[67] Prescott was described by a 'senior Kinnock aide' as 'treacherous' 'self-indulgent' and motivated solely by ambition.[68] Cook was depicted as 'a loose cannon', 'slippery' and 'untrustworthy', a 'Lenin without the human touch' who 'wants to be leader' despite the fact that 'plastic surgery hasn't got that far'.[69] Initially Mandelson was acting on Kinnock's behalf but increasingly he followed his own agenda as he 'concentrated on clearing the way for the eventual succession' of his allies Brown or Blair, 'by undermining as much as possible, the credibility of other possible contenders' notably Cook and Gould.[70] Indeed, 'every time Gould or Cook went on TV it was portrayed back to friendly journalists as a gaffe.'[71]

Finally, Kinnock's reliance on the soft left began to diminish by the end of the decade. The weaker the threat from the hard left, the more dispensable the soft left became. An array of factors (including the crushing of Tony Benn and Eric Heffer after their ill-thought-out decision to challenge for the leadership and deputy leadership, the growing use of OMOV in internal party elections and the general drift of the party to the right) remorselessly gnawed at the hard left's power base. By 1990 Kinnock had secured a tight grip on both the NEC and the Shadow Cabinet, and the soft left had lost virtually all leverage. The highly pluralistic, deeply polarised party characterised by the institutionalised dispersal of powers and weak central authority evident in the early 1980s had been replaced by a powerful central authority exercising tight control over all aspects of organisational life. The decomposition, fragmentation and demoralisation of the left, the increasingly supportive role played by the unions, the impact of rule-changes such as the extension of OMOV coupled with Kinnock's assertive leadership culminated in the emergence of a much more centralised party. This was the indispensable condition for the leadership's drive – commenced by Kinnock and completed by Blair – to transform the party.

The 1992 Election

For the first couple of years after 1987 Labour limped in the polls but by 1990 with the onset of a major recession and massive resentment over the imposition of the poll tax Labour leapt into the lead. Splits over economic policy and the European Union and the resignation of two senior Cabinet ministers, Nigel Lawson the Chancellor and Sir Geoffrey Howe, the Foreign Secretary followed, culminating in the ousting of Mrs Thatcher. The delight of Labour supporters was short-lived. She was replaced by the reassuringly mild-mannered and quietly-spoken John Major, the poll tax was abolished and almost immediately, Labour's handsome lead evaporated. Notwithstanding, it stayed marginally ahead in the polls and it was in an optimistic frame of mind when the campaign for the 1992 election opened.

To a large extent the campaign proceeded as planned and it seemed – according to the opinion polls – to be effective. There were, however, some serious mistakes. The health issue came to be overshadowed by a controversial party election broadcast designed to show how a cash-starved and mismanaged NHS caused lengthy waiting lists whilst private patients secured immediate treatment. But its impact was totally nullified when the issue was side-tracked by 'the war of Jenny's ear': the row over the 'real-life story' upon which one Labour official carelessly stated the broadcast was based. The end-result was to distract attention from one of Labour's strongest cards. The huge and elaborately organised Sheffield 'mega-rally' designed to give a final boost to the campaign also proved an embarrassment. Years of incessant and often vicious attacks by the right-wing tabloids had severely damaged Kinnock's standing in the public's eye.[72] His grasp of issues – particularly economic ones – never appeared convincing, he struggled with a reputation as a 'windbag', a 'lightweight' who simply was not up to the job of being Prime Minister. Unfortunately, at the Sheffield rally Kinnock himself revived doubts about his suitability, greeting his wildly cheering audience like a preacher at a Deep South revivalist meeting.[73]

Further, the Conservative campaign may have seemed less professionally organised than Labour's but it was far more successful in communicating its key messages. Labour, the Conservatives and their tabloid allies hammered away, would raise tax by a huge £35 billion – the figure which having proved so effective in the last election was recycled for this one. Allegedly, this would cost everyone an extra £1,200 in taxes. In fact, Labour's plans were quite modest. Only two significant expenditure pledges were made, to raise child benefits and pensions. These were to be financed by raising the upper band of income tax from 40 per cent to 50 per cent and by abolishing the upper limit on National Insurance contributions (which meant an effective top rate of direct tax of 59 per cent) According to the highly regarded Institute for Fiscal Studies four out of five families would gain from these plans, and only 9 per cent (those earning over £30,000 at 1992 prices) would lose.[74] Modernisers later asserted that the Smith tax proposals had been the single most decisive factor in destroying Labour's prospects: they blamed Smith who had refused to budge though strongly pressed by Kinnock to do so. Although the proposition has now entered the annals as established wisdom, Heath, Jowell and Curtice, however, found 'very little evidence' to support it. According to the polls, the damage was inflicted because many voters believed what the Tory/tabloid *claimed* Labour's policy to be, rather than what it *was*.[75]

Until the last moment, the polls indicated that Labour would scrape together enough seats to form a minority government. But the polls were wrong. With the country trapped in a serious recession the additional 3.6 per cent share of the vote it received to bring it to a mere 34.4 per cent, well behind the Tories, was a crushing blow.[76] Major retained power with a majority of 21, large enough to carry him through to the next election.

The Smith Interregnum

Kinnock immediately indicated his intention to resign. Smith was the obvious *dauphin*, the heir in waiting. Notwithstanding,

Gould, who had clashed continuously with him over macro-economic policy and the ERM, decided to throw his hat in the ring. It was an unwise decision. Gould was warned by Kinnock: 'Smithy has got it all sewn up. You'll get only a fraction of the vote. Better to leave it to him,' adding, somewhat cryptically, 'he won't last the course. It's important that you're there to pick up the pieces.'[78] However, he would not be swayed, arguing that the contest must be used to raise issues (like the ERM) which to preserve party unity had not been openly discussed before. Predictably Smith overwhelmed his opponent, scoring 90.9 per cent of the electoral college to Gould's 9.1 per cent. In the trade union section he won 38.5 per cent of the 40 per cent granted to the unions, in the constituencies 29.3 per cent and in the PLP 23.1 per cent. In fact, the scale of the victory was exaggerated by the fact that both unions and CLPs voted as blocs. The deputy leadership contest was more open. Of the three contenders, Gould, Prescott and Beckett, the former had no chance because of his decision to compete also for the leadership whilst the latter soon emerged as the favourite, in part because she had the (unofficial) support of Smith. She won easily on the first ballot gaining 57.3 per cent compared to Prescott's 28.1 per cent and Gould's 14.6 per cent.[79]

The Clash Over Parliamentary Selection

Smith adopted a much more collegial, tolerant and consensual approach to leadership than Kinnock. He was widely liked and admired in all wings of the party and had remarkably few political enemies. He dispensed with the heavy-handed methods of control used by his predecessor (and successor) and treated critics with respect.[80] It was ironical, therefore, that his leadership almost came to grief in a fierce battle over a matter, party rules, to which he had in the past attached little importance. He had indicated in his campaign for the leadership that he favoured various organisational reforms, such as the reduction of the union vote at conference and the extension of OMOV to the election of the leader and to the selection of parliamentary candidates but had not anticipated they would assume so much significance.

The first two issues were in fact resolved, as he had anticipated, in an amicable manner. The NEC's recommendation to reduce the union vote from 90 per cent to 70 per cent (with the possibility of a further cut to 50 per cent if constituency membership reached 300,000) had been approved with little opposition at the 1990 conference. Its implementation deferred until after the next election it was finally incorporated in party rules at the 1992 conference. The second issue was also settled without too much difficulty.There was a widespread feeling that future elections for the leadership should be decided on the basis of one member, one vote (OMOV). After consultation indicated support for continued union involvement it was agreed that the size of the union vote be cut from 40 per cent to one-third, equal to that of the constituency parties and the PLP. Ballots were to be conducted on a one member one vote bases with the results then aggregated in each section. In the union section, the right to vote was restricted to those political levy payers who indicated their support for the Labour Party. The third issue, parliamentary selection procedures, caused – to Smith's surprise – much more of a headache, and indeed at one point seemed to threaten an end to his leadership.

The Shadow Cabinet and the bulk of Labour MPs had never been reconciled to mandatory reselection and wanted to dilute the influence of activists by introducing some form of OMOV. The issue was first raised in 1984 when Kinnock, wary of the opposition to outright OMOV, opted for a compromise system of 'voluntary OMOV' in which General Committees could, if they so choose, delegate the right to determine the fate of a sitting MP to party members as a whole. The scheme, however, was attacked as half-baked and ill-thought out and was rejected at conference that year by 3,992,000 votes to 3,041,000.[81] He revived the question in 1987 with the next round of reselections beckoning. There was now a growing suspicion that OMOV was designed to reduce the input into the party of the unions as well as activists, which stiffened the former's opposition. Once more Kinnock was forced to compromise. He proposed an electoral college which included all individual members but gave up to 40 per cent of the vote to the unions whilst the rest of the vote was to be cast by individually-balloted rank and file members, The scheme was overwhelmingly adopted by conference by 4,545,000 votes to 1,608,00.[82] But it satisfied few, being cumbersome, difficult to operate and open to manipulation and there was soon general agreement that it should be scrapped.

The 1991 conference once more rejected OMOV preferring another complicated procedure that proved so impracticable that it, too, soon fell by the wayside. Though a strong body of opinion now favoured a straightforward, simple to operate system of OMOV a powerful group of unions, including the TGWU, the GMB and NUPE were insistent on preserving their role. In 1992, the question was referred to the recently-established Labour Party–Trade Union Links Review Group. After protracted discussions Prescott introduced a compromise, the so-called 'levy-plus' scheme by which political levy payers could participate in selections if they joined the party at a discounted rate. The NEC approved the scheme in July 1993, but the majority of unions continued to resist. Smith, facing imminent defeat at the 1993 conference, then raised the stakes by warning that, if beaten, he would resign

Why were so many unions – including those like the GMB with a tradition of leadership loyalism – so obdurate over an issue about which few voters cared, and fewer understood, whilst having so willingly compromising over others? It seems likely that the main reason was that it became a lightning conductor for a general sense of grievance. Trade union leaders were indignant over a spate of reports which appeared in the press the previous year highlighting private research conducted for Labour which (allegedly) blamed the unions for the electoral defeat. In fact, the party's post-election research hardly mentioned the unions: exploiting their close links with well-disposed and compliant journalists modernisers' such as Mandelson had planted the stories.[83] The ploy worked since, despite the dearth of evidence, the claim soon attained the status of (endlessly recycled) media lore. Union leaders, who had assiduously kept a low profile during the election campaign greatly resented being scapegoated and reports that the ultimate purpose of the modernisers was an end to the union connection further fed their suspicions.

Whatever the reasons, the TGWU and the GMB were playing with fire and the party only avoided a grave embarrassment by a hair's breadth. The result of the vote remained uncertain until the very last moment, when the NEC motion was carried by 47.5 per cent to 44.4 per cent. (Voting at conference was now conducted by percentages rather than numbers, for presentational reasons.) Until the last moment defeat seemed certain until some smart foot-work persuaded MSF to switch from opposition to abstention[84] and Prescott rallied delegates by a rousing defence of the party-union link. If Smith had lost the vote he intended to call for another one the following day and turn it into a vote of confidence – which almost certainly he would have easily won.[85]

Once resolved, tensions ebbed rapidly and Smith's immense skill in managing the party produced an unusual period of harmony. The main source of disagreement, bubbling below the surface, was the impatience of leading modernisers, such as Blair, Brown and Mandelson, with the pace of change. They were convinced that further sharp moves to the right were essential if the party was to regain the electorate's trust, and felt the leader was unduly sanguine over the next election.[86] Though on most key items of policy which divided the modernisers from the left, Smith was more sympathetic to the former (especially on economic policy) he did not believe that any further dramatic alterations in policy were needed: the indispensable condition for victory at the polls had been met, he felt, when he had replaced Kinnock as leader. His sudden death from a massive heart attack on 12 May 1994 meant that this proposition would never be tested.

Notes

1   David Denver 'Great Britain: From Opposition with a Capital 'O' to Fragmented Opposition' in Eva Kolinsky (ed.), *Opposition in Western Europe* London, Croom Helm, 1987 p88.

2   David Easton, *A Systems Analysis of Political Life*, Chicago, John Wiley and Sons 1965 p193.

3   Ivor Crewe and Tony King, *The Social Democratic Party* Oxford, Oxford University Press, 1995 p75.

4   *Ibid.* pp76-84.

5   Lewis Minkin, *The Contentious Alliance: Trade Unions and the Labour Party*, Edinburgh, Edinburgh University Press 1991 pp202-204, 325.

6   Michael Crick, *The March of Militant*, London, Faber and Faber, 1986

7   For a detailed account, see Eric Shaw, *Discipline and Discord in the Labour Party*, Manchester University Press, Manchester.

8   Martin Linton 'Disaster Snatched from the Jaws of Defeat', *The Guardian* 30 June 1983.

9   David Butler and Dennis Kavanagh, *The British General Election of 1983* London, Macmillan 1984 p274.

10 *Ibid.* pp300, 119.

11 See eg Ivor Crewe, 1 'The Disturbing Truth Behind Labour's Rout', *The Guardian* 13 June 1983 ; Ivor Crewe, 'How Labour was Trounced all Round', *The Guardian* 14 June 1983; Ivor Crewe, 'The Electorate: Partisan Dealignment Ten Years On' *West European Politics* Vol. 7 1984; Anthony Heath, Roger Jowell R, John Curtice, *How Britain Votes* Oxford, Pergamon Press, 1985.

12 Crewe, 'The Disturbing Truth'. Using Heath, Jowell and Curtice's categories, Labour's share of the working class vote fell from 55 per cent in 1979 (itself a decline in 9 per cent since 1974) to 49 per cent; of the routine non-manuals from 32 per cent to 29 per cent, and of the salariat from 22 per cent to 13 per cent. Heath, Jowell and Curtice, *How Britain Votes,* p68-9.

13 Labour Party Conference Report 1983 p29.

14 Neil Kinnock, 'Reforming the Labour Party', *Contemporary Record,* Vol.8 No.3 1994 p.553.

15 Minkin, *The Contentious Alliance* p401.

16 *Ibid.* p409.

17 See, for example, Peter Jenkins, *The Thatcher Revolution* London, Cape 1987 pp.251–53; Tudor Jones, *Remaking the Labour Party:*

from Gaitskell to Blair, London; Routledge, 1996; Martin Smith, 'Neil Kinnock and the Modernisation of the Labour Party', *Contemporary Record,* Vol.8, No.3, 1994.

18 TUC-Labour Party Liaison Committee, *People at Work: New Rights, New Responsibilities* London, Labour Party, 1986; Michael Leapman, *Kinnock* London, Unwin Hyman, 1987, pp136-7; *The Guardian,* 14 August 1986.

19 Roy Hattersley, *Economic Priorities for a Labour Government* London, Macmillan, 1987 p28.

20 *The Guardian,* 5 August 1985.

21 Minkin, *The Contentious Alliance* pp409, 402.

22 Labour Party NEC, *New Industrial Strength for Britain,* London, Labour Party, 1987.

23 Labour Party NEC, *A Future That Works,* London, Labour Party, 1984.

24 *Social Ownership,* London, Labour Party, 1986.

25 Interview, *Kinnock: The Inside Story* ITV 25 July 1993.

26 Kinnock, 'Reforming the Labour Party', p538.

27 Blunkett, Interview in *Kinnock: The Inside Story* ITV 26 July 1993.

28 Interview with David Dimbleby in *Neil Kinnock – The Lost Leader,* BBC 2, 5 December 1992.

29 Labour Party Conference Report, 1984 pp55, 102.

30 According to Meacher, 'the hostility of the Shadow Cabinet [at a meeting in September 1984] to the miners was unbelievable.' Tony Benn, *The End of an Era Diaries 1980-1990,* London, Hutchinson 1992 p.374.

31 Richard Heffernan and Mike Marqusee, *Defeat from the Jaws of Victory: Inside Kinnock's Labour Party,* London, Verso, 1992, p61.

32 NEC minutes 12 Dec. 1984.

33 Leapman, *Kinnock* p149.

34 Colin Hughes and Patrick Wintour, *Labour Rebuilt: The New Model Party* London, Fourth Estate, 1990, pp51-52. The key participants were Mandelson, advertising executives Philip Gould and Deborah Mattinson who alone were placed on the party's payroll), Chris Powell and others from the BMP advertising agency, and Patricia Hewitt and Charles Clarke representing the leader.

35 For detailed accounts, see Eric Shaw, *The Labour Party Since 1979: Crisis and Transformation* Routledge, London, 1994 and in particular Philip Gould, *The Unfinished Revolution: How the modernisers saved the Labour Party,* London, Little, Brown and Co., 1998.

36 David Butler and Dennis Kavanagh, *The British General Election of 1987* London, Macmillan 1988 p103.

37 Labour Party NEC Report 1987 p3.

38 Ivor Crewe, 'A New Class of Politics', *The Guardian* 15 June 1987; Ivor Crewe, 'Tories Prosper from a Paradox', *The Guardian* 16 June, 1987.

39 Fritz Scharpf, *Games Real Actors Play: Actor-centred institution-alism in Policy Research* Oxford, Westview, 1997, p19.

40 Gould, *The Unfinished Revolution* p86.

41 *Ibid.* p49.

42 i.e. ethnic minorities, though this was not spelt out, as it might have been thought indelicate.

43 Cited in Gould, *The Unfinished Revolution* pp49-54, 121; *Labour and Britain in the 1990s,* London, Labour Party.

44 Since their focus group records have never been made public, there is no way to judge the validity of the inevitably subjective inferences drawn by SCA members. Assuming nevertheless that the portrayal of voter perceptions drawn was an accurate one, it is worth noting, firstly, they reflected a high level of prejudice, ignorance about the party and policy issues whilst clearly echoing the views which had been assiduously disseminated by the right-wing tabloids since the early 1979's See, e.g., Philip Golding and S Middleton *Images of Welfare* Oxford, Martin Robertson, 1982. This might have raised a series of political and ethical dilemmas about how the party should respond, but never did. Secondly, it was assumed – with a great leap of logic – that since the impressions of the party of the party were widely and deeply held, therefore *they must be true* – that the party was indeed biased towards the 'minorities', profligate in its attitude to tax and spending, run by the unions and so forth: hence the only effective way Labour could rebuild trust was by shedding policies that could give any credence to these beliefs.

45 For a fuller account, see Shaw, *The Labour Party Since 1979.*

46 The first, *Social Justice and Economic Efficiency,*London, Labour Party,1988, was a general overview and soon forgotten.

47 *Meet the Challenge, Make the Change,* London, Labour Party,1989; *Looking to the Future* London, Labour Party, 1990 and *Opportunity Britain* London, Labour Party.

48 See, e.g., Martin Smith and Joanna Spear, *The Changing Labour Party* London, Routledge, 1992.

49 Hughes and Wintour, *Labour Rebuilt* p149.

50 Interview party official.

51 Minkin, *The Contentious Alliance* pp467, 479.

52 *Independent,* 13 February 1988.

53 *The Guardian,* 2 October 1987.

54 *The Guardian,* 11 June 1988, *The Guardian,* 7 October 1988.

55 Hughes and Wintour, *Labour Rebuilt* pp121-122, 126.

56 Ian Aitken, *The Guardian* 1 October 1990.

57 *New Statesman & Society,* 2 January 1993.

58 Stephen Wilkes, 'The Conservative Government and the Economy', *Political Studies* Vol. 45 No.4, 1997, p692.

59 *Tribune,* July 1990.

60 *The Guardian,* 26 August 1991.

61 *Independent on Sunday,* 6 May 1990.

62 National Institute of Economic and Social Research, 'Policy Options Under a Labour Government', *National Institute Economic Review* Nov. 1990 p52.

63 Kinnock, 'Reforming the Labour Party', p550.

64 Andy McSmith, *Faces of Labour* London, Verso, 1997 p144.

65 Bryan Gould, *Goodbye to all That*. London, Macmillan, 1995, p215.

66 Cited in McSmith, *Faces of Labour* p132.

67 Minkin, *The Contentious Alliance* p468. Sawyer resigned from the NEC in 1994 on being appointed General Secretary of the party a post he held until 1998 when he was ennobled. He was re-elected to the NEC in 1999.

68 Interviews with party officials and MPs. Gould, *Goodbye to all That.* pp217-8

69 *Observer,* 10 February 1991.

70 John Kampfner, *Robin Cook,* London, Gollancz, 1998, p81.

71 Gould, *Goodbye to all That,* p226.

72 Former aide to Cook, cited by Kampfner, *Robin Cook,* p82.

73 Bill Miller *Media and Voters*, Oxford, Clarendon Press, 1991, pp171-2, 175-6

74 David Butler and Dennis Kavanagh, *The British General Election of 1992* London, Macmillan 1993 p125.

75 Ken Newton, 'Caring and Competence: the Long, Long Campaign' in Tony King *et. al. Britain at the Polls, 1992*, Chatham, New Jersey, Chatham House, 1992, p145.

76 Anthony Heath, Roger Jowell and John Curtice, *Labour's Last Chance?* London, Dartmouth, 1994 p292; Crewe, 1992: 7-8. Figures cited from NOP and Harris exit polls.

77 Labour performed best amongst AB's professional and managerial gaining 10 per cent, and the DE's (semi-skilled and unskilled) at 8 per cent but amongst C1's (clerical workers) and C2's (skilled manual) the increase was only 4 per cent. Ivor Crewe, 'Why did Labour Lose (Yet Again)?' *Politics Review* Vol. 2 No. 1, 1992, pp7-8. Figures cited from NOP and Harris exit polls.

78 Gould, *Goodbye to all That.* p253. If he had followed the advice, and stood for the deputy-leadership – which he probably would have won – the eventual succession to Smith *might* have been different: according to a former senior Kinnock aide, Gould was the only person who could have beaten Blair. Interview 1998.

79 Keith Alderman and Neil Carter, 'The Labour Party Leadership and Deputy Leadership Elections of 1992', *Parliamentary Affairs*, vol. 46 no 1 1993.

80 Andy McSmith, *John Smith* London, Verso, 1994, p180.

81 Labour Party Conference Report 1984 p66.

82 *The Guardian* 29 September 1987.

83 'What was striking about the actual poll was the virtual absence of any direct association between voting and the union link.' Keith Alderman and Neil Carter, 'The Labour Party and Trade Unions: loosening the ties', *Parliamentary Affairs*, vol. 47 no 3 1994.

84 Party and union leaders persuaded the MSF delegation that by defeating OMOV they would also throw overboard moves to further the union's policy of increasing the number of women MPs.

85 Andy McSmith, *John Smith* p311.

86 Gould, *The Unfinished Revolution* p191; McSmith, *John Smith,* p313–4.

Tony Blair and the Transition to New Labour: 1994-2000[1]

Martin J. Smith

From its electoral nadir of 1983, Labour has transformed itself from a factional minority party, which appeared in terminal decline, to a government that is able to maintain higher support than any previous administration. Under Tony Blair the party looks to have achieved Harold Wilson's aim of making it the natural party of government and indeed with the routing of the Conservatives outside of England, the only truly national party. In the 1970s and 1980s Labour was faced with four interconnected problems: electoral support appeared to be in long-term decline with its natural supporters apparently not agreeing with a number of central policies;[2] from the early 1970s there were growing conflicts between the party leadership and the party membership over party policy and internal democracy; by the late 1970s the alliance with the unions which had done so much to support the party leadership was under increasing stress and to some extent breaking;[3] and the Labour governments of 1964–70 and 1974–79 suffered severe policy failure. They were unable to deliver on their economic and social policy goals and in 1976 they effectively abandoned Keynesian demand management in the face of rising public expenditure, high unemployment, and an unprecedented inflation rate.[4] Once 'the party was over', a hole was created in Labour's governing strategy; it appeared to lose a mechanism for providing economic growth and social justice. Consequently, it was losing its claim to governing competence.

The essence of Blair and New Labour is an attempt to resolve these problems: to end electoral decline; to reduce the potential for party conflict; and to provide an ideology which can retain some of Labour's historical commitments to social justice without alienating the middle income support necessary for electoral victory. Consequently, New Labour has three elements to its strategy for filling the gap left by the absence of Keynesian social democracy. They are electoral, party and governmental. However, the strategy of Blair and his supporters raise a number of important questions. How new is New Labour? Is Labour under Blair offering anything other than Labourite Thatcherism? If so, what is the nature of New Labour ideology under Blair?

Blair's Strategy for New Labour

Electoral

It is impossible to understand New Labour without comprehending the severe impact that Labour's electoral failure had on the party. Five points need to be made about Labour's electoral failure. First, Labour's vote declined steadily from 1951 to 1983 indicating that the loss of support was structural, as well as political. Second, the scale of the defeat in 1983 was such that it devastated the party, leadership and in particular the left. The 1983 defeat highlighted the scale of the electorate's disillusionment with the party, and more importantly, it undermined any legitimacy the left had in claiming the party's loss of support was indication of the drift to the right. Third, the policy changes undertaken by Neil Kinnock between 1987 and 1992 were not sufficient to ensure Labour's electoral victory and suggested that Labour needed more radical changes in policy if it was to retain power. Fourth, the policies of Labour and the views of the electorate diverged significantly throughout most of the 1970s and 1980s. Fifth, the post-war period has seen significant social change. The size of the skilled manual work has declined whilst there has been a growth in clerical occupations. In 1961 2.7 per cent of the population were employed in managerial occupations compared to 11 per cent in 1990. 8.7 per cent worked in the professions compared to 21.8 in 1990 and those occupied in crafts and operators declined from 43.1 percent to 22.3.[5] Moreover, the structure of work has changed greatly with many more people working part-time and substantially more women working. In addition, the standard of life of 'ordinary' people has been transformed and their interests and desires are not what they were in 1945. In order to win Labour had to attract a different electorate whose aspirations no longer centred on the primary goals of job security, access to health care and relief from poverty. Instead, concerns were with quality of life and limiting tax liabilities.

The problem for the Labour Party is that its electoral position has always been, and still is, precarious. A convincing electoral victory has required the votes of its core working class support coupled to a significant middle class vote. Electoral and social change has made the winning of middle class votes even more urgent. But the party has only successfully attracted this coalition in two elections 1945 and 1997 and even these 'landslide victories' were built on sand.[6] In 1945 Labour won 63 per cent of the middle class vote.[7] In 1997 32.2 per cent of Labour's vote came from the salariat, compared to 31.4 for the Conservatives and 37.5 per cent from white-collar workers compared to 24.9 for the Conservatives.[8]

Therefore central to Blair's vision of New Labour is a strategy for permanently linking the working class, the lower middle class and a significant element of middle class support. Such a bloc is the mechanism for ensuring that Labour can be a serious governing party for the foreseeable future without following the precarious and divisive path of proportional representation. Blair's vision of Labour is very much of a party that can place itself in the centre and consequently build a wide coalition of support. Blair is conscious that:

With the possible exception of 1964, Labour has hitherto been unable to recreate the strong consensus of 1945. The truth that we must take seriously is that 1945 was the exception not the rule.

Blair's concern is to create a permanent coalition and this goal, which is an artefact of electoral necessity, provides a great constraint on Labour's policies. It explains the need to overcome traditional antagonisms, the reclaiming of patriotism and why certain policies such as high marginal rates of taxation, the abolition of private schools and nationalisation are no longer an option. This is not an acceptance of a Thatcherite agenda but awareness that certain Thatcherite policies were popular and their continuation is necessary for building a wide electoral coalition. Central to the electoral strategy is the party strategy.

Party

One of the central problems both for the electoral strategy and the governing strategy was the role of the party. There was a belief that the divisions in the party, the strength of party activists and conflicts between the party and the leadership (and, of course, a section of the party breaking away to from the SDP) were both undermining electoral support and creating perceptions of governmental failure. The belief of leaders as far back as Hugh Gaitskell was that activists wanted policies that were not supported by the electorate and that activists through accusations of betrayal were creating expectations of a Labour government that could not be met in the 'real world'. These problems were exacerbated in the 1980s when party activist increased their say over party policy, the selection of candidates and the election of the leader. The fear of the party is emphasised by the famous leaked memo by Patricia Hewitt that stated:

It is obvious from our own polling, as well as from the doorstep, that the 'London effect' is taking its toll: the gays and lesbians issue is costing us dear among the pensioners, and fear of extremism and higher taxes/rates is particularly prominent in the GLC area.[9]

Thus Blair's party strategy has been concerned with reasserting central control and moderating party policy; in essence modernising the party, its policies and its structures.

It is important to note that Blair was not the first Labour leader with the aim of modernising the party. Gaitskell was acutely aware of the need to change Labour's ideology and policy in the light of economic and social change.[10] Wilson wanted to present Labour as a modernising party and clearly saw the role of nationalisation as a means rather than end. Finally, as we shall see below, Neil Kinnock initiated the process of modernisation that has been carried further by Blair. However, what makes Blair's modernisation different is that it is more fundamental than previous attempts, that it tackled the issue of Clause IV, and it is linked with electoral success.

A central and defining component of Blair's modernising project was the reform of Clause IV of the Labour Party constitution. Blair quickly decided that he would drop Labour's commitment to common ownership of the means of production.[11] The impact of the decision was far-reaching. Blair was demonstrating a break with the past and symbolic ending the link that Labour had with state ownership (and distinguishing himself from the modernisation projects of Kinnock and Smith). This was a confirmation of a fundamental change in the ideological position of the party. The party was unconditionally disassociated from state socialism and the myth was dispelled that Labour 'would nationalise everything'. It was intended to send a clear message to voters about how Labour had changed. It also indicated in an unambiguous way that key elements of the party ideology would change. By giving the leader a mandate it stamped Blair's authority on the party. In supporting the reform of Clause IV the party was supporting Blair's whole programme of modernisation. Yet Blair was concerned with reassuring the party:

The process of what is called 'modernisation' is in reality, therefore, the application of enduring, lasting principles for a new generation – creating not just a modern party and organisation but a programme for a modern society, economy and constitution. It is not destroying the left's essential ideology: on the contrary it is retrieving it from an intellectual and political muddle.[12]

Once Clause IV was reformed Blair quickly consolidated the reforms to the party machinery that Kinnock had begun. Blair strengthened one member one vote and through the development of the policy forum he effectively undermined the role of conference in policy making. Likewise, the NEC which at times had been a troublesome critic of the leadership became increasingly Blairite whilst its policy role was significantly reduced.

The aim of these reforms has been both to reduce the influence of party members and to re-educate them. The party leadership can offer policies that are attractive to voters rather than the party and in pursuing such polices not be accused of betrayal. Central to Blair's strategy is an attempt to eradicate the 'culture of betrayal' by pointing to the political and economic constraints which will prevent Labour achieving many of its policies in the short term. In an article in the *Guardian* of July 1995 he urged members to be realistic about what can be achieved:

With the ideological and organisational change, there has to come the attitude of mind of a party to govern. Part of this means activists should not raise to every bait held out by the press or revive the old 'betrayal' psychology that has dogged the party before.[13]

Central to this process is the creation of the rhetorical device of old/new Labour. One dichotomy that remains in Tony Blair's philosophy is that between old and new Labour.[14] If there is an enemy left and one that is strongly identified by certain elements in Blair leadership it is 'Old Labour'. The reality of old Labour is that it is a combination of the right of the party, the left and dissidents but its rhetorical importance is that it is a way distancing new Labour from its past and indicating to the electorate that the party has changed fundamentally. Consequently, the negation of old Labour is an important element in shaping what is new. The problem, of course, is that the dichotomy is false and many of the concerns, if not directly the policies, of the present government are similar to previous Labour governments. All past Labour administrations have been concerned to find a middle way between free market capitalism and state-centred socialism and have effectively attempted to run the British economy successfully in order to produce some fruits for redistribution. Other 'new Labour' themes like the importance of education, traditional values and law and order have been important for past administrations, particularly the socially conservative Callaghan administration. New Labour is not free from its traditions and themes of social conservatism, and social justice that reoccur in new Labour have a strong resonance with the past.[15] Moreover, the appeal to realism in the membership is a theme that has reoccurred in Labour administrations. This invocation of realism in the party is central to Labour's governing strategy.

Governing

Labour's statecraft[16] is essential to new Labour's ideology. Labour has to govern in a way that does not undermine its electoral coalition (thus enabling a second term) and therefore it is important that party criticism does not undermine its essentially conservative governing strategy. Blair and Brown have explicitly attempted to locate Labour's position in office in the context of globalisation. There is a considerable debate concerning whether globalisation is real or a discursive construct.[17] Whether or not it is real, it is clear that there have been major changes in the nature of economic production and the relationships between states in the international system. International trade has grown, the size of currency markets has increased exponentially, the number of multinational corporations has risen dramatically and the development of telecommunication and computer networks have intensified the quality and frequency of international exchanges.[18] In addition, and what cannot be denied, is that there is now a transnational layer of government which directly constrains the actions of nation states. For Britain, the EU, World Trade Organisation and NATO effectively make decisions on a range of economic and social issues that cannot be ignored at national level.

The crucial point is that Blair and Brown believe that the economy is becoming globalised. According to Blair, 'The driving force for economic change today is globalisation'.[19] The perception of a globalised economy frames the choices that the New Labour government makes. This is most clearly apparent in two areas. Public expenditure policy is made within the context of not wishing to upset the global currency markets. Even before globalisation previous Labour governments were constantly constrained and undermined by currency speculation. Often public expenditure cuts were forced on Labour in order to reassure the markets.[20] Blair and Brown have been concerned to reassure capital not because they are selling out (although they may be) but because they have little option. In capitalist systems the interests of business are privileged[21] and if Labour has rejected socialism it has little choice but to provide, as far as possible, the private sector with the conditions for economic growth.

The combination of economic crisis and globalisation has created one of the most problematic issues for Labour: the relationship between taxation and spending. Labour's problem is that at its core is a belief in social justice and greater equality and the means of improving social justice has traditionally been to tax in order to increase welfare spending. The problem was that government had on one side reached the limit of spending that markets were prepared to accept and voters had reached the limit of taxation that they were prepared to pay. Despite polls revealing voters would pay more tax for welfare services, Labour's own evidence suggested otherwise.[22] However, even with the evidence and economic circumstances it was very difficult for Labour to cut this Gordian knot. Both Kinnock and Smith were committed to increased welfare spending. In order to meet Labour's commitments there had to be a source of income and hence in 1992 Labour had limited plans for increased taxation. Whilst these proposals for increased taxation only affected people on higher salaries, there was little faith amongst the electorate that they would not increase everyone's tax bills and this view was reinforced by the Tories effective Tax Bombshell campaign.[23] More people thought that they would be better off under the Conservatives than Labour.[24]

In creating New Labour Blair and Brown sought to resolve the paradox of increasing spending on welfare whilst reassuring voters that they would not increase income tax. The core of the project is a commitment to lowering income tax whilst finding new sources of income to fund welfare. In order to do this Labour economic policy is based on:

- Fiscal conservatism which meant accepting Conservative spending plans for the first two years and balancing budgets over the medium and long-term.
- Cutting income tax rates and not increasing higher rate taxation.
- Finding new sources of finance through the comprehensive spending review which redistributed existing money within government.
- New sources of taxation through changing the married allowance, reducing mortgage tax relief and closing other tax loopholes in areas of capital gains and other taxes.
- Aiming at low inflation and economic growth so that more money is generated in the economy.
- Windfall tax from privatised utilities to fund health and education.

The principal aim of new Labour is to eliminate the tax and spend problem by ensuring greater social justice without increasing income tax. The Labour leadership feels that for reasons of international economy and electoral expediency it has little choice but to be fiscally conservative. However, it still intends to redistribute wealth to poorer rather than richer sectors of society.

Moreover, by shifting decisions on interest rates to the monetary policy committee (and perhaps ultimately to the European Central Bank) an important element of statecraft involves dispensing with culpability for economic problems.[25] The governing strategy reinforces the electoral strategy by reassuring middle income earners that they will not be taxed. More importantly, it avoids the problem of governing failure that wrecked Labour in 1970 and 1979. Labour has been careful not to promise anything it cannot deliver thus reassuring the electors it has not failed and the party it has not sold out. In addition it has been careful not to offend capitalists or global currency markets thus preventing the runs on the pound that damaged the party in 1966, 1969, 1975 and 1976. Blair's crucial strategic insight which separates him from previous Labour prime ministers is to incorporate the constraints of the financial markets into Labour's policy and so circumvent the currency crises that paralysed previous administrations.

How New is New Labour?

As was indicated above Blair and his supporters are careful to maintain a distinction with old Labour and present their project as new and in some ways a clean break with Labour's past. According to Mandelson and Liddle:

New Labour is fundamentally different from old Labour in its economic, social and political approach. It goes well beyond the battles of the past between public and private and about the role of the unions and the relevance of public expenditure, to the achievement of a more equal society.[26]

Nevertheless, Mandelson and Liddle place Labour within the social democratic tradition whilst Blair goes further. He has appealed directly to Labour's past and particularly to the 1945 government as a source of legitimacy for his actions. As Blair said in a speech to commemorate the 50th anniversary of Labour's election in 1945: 'To create the conditions in which Labour is once again capable of leading a governing consensus – in which it is truly the "people's party" – we have to learn the lessons of 1945'.[27] More recently he has declared that, 'The Third Way stands for a modernised social democracy, passionate in its commitment to social justice and the goals of the centre left'.[28] Blair is concerned to link Labour with its previous glories and traditions whilst at the same time distancing his party from the failures of the past.

New Labour is linked to its past in both policy and ideology. It has a number of direct links with previous governments and traditions within the party. All Labour governments –

particularly those of Wilson and Callaghan – have been pragmatic, centrist, concerned to work with capital and hopeful of building a sufficient electoral coalition to remain in office. Many of the policy goals of previous administrations are consistent with the goals of the current Labour government. One clear example is education. Callaghan initiated the 'Great Debate' on education because like Blair and Blunkett he was concerned with falling standards and the impact of 'trendy' teaching methods on the education of children.[29] Similarly, previous administrations were concerned with containing the cost of welfare policy – and where possible reducing universalism – whilst retaining the commitment to social justice and the poorer sectors of society.[30] Some of the ideological positioning on the role of the state, the role of the private sector and issues of taxation are probably less distinct from old Labour governments than Blair would like to admit.

At a more ideological level New Labour has not completely abandon traditions that have existed within the party.[31] As Marquand has suggested, the progressive tradition in Britain developed from the fusion of liberalism and socialism and it was the division of these traditions into two parties that gave the 20th century to the Conservative party.[32] Blair wants to recapture that tradition and incorporate the 'New Liberalism' and to reincorporate traditions of community and Christian socialism. More particularly, Blair and New Labour can be placed within the lineage of revisionism. As David Lipsey points out, revisionism is not a doctrine or body of ideas but 'Revisionists revise' and Blair is in the tradition of Gaitskell and Crosland which was concerned with changing Labour's policies to fit changing circumstances.[33]

Finally, there is the question of whether Blair continued the modernisation undertaken by Kinnock or whether under Blair there was a qualitative shift in the trajectory of modernisation after Kinnock? Kinnock clearly sees Blair following in his footsteps.[34] Similarly Blair has acknowledged the debt to Kinnock:

With Neil Kinnock's election as leader we began a long march of renewal. That project was taken forward by John Smith. We owe it to them both, and above all to the people who most need a Labour government, to finish the journey from protest to power.[35]

However, there is some feeling that with Kinnock's links to the traditional old Labour heartland of the Welsh valleys, to the left and to the trade unions, he was unable to make the sort of radical break that was required and so failed to change the party enough.[36] It is true that in 1992 Labour retained commitments both to increased taxation and spending. There were also commitments to industrial intervention, full employment and a continued role in a variety of forms of some type of public ownership.[37] One proposal was for an enhanced DTI and a British Technology Enterprise to encourage industrial investment.[38] Consequently, in policy terms there are significant differences between Kinnock and Blair. The New Labour government is committed to fiscal conservatism, reform of social security, a reduced role for the state and more traditional policies on the family, law and order and education. The point emphasised by Pannitch and Leys is that Blair 'was almost completely free from the influence of the party's traditional "labourist" ethos' and consequently could make a break with the past that was not open to Kinnock or John Smith.[39]

Yet there is a clear progression between what Kinnock was trying to do and the developments under Blair. In terms of the party, there is a direct lineage between Kinnock's moves to One Member One Vote and reducing the size of the bloc vote and Blair. Kinnock shifted policy making away from activists by ensuring it was made in joint policy committees of NEC and the Shadow Cabinet. The creation of policy reviews was a masterful way of ensuring that changes in policy came from the leadership rather than the membership. In terms of policy, Kinnock made significant changes in abandoning unilateral disarmament, withdrawal from the European Community and dropping the commitment to renationalise privatised industries. Kinnock also initiated the changes on welfare and economic policy and more importantly repositioned Labour's relationship both to the state and the market. Kinnock first highlighted the notion of the enabling state rather than the interventionist state and made it clear that Labour could be reconciled with capitalism.[40] Whilst Kinnock, because of personal history and organisational inertia, had more ties to Labourism than Blair, it cannot be denied that without Kinnock's changes there would not have been a Blair revolution. Kinnock changed the expectations of the party and slayed a number of important dragons. Perhaps more importantly, he marginalised and divided the left thus creating the necessary support to carry modernisation through. Like a De Clerk or a Trimble, Kinnock had enough legitimacy with the old regime to bring a majority with him[41] and thus change the party in the 1980s to an extent that would have been impossible for someone from the right.

There are also important ideological similarities between Blair and Kinnock. Like Blair, Kinnock was concerned to emphasise the importance of the individual within the collective and thus the emphasis of welfare policy was on social justice and greater equality rather than any absolute equality. Kinnock also emphasised a changing role of the state in recognition of the failure of the big state to meet the needs of ordinary people. Again, this continuity emphasises the way that the revisionist approach has been a consistent trend in the party since the 1950s and Blair is not without some ties to party history and ethos.

New Labour as Thatcherism

For a number of commentators new Labour is simply Labour's accommodation to Thatcherism.[42] For Hay, Thatcherism created a new state regime based on the dismantling of corporatism, the abandonment of full employment, a shift to the private provision of public goods, and the centralisation of power in the state. Blairism is thus the consolidation of the regime with any policy changes being 'minor tinkering' or crisis management rather than an attempt to forge a new state regime.[43] For Hay, the policies of the Labour party in the Blair era are an indication of the success of the Thatcherite hegemonic project that is indicated by:

(a) the extent to which we are witnessing the consolidation of a 'one vision democracy'; (b) the degree of convergence between the parties around a Thatcherite agenda; and (c) the extent to which this represents a departure from the politics of consensus which characterised the post-war settlement.[44]

However, it is possible to take issue with each of these indicators. Thatcherism and Blairism share some elements of a vision of democracy that is essentially elitist, closed and executive centred. However, these elements are not Thatcherite but belong to the British political tradition and thus have infected all governments since the 1850s.[45] In other areas of democracy New Labour and Thatcherism are very different. Thatcherism is essentially monotheistic and individualistic; government is based on the unity of executive sovereignty, which is maintained by election through individual voters. The civil society-state link is between the governors and the individual and it is not mediated by groups or other layers of administration. Labour's vision of democracy, especially as espoused in its constitutional reform programme, is quite different. Blair's notion of individualism – which is central to his political creed – is based on a belief:

that we can only realise ourselves as individuals in a thriving civil society, comprising strong families and civic institution buttressed by intelligent government. For most individuals to succeed, society must be strong. When society is weak, power and rewards go to the few not the many.[46]

Unlike the Thatcherite view, it is not a case of the individual against the group. New Labour's vision of democracy is also underpinned by a notion of pluralism in which there cannot be a single correct path nor a single source of policy. Such a view has seen realisation at different levels of politics from the adoption of task forces and people's panels, and including Liberal Democrats in a cabinet committee at central government level to devolution at regional level and the creation of a London authority at local level. As Blair has said:

...we need to move decision making back closer to the people by decentralising government and giving local government more power. I know that it is easy to talk about pluralism when in opposition but much harder to give up when in government. I am determined that we should do so.[47]

Whatever the limitations on Labour's pluralism in office, its constitutional programme is extremely radical by British standards and far removed from a Thatcherite vision of democracy. There is a notion that power should be dispersed and that democratic rights can belong to collective identities. New Labour is looking to re-establish the intermediate institutions that the Conservatives either bypassed or destroyed.

The second element of Hay's hegemonic success is policy convergence around a Thatcherite agenda. In a range of policy areas there has been significant policy convergence and examples include elements of economic policy; the cuts in lone parent benefit and the continuation of private prisons. However, the reasons for policy convergence are complex. It takes considerable time to change policy. For example the Conservatives maintained a liberal criminal justice policy (despite ideological rhetoric) until the appointment of Michael Howard[48] because there are major financial, political and institutional constraints on what governments can do.[49] There has always been some policy convergence between succeeding governments partly because they are both in the same context and partly because change takes time. In other areas it is clear that the policy agenda and the capabilities of the state have changed and to some extent the Labour government has accepted the world that it has found. It would be very difficult for Labour to return to the sorts of industrial policies that existed in 1979. This may be because of Thatcherite hegemony but it may also be because the world has changed.

Any government has little choice but to accept the institutional framework that exists when it gains office. The state in 1979 was very different to the state in 1997. In 1979 the number of civil servants was 565,815; by 1997 it was 430,335 of which 256,935 worked in next steps agencies.[50] In 1979 the state had a range of mechanism, in addition to a large nationalised sector, through the 1972 and 1974 Industry Acts and the creation of the National Enterprise Boards and Sector Working Parties which enabled the state to intervene directly in the production process. These mechanisms were reinforced by a range of corporatist institutions such as the National Economic Development Council, the price commission, the Manpower Services Commission, Incomes and Prices Board which ensured capital and labour institutionalised contact with government and the potential to influence policy outcomes. The Thatcher government effectively dismantled all this machinery even abolishing sponsorship departments within the DTI (they were later recreated) which gave departments contact with key industrial sectors. The DTI was effectively emasculated in the Thatcher years. Its expenditure was cut dramatically and it shifted from an industrial department to one concerned with trade, the single European market and deregulation.

Consequently, Labour inherited a state that did not have the ability to intervene in the way it had in the 1960s and 1970s. To re-establish such a state would involve tremendous costs and time. It took the Conservatives at least ten years to abandon just some of the vestiges of the post-war state. Moreover, the incentives for re-creating such a state are very low. Effectively both corporatism and state intervention failed either to provide political stability (or legitimacy) or economic success. The collapse of the Labour government in 1979 was linked closely to the failure and collapse of the corporatist, interventionist state. New Labour's interventionism is not, therefore, based on the types of structures that existed previously. It has adapted many elements of the Thatcherite state including public/private partnership, multiple-service delivery and intervention through incentives rather than abandon the new administrative machinery and managerial mechanisms.[51] Nevertheless, what Labour had done is to de-ideologise these elements of new right thinking and incorporate them into government policy. Labour's use of these mechanisms is not part of a strategy to marketize and dismantle the state but a belief that the market should be used where it is more effective. Moreover, a distrust of the state is no longer a provenance of the right. Increasingly thinkers on the left are suggesting that social problems need much more complex solutions that the state can provide.[52]

More importantly there are a whole range of policy areas where Labour is adopting distinct policies.

Public expenditure

Whilst in the first two years of the Labour government, Labour stuck to the Conservative spending plans, over the next three years the government aims to increased expenditure by 2.25 per cent in real terms. Even these limited increases can be contrasted with Thatcherism which saw public expenditure as anathema and, at least in its initial phase, promised to reduce public expenditure in real terms. More importantly, spending increases are not to be generalised but spending will be reallocated 'to key priorities'.[53] Expenditure will rise on education by 5.1 percent and on health by 4.7 per cent.

The increases in these areas show two important differences from the Thatcherite agenda. First, a commitment to policy areas that are linked to themes of social justice and welfare. Second, a belief that state provision, and the state more generally, is an important element in the delivery of welfare and other public goods. Whilst Labour have accepted many elements of the Thatcherite institutional settlement (reduced numbers of civil servants; privatisation, managerialism and next steps agencies), Labour's vision of the state is diametrically opposed to that of the Conservatives. Blair accepts that the era of big government is over (although we still have 'big government') but sees new Labour as using the 'power of government to promote the common good'.[54] For Blair:

Big government is dead. The days of tax and spend are gone. Much of the deregulation and privatisation that took place in the 1980s was necessary. But everything cannot be left to the market. We believe that there is a role for active government. But it is a modern government that does things in different ways.[55]

The notion that the state is a force for bad and undermines the common good was central to Thatcherism and the New Right perspective. As the *Modernising Government* white paper indicates:

There has been a presumption that the private sector is always best, and insufficient attention has been given to rewarding success in the public service and to equipping it with the skills required to develop and deliver strategic policies and services in modern and effective ways.[56]

Many of Labour's policies are highly interventionist. Welfare to work involves the state deeply in the process of finding work and forcing on individuals the requirement to work. Labour's family policy is concerned with providing state incentives to maintain traditional families and ensure some redistribution of wealth to the poorest family units. Even in the economic area, the minimum wage (whatever its level) is a determinedly anti-market policy and Labour direct intervention in the Rover/BMW issue (and provision of a subsidy to BMW) is reminiscent of some of old Labour's crisis management. Labour's commitment to a minimum wage and higher levels of employment indicate Labour has abandoned the key nostrum of monetarism that there is a natural level of unemployment and it is committed to a very different labour market policy. In addition, linked to labour marked polices are issues of social justice. According to Gordon Brown, 'Our commitment to equality is as strong as ever' and it cannot be denied that the 1999 budget contained a significant element of redistribution.[57] Moreover, by accepting the social charter, the government has indicated an important break with Conservative labour policy. New Labour may be accepting most of the state structures created by the Conservatives but unlike Thatcherism, they retain a positive notion of the state.

The European Union and the Single Currency

Britain's relation to Europe and monetary union is central to conceptions of the role of the state, sovereignty, and the fundamental political economy of government. The Conservatives' opposition to EMU and sceptical position on the EU in general indicates a different narrative for Britain's economic future. Labour, by apparently moving toward membership of EMU, sees the EU as providing a framework for financial stability and economic growth. Labour's vision of political economy is hence internationalist and to a degree interventionist in the sense of ascribing to European initiatives on regional, employment and social policy. For the Conservatives, a sustainable economy has to be nationally based and Britain's economic success will be based on retaining our own currency and providing a cheap and deregulated labour market which will be able to undercut expensively produced Euro-area goods.

At the core of New Labour and Thatcherism are diverse visions of political economy. For the Conservatives, Britain's future relies in using economic sovereignty to undercut labour prices and currency prices in the Euro bloc. With the access that the Single Market guarantees Britain will be able to trade freely in Europe with much reduced production costs (through keeping down labour costs and not subscribing to the social cost which derive from the social compact). This will make Britain an offshore haven that will prove attractive to foreign investment looking for access to the EU market. For the Conservative a laissez-faire state will allow Britain to undercut its competitors.

For New Labour, the EU is a means for providing price stability, a European market, social benefits, modernisation of the economy and a strategy for dealing with the impact of globalisation. Rather than a free market strategy it is ultimately a transnational state-led strategy which involves a considerable loss of economic sovereignty with the added benefit of allowing government to absolve itself of difficult economic decisions.

Defining New Labour

Whilst there remain many disputes over the nature and causes of Thatcherism, there was a general consensus over its main ideological principles. It says something about the nature of New Labour's that there is no similar consensus in defining the key ideological features of its ideology. It is seen as social democratic, conservative, Thatcherite or a third way. This definitional ambiguity is partially a result of how New Labour has been presented; it is concerned with building a broad coalition and thus Blair is eager not to offend. Moreover, as part of the electoral strategy New Labour has been concerned with challenging many of the traditional boundaries that have defined previous ideologies such as individual/community, market/state, nationalism/internationalism and wealth creation/social justice.[58] In all these areas, Blair believes that it is possible to turn these apparently antagonistic relationships into dependent relationships and in this way build a coalition of support that is based on both sides of the class/ideology debate. As he said:

My vision for the 21st century is of a popular politics reconciling themes which in the past have wrongly been regarded as antagonistic - patriotism and internationalism; rights and responsibilities; the promotion of enterprise and the attack on poverty and discrimination.[59]

This project then can be no mere reflection of Thatcherism, which by its very nature had distinct positions of each of these binary antagonisms. New Labour's ideology can be categorised as inclusionary (with others like one nation Conservatism and fascism) rather than exclusionary (such as Marxism and Thatcherism). Within this context the importance of Labour's policy of social inclusion becomes apparent. (It should be noted that such an inclusionary strategy is not new for Labour. It was partly the appeal of the Attlee Labour government, which was elected around the issue of rebuilding a fairer and more modern

Britain after the war, and Wilson's goal in the 1960s was to turn Labour into the Natural Party of Government.) This inclusionary ideology provides both an important governing code and electoral strategy for the Labour party but it does however contain a number of problems and contradiction. For while ideology may be able to overcome the distinctions between markets and states or wealth and poverty, the reality of government is that choices between these options often have to be made and making the choices in government may make it difficult to retain the electoral coalition.

The inclusive ideology is based on a number of important and recurring themes. Central to Blairism is populism. Labour is not presented as a class party but a party that is attempting to attract votes across the social spectrum and is prepared to listen to the demands of voters in order to achieve that goal. Linked to populism is a reoccurrence of the attempt to regain patriotism for the Labour party. Thus nation and an identity which is bound to nation has be reclaimed by new Labour. For Blair, patriotism underlines one of his key beliefs: the importance of community - a sense of belonging to a wider social unit than the family. New Labour rejects the individualism of the new right without embracing the collectivism of old Labour. It is through the community that social support and some social justice can be achieved and thus community can assume some of the functions of the state. New Labour does marry the Thatcherite world it found with some of the traditional concerns of the Labour party. It adopts individualism and patriotism but within a context of community and the European Union making it a complex and to some extent ambiguous and changing set of ideas.

Notes

1 I would like to thank Dave Richards for his comments on an earlier draft of this paper.

2 Ivor Crewe, 'The Labour Party and the Electorate' in Dennis Kavanagh (ed.) *The Politics of the Labour Party*, London, George Allen and Unwin, 1981; Anthony Heath *et al, Understanding Political Change*, Oxford, Pergamon; Paul Whiteley, *The Labour Party in Crisis*, London, Methuen, 1983.

3 Patrick Seyd, *The Rise and Fall of the Labour Left*, Basingstoke: Macmillan, 1987; Steve Ludlam, 'New Labour and the Unions: the End of the Contentious Alliance' in Steve Ludlam and Martin J. Smith (eds), *New Labour; Party, Policy and Ideology*, London, Macmillan, 2000.

4 Steve Ludlam, 'The Gnomes of Washington: Four Myths of the IMF Crisis', *Political Studies*, 40, 1996; and James Callaghan, *Time and Chance*, London, Fontana, 1988.

5 Manuel Castells, *The Rise of the Network Society*, Oxford, Blackwell, 1996, p. 307.

6 *Guardian*, May 26 1999.

7 Figures from Ivor Crewe, *Political Studies*, 34, 4, 1986; *New Statesman*, May 1997, Special General Election Edition.

8 Thanks to Paul Whiteley for supplying these figures from the British Election Survey 1997 Data Set.

9 Quoted in Philip Gould, *The Unfinished Revolution*, London: Little, Brown, 1999.

10 Brian Brivati, *Hugh Gaitskell: A Biography*, London: Richard Cohen Books; Michael Kenny and Martin J. Smith, 'Discourses of Modernization: Gaitskell, Blair and the Reform of Clause IV' in Charles Patie, David Denver, Justin Fisher and Steve Ludlam (eds.) *British Elections and Parties Review*, Volume 7, London, Frank Cass, 1997. David Lipsey, 'Revisionist Revise', in Dick Leonard, (ed.) *Crosland and New Labour*, London, Macmillan, 1999.

11 Gould, *Unfinished Revolution*.

12 Tony Blair, *New Britain, My Vision of a Young Country*, London: Fourth Estate, 1996, pp.221-2.

13 See Michael Kenny and Martin J Smith, '(Mis)understanding Blair', *Political Quarterly*, 68, 1997, p. 227.

14 See also Colin Hay, *The Political Economy of New Labour: Labouring under False Pretences?*, Manchester, Manchester University Press, 1999.

15 Michael Kenny and Martin J. Smith, Blair, 'New Labour and Ideology' in Ludlam and Smith, *New Labour.*

16 See Jim Bulpitt, 'The discipline of the new democracy: Mrs Thatcher's domestic statecraft', *Political Studies*, 34, 1986, pp.19-39.

17 Anthony Giddens, *The Third Way*, Cambridge, Polity 1998; Paul Hirst and Grahame Thompson, *Globalization in Question*; David Held, Antony McGrew, David Goldblatt and Jonathon Perraton, *Global Transformations*, Cambridge, Polity, 1999.

18 David Held *et al*, *Global Transformations*, Cassells.

19 Blair, *New Britain*, p.118.

20 See Harold Wilson, *Labour Government 1964-70*, London, Weidenfeld and Nicolson, 1974.

21 Charles E. Lindblom, *Politics and Markets*, New York, Basic Books, 1977.

22 Gould, *The Unfinished Revolution*.

23 Gould, *The Unfinished Revolution*, pp. 124-127.

24 David Sanders, 'Why the Conservative Party Won – Again' in Anthony King (ed.) *Britain at the Polls 1992*, New Jersey, Chatham House, 1992.

25 Hay, *The Political Economy of New Labour*; Bulpitt, *The discipline of the new democracy*.

26 Peter Mandelson and Roger Liddle, *The Blair Revolution: Can New Labour Deliver?*, London: Faber and Faber, 1996.

27 Blair, *New Britain*, p.13.

28 Tony Blair, *The Third Way: New Politics for the New Century*, London: Fabian Society, 1998, p.1.

29 For the detail see Colin McCaig, 'Education, Education, Education', in Ludlam and Smith, *New Labour*.

30 See Tim Bale, 'Sacred Cows and Common Sense: The Symbolic Statecraft of the Political Culture of the Labour Party', Unpublished Ph.D. thesis, University of Sheffield, 1997.

31 See Michael Kenny and Martin J. Smith, Blair, 'New Labour and Ideology' in Ludlam and Smith, *New Labour*.

32 David Marquand, *The Progressive Dilemma*, London, Heinemann, 1991.

33 David Lipsey, 'Revisionists Revised' in Lipsey and Dick Leonard (eds), *The Socialist Legacy: Crosland's legacy*, Cape, 1981.

34 Interview conducted with Neil Kinnock by author September 1997.

35 Blair, *New Britain*, p.3.

36 Gould, *The Unfinished Revolution*, p.158.

37 Labour Party, *Meet the Challenge: Make the Change: A New Agenda for Britain*, London, Labour Party, 1989.

38 Andrew Gamble, 'The Labour Party and Economic Management', in M. J. Smith and J. Spear (Des), *The Changing Labour Party*, London, Routledge, 1992.

39 Leo Panitch and Colin Leys, *The End of Parliamentary Socialism* London, Verso, 1997, p. 227.

40 Martin J. Smith, 'Neil Kinnock and the Modernisation of the Labour Party', *Contemporary Record*, 1994, 8, pp. 555-566.

41 Panitch and Leys, p. 219.

42 For examples see Panitch and Leys, *The End of Parliamentary Socialism*; Richard Heffernan, *New Labour and Thatcherism*, London, Macmillan 1999; Richard Heffernan and Colin Hay, 'Labour's Thatcherite Revisionism: Playing the Politics of Catch-Up', *Political Studies*, 1994, pp.700-7; Hay, *The Political Economy of New Labour*; Paul Foot, 'A Labour Party Thatcher can be Proud of', *The Guardian*, 26 March 1996.

43 Colin Hay, pp. 151-165.

44 Hay p. 130.

45 David Richards and Martin J. Smith, 'New Labour, Whitehall and the Reform of the Constitution', in Ludlam and Smith, *New Labour*; Martin J. Smith, *The Core Executive in Britain*, London, Macmillan, 1999.

46 Blair, *The Third Way*, p.3.

47 Blair, *New Britain*, p. 262.

48 David Richards and Martin J. Smith, 'How Departments Change: Windows of Opportunity and Critical Junctures in three departments', *Public Policy and Administration*, 12, 1997, pp.31-50.

49 Richard Rose, *Inheritance In Public Policy: Change without Choice in Britain*, New Haven, Yale University Press, 1993.

50 *Civil Service Statistics*, 1998, http:/www.cabinet-office.gov.uk/civil service, 1999/cental/statistics/summary.htm

51 Blair's attitude to reforming Whitehall is clearly presented in his speech on 'Modernising Central Government', Senior Civil Service conference, October 1998.

52 For example, see Paul Hirst, *From Statism to Pluralism*.

53 *Comprehensive Spending Review*, CM4011, HMSO, London, 1998: 13.

54 Blair, *The Third Way*, p.15.

55 Blair, 'Modernising Central Government'.

56 *Modernising government*, Cm 4310, London, The Stationery Office, 1998, p. 11.

57 Gordon Brown, 'Equality – Then and Now', in Leonard, *Crosland and New Labour*, p.47.

58 See Chantal Mouffe, *Dimensions of Radical Democracy*, London, Verso, 1992.

59 Blair, *The Third Way*, p.1.

Part II
Centenary
Reflections

In Defence of New Labour

Denis Healey

The key question is not what Tony Blair has done to the party, but has the party changed as society, from which it grows and it changes, has altered? Moreover, the decisions which have changed the party's constitution, structure, and policies, really all started in the days of Neil Kinnock. The process of change was carried much further – practically into Blairism – by John Smith and it was only his very tragic and early death that prevented him being the great leader. Blair has adapted the party still further as society itself has changed. The fact that he has done the right thing is proven by the fact that the Labour Party is much more popular now after being two years in power than it was when it won an exceptionally large majority in the last general election.

You have got to see the Labour Party as reflecting – sometimes with dangerously long time lapses – changes in the structure of society. The Labour Party was founded by a very odd coalition of mainly middle class intellectual socialists who belonged to the current which was launched in 1848 when revolutionary movements swept the whole of Europe, and by people like Keir Hardie and trade unionists who wanted a better standard of life for working people. Rather than power – they were not interested in power in society except in so far as it would help them to improve their living standards – the trade unions wanted to have some direct representation. They were quite prepared to work along with the middle class intellectuals who were socialists, though of course there were a lot of quite outstanding working class socialists like Keir Hardie who was the founder of the party.

When I was a student in the sixth-form in Yorkshire I knew two old men in their sixties who had been at the founding conferences of the party in 1903 and 1908. Talking to them convinced me that it was really working people trying to find their place in the sun and allied with the socialists who gave them a coherence of policy. Compared with the parties in the continent which regarded policy as a guiding star, the interesting thing in Britain, has been that on the whole the party has never aimed at more than it believed it could achieve. In the inter-war years particularly following the great slump, the demands of the unions for a powerful role became important and of course they produced some outstanding leaders: Bevin was one of my idols and I still regard him as, with Roosevelt, one of the two greatest democratic politicians in the 20th century.

When Attlee won the election in 1945, on what was openly a socialist manifesto, he carried out his program - one of the few governments which has actually done what it set out to do. Even if what he set out to do was not quite revolutionary by the standards of the time it was overwhelmingly for rapid and substantial change. He did change everything. Attlee was extraordinary wise and intelligent, comparably in many ways with Eisenhower in the US in so far as neither of them talked at any great lengths about what they wanted to do but they did very dramatic and necessary things. Essentially Attlee aimed to end the class war not to win it, and to a very large extent he did end it at least as it then existed. What he did not do, however, was to change the constitutional structure of the party so that it was able to represent the views of the people as a whole. He did not want the Labour Party to be only a working class party - he himself was at a public school and had a personal tenderness for people who had been at his public school when he was PM. The change in the party structure became essential as we lost election after election through the 1950s and we were dogged, when we were in opposition during those years by a civil war between the unreconstructed left, which in the post war period was very much influenced by Trotskyites and communists, and the trade union wing which was very unrepresentative of its own members because very few trade union executives which took the decisions consulted their members in the important issues; the narrowness of the vote between me and Benn for the deputy leader was a very good example of that. Finally it was Neil Kinnock as leader who realised the need for a complete change in approach.

Earlier Gaitskell had tried to do too many things too fast at once. It was Cousins who said when he spoke at the Scarborough conference when Gaitskell made his speech in favour of getting rid of Clause Four: 'I would not be opposing you on this if you were not in favour of keeping nuclear weapons'. Gaitskell was trying to do everything at once. Clause Four was rather like with the doctrine of the Trinity in the Christian church: how much people in the church really believe in it is very uncertain, but if you want to strike it out of the canon you get tremendous opposition. There was an element of almost religious utopianism about it. Indeed on the whole in democracies ever since the French Revolution there has been a struggle between the ideologists and the utopians;

when you get an utopian ideology, as sometimes you get in the Labour Party, boy, you are in trouble.

The very striking thing about the Labour Party today – the Blair Labour Party – is the extent to which it is run by Scotsmen. John Smith was a very good example, and then you have Donald Dewar, George Robertson, and of course Blair himself, and Gordon Brown. Gordon is the guts of the party though he is not too good on television because he has one bad eye. Frankly no PM can succeed with a bad Chancellor.

It is 45 years since I wrote an article for a Norwegian paper which was pure Blairism. It said don't imagine that everybody is going to be in favour of expanding the welfare state because now it is the mass of the people who are paying for it. Nationalisation is no longer a relevant way of dealing with industry because it is how you manage it, not who owns it, that matters. I think that a lot of people in the party would have agreed with me even then but the party was very slow to change because all institutions are slow to change, there is an institutional inertia and the vested interests are powerful in any institution which is threatened by change.

Had John Smith lived he would have moved not quite as fast as Blair because he would have wanted to retain the support of Old Labour which Blair appears totally lacking in interest in. In fact if anything Blair regards Old Labour as an embarrassment and its public support as embarrassing. Blair has done a very good job. His government is the first one to be more popular two years after having won a big victory in the election but he is mainly concerned with running the country well and having a sensible foreign policy. I do not think his foreign policy is quite so well constructed as his domestic policy because the present generation of politicians in all parties who did not serve in the last war do not have much of a sense of history. The USA has reached such a situation very much sooner. It is still a fluid equilibrium but I think that certainly the class war is not going to dominate it. There will be big arguments about the extent to which you interfere with the market in order to achieve fairness and other social objectives. But most of the decisions were really made in the Attlee period when we adopted the Welfare State which was proposed during the war by a liberal Beveridge. Today's questions are no longer seen as so agonisingly important and this was reflected in the very low vote in the European elections in 1998.

The Legacy of the SDP

David Owen

In my autobiography, *Time to Declare*, published in 1991, I wrote that it would only be historians in the 21st century who would be able to determine how successfully the SDP contributed to a change in political attitudes. But that if coalition politics did ensue that would prove to be a more lasting legacy than our considerable impact on reforming the Labour Party. I still think it is too early to make a final judgement on this aspect. In 1982, a year after the SDP was launched, when I was already very concerned about a takeover by the Liberals, I said 'Our epitaph might be that we had saved the Labour Party' and added that 'there were worse fates than that'. After the tenth anniversary of the founding of the SDP in 1991 the *Times* in an editorial, 'To the Four's credit', disinterred that quotation and concluded it was indeed our epitaph.

A premature conclusion was made in 1995 claiming that the wholesale recasting of the Labour Party owed almost nothing to the SDP'.[1] Largely written during John Smith's period as leader of the Labour Party, it was nonsense when published and manifestly absurd as judged in 1999 against the first two years of Tony Blair's prime ministership. Academics are often not very good at making contemporary political judgements. For example, Tony King strongly advised Shirley Williams not to contest the Warrington by-election, a decision that did more damage to her leadership prospects and thereby to the Social Democrat cause than anything else in the SDP's short history.

I have always been a social democrat. For me, while I prefer social democrat, the term democratic socialist, as in continental Europe, is interchangeable. I have no wish to repudiate the great body of socialist thinking and writing about egalitarianism and its linkage to an individual's freedom. British socialists, like Robert Owen, William Morris, Professors Tawney and Titmus, G D H Cole and Tony Crosland have made a profound contribution to political thought and I will not denigrate their memory by decrying socialism. The SDP interestingly did contemplate calling itself New Labour among other names like the Radicals and we would have joined Socialist International early on had the Labour

Party not blocked our membership. There was considerable understanding for our policy position abroad amongst social democratic political leaders like Helmut Schmidt and Willy Brandt. After leaving the shadow Cabinet in November 1980 had the SDP not been formed I would have given up my seat in Parliament rather than fight the 1983 election on Labour's manifesto. It was an essential element in Labour's 100-year history that some of its members in 1981 insisted that principles on vital policy questions came before party.

The all-important change to Labour's suicidal political stance on defence and Europe in the 1980s was the SDP's capacity to capture Labour votes in Labour-held constituencies in both 1983 and 1987. Few things shook Michael Foot more in the 1983 election campaign than touring Plymouth Devonport's post-war council estates in the last week of the campaign where he had been used to seeing his own Labour posters in 1945–59 and instead seeing in virtually every house SDP posters. Labour's commitment to come out of the European Community without even a referendum and to abandon nuclear deterrence was totally unacceptable to millions of Labour voters. But the nature of politics is that such realities have to be expressed first in the ballot box. Losing votes to the Tories could have been explained away; losing votes to the hated SDP was a humiliation that had to lead to a fundamental policy rethink.

Many in different parties and none contributed to the all-important replacement of the old state control/free market polarisation of the 1970s and 1980s culminating in Labour, Liberal Democratic and Conservatives accepting the market economy, but it takes a highly prejudiced mind to deny the role in that process of the SDP. First the SDP had to have an argument within itself, which was finally resolved at our 1985 conference in Torquay. It took Labour a further ten years to dump Clause Four in its constitution, to really accept the reforms of trade union law, to welcome profit motivation, private enterprise and accept the need for incentives.

Labour started on the road back to government when Neil Kinnock had an oratorical triumph against the hard left at their 1985 conference in Bournemouth savaging Derek Hatton and the Liverpool Labour Party. Prior to the Kinnock speech the SDP/Liberal Alliance was ahead in the opinion polls and one poll had us 9.5 per cent ahead of Labour with the Conservatives third. After hearing that speech I knew that Labour were pulling back from the brink.

The new Labour Government's constitutional reforms of 1997–99 arose out of the 1980s debate. Although long espoused by the Liberal Party, it was not untl the SDP leaders used their recent experiences in government to develop a coherent programme of devolution to Scotland, Wales and Northern Ireland, and adopting the European Convention on Human Rights, electoral reform and freedom of information, that a cross-party body of opinion began to build up, sufficient to overwhelm by the middle 1990s the constitutional conservatism of John Major's government.

It was, however, for the championing, from our earliest days, of an anti-poverty strategy that the SDP deserves to be remembered sympathetically by its critics on the left. The SDP policy of integrating the tax and benefit system challenged all parties to think more deeply about welfare reform. Making our own middle class supporters face up to the justice of abolishing the married man's tax allowance, of substantially increasing child allowance and of ending mortgage tax relief was, throughout the 1980s, crucial to the 1990s reforms. All were initially unpopular but right and the SDP paved the way for the changes made first by the Conservative government and now by the Labour government.

Sadly the SDP was unable to capture enough seats in the House of Commons in the all-important 1983 election to survive as an independent force. Once Labour began to lose its extremist policies and image the task was even harder. I still believe had the SDP/Liberal Alliance held together until 1992 we would have held the balance of power with the 40+ seats the Liberal Democrats got in 1997. In 1992 Labour was desperate for power and we could have extracted PR for Westminster elections from Neil Kinnock as the price for Labour returning to government. The bargaining counter would have been PR for Europe and possibly local elections from John Major.

After Labour's fourth election defeat in 1992 Tony Blair was one of the few Labour leaders to recognise that Labour's rethinking had not moved anywhere near far enough to win the trust of sufficient voters and something far more radical had to come. After having listened to SDP policies for his first nine years in Parliament he chose, when he became leader, not just to adopt almost every single one of them but also, more importantly, to talk the language of political co-operation, not merging, across the party political divide. Some of the most progressive SDP thinking all adopted by new Labour came from the small SDP that was left after the break-up of the party and the forming of the Liberal

Democrats in 1987. On education we espoused self-managing schools, we advocated welfare at work, the separation between providers and purchasers in the NHS, elected mayors and independence for the Bank of England. The SDP however by then was dying and becoming more a think tank. That legacy has in part been taken over by the Social Market Foundation.

Whether new Labour adopts the long-standing Liberal Party commitment to Eurofederalism remains an open question. It is an important political fact, however, that the SDP while firmly committed to British membership of the European Community never adopted Liberal policy to the European Community within the Alliance. Indeed the SDP's last party political broadcast in September 1991 was to alert people to the danger of losing Britain's identity as a self-governing nation, a very real danger now were we to rush into Euroland. The sensible policy on the euro is not to rush into a referendum in 2001 or 2002. That would be a profound mistake by Tony Blair and the Labour Party. The immediate downside risks, economic and political, are far, far greater than the upside gains.

The modernisation of Britain to develop a more open, intelligent, fairer, classless, innovative and risk-taking society is essential. Good government eschews ideology but it needs a political philosophy. The problem facing social democrats is that ours is a philosophy constantly evolving to grapple with a complex world. Social democrats readily admit that most decisions are taken on the balance of advantage 6:4 or 7:3 and that only rarely are issues so clear cut that one can argue the case 10:0. Social democrats sense that there has to be a broader background to develop a fair society than just a market economy. Market principles have to be checked and balanced against those of a value-based society. Two key values of social democracy are the spirit of generosity and the spirit of solidarity. It is not possible to be a social democrat without a fairly deep attachment to the virtue of collective conscience, acting to achieve social justice.

Note

1 *SDP: The Birth, Life and Death of the Social Democratic Party*, Ivor Crewe and Anthony king, OUP, 1995.

A Tory View of 1964–70

Lord Biffen

Labour won a narrow but well-judged election victory in 1964, which was reinforced eighteen months later. The theme was that modern socialism by the use of planning and partnership between government and industry could raise national output and improve the welfare state.

The Tories viewed this with a mixture of political hostility and appreciation. Labour's programme was not so different from that followed by the Tory Chancellor, Reginald Maudling. This had, in turn, caused anxiety amongst the party's economic liberals – notably Enoch Powell.

On the whole the Tory liberals and not the Edward Heath leadership made the running in the opposition to the Wilson government. They believed they were justified by events.

The National Plan was a somewhat tepid programme of voluntary targets and growth forecasts. The project lived an uncertain political life and died in ignominy with the devaluation of sterling. Its demise also affected the reputation of the ebullient Labour deputy leader George Brown. The episode confirmed the liberal Tory instinct that political planning was a sham, and that the need was for greater reliance on market forces.

Prices and incomes policies were even more at the heart of Labour's policy. Essentially they were voluntary in concept and enforcement but there was a statutory 'long-stop' which was given parliaments legal authority. This was a dubious tactic. It meant that the policy was given a high legal profile and was constantly debated in parliament. Conservatives had no qualms about joining forces with Labour dissidents, including, trade unionists, in opposing a policy that seemed simultaneous nit picky and heavy handed. Eventually the policy was abandoned but not before a major trade union leader, Frank Cousins, had resigned in disillusion from the cabinet and parliament. Once again the Tory liberals felt vindicated in opposing a policy that was economically lacklustre and politically an albatross.

Labour's plans to revitalise industry were regarded by the Tories with cynicism rather than hostility. Their general view was that there was no great shortage of capital for business and that the city could best allocate it. Labour proposed a modest state inspired merchant bank - the Industrial Relations Corporation. Politically it made little impact, but neither did it provide the acute problems that undermined the National Plan and the Incomes Policy.

Labour's final attempt to restructure the economy was an ambitious plan to reform the trade unions. The task was entrusted to Barbara Castle who grandly entitled her plans *In Place of Strife*. Discord never left the Cabinet room.

Labour's economic policies provided easy targets for the Tory liberals who included such young 'high fliers' as Geoffrey Howe, Terence Higgins and Patrick Jenkins, but they only just reaped an election victory in 1970.

Devaluation and the Treasury leadership of Roy Jenkins enabled Labour to make a substantial recovery. It was not enough to deny Edward Heath the premiership. Once installed he eventually introduced price and income controls, greater state subsides for industry and an aborted law on trade union reform. His critics bewailed it was old Labour writ anew and not much better. In truth the political carousel still had not turned to liberalism, and did not do so until the 1980s.

The Challenge of Co-operation

Calum MacDonald MP

Labour's first century saw only spasmodic electoral success. By the 1980s, the party appeared doomed to permanent opposition. In a dramatic turnaround, however, Labour was reborn in the 1990s, emerging as one of the fastest growing parties in Europe, capturing the largest number of seats in its history and enjoying the most successful beginning to any of its periods in Government. It remains to be seen whether this will prove just another of its occasional spasms of success or, alternatively, the start of a new era of political hegemony. Secondly, and just as important, can this electoral success, if sustained, produce a record of social and political achievement to stand comparison with the best in the party's past? Answering these two questions in the circumstances of the 21st century will take the Labour Party into new and uncharted waters.

Electorally, Labour has done best either when it has enjoyed a complete monopoly of the centre-left, as in 1945, or else when it has engaged in explicit co-operation with the Liberal Democrats, including tacit tactical voting, as in 1997. Monopolistic politics ceased to be possible on the progressive left when the Liberals began their national revival in the 1970s. It is the new politics of centre-left co-operation which will have to underpin Labour's electoral strategy in the 21st century.

New thinking on policy, as well as on strategy, will be required to answer the second question and make Labour's future governments a success. The party's core mission has always been to tackle what we now term social exclusion, encouraging a fair distribution of the nations prosperity and helping the casualties of the market economy re-establish themselves within the community as a whole. The context in which that is done has changed greatly, however. In particular, today's political agenda has ceased to be purely domestic and, more and more, requires co-ordinated action at the European level. In government, as well as in campaigning, Labour's politics in the new century will need to be very different from the old.

Although Labour is now in the electoral ascendant, many of its traditional policies have been jettisoned. The talk is of new forms of privatisation, not nationalisation. The tripartite consensus of corporatism has been replaced by the language of entrepreneurship and competition. The welfare state is being reformed, away from universalism and paternalism, and towards targeted assistance and the rhetoric of self-help and responsibility. At the same time, the established power structures of the British state, which old Labour defended, are being broken up and dispersed through a programme of radical constitutional reform. These are profound changes. The political routines, organisational practices, membership attitudes and social culture which comprised 20th century Labourism are being rapidly and determinedly discarded. In a sense, the Labour Party itself is being hollowed out, even as it increases its membership. New Labour is such a successful slogan precisely because it has the merit of being true.

Changes as profound as these made it all the more important to articulate the core purpose and values of the Labour Party, the raison detre that distinguishes it from rival election machines. The debate over Clause 4 was seminal because it spelt out to the Party and to the wider public what was really fundamental. The concepts of community and fairness, of individuals being bound together by shared values and mutual responsibilities, emerged as being at the core of Labour's beliefs. These values are distinctively different in their emphasis from the key liberal concerns of rights and individual freedom, although not necessarily in conflict with them. The new expression of these values is also quite different from the old language of class interest and struggle. They reach back beyond Labour's Victorian birth to a much older philosophical tradition, centred on notions of the good society where everyone is treated as being of equal moral worth.

These values will determine the policy agenda of Labour's second century, just as they did the first. The jargon may have changed but social inclusion is a recognisable and distinctive Labour concern that spans the decades. The worst off are excluded not just from money but from work, leisure, health and learning.

At the other end, the rich exclude themselves with private schooling, private health care and private security around their houses. New Labour may have begun in Government with a determination to prove its economic competence but, very quickly, the test of Labour's success has become its ability to restore public confidence in political action to realise these timeless social values.

Delivering on these concerns cannot be done by an occasional Labour Government, no matter how valiantly it strives in its brief periods in office. For most of Labour's first century, the party has been adrift in opposition. The Conservatives dominated government for 70 of the 100 years up to 1997, largely because of the centre-left split over that period. Since the Cook–Maclennan pact of 1996, however, there has begun an unprecedented level of dialogue and co-operation between Labour and the Liberal Democrats. The centre-left commands majority support amongst the electorate. It is the Tories who now appear isolated and if co-operation can be sustained, then the new century could well see the hegemony of progressive politics to which Tony Blair aspires.

The centrifugal forces in British politics are powerful, however, especially for parties operating in the eye of government. If co-operation is to withstand both the pressures of government and the scepticism of the media, it will have to become considerably stronger than these tentative beginnings. In particular, to succeed in the long-term political co-operation must become rooted in the cultures and instincts of both parties, at all levels, and not just be seen to be driven from the top. If co-operation does not deepen in this way, then the tensions inevitable in government will lead to faction and division, and division in turn will lead to long-term political defeat. It is impossible at this point to predict whether political co-operation will grow stronger or weaker but we can say it will be crucial in shaping Labour's fortunes in the new century.

The other essential difference between the past century and the new is the policy environment within which future Labour governments will operate. We no longer have a closed, national, social and economic system, where the key variables are, in principle, at least, controlled by domestic governments. Britain is open, more than ever before, to international forces of trade, culture and communication. For most of Labour's first century, Europe was important only as it directly affected Britains security. The last three decades, however, have seen an enormous change.

The question of our relationship with Europe has become of central importance to our domestic politics, spilling over to affect a wide range of policy areas. In the new century, the importance of Europe will increase further, from occupying the centre of the national stage to becoming that stage itself for our party politics. Europe will no longer be seen as a separate issue, albeit one of great salience and complexity. It will become instead the main forum, the determining environment, for almost all important political questions.

Joining the single currency will mark a fundamental change. Arriving at an appropriate interest rate for the entire euro zone is not necessarily going to be any more fraught or complex than finding one suited to the wide internal diversity of individual national economies. What will be unprecedented, however, will be the degree of co-ordination, in fiscal and macro-economic policy, that will be required of the 12 governments of the euro zone.

How will the 12 governments come to a collective view? How will the dialogue between the collective governments and the European Central Bank be handled? What will be the relationship between the monetary strategy for Europe and the fiscal policies of the national governments? Running EMU is going to be a completely different task from simply achieving it. Developing a system of European economic co-ordination which can deliver social objectives as well as economic, and do so during times of recession as well as in periods of growth, will be the single biggest economic policy challenge facing the British Labour Party in the opening years of the 21st century.

Economic policy is not the only area where the European dimension will come to shape and determine domestic politics. Perhaps the single biggest challenge to the familiar 20th century practice of national decision-making will be the accelerating development of a European defence identity. It is a striking illustration of the difference between new Labour and old that this debate is being driven forward by the British Government, spurred on by the recent conflicts in the Balkans, and with its European partners running to catch up. The key point for present purposes is, again, that helping to co-ordinate these crucial policies on a European scale will create a working environment for the Labour Party quite different from its experiences over the last 100 years.

Political co-operation on the centre-left within Britain, and inter-governmental co-operation across Europe. These are the two big challenges facing Labour at the start of the new century. If Labour succeeds in meeting both of these, it will enjoy an era of achievement greater than any in its past.

The Global Future

Clare Short MP

In 1849 in Surrey life expectancy was 45, in London 37, and in Liverpool just 26. The conditions that were then common across the UK – low life expectancy, high infant mortality, child labour, illiteracy, squalor and malnourishment are still being experienced by the mass of the people in the poorest countries. In fact one quarter of humanity still live in these conditions. I believe that this reality clarifies the achievements of the Labour Party in the past and the challenge for the next century.

As industrialisation gathered pace in Britain, it led to a massive change in society. People moved in large numbers from the countryside to the cities. They had lived with poverty and deprivation in the countryside but now they faced a different reality. It was clear that their work was creating great wealth. A new working class and middle class identity was born. The old deference to the land-owning classes was in decline. But the massive wealth being generated by industrialisation was not being equitably distributed. Squalor lived side by side with plenty. These were the conditions in which the Labour Party grew and came to maturity. Half way through the century we formed our first majority government which created a major new settlement with a commitment to full employment and the welfare state that subsequent Tory governments did not dare to challenge and unravel. This was the length of time it took to create a new set of values, a political alliance, and a new consensus that the wealth generated by industrialisation should be used to create the conditions that would lift the whole population of the country out of poverty.

Obviously prior to the advent of industrialisation, there had been many thinkers who espoused socialist ideas. There had also been a trade union movement made up of craft unions trying to ensure that their interests were properly represented in relation to their employers and in society more broadly. And there were alliances between the Liberal party and trade union sponsored candidates in elections. But it was industrialisation that created the conditions where wealth was available, people came together in towns and generated a new consciousness, and where all workers, including unskilled workers, started to organise in trade unions that made it possible for the Labour Party to become a party capable of taking power.

The first instinct of the new working class was to organise in trade unions in order to achieve fair treatment at work and reasonable wages. But it was soon clear that society would not be civilised through trade union actions alone. Decent housing, education for all children, health care and sewage systems required the effective use of the resources of the state and that required political organisation.

For the Labour Party to succeed its appeal had to reach beyond its base in the trade union movement. The Labour Party was a broad alliance drawing on the Fabian tradition, the Methodist religious and social reform tradition, the co-operative movement and other progressive forces. But it was industriali-sation, the new wealth it created and the new class consciousness it generated, that made possible the rise and rise of the Labour Party which reached its high point in laying down the post war settlement. This settlement was maintained even though the Conservative Party held power for most of the second part of the century. This was a narrow political failure rather than a failure of Labour's project as the Tory party did not dare – at least not until the advent of Thatcherism – to challenge the commitment to full employment and the welfare state.

The challenge for the Labour Party at the beginning of our second century is to understand the way in which history is unfolding and shape it once again for the benefit of humanity.

Globalisation – the rapid movement of information and capital around the world – is reshaping all our economic arrangements and changing the role of the nation state. It is also generating a massive increase in wealth. But that wealth is not being equitably distributed. We are seeing a growth in inequality and instability within and between countries. We are also living at a time of growing inequality between individuals, with the world's wealthiest 285 people owning more wealth than the total annual income of the poorer 47 per cent of humanity.

The challenge for the Labour Party in the next century is to create new political alliances with our sister parties and other progressive forces across the globe. To ensure that the new wealth being generated by globalisation is equitably distributed – so that the quarter of humanity who still live with squalor will be given the chance to lift themselves out of poverty in the early years of the next century.

Reinterpreting Labour's History of Failure

Austin Mitchell

Changing Old Labour to New, deeper than a make-over but not total transformation, makes the party more like the Liberals at the start of century: un-ideological, inclusive, practising the 'big tent' politics of working with other parties to re-create their broad coalition of progressive forces.

These changes were necessary because Labour has been the century's least successful major party. In power for 23 of the 65 years we have been one of the big two, a worse performance than the Liberals before their 1916 split relegated them to third party status. Even on the occasions, 1945, 1966, when Labour won a big majority, it quickly lost it. So New Labour is attempting to escape from that record by not only winning power, but keeping it.

The inferiority complex which motivated this project was justified but in writing off the past we forget that failing to win power and losing it quickly are different problems springing from different causes. The first comes from fear of our intentions amplified by internal rows and the threat of a looming Left, and enormously exacerbated by a hostile media. Yet such fears did their worst damage at elections Labour stood no chance of winning: 1955, 1983 and 1987. Even when we had higher hopes in 1959 and 1992 the odds were against us for the electorate's desire for change had been met by Tory changes of leader two years before the poll. The fear of frightening people really arises from a belief that the pendulum would swing to us if we didn't stop it. Yet, in fact, long incumbencies are the norm. So we have won only when Tory governments fail monumentally as in 1945 and 1997, more marginally in 1964 and 1974.

Thus the real problem has been an inability to win second terms, a failure caused neither by frightening people, nor by any excess of socialism, but by an inability to manage the economy in such a way as to improve the lot and the living standards of the mass of the people. The Tories, from whom electors expect less, have delivered more, particularly in 1959 and 1987, and are, in any case, less harshly judged when they don't. Labour, expected to deliver to the many not the few, has a more difficult task, and hasn't performed it well.

This is not a failure of socialist economics. They don't exist and we've never tried to develop them. Nor is it a failure of competence. Labour Chancellors have been an impressive breed and the clever party absorbed Keynes first. It is one of confidence and priorities. Members and MPs are inevitably preoccupied with spending on housing, health, education and welfare, and less interested in wealth generation and economics but the party and its leaders have not only not remedied this deficiency but been deeply deferential to economic and financial orthodoxies, particularly those preached by finance and the City institutions, of which Labour always stands in awe. We once, though no longer, had a fight with industrial capitalism. We have always viewed finance capitalism and the City as arcane mysteries and liked them to pat us on the head.

Always disproportionately powerful and concentrated in the City close to the heart of government, finance capitalism has been well served by Labour. Our governments have accepted its orthodoxies and striven to show themselves respectable by defending its interests to a bitter end, which has usually been that of Labour governments.

That of 1929–31 set the pattern breaking itself defending a gold standard which the incoming National Government promptly abandoned to baffled Labour complaints of 'they never told us we could do that'. The resulting devaluation triggered the fastest growth and the biggest fall of unemployment of any industrial country but taught no lessons to Labour.

Our great post-war government, radical in building a welfare state and a new post-war settlement tilted to the people, was still orthodox in economic policy, except for the use of direct controls it inherited from war. As the City wanted, it went back to an untenable prewar parity against the dollar. It then clung to that for too long, devaluing only in 1949 so the economic boost came too late to save Labour, handing its benefits to the Tories who'd never had it so good. Or so long.

The next government from 1964 began with a National Plan to get the growth its every promise and prospect depended. Yet defending an untenable exchange rate on behalf of the City quickly had a higher priority than plan growth or promises which only a competitive exchange rate could fulfil. Devaluation was forced on Labour in November 1967, once again in time to get us thrown out because of the stern disciplines which followed. Again we handed the benefits to the Tories to squander as they pleased.

The 1974 government was less culpable but fought a brave rearguard action to defend the post-war settlement, capitalism as it knew it, and the City and its interests. The sacrifices they involved were placed on Labour's people because it used incomes policy to defeat inflation and high taxation to keep up spending. Even though exchange rates now floated, Labour struggled to keep the pound high to check inflation, defending it by cuts in spending in 1976. Then Denis Healey uncapped it, encouraging an appreciation which checked growth and prevented manufacturing seizing the better prospects, both processes then boosted by the Tories. They followed our practice of using a high exchange rate to discipline the economy and break inflation, though they added unions, manufacturing and basic industries to the list, damaging all by depression and deflation.

So in every case Labour paid the price of orthodoxy and its loyalty to the interests of the few and their money rather than the many and their needs. In 1931 it was decimated at the polls. In 1951 it lost to Tories promising to make people richer quicker. In 1970 disappointed supporters failed to turn out because Labour hadn't delivered. In 1979 Labour was punished for the pain it had inflicted by using taxes and cuts in real incomes to defend the status quo rather than going for growth. Labour had proved as adept as Tories, in some respects more so, at cutting public spending, living standards and jobs to check inflation.

In each case the price of failure was electoral relegation. Yet it was this which brought the enfeebling rows and the usual attempt of oppositions to make themselves perfect by in fact making themselves sects. From these processes Labour then has learned the wrong lessons. To escape from opposition's miseries, principles, images and history were all chucked overboard to make the party more acceptable. Yet the deference to economic orthodoxies which had caused the failure in the first place was not only never questioned but actually compounded. In Britain orthodoxy is respectability. So in the 1990s we embraced the instrument of our previous defeats as the prime objective and the central commitment of government. We were more orthodox, more respectable than irresponsible Tories.

In fact, 18 years of Tory government had ended in failure because they embraced the more punitive orthodoxy called monetarism lock, stock and wage cut, using unemployment, dear money and a high exchange rate to counter inflation, closing down large sections of manufacturing, boosting unemployment massively and producing two deep and self-inflicted recessions, then increasing both taxes and public spending to pay for the social security costs resulting. Orthodoxy wasn't working but instead of developing our own alternatives, combining state and market, or planning for policies to boost growth and jobs, Labour desperate for power, suffering from a galloping inferiority complex and obsessed by the need to make itself respectable and avoid the hostility of finance and of a media which amplified its concerns, endorsed the Tory techniques and implicitly much of their record. We even tied our own hands against any departure from orthodoxy offering only a kinder monetarism.

So the party of the people, defeated in 1931, 1951, 1970 and 1979, because it hadn't advanced the many, has strengthened its attachment to the economies of plutocracy benefiting the few and espoused policies which are better for wealth than jobs, money than production, finance than people and the City rather than manufacturing, heavy industry or the regions from whence Labour sprang. 'Modernisation' has been pursued obsessively everywhere. Except in economic policy. There it is seen as going back to Gladstonian liberalism.

Thus we have disavowed objectives central to the party, abandoning growth for 'stability', full employment as an objective for low inflation, Keynes for monetarism, demand management for 'hands off', betterment for confidence, management for markets, deficit spending for a surplus, and public spending and borrowing for the privatisation of credit and the PFI, coupled with an asset inflation to provide the (privatised) Keynesian boost to demand, neither public spending nor government macro policies can. The Bank of England was given powers unheard of since Montague Norman, keeping interest rates high in both real and intentional terms and making an exchange rate more overvalued than 1945–9, 1964–7, 1977–9 or in the bitter ERM experience, the instrument of inflation control. Ending boom and bust, which really means avoiding the risk of growth, have ensured that growth rates, lower than past norms and much lower than competitors, are rated as real achievements. Britain has a historic opportunity to boost growth because inflation is dead. Government will not seize it.

Will policies forced on post Labour governments be the salvation of a new government which has made them central? Parties which don't do too much damage but manage the economy 'sensibly' and the media better can have long tenures in consumer democracy until boredom, degeneration or time for a change undermine. People do expect more of Labour and it's always harder to deliver to the many than the few. Yet the British are a nation with low expectations. So not making things worse could look like triumph. Especially for Labour unless it grows a confidence it didn't come in with.

Yet it may not work. We have already damped inherited growth. There is much ground to be made up in a nation which has lagged for so long. After decades of cuts, health, education, welfare and local services are run down. Real improvement requires far more public spending than can be provided without substantial increases in taxation, plus fast and sustained growth. Yet we are committed against both.

Through this last century Labour has shaped Britain's welfare society and delivered the people from Tory failures. Yet it hasn't been as successful as the centre-left parties in advanced industrial countries while Britain has delivered less than most to its people in terms of growth, higher living standards, better services and general betterment. Yet paradoxically Labour ends the century more deeply attached to the economic policies which have led to this failure than other parties of the left, preaching the market to disbelieving Social Democrats overseas because the policies leading to past failures are now viewed as the only available instruments for future success.

Much has changed on the political left, some of it through failure, some through fashion. Labour's evangel has changed from class-based creed to appeal to the altruism in all; its instruments from the state planning, and the managed, mixed economy, to markets, rights, and empowerment; to build for the many the platform, wealth, education and privilege give to the few. Yet no change has been greater than the abandonment of the old simple objectives of full employment, economic well-being, equality and the higher public spending a strong economy generates. Having misread the past and despaired of any ability to build socialism, even social democracy, in one country we have effectively abandoned the need to keep the interests of the people paramount and made virtues of orthodoxy, respectability and the polite applause of wealth. We will grow if the world grows, fail if it fails, but always tagging along behind doing little but tinker for ourselves and unable to deliver on Tony Crosland's vision of a society liberated by growth lifting all boats, permitting painless redistribution and generating the public spending necessary to better the lot of all. The many, and the few.

An End of Century Report Card

Angela Eagle MP

A century on from the inaugural meeting in the Memorial Hall, Farringdon Street, London, what has the Labour Party ever done for us?

The National Health Service, educational opportunities, decolonisation and significant progress towards a fairer more equal society for a start.

At the turn of the century it is fashionable for some to declare the end of history and the triumph of one system, globalised capitalism. I am not so pessimistic.

Everywhere when I visit societies that do not have a strong social democratic presence I see its consequences. Huge disparities between rich and poor. Excess and affluence for the few alongside lack of opportunity and waste of potential for the many. Yet the aspirations of ordinary people in these societies closely match Labour's historic purpose. The lack of a Labour Party to express them is a crucial gap. The consequences of untrammelled free markets are poverty, exploitation and environmental degradation.

People who perceived these dangers and were determined to fight them created the Labour party to be a vehicle for progressive socialist change in the first industrialised society. It was and is the voice of the ordinary person ensuring political representation for their needs and aspirations. The most surprising thing is how many of these threats have persisted through the century and still present a real challenge to us today. We have a record to be proud of in our first hundred years but we haven't been so successful that we can have a centenary celebration and all go home.

Just as the suffragettes somewhat naively took it for granted that the extension of the franchise to women would largely solve questions of equal rights and opportunities, perhaps we have underestimated the tenacity of the forces, which drive societies to exploitation and division. The cul-de-sac of Soviet Communism also hindered our cause creating a terrible example of tyranny in the name of workers power.

Its dramatic collapse provided us with an opportunity once more to focus on the importance of harnessing the forces of global capital for the good of all humanity rather than the enrichment of the lucky few.

Freed from the Soviet yoke the Baltic States openly admired Thatcherism and decided to opt for an American rather than a Swedish style market economy. Nearly ten years and many privatisations later as they contemplate the widening gap between the very rich and poor they are regretting their enthusiasm and searching for a better balance.

In his book *The Future of Socialism* Crosland chartered the transformation of the market system into something he believed harnessed the dynamism of markets with the interests of all the people. He believed there was much work still to do not least on equality, but that the major battles were won. I read this with much irony in the middle of the Thatcherite onslaught with no end to it in sight. He would scarcely have believed the return of capitalism red in tooth and claw.

But this teaches us all a valuable lesson. Never take progress for granted. Work to entrench it but never stop making the basic case for the principles Labour believes in.

Despite achieving power for only 30 of our first hundred years we have helped to make our country a better place. Before the creation of the NHS childbirth was the most common cause premature death for women in Britain. Rates, which had remained unchanged for 100 years, improved suddenly and dramatically after Bevan had done his job. Such examples are legion and we should reclaim them and take credit for them too.

In our first century our influence has been out of proportion to our years in office and we have much to be proud of. At the beginning of our second century we have yet to complete our fight to end poverty.

The world is becoming a smaller more interdependent place. It is also a more fragile place ecologically. The threat posed to the earth's climate by greenhouse gases places a priority on international planning for sustainable development and a fairer sharing of the burden between developed and developing countries.

At the same time new technology is making global communications and information flows almost instantaneous. This has the potential to make political censorship and repression very much harder to achieve than it was in the twentieth century. This technology could strengthen the forces of democracy and transparency and improve accountability too.

However, unchecked, these globalising trends also have the potential to enslave rather than free humanity. We have to ensure that there is more on the world agenda than gigantic multinational power plays, which treat employees, as a commodity to be disposed of at will. Co-operation at a supranational level and systems of international regulation will need to be developed to minimise this threat.

We also need to ensure that no one is left out of the digital revolution and denied access to the new technologies and the benefits they can bring. The Labour government has already begun a determined effort to ensure that there is equality of access in the UK but achieving this aim worldwide is a very challenging and vital task.

Far from being the end of history, I think that we are embarking on another exciting chapter. One where Labour's key values are as important and relevant as ever. As for our end of century report card, 'has worked hard and made good progress but still has a lot to do!'

Part III
Themes in
Labour's First
Century

Trade Union Freedom and the Labour Party: Arthur Deakin, Frank Cousins and the Transport and General Workers Union 1945–64

Robert Taylor

'No union has contributed more in organised strength, in practical wisdom and in imaginative vision to the success of the Labour party than the Transport and General Workers union.'   Clement Attlee, 1947[1]

'Brothers, we have got to recognise the difficulties that confront us and act with a sense of responsibility, while expressing our determination to secure those conditions that will make for a reduction in the prices level and increase the level of the wages that we get.' Arthur Deakin, 1949 TGWU biennial delegate conference.[2]

'The general executive council of my union firmly believe that its job is to improve the standard of living of our people. We are not satisfied even to maintain it. We know the economic struggle that the country is facing but we also know that we are governed by a body which advised us that we were coming into an era of prosperity in an atmosphere of free for all. We have said and we mean it that if it is a free for all, we are part of the all.' Frank Cousins, May day in Glasgow 1957.[3]

The Transport and General Workers was always the colossus of the Labour Movement from its formation through mergers in 1922 under the visionary leadership of Ernest Bevin.[4] During the period immediately after the Second World War, it was the largest trade union in the western industrialised world, claiming over 1.3m members by the middle of the 1950s. The TGWU's massive block vote was used ruthlessly to dominate policy-making at party conference and to decide who sat on the National Executive as well as the all-important Conference Arrangements Committee. Labour leaders always tried to make sure the TGWU was on their side in their inner-party battles. In power and influence, it towered over the other trade unions affiliated to the party. Only the National Union of Mineworkers enjoyed comparable strength and that union's importance went into serious decline during the 1950s in line with the loss of jobs in the contracting coal industry. The pivotal role played by the TGWU in Labour party politics, however, was not simply due to the sheer size of its mass membership translated into a huge block vote. Its strategic position also owed a great deal to the strong character and robust opinions of successive general secretaries.

Bevin deliberately created a highly centralised trade union, designed to unify the often conflicting sectional interests that existed between its disparate members. Its sense of purpose and direction therefore came primarily from the personal abilities of the man at the top of the union. The authority he wielded was strengthened enormously by the fact that the post of general secretary was the only one in the TGWU elected through a branch ballot vote of the entire membership. 'The general secretary represented the unity of the union', explained Lord Bullock in his biography of Bevin. 'He was the man who held it together and resisted the particularist tendencies of the trade groups. It was to the general secretary that the executive looked for guidance in formulating policy and under his supervision that the officers carried out the executive's decisions'.[5]

The union's structure reflected Bevin's personal domination. He used it to make himself the indispensable figure both in the modernisation of the TUC with its general secretary Walter Citrine after the 1926 general strike as well as in the return of the Labour party to the mainstream of national politics in the aftermath of the 1931 electoral disaster. Without the TGWU's moderating influence, it is doubtful whether Labour would have accomplished even a limited electoral recovery during the years leading up to the outbreak of the Second World War. However, the TGWU often looked to the outside world as little more than Bevin's creature. He seemed to control or at least dominate its internal proceedings through both the union's the general executive council and the biennial delegate conference by sheer force of a dynamic personality. But in May 1940 Bevin was seconded from the TGWU by Winston Churchill to join his coalition government as Minister of Labour and National Service with the task of mobilising Britain's workers for greater production in the total war against Nazism. He turned out to be one of the great successes of that administration in the eventual achievement of victory. After 1945 Bevin, as Foreign Secretary, was to became an impressive guarantor of Labour's peacetime programme with its commitment to full employment, the creation of a national health service and the nationalisation of key industries like coal, the railways and iron and steel.

The history of the TGWU between 1945 and 1964, however, suggests that the union did not require a larger than life figure like Bevin in order to exercise effective power and influence over the rest of the Labour Movement. Both Arthur Deakin, general secretary from February 1946 until his death on May day 1955 and Frank Cousins who held the post from March 1956 until June 1969 were to demonstrate in their contrasting ways just how important the TGWU continued to be after Bevin's departure in ensuring the party's political success as well as its internal cohesion.

Deakin's posthumous reputation has suffered badly, especially at the hands of his own union. He is invariably portrayed by the TGWU as a tyrannical figure of 'darkness', an anti-communist autocrat who tried to dominate the union with a rod of iron against an increasingly restive rank and file hostile to wage restraint. 'In running the union Deakin resembled a small businessman in outlook, rather than the leader of hundreds of thousands of industrial workers', wrote future TGWU general secretary Jack Jones, who disliked Deakin's right-wing anti-Communist Labour politics, perhaps more than his autocratic style of running the union.[6] Geoffrey Goodman – no enthusiast – wrote in his biography of Frank Cousins that Deakin was 'a strange mixture'. Outwardly he was a 'hard, ruthless, blustering, bully-like man' but behind the 'iron mask was an unexpectedly sensitive and generous human being'.[7] Michael Foot – from a hostile Bevanite perspective – described Deakin as 'a fierce, breezy, irascible, stout-hearted bison of a man who genuinely believed that any proposition he could force through his union executive must be the will of the people and more especially the will of Ernest Bevin whose requirements he had normally taken the precaution of finding out in advance.' Foot also believed he 'lacked Bevin's redeeming powers of imaginative rumination'.[8] It is true Deakin was no Bevin but then there has never been anybody else like Bevin in the trade union movement. However, when judged by any other standard, Deakin was an impressive and effective general secretary who maintained the TGWU as a powerful and responsible force in the period that turned out to be but perhaps did not seem so at the time – Labour's only golden age. It is no exaggeration to assert that it was the TGWU under Deakin's leadership that helped to save the Attlee government from economic disaster. Between February 1948 and the summer of 1950 Deakin – at first with reluctance and then with characteristic enthusiasm – took the lead inside the Trades Union Congress in trying to restrain pay demands among the rank and file at a time of full employment.

Deakin was one of the most belligerent champions of Labour's post-war social settlement. Professor Hugh Clegg believed Deakin equalled Bevin in his courage and 'came near to him in force of character', while sharing most of the same values, although he lacked Bevin's genius for 'an intuitive grasp of situations and problems and how they could be handled'.[9] Philip Williams described Deakin in his biography of Hugh Gaitskell as: 'one of those vigorous, boisterous, extroverted and intolerant working-class characters whose bullying and crudity are readily excused by intellectuals who like their politics but never forgiven by those who do not'. But Deakin belonged to that small group of post-war national trade union leaders who 'in the precarious economic situation after the war used their great bargaining power with restraint'. Despite persistent left-wing criticism Deakin and others like him, wrote Williams, 'improved their members' real standard of living substantially without imposing the arbitrary injustice of inflation on the poor and weak and they made it possible under the Attlee Cabinet to reconstruct the economy and lay the foundations for lasting prosperity on which future governments failed to build'.[10]

Deakin was acting TGWU general secretary during Bevin's absence at the Ministry of Labour between May 1940 and July 1945. It was under his leadership that the TGWU grew in membership during the Second World War. There is no reason to believe he was anything less than competent and diligent both in managing the union and acting on its behalf in the mobilisation of the organised working class under crisis conditions. The shopfloor war effort owed much to the work of the trade unions, and not least to the TGWU. Deakin played a key role among that remarkable generation of Labour Movement leaders who helped to defeat Nazism and prepare for post-war reconstruction. Whatever his personal feelings might have been towards Bevin, Deakin remained publicly his faithful and able lieutenant. But it was in the immediately post-war period that he came into his own and out from under Bevin's massive shadow. Between July 1945 and his sudden death from a heart attack on May Day 1955, Deakin proved to be a passionate and loyal defender of Labour's cause whether the party was in government or opposition. It is true he would often wield his union's huge block vote at party conferences to obstruct the party's increasingly vociferous left-wing. In alliance with Will Lawther, president of the National Union of Mineworkers and Tom Williamson, general secretary of the General and Municipal Workers, Deakin became a pivotal figure in the so-called TUC junta. This group acted as a formidable praetorian guard, protecting the Labour leadership from its party enemies. The unswerving support given by the TGWU leadership to the post-war Labour government, both inside the TUC as well as the party, was undoubtedly a crucial factor in consolidating its overall achievements. Vic Allen in his portrait of Deakin went so far as to suggest he occupied the role Walter Citrine had played when strategically-minded TUC general secretary until his departure to the National Coal Board in September 1946. He was 'the central figure of a small but influential group of union leaders whose unions accounted for almost half the total affiliated membership of the TUC'.[11] During the period of the Attlee government it was Deakin – with occasional interventions from Bevin at the Foreign Office at times of national emergency – and not the mediocre TUC general secretary Vincent Tewson who played the dynamic role in the development of a vital political and social network of power and influence, which was established between senior cabinet ministers and union leaders that underpinned the stability of the Labour government. Deakin was delighted at the degree of access to government departments that the trade unions gained for the first time during those years. 'We have an open door in relation to all state departments and are thus able to get our difficulties examined in such a way as would not have been possible with any other party in government', he told Allen.[12] Deakin was an active member of a number of tripartite organisations that continued to function after the war including the National Joint Advisory Council and the Joint Consultative Committee. The Economic Planning Board, established in 1947, also provided senior union leaders with the direct opportunity to influence government policy. But the TUC did not enjoy unquestioning access to ministers for the implementation of policy. There was no general right for the TUC to be consulted on the drawing up of legislation for taking private industries into the state sector. As Norman Chester wrote in the official history of nationalisation: 'The TUC and the unions found the fact that a Labour government was in power did not eliminate the need for formal consultative machinery. Indeed, at first they had to fight hard for the principle of being consulted on those matters which were directly within their sphere of interest'.[13] But for the most part the TUC and the government worked in harmony together. The common understanding between the ideology and instincts of the party and the trade unions during those years owed much to Deakin's steadfastness under external as well as internal union pressures.

Kenneth Morgan suggested 'the Labour government's unity was based, more than at any other time in history, on the projection of a traditional programme of protection for the working class and recognition of the unions as a new estate of the realm.'[14]. This did not mean the government-trade union relationship was not without its strains. Some cabinet ministers, notably Emanuel Shinwell as Minister of Energy and Herbert Morrison, were less than punctilious in drawing union leaders into the policy-making process or even keeping them informed on what they were doing. No formalised structure of liaison was created to keep the government and the TUC in close touch. As a result. the TUC complained about the lack of ministerial consultation on a number of occasions. But in a very deep and personal way the emotional ties between the party and the big trade unions like the TGWU are crucial to an understanding of the strengths and weaknesses of the Attlee government.

The importance of Deakin to the success of the special relationship between the party leadership and the unions can be gleaned from a variety of sources but especially from his many verbal interjections at the union's biennial delegate conferences, in his signed articles in its monthly journal – The TGWU Record – and above all in his quarterly reports to the union's general executive council. Despite his bluster and notoriously short temper he could be a persuasive and thoughtful advocate of what was a new kind of trade unionism. This sought to transcend the industrial politics of collective bargaining and to concentrate on extending the power and responsibilities that Deakin believed organised labour ought to exercise in the interests of an economic strategy that sought to create full employment, more social justice and greater equality. The resulting social contract of the 1940s may have fallen far short of the centralised national co-ordination practised successfully by Social Democratic governments in Scandinavia with their trade union allies during that period but it still represented a significant modification to the traditional British system of voluntarism, where trade unions – outside the exigencies of wartime conditions – sought to keep the state away from their bargaining activities with employers. The impressive unity displayed by the 'contentious alliance' between 1945 and 1951 was based on a deeply shared sense of working class solidarity. By contrast the tangled relationship between Labour governments and a more decentralised trade union movement during the 1960s and the late 1970s was to prove more difficult to sustain when compared to the Attlee years. Of course, the social circumstances of the period immediately after the end of the war encouraged greater working class cohesion. Faith in voluntarism and rank and file support in the trade unions for the first majority Labour government in history was of crucial importance in ensuring the defence of its achievements. But it would be churlish to ignore the enormous contribution proletarian patriots like Deakin made to Mr Attlee's overall success.

Deakin himself always took collective loyalty to the Labour Movement seriously. As he explained in his quarterly report to the union's general executive council shortly after the party's 1945 election victory: 'We must realise the new government will require all our assistance and understanding in the tasks that lie ahead. Very clearly, if we are to bring about economic security and a great measure of social reconstruction it will be necessary for everyone to pull their weight; in other words, we have got to work well to live well.'[15] The TGWU had strengthened its own position in the parliamentary Labour party at the 1945 general election. Not only was Bevin appointed foreign secretary. Others from among the union's sponsored MPs were also given senior positions in the new government with Sir Ben Smith as Minister of Food and W J Edwards as Civil Lord of the Admiralty. In addition, the TGWU was proud to proclaim its parliamentary under-secretaries at the Home Office and Colonial Office and a parliamentary secretary at the Ministry of Health. As many as 39 of the Labour MPs in the 1945 Parliament were directly sponsored by the TGWU.

Deakin called on workers to demonstrate their loyalty to their trade unions as well as the Labour government. 'Nothing could be more fatal to the restoration of our economy and to the creation of the new wealth we must have if we are to have higher standards of living than a repetition of the unofficial strikes we have witnessed during the past month, particularly in the docks', he told his general executive council in December 1945.[16] He attacked unofficial strikers, suggesting their behaviour played 'into the hands of reactionary elements'. Deakin believed in what he called 'an orderly society' through an acceptance of voluntary negotiation based on collective bargaining through industry-based joint councils.[17] He understood and sympathised with the Labour government's efforts to restore Britain's war-shattered economy to peacetime conditions. Deakin urged the union's members to back the 'great drive for exports' and to show the 'greatest possible measure of loyalty, self-discipline, patience and restraint on the part of the public generally'.[18] 'If we are to make up the goods in short supply and at the same time develop our export trade to the greatest possible extent, it can only be done by a measure of control within a planned economy', he explained in his spring 1946 executive council report. 'If we fail to do this then I am convinced that we shall repeat the errors of those fateful years between 1921 and 1933 which followed from the false prosperity arising from our failure to grapple in a practical way with the conditions that obtained at the end of the first world war.'[19] Deakin warned his members of the economic rigours that lay ahead and said he was disturbed at the way in which they accepted 'the propaganda carried on against the continuance of controls'. 'Whilst this form of restraint is naturally irksome and repressive in wartime it is, in my view, very necessary and we should accept for a considerable period of time ahead that orderly approach to our economic problems which will enable us to gradually get back to our normal trade both in the home and export markets'.

Deakin was never Labour's fair-weather friend. He believed his union must defend and fight for the party against its innumerable enemies in bad as well as good times. However, he was always keen to try and ensure the political and industrial objectives of the Labour Movement were kept separate. Deakin never held a high regard for most politicians and was keen they should keep their noses out of internal trade union affairs. This often led to an apparent confusion. At the 1946 party conference he moved a resolution urging the Labour government to 'require all employers to negotiate the introduction of the 40-hour working week with the trade unions' in line with TUC policy. During his speech Deakin suggested the trade unions did 'not want to use the political organisation' of the party to secure a reduction in working hours, arguing that it could be 'best achieved through our industrial machine and through the usual channels of negotiation'.[20] However, Deakin went on to demand that George Isaacs, Minister of Labour, be given enabling powers to force employers and unions to bargain together over the working hours issue. This would enable him to tell both sides of industry: 'Get together. Shorten the hours of work within a reasonable period of time'. Deakin argued that a shorter working week was 'an indispensable condition to our industrial progress and to the promotion and maintenance of high efficiency in industry'.

But as an increasingly important figure on the TUC's economic committee, he was also painfully aware of the mounting economic troubles confronting the Attlee government. Deakin welcomed the TUC's growing involvement in discussions with the Treasury on macro-economic policy. 'The trade union movement at this time is developing a wider sphere of activity and is required to assume a greater degree of responsibility than at any previous time in its history', he told his general executive council in his fourth quarterly report for 1946.[21]

It might be said that the function of the trade union movement is changing considerably. We are no longer confined to the limited function of dealing merely with wages and ordinary conditions of employment. Trade unions have a part to play in the planning of that economy which will provide full employment and rising standards of life, developing a relationship within socialised services which calls for a new approach and understanding with an acceptance of responsibility to the masses of the people. The acquisition of power leaves us with no middle course. We must face up to the fact that power carries with it responsibility.

At times Deakin often gave the impression that the TGWU alone was carrying all the burdens of the post-war economy on its massive shoulders. As he explained to his executive council:

We are now facing the most critical period following the war. The government cannot alone solve those pressing problems with which we are faced. Production and nothing short of maximum effort on the part of all concerned will bring about those conditions which will enable us to produce the goods we require and maintain those services which are essential to our national development, with the realisation of our policy of full employment and rising standards of life...
We must face up to our responsibility, leaving our members in no doubt whatsoever that it all depends upon them. There must be no side-stepping of responsibility or refusal to face up to the obvious. Nothing else but an all-out effort will pull us through.[22]

Deakin was prepared to go a long way in support of the government in his calls for higher productivity and an improvement in workplace efficiency. As a member of the Anglo-American Council on Productivity, established by Chancellor Sir Stafford Cripps in 1948, he was an enthusiast for a better utilisation of labour, the introduction of new production techniques and more industrial investment. Deakin was not opposed to a revival of the joint production committees, which had been so important during the war. 'This type of joint consultation is essential and should be developed', he wrote in the TGWU *Record*.[23] But he argued this should be done without involving such bodies in wage bargaining. Deakin remained ferociously hostile to unofficial strikers and sought to prevent the breakdown of recognised industrial relations procedures, especially in the docks where he found himself at loggerheads with the union's militants in ports like Liverpool, Hull and London. He was always suspicious of the behaviour of shop stewards, regarding them as too often a disruptive and disobedient Communist menace and with the coming of the Cold War as part of a wider political conspiracy to subvert the economy. As President of the World Federation of Trade Unions between 1946 and 1949, he also became increasingly aware of the Communist domination of that organisation. In early 1949 Deakin and the TUC walked out of the WFTU and helped in July to found a new anti-Communist international body – the International Confederation of Free Trade Unions. It was during that same year that Deakin also led the way to suppress Communist activism in the TUC and affiliate unions, not least his own where an estimated nine Communists sat on the TGWU's 34-strong general executive council and three of the eight-strong finance and general purposes committee were Communist party members. At the union's 1949 biennial conference Deakin took the lead in having Communists and Fascists banned from holding office in the TGWU. Such illiberal behaviour reflected the feelings of the time. International events such as Stalin's blockade of west Berlin and the capture of power by the Communists in Czechoslovakia did much to alienate Labour movement sympathies for the Soviet Union.[24] But Deakin's anti-Communist tirades were over-zealous and simplistic, especially during the unofficial dock strikes of the period. The most authoritative account of that industrial conflict carried out by K G J C Knowles suggested Communist strength was due to weaknesses in the TGWU structure which failed to articulate genuine grievances. 'The history of all these strikes reveals not only a resentment by the dockers of the tight discipline necessitated by decasualisation of the industry but also an enduring suspicion of their own main union which seems to have been aggravated by union participation – however defensible – in the managerial functions of the Dock Labour Board.[25] A study of the internal affairs of Deakin's union by a young American Joseph Goldstein, published in 1952, characterised the TGWU as 'an oligarchy at every level of its structure, failing to elicit the active participation of its members'.[26] Although any similar analysis in other unions would have probably revealed the same representation problem, it is clear that the TGWU was suffering from atrophy although it seems improbable to believe the rank and file was to the left of Deakin, at least on international issues. However, his anti-Communism was often extreme and unconvincing, even by the standards of his day. He even blamed a Communist 'fifth column' for the loss of some Labour parliamentary seats in the 1950 general election such as Bexley, Shipley and Glasgow Scotstoun and Govan.[27]

Deakin was by no means a sturdy champion of freedom in industrial relations despite his hatred for Communism. He was quite ready, for example, to throw his formidable support behind state regulations to control the movement of workers to meet supply bottlenecks caused by labour shortages. He also accepted the continuation of the National Arbitration Order 1305 imposed by the government in 1940 after the end of the war. This was supposed to outlaw strikes through the imposition of compulsory arbitration. Deakin also favoured other forms of government control to manage the economy such as the regulation of trade, rents, dividends and profits. He was an enthusiastic supporter of the Labour government's industry nationalisation programme, at least until 1949.

But for a long time Deakin remained implacably opposed to any form of national wage restraint based on government action. Even as late as the summer of 1947 Deakin continued to oppose the idea of an incomes policy which was still at that time a popular cause on the Labour left. 'I know there are people crying out for a wage policy, that is, a revised version of the Marxist theory – to each according to the service rendered to the state', he told the union's biennial conference.[28] Employers also favoured a wages policy, added Deakin pointedly. They did so because it would help them to increase their profits at the expense of workers' pay. 'Neither point of view is acceptable', he declared. 'No point of view which strives to secure that one industry or a section of industry shall get a privilege over the others, will work or prove acceptable to our people in this country'.

Deakin was keen to see an improvement in annual labour output but he did not believe this should directly involve any intervention by the state. 'The question of incentives, wages and conditions of employment are questions for the trade unions and the sooner some of our people on the political side appreciate that and leave the job to the unions the better the battle for production.' However, he also told the 1947 Labour party conference that his union would continue to oppose any suggestion of a national incomes policy. 'We will have none of that. Under no circumstances at all will we accept the position that the responsibility for the fixation of wages and the regulation of the conditions of employment is one for the government.'[29] Deakin's views on voluntarism may have been instinctive and traditional but they were based on hard, practical experience in representing TGWU members. There could be no state intervention into collective bargaining that would involve any preferential treatment for some workers with skill and who were in demand at the expense of the rest of the working class. 'The people I represent are not prepared to play second fiddle', he warned. 'Any attempt to alter the method of negotiation within industry would be fatal. You will not get the necessary production in the next eighteen months if you destroy confidence in our negotiating machinery, in our established procedure in industry'. Deakin pleaded with delegates at the 1947 party conference to reject a statutory incomes policy. 'It would be disastrous, it would create chaos and conflict amongst the rank and file and this would be destructive of the economy of the country'.

In a debate on a left-wing motion from Rushcliffe constituency party calling for a comprehensive policy from the government on wages, hours and the distribution of the national income, Deakin expressed his hostility to any state involvement in pay determination. As he explained:

Do we want a pay policy in this country that attempts by a declaration to determine what is the right wage in a particular industry? Are we seeking to set out the order in which wage policy shall be applied to industry? If you accept this policy then you will rue it. We shall quickly reach that inflationary stage which we have sought to avoid. You will have such strife and conflict within your ranks that no power can restrain the demand for wages and the production of those conditions which will result in inflation. What we have got to strive for is to make wages of real value, increasing the purchasing power of the wages we have got. By that method we shall strike a balance in our industries which will enable us to build up a standard of life to get the goods so necessary at this time.[30]

As late as October 1947 he continued to resist the idea of wage restraint emanating from the state. In a speech as TUC fraternal delegate to the American Federation of Labor in San Francisco, Deakin told delegates the British government had established a new section of the Ministry of Labour to collect and collate wage data with the intention of presenting such material to wage tribunals and other negotiating bodies to help them assess the sense of wage claims. 'We are not prepared to allow this to go further than a fact finding apparatus', he added. 'We should resist any claims on the part of the government concerned, even to offer an opinion as to whether a particular wage claim should be conceded or turned down'. But Deakin added the British unions themselves needed to consult among themselves on pay and develop machinery to do this. At the same time the government would have to act more decisively on keeping down price increases to avoid an inflationary spiral.[31]

It was therefore with genuine reluctance that Deakin dropped his instinctive opposition to any form of government intervention over pay bargaining. However, as chairman of the TUC's special committee on the economic situation, he knew full well how close the British economy was coming to collapse by the end of 1947. Deakin and his TUC colleagues were kept fully informed by Hugh Dalton and then by Stafford Cripps as Chancellor of the Exchequer about the country's perilous position. The tone of his quarterly reports to the union's executive council do not suggest Deakin needed much convincing that this was no time for complacency and self-congratulation. 'We shall not find any solution to our present difficulties by burying our head in the sand and refusing to face up, in a realistic way, to the intricate and serious problems confronting our country at this time', he explained to members.[32] But Deakin – like other loyal national union leaders – disliked the government's lack of consultation before publishing its White Paper on personal incomes, costs and prices in February 1948. This threatened vaguely to introduce direct state intervention in wage bargaining unless the unions stopped making pay demands that might add to business costs and lead to price rises. It is true the document did not propose the introduction of a fully-blown national incomes policy like those in the 1960s and 1970s but it did represent a significant breach in the voluntarist tradition of pay bargaining. Unfortunately the emphasis was on wage self-restraint alone and the government did not seek to use the opportunity to develop a wider strategy of manpower planning with long-term objectives. The White Paper warned no wage rises were justified that were not earned through a 'substantial increase in production'. It added the government would be guided by that principle in its own behaviour as an employer. The White Paper also argued any rises in production costs due to wage increases should not be taken into account in any proposed price rises. Under such pressure and with obvious misgivings the TUC agreed, at a special conference of affiliate union executives in March 1948, by 5,421,000 votes to 2,032,000 against to co-operate with the government on wage restraint. However, the size of the minority trade union vote was a clear warning that many unions resented what they believed amounted to a government-imposed policy which would restrain their freedom to negotiate. In fact, the TUC was successful during intensive negotiations with Cripps in winning reassurances from the Treasury that the new wages policy would still enable low paid workers to gain higher rises, allow companies in undermanned essential industries to meet labour shortages through better pay offers and recognise the key role of intra-industry wage differentials based on craft skills, training and experience. On the face of it, those caveats could have been loopholes that might have led to the early collapse of the policy. But in practice Deakin and other national union leaders issued restraining instructions to their negotiators that proved effective in holding back wage rates, at least for a time.

In his quarterly report in the spring of 1948 to the general executive council Deakin explained his own conversion to the need for wage restraint. 'We must have a measure of stability in relation to wages and prices and take those steps which will avoid inflationary tendencies', he argued. 'This means trade union executives have got to accept a measure of responsibility and guide policy. It is not sufficient to be swept along in a clamour of wage increases. If we accept a position of that kind it simply means that we would be assisting in creating those conditions which would ultimately destroy the real influence of the trade union movement'.[33] Deakin's loyalty to the TUC's national wages policy was also evident at the 1948 party conference. Defending the government's economic strategy he praised Labour's welfare reforms and called for absolute support for ministers:

Let us make up our minds that we say nothing which will prevent our people from pulling their full weight. I would say to the political theorists: 'Beware of stepping out in such a way that you hinder rather than help the programme of the government at this time'. I know there is a disposition on the part of some of our friends in the political movement to make specious promises and to say we must change this and the other but we must have regard to the economic facts.[34]

It was Deakin too who moved the key composite motion on the control of wages, prices and profits, calling on the conference to welcome the government's economic strategy as long as it was based on a determination to stabilise the cost of living. He did so by emphasising the assurances the government had made to the TUC over dealing with excess profits. Deakin was sensitive to the charge that he had changed his position over wage restraint because of his unthinking loyalty to the government. 'I do not want anyone to tell me that I have changed my ground; that I was opposed to a wage policy', he insisted. 'I was and still am in relation to any proposal which would leave the government with the responsibility for fixing a minimum standard of life. We welcome the policy for the reason that it leaves us freedom for negotiation and some of us have not be unsuccessful up to the present in securing the consideration that was our entitlement even in the face of the White Paper.'[35] Deakin pointed out the government's policy provided 'an opportunity for claims on behalf of people who increase their productive capacity'. 'We recognise the difficulty of the government. A change over in principle of the character involved in this policy cannot be accomplished overnight', he admitted. 'We have to be a little patient'. Deakin made it clear he expected the TUC 'as the responsible instrument for the negotiation of wages and conditions' to keep a 'tight hold on the position and see to it that the assurances and the guarantees' given to them were fully carried out'.

By the late summer of 1948, however, Deakin was less defensive in his support for the wages policy and lectured his executive council on the changing role of the trade unions in their relations with the state. As he told them in his August report:

The trade union movement is faced with problems which need a reorientation of our point of view. With Labour in government, socialisation of industry, control and supervision of industry, the incidence of taxation and of governmental policy designed to limit the activities of the money interests, we must condition our approach to the changed conditions with which we are faced. We have got the power but with it we have the responsibility calling for clear insight and a conception of the new order. The trade unions have an ever-increasing importance in developing the new social order. We must act with wisdom and discretion. not at any point sacrificing our principles or the interests of the people we represent but in a constructive manner and with a sense of dignity and understanding.[36]

Deakin believed the TUC wages policy had helped to save the British economy from collapse. As he told his executive council in his last quarterly report for 1948:

Whilst the question of wages, profits and prices has inevitably caused us some concern and poses a policy which is not readily understood it would not be too much to say that the restraint that has arisen from the acceptance of this policy has possibly saved us from a depression and a worsening of our standard of life which could, and would in my opinion, have followed any refusal on our part to face up to practicalities.[37]

By the time of the 1949 Labour conference he had turned into a passionate advocate, condemning his critics for 'arguing a policy of despair'. However, he continued to battle for the protection of the low paid even in a period of wage restraint. 'We believe there is justice due to the people engaged in vital services who are contributing substantially to the economic recovery that is taking place. They are entitled to more consideration than they are getting.' But Deakin was convinced the government's restrictive approach remained necessary. 'If you lift the limit at this time you create a condition which will react very unfavourably upon the minds of wage earners', he concluded. 'Are we striving to attain the policy that this Movement has declared so long or are we striving to create chaos and confusion?. Do not forget there are people who say we cannot succeed unless we produce that condition where unemployment and under-employment prevails. That is a distinct challenge to our purpose and unity'.[38]

It was during his passionate defence of the TUC wages policy at his own union's 1949 biennial conference that Deakin explained why he believed the unions had faced no credible alternative but to back the government's efforts to restrain wage demands. As he told the delegates:

I do not say there is an easy way, any early solution to the problems with which we are confronted, but at least I am satisfied of this, that if we take the same course, exercise restraint, accept a measure of stability, I am perfectly sure that we shall avoid those economic consequences that attended our efforts in 1922 to 1932. Seared in my soul is a remembrance of the want, the suffering and privation that came our way following the depression of 1922, bringing with it those vast tracts of depressed areas and a great army of unemployed.[39]

It was his personal fear that the current economic troubles could precipitate a return to the desperate conditions suffered by the working class during the inter-war years that shaped Deakin's attitude. His 1949 speech to the biennial conference on the need for voluntary pay restraint was one of the most impressive he ever delivered to his union. He called for loyalty to Labour at a time of national crisis. As Deakin explained:

It is no use anyone trying to fool you at this time and say that we can promote and succeed with extravagant wage claims or even modest wage claims in some of the better paid industries with which we are dealing. In point of fact I am going to be brutally frank this morning. I doubt whether at this time we can get wage increases at all. I am going to be no party to misleading the members of this organisation into a belief that we can do those things in face of the circumstances which confront this country at this time. That, I suggest to you, is not leadership. It means that you are fooling people into the belief that you can do things which you cannot. You are creating a condition of unrest in the minds of people which is absolutely and completely unjustifiable. I am not a person who advocates a policy of despair. I believe we have achieved solid results during the years when Labour has been governing this country. (Hear, hear.) I want to see that position consolidated. I know there is a popular idea running around that you have to keep people in a continual state of agitation if you are to maintain their economic position. I do not believe it. I believe that if you do that, if you follow that line of country, you are rendering lasting disservice to the people whom we represent.

In the aftermath of the government's September 1949 devaluation of sterling, Deakin told his members 'there was an even greater need for trade unions to exercise restraint in their right to pursue wage claims.' He was convinced there was no alternative but to tighten up the TUC's existing voluntary wages strategy. 'Unless we accept a measure of restraint within the limits proposed by the TUC then we have not even a fighting chance of averting the crisis which faces us', he added.[40] But the mood among many unions was growing hostile to any more self-restraint in pay bargaining. They only backed narrowly by

4,263,000 votes to 3,606,000 against, the tougher pay policy agreed after devaluation. The new policy argued that wage rates must be held stable while the interim retail price index which then stood at 112 remained between an upper and lower limit of 118 and 106. If the figure reached either limit, then the TUC said there should be a resumption of voluntary bargaining. The formula also insisted sliding scale arrangements, which provided back-dated adjustments to cover rises in living costs, should be suspended. The policy was supposed to last under January 1951. But within a few months it was no longer credible as union after union rejected it in the face of rising prices. By June 1950 the TUC had abandoned the policy, leaving it to the 'good sense and reasonableness' of the unions to determine their wage claims. Deakin continued to exhort support but his was becoming an increasingly lone and beleaguered voice. The 1950 Congress buried any further commitment by the unions to wage restraint by refusing to accept further support for wage restraint by 3,898,000 votes to 3,521,000 against despite Deakin's assertion that its opponents favoured a policy of 'smash and grab'.[41] It was the first defeat the TUC general council had suffered since 1945.

Was the temporary trade union self-sacrifice important in preventing an economic collapse? In his history of British economic policy during the period, Sir Alec Cairncross acknowledged that between June 1945 and June 1947 average hourly wage rates went up by 9 per cent in the first twelve months and by 8.5 per cent in the second. Over the next nine months to March 1948 wages grew on average by almost 9 per cent. But from then until the September 1949 devaluation the annual rate of wage increases actually fell to 2.8 per cent and dropped further to not much more than one per cent in the twelve months following devaluation. By contrast, retail prices rose during that same period, with a sharp 5 per cent annual growth rate in food prices in the period up to devaluation. 'That money wages rose so little when real wages were stationary or falling and unemployment was down to 300,000 is striking testimony to the influence of the trade union leaders', wrote Cairncross.[42] Kenneth Morgan has written of the 'remarkable abdication of their roles by the unions, unique in times of peace. The general effect of the wage freeze policy was remarkably successful in the fragmented, adversarial world of British labour relations and a political triumph for Cripps'.[43] To Peter Hennessy it was 'a measure of the never-to-be repeated unity of the Labour Movement in the late 1940s.'[44]

But it is also true that the trade unions could not continue to restrain the wage demands coming from their members indefinitely despite pleas by government ministers about the national interest, particularly with the deterioration in the economy due to an increasing balance of payments deficit and the threat of inflation due to rising commodity prices with the onset of the Korean war. Deakin may have convinced himself that wage moderation was vital to the achievement of economic success but he found it increasingly difficult to ensure many negotiators in the TGWU that this was any longer a sensible strategy to pursue in the face of shopfloor frustrations. Throughout 1950 and the first ten months of 1951 the Treasury continued to hanker after some form of institution like a central wages board to oversee pay trends without compulsion. Deakin may well have gone along with this if the government had decided to introduce such a policy but it is unlikely the TUC would have agreed even if Labour had won the 1951 general election. Overwhelmingly members of the TUC general council accepted they could no longer uphold a so-called national wages policy. Deakin was unhappy at the growing opposition to wage restraint inside many unions. But he acknowledged the TGWU could not stand against the tide. 'We cannot permit the interests of our members to be lost sight of in the general trend of events', he acknowledged to the executive council in August 1950.[45] 'If the Movement will not exercise restraint and good sense it is too bad. On the other hand, we have a job of work to do on behalf of our members. If the great measure of stability that we have secured is undermined, then those who have advocated a policy of disregarding economic facts will have something to answer for'. Deakin continued to believe the TUC's rejection of the principle of restraint was 'a great mistake'. From his sick bed in the Manor House hospital in November 1950, he insisted that while the union would accept the TUC position this 'did not mean the end of wage restraint.' 'It simply means a shifting of responsibility', he explained. Instead of the TUC, the affiliate unions would have to pursue restraint in their own way or there would be a 'policy of drift' which would precipitate 'an inevitable collapse of the nation's economy'. Deakin expressed opposition to submitting 'fantastic wage claims'. 'The sensible line to take is to submit open applications where considered justified, leaving it to the ability and wit of the negotiators to produce the best possible result.'[46] He believed a 'smash and grab' policy never achieved anything of lasting value anywhere. It only creates a feeling of 'you wait until our opportunity presents itself and we will get our own back' which is not the right atmosphere within industry.[47] Deakin was also as convinced as ever that 'to merely strive for increased wages which quickly disappear as a result of increased prices is no solution to the working-class problem. What we must all be fearful of is, creating that condition which will result in an uncontrollable inflationary spiral. If this happens, then I feel nothing can save us. The clock would be set back for many decades; in fact, we should not recover during the lifetime of the present generation', he told his executive council in June 1951.[48]

Despite the serious division of view over pay between the government and the unions, Deakin made a rallying call for unity in the pre-election 1951 party conference. 'We have had our grouse but at the bottom of the hearts of our people is the recognition that never before in the history of government in this country have we had a better deal than we have had from the Labour government during the last six years. We know as trade unionists, how great is the value of the support and consideration that we have had'. Deakin expressed trade union appreciation for government successes in maintaining full employment and introducing measures of social justice.[49]

Labour's narrow defeat at the polls was followed by a period of bitter inner-party conflict in which Deakin played a prominent role. He seemed to devote much of his time to an endless and negative struggle against those he saw as his implacable enemies on the left. In alliance with Williamson and Lawther, he sought to protect Attlee and his government's legacy against the challenge from the brilliant but mercurial Aneurin Bevan. At the raucous 1952 Morecambe party conference Deakin provoked uproar among delegates with an outspoken attack on the Bevanites in his speech as TUC fraternal delegate. He accused them of forming an inner party caucus and 'creating a mistrust which will destroy the confidence of the people in the Labour party as an effective instrument of parliamentary government'. Deakin called for a 'complete disbandment' of the party's 'dissident element'. He bellowed over a rising chorus of boos; 'Let them get rid of their whips; dismiss their business managers and conform to the party constitution. Let them cease the vicious attacks they have launched upon those with whom they disagree, abandon their vituperation and the carping criticism which appears regularly in *Tribune*.' He said they needed to realise ordinary trade union members and the party rank and file had 'no time or use for such tactics or for their disregard of those principles and loyalties to which our Movement has held so strongly throughout the whole course of its existence'.[50]

Later at the same conference Deakin erupted in fury against a left-wing attempt to win support for the use of industrial action for political purposes. The following exchange, recorded in the annual conference report, speaks for itself:

Deakin: 'I think it is time conference came down to earth on this matter and appreciated the significance –' [at this point the speaker was interrupted by shouts from a section of the conference.]
Chairman: 'Will delegates please listen to the speaker on the rostrum.'
A Delegate: 'We have heard him once.'
Mr Deakin: 'You know you would listen if you wanted to get money from the trade unions.'
A Delegate: 'Who is buying his way now?'[51]

But Deakin was unintimidated by the delegates and concluded with the assertion that the trade unions would not back any incitement to foment political strikes. 'We believe in parliamentary democracy. We know perfectly well who has got to carry the baby when trouble of that character comes and if you want to destroy the future prospects of this party and delay the day when Labour is returned to the government of this country, then pass this resolution'.

Not even the Morecambe conference went so far as to encourage the use of political strikes to topple a democratically elected government but Deakin's extraordinary behaviour reflected the belligerent mood of the trade union right, forced onto the defensive in the face of growing resistance to the party leadership from many constituency activists. Morecambe's aftermath was significant because it revealed Deakin's preference for whom he believed should succeed Attlee as party leader. At a speech in Stalybridge former Chancellor of the Exchequer Hugh Gaitskell questioned how many Communist or Communist-inspired delegates had been attending the Morecambe conference and called for an end to 'the attempt at mob rule by a group of frustrated journalists' with the restoration of the 'authority and leadership of the solid, sound, sensible majority of the Movement'.[52] Such robust remarks impressed Deakin and he began to mobilise the trade union block votes behind Gaitskell. This led to Gaitskell's triumph over Bevan for the party treasurership in 1954, seen as a necessary stepping-stone to the position of party leader. Without Deakin's support, Gaitskell would have found it more difficult to make an impact among the trade unions. It is true union backing was not a prerequisite to be elected party leader. The parliamentary Labour party held the exclusive franchise. But Gaitskell's close relations with union bosses like Deakin did him no harm on the party's centre-right and especially among the trade union group who made up an estimated third of the Labour MPs who almost all voted for him.

Although he might have suggested the unions should not interfere directly in the party, Deakin believed the trade unions should not restrain themselves from expressing their collective opinion on party policy. 'The trade union point of view must be considered at all times and the trade unions be given the opportunity to take full part in developing those policies which we regard as of prime importance to the members we represent,' he told delegates to his union's 1953 biennial conference.[53] 'We are not prepared to accept the view that all the sense and judgement rests in the political movement of this country. We have hard experience, we are not mere theorists. We have got to face hard, matter of fact, day to day problems'.

However, while Deakin remained resolute in his defence of the party's right-wing leadership, he was not ready to welcome or participate in any public debate on how Labour should modernise its policies to regain political power. Deakin was never a revisionist. He continued to articulate a traditionally pragmatic trade union position. He did not show much obvious interest in a wider employment agenda either. It is true he opposed the shopping list approach of the left to the nationalisation of specific industries and favoured a period of consolidation before any more were taken into state ownership. But this did not mean Deakin was ready to question Labour's traditional commitment to nationalisation.

On the other hand, he was not prepared to oppose the Churchill government on principle on everything they did. Indeed, Deakin and the other right-wing members of the TUC Junta established friendly relations with the Prime Minister and the conciliatory Sir Walter Monckton, Churchill's Minister of Labour. Deakin remained anxious about the dangers of any wages free-for-all in a time of full employment. 'There still prevails in some sections of our movement the idea that all they have to do is to continually seek wage increases regardless of consequences', he told a conference of tin-plate workers in May 1954.[54] He insisted the Labour Movement had 'moved on from the propaganda stage to the point where we must of necessity be prepared to accept a great measure of responsibility. Our duty is to take care of the wages and well-being of the members we represent, to do that as effectively as possible and not to allow at any time political considerations to obscure our day to day responsibilities'.

Deakin opposed the suggestion that trade unions should seek to maximise their bargaining strength whenever possible by taking advantage of any shift in the industrial power balance. As he told his union's Irish delegate conference in Belfast in October

1954; 'It should not be the policy of any single trade union or group of unions having a privileged position to pursue policies to the disadvantage of the interests of the community. If the trade unions are to maintain that influence and position in the economy which they claim, the pattern of their policy must be related to the needs of the community at large in addition to serving the intrests of the people they represent.'[55] Deakin insisted that under his leadership, the TGWU would continue to exercise restraint and not pursue wage claims to exploit the position of a particular group or for the sake of it.

But this did not mean he was ready to discuss the possible creation of an incomes policy under any future Labour government. As he told his executive council in June 1952: 'It is not practicable to switch over to a firm policy of fixing wages on a national basis by relating the wages paid in one industry to those operating in another, without creating a measure of industrial unrest which would add considerably to our difficulties at the present time.'[56] An attempt was made at the 1952 Trades Union Congress to create a review of wage-fixing and negotiating machinery, with the aim of deciding whether it was 'desirable' to have greater co-ordination 'with a view to providing greater equity and fairer relativities'. Although TUC chairman on that occasion and therefore unable to speak himself, Deakin made his views known by telling the mover of the motion it would be a 'sheer waste of time' for him to exercise his right of reply to the debate.[57]

But Deakin also found himself pushed onto the defensive in his advocacy of voluntary wage restraint in the national interest and in opposition to what he saw as the growing dangers of wage-push inflation through workplace extremism fuelled by militant shop stewards. In his final years Deakin seemed to be a bitter, frustrated man at odds with the times. He grew increasingly critical of the mass media which he believed was unfairly giving the TGWU a bad name through abuse and misrepresentation. But he was also exasperated by what he regarded as the wrecking tactics of the Communist party inside the union, especially in the docks and the passenger transport industry. Deakin was determined, as far as he could, to ensure the union's industrial activities were kept rigidly separate from its political aspirations. 'I will be no party under any circumstances so far as I can influence the position, to sacrificing the industrial welfare of our people on the altar of political expendiency', he told a Scottish delegate conference in July 1954.[58] By the time of his fatal heart attack, however, Deakin sounded like an embattled figure from the past, defending a post-war social settlement that was starting to disintegrate in some industrial sectors under the pressures imposed by workplace bargaining and full employment.

In fact, within seven months of his death Deakin's union began to move in a different political and industrial direction. This had little to do with any rank and file revolt. The election of the left-wing Frank Cousins as TGWU general secretary in May 1956 was more the result of fortuitous events than due to a revolt from below. Deakin's chosen successor had been the moderate Jock Tiffin but he was already a sick man when elected and he died in December 1955. By that time Cousins had been appointed assistant general secretary by the union's executive council. No doubt, ability played an important part in his meteoric rise to the top of the TGWU but as Geoffrey Goodman explained – that if Harry Nicholas had not been found inadvertently in arrears in his membership subscription when his wife was in hospital he would probably have occupied the second most important position in the TGWU from 1948 instead of Tiffin and therefore been ready to succeed Deakin in 1955.

From the moment of his surprise arrival at the top of Transport House, Cousins began to turn the union away from what he regarded as the political excesses of Deakinism. This did not mean democratising the TGWU's structure. As general secretary, Cousins was as keen as his two predecessors to ensure he held on to all the power and authority that came with what was the most important trade union job in the Labour Movement. Indeed, Cousins was viewed with some initial suspicion not only by the party's right-wing but also by the Bevanites. Bevan himself never found Cousins an easy man to deal with, suspecting he was a syndicalist at heart. His acolytes Richard Crossman and Barbara Castle were more sympathetic but somewhat equivocal about the Cousins approach. Indeed, the TGWU general secretary – described as the 'awkward warrior' by his sympathetic biographer Geoffrey Goodman – found himself very much an isolated figure both in the TUC and the Labour party. He was unpredictable and awkward, quick to take offence and often difficult to fathom. It is untrue the TGWU under Cousins went left-wing over night. While his union could no longer be relied upon to be part of any Pretorian guard protecting the leadership, it was not a consistently reliable supporter for a left-wing agenda either. As Martin Harrison explained: 'The problem that Mr Cousins and his union set the party is not that they have gone into systematic opposition but that their support can no longer be depended on as it was in Deakin's day.'[60] Certainly the TGWU was now a source of genuine anxiety to Gaitskell as he sought to find a way for the party out of the political wilderness. Cousins and his union became the bogeymen of the right-wing tabloid press and were therefore seen as a liability and not an asset in Labour's hopes of electoral recovery.

Cousins also turned out to be as much an autocrat as Deakin. It is debatable whether his strongly-held left-wing political beliefs were shared by the majority of his union's rank and file. Certainly his emotional commitment to unilateral nuclear disarmament did not reflect the views of the membership. And yet he was able to change TGWU defence policy within two years of his election as general secretary. The union has remained in favour of unilateral nuclear disarmament ever since into the age of Tony Blair.

Cousins was determined to exercise control over Labour MPs who were sponsored by the TGWU. David Buckle, the union's district secretary in Oxford for 27 years records in his autobiography of his interview with Cousins when he sought his union's financial support as a parliamentary candidate. On that occasion Cousins made it clear he expected Buckle to give him a personal undertaking that he would neither ask any questions or make any speech in the House of Commons if elected on any matters relating to the TGWU or industrial relations without first consulting him. Buckle replied that he could give no such assurance because he would regard himself as the representative of the constituency which elected him and not a delegate of the TGWU.[61]

However, perhaps the most important difference from the Deakin years came with Cousins's outspoken repudiation of any form of wage restraint. The change of attitude in the TGWU was clear from the general executive council's declaration in December 1955 with its opposition to holding back on pay demands. 'We are not prepared that our members should stand still whilst the government continually hand out largesse to those who are more favourably placed', acting general secretary Cousins explained in the union journal. He made it clear the TGWU in future was not 'prepared to accept the principle that the proper living standards of the members of the unions shall wholly be dependent upon higher productivity'.[62]

Cousins burst dramatically onto the public scene with an aggressive speech to the 1956 Trades Union Congress that upset many on the TUC general council with a blunt repudiation of wage restraint. 'We accept that in a period of freedom for all we are part of the all', he told delegates. 'We are not going on the rampage. We are not going to use our organisational strength to prove that the TGWU are first and the rest can get where they like. What we are saying is that there is no such thing in this country as a place where you can say "wage levels stop here" and that we ought to be content even if things remain equal'.[63]

His speech may seem muddled when read today but it left a distinct impression that Cousins and his union were in the mood for a wage confrontation with both the government and employers. However, his TUC declaration was more of symbolic than substantive value. It made it clear that Deakinism with its emphasis on responsibility and cooperation with employers over wage bargaining was over. From now on, the TGWU would adopt a much more militant wages strategy in line with the angry frustrations of the shopfloor. In practice, Cousins turned out to be much less combative than his confused but threatening rhetoric might have suggested, at least when it came to confronting employers at the bargaining table. The 1958 London transport bus strike turned out to be a seminal event in the humbling of Cousins as a trade union militant when his members went down to humiliating defeat after the TUC general council refused to throw its weight behind the TGWU cause.

But Cousins enjoyed much more success as TGWU leader inside the Labour party. It was soon clear that he had little time for the efforts of the modernisers who wanted to make Labour more electorally popular. Cousins was an old-style authoritarian socialist who believed unquestioningly in the state nationalisation of large sectors of industry. 'We still think of nationalisation as an instrument of economic power for the government', he told his union's biennial conference in 1957. 'We do not think it right that industries which have the power of control over the livelihood of the people should be subject to the whims of the persons engaged in them only for the sake of making profits and able to determine our standard of living, leaving us in the position of redressing the balance through our trade union organisation'.[64] As he told the 1959 party conference: 'There are five or six million people who are socialists in embryo waiting for us to go out and harness them to the power machine we want to drive'.[65] Cousins may have endorsed the party's moderate 1958 statement on *Industry and Society* but he was at the forefront of the opposition to Gaitskell's ill-fated attempt to revise clause IV section 4 of the party's constitution. The TGWU even voted alone against the compromise statement of aims that ended that crisis.

Cousins was also more political in his advocacy of unilateral nuclear disarmament although it remains difficult to fathom what he actually wanted. His emotional hostility to all nuclear weapons was self-evident and so was his belief that Britain should set an example to the world and abandon its own nuclear deterrent. What remained unclear was whether Cousins also wanted Britain to withdraw from the US-dominated North Atlantic Treaty Organisation, demand the closure of all US nuclear bases in the country and declare itself to be a neutral country. Initially, Cousins called for an end to all hydrogen bomb tests for ever, an immediate pledge that Britain would not be the first to use nuclear weapons in the event of a war and that a future Labour government would ban the manufacture of nuclear weapons. In a letter to Gaitskell in June 1956 he suggested it was 'absolute nonsense' that he wanted unilateral renunciation of the bomb and an end to Britain's NATO membership.[66] A month later his union's conference voted for a composite resolution that called for resistance to all missile bases in the country and the prevention of all planes carrying nuclear weapons using UK bases.

It is true that during the spring and summer of 1960 a number of unions joined the TGWU in the unilateralist camp, including USDAW and the AEU. But Cousins was unclear over what he wanted. In his 1960 conference speech he tried to explain to delegates whether the unilateralist strategy meant Britain would have to leave NATO. 'If the question is posed to me as simply saying, am I prepared to go on remaining in an organisation over which I have no control, but which can destroy us instantly, my answer is Yes, if the choice is that. But it is not that'.[67] Cousins and the TGWU continued to oppose the party's defence policy but after their defeat over the issue when Gaitskell reversed the Scarborough decision at the 1961 conference it seemed unlikely they would be able to stage another successful offensive. In the autumn of 1962 Cousins found himself in full accord with Gaitskell's anti-European Common Market stance and for the first time since his accession to the TGWU leadership it seemed the union and the party were in harmony. Nonetheless, the accession of Harold Wilson to succeed Gaitskell who died suddenly in January 1963 brought an even warmer relationship. Wilson made a speech to the union's biennial conference that summer which was well received by delegates. In it he denounced unofficial strikes and out-dated restrictive practices. He also warned that Labour would require a restraint on pay if elected to government.

Cousins was ill and could not preside at the 1963 biennial conference but his views about incomes policy was the most troublesome for the Labour leadership. On this issue, however, he spoke for his mainly unskilled manual worker members. As he told the 1958 Trades Union Congress his union would accept no form of wage restraint. If they did they would be entitled to be called 'an industrial mouthpiece of a political party'.[68] But Cousins said they were 'trade unions representing the workers and we shall continue to do that whatever government is in power because that is democracy'. As he explained in the TGWU Record in October 1963: 'If we do not fulfil the purposes for which members join unions, to protect and raise their real standard of living, then the unions will wither and finally die. We can give leadership, we can persuade but basically we must serve trade union purposes.'[69] In a speech in Oxford in June 1964 Cousins expressed similar sentiments. 'It is not the intention of the trade union movement to hold back its members' wage claims if they are justified. It is our purpose to sell our labour and our skill in the open market to the best of our ability while we live under the present system'.[70] Such views were unexceptional among union negotiators. But they suggested that under any government not only that organised labour should be allowed to practise collective bargaining free of state intervention but also not even agree to any voluntary approach that involved wage restraint. However, Cousins was prepared to accept what he described as a 'planned growth of wages' at the 1964 Trades Union Congress, perhaps more through a willingness to ensure unity on the eve of the general election than any genuine change of attitude to pay policy.[71] Surprisingly he accepted a Cabinet post in the Labour government elected a few weeks later and became Minister of Technology. It was not a successful move from the trade union world to parliamentary politics. In July 1966 Cousins resigned in protest at the introduction of wage restraint to deal with the financial crisis and went back to his old job at the TGWU, preparing the way for the succession of Jack Jones three years later.

Cousins told the 1959 TGWU conference that he believed 'the most important thing in our lives was to elect a Labour government determined to carry out a socialist policy'.[72] However, his behaviour as general secretary compelled the party leaders to reassess what the relationship between Labour and the trade unions ought to be. As Gaitskell explained to the 1959 Trades Union Congress: 'We are comrades together but we have different jobs to do. You have your industrial job and we have our political job. We do not dictate to one another. Any leader of the Labour party would not be worth his salt if he allowed himself to be dictated to by the trade unions'.[73] For his part, Cousins in 1956 had assured the party conference that 'I told you last year not to tell the unions how to do their job and I am certainly not going to tell the Labour party how to do its job'.[74] In practice, he violated his own recognition of that tacit understanding about spheres of influence that implicitly determined how the party and the unions conducted their affairs. The very public conflict between Cousins and Gaitskell helped to highlight the difficult nature of the party-union relationship. Allan Flanders in his brilliant essay on trade unions and politics written at the height of the conflict over defence explained the nature of what he called 'that silent self-denying ordinance practised by the trade unions within the Labour party', which Cousins had brought temporarily into question.[75]

But it was not so much the controversy over defence that threatened to bring the party-union marriage into question. Under both Deakin and Cousins the TGWU had revealed the more fundamental tensions that lay at the heart of the party-trade union connection which focused on the nature of collective bargaining in a market economy in relation to a party committed to planning, social justice and economic growth. The two men did not share common political views on most issues. Deakin was a working class patriot, who believed in the mixed economy, order and responsibility and managed his union with increasing difficulty in the face of rising shopfloor discontent. Cousins was a muddled, emotional but incorruptible man who often seemed more interested in developing a political than an industrial agenda. Both men were authoritarian, hostile to dissent within their union and convinced of the rectitude of their own positions. They also shared an understandable pride in the power and influence that the TGWU was able to exercise over the rest of the Labour Movement. They also held similar instinctive and traditionalist views about voluntarism in industrial relations. They were not modernisers, though sympathetic to the challenge of automation and the need for greater productivity. They were above all both believers in free collective bargaining. Deakin's passionate views on that subject between July 1945 and February 1948 were mirrored by those of Cousins after 1956. It is true Deakin came to support wage restraint and persisted with his concern to hold back sectionalist demands even when the Labour party was in opposition. He seems to have genuinely convinced himself that a wages free for all would ignite inflation and wreck the economy, plunging the country back to the dreadful conditions of the inter-war years with the return of mass unemployment. Cousins was uninhibited, at least in theory, about the need for

TGWU members to be part of the all. In his often angry way, he reflected the frustrations and aspirations of a growing number of manual workers in what was becoming the age of affluence. Although in practice he was no militant, perhaps chastened by the searing experience of the 1958 London busmens strike, Cousins remained instinctively hostile to any form of national incomes policy. He was persuaded to join Harold Wilson's cabinet in October 1964 as Minister of Technology. But after much frustration with political life, he resigned in July 1966 in protest at the government's decision to introduce wage restraint in the midst of a financial crisis. Returning to his union, Cousins prepared the succession for Jack Jones but he did not launch a raging campaign against the incomes policy in the period up to his retirement in 1969.

The history of the Deakin and Cousins years reveal how difficult it was to reconcile a belief in economic planning and collectivism under a Labour government with free collective bargaining in a segmented, decentralised market economy. Labour leaders from Attlee to Wilson sought to find ways of reconciling that contradiction. Despite their genuine loyalty to the party and the principles of democratic Socialism, both Deakin and Cousins showed the severe limitations imposed on them by industrial realities to unify their trade union and political aspirations in a coherent approach. Even the implied contract of 1945 that did so much to ensure the cohesion and self-confidence of Mr Attlee's government could not withstand the fissures produced by an industrial relations system that thrived on inter-union competitiveness and sectionalist pay bargaining. This was a dilemma which was well explained by Professor Jean McKelvey an American academic in 1953. She wrote:

What the British experience indicates most sharply is the essentially conservative nature of the trade union movement. This is not meant as either praise or criticism but simply as a statement of fact. So long as unions remain independent interest groups in a free society, they must function as associations whose primary concern is that of protecting their own members. No matter how much rhetoric is used about the new functions of the trade unions, the fact remains they are sectional bodies pursuing special interests.[76]

In fact, the economic and social conditions of post-war Britain made it impossible to reconcile laissez faire and statism in industrial relations. Deakin was wrong to think the problem was caused by the Communist menace among the shop stewards. The far left was able to exploit the instabilities caused by pay bargaining in a disintegrating and disorderly labour market experiencing full employment. Deakin's frenzied appeals for responsibility and order from his rank and file members could not succeed because most of them were never going to subordinate their bread and butter demands for the needs of a Labour government in trouble. Wage restraint could work for only a limited period without provoking severe tensions and conflict inside increasingly fossilised union structures like that of the TGWU. On the other hand, it was Deakin and not Cousins who was aware of the wider demands imposed on the Labour Movement by efforts to save an increasingly vulnerable economy in relative decline from international financial pressures. In his valiant but ultimately thankless efforts to support wage restraint in the national interest as defined by a Labour government, Deakin resembles a later TGWU general secretary. Jack Jones during the Social Contract of 1975–77 recognised the perils of hyper-inflation and the devastating impact economic collapse would have on the living standards of his members. Like Deakin he was also eventually convinced that free collective bargaining was a threat not only to the introduction of democratic socialism but to the long-term well-being of the economy and therefore their members. They also shared a similar fear that a free for all could bring a return of the poverty and despair experienced by many of Labour's core voters among the manual working class between the wars. Of course, their politics were quite different. However, the TGWU after Bevin, demonstrated through the calibre of its leaders that its behaviour was vital to the party's success and failures. Inside that mighty organisation the tensions and dilemmas that troubled the Labour party over regulation and voluntarism in the immediate post-war years were debated but they were not really satisfactorily resolved. Perhaps they never could be in a democratic society dominated by a culture of laissez-faire individualism.

Notes

Two books were of immense value in writing this essay. Vic Allen's *Trade Union Leadership*, London 1955 on Deakin and Geoffrey Goodman's *The Awkward Warrior*, London 1979 on Cousins were indispensable. I am extremely grateful to Ray Collins and Regan Scott at the Transport and General Workers union for allowing me access to the union's archives in London and to the Modern Record Centre at Warwick University. The verbatim records of the union's biennial delegate conferences are kept locked away in a safe in headquarters. They are the only copies available and provide a fascinating picture of both Deakin and Cousins in action as they dominated those conferences from start to finish. Useful insights of Deakin can also be found in a sympathetic portrait in the *Dictionary of*

Labour Biography Volume Two edited by Joyce Bellamy and John Saville. There is a short biography on Cousins written by Margaret Stewart, just after his retirement in 1969 which is also of interest.

Other works worth consulting include J Tomlinson, 'The Labour Government and the Trade Unions' in N Tiratsoo (ed) *The Attlee Years*, London 1991; J Hinton, *Shopfloor Citizens*, London 1994; K Middlemas, *Power,Competition and the State Vol 1 1940-1961*, London 1987 and H Pelling, *The Labour Governments 1945-1951*, London 1984.

1 TGWU Record January 1947
2 BDC verbatim report 1949.
3 TGWU Record June 1957.
4 The history of the trade union's origins can be found in K Coates and T Topham, *The Making of The Labour Movement: The Formation of the TGWU 1870-1922*, Nottingham 1994, and A Bullock, *The Life and Times of Ernest Bevin Vol 1 Trade Union Leader 1881-1940*, London 1960 pp 180-220.
5 A Bullock, Vol 1 p 205.
6 J Jones, *Union Man*, London 1986, p 132.
7 G Goodman, *The Awkward Warrior, Frank Cousins: His Life and Times*, London 1979, p 100.
8 M Foot, *Aneurin Bevan*, Vol 2 1945-1960, London 1973, p 353.
9 H Clegg, *A History of British Trade Unions since 1889* Vol 3 1934-1951, Oxford 1994 pp 363-4.
10 P Williams, *Hugh Gaitskell*, London 1979, pp 335-336.
11 V L Allen, *Trade Unions and The Government*, London 1960, p 288.
12 V L Allen, *Trade Union Leadership*, London 1957 p 150.
13 N Chester, *The History of Nationalisation*, London 1975, p 79.
14 K Morgan, *Labour in Power 1945-1951*, Oxford 1984, p 81.
15 A Deakin, Quarterly Report to GEC June 1945. TGWU Archives.
16 A Deakin, Quarterly Report to GEC December 1945. TGWU Archives.
17 'The Nation's Fight for Economic Survival', *TGWU Record* November 1945.
18 'Full Ahead in The Great Drive for Exports', *TGWU Record* September 1945.
19 A Deakin, Quarterly Report to GEC March 1946. TGWU Archives.
20 Labour Party conference Report 1946 pn 135-136.
21 A Deakin, Quarterly Report to GEC December 1946. TGWU Archives.
22 A Deakin, Quarterly Report to GEC March 1947. TGWU Archives.
23 'The Need for Increased Productivity', *TGWU Record* December 1948.
24 J Phillips, 'Labour and The Cold War: The TGWU and the politics of anti-Communism 1945-1955', *Labour History Review,* Vol 64 No 1 Spring 1999. Also see J Phillips, *The Great Alliance,* London 1996; P Weiler, *British Labour and The Cold War*, Stanford 1988; N Fishman, *The British Communist Party and The Trade Unions*, London 1995.
25 K G J C Knowles, *Strikes*, Oxford 1952 p 39.

26 J Goldstein, *The Government of British Trade Unions*, London 1952 p 271.
27 'The Election: An Analysis and Lessons for The Future', *TGWU Record,* March 1950.
28 Biennial Delegate Conference Verbatim Report 1947. TGWU Archives.
29 Labour Party conference report 1947 p 144.
30 *Ibid.* p 156.
31 TGWU Record November 1947.
32 TGWU Record January 1948.
33 A Deakin, Quarterly Report to GEC March 1948. TGWU Archives.
34 Labour party conference report 1948 p 142.
35 *Ibid.* p 142.
36 A Deakin, Quarterly Report to GEC August 1948.
37 A Deakin Quarterly Report to GEC December 1948
38 Labour party conference Report 1949 p 142.
39 Biennial Delegate Conference Verbatim Report 1949. TGWU Archives.
40 *TGWU Record* November 1949
41 Trades Union Congress Report 1950 p 471.
42 A Cairncross, *Years of Economic Recovery, British Economic Policy 1945-1951*, London 1987 pp 405-6.
43 K Morgan, *Labour In Power 1945-1951*, Oxford 1984 p 378.
44 P Hennessy, *Never Again, Britain 1945-51*, London 1992 p 382.
45 A Deakin, Quarterly Report to GEC August 1950. TGWU Archives.
46 A Deakin Quarterly Report to GEC November 1950 TGWU Archives.
47 A Deakin Quarterly Report to GEC March 1951. TGWU Archives.
48 A Deakin Quarterly Report to GEC June 1951. TGWU Archives.
49 Labour party conference report 1951 p 92.
50 Labour party conference report 1952 p 125-7.
51 Ibid p 78.
52 P Williams, p 304-8.
53 Biennial Delegate Conference Verbatim Report 1953. TGWU Archives.
54 *TGWU Record* April 1954.
55 *TGWU Record* November 1954.
56 A Deakin Quarterly Report to GEC June 1952, TGWU Archives.
57 Trades Union Congress Report 1952 p 508.
58 *TGWU Record* August 1954.
59 G Goodman, *The Awkward Warrior*, London 1979 p 80-81.
60 M Harrison, *Trade Unions and The Labour Party since 1945*, London 1960 p 135.
61 D Buckle, *Hostilities Only*, Oxford 1999 p 66.
62 *TGWU Record* January 1956.
63 Trades Union Congress Report 1956 pp 398-400.
64 Biennial Delegate Conference Verbatim Report 1957, TGWU Archives.
65 Labour party conference report 1959, p 131.

66 G Goodman, pp 215-218.

67 Labour party conference report 1960 p 180.

68 Trades Union Congress report 1958 p 434.

69 *TGWU Record* October 1963.

70 *TGWU Record* August 1964.

71 G Goodman p 372.

72 Biennial Delegate Conference Verbatim report 1959, TGWU Archives

73 Trades Union Congress report 1959, p 460.

74 Labour party conference report 1956, p 82.

75 A Flanders, *Trade Unions and Politics in Management and Unions*, London 1970, p 34-36.

76 J McKelvey, 'Trade Union Wage Policy in Post-War Britain', *Industrial and Labor Relations Review* No. 6, 1952 p 19. Also see B Roberts, *National Wages Policy in War and Peace*, London 1958.

77 This debate is touched on in D Marquand's brilliant *Unprincipled Society*, 1988 as well as by A Fox in his perceptive *History and Heritage*, London 1985.

Norms and Blocks: Trade Unions and the Labour Party since 1964

Steve Ludlam

In 1971, following bitter rows over Labour's industrial relations white paper, *In Place of Strife*, TGWU general secretary Jack Jones explained union attitudes to the party–union link by citing someone asked, after 50 years of marriage, if divorce ever crossed his mind: 'Divorce never, murder, often'.[1] No period in Labour's first century witnessed more murderous disputes than that after 1964. In the 1960s Labour governments imposed a state of emergency on strikers, and threatened penal sanctions against strikes; in the 1970s they used troops to break strikes; and in the 1980s withheld unconditional support from the miners' epochal strike. Unions were blamed for the election defeats in 1970 and 1979, and for the party strife that followed, and repeatedly accused of exerting excessive power inside the party, with damaging electoral results.

The link survived to celebrate its centenary in Downing Street, yet divorce was again rumoured, the link condemned by 'ultra-modernisers' as the last obstacle to rebranding Labour as a classless, progressive electoral vehicle. Trade unionists, on this view, should influence the 'new middle class' party as individual members, not through affiliated organisations.[2] Blair's shadow employment secretary infuriated unions, briefing journalists during the 1996 TUC that Blair wanted to break the link. James Callaghan, politically destroyed by the 'winter of discontent', nevertheless responded that it was, 'part of our heritage and it is instinctive in our party and movement that we should keep the link. Anyone who doesn't believe that doesn't understand our history or the natural foundation of our party.'[3] The link is multi-faceted, and active at national and local levels. But most of this activity assumes the centrality of Westminster and Whitehall, so this chapter considers the strains on the national alliance, the dilemmas of economic management in office, of reconstruction in opposition, and the question of whether the labour alliance's first century may be its last.

Centrifugal Forces and Political Economy

Several general factors producing contention stand out. Ideological struggles that split foreign labour movements into competing organisations have, historically, been conducted overwhelmingly inside the Labour Party and a unified union movement. Within a 'labourist' tradition of parliamentary methods and industrial voluntarism, socialist and social democratic groupings have battled over ideology and policy, occasionally undermining the party's electoral effectiveness and unions' internal stability. Secondly, tensions have arisen from Labour's constitution, in which individual unions affiliate as organisations – uniquely among Europe's governing parties by the century's end. Labour's conference remains dominated by massive union block votes – the 'dead souls of Labourism' as one critic tagged such 'indirect' members.[4] Until 1998, block votes elected the majority of the party's executive committee (NEC). Unions have, in consequence, been praised and cursed according to how they have voted. Tension has been fierce, thirdly, when Labour pursued incomes policies, in response to the economic consequences of imperial decline. 'It almost appears', one study noted, 'as if the objective economic historical role of the British Labour party is to do (no doubt despite itself) those things to the workers that Conservative governments are unable to do.'[5]

Each of these sources of tension complicated the labour alliance's ambiguous demarcation between industrial and political arenas, especially, as the TUC told a Royal Commission, when Labour started to form majority governments.[6] Unions supposedly concerned themselves primarily with protecting unions and industrial relations from state interference; party leaders controlled wider electoral and parliamentary politics. Conformity to unwritten rules of union self-restraint, granting the parliamentary leadership *de facto* autonomy, has been the norm, though less than universal during conflicts over fundamental purposes.[7] Territorial incursions in either direction account for the labour alliance's worst conflicts.

The crucial contextual factors have been the interrelated crises of Britain's political economy and the postwar consensus. Until 1979, governments generally accepted responsibility for sustaining full employment by Keynesian demand management. Supply-side costs, notably wages, were held responsible for inflation. Tripartite institutions incorporated unions and employers into government economic strategies intended to enable unions deliver wage restraint. From 1979 Conservative governments, rejecting Keynesianism and tripartism, turned to neo-liberal political economy. Unemployment was seen as resulting not from defective demand management, but from supply-side factors, notably monopolistic unions. Inflation resulted from profligate demand management, not wage militancy. Union-government relations now turned on policies and legislation designed to cripple unions. Union membership began a long decline. Union-party links, after a period of upheaval in the party, revolved around Labour's long struggle to regain electoral credibility by adapting policy to neo-liberal business opinion and voters' preferences, not least by reforming the union role in the party.

In Place of Planned Growth of Incomes

After 13 'wasted years', the goodwill that greeted Harold Wilson's 1964 victory contrasted strikingly with the ill-will of his final year in office which produced, in Denis Healey's words, 'six months of civil war throughout the Labour movement ... nearly bringing the Government down'.[8] What had so disrupted the alliance? Two factors were central. Union acquiescence in wage controls became central to Labour's economic policy. Its manifesto promised an incomes policy for a 'planned growth of incomes'. The TUC's agreement, 'entirely foreign to trade union tradition and practice', was aimed at influencing wider policy outcomes: 'Any agreement, within the framework of economic planning, on a wages strategy which involved unions in modifying their own bargaining objectives could only be reached within the context of more general agreement on national economic and social priorities.'[9] The new Department of Economic Affairs, National Plan, and Prices and Incomes Board promised harmonious progress on this wider agenda. Wilson, however, prioritised defence of sterling and Britain's imperial role, borrowing from the US on secret conditions including costly military commitments, not devaluing sterling, and statutory wage controls.[10] 'Planned growth of incomes' turned into emergency wage freeze, deflationary policy wrecked the National Plan. When devaluation became unavoidable in 1967, the unions were already abandoning incomes policy. In 1965 the TUC voted heavily in favour; in 1966 TGWU leader Frank Cousins quit Wilson's Cabinet in protest, but the a bare TUC majority voted for the incomes policy; in 1967 it rejected it, again in 1968 by almost eight to one.[11] Average real incomes, the TUC discovered, had barely risen and for many groups, 'the level of real wages actually fell in the years 1965-69.'[12] Labour's strategy, one study suggested, had become 'socialism in one class'.[13]

The second factor that undermined relations was the incorporation, in the industrial relations white paper *In Place of Strife*, of powers to interfere with unions and free collective bargaining, including penal sanctions against unofficial strikers. The Royal Commission on Trade Unions and Employers Associations opposed such sanctions, but Wilson was determined to be seen to act against politically damaging unofficial strikes.[14] As the incomes policy legislation lapsed, Cousins' successor observed, Wilson, 'sought to control the trade unions by other means'.[15] The TUC voted against the white paper by eight to one. Nearly 100 Labour MPs rebelled, as the PLP trade union group mobilised.[16] The PLP chairman and the Chief Whip warned Wilson they could not get penal sanctions through parliament. The NEC voted sixteen to five to reject sanctions, the rebels including Home Secretary James Callaghan.[17] Wilson dropped the white paper, accepting a 'solemn and binding' TUC undertaking to control unofficial strikes.

'Permanent damage' had been done, in Healey's view, to union-party relations.[18] Trade unionism had been intensely politicised: every wage dispute challenged the state; proposed penal sanctions threatened to criminalise union activity, prompting mass protests. The unwritten rules of the alliance had been violently breached by Wilson, whose economic policy had 'shattered the protective demarcation between the industrial and the political.'[19] Most union votes in the NEC and the party conference turned against the party leadership; some realigned with the party's left wing to recast policy.[20] Leftwing union leaders took office, the media's 'terrible twins', Jack Jones (TGWU) and Hugh Scanlon (AUEW), carrying nearly a third of party conference votes. The trade union group in the PLP, previously barely functioning, had been mobilised against the leadership.[21] The Conservative Industrial Relations Bill, however, soon provided the impetus for mending fences and seeking a new accommodation.

The Rise and Fall of the Social Contract

The period of the Heath government provides an extraordinary contrast. Massive industrial unrest, factory occupations, flying pickets overwhelming the police, union activists imprisoned, then freed by solidarity strikes, looked like open class warfare. Ministers compared defiant strikers to IRA bombers; retired generals formed private armies to defeat strikes; the government used the public army and secret police. It is hard to exaggerate the intensity of these years.[22] Yet in the union-party relationship, a new calm prevailed.

The labour alliance's internal settlement produced in the social contract, 'the most comprehensive and coherent set of political demands developed by the labour movement for a generation.'[23] A new TUC–Labour Party Liaison Committee was created, with six representatives each from the PLP, TUC, and NEC; it would continue to monitor and develop policy if Labour won office. Several factors explain the emergence and form of the social contract. Both sides wanted unity. The unions' initial objective, soon agreed, was to repeal Heath's Industrial Relations Act. Both sides sought electoral credibility, the 'ultimate rationale' for the contract.[24] Party leaders' urgently needed a credible wages pact. The longstanding trade-off formula was adopted, a broad policy agreement that would 'make it possible to reach the wide-ranging agreement which is necessary to control inflation and achieve sustained growth in the standard of living.'[25] The NUM, suspicious of wage restraint, agreed, 'to give the Labour Party as much of a chance as possible'.[26] Jack Jones wanted a programme, 'to which the Labour Party would be tied when it was next elected'.[27] *Economic Policy and the Cost of Living* thus contained the extraordinary promise that, 'the first task' of a Labour government would be, 'to conclude with the TUC, on the basis of the agreements being reached on the Liaison Committee, a wide-ranging agreement on the policies to be pursued in all these aspects of our economic life and discuss with them the order of priorities of their fulfilment.'[28] Such commitments, covering not only industrial relations law reform and counter-inflation policy, but interventionist industrial strategy, the Common Market, and commitments to enhance social and other public expenditure programmes, constituted the 'wider social contract' beyond the implied wage policy.

Initially, the deal worked. Re-united, Labour was re-elected. The Industrial Relations Act was repealed, and new employment legislation drafted, largely by the TUC. Price controls were introduced, pensions increased. Unions delivered wage restraint, conforming to Heath's wage limits until the TUC agreed a freeze in real wages for 1974/5.[29] The conventional wisdom that this agreement deal collapsed in a scrummage of 30 per cent settlements is highly misleading. Four per cent real increases in 1974 were lower than preceding years, real incomes fell absolutely in 1975 (Table 1). In response to 1975's sterling crisis, unions agreed the £6 limit that began three years of unprecedented wage cuts. Out of political loyalty, unions were 'legislating for lower standards of living, the recommended settlements were substantially below the rate of inflation.'[30] On one account, Labour performed 'a political miracle – winning trade union support for wage cuts and unemployment, and ending abruptly the highest level of industrial militancy since 1926.'[31] So why did the alliance collapse in the 'winter of discontent'?

Table 1: Labour and the Unions: Incomes Policies 1964–79[1]

Period	Party in office	Legal status	Wage increases permitted	% change, weekly earnings (inflation adjusted)
65-66 – 1	Labour	Voluntary, TUC support	3%-3.5%	+3.7 (65)
66-67 – 2		Compulsory, TUC support	0%	+0.3 (66)
67-68 – 3		Voluntary, some compulsion; TUC support voluntary, reject conpulsory elements)	0%	+3.3 (67)
68-69 – 4		Voluntary, compulsory 12 month delay, TUC reject	0% to 3.5%	+3.1 (68)
69-70 – 5		Voluntary, some compulsion, TUC reject	2.5% to 4.5%	+2.7 (69)
70-72	*Conservative*	*Voluntary, enforced in public sector, TUC reject*	*1% reduction from agreements ('N-1')*	*+7.1 (70)* *+1.7 (71)*
72-74 – 1	*Conservative*	*Compulsory, TUC reject*	*0%*	*+8.6 (72)*
– 2		*Compulsory, TUC reject*	*£1+4% maximum*	*+5.9 (73)*
– 3		*Compulsory, TUC reject*	*7% maximum*	
74-75 – 1	Labour (Social Contract)	Voluntary, TUC support	0% real earnings	+4.0 (74)
75-76 – 2		Voluntary, reserve powers, TUC support	£6 maximum	-0.8 (75)
76-77 – 3		Voluntary, TUC support	5%, £2.50-£4.00	-3.3 (76)
77-78 – 4		Voluntary, linked tax cuts, TUC informal support	10%	-7.2 (77)
78-79 – 5		Voluntary, sanctions on employers, TUC reject	5%	+5.5 (78)

1   The periods covered by successive polices do not correspond to calendar years, so the figures for changes in weekly earnings do measure precise effects of such policies (nor do they take into account tx rates).

Sources: R. Tarling, and F. Wilkinson, F., The Social Contract: Postwar Incomes Policies and Their Inflationary Impact', *Cambridge Journal of Economics*, Vol 1 No 4 1977; Robert Taylor, *The Trade Union Question in British Politics: Government and Unions since 1945*, Oxford: Blackwell 1993; Robert J. Flanagan, David Soskice, and Lloyd Ullman, *Unionism, Economic Stabilisation and Incomes Policies: European Experience*, Washington: Brookings Institution 1983.

The concern here is not with every destructive myth about the disputes of that winter.[32] One requires comment here: the notion that 'the unions' launched a surprise attack on the government. In fact all sections of the movement were split over policy by 1978. Unions warned repeatedly that workers would reject further wage controls, and the 1978 party conference voted by two to one against such controls. The party's general secretary told the 1979 conference, 'Why was there a winter of discontent? The reason was that, for good or ill, the Cabinet, supported by MPs, ignored Congress and Conference decisions.'[33] Labour backbenchers scuppered Callaghan's sanctions against employers breaching his five per cent limit; his own chancellor thought the limit 'provocative as well as unattainable'.[34] The TUC was paralysed, the crucial General Council vote on a compromise wage package, split 14 to 14, and was declared 'not carried', to the relief of general secretary Len Murray who believed the package 'would have evaporated within a fortnight'.[35]

Conventionally, the social contract's disintegration is blamed on the severity of the incomes policy. One expert observed, 'the average wage earner has suffered the biggest cut in his standard of living since before the industrial revolution.'[36] But for four years the wage deal had held, even if some skilled workers eventually revolted. Clearly, the form the collapse took was wage militancy, but the point frequently neglected is that wage restraint was a *quid pro quo* for the 'wider social contract'. Callaghan himself had insisted at the 1974 TUC, 'The social contract was devised as a whole, and it will stand or fall as a whole. No one ... is entitled to say that he accepts the part that pleases him but rejects the rest.'[37] Union disappointment subsequently grew over the dilution of price controls and the industrial strategy, over Europe, and over progress towards industrial democracy. Another specialist noted, 'The single most striking feature of the relationship between the Labour Party and the trade unions in this period is the gap between the public *image* of trade union power and the private *reality* of waning trade union influence over public policy.'[38] In retrospect, Len Murray agreed,

It may sound paradoxical but the government had a bloody sight more access to the trade union movement than we had access to the government. I am perpetually astonished by the belief that we went in and demanded things of Callaghan. It was much more them putting stripes on our backs, and we were agreeing to things that we didn't particularly want to fight for.[39]

By far the greatest source of bitterness was deflationary fiscal policy in the 1975–77 period. The rapid doubling of mass unemployment to over 1.3 million by 1976 appalled union leaders. Yet from 1974, Healey's budgets deliberately increased unemployment when it was already rising. Other deflationary policies, cash limits on public spending, money-supply targeting, and public spending programme cuts, began long before the IMF arrived in December 1976.[40] Far from protecting the 'social wage', Labour made 'the largest cuts in real public expenditure that have occurred in the last fifty years.'[41] This undermined the cohesion of the union-party link in two crucial respects.

First, as one insider account notes, 'The issue of cuts brought about a major split within the trade union movement.'[42] Public service unions rejected the divisive ideological argument, voiced in manufacturing unions, that public spending was 'crowding out' the 'wealth creating' sector. Setting up an unprecedented ginger group in the TUC, they noted that,

This argument has been used by the Government to divide the trade union movement. Cut back on the public sector, argues the Chancellor, and there will be more investment and therefore more jobs for trade unionists and the unemployed in the private manufacturing sector. Clearly the argument has been used not only as a convenient justification for the cuts in the social wage, but also as an attempt to neutralise the influence of the TUC in opposing the Government's strategy.[43]

TUC motions from 1975 on opposing cuts and cash limits were routinely passed but ignored, as the TUC's senior leadership appeared to endorse Healey's cuts, and isolated NEC members on the Liaison Committee who opposed the cuts. Jones was unhappy about the cuts, 'but keeping the Government in office was still more important.'[44] Given the exclusion of the giant public service unions from the TUC's most powerful committees, resentment was inevitable.[45] Jones's successor recalls that by 1978, 'There was so much suspicion that the whole of the General Council would have to turn up to meet the Prime Minister and the Chancellor of the Exchequer.'[46] The resulting divisions cut across older left-right loyalties and realigned TUC politics, undermining the TUC's authority and dislocating union voting in the party.[47]

Secondly, the cuts removed the rationale for wage restraint (Figure 1). In 1974 and 1975, unions repeatedly stressed the 'social wage' to secure acquiescence in wage controls. TUC and union debates and records reveal growing frustration with the impact of fiscal deflation on full employment and the 'social wage'; the first cuts package almost overturned TGWU approval of the £6 policy within a day. TUC motions were carried attacking cuts and cash limits, warning that they breached the social contract. Cabinet ministers knew the risks, as their memoirs and diaries attest.[48] Callaghan himself warned the IMF that more cuts would wreck the wage policy.[49]

Figure 1 Impact of Public Spending Cuts on the Social Contract

'Because the Social Contract has been regarded as a trade-off between the trade union Movement and a Labour Government, and because the Government has failed to meet the expectations it raised among workers when it entered into the bargain, the Social Contract has been transformed, in the eyes of trade unionists, from an agreement about economic and social priorities into a vehicle for implementing a policy of wage restraint – and nothing more.' National Union of Public Employees, 1977.

'When the Government was anxious to secure and maintain the support of the Labour and Trade Union movement for a policy of limiting wage increases, the concept of a social wage was paraded like a crusader's banner. Government supporters stated that unless strict limits on money wages were accepted it would be necessary to cut the social wage. ... We all know what happened since that time. We had massive cuts in public expenditure.' National Union of Mineworkers, 1977.

'You couldn't actually see the social policy being delivered. We know aspects of it were being delivered, but also publicly, and to a large extent in real terms, the Government's direction was to cut public expenditure covering those aspects of the social wage. So there was every reason for everybody getting pissed off, and "one more year" gradually lost its credibility.' Larry Whitty, General and Municipal Workers Union National Officer.

'The principle cause of undermining any sort of hope in a Social Contract with the government or any sense of understanding were the terms agreed by Denis Healey with the IMF ... which meant that policies on pensions, promises on other things like other benefits would not materialise, neither would some of the other public spending programmes, whether it be national health, building, things like that – there were severe cutbacks. This disillusioned lots of people.' Moss Evans, General Secretary, Transport and General Workers Union.

'In the end, it was the decision to batten down the hatches in the public sector that led to the uprising, to the so-called Winter of Discontent. That was the strongest thing" Len Murray, General Secretary of the Trades Union Congress.

Source: Steve Ludlam, 'The Impact of Sectoral Cleavage and Public Spending Cuts on Labour Party/Trade Union Relations: the Social Contract Experience', in David Broughton, David Farrell, David Denver, and Colin Rallings (eds.) *British Elections and Parties Yearbook 1994*, London: Frank Cass 1995.

There was, then, no sudden degeneration of millions of ordinary workers into what one Cabinet minister calls 'collective barbarity'.[50] What degenerated was agreement between unions and government, without which, Callaghan then told his party, 'a Labour Government cannot, in the long run, survive.'[51] There were two principal outcomes for the union-party link. The electoral effect was that Labour spectacularly lost its special claim to hold the key to industrial harmony. Secondly, key unions moved into opposition to the parliamentary leadership, and into alliances with party rebels.

Civil War

Between 1964 and 1979, the most important factors disrupting the link's traditional demarcations had been ideological and economic: the shifting left-right alignments of key unions, the attempts to resolve economic problems by limiting free collective bargaining. In the period after Thatcher's election victory, it was the constitutional factor, combined with factional alignments of union affiliates, that dominated the relationship. The election of 1979 ended the era dominated by wage controls and Keynesian political economy. It opened a period of multiple political and economic traumas for the labour movement. The new Conservatism was unremittingly hostile to trade unionism, in its legislative attacks, rejection of tripartism, and creation and tolerance of mass unemployment. Union strongholds in industry and mining were wiped out, activists demoralised, and membership began a steep decline that had barely halted as the century ended. Labour struggled to regain electoral success, weakened unions bailing out the party financially, even as the parliamentary leadership felt obliged, to woo back Tory voters, to sideline unions' objectives and their role in the party (Figure 2). Before this 'modernisation' began, though, a civil war erupted that was 'unlike anything known before in Labour Party history ... an unprecedented internal schism over party democracy.'[52] The link was under the spotlight as key unions moved not just, as after 1970, to reconstruct policy, but also to reform the party constitution to limit the autonomy of the PLP.

The Campaign for Labour Party Democracy (CLPD) secured two of its three target reforms: ending the PLP's monopoly on electing the leader, introducing automatic re-selection of sitting MPs, but not changing control of the manifesto.[53] The unions' role is subject of historical controversy. One view portrays the massed unions invading the PLP's territory. 'The changes,' on this view, 'were brought about by a union decision to move into Labour Party politics more decisively than ever before, and to throw their weight heavily against the parliamentary leadership.'[54] Others challenge this view. A contemporary study noted CLPD's difficulties in mobilising union support.[55] Some unions certainly did engage. NUPE's deputy leader, a vice-president of CLPD, recalled one of his research officers being virtually seconded to CLPD work.[56] No union motions at the 1979 party conference raised the reforms. Only three unions, albeit large ones, consistently voted for all three reforms. Crucially, the decisive votes were extremely close, suggesting that union majorities did not exist for any of the reforms.[57] There was, therefore, no massed union assault, but sufficient division to leave constituency votes decisive.

Indeed, the period produced intense union factionalism.[58] Rifts on the right were overcome, as the ginger group Trade Unions for a Labour Victory (TULV) was accused by the left of organising a 'counter-revolution'.[59] The GMWU pressed postponement of voting on the structure of the new electoral college, allowing MP's to elect Michael Foot under the old rule (Healey was expected to win); only the AUEW's tactical ineptitude subsequently enabled the left to win the 40–30–30 formula giving the unions the largest vote.[60] The 1981 NEC election results revealed early successes for the union right, which, by 1982, had removed all its target NEC leftwingers, who had helped secure the reforms.[61] Benn's 1981 deputy leadership challenge secured only 15 per cent of union votes on the first round, 35 per cent on the second. The union left, like the PLP Tribune Group, was now fracturing into 'soft' and 'hard' wings. Alarmed by the party's condition, by Thatcher's anti-union laws, and by the breakaway SDP's threat to Labour's re-election hopes, TULV brokered the so-called 'Peace of Bishop's Stortford'. The left would not use the electoral college to challenge the leadership; the right would not reverse the reforms.[62] The unions, by implication, would punish any faction that broke ranks.

Reconstruction

The unions' block votes became increasingly controversial, not least because of the autocratic manner of their deployment. The GMWU's leader told another general secretary, 'I fill in the voting form at the TUC and Labour Party and I don't have to show it to anyone.'[63] For decades party leaders welcomed the protection of block votes. With loose union cannons careering across the PLP's decks, protests were now voiced – even more loudly when union leaders quickly ditched Foot and levered in the Kinnock-

Hattersley 'dream ticket'. Kinnock moved to reform the union votes too quickly, his defeat over 'one member, one vote' (OMOV) described by one New Labour pioneer as having 'set back modernisation by ten years'.[64] Kinnock recalled, rather, that it taught him to secure union votes in advance.[65] Peter Mandelson acknowledged at the 1998 TUC that unions, 'helped Neil Kinnock save the Labour Party in the 1980s.'[66] Union backing was crucial to expelling Militant and passing Kinnock's wide-ranging Policy Review.[67]

The unions' self-restraint was driven by desperation to see Labour re-elected, given the devastating impact of Thatcher's economic, and industrial relations policies, of mass unemployment and industrial closures, union-busting legislation and full deployment of the state against strikers.[68] The net effect was most brutally apparent in the miners' strike, for Kinnock 'a lost year' delaying modernisation.[69] The labour movement's response demonstrates again the foolishness of viewing the link as simplistically bi-polar. Kinnock was widely condemned, not least by his party Chairman, for failing to give the miners full support and for attacking its leadership at the 1985 party conference.[70] But the unions were just as divided, nearly three million union votes were cast at the 1985 party conference against the NUM resolution seeking retrospective compensation.

In Minkin's view nothing better demonstrates the unions' sensitivity to Labour's image requirements than Policy Review process after 1988.[71] Union general secretaries, traditionally kept at arm's length from the NEC policy machinery, were brought onto the review groups. The only group that caused Kinnock trouble was the People at Work group covering industrial relations. The 'new realist' TUC stopped short of demanding repeal anti-union laws covering picketing, solidarity action, the definition of a lawful strike, loss of legal immunity, accepting polling evidence that a majority of trade unionists supported such limitations on unions.[72] The TUC's new stance, 'amounted to a revolution in trade union perspectives on industrial relations policy.'[73] But Michael Meacher, chairing the group, proposed statutory union recognition, legal solidarity strikes, and legal immunity from damages. Kinnock's office simply took over the People at Work group's brief, and after much arm-twisting secured the TGWU's acquiescence to the loss of immunity.[74]

After the 1984 setback, Kinnock only slowly reformed the union role in the party (Table 2). On one view, his failure to break the link was a major failure of his modernisation.[75] Others point to his *de facto* achievement. One argues that the power relationship between unions and party was 'all but completely reversed' by 1990, 'a major unsung achievement'.[76] The parliamentary leadership was now 'less restricted ... than ever before'.[77]

Table 2: The Link since 1979: Industrial Relations Policy, and the Labour Party Constitution

Party policy on industrial relations	*Unions' constitutional position in party*
1983 manifesto: repeal all Conservative anti-union laws; 'discuss' national minimum wage; radical extension of industrial democracy; national economic assessment, no return to 'old policies of government-imposed wage restraint'.	1981 New electoral college for leader and deputy: unions 40% of vote, MPs 30%, constituencies 30%
1987 Manifesto: Keep Thatcher laws on strike and union election ballots; new laws on worker and union rights; national minimum wage (no figure); industrial democracy dropped; national economic assessment to 'identify the concerted action' needed to 'contain inflation'.	1984 Kinnock's attempt to introduce One Member One Vote in MP selection defeated by union votes
	1987 Trade union votes in constituency selection of MPs limited to maximum 40%
1989 Policy Review Switch from collectivism to 'positive framework of law'; keep Thatcher laws on strike and union election ballots; legalize limited secondary action; end sequestration of union funds; national minimum wage at 50% of median wage; reject 'pay policy or any form of pay norm'.	1989 TUC/Labour Party Liaison Committee ceases to meet.
1989 Blair announces Labour will not restore legality of 'closed shop'.	1990 Conference vote in principle to reduce overall union vote at Conference from 90% to 70%; National Policy Forum created.
1992 manifesto: a 'fair framework of law ... no return to the trade union legislation of the 1970s', keep Thatcher laws on ballots for strikes and elections, on and picketing; national minimum wage promised at 50% of median wage; national economic assessment to become 'an important influence on collective bargaining'.	1992/3 review of union link produces One Member One Vote for MP selection; union share in leadership electoral college vote cut to 33%, unions required to ballot members and divide votes according to of members' preferences; union vote at Conference reduced to 70% immediately, falling to 49%; trade union membership no longer obligation on eligible party members.
1997 manifesto: 'The key elements of the trade union legislation of the 1980s will stay on ballots, picketing and industrial action'; 'where a majority of the relevant workforce vote in a ballot for the union to represent them, the union should be recognised'; national minimum wage promised, at 'sensibly set' rate.	1995 Union sponsorship of individual MPs abolished.
	1997 'Partnership in Power' reforms of party constitution. On NEC, unions keep 12 NEC seats, but lose majority control through block vote of 18 out of 29 seats, retain 12 union seats in NEC expanded to 32. On National Policy Forum, unions have 30 out of 175 seats.
1998 *Fairness at Work* white paper (see below)	

Table 2: continued

1999 national minimum wage at £3.60 per
hour (approximately £1 less than TUC
demand).

2000 Employment Relations Act based on
Fairness at Work: union recognition automatic if 50%+1 in membership, subject to
appeal, by ballot providing 40% of relevant workforce vote yes; right to be accompanied in disciplinary and grievance
cases; unlawful dismissal rights for strikers for 8 weeks; discrimination against
trade unionists illegal; individual EU
work rights incorporated.

After 1989 Kinnock was defeated only once, on a minor policy issue. As a result of 'systematic' meetings with union allies, Kinnock recalled, 'I could guarantee before every meeting what would happen.'[78] By 1990, the TUC-Labour Party Liaison Committee had stopped meeting, high-level links moving into a private 'contact group'.

Of Thatcher's attacks on the labour movement, only that on union political funds back-fired badly. A Trade Union Co-ordinating Committee (TUCC) was established, playing down the Labour link. Its tactic of loyal unions voting first to create a bandwagon, triumphed.[79] Every Labour-affiliated union voted to retain its fund; 20 other unions voted to set one up.[80] TUVL then merged with TUCC, creating Trades Unions for Labour (TUFL) to maximise union support in general election, especially in key seats. Labour's share of the union vote in general elections had slumped from 73 per cent in 1964 to 39 per cent in 1983.[81] It would rise to 46 per cent by 1992, before recovering to 57 per cent in 1997. Unions increased their material support, while consciously lowering their campaign profile. Paradoxically, as Labour's appeal grew, so did the electoral significance of the link. Union economic power barely registered as an issue in 1992, but union domination of Labour remained the third most important reason voters gave for not voting Labour, behind tax fears and Kinnock's image. Before the 1997 election, though, New Labour's popularity left 'Labour is in the pockets of the trade unions' the main reason given for not voting Labour.[82]

The union issue re-ignited after the 1992 defeat. Kinnock's media managers commissioned research showing Labour lost, 'because it was still the party of the winter of discontent; union influence; strikes and inflation; disarmament, Benn and Scargill.'[83] Again voices demanding divorce were amplified by anger that unions had again stitched up the leadership succession. A review group on the link was established. John Smith was 'relaxed in his defence of the link', but called for OMOV in parliamentary candidate selection, for unions to quit the electoral college, and for the block vote to be reformed. He reflected party attitudes revealed in the first mass survey of Labour members: 81 per cent favoured OMOV for electing leaders, 72 per cent felt block votes brought the party into disrepute, though only 43 per cent thought unions had too much power in the party.[84] Three crucial proposals emerged, all adopted. The total union conference vote was cut to 70 per cent, to fall to 49 per cent as mass membership rose. The block vote was abolished: in future a union's conference delegates would each hold an equal share of its total vote, and could cast their share independently. In the leadership electoral college, the union vote was cut to a third. Finally, a modified OMOV system for candidate selection passed after a dramatic last-minute decision to abstain by a union delegation mandated to vote against.[85] Unions believed modernisation of the link was now complete. Blair and his close allies did not.

New Labour, New Labourism?

Since 1985 Labour's electoral strategy had been to recapture floating voters.[86] In the 1990s these key voters remained obsessed with the union link. Blair's private pollster told him that New Labour was defined by his 'willingness to take on and master the unions. In focus groups the switchers spoke of little else.'[87] In the pre-election period, Blair repeatedly offered reassurance: 'We changed the Labour Party, changed the way our members of parliament are elected, changed our relationship with the trade unions. We have changed our policymaking. We have doubled our membership. We have rewritten our basic constitution. Why? To make a New Labour Party that is true to its principles and values and is going to resist pressure from them or anyone else.'[88] In 1995 he ended the practice of unions sponsoring MPs.

In 1997, for the first time, Labour's manifesto commitments on industrial relations were not the product of an agreement with the TUC. Blair promised, 'We will not be held to ransom by the unions. ... We will stand up to strikes. We will not cave in to unrealistic pay demands from anyone. .... they will get no special favours in a Labour Government.'[89] The union question barely surfaced in the campaign, until Major attacked union recognition proposals. Blair's focus groups were alarmed, 'because: unions plus Labour equals danger. Union domination is people's core fear of Labour.' The next morning Blair reiterated that, 'Anyone who thinks Labour has made changes in the party to give it all away to the unions or anyone else does not know me.'[90] The issue did not resurface.

Unlike the message, policy was less than novel. Dumping Smith's pledge to abolish the qualifying period for employment rights was new, as were Blair's criticisms of the European social model. But the promise to retain anti-union laws, the commitments to statutory union recognition rights, a national minimum wage, and the EU social protocol, were all legacies of the Kinnock-Smith modernisations. The TUC had already shifted. The 1996 New Unionism project followed a long series of TUC modernisation initiatives.[91] Indeed New Unionism represents a re-orientation as radical as New Labour, notably the shift from voluntarism to legally enforceable rights.[92] All three primary union expectations of New Labour – national minimum wage, union recognition rights, and signing the EU Social Protocol – were, significantly, guaranteed by law, not collective bargaining. So, how likely is link to survive, in its present form, into the 21st century?

Minkin's monumental study summarised the factors securing the link. He identified four advantages to the party: funding, stability, mutual education, and the 'people's party' image.[93] Of these, only the first remains important to New Labour. Certainly, Blair has benefited from the unions' stabilising role: their votes disposed of Clause IV, continue to block unwelcome conference resolutions, and delivered the Welsh leadership election to Blair's candidate. But his reforms of party policymaking and candidate selection are designed to render such dependence obsolete. Crucially, there is no place, in Third Way 'flexible labour markets', for national incomes policies, and no need for loyal unions to police them. 'Mutual education' is redundant, as focus groups and private polling reveal working class preferences to the leader's office. As for the image of the people's party, Blair sees unions as counter-productive.[94]

Union funding, however, remains vital, as union leaders alarmed by 'ultra-modernisers' frequently point out. Estimates of the value of union backing from 1979 to 1997 run as high as £250 million. Proposed alternatives have failed: Blair has ruled out state funding as offensive to taxpayers; mass membership subscriptions have proved insufficient, though by 1998 they contributed 40 per cent of party income – more than unions for the first time. Blair, though, has also courted the rich. In 1998 'high value donors' contributed a fifth of party income, helping reduce the union share to the lowest ever level, 30 per cent. A few millionaire donors at elections could make a significant difference, especially if Labour legislates to cap election expenditure, as one minister put it, to make it 'far easier for us to cut the umbilical cord with the unions'.[95] Nevertheless, a millionaire-funded media campaign cannot simply replace the 10,000 activists and vast material resources the unions put into the 1997 election.[96] Unions remain important to getting the vote out, union members remain a bedrock of Labour's vote. New Labour still needs union money and infantry, and is unlikely, before the next election, to test how much it would still get if it broke the link.

Since the unions' constitutional position prevents their simple expulsion, how likely are they to withdraw? Minkin identified four factors binding unions to the party: 'Movement consciousness'; conventions of solidarity; access to the policymaking process; and 'shared historical projects'.[97] How many still matter? Blair simply dismissed 'movement consciousness' at the 1996 party conference, 'The Labour government is not the political arm of anyone today other than the British people ... Forget the past.'[98] By 1997, only 34 per cent of party members belonged to unions, down from 64 per cent in 1990.[99] New Labour's restoration of union rights at GCHQ was a deeply appreciated symbol of conventional solidarity. But TUC leaders were appalled to hear that Blair's advisers encouraged the CBI to be tougher over *Fairness at Work*, and pressed German employers to block EU legislation on works councils, a government officer explaining, 'The government does not want to encourage the spread of trade unionism.'[100]

Unions had discounted these two factors by 1997, but the third, access to government policymaking remained a high priority. Union access to ministers and Whitehall improved immeasurably, but only six per cent of appointments to Blair's policy taskforces were trade unionists.[101] No consultation with unions preceded the Royal Mint and air traffic control privatisations, but Blair granted them procedural rights to vet tenders for Private Finance Initiative projects. After years of exclusion, any access was progress. What of indirect influence through party policymaking? Blair told the TGWU, 'There was a time when a large trade union would pass a policy and then it was assumed Labour would follow suit. Those days are over. Gone. They are not coming back.'[102] In 1996, Blair launched *Partnership in Power*, the most comprehensive party reforms since 1918, immediately interpreted as an attack on unions (Figure 2) But the new policy forums and commissions could give unions more effective influence in the 'rolling' policymaking process, as both Blair's advisers and union leaders have suggested.[103] And unions still greatly value the PLP trade union group, whose influence produced crucial last-minute concessions in *Fairness at Work*.

What of Minkin's final binding factor – 'shared historical projects'? New Labour has never promised full employment, but its 'full employment opportunity' rests on economic policy assumptions to which the TUC's New Unionism has adapted. Some unions expressed concern at 'targeted' rather than universalist, welfare policy; others supported it, and most accepted the election pledge to stick to Conservative spending plans until 1999, welcoming subsequent increases for health and education. The 'welfare-to-work' and 'lifelong learning' training initiatives offered union participation and a 'union learning fund' subsidising union involvement. And when invited to accept that the universal state pension would never be enough to live on, and to encourage private 'stakeholder' pension schemes, the TUC responded enthusiastically, and the AEEU immediately launched one.

But such opportunities are of marginal significance in face of the historic crisis of falling union membership. TUC-affiliated membership fell to 6.6 million in 1997, from 12.2 million in 1979. The proportion of eligible workers in unions fell to 30 per cent by 1997, from 53 per cent in 1979; among workers aged under 20 to 6 per cent.[104] John Monks repeatedly stressed, 'Trade union recognition is the key. We will judge the government, in terms of its relationship with the trade unions, over how it responds to this issue. This is a defining issue for trade unionists.'[105] It soon emerged that Blair shared the CBI interpretation of Labour's manifesto commitment that, 'where a majority of the relevant workforce vote in a ballot for the union to represent them, the union should be recognised.' On this view, a ballot 'majority' meant 50 per cent of the workplace electorate not just of those voting. A long war of words ensued. The TUC eventually accepted a 30 per cent threshold; *Fairness at Work* proposed 40 per cent. Other rights for employees and union members were included, but five million workers in small firms were excluded. But there was enough to satisfy the TUC and avoid a backbench revolt. The crucial concession, pressed by backbench allies, was automatic recognition where unions recruited 50 per cent 'plus one' of the workforce. Blair had earlier rejected this. Employers were furious, and procedural obstacles were later incorporated. But the TUC insisted that the balance of power had tilted back towards unions. The recruitment implications were universally welcomed.

The national minimum wage package also contained compromises, with a low adult rate, but one subject to future review. Monks welcomed it as typifying Blair's 'quiet revolution' helping the unions.[106]

So, there is clear evidence that a new 'shared historical project' is possible. Key unions accept enough of New Labour's economic strategy, want to be training and welfare agencies, and welcome recruitment openings, to suggest that a 'supply-side New Labourism' can emerge. If not, or if 'ultra-modernisers' force a split, are there viable political alternatives for unions? Minkin suggested two: non-partisan campaign politics, and other parties.[107] He thought the first unlikely, but in 1994 the TUC relaunched itself as a more independent campaign group, and in 1997, for the first time, did not call for a Labour vote. Robert Taylor advised unions to divorce Labour, pointing to the resources available for such work if they stopped 'pouring millions of pounds into the coffers of an ungrateful party'.[108] A repositioned TUC, and pressure group activity, remain compatible with individual unions remaining in the party: unions need legislative allies. What of other parties? Minkin dismissed Britain's small, electorally irrelevant, far left parties. The Socialist Labour Party has since split from Labour, led by Arthur Scargill and several other senior union leaders. But no national unions have affiliated to the SLP, and, crucially, its electoral impact has been negligible.

However, interesting new possibilities, over the horizon when Minkin wrote, are appearing, consequences of dispersing UK legislative sovereignty. The more worker rights are Europeanised, the less unions need domestic allies; if Blair resists the 'social dimension' unions might even seek other European Parliament allies. Devolution reforms suggest further fragmentation. Partial legislative autonomy in Scotland is the most immediate case; others will emerge in Wales, the English regions, and directly elected, executive city mayors. Proportional representation and coalition government in Soctland and Wales, and perhaps eventually in Westminster, may induce some unions to back different party horses for different legislative courses. Labour's monopoly is likely to slowly weaken.

Conclusions

Peter Jenkins observed, after the battle over *In Place of Strife* in 1969, that 'The Social Democratic dilemma – how to contain the interests of organised labour within a broadly based political party, and how to combine free trade unionism with the efficient management of a mixed economy – remained unsolved.'[109] Many hoped the social contract might square both circles. Its collapse ended the party leadership's conviction that the union-party link could be an electoral advantage. The Thatcher years' impact on the link was profound. After a brief return to the radical interventionism of the alternative economic strategy, Labour leaders' gradual acceptance that tripartism and incomes policies had gone for good released the labour alliance from the corporatist vice that crushed it between 1964 and 1979. Half of Jenkins's dilemma had disappeared. The other, uncoupling the party's appeal from organised labour, was greatly eased. However much the party depended on their money, unions were weakened industrially to the point of accepting virtually any party reforms, policy or constitutional, that might unseat the Conservatives. At the end of Labour's first century, the ties that bind the party to the link are weaker than ever, and will dissolve if financial independence is achieved. But there is little enthusiasm in the party for acrimonious divorce, only 19 per cent of members, and only 10 per cent of Labour MPs want to end the link.[110] And the final decision will rest with the unions.

The labour alliance has often been more anguished, but rarely has the relationship's fundamental rationale been weaker. Yet the three key factors that have strained the alliance have become very much weaker. Thanks to expulsions, withdrawals, and 'control freakery', ideological tension, though still present cross the alliance, is very subdued. Constitutional conflicts have been removed from the NEC and conference where the union role was once so controversial, into the safer and mainly private arenas of the new policymaking forums, where unions are a minority. The principal sources of economic policy tension, tripartite planning and incomes polices, are long since disowned; unions worried about deflation now picket the 'independent' Monetary Policy Committee at the Bank of England, instead of heckling Denis Healey. Minkin argues that, 'the protection and advancement of labour's industrial interests was the anvil upon which the 'labour alliance' was forged, it was the basic and unifying purpose of the Labour Party.'[111] This has long ago ceased to be the case, as occupying Downing Street became the party's basic purpose. Of the greatest significance now, though, is the fact that the party leadership no longer accepts the primacy of the unions in determining party industrial relations policy, or even feels an obligation to consult with unions any more than with business leaders. The pivotal demarcation of territory between the industrial and the political is no longer conceded by New Labour's leaders, the boundary is no longer recognised.

However, a majority of key union leaders accept New Labour's political and economic strategy, and have abandoned voluntarism in favour of legal employment rights. New Labour has delivered some such rights, and should help unions reverse falling membership rolls, which finally stabilised in 1999. And in New Labour's 'flexibility-plus' labour market vision, New Unionism sees opportunities to supply the 'pluses' of workplace rights and training, an agenda for a supply-side New Labourism, a new, if much narrower 'shared historical project'. Similarly, New Labour's reformed party structures deprive unions of their earlier dominance, but offer new influence in the rolling policy programmes. It is an enormous risk for unions to write off a century of investment in Labour without a clear alternative and such alternatives as exist imply only limited disengagement. Pressure group activities, devolution and electoral reform bringing other sympathetic parties in office, these may slowly realign unions' political affiliations in the medium term, especially if Labour and Liberal Democrats grow closer nationally. In the union-party marriage, differences are not yet irreconcilable, but gradual separation looks inevitable. Unions and New Labour will eventually evolve a new partnership, beyond federal affiliation. They will become just good friends.

Notes

1   Leo Panitch, *Social Democracy and Industrial Militancy: the Labour Party, Trade unions and Incomes Policy, 1945–74*, Cambridge: Cambridge University Press 1976, p. 258.

2   Philip Gould, *The Unfinished Revolution: How the Modernisers Saved the Labour Party*, London: Little, Brown 1998, pp. 396–7; Peter Mandelson and Roger Liddle, *The Blair Revolution: Can New Labour Deliver?* London; Faber and Faber 1996, 226.

3   *New Statesman*, 20/12/96.

4   Tom Nairn, 'The Nature of the Labour Party', in Perry Anderson *et al, Towards Socialism*, London: Fontana 1965, pp. 179–80.

5   D. Jackson, H. A. Turner, and F. Wilkinson, *Do Trade Unions Cause Inflation?* Cambridge: Cambridge University Press 1972, p. 114.

6   Trades Union Congress, *Trade Unionism*, London, HMSO 1966, p. 132.

7   Lewis Minkin, *The Contentious Alliance: the Trade Unions and the Labour Party*, Edinburgh; Edinburgh University Press 1992, pp. 461–2.

8   Denis Healey, *Time of My Life*, London: Penguin 1990, p.341.

9   Trades Union Congress, *Annual Report of the Trades Union Congress 1963*, London: Trades Union Congress 1963, pp. 391, 494.

10 Clive Ponting, *Breach of Promise: Labour in Power 1964–1970*, London: Penguin 1989, p. 52.

11 For detailed accounts see Panitch, *Social Democracy,* pp. 63–165; Robert Taylor, *The Trade Union Question in British Politics: Government and Unions since 1945,* Oxford: Blackwell 1993, pp. 134–44.

12 Trades Union Congress, *Inflation,* London: Trades Union Congress 1970, no pagination.

13 Panitch, *Social Democracy,* p. 244.

14 The Royal Commission in Trades Unions and Employers Associations 1965–1968, *Report,* London: HMSO 1968, p. 267; Harold Wilson *The Labour Government 1964–70: a Personal Record,* Harmondsworth: Penguin 1971, p. 746.

15 Jack Jones, *Union Man: an Autobiography,* London: Collins 1986, p. 202.

16 Eric Heffer, *The Class Struggle in Parliament,* London: Dent 1972, pp. 124–34.

17 James Callaghan, *Time and Chance,* London, Collins 1987, p. 273.

18 Healey, *Time of My Life,* p. 341.

19 Martin Harrison, 'Trade unions and the Labour Party', in Richard Kimber and Jeremy Richardson (eds.), *Pressure Groups in Britain,* London: Dent 1974, p.79.

20 Lewis Minkin, 'The Party Connection: Divergence and Convergence in the British Labour movement', *Government and Opposition,* Vol 13 no 4 1978, p. 471; Mark Wickham-Jones, *Economic Strategy and the Labour Party: Politics and POlicymaking, 1970–83,* Basingstoke: Macmillan 1996, pp. 135–6.

21 Irving Richter, *Political purpose in trade unions,* London: George Allen & Unwin 1973, pp. 162–4.

22 For an account, see Chris Harman, *1968: the Fire Last Time,* London: Bookmarks, 1988, pp. 233–70.

23 J. Clarke, H. Hartmann, C. Lau, and D. Winchester, *Trade Unions, National Politics, and Economic Management,* London: Anglo-German Foundation 1980, p. 30.

24 Andrew J. Taylor, *The Trade Unions and the Labour Party,* London; Croom Helm 1987, p. 28.

25 Trades Union Congress, *Annual Report of the Trades Union Congress 1973,* London: Trades Union Congress 1973, p.315.

26 Joe Gormley, *Battered Cherub,* London: Hamish Hamilton 1982, p. 160.

27 Jones, *Union Man,* pp. 279–80.

28 Trades Union Congress, *Annual Report 1973,* p. 315.

29 Trades Union Congress, *The Development of the Social Contract,* London: Trades Union Congress 1975.

30 Hugh Scanlon, *Interview with Author,* 1992.

31 David Coates, *Labour in Power? Study of the Labour Government 1974–1979,* London: Longman 1980, p. 25.

32 For a discussion see Steve Ludlam, 'The Winter of Discontent', *Politics Review* No 3 1999.

33 Labour Party, *Report of the Annual Conference of the Labour Party 1979*, London: Labour Party 1979, p.198.

34 Healey, *Time of My Life*, p. 462.

35 Lionel Murray, *Interview with Author*, 1992.

36 Robert Taylor, 'The Voluntarist Tradition: British Unions and Incomes Policy', *Socialist Commentary*, March 1977, p. 10.

37 Trades Union Congress, *Annual Report of the Trades Union Congress 1974*, London: Trades Union Congress 1974, p. 396.

38 Coates, *Labour in Power?* p. 82.

39 Murray, *Interview.*

40 Steve Ludlam, 'The Gnomes of Washington: Four Myths of the IMF Crisis of 1976', *Political Studies*, Vol 40 No 4 1992, pp. 713–727.

41 Peter Jackson, 'Public Expenditure', in Michael Artis and David Cobham, (eds.), *Labour's Economic Policies 1974–79*, Manchester, Manchester University Press 1991, p. 73.

42 David Hall, *The Cuts Machine: the Politics of Public Expenditure*, London: Pluto 1983, p. 10; see also Robert Fryer, 'British Trade Unionism and the Cuts', *Capital and Class* No 8 1979.

43 National Steering Committee Against Cuts, *Breakdown: the Crisis in Your Public Services*, London: National Steering Committee Against the Cuts 1977, p.18.

44 Jones, *Union Man*, p. 304.

45 Bernard Dix, *Interview with Author*, 1992.

46 Moss Evans, *Interview with Author*, 1992.

47 Steve Ludlam, 'The Impact of Sectoral Cleavage and Spending Cuts on Labour Party/Trade Union Relations: the Social Contract Experience', in David Broughton, David Farrell, David Denver, and Colin Rallings (Eds.) *British Elections and Parties Yearbook 1994*, London: Frank Cass 1995.

48 Healey, *Time of My Life*, p. 410; Joel Barnett, *Inside the Treasury*, London: Andre Deutsch 1981, p. 64; Barbara Castle, *The Castle Diaries 1974–76*, London: Weidenfield & Nicholson 1980, pp. 52, 352; Susan Crosland, *Tony Crosland*, London: Jonathan Cape 1982, pp. 355, 377.

49 United States Senate, *US Foreign Economic Policy Issues: the United Kingdom, France, and West Germany.* Washington: United States Government Printing Office 1977, p. 8.

50 Peter Shore, *Leading the Left*, London: Weidenfeld and Nicolson 1993, p. 118.

51 Labour Party, *Annual Report 1979*, p. 227.

52 Minkin, *Contentious Alliance*, p. 126.

53 See Patrick Seyd, *The Rise and Fall of the Labour Left*, London: Macmillan 1987, pp. 100–36.

54 Ben Pimlott, 'Trade Unions and the Second Coming of CND', in Ben Pimlott and Chris Cook, *Trade Unions in British Politics: the First 250 Years*, London: Longman 1991, p. 217.

55 David Kogan and Maurice Kogan, *The Battle for the Labour Party*, London: Fontana, 1982, pp. 41–5.

56 Dix, *Interview*.
57 Minkin, *Contentious Alliance*, pp. 195–8.
58 A. Taylor, *Trade Unions*, pp. 132–42.
59 Leo Panitch and Colin Leys, *The End of Parliamentary Socialism: from New Left to New Labour,* London: Verso 1997, pp. 199–206; also Richard Heffernan and Mike Marqusee, *Defeat from the Jaws of Victory: Inside Kinnock's Labour Party,* London: Verso 1992, pp. 149–51; Ken Coates and Tony Topham, *Trade Unions and Politics,* Oxford: Basil Blackwell 1986, pp.181–1.
60 Seyd, *Rise and Fall*, pp. 118–21.
61 Minkin, *Contentious Alliance*, p. 325; Panitch and Leys, *End of Parliamentary* Socialism, p. 200.
62 A. Taylor, *Trade* Unions, pp. 142–5.
63 Clive Jenkins, *All Against the Collar: Struggles of a White-Collar Union Leader*, London: Methuen 1990, p. 224.
64 Gould, *Unfinished Revolution*, p. 43.
65 Neil Kinnock, 'Reforming the Labour Party', *Contemporary Record* Vol 8 No 3 1994, p. 538.
66 Peter Mandelson, *Speech to the 1998 Annual Trades Union Congress*, London: Trades Union Congress 1998.
67 Eric Shaw, *Discipline and Discord in the Labour Party*, Manchester: Manchester University Press 1988, pp. 257–90; Gerald Taylor, *Labour's Renewal? The Policy Review and Beyond,* Basingstoke: Macmillan 1997 pp. 48–9.
68 For an account see David Marsh, *The New Politics of British Trade Unionism: Union Power and the Thatcher Legacy*, Basingstoke: Macmillan 1992.
69 Kinnock, 'Reforming', p. 542.
70 Eric Heffer, *Labour's Future: Socialist or SDP Mark 2,* London: Verso, 1986, p. 63.
71 Minkin, *Contentious Alliance*, p. 476.
72 A. Taylor, *Trade Unions*, pp. 159–68.
73 Minkin, *Contentious Alliance*, p. 473.
74 Colin Hughes and Patrick Wintour, *Labour Rebuilt: the New Model Party*, London: Fourth Estate 1990, pp. 144–52.
75 Martin J. Smith, 'Neil Kinnock and the Modernization of the Labour Party', *Contemporary Record*, Vol 8 No 3 1994 p. 563.
76 Philip Basset, *Strike Free: New Industrial Relations in Britain*, London: Macmillan 1991, p. 308.
77 Minkin, *Contentious Alliance*, pp. 478–9.
78 Kinnock, 'Reforming', pp. p 542–3, 550.
79 For accounts, see Paul Webb, *Trade Unions and the British Electorate*, Aldershot: Dartmouth 1992, pp. 27–30; Coates & Topham, *Trade Unions and Politics*, pp. 147–65;
80 Minkin, *Contentious Alliance*, pp. 564–5; R. Taylor, *Trade Union Question*, p. 301.
81 John McIlroy, *Trade Unions in Britain Today*, Manchester, Manchester University Press 1995, p. 287.

82 Anthony King, 'Why Labour Won – at Last', in Anthony King *at al*, *New Labour Triumphs: Britain at the Polls*, Chatham, New Jersey: Chatham House 1998, p. 204.

83 Gould, *Unfinished Revolution*, p. 158.

84 Patrick Seyd and Paul Whiteley, *Labour's Grassroots: the Politics of Party Membership*,Oxford: Clarendon Press 1992, pp. 50–1.

85 On the union link review, see Paul Webb, 'Reforming the Labour Party-Trade Union Link: an Assessment', in David Broughton, David Farrell, David Denver, and Colin Rallings (eds.) *British Elections and Parties Yearbook 1994*, London: Frank Cass 1995.

86 For analysis and insider insights respectively, see Eric Shaw, *The Labour Party since 1979: crisis and transformation*, London: Routledge, 1994; Gould, *Unfinished Revolution*.

87 Gould, *Unfinished Revolution*, pp. 257–8.

88 *Guardian*, 11/04/97. For other examples see Paul Anderson and Nyta Mann, *Safety First: the Making of New Labour*, London: Granta 1997, pp. 323–5.

89 *Financial Times*, 07/04/97.

90 Gould, *Unfinished Revolution*, pp. 353–4.

91 Trades Union Congress, *TUC Towards 2000*, London: Trades Union Congress 1991; Trades Union Congress, *Campaigning for change: a new era for the TUC*, London: Trades Union Congress 1994.

92 Robert Taylor, *The Future of the Trade Unions*, London: Andre Deutsch1994, 197–216.

93 Minkin, *Contentious Alliance*, pp. 647–9.

94 Tony Blair, *Speech to the 1995 Annual Conference of the Labour Party*, London: Labour Party, 1995.

95 *Financial Times,* 17/10/97.

96 National Trade Union and Labour Party Liaison Committee, *We did it*, London: Labour Party 1998.

97 Minkin, *Contentious Alliance*, pp. 653–5.

98 Tony Blair, *Speech to the 1996 Annual Conference of the Labour Party*, London: Labour Party 1996.

99 See the results of the survey by Patrick Seyd and Paul Whiteley in Steve Ludlam (Ed.), *New Labour and the Labour Movement: Proceedings of a Conference Held in Sheffield, June 1998*, Sheffield: University of Sheffield Political Economy Research Centre 1998, p. 68.

100 *Financial Times*, 01/12/98.

101 Steve Platt, *Government by Task Force: a Review of the Reviews*, London: The Catalyst Trust 1998, p. 10.

102 Tony Blair, *New Britain: My Vision of a Young Country*, London: Fourth Estate 1996, p.133.

103 For advisors remarks, see the paper by John Cruddas and Matthew Taylor, 'New Labour, New Links', London, *Unions 21* 1998; for union leaders see Bill Morris in *Tribune* 02/10/98 and Diana Jeuda, in Ludlam, *New Labour and the Labour Movement*, pp 44–7.

104 *Labour Research*, August 1998.

105 *New Statesman*, 27/02/98.

106 *Financial Times*, 24/06/98. For early reactions see constributions in Ludlam, *New Labour and the Labour Movement*; for analysis see Robert Taylor, The *Fairness at Work* White Paper, *Political Quarterly* Vol 69 No 4 1998, pp. 451–7.

107 Minkin, *Contentious Alliance*, pp. 655–6.

108 *Tribune*, 22/05/98.

109 Peter Jenkins, *The Battle of Downing Street*, London: Charles Knight 1970, p. 166.

110 Seyd and Whiteley survey, in Ludlam, *New Labour and the Labour Movement*; *New Statesman*, 03/07/98.

111 Minkin, *Contentious Alliance*, p. 11.

Leaders and Followers: The Politics of the Parliamentary Labour Party

Richard Heffernan

'As long as I hold any position in the Parliamentary Labour Party – and I know I can speak for my colleagues also – we are not going to take instructions from any outside body unless we agree with them.' Ramsey MacDonald, speech to the Labour Party conference, October 1928.

'Unity and the ability to act in concert is, and always has been, the cornerstone of Labour movement power. It will be no different in the government led by Tony Blair.' Private Memorandum, Labour Whips Office, October 1996.

Conceived as a vehicle through which the Labour movement could use Parliament to pursue political influence, the Labour Party has always utilised the existing constitution as the means of its advance, prioritising the election of Members of Parliament and placing great authority in the hands of its Parliamentary leadership. As a left-right political coalition fashioned by its labourist political culture and copperfastened by the disciplines imposed by a plurality electoral system, the Parliamentary Labour Party that has emerged over the course of the 20th century is a centralised institution defined by its partisan interest.[1] The historical division most often alluded to is that between a majority right and a minority left, most recently modernisers and traditionalists in new and old Labour, but another significant distinction is that between Labour frontbencher and backbencher, the Parliamentary leadership and the Parliamentary party. As well as being a centrist, indeed predominately right-wing institution, Labour's Parliamentary party is an organisational hierarchy – a leadership support base – presided over by a quasi-collegial leadership within the Cabinet or the Shadow Cabinet.

In the interests of co-ordinating Labour's message and strengthening its appeal, the contemporary Parliamentary party is run as a very tight ship. Party managers go to great lengths to restrict backbench dissent, ensuring Labour MPs speak with one voice, applying necessary incentives when required. The image of today's 'on-message' backbench Labour MP, the 'Millbank clone' eager to trumpet the leadership's message and unwilling to brook deviation from the party's line, is well established, a critic's illustration of a 'control freakery' that lies at the heart of New Labour. In striving for a unitary party, the Blair leadership is determined the Parliamentary party march to the frontbench tune. For their part, a great many Labour MPs are more than happy to do so, usually out of genuine agreement with government policy, or else the recognition that backbench disloyalty is not the best way to work a prized frontbench ticket. Press releases, Parliamentary questions, and even suggestions for speeches can be all pre-prepared by the Labour machine as whips and ministerial aides brief MPs in advance of House of Commons business ensuring supportive speeches are delivered and friendly questions asked of ministers. Given the strictly partisan atmosphere of the Commons, MPs need little encouragement to cheer on 'their minister' against 'his or her opponent', but planted questions now surface with such regularity, one wag has suggested Prime Minister's Question Time be renamed Gardeners Question Time.

Naturally, Labour cares little in government about the legislature's role as a check and balance on the executive. Prioritising the party's political and electoral well being requires MPs to tow the party line: MPs have been instructed not to respond to journalist's enquires, appear on television or radio news programmes, or even reply to questionnaires (an rule also applying to their spouses) without the permission of the Whips Office. While these edicts are ignored by MPs from all parts of the party spectrum, they are adhered to by the loyal, the fainthearted and the unscrupulously ambitious. One backbench MP, a medical doctor before entering Parliament in 1997, recently refused to grant a media interview on the medical perils of smoking until he had secured the permission of the whips to do so. Of course, the instillation of discipline is a short step away from the imposition of control. While issuing MPs with pagers to allow whips to issue instructions and advice in regard to Commons business helpfully keeps Labour's Parliamentary troops in touch with their Parliamentary commanders, the recent decision to compile a database of MP's votes, speeches, published quotes, published articles and expressed opinions, on Excalibur, the Millbank computer, perhaps has more to do accumulating 'evidence' for the 'prosecution' of rebel MPs, and certainly is intended to deter other would-be rebels.

Cynics or realists suggest that far from confining their role to 'heckling the steamroller', the traditional role meted out to powerless backbenchers as described by Austin Mitchell, present-day Labour MPs more often than not see their function as 'praising its drivers'. But, such is the partisan nature of British Parliamentary politics, all political parties are loath to allow backbenchers to speak their minds, and always have been. Thus, while their Parliamentary vote is their own, Labour MPs have always been expected to exercise it in a partisan spirit. Other than matters of conscience such as abortion, capital punishment, and other such moral questions, Parliamentary leaderships never fail to lay down a party line, one enforced by threat of punishment and/ or promise of reward. The majority of Labour MPs follow the lead of their leaders because they wish to do so, either out of a sense of self interest, or because they are in agreement with the policy. Where pure partisan loyalty requires reinforcement, carrot more than stick, reward rather than punishment, are the time honoured methods promoting discipline within the Parliamentary party. There is nothing new in the efforts of Blair-led Labour to control its backbenchers, but the attempt to secure a centralised control has certainly been taken to new heights in recent years.

Yet, while not necessarily completely docile, rank and file backbench Labour MPs have surprisingly little impact upon the Parliamentary leadership or the wider party. At best, they are able to rock the boat by sporadic, minor rebellions usually comprising a minority of MPs. Rather than being participants in major political events, MPs often find themselves spectators of them. On the outside looking in, backbenchers have been able to comment on events played out at the top of the Parliamentary hierarchy, but usually exert little impact on them. With regard to lines of communication between frontbench and backbench, backbench opinion may be represented less effectively within Labour's Parliamentary party than in the Conservative Parliamentary party. Labour's Parliamentary party has nothing remotely resembling an equivalent of the Conservative 1922 Backbench Committee, an institution which jealously guards its independence from the Tory frontbench. Drawn from and elected by backbenchers, the 1922 champions backbench opinion and, while the leadership can make its wishes known through the 1922 in addition to the traditional means of the whips office, the 1922 Committee represents the collective views of backbenchers to the frontbench, and can do so quite forcibly at times. In contrast, while the Parliamentary Labour Party is a significant sounding board making the frontbench aware of MPs' opinions, its weekly meetings are never independent of the leadership and more likely offer a forum for the leadership to represent itself to the

Parliamentary party rather than the other way round. Labour's frontbench communicates with its backbenchers primarily through the leadership-controlled whips office, and does so on a individual, rather than a collective basis.

In addition, unlike the Conservatives, Labour's Parliamentary party has consistently failed to challenge a unpopular and underperforming leader. While many disgruntled MPs made clear their strong disapproval of, say, Harold Wilson in 1968–69, Michael Foot in 1982–83 or Neil Kinnock in 1988 and 1991–92, they did so mostly in private and only indirectly in public. No real challenge was ever pressed home. In contrast to Labour's forbearance, the political culture of the Conservative Parliamentary party is altogether more ruthless: Labour MPs have never attempted to emulate the 1975 sacking of Edward Heath or the dramatic 1990 dismissal of Margaret Thatcher. Excepting sporadic left-wing sniping against Labour governments in 1948–51, 1966–70 or 1974–79, no Labour grouping has mounted a sustained challenge to its leadership. While the Conservatives are no paragon of democratic virtue, the Tory backbenches have consistently taken on their frontbench over innumerable political issues: tariff reform persistently divided the Parliamentary party from 1905–31; the Baldwin and Chamberlain governments were consistently challenged over appeasement in 1935–39; Neville Chamberlain's premiership was ended by the famous backbench revolt following the Norway debate of May 1940; Anthony Eden was brought down in the wake of the Suez debacle; an underperforming Harold Macmillan forfeited crucial backbench support in 1962–63; and, more recently, persistent Euro-sceptics destabilised Conservative governments in 1970–72, during the Maastricht 'rebellion' in 1992–93, and over the single currency in 1992–97. Indeed, nothing compares in Labour's Parliamentary history with the now famous 1922 Carlton Club revolt of Conservative MPs which ended the Lloyd George-led coalition and toppled Austin Chamberlain from the Conservative leadership.

Leading the Labour Party may not be the easiest job in the world (Neil Kinnock privately likened the task to 'nailing jam to the ceiling'), but Labour MPs have provided their leaders with a security of tenure denied their Conservative counterparts. All post-war Conservative leaders, with the exception of John Major who resigned the party leadership in the wake of the Tory defeat in May 1997, have found themselves pressurised to resign, or else have been publicly cast aside by their party. In contrast, overlooking the particular case of George Lansbury in 1935, no

Labour leader has been sacked since 1922.[2] On only four occasions has an incumbent leader faced a actual leadership challenge: Reluctantly egged forward by disgruntled elements of the PLP centre-left, Harold Wilson failed to unseat Hugh Gaitskell in 1960, Tony Greenwood offered a token challenge in 1961, Tony Benn unsuccessfully challenged Neil Kinnock in 1988. On all of these occasions, the challenger had no expectation of success. Only one Labour leader, JR Clynes, was turfed out of the leadership when he was replaced by Ramsey MacDonald in 1922. Most leaders have been able to choose the manner and moment of their departure: MacDonald cast the position aside when he formed the National Government in 1931; Michael Foot and Neil Kinnock stood down in the immediate wake of electoral defeat in 1983 and 1992;. and Clement Attlee in 1955, Harold Wilson in 1976 and Jim Callaghan in 1980 all chose to retire at the time of their own choosing. Of course, two other leaders, Hugh Gaitskell in 1963 and John Smith in 1994, died in office.[3]

The Parliamentary and the Extra-Parliamentary Party; the Parliamentary Leadership and the Parliamentary Party

Theoretically, power within Labour's pluralist and federal structure is shared between the Parliamentary leadership and the extra-Parliamentary party in the form of the National Executive Committee (NEC) and the annual conference. Under the 1918 constitution, the NEC and the Labour conference formulated policy, while the Parliamentary party implemented it. On occasion, competitive tensions between the Parliamentary and the extra-Parliamentary party have certainly destabilised the party. In times of considerable intra-party tension, such as 1931–35, 1951–55, and 1970–83, when left and right urged alternative courses of action on the party, the Parliamentary party more likely favoured a different course of action to the one urged by the extra-Parliamentary party. In practice, Labour has been dominated by its Parliamentary leadership for most of its history and past political divisions between the party in Parliament and the party in the country have been exacerbated by the fact that the extra-Parliamentary party, particularly constituency parties, the vast majority of active members and, less frequently, affiliated trade unions, were invariably of the Labour left, while the Parliamentary party remained the firm redoubt of the Labour right.

As an opposing centre of authority to the Parliamentary leadership, the extra-Parliamentary party has been used to great effect by critics from the left and centre left of the party. One major issue of contention within the party focused on the extent to which Labour MPs should be considered delegates of the party, or representatives able to act on their own opinion. The lesson drawn by the extra-Parliamentary left in the wake of political setbacks and defeats suffered in government in 1929–31, 1964–70 and 1974–79, was that Labour's Parliamentary leaders had to be controlled through accountable structures granting power to the NEC and the conference. This was principally directed against the Parliamentary leadership but, given the Parliamentary party is the institution from which the leadership obtains power and authority, it was interpreted as an attack on the privileges of a Parliamentary party which jealously guards its autonomy from the extra-Parliamentary party. Back in 1907, Kier Hardie objected to conference attempts to force Labour MPs to support women's suffrage. In 1960, Hugh Gaitskell made clear Labour MPs' determination to ignore a conference resolution in favour of unilateral nuclear disarmament: 'What sort of people do you think we are? Do you think we can simply accept a decision of this kind? Do you think we can become overnight the pacifists, unilateralists and fellow travellers that other people are? How wrong can you be?'[4]

As Robert McKenzie first suggested back in the 1950s, Labour leaders are obliged to take note of views expressed within the wider party, but 'effective decision making authority will reside with the leadership groups thrown up by the parliamentary parties (of whom much the most important individual is the party leader); and they will exercise this authority so long as they retain the confidence of their parliamentary parties'.[5] While theoretical differences between Labour and Conservative were often contrasted – the claim Labour is a plural democracy, the Conservatives an elitist oligarchy – MacKenzie argued they were practically similar. Provided the Parliamentary elite is not divided and the majority of the Parliamentary party agree, the Tory leadership has sole responsibility for formulating policy, drawing up the programme of the party and determining electoral strategy in government or opposition. While democratic structures impel Labour's Parliamentary leadership to seek the agreement of the wider party in opposition and, less frequently, in government, its Parliamentary leadership actually enjoys the same privileges as its Conservative counterparts: Its leaders have 'repeatedly refused to accept external direction'.[6] Provided the Parliamentary elite is relatively united, the support of the Parliamentary party majority is forthcoming, and the agreement of the extra-Parliamentary party can be secured, it too has the de-facto authority enjoyed by Conservative leaders: 'The leaders of the Parliamentary Labour Party (through the NEC) advise the Party Conference as to what the Conference should advise the Parliamentary Labour Party to do. When the leaders are in substantial agreement they can be reasonably sure that they can (with the aid of a majority of the trade unions) get the conference to advise them to do what they want to do anyway.'[7]

While the extra-Parliamentary party can at times significantly restrain the Labour leadership,[8] Labour's constitution also provide the means for the leadership to face down extra-Parliamentary criticism or pressure.[9] Historically, with over 90 per cent of the vote at all Labour conferences, the trade union block vote determined conference policy. Between 1950 and 1991, Labour's parliamentary leadership could win any conference vote provided it had the support of the four largest trade unions: For example, at the 1990 conference, the TGWU, the GMB, NUPE and the AEU together cast 3,258,000 votes out of 6,038,000.[10] This block vote usually delivered the conference decisions the Parliamentary leadership wanted, providing the 'praetorian guard' protecting them from the extra-Parliamentary party. Of course, the trade union vote could on occasion become 'detached' from the leadership, as happened on unilateral nuclear disarmament in 1960 and on a whole range of policy issues between 1966–70 and 1974–82. When unable to instruct the conference and the NEC, party leaders have chosen to ignore it. However, should the NEC fall under the control of a different faction from the majority of Cabinet or the Shadow Cabinet, as happened in 1975–81, the ability of the Parliamentary leadership to lead Labour may be severely impaired.

Yet, despite the past ability of the extra-Parliamentary left to use the trade union block vote and the NEC to tussle for control of the party, domination by the Parliamentary leadership is the rule, not the exception. Periods of leadership dominance include: 1922–31; 1935–51; 1962–70; and 1987 to date; Periods of significant extra-Parliamentary influence include: 1931–35; 1978–82; Periods of protracted conflict include 1951–55; 1974–78; and 1982–87. Of this last category, 1951–55, the Bevanite ascendancy was essentially a sporadic intra-Parliamentary party revolt spearheaded by a minority of left-wing MPs associated with Aneurin Bevan cheered on by rank and file constituency parties. Excepting the 1951 Morecambe conference, the Scarborough conference of 1960 and one or two other occasions, the principal institutions providing for the expression of extra-Parliamentary opinion, the NEC and the conference remained firmly under the command of the Attlee and Gaitskell leadership. It was only after 1970 – and specifically, after 1978 – that the leadership's hold on the party was really tested amid the left-wing upsurge headed by Tony Benn. In recent years, however, it appears the perpetual conflict between the Parliamentary and the extra-Parliamentary party, which has 'varied over time' but 'never been definitively resolved'[11] has now been definitively resolved in favour of the Parliamentary leadership, if not the Parliamentary party itself.[12]

While the Parliamentary and the extra-Parliamentary party should be distinguished, it is also important to disentangle the Parliamentary party from the Parliamentary leadership. Where McKenzie claimed '[l]ike Bagehot's constitutional monarch, the annual [Labour] Party Conference has the right to be consulted, the right to encourage and the right to warn. But this is not to say that the members of the mass organisation have the right, under the British parliamentary system, to control or direct the actions of their parliamentary leaders',[13] similar may be said of Labour's Parliamentary party. In reality, while theoretically in charge, Labour MPs have 'the right to be consulted, the right to encourage and the right to warn', but the limited opportunity, 'to control or direct the actions of their parliamentary leaders'. While providing Labour's representation within Parliament, the Parliamentary Labour Party makes little *direct* contribution to determining party policy or deciding its political direction. Its *indirect* role has always been to provide the *personnel* from which the party leadership is drawn and the *political base* upon which they rely. Policy-making has never been the prerogative of backbench MPs, nor even the responsibility of a great many frontbench MPs. The higher up the Parliamentary hierarchy an MP climbs, the more influence they accrue. Obviously, the Cabinet or the Shadow Cabinet (or, increasingly, the party leader's innermost circle) is where power and authority is found. The authority of Labour's leadership arises not just from the weakness of the extra-Parliamentary party, but from the restricted autonomy of the wider Parliamentary party as well. In opposition and in government, all party leaderships hold considerable formal and informal powers, a fact reflecting their centrality within the British Parliamentary system.

Excepting the pre-1983 constitutional reform agenda championed by the left to fetter the Parliamentary leadership, Labour had been notoriously conservative in regard of modernising its constitution, favouring incremental, piecemeal alteration over dramatic or radical change. However, since the mid-1980s the constitution has been altered to enhance the executive power of the leadership. The freedom of action of nominally autonomous party bodies such as the Shadow Cabinet (and now the Cabinet), the NEC, and the party conference have been increasingly limited as power has been increasingly hived off to an inner circle comprising the leader, his private office, trusted campaign professionals, as well as other leading members of the Parliamentary party. This has been at the expense of the extra-Parliamentary party, but also of backbench MPs as well. In response to its electoral crisis of 1979–97, Labour enabled its leadership to impose the political prescriptions it deemed necessary to cure the party's electoral ills and deal with its attendant ideological crises. This has instituted the strongest, most centralised, leadership Labour has known; more powerful than the 'social democratic centralism' of 1930–70.[14] As party leader since 1994, Tony Blair's freedom to lead – not outright command – his party is one predecessors such as Hugh Gaitskell, Harold Wilson and Jim Callaghan could only have dreamt of.

The Parliamentary Party: Structure and Organisation

Conversely, having come to Westminster to represent a collectivist movement, Labour MPs rarely act collectively, excepting voting the party line in Commons divisions or signing Early Day Motions and other such Parliamentary petitions. Backbenchers largely pursue their own interests, dealing with whips on a one to one basis, only occasionally joining together in large number to press a particular course of action on a Labour minister or attempt to dissuade him or her from doing something. MPs climb the Parliamentary hierarchy individually, albeit often as members of a coterie, attracting support and organising their own coterie as they do. Fashioned by partisanship, hierarchy, loyalty, ambition and patronage, the political culture of Labour's Parliamentary party has always underpinned the frontbench/backbench–leader/follower divide. While backbenchers possess only a theoretical power of veto, frontbench MPs outside the Cabinet, and many lower-ranking ministers within the Cabinet, also exercise less influence over Labour's deliberations. Collective Cabinet responsibility, rigorously enforced by all British Parliamentary parties, requires frontbench members to support the decisions of the frontbench even when these decisions have not been collectively reached. Unhappy ministers and/or shadow ministers are obliged to publicly put up and shut up and vote the party line (although, by the well-established process of leaking and briefing in the Parliamentary Lobby, their private disagreement may anonymously be made known). The fact that the overwhelming majority of Labour's frontbenchers outside the Cabinet or the Shadow Cabinet have been more than content to support decisions of the Parliamentary elite, should not detract from the fact they have no formal – and few informal – opportunities to affect or otherwise influence the decision making process outside of the departmental issues they may be given responsibility for.

While Labour's frontbench has long been bound together by collective responsibility, it is no secret the Labour hierarchy would dearly love to extend this requirement to backbench MPs as well; in May 1999, responding to criticisms from a minority of his backbenchers relating to Labour's welfare reform programme, Tony Blair argued that Labour MPs were expected to rally public support for the government, explaining what it was doing and why: 'MPs have got to realise they're not just a pressure group to pass concerns on to government ... they're also ambassadors for the government'.[15] In more genteel terms, these remarks echo Harold Wilson's 1967 criticism of disloyal MPs when he observed that every dog was allowed one bite, but should it become a habit its owner might have doubts about renewing its licence when it falls due.[16]

For a variety of reasons, chief among them partisanship and party loyalty on the part of government backbenchers, British MPs invariably offer an inadequate check and balance to the over-powerful British executive. Backbench MPs are also so poorly resourced they are ill-equipped to hold the government effectively to account; frontbenchers enjoy the use of infinitely more resources than backbenchers. When Labour is in opposition, state funding of political parties, the so-called Short Money, goes not to Labour's Parliamentary party but to Labour's frontbench in addition to other funding sources such as company donations, trade union loans, and 'blind office trusts'. These all provide the frontbench with a veritable army of researchers, advisers, assistants, press officers, and assorted gofers. In government, the frontbench enjoys access to far wider ministerial resources. Indeed, rather than provide Labour backbenchers with the resources to scrutinize government activity, the current government seeks instead to ensure they are fully briefed on government policy and primed to support ministers from the backbench and offer possible rebuttals for opposition attacks on the government.

The regular weekly meetings of the Parliamentary party, held every Wednesday morning when the Commons is in session, are often able to discuss political matters, but rarely to decide them. Compared to the deliberative meetings of a Labour group on a local authority, these formal meetings – and the backbench 'Subject Committees' the Parliamentary party organises – have little policy impact. At best they provide a forum for the expression of backbench discontent (or support for the leadership), if not necessarily its resolution. As is vividly recalled in the diary accounts of Tony Benn and Dick Crossman, the Bevanite revolts were played out in meetings of the Parliamentary party, and in 1970–72, the Parliamentary party played an important role in determining Labour's opposition to the Heath-led entry into Europe, 'on these terms, at this time'. Here, the leadership's position was ambivalent, the Shadow Cabinet divided, and the pragmatically anti-Europeans led by Wilson required majority opinion among MPs to underpin their final decision as to where Labour would stand on the issue. In 1986, at a more mundane level, MP criticisms of Harriet Harman's decision to send her child to a selective school was so widespread, Tony Blair was obliged to speak up in her support at a Parliamentary party meeting. Nonetheless, unless an acute political crisis captures the attention of MPs, weekly meetings of the Parliamentary party are sparsely attended. Even important meetings are poorly attended. For example, when the first reforms of standing orders in 30 years were proposed in 1996, only 113 MPs actually turned up.[17] In the wake of a 1997 backbench rebellion over lone parent benefits, only 200 out of 419 MPs chose to attend a party meeting addressed by Tony Blair. On the very rare occasions a Parliamentary party meeting has the opportunity to vote on something substantive, the 'pay roll' vote of Ministers or shadow Ministers turns out to support the frontbench line. Given the size of the Labour frontbench – in 1990 it comprised 90 out of 228 MPs, some 40 per cent of the Parliamentary party – it provides the leadership with a reliable block vote.

Party management is discharged through the well-resourced Whips Office, rather than the formal structures of the Parliamentary party. Appointed by the party leader in government, the party's Chief Whip was elected by Labour MPs in opposition until Tony Blair won approval to appoint his own candidate in 1996.[18] Party whips are the Labour leadership's Parliamentary policeman and the chief resource for instilling order and discipline among Labour MPs; but they are also an early warning system alerting the Parliamentary hierarchy to backbench complaints and concerns. Under the standing orders of the Parliamentary party the whip may be withdrawn at the discretion of the Chief Whip from any Labour MP who fails to follow majority decisions of the Parliamentary party. While imposing Labour's line is one thing; actually deciding the line is another. Weekly meetings of the Parliamentary party do not determine the stance Labour MPs take on Commons business. Instead, the whip is drawn up by the 'Parliamentary Committee', the Cabinet or the Shadow Cabinet (more usually by the leader's 'kitchen cabinet' or 'inner circle'), and reported to Labour MPs at a routine business meeting of the Parliamentary party. Since 1923, Labour's Parliamentary Committee has been elected by Labour MPs when the party is in opposition. In government, appointment is the leader's prerogative, as is always the case regarding the allocation of portfolios and the appointment of the frontbench outside the Cabinet or the Shadow Cabinet. This annual election grants some power to backbenchers, but once elected the Shadow Cabinet/ Cabinet oversees Labour's Parliamentary activities through its Parliamentary business managers and the Whips Office, both of which are appointed by the leadership, not the Parliamentary party, reporting upwards to the leadership not downwards to the Parliamentary party.[19]

For MPs to collectively debate legislative issues and arrive at a majority position is very much the exception. Backbench MPs usually make individual rather than collective representations to the leadership through their party whips. Of course, it would be wrong to conclude that Labour MPs are entirely powerless. In theory, able to make and unmake governments by a Parliamentary vote, they possess great power. In practice, this power is neutered by partisan interest. Yet, the fact that Labour MPs are very important, if informal, 'sounding boards' should not be overlooked. While they are individually rarely able to decide policy, Labour MPs can individually – and collectively – advise and warn government, particularly by exerting private pressure behind the scenes. Given that ministers do not like internal differences made public, the un-codified practice of *anticipated reactions* plays an important part in Parliamentary politics. The prospect of rebellion can deter the frontbench from pursuing a particular course of action, particularly if critics are many in number and comprise leadership loyalists not drawn from the list of 'usual suspects' of backbench rebels. Thus, the Parliamentary leadership will not always press issues it knows backbenchers cannot easily support; it may think again. While the ambitious MP will reply 'how high', when asked to jump, a great many

Labour MPs, while preferring to keep their head well below any parapet, may find that proverbial straws can and do threaten to break the camel's back. MPs cannot endlessly be dragooned into a voting lobby on promise of reward or threat of punishment; frontbenchers recognise that as valuable a resource as backbench goodwill can be easily eroded by resentment.

While successful rebellions – those which defeat the frontbench – are unheard of, revolts happen. In 1943 97 MPs voted against the decision of Conservative and Labour Ministers in the Churchill-led Wartime Coalition to postpone the introduction of the Beveridge Report until after the war; Bevanite inspired rebellions saw 57 MPs break the whip on the defence estimates in 1952 and 61 MPs abstain on a Labour amendment supporting the manufacture of the hydrogen bomb in 1955; 60 MPs abstained on a pro-nuclear weapons Labour amendment in 1960 and Michael Foot and four other MPs had the whip withdrawn for voting against the Defence Estimates in 1962; the defection of two right-wing MPs temporarily derailed the re-nationalisation of the iron and steel industry in 1964–66; during the 1966 Parliament there were several backbench rebellions on defence issues, foreign policy, entry into the EEC, incomes policy, and obstructing House of Lords reform, topped by 55 MPs voting against the 1969 White Paper, *In Place of Strife*, amending the immunities enjoyed by trade unions, while 40 abstained; in 1971 69 MPs, led by the deputy leader, Roy Jenkins, voted against the Labour whip opposing EEC entry and another 20 abstained, providing the key to Heath's majority and staving off the Tory government's defeat; the 1974 Parliament witnessed backbench rebellions on numerous issues when only 19 per cent of Labour MPs failed to cast at least one dissenting vote against the Wilson and Callaghan governments,[20] indeed, once the government's majority disappeared in 1976, the government was defeated 42 times, on 23 occasions because Labour MPs voted in the opposition lobby.[21]

Given the House of Commons is a reactive legislature, MPs are able only to endorse, modify, or reject proposals laid before it by the government of the day. When they occur, backbench rebellions are inevitably attempts to exercise a negative veto against something the government is doing, has done, or intends to do, rather than being a positive recommendation for action. Even in Blair's tightly run ship, significant rebellions have taken place, although the government's legislation has been unscathed. In December 1997, 47 MPs voted against cuts in lone parent benefits and another 25 abstained (and 120 signed a private letter of protest); 16 MPs voted against the Terrorism and Conspiracy Bill in September 1998; and, most significantly, in May 1999, 67 MPs voted against means-testing and restricting access to incapacity benefits and another 39 abstained, reducing the government's 179 Commons majority to 40. In June 1999, backbench criticism of the Asylum Bill led ministers to offer concessions and, despite considerable misgivings of the part of ministers, the degree of backbench support for the passage of a bill banning the hunting of foxes is likely to oblige the Labour government to stand by its manifesto commitment. Although 184 Labour MPs also voted at least once against the leadership line in 1992-96 on a range of issues including (principally) Europe, economic policy, foreign policy, welfare policy, and law and order,[22] these votes are for the most part expressions of opinion, rather than organised attempts to defeat the frontbench. While not encouraged, rebellions by the 35-odd left-wing Campaign Group MPs have usually been disdainfully tolerated – tolerated in the sense they have been ignored – and deemed to be of no consequence.

A collegial leadership?

Of course, even amid the on-going 'presidentialisation' of Parliamentary government, the elite of Labour's Parliamentary party remains collegial, its leadership to an extent plural and collective while power and authority are still exercised hierarchically. British Parliamentary parties can be structurally represented as a set of concentric circles; at the centre lies a small inner core elite and at the margin is found a much, much larger peripheral elite in which the majority of backbenchers are located, both mediated by other circles. Power is locational: the closer to the centre the player, the more power and influence they have. Obviously, the party leader and his closest – elected and non-elected – associates are to be found in the innermost concentric circle. To some extent, the collegial leadership, in the form of senior party figures within the inner and outer core elites, can check and balance itself, depending on how powerful the leadership is, and if the party is in government or opposition.

By overcoming constraints faced by resources possessed, leaders carefully bargain for the support of influential figures inside the Cabinet, the Shadow Cabinet, and, in the past, NEC members and trade union leaders. The ability to lead is contingent on a variety of resource factors such as party standing, Parliamentary base, policy success, electoral popularity, public visibility, media profile, or party contentment at the prospect of up-coming electoral success. Leaders find their authority generally ebbs and flows, but generally speaking, strong leaders have included MacDonald, Gaitskell, and Blair; weaker leaders, Lansbury, Callaghan, and Foot; intermediary leaders, Wilson and Kinnock; and genuinely collegial leaders, Attlee and Smith.: While power has shifted towards key central actors, it is by no means held by the party leader alone. Senior party figures deemed likely to offer some form of possible threat to the leader and/ or who have an independent Parliamentary party base of their own, also find their way up the party hierarchy. Thus leader's wisely apply the crude but apposite principle enunciated by Lyndon Johnson: keeping potential party rivals 'inside the leadership tent pissing out', rather than having them 'outside the tent pissing in'.

Factions, Groups, Expulsions and Defections

Personal and political factionalism are common to all political parties, none more so than within Labour's broad church. While partisanship fosters party unity, personal feuds, individual jealousies and political disagreements, both systemic and occasional, are also woven into Labour's history. For example, when it was suggested to him that Herbert Morrison was 'his own worst enemy', Ernest Bevin replied 'not while I'm alive', such was his antipathy to a man he scornfully dubbed the 'little cockney'. In a private conversation with Dick Crossman, not, it should be admitted, the most reliable of diarists, Hugh Gaitskell likened Nye Bevan to Hitler in 1955, indicating a then hatred and distrust heartedly reciprocated by Bevan. Numerous other examples abound. However, differences that significantly destabilise the party (as in the Bevan-Gaitskell clash of 1951–55; or the Benn-led campaign to turn Labour to the left in 1974–81) are invariably political, not necessarily personal. Personal differences are more easily managed given the obligation to compromise partisanship imposes when Labour MPs are 'obliged to hang together, for fear of hanging separately'. Nonetheless, the not infrequent absence of fraternity and sorority within the Parliamentary Labour Party can bring to mind the old Churchillian adage that MPs sit in the House of Commons facing their political opponents, but are surrounded by their political enemies. Of course, it was ever thus. Few administrations or parliamentary groups are composed of chums who are ever the best of pals, but contain co-operating factions, individuals and groupings competitively divided in their differing personal aspirations, political ambitions or ideological proclivities.

Would-be Labour leaders try to organise – or have organised for them – some base of support, large or small, within the Parliamentary party to advance their interest, facilitate politicking and allow them to collect troops. Narratives of Labour Party history are replete with references to personal coteries, invariably political in orientation, such as Gaitskellites, Bevanites, Jenkinsites, Bennites, Kinnockites and, more recently, Blarites and Brownites (although little mention is made of, say, Wilsonites, Callaghanites, Attleeites, or Smithites). Today's Parliamentary party contains personal supporters of both Tony Blair and Gordon Brown, majority 'Blairites' and minority 'Brownites', broadly sharing the same policy agenda and coexisting relatively harmoniously despite occasional spats. The deputy leader, John Prescott, also has his own, much, much smaller, personal grouping. Noteworthy past examples of leading figures with partisan coteries include: Herbert Morrison in 1944–46; Hugh Gaitskell and Nye Bevan in 1951–55 and, in Gaitskell's case, beyond; George Brown, briefly in 1960–63; and Roy Jenkins, definitively, in 1968–76. Some prospective leadership candidates, Tony Benn, Denis Healey, Tony Crosland and Robin Cook all come immediately to mind, often fail miserably at organising a personal coterie; others, notably Clement Attlee, Harold Wilson, Jim Callaghan, and Michael Foot, succeed to the leadership by attracting rather than organising support at a key, opportune moment. Indeed, Neil Kinnock won the leadership in 1983 in spite of a weak Parliamentary base at a time when affiliated trade unions and constituency parties cast 70 per cent of the leadership vote.

Parliamentary pressure groups, ginger groups, political campaigns and factional organisations are also a way of political life. They link MPs with the extra-Parliamentary party, but also reflect and encourage continuing intra-party disputes, usually between Labour's left and right. Over the years Parliamentary groups such as the ILP; the Clydesiders; the Socialist League; Keep Left; Keep Calm; Gaitskellites; Bevanites; Victory for Socialism; the Tribune Group; the Campaign for a Labour Victory; Labour Solidarity; the Socialist Campaign Group, have jostled for position and influence within the Parliamentary party, as have informal groupings such as Parliamentary CND; pro-and anti-Europeans, and, more recently, the competing First Past the Post and Fair Votes lobbies opposing or else supporting reform of Britain's electoral system. The once all-important Parliamentary grouping, the Trade Union Group comprising the archetypical unambitious, worthy working class MPs, for years provided the ballast of the Parliamentary party; should an issue play with this 'tea room' vote, the leadership knew Labour MPs would be sure to wear it.

If the majority of MPs are loyal to the leadership in public, if not necessarily in private, protest, dissent and factionalism are a feature of Labour politics. Left-wing extra-Parliamentary party revolts have usually found dissident MPs to champion their cause within the Parliamentary party, and dissident MPs also fashion their own party rebellions and factions, attracting support from the non-Parliamentary party. The ILP organised itself as Labour's left-wing Parliamentary conscience in the 1920s; a number of MPs were attracted by the radical appeal of the pre-fascist Oswald Mosely in 1930–32; Nye Bevan and Stafford Cripps helped organise the Socialist League in 1937–39; pre-Bevanite MPs like Michael Foot, Dick Crossman, Ian Mikardo led campaigns critical of the Attlee government in 1948–51; Bevanite MPs, in alliance with an extra-Parliamentary left around the Tribune newspaper, flew the flag for the left within Parliament in 1951–55, and beyond; MPs in the Tribune Group did likewise in the 1960s and 1970s; as did the Socialist Campaign Group of Labour MPs in the 1980s and 1990s. Able to command key elements of the official Labour Party machine, the Labour right has never felt a similar urgency to organise factions but Hugh Gaitskell's supporters helped organise the anti-left Campaign for Democratic Socialism in 1960–62; the Jenkinsite remnants of Gaitskellism set up the Campaign for a Labour Victory in 1977, an organisation paving the way for the SDP secession of 1981; Labour Solidarity was established in 1982 to combat Bennism; and since 1985, Labour modernisers, Kinnockites and Blairites in Parliament and outside, have organised the reconstruction of old Labour into new.

As a reaction to Bevanism, described by Hugh Gaitskell as an 'organised conspiracy' to seize the leadership, MPs expressly prohibited organised factions within their ranks in 1953. While this decision at the time denied Bevanite MPs the opportunity to advance their campaign, political groupings have continued to be tolerated, although political disagreements have often provoked the threat of disciplinary measures. The withdrawal of the whip and/ or the threat of expulsion from the party itself is the ultimate sanction the leadership can use against recalcitrant MPs. Obviously, the fewer in number they are, the more likely the discipline. While Bevan, Cripps and George Strauss were expelled from the party in 1939, the withdrawal of the whip has usually been temporary and not involved expulsion: Having had the whip withdrawn by a 141–112 vote in the Parliamentary party for challenging Attlee's authority in the Commons over the nuclear deterrent in 1955, Bevan was famously saved from expulsion by one vote on the NEC. Excepting the late 1940s expulsion of fellow-travelling MPs such as John Platt-Mills and Konni Zillicus and that of Militant-supporting Terry Fields and Dave Nellist in 1991, the whip has more usually been withdrawn from MPs guilty of misdemeanours or accused of other wrongdoings, rather than because of political activity or belief.[23] Generally, given the political difficulties arising from charges of control freakery, expulsions may prove more trouble than they are worth. Recalcitrant MPs can win the backing of their constituency parties or wider forces within the extra-parliamentary party.[24] Expulsion has not usually been the first resort of the leadership: The implicit threat suffices to enforce order and forestall significant Parliamentary revolts; appeals to party loyalty usually ensure rebellions are limited to a size that may embarrass the Labour frontbench, but do not bring about its downfall. Historically, the size of the Parliamentary party has been reduced more as a result of defections from its ranks than from expulsions.[25]

Conclusions

There have been all sorts of Labour MP in Labour's first century: effective or ineffective, talented or time-serving, wannabe, has-been or never-likely-to be. The principal distinctions within the Parliamentary party remain that between frontbencher, backbencher and eager-to-be frontbencher, leadership loyalist, critic or would-be critic, all overlaying the traditional left/right/centre divide and significantly affecting the political culture of the Parliamentary party. Despite the prestige conferred by election to Parliament, newly elected Labour MPs often discover the average backbencher has far less actual power and influence than, say, senior councillors or leaders of major local authorities. While a number of MPs distinguish themselves as permanent backbenchers (Sydney Silverman and Tam Dalyell come to mind), the route to power and influence most choose is becoming tomorrow's frontbencher, making their way up the Parliamentary greasy pole. All too often rank and file MPs are spectators of major political events rather than participants in them; able to comment privately, indeed, to gossip incessantly, but less willing or able to speak publicly about events played out at the top of the Parliamentary tree they are rarely able to influence directly. For example, in both the collapse of the second Labour government in

August 1931 and the IMF crisis of September to December 1976, backbenchers exercised little impact on the eventual outcome, their influence restricted to cheerleading the relevant leadership faction they felt an affinity with. For its part, the leadership is forever eager to restrict what little autonomy Labour MPs do have available to them, seeking to prevent whenever possible even a minority of backbenchers rocking the frontbench boat.

Although the projection of 'Labour' as its 'leadership' is a long established practice, it has become an ever more central component of the party's public profile, as with all political parties.[26] Every party issue is now cast as an issue of confidence in the leadership. As the projection of the leadership has become the central feature of Labour's modern electioneering efforts, favourable or critical news media reportage helps root the Parliamentary hierarchy ever more at the centre of the political process. The Parliamentary party is divided into those who 'follow' and those who 'lead', as well as being sub-divided into leadership 'loyalists' and 'critics'.[27] Periodic 'revolts' of the extra-Parliamentary party have usually been provoked by the perception that Labour has failed to promote radical reform when in office (as in post-1931, post-1951, post-1970, and post-1979), political change within the party is usually promoted by a pre-eminent leadership able to sponsor programme change by utilising its control over the party apparatus. The party increasingly sees enormous benefit in being led by its leadership from the front and, as importantly, controlled from the top down. Over time, this has served to empower the Parliamentary leadership, not the Parliamentary party.[28]

In contrast to past left-wing revolts seeking to hone the party's policy agenda to prepare the party for government, leadership sponsored programmatic change is often a response to electoral difficulties, a determination to prioritise successful office seeking over policy seeking. For the leadership to be successful in its endeavours, programmatic renewal needs the endorsement of the collegial leadership, the agreement of trade unions leaders and, last and least, the acquiescence of the party membership. Crucially, it has also to draw support from the bulk of the Parliamentary party, even if the degree of that support is passive and acquiescent. Thus, partisanship, patronage, hierarchy, loyalty, and ambition bind MPs together, helping ministers, would-be ministers and backbenchers comply with the leadership's preferred agenda. Because professional politics remains a matter of climbing the greasy pole, Labour's Parliamentary party is simultaneously a pole as well as the ladder assisting ascent. Personal progression within political parties is so often determined by the Disraelian adage, 'damn your principles and stick to your party', in its first century, the Parliamentary Labour Party has been no different.

Notes

1 Over time, the demographic composition of the Parliamentary Labour Party has altered as the percentage of manual workers on the Labour benches has fallen from 72 per cent in the 1920s and 1930s to 36 per cent in the 1950s to 29 per cent in the 1980s. Of course, gradually, the number of women MPs has increased, with 101 women (out of 419 Labour MPs) entering Parliament at the 1997 general election.

2 Indeed, the only time a leader really came close to be toppled was in 1968–9 when rebel MPs on the right of the party endlessly plotted to get rid of Harold Wilson. On that occasion, the two contenders best placed to replace him, Roy Jenkins and Jim Callaghan, ultimately refused to endorse the effort, each afraid the other would benefit should the adage 'he who wields the dagger, never wears the crown' apply.

3 Cf Leonard Stark, *Choosing a Leader: Party Leadership Contests in Britain from Macmillan to Blair*, London, Macmillan 1996 pp36-40

4 Labour Party Annual Conference Report, 1960.

5 Robert McKenzie, *British Political Parties*, London, Heinemann, 1964, p 635.

6 *Ibid.* p 640.

7 *Ibid.* p 426.

8 Lewis Minkin, *The Labour Party Conference*, Manchester, Manchester University Press 1980.

9 Cf R H S Crossman, 'Introduction' to Walter Bagehot, *The English Constitution*, London, Fontana, 1963.

10 Lewis Minkin, *The Contentious Alliance: Trade Unions and the Labour Party*, Manchester, Manchester University Press 1991.

11 Eric Shaw, *The Labour Party Since 1945*, Oxford, Basil Blackwell, 1996, p 59.

12 The party conference's lack of deference to the Parliamentary party was historically symbolised by the reservation of the platform for members of the NEC; if called in debate, Ministers and shadow Ministers not on the NEC had to speak from the floor. However, since the late 1980s, the conference platform has been exclusively given over to Ministers and shadow Ministers at the behest of the leadership. Labour's leaders now address their conference in the time-honoured fashion of their Conservative counterparts.

13 McKenzie, *British Political Parties, op. cit.* p 636.

14 Eric Shaw, *Discipline and Discord in the Labour Party*, Manchester, Manchester University Press, 1988.

15 *The Guardian*, 26 May 1999.

16 Philip Ziegler, *Wilson: The Authorised Biography*, London, Harper Collins, 1993.

17 *The Daily Telegraph*, 5 December 1996.

18 Labour Whips do not enjoy the same status as Conservatives whips. The Conservatives Whips Office has been a training ground for those most likely to comprise tomorrow's party leaders; John Major's first frontbench post was as a government whip, and former Chief Whips such as Edward Heath, Willie Whitelaw and Francis Pym all went on to hold high office in the Conservative Party and in government. 'NCO's' rather than 'officer material', Labour Whips, often trade union MPs, have little chance of serving in a Labour Cabinet. With exceptions such as John Silkin, Ted Short and Donald Dewar, Chief Whips, such as William Whiteley, Herbert Bowden, Bob Mellish, Michael Cocks or Derek Foster, have not gone on to higher office.

19 Since the party leader ceased being chairman of the Parliamentary Labour Party the post has had little significance. Incumbents are usually worthy, well regarded centre-right figures such as Glenville Hall, Cledwyn Hughes, Jack Dortmund, Stan Orme, or Doug Hoyle, perennial backbenchers or former frontbenchers on their way out rather than up, with little ambition and less influence. While the only seriously anti-leadership figure to secure the post, Manny Shinwell, detested the party leader, Harold Wilson, and was an active participant in backbench intrigues against him, others have been more likely to make representations for the leadership to Labour MPs, rather than the other way round. The present holder, Clive Soley, is criticised for being a leadership cheerleader, speaking on behalf of the government in the news media and backing ministers in their infrequent disputes with backbenchers, but Soley makes no bones of being a fully paid-up leadership loyalist, claiming his concern for party unity is such he represents the views of critical or concerned backbenchers in private rather than in public.

20 Backbench dissent was most frequent in the 1974 Parliament. 40 MPs cast more than 50 dissenting votes in the 1974 Parliament, and 9 MPs cast over 100. In the 1978–79 session, 45 per cent of whipped divisions saw Labour MPs vote against the government.

21 Philip Norton, *Dissension in the House of Commons, 1974–79*, Oxford, Oxford University Press 1989.

22 Philip Norton and Philip Norton, *Blair's Bastards*, Hull, Centre for Legislative Studies 1996.

23 Eric Shaw, *Discipline and Discord in the Labour Party, op. cit.*

24 A recent example is that of the Labour MP Dennis Canavan. Denied the opportunity to stand for the Scottish Parliament in the constituency he had represented at Westminster since 1974, Canavan declared his intension to stand as an independent and was expelled from the party. At the election in May 1999, he trounced the official Labour candidate to take a seat in the Holyrood Parliament.

25 Major organised defections include: Ramsey MacDonald leading 14 MPs into the ranks of 'National Labour' on setting up the National

Government in August 1931; the Independent Labour Party disaffiliating in 1932 and five MPs ceasing to be Labour MPs; and 17 MPs, some 10 per cent of the Parliamentary party, defecting to the SDP led by Roy Jenkins, David Owen, Shirley Williams and Bill Rodgers in 1981–82. Noteworthy individual defections include: Oswald Mosley leaving to found the New Party in 1931; Ray Gunter resigning the Labour whip in 1972; Dick Taverne resigning from Parliament to fight and briefly win his Lincoln seat as an independent in 1973; Christopher Mayhew joining the Liberals in 1974; Jim Sillars and John Robertson defecting to found the Scottish Labour Party in 1976; Reg Prentice leaving the Labour Cabinet to join the Conservatives in 1977; and Dick Douglas joining the SNP in 1991.

26 Angelo Panebianco argues that party memberships have been replaced as the cornerstone of party organisations by powerful internal interest groups, foremost of which will be a pre-eminent leadership able to determine programme and strategy through a cadre of powerful electoral-professional organisers, all of whom are loyal, first and foremost, to the party leader. Panebianco, *Political Parties*, Cambridge, Cambridge University Press, 1988.

27 Critics can become loyalists: In the 1974 Parliament, Neil Kinnock, a left-wing backbencher yet to re-invent himself as the keen disciplinarian he became when leader, frequently voted against the Labour government, helping propel himself to prominence within the party and securing a place on the NEC in 1978 alongside other more consistent Parliamentary rebels such as Eric Heffer and Dennis Skinner.

28 In the late 1970s and early 1980s, the extra-parliamentary left successfully pursued two constitutional reforms intended to fetter the power of the Parliamentary leadership: the re-selection of Labour MPs each Parliament and the election of the leader and the deputy leader under a wider electoral franchise beyond that of Labour MPs. Yet, re-selection did nothing to alter the political composition of the Parliamentary party, disappointing radical activists who hoped right-wing MPs could be replaced with left-wing alternatives. The wider franchise under which the Labour leader is elected ultimately benefited not Tony Benn as was intended, but Neil Kinnock, and, in time, Tony Blair: '[T]he party leader's power has been greatly enhanced by the fact he is chosen by the electoral college and not just the PLP. This has allowed Kinnock, Smith and Blair to claim their views have strong support in all sections of the party.' Stark, *Choosing the Leader, op. cit.* p.66.

Crimes and Misdemeanours: Managing Dissent in the Twentieth and Twenty-First Century Labour Party

Tim Bale

Let me make something clear at the start. If the charge is wanting our party to be successful and our government to continue concentrating all its energy on delivering our promises, then I plead guilty. And if that means wanting us to be a modern, disciplined party with a strong centre, I'd like that offence to be taken into account as well....Of course the Tories and the media preferred it when the Labour Party was divided, disunited and incapable of putting over a coherent case to the people. I am sorry to disappoint them; but those days are gone, and they are not coming back. Tony Blair, *The Independent*, 20 November 1998.

Throughout the 20th century, European parties of the left have had to deal with the tension between their leaderships' need for freedom of manoeuvre and their activists' insistence that those leaders display continued commitment to party democracy and party principles. Arguably, this tension has grown as an increasingly volatile electoral, parliamentary and economic environment has put an even greater premium on leadership flexibility.[1] Things are also worse because media coverage of politics has grown ever more obsessed with intraparty splits and spats. These, after all, are conflicts supposedly rooted in the ideological zeal of increasingly eloquent and resourceful party activists, on the one hand, and, on the other, in the disciplinary zeal of leaders now equipped with technology that enables them to police and punish dissent as never before.

The British Labour Party is no different from its continental counterparts in facing such tension. Perhaps, indeed, it is one of the parties most prone to it: its constitutional development has not kept pace with the gradual accretion of power to its parliamentary leaders to which its trade union backers have largely given their consent.[2] This combination of *de facto* centralisation and a still nominally confederal structure would have been problematic enough on its own. But things have been made even more awkward by the fact that the Labour Party has traditionally fought shy of establishing a sufficiently explicit 'core body of principles, setting the fundamental principles of the party, which could thereby define the outer limits of the ideologically permissible'.[3]

In short, both Labour's foundations and its external walls have historically been pretty shaky, and this has rendered its ongoing efforts to cope with the inevitable tension between leaders and followers particularly difficult. Certainly pronouncements that such tension has somehow been finally resolved in favour of one side or the other are nothing new and are highly likely to be proved wrong almost as soon they are made. Today's media headlines provide an instructive paradox: they present an image of increasing central control of the party by the leadership at the same time as uncovering incidents aplenty that would appear to undermine the image. For the suspicious this might point to a leadership both highly skilled in media manipulation and keen to legitimise its new disciplinary apparatus. More likely, though, it points to something more mundane but also more important – namely that the potential for tension between sections of a political party is ever-present, but (and also because) the nature of that tension and its exact location will change over time.

Labour's problems date from the moment of its conception. The agreement in February 1900 between the TUC and socialist and co-operative societies to which the party owed its existence committed the partners to establish 'a distinct Labour group in Parliament, who shall have their own whips, and agree upon their policy'. The autonomy of the Parliamentary Labour Party (PLP), if not guaranteed, was thereby legitimised. The fact that it was actually exercised almost from the outset soon led to trouble. From 1906 onwards there was a move on the part of some ordinary and affiliated members, worried that those at Westminster were a little too cosy with their Liberal counterparts, to insist that they act as delegates of the party rather than representatives of their constituents. This was vigorously resisted, yet only partly resolved in 1907 by a compromise that gave conference responsibility for party policy but guaranteed that Labour MPs should be able to decide on how to pursue its timing, priority and implementation. The compromise, however, has to be seen in the long-term less as a solution than as an excuse or a euphemism for one: as Shaw stresses, conceptions of the relationship between the parliamentary and extra parliamentary party have 'varied over time', and have 'never been definitively resolved', thereby ensuring that 'endemic tensions [have] frequently enveloped' not only Labour's policy but its policy making.[4]

To some extent, however, these early tensions were temporarily obscured by the emergence of the charismatic Ramsey MacDonald as Labour's leader. Things were also made easier by the fact that for over a decade, despite the increasing electoral strength of the party, Labour MPs were not called on to make actual governmental decisions rather than oppositional stands. Even when the situation changed with the brief occupation of office by the first, largely ineffectual, Labour government of 1924, extra parliamentary recriminations, if not absent, were rather muted. MacDonald was able to point to the administration's minority status and also deflect blame for its defeat onto the right wing media's focus on the forged Zinoviev letter. In any case, those trade unionists who might have rendered criticisms of the political leadership's timidity more effective were soon distracted and chastened by their own rather more direct defeat at the hands of capital in the General Strike of 1926.[5]

They were also increasingly preoccupied by the perceived need to do something about the 'Red Menace' within both their own ranks and, by extension, those of the Labour Party. The British Communist Party (CPGB) first applied for affiliation to Labour in the year of its formation, 1920, but this and a further application were both rejected by Labour's National Executive Committee (NEC). The NEC, partly under the influence of its union representatives, was becoming steadily more concerned about the presence of Communists not only in the constituencies but also in its own parliamentary ranks. At the 1924 conference it was decided to ban Communists from individual membership of the party. In the following five years, the NEC took steps to disband and reconstitute local parties that it regarded as either run by, or soft on, CP members, who at the time were under Comintern instructions to make common cause with (if not necessarily to infiltrate) other left-wing movements.[6] The leadership, working through the NEC, also took the opportunity to exploit the willingness of some on Labour's left, and in particular the Independent Labour Party (ILP), to heed the calls for a 'popular front' in order to discredit them.

The party and union fight against Communist influence and infiltration, after gathering strength throughout the 1920s, culminated in 1929 in a major revision of Labour's constitution whereby the NEC's formal managerial authority was boosted, its regulatory powers were augmented and it was equipped with more potent disciplinary sanctions. After 1929 the NEC was given not only the power to interpret the party's rules, constitution and standing orders, but also the right – without prior approval by conference – to expel or block the candidature of individuals and declare ineligible for affiliation (i.e. 'proscribe') organisations that, in its judgement, did not 'accept and conform to the Constitution, Programme, Principles and Policy of the Party'.[7] The NEC was also empowered to expel an MP who failed to act according to the Standing Orders of the PLP. This last development was to assume importance within less than a decade. It was of little relevance, however, when just two years later, in 1931, the Labour Party was engulfed by the most serious political crisis to have hit it since its birth.

Leadership is always a ´thorny issue in parties of the egalitarian left and Labour proved to be no exception, especially early on in its life. It took the fledgling PLP over a decade before it felt able to commit itself to the leadership of one man, Ramsey MacDonald – only for that same man, as Prime Minister in 1931, to perpetrate an act of betrayal so breathtaking that it was to turn the inherent ambivalence towards leaders felt by many socialists into outright and long-lasting distrust. On the other hand, the events of 1931, although they were in part responsible for stalling 'the forward March of Labour' for a decade, did at least show that the movement – both party and unions – were bigger than any one man. MacDonald's 'National Labour' attracted only a handful of MPs beside the other Cabinet members who had jumped ship, and no constituency party or trade union joined them. Indeed, one of the most significant outcomes of the debacle of 1931 was a strengthening of the relationship between the industrial and the political wings of the Labour movement. The former – personified by Ernest Bevin – was determined to ensure, through union majorities on the revivified National Joint Council (later the NCL), that the party would never again enter office so ill-equipped in terms of both policy and institutionally-rooted support.

Bevin's efforts were made easier by the fact that the ILP chose in 1932 to disaffiliate from the Labour Party in disgust. Many left wingers preferred to stick with the latter rather than follow the former into the political wilderness, but they did not necessarily have an easy time of it – particularly if they were active in the Socialist League that 'aimed to replicate the role of the 'old' ILP within the Labour Party, and be a force for radicalism and not for disloyalty'.[8] Such hopes were dashed by the increasing grip of the trade unions – and therefore the union ethos of discipline, loyalty and majority rule – on the party and by the untimely reconversion of the CPGB to the popular front policy that saw so many who chose to co-operate with it branded 'fellow-travellers'. The fruit of the policy, the so-called 'Unity Campaign' that was launched in 1937 and included both the ILP and the Socialist League, led swiftly to the voluntary dissolution of the latter in the face of a decision by the NEC to disaffiliate it. This did not, though, prevent some of its leading lights continuing to argue for 'anti-fascist' and 'anti-war' co-operation with other Leftists. It is well known that in 1939 this argument saw both Stafford Cripps and Aneurin Bevan expelled from the party. What is less often recalled is that both expulsions were heavily supported by delegates to that year's annual conference who not only felt that alignments with more extreme groups would do Labour no good, but also frowned on the two's obvious incapacity to abide by majority decisions.[9]

The war years served to increase the grip of the leadership on the party. With regard to the extra-parliamentary party the process began with the NEC taking the opportunity to expel individuals and disband CLPs whose defence of the indefensible (namely the Nazi-Soviet pact and the invasion of Finland) marked them out as 'fellow travellers' of Communism. Meanwhile at Westminster, criticism of the government, of which Labour was of course a powerful part, was muted. One of the few exceptions was the decision of almost one hundred Labour MPs in February 1943 to call a Commons vote and defy the official whip in support of the party's campaign for implementation of the Beveridge report on the welfare state. Interestingly, there was little long-term fall-out from this rebellion: indeed one of its leaders, the readmitted Bevan, went on to become a crucial part of the postwar Attlee government. This was due partly to the fact that numbers always provide protection for dissidents, but mostly to the fact that, by allowing the party to appear at once responsible and radical, the rebellion allowed Labour to have its cake and eat it too.

It is still widely assumed that the Attlee government between 1945 and 1951 suffered relatively little from the strife that became characteristic of later Labour administrations. According to this orthodoxy, any problems in parliament were largely caused by rogue individuals on either the extreme right or (pro-Soviet) left of the PLP. Alfred Edwards, expelled for his vehement opposition to the nationalisation of steel and the right to strike, and John Platts-Mills, expelled for persistent dissidence on both domestic and foreign policy, are often offered as paradigmatic examples. These are then counterposed with the suspension of the disciplinary code covering MPs, the PLP's standing orders, for the duration of the government, and with the fact that the government (bolstered by trade union support) not only delivered on a radical agenda, but also took care to involve backbenchers in its work via various liaison committees.[10]

While this picture is by no means a total misrepresentation, it is in danger of understating the extent and the depth of dissent during the period, particularly after 1949. The government was more than aware of the criticism that its policy (and in particular its foreign policy) attracted both inside and outside Parliament – and of the links between critics in the two locations, especially after the resignations from Cabinet of Wilson and Bevan in 1951. It also took tentative – though largely unsuccessful – steps to mute that criticism by, for instance, attempting to disrupt the communication between constituencies over resolutions to the annual conference. True, there was considerable comfort in the fact that those actively critical of the government 'saw themselves as the keepers of Labour's conscience rather than as an alternative leadership of their party'.[11] Nevertheless, that there was 'a significant level of protest and alienation'[12] during the Attlee era is undeniable and helps to explain the problems of the 1950s which would otherwise seem to come out of nowhere.

Open factional war was declared almost as soon as Labour lost office in 1951 because it had already been going on for sometime, just less publicly. Only this explains the reimposition of the PLP's Standing Orders (and in particular the threat of withdrawal of the whip for failing to stand by majority decisions of the PLP meeting) in the spring of 1952, following a vote on German rearmament that might otherwise have been seen as an isolated incident. And only this explains why the left was able to mount a campaign that saw it capture six out of the NEC's seven constituency seats at the Morecombe conference later on in the same year – a move that threatened (though as yet that was all) the NEC's *de facto* status as 'the extra parliamentary arm of the Cabinet' or Shadow Cabinet (known then as the 'Parliamentary Committee).[13] Some were capable of realising that this victory for the left would prove less than unalloyed since the new standard bearers were bound to be 'compromised to some extent through their formal responsibility for the pronouncements of a body where they were in a minority'.[14] For those with hotter heads, however, the result was a call to arms. The sweeping away of stalwarts who had long provided a crucial overlap between Cabinet and NEC, such as Morrison and Dalton, provoked Labour's future leader, Hugh Gaitskell, into an intemperate attack on the supposedly pro-Communist left in the Labour Party. It also prompted the overwhelmingly centrist and right-wing PLP to expressly prohibit, at Attlee's reluctant request, the existence of any organised faction within its ranks, thereby putting an end to some of the more ambitious projects of the so-called Bevanite MPs.

But while the leadership could get such disciplinary measures passed, it could only do so in a period of perceived crisis and by making them an issue of confidence. Even then, most of the measures involved more compromise than is often acknowledged because only a very few MPs were keen to provide the leadership with powers whose use might result in a full-blown split or at least affect them personally if ever they were to rebel.[15] The existence of this temperate, tolerant rump helps explain how Bevan was able to secure sufficient support from his colleagues at Westminster to scrape into the Shadow Cabinet. But Bevan – consumed as he was by his political convictions, his personal ambitions to beat Morrison and Gaitskell to the leadership, and by the feeling that the mass party was behind him – spurned any opportunity thus given to him to mend fences. In April 1954 he walked out of the Shadow Cabinet over a vote on defence co-operation with the USA in South East Asia (only to have his place taken by someone he regarded as very much a lieutenant, Harold Wilson) – disloyalty which no doubt contributed to Bevan's trouncing at the hands of Gaitskell when the two competed later on in the year for the post of Labour Party Treasurer. Indeed that result merely confirmed what many had known for years. The most powerful trade union leaders – and in particular Arthur Deakin of the Transport Workers – despised Bevan, believing his supporters were (or were little better than) the communist unionists they themselves had to deal with, and were looking for an opportunity to take the troublesome Welshman out of Labour politics altogether.

They got their chance in the spring of 1955 when Bevan publicly taunted Attlee over the Shadow Cabinet's acceptance of the Conservative government's plans to manufacture Britain's own hydrogen bomb, and then led a backbench revolt on the issue. Bounced by a Shadow Cabinet threat to resign unless backed, the PLP narrowly voted to withdraw the whip from Bevan and to order him to appear before the NEC to explain his conduct – a process from which Bevan was lucky to escape without expulsion.[16] Following this incident, the general election defeat of the same year, and his overwhelming defeat by Gaitskell in the race to replace Attlee, Bevan settled down in to playing (at least in public) a loyal second fiddle to his nemesis – a role he first took on when at the Brighton conference in 1957 he laid into the 'emotional spasm' that was unilateralism, and a part he continued to play until his death in 1960. Certainly Bevan had little time for Victory for Socialism, the left-wing ginger group that for a few years after 1956 attempted (with limited success and even fewer organisational resources) to revive Bevanism and preach unilateralism in the constituency parties

Transport House and the NEC were concerned about Victory for Socialism – but only to the extent of keeping an eye on it and circulating (presumably fairly effective) warnings that it would act should there be any evidence that VFS intended, for instance, to set up branches. Meanwhile, however, it turned a blind eye to local parties in cities like Liverpool and Glasgow which combined right wing attitudes with practices and habits that were anything but inclusive and democratic. Indeed, if they and the NEC did interfere in local politics, it was normally (as with MPs) to protect councillors being disciplined (for example, by deselection) by local parties angry that they had departed from 'left-wing' established policy or principles; in Nottingham in the 1960s they even went so far as to try to discipline and expel some local party members, including Ken Coates.[17] At the same time they also took no action whatsoever against the Campaign for Democratic Socialism (CDS), founded in 1960 to support Gaitskell's call to 'fight, fight and fight again' to save Labour from the unilateralists who had proved victorious at the conference that year. This was despite the fact that the CDS was clearly an organisation dedicated to the promotion not just of ideas but also party candidates and office holders. It is hard to believe that had VFS behaved in the same way, the leadership would have been so lenient.[18]

True, the reach of Transport House, run until well into the 1960s by the dedicatedly right-wing Sara Barker and Morgan Philips, can be overstated: as Shaw emphasises, the centre was inevitably constrained by such things as 'the scarcity of organisational resources, the jealous defence of trade union prerogatives, the reliance upon voluntary electoral labour in single-member constituencies and the strength of particularistic sentiments in the provinces'.[19] There is no doubt, however, that party officials both in London and in the regional centres exercised a powerful degree of pre-emptive control, particularly in the crucial area of candidate selection. They also supported (though not it must be said with much manpower or money) attempts to enforce the so-called 'Proscribed List' of organisations declared ineligible for affiliation to the Labour Party. 1962, for instance, saw the NEC try to expel a number of prominent unilateralists, including Bertrand Russell, only to find that its power to do so was in fact limited both by party opinion and by its own constitution, which restricted such action to members (as opposed to just associates) of proscribed organisations.[20] Partly as a result, the Proscribed List fell into desuetude long before it was formally abolished in 1973.

The 1960s began badly for Labour, especially at Westminster. Although Bevan had persuaded his Shadow Cabinet colleagues to suspend Standing Orders in a spirit of unity (they were replaced by a Code of Conduct), the spring of 1961 saw five MPs, including Michael Foot, being deprived of the Labour whip (for which read expulsion from the PLP) after a vote against the defence estimates – action which was followed in December by the reinstatement of Standing Orders. Whether this had much to do with the tight discipline demonstrated by Labour backbenchers between the party's wafer-thin election victory of 1964 and the election of 1966 is, however, a moot point. The sheer paucity of Wilson's majority in any case almost guaranteed that even the most rebellious MP (on the left at least) would pull back from the brink of action that might endanger the life of the government.

The 1966 general election gave Labour both a huge parliamentary majority and a huge disciplinary headache.[21] Rebellious behaviour increased with both the occupation of office and the size of majority, in keeping with the trend for the Labour Party between 1945 and 1974 (when the second part of the correlation broke down).[22] But it was not just the sheer size of the new intake that was important. It was also a question of its perceived characteristics. The new members were younger, better educated, more impatient and more assertive. They were therefore vulnerable, once they discovered how little real influence they had, to rapid disillusionment and possibly recruitment by the left, whose attitudes on issues like race, colonialism and moral issues they shared. Moreover, many were surprised to be elected in the first place, knew they were unlikely to be elected in the same constituency at the next election, and were well aware that they would need to make a name for themselves in order to boost their chances of selection for a safer seat next time around. Wilson's solution was to reject the pleas of traditionalists for a return to the hierarchical certainties of Standing Orders and instead to plump for a new, 'looser rein'.[23] This would be held by Dick Crossman as Leader of the House, John Silkin as Chief Whip, and, to a lesser extent, by Douglas Houghton, who replaced 'that bad tempered antique' Manny Shinwell as Chairman of the PLP.[24]

In fact, is all too easy to exaggerate the extent to which the 'old regime' played by the book rather than relying on more informal, discretionary, and often more manipulative, means.[25] By the same token, it is easy to overdo the liberalism of the liberal regime. Actually, the latter was still at heart part of a managerial strategy. It was just that the incorporation of what was seen to be a greater variety of voices was to be achieved not by giving orders to follow the leader, but by increasing the extent of specialisation and division of function within the PLP. The new regime was indeed characterised by increasing tolerance of dissent, but only in the sense that the number of reserve areas in which 'conscience' would be allowed to hold sway was broadened at the discretion of the leadership in return for loyalty when it really mattered.

At first, the regime seemed to prove its worth as a number of backbench rebellions, notably on defence, foreign and incomes policy passed off without seeming to seriously damage either party or government. Underneath, however, the supposed leniency of Silkin and Crossman was fuelling resentment not just among ministers like Healey, Crosland and Jenkins, but also amongst those backbenchers who routinely backed the government and sometimes suffered for it in their constituencies. This resentment, combined with Harold Wilson's need to demonstrate his grip on both the party and the economy, led in early 1968 to a full-blown disciplinary crisis when, following a large rebellion against a package of spending cuts designed to support sterling at its new (devalued) level, Silkin attempted to summarily suspend the rebels from all PLP activities.[26] After a period of turmoil the move was only narrowly approved by the PLP, which a few weeks later went on to approve – again not without argument – a new Code of Conduct. The new Code was important not just because it the sanction of suspension allowed the PLP to administer what Crossman called 'something between a mild rebuke and "capital punishment"', but also because it contained the first ever reference within the rules of the PLP to a Labour *government*, making it crystal clear that abstention from a vote of confidence in that government was 'a serious offence with no excuses or concessions to conscience'. It also clearly signalled that, however liberal the regime, it would not tolerate repeated dissent and that the latter would end in expulsion.

The risk of being forced into secession from the PLP was not, of course, one which many members of the left-wing Tribune Group wished to court. Nor of course, it must be said, was it one which – in their calmer moments – many in the leadership looked forward to. Even if they managed to secure the expulsion of the

PLP's left-wingers, they could not rely on the NEC expelling them from the party and/or withdrawing its endorsement from such a large group of sitting MPs at the next election – especially when those MPs were backed by their constituency parties. Labour's majority from the 1966 was huge; but it was likely to be lost or at best severely reduced next time around; the continued PLP membership of left-wingers in rock-solid seats was therefore vital. In any case, as the climb-down over its proposed new settlement for industrial relations, *In Place of Strife*, demonstrated, the government could no longer rely on those it had previously thought of as loyalists.

Outside Parliament in the late 1960s the issue for the party was not so much one of discipline as staunching the outflow of ordinary, often very moderate, members disillusioned by the government's reneging on so many promises.[27] This development, because it rendered increasingly moribund constituency organisations ripe for take-over by more radical rank and filers, was (as we shall see) to have considerable long-term implications. Something else that had equally important long-term implications was the so-called Pembroke judgement, originating from the expulsion of maverick right-wing MP Desmond Donelly. Following the judgement, the NEC was forced into having to give dissident CLPs or individuals the right to a hearing by an unbiased tribunal, knowing that if due process and natural justice were not followed its rulings could be contested in the civil courts.[28] The other significant shift was at Transport House where Len Williams and Sara Barker at last gave way to fresher, rather more liberal, faces, including Ron Hayward, who became National Agent and then General Secretary.

Underneath Prime Minister Harold Wilson's rhetorical insistence that 'the government must govern', profound changes were occurring. These changes would threaten the 'structure of integrated organisational control which enabled the parliamentary leadership to amass the powers that were constitutionally divided amongst a range of institutions', but which actually 'rested to a significant degree on contingent factors which might not always be present'.[29] By the late 1960s, as an increasingly desperate Labour leadership contrived to alienate almost all sections of the movement, there were no longer 'concurrent majorities in virtually all key institutions (the NEC, the ... Cabinet, the PLP, the major unions, conference)', nor indeed was there a consensus on the general ideological or policy direction of the party.[30] Perhaps this situation could have continued, although hardly without conflict, had Labour won an unprecedented third term. Unfortunately, of course, it did not.

Until the general election defeat of 1970, the Labour right had generally been able to use its grip on the key components of the party's structures to discipline the left. Now, though, the tables were turning as the latter, exploiting disenchantment with Labour's performance in office, began to win control of major trade unions. The left's clout on the NEC and its block votes at conference were used to influence policy, resulting, for example, in the impossibly radical *Labour's Programme 1973*. They were also used to soften the sanctions handed out to dissenters, and press for organisational change along the lines of that advocated by internal pressure groups like the Campaign for Labour Party Democracy (CLPD). Such change took a decade or so to come about, and the leadership's relationship with the unions naturally improved in the face of Ted Heath's 1971 Industrial Relations Act. But the left was at least able to ensure that the party's machine and procedures were not used either to promote the interests of right wing candidates or MPs above those of members active in the campaign for constitutional change.[31] It was also able, in 1973, to persuade the NEC symbolically to abolish the Proscribed List. This last move made little substantive difference at first,[32] but arguably rendered the party more vulnerable to entryism by other organisations in years to come.

Because the number of rank and file members fell precipitately from the late 1960s, left wing activists found it easier in the early 1970s to take control of CLPs and therefore to ensure a left-wing majority in the National Executive's constituency section. As a result, the NEC, when on the same side as the trade unions, was to cause the 1974–79 Labour government a great deal of trouble. Even before that government assumed office, however, a feeling took hold that the only way to break out of the pattern whereby moderate parliamentarians simply ignored a radical manifesto was to hold them properly to account.[33] In 1973, the local party in Lincoln refused to readopt Dick Taverne, who, having failed in his appeal to the NEC, promptly fought a by-election in protest and – most unusually in British politics – achieved an embarrassing victory as an independent.[34] In 1975 local party members attempted (in the end successfully) to remove a Labour Minister, Reg Prentice (who later crossed the floor to become a Conservative). Such incidents may have been rare, yet they reflected a growth in support for the kind of mandatory reselection procedure that was later proposed (though defeated) at Labour's 1978 conference. Many MPs –

especially on the social democratic right of the party – began to fear for their political careers: even if they managed to survive the loss of the coming general election, they risked being deprived even of the chance to stand at the next one.

The eventual defection of the social democrats, of course, occurred only once the left was able to move on to the offensive after the defeat of 1979. The movement leading up to the split, however, predated this power-shift. Aside from the left's growing power in the constituencies, things began to fall apart in Parliament even before Labour re-entered government in 1974. Problems began in earnest as Labour struggled with the question of Europe. In October 1971, those who were to become the 'Gang of Four' led a large rebellion (69 voting against the Labour whip and 20 abstaining in defiance of it) in support of Heath's agreement to join the EEC, with Roy Jenkins almost forfeiting his deputy leadership post as a result. Six months later Jenkins and three others did resign from the frontbench in disgust at Wilson's decision to make a referendum on Britain's membership Labour policy, though Jenkins returned to the Shadow Cabinet in October 1973 agreeing to abide by the plan. The eventual outcome of the process – a huge public majority to stay in on renegotiated terms in June 1975 – did little to heal the divide. Indeed the highly unusual 'agreement to differ', which allowed both front and backbench politicians from the same party to argue on one side or another, may well have given Jenkins and others a taste for 'breaking the mould'.

Labour's parliamentary disciplinary problems in the 1970s were not, unsurprisingly, confined to Europe. Indeed the 1974–79 government had to contend with one of the most fractious parliaments in British political history. Major and minor rebellions occurred on a bewildering variety of issues, but both Wilson and Callaghan found themselves virtually powerless to act since their majorities were so low as to rule out expulsion or even other, lesser sanctions.[35] Callaghan, determined not to let public sector wages rip once the economy began to improve after a period of anti-inflationary austerity, also proved incapable of preventing the collapse of the 'social contract' strategy as trade unionists on the ground began defying not just the pleas of Michael Foot (the government's industrial relations Mr Fixit) but also their very own leaders. The resultant 'Winter of Discontent' helped ensure Labour's defeat at the 1979 general election and ushered in a period of ideological and institutional infighting against which all the party's previous disciplinary struggles – especially outside parliament – were to pale in comparison.

Loss of office by a Labour government had of course led to recriminations before. This time, however, the left in particular pursued a 'don't get mad, get even' strategy – an approach made all the more possible by the influence of figures like Tony Benn and Eric Heffer on the NEC. At the 1979 and 1980 conferences left wingers exploited both constituency and union frustration with the leadership to push through – albeit on very narrow majorities – the mandatory reselection of sitting MPs and an electoral college system for the party's leadership elections. The effect of the latter can be overstated.[36] But the impact of the former – for a while and psychologically at least – was quite profound. The left liked the system *per se*, but also because it vested control of the process (like most things at CLP level) in constituency General Management Committees. According to the common wisdom, GMCs were chock full of activists who had joined the party comparatively recently and, as a result of their educational and occupational backgrounds, were unsocialised in the 'traditional labourist norms of loyalty and solidarity'.[37] Left ascendancy was apparently assured.

Yet the left of the Labour Party ended the 1980s not just in a weaker position than it had begun them, but in perhaps in its worst shape ever. In part this was because it suffered a backlash from the bitterly divisive deputy leadership battle between Benn and Healey. And in part it was because Labour's parliamentary heavyweights were able to blame the party's catastrophic general election defeat in 1983 not on themselves but on a manifesto that embodied so many of the left's long-cherished goals – unilateralism, EC withdrawal, and a protected, state-enhanced economy. But it was also because the left, as much through its own desperation to build an anti-Thatcherite 'popular front' as its opponents' tactics, allowed itself (in an echo of the 1930s) to become tarred with the same brush as an organisation that did pose a genuine threat to the institutional and ideological integrity of the Labour Party – the Militant Tendency.

Militant, despite its claim that it was simply a ginger group with its own newspaper, was a Trotskyite entryist organisation intent on using the Labour Party as at the very least a vehicle at least for publicity, if not full-blown power. While it came nowhere near the latter – at least on a national level – its antics in a handful of CLPs and Labour-held local authorities ensured it a great deal of the former. This was due partly to the left-wing NEC's refusal to back constituencies and organisers who tried to combat what they saw as infiltration,[38] but mostly to the hunger displayed by Conservative tabloid newspapers for 'loony left' stories which would discredit Labour as a whole. This tactic proved incredibly effective at by elections in Bermondsey (1983) and Greenwich (1987) when local party activists exercised their independence from the leadership by selecting so-called 'hard-left' candidates – and in the first case were supported to the hilt by an NEC seemingly oblivious to how badly such support undermined the already shaky authority of the party leader. Prior to the 1983 election, the Labour left's (and Michael Foot's) tolerance and commitment to pluralism,[39] as well as its fear of provoking a general witch-hunt, ensured that the party's NEC (moving rapidly rightward after the Benn-Healey deputy leadership contest) had to be content with proscribing the organisation and expelling only Militant's five-member 'editorial board'. Although these measures were, it should be noted, overwhelmingly supported by conference, the NEC could do no more – partly because the upcoming general election demanded unity and partly because it found itself stymied by judicial rulings. These rulings, particularly one which forced the NEC into humiliating climb-down on its plans to use the so-called Register to ban Militant, obliged it to act only within a strict interpretation of party rules and to ensure its procedures accorded with natural justice.[40]

Following the general election defeat of 1983, the case for further action, whatever the difficulties involved, became ever more pressing. It came in the shape both of procedural action and a public show of strength by a new leader. Neil Kinnock was desperate, firstly, to emphasise Labour's moderation and, secondly, to escape from the image of impotence created by his being caught between a rock and a hard place during the Miners' Strike. At the 1984 conference, Kinnock had suffered an embarrassing reverse when his proposal to introduce one-member-one-vote in order to offset the power of CLP activists in parliamentary selection procedures was rejected. At the 1985 annual conference, however, Kinnock launched a scathing attack on the Militant-inspired Liverpool city council, earning him plaudits in press and party alike. Following an investigation soon afterwards, the Liverpool District Labour Party was suspended by the NEC following an investigation pressed for by prominent soft-leftists like David Blunkett and trade unionists like NUPE's Tom Sawyer, all of whom were now convinced that their earlier attempts to mediate had been cynically manipulated by Militant. Then began a nationwide campaign to rid Labour once and for all of Militant. In Liverpool, the infamous Derek Hatton and other

Militant supporters were expelled from the party in the summer of 1986.

Things did not always go smoothly. The rooting out of Militant, indeed, imposed 'a considerable cost in scarce time, energy, and organisational and financial resources', not least because the leadership once again found itself up against legal restraints on its freedom to discipline its own members.[41] So serious were these that the party opted (at the 1986 annual conference that also backed the expulsions in Liverpool) to contract out the disciplinary functions of the full NEC to a newly established National Constitutional Committee. The NEC, on the other hand, was able to use its existing powers in both 1986 and 1987 to block the parliamentary candidatures of activists it considered beyond the pale.

In 1988 Tony Benn and Eric Heffer made a doomed leadership bid. By that time, however, both Militant and the non-entryist 'hard left' that had coalesced around CPLD and the Campaign Group of the PLP were severely weakened. This weakness was reinforced as it became apparent that the 'soft left' – the Labour Co-ordinating Committee, the (now milder) Tribune Group of the PLP and major NEC players like Blunkett, Meacher and Sawyer[42] – had moved towards those who argued that their more extremist counterparts were in fact an alien force that had no place in the party. By the late eighties, then, Kinnock had gained firm control of the NEC, had begun to shift the party towards policies which accepted the permanence of at least some of Margaret Thatcher's changes, and had even begun to undo the progress towards 'activist democracy' achieved by the left at the beginning of the eighties. The reselection of MPs, for instance, was no longer controlled by GMCs, and there was growing use of OMOV (one member one vote) for elections throughout the party.

This trend has continued and even accelerated throughout the 1990s. Indeed, if the modernisers – and paradoxically their most implacable left-wing opponents – are to be believed, the New Labour government exercises unparalleled party discipline. Apparently the leadership, and its machine located at Millbank opposite the Palace of Westminster, effectively controls not just the party's parliamentarians, but also the NEC and as a result both the official policy-making process and disciplinary machinery. It has also taken steps, we are told, to ensure that important new developments in British politics, such as Scottish and Welsh devolution, the increasing importance of Europe, and the election of a mayor for London, do not pose a threat to its position. Yet this picture merits some qualification. While the leadership, aware of the media's insatiable appetite for stories of internal splits, may indeed be keener than ever to suppress and punish dissent, tales of its total control tend to ignore the importance of sheer contingency and what are still some crucial constraints.

At Westminster there is understandable concern that the leadership is now using the *Excalibur* database that Labour so effectively deployed against the Conservatives in the run up to the 1997 general election in order to keep tabs on its own more outspoken, dissenting MPs. The Whips Office has also decided to send reports on troublesome MPs to their constituencies, the argument being that those MPs should be accountable for their behaviour to those who have the power to deselect them. The criteria for judging such behaviour – largely an MP's 'voting record' – is of course open to dispute. Few would object perhaps to CLPs being alerted to poor attendance, but the highlighting of incidences where the member has not voted the government's way is a worrying development for many – particularly on the left, with vocal dissenters like Alan Simpson and Diane Abbott singled out early on for this kind of attention. On the other hand, those who mistrust the leadership cannot have it both ways: another reform introduced is to insist on a one-member-one-vote constituency 'trigger' ballot before any contest which may involve the deselection of a sitting MP can even take place; traditionally this would have been seen as a ploy by the right to undo what the left worked so hard to achieve in the 1970s and early 1980s; now it may serve to protect left-wing MPs against 'loyalist' constituency activists. When it comes to selecting new candidates or reconsidering existing MPs, however, the new system, whereby the NEC vets all potential parliamentary candidates is clearly one way in which the leadership (as long as it controls the NEC) can ensure a future stream of ideologically acceptable, well-behaved MPs. True, CLPs are not obliged to choose from the panel drawn up by the NEC, but in such cases their choice will be interviewed by the NEC before being confirmed.[43]

Historically, rebellious Labour MPs had found it possible to cause further problems by getting themselves elected to the NEC and using it as a base with which to lend legitimacy and authority to their attacks on the leadership. To prevent this, the leadership successfully pushed through a reform to the composition of the NEC which barred MPs from standing for election to the Constituency section of the newly expanded NEC, though they could stand for the three places allocated to and voted on by the PLP. Despite a controversy surrounding the balloting arrangements for the latter section, candidates acceptable to the leadership ended up defeating long-time NEC stalwarts of the left like Dennis Skinner. In the constituency section, however, the new rules did not produce an entirely satisfactory result, with the leadership-backed 'Members First' slate gaining only two of the six CLP places, with the rest going to members of the 'Labour Grassroots Alliance'.[44] One of the latter was the very same Liz Davies who before the 1997 general election had been removed as Labour candidate for Leeds North East ostensibly for her refusal to give a guarantee that she would be bound by the Labour whip, but also for a long history of left-wing dissent – another example of the difficulty of excluding permanently anyone who combines an ability not to stray too far ideologically with both persistence and an excellent knowledge of the party's rule book.

In Scotland, the Labour government faces two challenges. First, it is having to deal with a legacy of dodgy dealings and in-fighting within Labour local authorities and groups that has extended itself even to Westminster. As in the past, the party has not found it as easy as it might have hoped to intervene in response to media calls for firm action, despite having redesigned its disciplinary procedures by creating the quasi-judicial National Constitutional Committee supposedly at arms-length from the NEC. Such procedures can do little where, as in North Lanarkshire for example, the majority local Labour Group clearly rejects the leadership's preference for the removal of certain members. Nor are such procedures necessarily legally more fireproof than their predecessors when it comes to legal challenge, as the case of Pat Kelly, Provost of Glasgow, has showed. And when they do eventually seem to have achieved the desired result, as in the case of Tommy Graham MP (whose alleged bad behaviour in a number of areas made him *persona non grata* at Westminster) that result can still take an inordinately long (and in media terms damaging) time to achieve. The origin of the Graham case, of course, lay not just in local Scottish politics, but in a scramble for seats among sitting MPs following boundary reorganisation. This does not bode well for the future if that future includes the introduction of mixed PR for Westminster elections: the consequent reduction in Scottish (and other) seats, especially if combined (as it surely will be) with a reduced vote for Labour seems likely to make competition between its parliamentarians for a constituency even more intense.

That competition could also include a fight for a place on a possible party list, which brings us naturally to Labour's second challenge in Scotland, namely the establishment of a devolved parliament. Even before its inauguration, Labour had to deal with myriad complaints and problems surrounding the composition of the party lists for the first Scottish election. According to opponents of the leadership, the decision to choose a closed-list system, where candidates and their rank order are decided by the party rather than the voter, was itself a means of establishing central control over the process. The vetting procedures used to draw up the lists and the order thereon, it was claimed, gave the leadership (via the 'Blairite' and trade union dominated Scottish and National Executives) the opportunity to stymie the ambitions of a range of 'usual suspects' (notably the left-wingers Dennis Canavan and Ian Davidson). The leadership's denials that it had any ulterior motives beyond amassing a slate of effective and presentable candidates were perhaps a little hard to swallow whole. However, it could justifiably point to the fact that other 'troublemakers' (such as John McAllion and Malcolm Chisolm) had made it through the initial filtering process in order to counter accusations that it, rather than regional party 'selectorates', was in complete control.

The media was not as interested in any similar problems in drawing up lists for the less influential Welsh assembly. It did, however, pick up on the alleged 'gagging' of anti-devolution MPs by threats of deselection and on the contest for the assembly's party leader. Interest in the latter was also given a new lease of life when the initial winner, the leadership-backed Ron Davies, was involved in a sex scandal. The affair re-opened not just the contest itself, but also a debate about the rules by which it should be conducted and the role of the trade unions in the internal workings of the party – a role which, for all the talk of 'an arms length relationship', continues to be both significant and highly supportive of the leadership.[45]

If the experience of other countries is anything to go by, however, in both the Scottish and Welsh cases, devolved representation is likely to lead to periodic conflicts between the government at Westminster and those newly installed in London, Edinburgh and Cardiff. Even if those governments are all Labour governments, the temptation to prove themselves autonomous and to demand a larger share of scarce resources is likely to prove strong, thereby adding a new dimension to intra-party dispute. Quite how these conflicts might take shape or be resolved is uncertain. Most obviously, they are likely to cover both policy – the Scottish Labour Party has already shown some impatience with Tony Blair's lack of socio-economic radicalism at a time when it feels outflanked on the left by the SNP[46] – and choice of coalition partners. Whatever, such conflicts are more than likely to open up a new dimension in intra-party discipline that will surely preoccupy both journalists and scholars in the future. The same can be said (and was perhaps more quickly and fully recognised by the politicians themselves) of the election of a London-wide executive mayor – hence the much-publicised efforts of the Labour leadership to prevent the man who seemed to be by far its most popular choice, the left-wing MP and former GLC leader, Ken Livingstone, from becoming the party's candidate in the capital.[47]

The trend, then, seems to be an attempt to prevent in the first place the occurrence of problems that may lead to disciplinary fall-out in the future. The leadership, following this trend, also seems to have come down hard and come down early on dissenters at the European level. First, it achieved the expulsion of MEPs Hugh Kerr and Ken Coates, both of whom were instrumental in a front-page newspaper advertisement that challenged Tony Blair's plans to change Clause IV. Second, it ensured that the new proportional system of election to the European Parliament would involve closed lists to be drawn up – once again – by the NEC. Despite the fact that this process has helped ensure that none of the signers of the Clause IV ad. made it through, it is still easy to imagine a range of potential conflicts occurring between the party's leadership in London and its representatives at Strasbourg as the European Parliament gains more power and the Labour contingent becomes ever more closely integrated with the transnational party groups that are slowly but surely taking on a more meaningful identity.[48] Already Labour MEPs are finding themselves cross pressured: many, for example, were clearly unhappy in late 1998 and early 1999 about being pushed, apparently on the orders of the Westminster leadership and against their better judgement, not to support motions censuring the European Commission – a course of inaction which then caused considerable embarrassment when the Commission soon afterwards resigned *en masse* in the face of a damning independent investigation into its financial and administrative shortcomings.

Developments in British and European democracy, therefore, provide new arenas for the perennial tension between leaders and led to express itself. And even if they did not, it would be a brave analyst indeed who, having examined the disciplinary ups and downs of Labour's first century, predicted a new millennium of plain sailing at Westminster and in the extra-parliamentary party. The party's leader at the end of that century and at the beginning of that millennium, Tony Blair, will of course continue to talk tough, reminding his troops that sloppy behaviour and picky introversion were the cause of the party's problems in the past and could still undo it in the future. And doubtless there will be no shortage of insiders and outsiders lining up to declare the triumph of 'modernisation'. In support of their claim they will cite not just the expanded disciplinary apparatus and selection powers of the leadership but also the constitutional reforms of the 1990s – including of course the change to Clause IV – as evidence that the party has finally adapted its rules to its practice and developed the ideological litmus test that for too long it lacked.

But all this is surely questionable. Consider the following: just before the 1997 election the PLP agreed a new 'code of conduct' prohibiting an MP from doing anything which 'brings the party into disrepute' – but only after passing the left wing Campaign Group's amendment (see 'Labour left softens new code', *Guardian*, 5 December 1996) that this 'shall not be interpreted in such a way as to stifle democratic debate on policy matters or weaken the spirit of tolerance and respect referred to in Clause Four of the [new] Labour Party Constitution'! This kind of human ingenuity, and the ever present power of 'events, dear boy, events', mean that reports of the death of dissent are much exaggerated. This is true for the party in the country and the party in Parliament, the initial quiescence of which should by no means be taken as a sign of things not to come.[49]

However, in refusing to buy too easily into the talk of leadership triumph, we should be careful not to underplay the potential impact of one of the wider constitutional changes already identified as altering the terms under which intra-party politics is conducted. If some kind of proportional electoral system is introduced for elections to Westminster, the British party system may well undergo, if not transformation, then at least significant reordering. On the right of the Labour Party there has long existed a feeling – normally articulated only in private and at times of extreme pressure in government – that the argument with the left needs to be 'sorted out' once and for all. For reasons described above, the current electoral system and the resulting parliamentary composition of the party makes this wishful thinking – unless of course one takes the long-term view that changes in selection procedures will finally so alter that composition that the left will disappear from the bottom up. Those wanting a swifter solution, however, may look to PR to precipitate the inevitable.[50]

As the experience of other countries (for example, New Zealand) shows, moves to a proportional system open up a newly viable political space into which those politicians and voters discontented with their old parties can move. If dissent *is* finally to disappear as a significant feature of Labour Party politics in Britain, its disappearance may be precipitated by the voluntary departure of the dissenters rather than by their suppression or expulsion by the leadership. Given the combination of Mr Blair's evident sensitivity to accusations of control-freakery and his deserved reputation for strategic brilliance, any apparently incidental departure of the left following a move to proportional representation may actually be all part of 'the project'.

Notes

1   Otto Kirchheimer, 'The Transformation of the Western European Party Systems', in J. LaPalombara and M. Weiner (eds.), *Political Parties and Political Development*, Princeton: Princeton University Press, 1966.

2   See Eric Shaw, *Discipline and Discord in the Labour Party: the Politics of Managerial Control in the Labour Party, 1951–1987*, Manchester: Manchester University Press, 1988. The author acknowledges his debt to Dr Shaw's pioneering work in this area and would like to thank him for his comments on an earlier version of this chapter. He would also like to thank Ann Wilson for help with proof reading.

3   See Shaw, *Discipline and Discord*, pp. 233–4.

4   Eric Shaw, *The Labour Party Since 1945. Old Labour: New Labour*, Oxford: Blackwell, p.59.

5   Andrew Thorpe, *A History of the British Labour Party*, London: Macmillan, pp.60–1.

6   According to Eric Shaw (*Discipline and Discord*, p.15) some 27 local party organisations were disaffiliated between 1926 and 1929.

7   Shaw, *Discipline and Discord*, pp. 15–19.

8   Thorpe, *History of the British Labour Party*, p.81.

9   Labour's annual conference in 1934 declared the NEC had the right to expel activists on the grounds purely of association with proscribed groups; strictly speaking, however, the constitutional position remained one of the right to expel members of such groups (see Shaw, *Discipline and Discord*, pp. 23).

10 Thorpe, *History of the British Labour Party*, pp.115–117.

11 Jonathan Schneer, *Labour's Conscience: the Labour Left, 1945–51*, Boston: Unwin Hyman, 1988, p.222.

12 Schneer, *Labour's Conscience*, p.164.

13 Shaw, *Labour Party since 1945*, p.59.

14 David Howell, *British Social Democracy: a Study in Development and Decay* (London: Croom Helm, 1981), p.184.

15 Howell, *British Social Democracy*, p.183.

16 Shaw, *Labour Party since 1945*, p.61–2.

17 See below and also Shaw *Discipline and Discord*, pp.70–71, 83–88, 95.

18 See Shaw, *Discipline and Discord*, pp. 53–55.

19 Shaw, *Discipline and Discord*, pp. 295.

20 Shaw, *Discipline and Discord*, pp. 57– 61.

21 When, just after the election, Wilson was interrupted by a visitor while practising his putting at Chequers and asked 'How's your handicap?', the Prime Minister is said to have replied (playing on the increase in his parliamentary majority) 'Gone up from three to ninety-seven.' See *Philip Ziegler, Wilson: the Authorized Life* (London: Weidenfeld and Nicolson, 1993), p.248.

22 Philip Cowley and Philip Norton, *Blair's Bastards: Discontent within the Parliamentary Labour Party* (Hull: Research Papers in Legislative Studies – 1/96), p.5.

23 Ted Short, *Whip to Wilson* (London: Macdonald, 1989), p.254–5.

24 Peter Slowe, *Manny Shinwell: an Authorized Biography* (London: Pluto Press, 1993) , p.281

25 See Robert Jackson, *Rebels and Whips: an Analysis of Dissension, Discipline and Cohesion in British Political Parties* (London: Macmillan, 1968), pp.32, 292, 301–2. See also Slowe, *Manny Shinwell*, p.284.

26 See Tim Bale, *Sacred Cows and Common Sense, the Symbolic Statecraft and Political Culture of the British Labour Party* (Aldershot: Ashgate, 1999), pp.169–70.

27 See Bale, *Sacred Cows and Common Sense*, Chapter 7.

28 Shaw *Discipline and Discord*, pp. 168–171.

29 Shaw, *Labour Party since 1945*, p. 64–5.

30 Shaw, *Labour Party since 1945*, p. 64–5

31 Shaw, *Discipline and Discord*, Chapter 9.

32 Shaw, *Discipline and Discord*, pp. 297

33 By far the best account of this period is still provided by Patrick Seyd, *The Rise and Fall of the Labour Left* (London: Macmillan, 1987).

34 Note that none of the expelled Labour MPs who stood as independents in the 1950 election came close to winning and in most cases achieved a very small, even derisory, share of the vote – a warning perhaps to their erstwhile colleagues of the dangers of complete rupture as opposed to simple rebellion

35 Philip Norton, *Dissension in the House of Commons, 1974–1979* (Oxford: Clarendon Press, 1980).

36 For a start, Jim Callaghan resigned before the system (finally decided on at a special conference in 1981) could come into operation, though he couldn't prevent Michael Foot robbing Denis Healey of his putative destiny. Secondly, Tony Benn's 1981 attempt, under the new system, to take the deputy leadership from Healey not only failed, but precipitated the split between the hard and the soft left that was arguably crucial to Labour's long term salvation. Finally, it is doubtful whether any subsequent leadership elections would have produced different results even under the old (exclusively PLP) franchise.

37 Shaw, *Labour Party since 1945*, p.170.

38 Shaw, *Discipline and Discord*, p.223.

39 See Shaw, *Discipline and Discord*, p.209.

40 Shaw, *Discipline and Discord*, p.299.

41 Shaw, *Discipline and Discord*, pp. 300–301, see also chapter 12.

42 Shaw, *Labour Party since 1945*, p. 174.

43 For more detail on changed selection procedures and how the unprece-dented control – if not full use – of them by the NEC reflects the move toward a leadership dominated party: see Eric Shaw, 'Organisational transformation in the Labour Party: the case of candidate selection – some preliminary findings', paper prepared for delivery at the 1999 annual meeting of the Political Studies Association, University of Nottingham, 23–4 March 1999.

44 This apparent backlash against heavy-handed leadership involvement in NEC elections meant, according to press reports, that its inter-vention in years to come would be much less explicit.

45 After some dispute, the contest was re-run and won by Davies's replacement as Welsh Secretary, the 'Blairite' Alun Michaels – whose victory was marred, however, by the fact that he was soundly beaten (64–36) in the constituency section of the electoral college by his opponent, Rhodri Morgan, and therefore had to rely on the votes of trade union leaders who, allegedly, had been 'leaned on' – as if that were necessary – by Mr Blair. Interestingly, the only union to have balloted its members, Unison, discovered that 74% of them backed Mr Morgan.

46 The Scottish Labour Party conference in March 1998 passed a resolution calling the Blair government's decision to implement a number of Conservative initiated benefit cuts 'economically inept, morally repugnant and spiritually bereft.'

47 The Labour leadership, the press reported, was united in wishing to prevent Mr Livingstone's selection but torn as to how to achieve it, the two options being, first, to rely on the panel convened to come up with a shortlist deeming him unsuitable or, second, coming up with an alternative who would beat Livingstone fair and square in the selection contest which would follow shortlisting.

48 See Simon Hix and Christopher Lord, *Political Parties in the European Union* (London: Macmillan, 1997).

49 Philip Cowley, 'The Absence of War: New Labour in Parliament' in Justin Fisher et al, (eds.), *British Elections and Parties Review Volume 9* (London: Frank Cass, 1999). At the time of writing it is also widely reported that the government was dropping plans to privatize air traffic control and beefing up its bill on Freedom of Information in order to stave off large scale rebellions.

50 Tim Bale and Petr Kopecký, 'Can Young Pups Teach an Old Dog New Tricks? Lessons for British Reformers from Eastern Europe's New Constitutional Democracies', *Journal of Legislative Studies*, Vol.4, No.2 (1998), pp.149–169.

Labour's Constitution and Public Ownership: From Old Clause IV to New Clause IV

Tudor Jones

In April 1995 the recently elected Labour Party leader, Tony Blair, succeeded in rewriting Clause IV, Part Four, of the Party's constitution, committing Labour to the common ownership of the means of production, which had originally been ratified in London in February 1918. To Blair and his supporters this change was a long overdue sign of Labour's modernisation and ideological revision. To the declining number of, nonetheless, fervent defenders of the original Clause IV, its recasting involved the removal of a statement of socialist principle that had helped it bind the party together, infusing it with a sense of common direction and purpose.

This chapter will seek to examine the main political and intellectual developments that led to the formulation and ratification of Labour's old Clause IV in 1917–18. In doing so, it will survey some of the most influential interpretations of those events in the relevant historical literature.

The first and, as it proved, unsuccessful attempt to revise the 1918 constitutional clause, by party leader Hugh Gaitskell in 1959–60, will then be considered within its own historical-both political and intellectual-context. The main reasons for his ultimate failure will be explored and assessed.

Finally, the chapter will identify the political and economic factors underlying Tony Blair's successful campaign 35 years later to rewrite the old Clause IV. Within a radically changed political climate, it will examine the various reasons why he eventually secured the widespread support of the party in April 1995 for his new Clause IV, the new Statement of Labour's Aims and Values.

Producing an Article of Faith: the Emergence of Clause IV, 1917–18

The year 1918 was a watershed in the history of the British Labour Party since it bought two major new developments. First, its annual conference adopted in February 1918 a new party constitution and organisational structure. Second, a further conference, held in June 1918, officially adopted a new policy statement, drafted by the leading Fabian socialist thinker Sidney Webb and entitled *Labour and the New Social Order*.

The new party constitution contained among other things an outline of the 'Party Objects', which included a brief statement, again largely drafted by Sidney Webb, of Labour's general purpose. Set out in what later became known as Clause IV, Part Four, this committed the party:

To secure for the workers by hand or by brain the full fruits of their industry, and the most equitable distribution thereof that may be possible, upon the basis of the common ownership of the means of production and the best obtainable system of popular administration and control of each industry or service.[1]

The second major development of 1918, the acceptance of the document Labour and the New Social Order, involved the publication of the party's first extended statement of aims. This committed Labour to the pursuit of such policy goals as minimum living standards (a 'National Minimum' in Webb's phrase); full employment; the nationalisation, or state ownership, of land, railways, canals, coal and electricity; progressive taxation together with a capital levy; and an expansion of public services such as education, housing and health-care to be financed through the combined effects of direct taxation and nationalisation.

Though radical in certain aspects, this programme had also been shaped by the immediate climate of wartime collectivism, by, that is, the experience of government control of key sectors of the economy – railways, mines, shipping, food importing, for instance – that had been established by Lloyd George's War Cabinet after 1916. However, Labour and the New Social Order also had a wider ideological significance that has been widely recognized by political historians. As GDH Cole later wrote, the document 'committed the party to a definitely Socialist objective and thus converted it from a loose federation of Socialists and Trade Unionists into a Socialist Party with Trade Union Support'.[2] Specifically, it committed Labour 'to the objectives of Fabian Socialism and to working for them by parliamentary democratic means, as the inheritor and fulfiller of the progressive Liberal tradition rather than as the initiator of any new revolutionary doctrine'.[3]

In similar terms, Samuel Beer regarded Labour's 1918 pronouncements, not only Webb's Labour and the New Social Order but also his earlier statement of 'Party Objects' contained in the new party constitution, as indications of 'a basic change in ideology' that involved a movement away from radical Liberalism towards acceptance of 'the comprehensive ideology of Socialism'.[4] Once those formal commitments had been made by the party, it was thereafter 'accepted and official usage to say that its ultimate aim was a new social order, the Socialist Commonwealth'.[5] That goal had been underlined in Labour and the New Social Order when it declared that 'what has to be reconstructed after the war is not this or that Government Department, or this or that piece of machinery, but so far as Britain is concerned, society itself.'[6] One of the main instruments of social reconstruction, and hence one of the central 'pillars' of the new social order, was identified as 'the Democratic Control of Industry', involving 'a genuinely scientific reorganisation of the nation's industry, no longer deflected by industry profiteering, on the basis of the Common Ownership of the Means of Production'.[7]

This same vision of a transformed economy had also been projected in the statement of 'Party Objects' contained in Clause IV, Part Four, of the new party constitution, adopted in February 1918. Establishing common or public ownership at the heart of that vision, Clause IV provided the only specific reference to the party's domestic aims to be found in the new Constitution. It appeared thereby to offer formal recognition of Labour's socialist identity and purpose, confirmed shortly afterwards in Labour and the New Social Order. As Henry Pelling maintained, Clause IV thus 'for the first time explicitly committed the party to a Socialist basis'.[8]

Together with other members of a sub-committee of Labour's National Executive, including Ramsay MacDonald and Arthur Henderson, Sidney Webb had helped to prepare the party's draft constitution in July 1917. Two alternative statements of 'Party Objects' had originally been prepared, the one drafted by Webb that was eventually adopted, and a second, milder version, probably drafted by Henderson,[9] which referred to the need:

To secure for the producers by hand or brain the full fruits of their Industry by the Common Ownership of all Monopolies and essential Raw Materials.

Why two drafts were considered necessary is unclear from the relevant documentary evidence.[10]

Webb explained the thinking behind his own proposed statement in these terms: This declaration of the Labour Party leaves it open to choose from time to time whatever forms of common ownership, from the co-operative store to the nationalised railway, and whatever forms of popular administration and control of industry, from national guilds to ministries of employment and municipal management may, in particular cases, commend themselves.[11] In other words, Webb's statement was designed to provide a broad and flexible or even, arguably, ambiguous and imprecise, formula suitable for a loose and developing political organisation.

The dominant idea within Clause IV, Part Four-the common or public ownership of the means of production-had nevertheless become established since the 1880s and 1890s as a central strand of British socialist thought. As Kenneth Morgan has observed:

At least as an aspiration, the public ownership of major industries, utilities and national resources was inseparable from the socialist idea in Britain from the foundation of Keir Hardie's Independent Labour Party in 1893 down to the Second World War.[12]

Indeed, the ideal of widespread public ownership manifestly formed 'the jewel in the crown for dedicated socialists, Marxists and non-Marxists alike'.[13]

Since the 1880s that central ideal had been promoted by British socialist thinkers in a stream of books, pamphlets, articles and speeches. The Fabian Society in its programme of 1887 thus sought to achieve 'the reorganisation of Society by the emancipation of Land and Industrial Capital from individual and class ownership, and the vesting of them in the community for the general benefit'.[14] A few years later Sidney Webb restated the Fabian belief that 'the main principle of reform must be the substitution of Collective Ownership and Control for Individual Private Property in the means of production'.[15] Those sentiments were echoed by the Independent Labour Party at its inaugural conference in 1893 when it announced that its central objective was 'to secure the collective ownership of all the means of production, distribution and exchange'.[16]

The Fabian socialists had advocated common ownership since 1884 as a remedy for what they considered to be the structural defects of a capitalist economy, notably its increasing tendency to monopoly power, with growing concentration of ownership in key sectors, and its anarchic nature which led, they argued, both to a colossal waste of productive resources and to economic inefficiency. In contrast, common or public ownership would, first, ensure that the 'rental income', and hence the economic surplus, derived from private monopoly ownership of industrial capital would be directly acquired for social use. Second, and as a consequence, common ownership would thereby bring about a major redistribution of wealth.[17]

In addition, the Fabians argued that common ownership would eliminate the waste and inefficiency endemic to capitalism by means of public organisation and control of the nation's economic activity in the public interest and for the sake of social need, rather than private profit. In Bernard Shaw's words, common ownership would thus allow 'organised co-operation' to be 'substituted ... for the anarchy of the competitive struggle'.[18]

Fabian socialists had thus since the 1880s built the case for common or public ownership upon the basis of both ethical arguments concerning equity, which presented common ownership as an essential means of achieving a more equitable distribution of wealth, and technocratic arguments concerning efficiency, which presented it as an essential means of removing the anarchy, inefficiencies and waste judged to be inseparable from the workings of an unregulated market economy. These distinct, but related, justifications for public ownership were with varying emphases, to underlie Labour thinking and policy-making throughout the party's development and, particularly, in the years after 1918.

On a practical policy level, public ownership had also been advocated since the 1880s within the developing British trade union movement. In 1887 Keir Hardie, then a Scottish miners' leader, had called for the nationalisation of mines, railways, minerals and land.'[19] His demands were later supported at the Trade Union Congress where, from the 1890s onwards, his list of suitable candidates for state ownership was extended in a series of resolutions.

It was not, however, until 1908 that a specific policy commitment, to state ownership of the railways, was approved by the Labour Party conference, with further commitments, concerning the waterways and coal mines, being undertaken by the party in 1910 and 1912. But it was more of a pragmatic than a doctrinal motivation that underlay the party's new policy orientation in those early days. For the most insistent pressures for public ownership of the railways and coal mines emanated from the railwaymen's and miners' unions, who were concerned, above all, with improvements in wages, hours and working conditions, and therefore viewed public ownership of their industries as a practicable collectivist means of securing those desired ends. Viewed from this perspective, public ownership could be seen as another aspect of the Labour Party's 'politics of interest',[20] embraced as a further development of its strategy of redressing trade union grievances that was consistently pursued between 1906 and 1914.

It is, then, within these broader intellectual and political contexts of both doctrinal arguments for public ownership advanced by socialist thinkers and pragmatic, collectivist arguments for it increasingly deployed by trade unionists that the formulation and adoption of Clause IV in 1917–18 should be considered. Moreover, in identifying the causes of its formal ratification, the distinction between long-term and immediate factors needs to be borne in mind.

With regard to the latter, political historians have stressed, in particular, the split in the Liberal Party after 1916 and the consequent need for Labour to sharpen its break with the Liberals as it asserted its growing electoral and parliamentary independence.[21]

A second immediate cause of Labour's adoption of Clause IV in 1918 was the climate of collectivism during the First World War and the trade unions' subsequent, generally favourable response to increased state control of the national economy. Their experience of wartime collectivism had itself been reinforced by the work of the War Emergency Workers' National Committee, on which Sidney Webb, Arthur Henderson and Ramsay MacDonald co-operated to produce a coherent programme for the Labour movement. Webb, as the leading member of that Committee and the principal author of its key proposals, had developed its campaign for a 'Conscription of Riches', involving the public ownership and control of vital sectors of the economy, and hence for the expropriation of capitalists' wealth and income.[22]

A third contemporary factor was the impact of the Russian Revolution of 1917. Labour's adoption of Clause IV took place as, Winter has observed, 'in the heady days after the Bolshevik Revolution when the scent of radical change was in the air throughout Europe'.[23] Arthur Henderson's visit to Russia in the spring of 1917 had convinced him of Labour's need for a moderate, parliamentary socialist alternative both to Bolshevism and, more widely, to the appeal of the far left to working-class opinion throughout Europe.

Henderson therefore wrote, in late 1917, that Labour, as the leading 'Allied' socialist party, had to demonstrate 'that the Democratic State of tomorrow can be established without an intervening period of violent upheaval and dislocation'.[24] To that end, he advocated 'the reconstruction of the Labour party with an ideological base as the bulwark of the British parliamentary system'.[25]

It was from this standpoint that Henderson joined Webb and MacDonald on the sub-committee of Labour's NEC that paved the way for the eventual ratification of Webb's statement of 'Party Objects' in February 1918. It would appear, then, to be the case, as McKibbin has maintained, that:

Fear of Bolshevism and the extreme left throughout Europe was almost certainly a preliminary to the new constitution, and international developments were the occasion for its drafting; ...[26]

In spite, however, of the impact of these immediate domestic and international factors, one should not overlook what Harrison has called 'the long birth of Clause IV behind the short-term conditions of its delivery'.[27] In particular, attention should be paid to the long-running influence of over 40 years of sustained argument for public ownership in the diverse writings of British socialist thinkers from William Morris and Robert Blatchford to Sidney Webb and Bernard Shaw.

Sidney Webb's statement of 'Party Objects' consisted of a broad and imprecise formula. Its ratification by the special party conference in February 1918, Harrison has stressed, 'did not imply that the whole membership came to have a common objective, but rather that an objective had been proclaimed which both accommodated and concealed a large diversity of particular concerns'.[28] That objective was therefore loosely formulated because it was designed to appeal to Fabian and ILP advocates of nationalisation and municipal ownership, to Guild Socialist supporters of workers' control, to members of the Co-operative movement, and to hard-headed industrial trade unionists.

In addition, the notion, implicit in Clause IV, of state control, or more precisely, of common ownership under the control of the central state, held considerable appeal for the rising clerical and administrative middle classes in Britain, whose ranks included the 65 000 governmnent officials who by 1918 were employed in the Ministry of Munitions.[29]

In broad, practical terms, too, the formal adoption of Clause IV should be understood as part of a new constitutional settlement within the Labour Party that bound together what had hitherto been a loose federal alliance of trade unionists and socialists. Indeed, underplaying the role of socialist ideas in the early development of the party, McKibbin has maintained that:

It is easy to be overimpressed with the socialist objective and to be unconcerned with the corpus of the 1918 constitution ... [which] embodied not an ideology but a system by which power in the Labour Party was distributed.[30]

That internal distribution of power had both reduced the organisational influence of the socialist societies and increased the trade unions' representation on Labour's governing body, its enlarged National Executive Committee. In return for their dominant position within the party, organisationally, numerically and financially, the unions were prepared to accept 'the socialist objective' embodied in Clause IV 'partly because they had always been collectivist, partly because they had advocated nationalisation of specific industries even before the war, partly to indulge the Fabians, and partly because they did not think it mattered very much.'[31]

Furthermore, the unions' willingness to 'indulge' the Fabians led them to concede the adoption of Clause IV as, in Pimlott's words, 'a consolation prize to socialists in a package of reform which actually reduced socialist influence in the higher party echelons'.[32] For although the clause gave the party 'an officially socialist colouring which had been rejected in 1900',[33] it formed part of a constitution that seriously weakened the organisational role of both the ILP, the main vehicle of the Labour left since 1900, and the Fabian Society. The new constitution had achieved this end by formally establishing in 1918 constituency Labour parties and by thereby eroding the socialist societies' previously dominant role in recruiting individual party members. In the light of these practical political realities, 'the socialist objective' embodied in Clause IV, and socialist ideas in general, were, in McKibbin's view, of secondary importance compared with the organisational changes to which Labour was committed in 1918. Clause IV itself, therefore, was formally adopted, McKibbin has argued, for essentially functional reasons. In the first place, it helped to underline the party's distinctive identity and purpose because it 'offered the electorate a doctrine differentiated from that of the other parties', thereby 'sharpening the break between the Labour and the Liberal Parties'. In addition, Clause IV was a unifying force; for 'precisely because of its vagueness and lack of rigour [it] paradoxically had an umbrella function: it was an acceptable formula in a party where there was otherwise little doctrinal agreement'.[34] Harrison, too, recognized this point, maintaining that Clause IV:

... did not indicate ... the presence of a coherent ideology. It is better understood as a rallying point around which the adherents of different ideologies and the representatives of different interests assembled.[35]

This functional interpretation is supported by Beer's view that the socialist statements of 1918 offered the means by which Labour for the first time asserted its independence of the Liberals. He thus argued that 'the adoption of Socialism as an ideology was functional to this choice of political independence.'[36] Labour's apparent ideological conversion, expressed in Clause IV and *Labour and the New Social Order* was therefore 'not so much a cause as an effect of the hardly avoidable break with the Liberals'.[37]

Beer, however, in his influential account also stressed the normative aspect of the 1918 pronouncements, regarding them as firm indications of a 'basic change in ideology' that involved a transition from radical Liberalism to 'the comprehensive ideology of Socialism'.[38] Once those formal commitments had been made by the party, it then came to embrace officially the ultimate goal of a new social order, the Socialist Commonwealth, founded on the idea and policy of common or public ownership, 'the ancient orthodoxy of Socialism'.[39]

This view of the normative significance of Clause IV was developed more explicitly by both Harrison and Winter, who emphasised the attempts of Sidney Webb and others on the War Emergency Workers' National Committee to develop a coherent socialist programme for the Labour movement.[40] Webb's eventual statements of socialist aims were based on 'an indictment of capitalism and offered a pledge to mitigate, if not to end, the inequality and deprivation it bred'.[41] Their underlying purpose was 'to make the choice among the parties one of conviction rather than just a comparison of personalities'.[42]

The statement of 'Party Objects' formulated and refined by Webb in 1917–18 was thus shaped by the experience both of wartime collectivism and of recent domestic and international convulsions. It was also attuned to the needs of a youthful political party gradually attaining independence. Yet it was a document that sprang, too, from Webb's own Fabian socialist beliefs, which had been strengthened by all those developments in a climate of ideological turbulence throughout Europe.

Both practical and doctrinal factors, therefore, and functional and normative causes, underlay and inspired the formulation and ratification of Labour's original Clause IV in 1917–18. Moreover, regardless of its underlying motives and purposes, and in spite of its lack of clearly indicated policy priorities, the statement did at least imply some kind of official socialist commitment, one that was to prove itself in the long term replete with symbolic significance for the party.

Challenging the Faith: Gaitskell's Attempt to Revise Clause IV, 1959–60

The established place of Clause IV, Part Four, within the Labour Party's constitution was not to be challenged openly until 1959 when Hugh Gaitskell, party leader since December 1955, put forward his highly controversial proposal to amend or revise the text of Clause IV at the post-election party conference of that year. Gaitskell's undertaking was formed in the face of Labour's third successive election defeat and in the light of major economic and social changes in Britain. It also represented the cumulative, practical expression of a school of revisionist socialist thought, to which Gaitskell adhered, that had been developing within the Labour Party during the 1950s.

Labour revisionism had originally emerged in the midst of the fierce ideological and policy debate that followed the fall of the Attlee Governments in the 1951 and the completion of their nationalisation and welfare programmes. That debate focused in particular on the future role of public ownership, and nationalisation as its most commonly practised form, within both Labour Party policy and democratic socialist ideology.

The 'revisionist' position in this debate was concerned not only with revising Labour's policies, but also with reformulating socialist principles through a new analysis of changed economic and social conditions in post-1945 Britain. After Hugh Gaitskell's accession to the party leadership in December 1955, revisionist ideas on public ownership and socialist strategy were developed by himself and his parliamentary supporters, notably Anthony Crosland, Douglas Jay and Roy Jenkins. Under Gaitskell's political leadership, and with Crosland providing the main intellectual thrust, most clearly in his *The Future of Socialism* (1956), the most coherent expression of British revisionist socialist thought in the post-1945 period, revisionist positions on both economic and social issues were steadily incorporated into party policy statements such as *Industry and Society* in 1957.

As a body of ideas, revisionism involved two highly controversial deviations from widely accepted orthodoxies within Labour Party thinking. First, it repudiated the traditional view that socialism could be identified with the public ownership of the means of production. It thereby rejected the post-1918 theoretical commitment to extensive public ownership as the essential condition for achieving all major socialist objectives.

Second, revisionism presented an ethical restatement of democratic socialism in terms of values and ideals such as personal liberty, social welfare and, above all, social equality. What was distinctively revisionist about this was not the ethical emphasis in itself, but rather the insistence that these ideal ends could be pursued, using appropriate fiscal and social policy measures, without a large-scale extension of public ownership and within the framework of a market-oriented mixed economy. Moreover, from this perspective public ownership was viewed by Labour revisionists to be merely one useful policy means among several others for realising socialist values and ideals. Certainly it was not to be regarded as the cornerstone of a future socialist society.

Gaitskell had advanced the case for public ownership in these pragmatic and instrumental terms since the 1930s, treating it with qualified approval as a useful means of pursuing not only the goals of economic efficiency and stability but also what he considered to be 'the central socialist ideal of equality'.[43] In his 1956 Fabian pamphlet *Socialism and Nationalisation*, for instance, he maintained that an extension of public ownership was 'almost certainly necessary if we are to have a much more equal distribution of wealth'.[44] He also believed that public ownership could help to promote both full employment and industrial democracy.[45] During his period as party leader Gaitskell therefore advocated the public ownership, and specifically the nationalisation, of a substantial part of the British economy, including the steel, road haulage, aircraft, chemicals and machine tools industries.[46]

After Labour's third successive election defeat in 1959, Gaitskell's revisionist view of public ownership, which had thus been selectively favourable as well as cautious and pragmatic, found its expression in his proposal at the 1959 party conference to amend Clause IV of the party constitution. His keynote conference speech, which concentrated on the issue of nationalisation, had been promoted by Labour's official 'post-mortem' inquest. The report of the party's General Secretary, Morgan Phillips, had emphasised the electoral damage caused by Labour's policy on nationalisation, specifically by its ambiguous plans for the state ownership of leading private-sector companies.

In his conference speech, Gaitskell therefore umderlined his belief that Clause IV, as it stood, was a source of misunderstanding and misinterpretation in so far as it appeared to commit Labour to the public ownership of the whole, or at least the bulk, of the British economy. By 1959 he had consequently reached the conclusion that, in order both to emphasize that this was not really Labour's overriding objective and to clarify the party's broader socialist aims, it would be necessary to amend Clause IV.

With little support from friends or colleagues,[47] Gaitskell delivered his conference speech at Blackpool in November 1959 as his own contribution to Labour's 'post-mortem' on its electoral defeat. While he expressed his support for varied forms of public ownership and for the idea of public ownership as a useful policy instrument, his principal revisionist argument, which drew upon the theoretical analysis which Crosland, Jay and he himself had developed during the 1950s, was for amending Clause IV and hence for relegating nationalisation to a lower status in Labour's policy, strategy and ideology.

Gaitskell believed that the experience of the 1959 election campaign had clearly indicated that nationalisation had been a vote-losing issue for Labour, first, because of the manifest, albeit sometimes undeserved, unpopularity of the nationalised industries, and second because of the widespread confusion and misrepresentation surrounding Labour's future policy on nationalisation. He therefore wanted to steer a middle course between, on the one hand, the complacent suggestion that the existing frontiers between the public and private sectors should remain fixed and unchanged and, on the other, the fundamentalist belief that nationalisation or public ownership was the be-all and end-all, the first principle and overriding aim of socialism, a belief that derived from 'a complete confusion about the fundamental meaning of socialism and, in particular, a misunderstanding about ends and means'.[48]

In order to dispel this ideological confusion, Gaitskell set out what for him were 'the basic first principles of British democratic socialism', which included a concern for the disadvantaged and oppressed; a belief in social justice and hence an equitable distribution of wealth', and a desire for a classless society without snobbery, privilege or restrictive social barriers. Public ownership should be regarded, Gaitskell maintained, as merely 'a means to realising these principles in practice'.[49]

Clarification of these fundamental issues, in Gaitskell's view, required a straightforward restatement of Labour's basic aims and principles, which in turn would entail revising Clause IV, the only specific yet inadequate reference to the party's domestic purpose, since:

standing as it does on its own, this cannot possibly be regarded as adequate. It lays us open to continual misrepresentation. It implies that the only precise object we have is nationalisation, whereas in fact we have many other Socialist objectives. It implies that we propose to nationalize everything, but do we? Everything? The whole of light industry, the whole of agriculture, all the shops, every little pub and garage? Of course not.
We have long ago come to accept... for the foreseeable future, at least in some form, a mixed economy.[50]

Gaitskell's main recommendation, the revision of Clause IV, was thus the cumulative expression of both practical and theoretical considerations, and more broadly, an attempt to follow through the implications of the revisionist view of public ownership. It was formally presented as part of a necessary process of ideological adaptation which Labour was required to undergo. Yet at Blackpool in 1959 the widespread response to his speech was a vehement defence of traditional socialist attitudes and an attack on what the Labour left derided as revisionist attempts to reform and civilize capitalism and to abandon in the process plans for further nationalisation.[51]

Gaitskell eventually retreated from his original objective of replacing Clause IV with a new statement of Labour's aims towards a compromise whereby the original clause would be left as it stood but augmented by a new text, the New Testament' as it soon became dubbed, setting out the 'basic first principles of democratic socialism' in more contemporary terms. By summer 1960, however, it was becoming clear that acceptance of this more up-to-date statement would be extremely hard to achieve within the party, particularly in view of the hostility of four out of the six major trade unions, namely, the Engineers', Transport Workers', Miners' and Railwaymen's.

At the 1960 party conference, therefore, Gaitskell's new statement of 'Labour's Aims' was merely approved as 'a valuable expression of the aims of the Labour Party in the second half of the 20th century',[52] without being formally accepted as an amendment or addition to the 1918 constitution. This inadequate compromise was unquestionably a setback for Gaitskell since the original Clause IV was to remain completely unchanged. The entire episode thus indicated, as Williams observed, that 'though Gaitskell's face was saved, he had lost the battle over Clause IV after all, because of a sudden change in the dynamics of the political conflict'.[53]

Gaitskell's attempt to amend Clause IV in 1959–60 has often been strongly criticized, both by political historians and commentators and by his own contemporaries.[54] Tactically, he clearly made a number of serious errors – in highlighting, for instance, in a public and divisive manner an issue which few voters or even Tory activists were even aware of; in antagonising the trade union centre of the party, which for some time had provided much of his power base; and in failing to secure majority support for his proposal on either the key union executives or Labour's own National Executive.

Strategically, too, so his critics alleged, he was planning to remove a useful piece of ambiguity whereby in the past Labour had combined a practical acceptance of a mixed economy with a constitutional clause that implied a commitment to wholesale public ownership. In addition, it has been argued, by opening up the Clause IV issue in a confrontational style and unleashing such fierce opposition, Gaitskell had thereby precluded the possibility of any discreet demotion of further nationalisation in the future and thus prevented a more subtle, indirect process of 'adaptation by stealth'.[55]

Many of Gaitskell's critics have also focused attention on a third, even more fundamental strategic error. They have claimed that he was, above all, insensitive to the symbolic value of Clause IV as Labour's 'rallying point'[56] since 1918, and hence to the widely perceived role of public ownership and nationalisation as, in Crosland's phrase, Labour's 'familiar mental street-anchor',[57] as, indeed, the foundation stone of an alternative, non-capitalist economic system and social order, the Socialist Commonwealth.[58]

In appearing, then, as Roy Jenkins put it, to have 'over-estimated the rationality of political movements',[59] Gaitskell thus failed to foresee that party and union activists would react with bewilderment and outrage to his plans for revising Clause IV, for 'taking down the signpost to the promised land'.[60] As his successor to the party leadership, Harold Wilson later recalled, well aware both of the symbolic significance of Gaitskell's challenge and of the functional value of Clause IV, '...we were being asked to take Genesis out of the Bible; you don't have to be a fundamentalist in your religious approach to say that Genesis is part of the Bible...'[61]

Such critical observations need, however, to be qualified. For Gaitskell did not lack awareness of the traditional symbolism represented by Clause IV.[62] Indeed, rather than misunderstanding the nature of the Labour movement, with its enduring attachment to such potent symbols, he really, as Marquand has observed, 'understood it only too well'.[63] His unyielding rationalism throughout this entire episode, which had expressed itself in a pragmatic and entirely non-visionary view of public ownership, thus led him to reject Wilson's instrumental view of Clause IV as a symbol worth retaining for the sake of party morale and unity. By contrast, Gaitskell was convinced that it was simply irrational to preserve a theoretical commitment, embodied in Clause IV, to a mainly collectivised economy. Such a position he considered incompatible with the practical requirements both of the party's future policy-making, which should rightly be based on an acceptance of a mixed economy, and of its future electoral success.

But in taking this rationalistic view, Gaitskell had thus challenged the status of Clause IV as the formal expression of Labour's socialist myth, of its inspiring vision of a transformed economy and society founded on the public ownership of the means of production.[64] In mounting that challenge and thereby seeking to change an important aspect of Labour's political culture, he believed that he was taking an initiative that was necessary for modernising the party and ensuring its electoral recovery.

Yet ultimately Gaitskell's undertaking proved abortive not just because of his own tactical and strategic errors and the internal politics of the Labour movement. He failed, too, because, whilst he was not insensitive to the symbolic force of Clause IV, he nonetheless underestimated it. The forces of change that had been gradually developing since 1945, of which he was acutely aware, had not yet reached the point in 1960 where they eroded the ideological conviction and sentimental loyalty that continued to sustain Clause IV, Part Four.

Abandoning the Faith? Blair's Revision of Clause IV, 1994–95

None of Gaitskell's successors as party leader was to openly challenge the status of Clause IV as the embodiment of Labour's socialist myth until Tony Blair's controversial party conference initiative in October 1994. Blair's campaign to revise Clause IV was, however, launched in radically changed political and economic circumstances. It had been conceived, too, within an historical context, both political and intellectual, that had witnessed a gradual demotion of the role of public ownership within the Labour Party's policies, strategy and ideology.

Labour's crushing electoral defeat in 1983 marked the end of the left's temporary ascendancy within the party, which, among other policy victories, had involved support for an Alternative Economic Strategy based on a substantial extension of public ownership and control. The policy statement, Labour's Programme 1982, which became translated into the election manifesto of the following year, 'the longest suicide note in history', in Gerald Kaufman's much-quoted description, had even declared in fundamentalist terms that 'our social and economic objectives can be achieved only through an expansion of comrnon ownership substantial enough to give the community decisive power over the commanding heights of the economy.'[65]

The electoral debacle of 1983, and Neil Kinnock's subsequent accession to the party leadership, heralded a gradual movement away from the advocacy of large-scale public ownership and even, after 1987, a clear and unequivocal endorsement of the market economy in Labour policy-making. These changes were apparent both in the Policy Review document of 1989, *Meet the Challenge,*

Make the Change, and in the 1988 *Statement of Democratic Socialist Aims and Values*, largely written by deputy leader Roy Hattersley with assistance from Neil Kinnock.[66]

The 1989 document in effect formalised the abandonment of public ownership as a major instrument of Labour policy and socialist strategy, without actually proposing to repeal Clause IV of the party constitution. In practical policy terms, this entailed a rejection of proposals either for renationalising privatised companies or for any new extensions of public ownership, together with a consequent switch of emphasis to public regulation or control. All of this was accompanied by an acknowledgement of the merits of a market economy that was unprecedented in the historical development of Labour policy, and which thus amounted to a major and historic ideological shift in the party's official, public stance.

Labour's movement away from public ownership after 1987, it is true, was to a large extent a response to the practical difficulties of restoring the privatised industries to the public sector. Yet it formed part, too, of a broader policy shift away from established forms of state intervention, including, in particular, demand management and indicative economic planning. In the first policy area, Keynesian macroeconomic techniques were no longer regarded as the key to the maintenance of full employment. In the second, there were growing doubts about the efficacy of the state as an agency for directing capital investment into particular industries or for encouraging regional development through the use of subsidies.[67] In place of these interventionist instruments, Labour increasingly embraced a strategy of 'supply-side socialism', in which government's role was conceived as one of, first, intervening selectively in a market economy by investing in skills training, infrastructure and research and development, and, second, establishing a policy framework of macroeconomic stability[68] based on low inflation, neutral interest rates and a stable exchange rate.

These policy developments had a deeper ideological resonance. In the first place, they were themselves symptomatic of what Geoffrey Foote has called 'an unprecedented collapse of ideological certainty on the socialist left'[69] in the face of the perceived failings of left-wing socialism, illustrated at home by the electoral disaster of 1983 and abroad by Mitterand's abortive socialist experiment of 1981–83 in France. The changes in Labour's economic strategy reflected, too, a growing recognition both of the constraints placed on national fiscal policy by domestic electoral pressures and global economic forces, and hence of the limitations of Keynesian social democracy in the face of those harsh realities.

It is, then, within this changed historical context that Tony Blair's undertaking to rewrite Clause IV in 1994–5 needs to be viewed. Before he became party leader in July 1994, following his predecessor John Smith's untimely death in May of that year, Blair's decision, in Patrick Seyd's words, 'to tackle the most symbolic of party icons'[70] had already been anticipated by a few Labour modernizers in the wake of the 1992 general election defeat. These included Jack Straw, Giles Radice and Neil Kinnock. In March 1993 Jack Straw, then Shadow Environment Secretary, had thus called in his pamphlet Policy and Ideology for a complete revision of Clause IV. He argued that there was 'a disconnection between Labour's stated ideology and its approach to policy' since the party's vision of society, as embodied in Clause IV, had 'failed to keep pace not only with prosaic changes to Labour policy, but with more fundamental changes in Britain and in the world as a whole'.[71] The only argument against revising Clause IV seemed to Straw to be a negative on, based on the assumption 'that it would be too difficult to effect, too divisive and that it is more sensible simply to let this redundant piece of ideological phraseology "wither on the vine".'[72]

Yet there were, in Straw's view, 'overwhelming, substantive objections to the Nelson's eye approach to Clause 4'. Quite apart from the fact that the clause had been prominently displayed on party membership cards since 1959, it had become, over the years, 'a shibboleth of socialist belief which had acquired 'some mystical significance'[73] never contemplated by its original authors in 1917–18 when they had composed it for practical political reasons. Indeed, for that reason it was hard even to discuss Clause IV within the party and there was 'fear of the charge of betrayal if any move is made against it'.[74] Straw argued, therefore, that the 'recasting of Clause IV' was needed in the 1990s if Labour was 'to refresh our appeal to the electorate as the governing party which takes Britain into the 21st century'. Moreover, the revised Clause IV should comprise only 'a statement of ends', leaving statements of means to the party's 'continuous process of policy formulation'.[75]

Straw's proposal, however, received no immediate support in 1993 from the party leadership. On the contrary, John Smith regarded this initiative with displeasure in view of both its potential divisiveness and its timing, since it coincided with his struggle to secure the backing of trade union leaders for the principle of 'one member, one vote' in 1993.[76] His preference, instead, was for supplementing and superseding Clause IV with his own statement of democratic socialist values.[77]

Nevertheless, Straw did receive backing for his views both from the MP Giles Radice[78] and from a Fabian Society review of the party constitution, headed by Lord Archer of Sandwell, which concluded 'that the existing Clause Four (Part Four) should be replaced, both to separate principles from policies and to reflect contemporary thinking'.[79]

Furthermore, Smith's predecessor as party leader, Neil Kinnock, later echoed Straw's recommendations when he, too, advocated the revision of Clause IV. Recognizing the original clause's mythic force and appeal, Kinnock obsened that Labour's 'tablet of stone' had acquired 'the status of political holy writ'. It had become 'a hallowed part of Labour's political culture', regarded by many as 'the ideological definition of the party's character' or even as 'its evidence of socialist identity'.[80] Yet, while he conceded that public ownership and nationalisation had once been 'central to my idea of socialism', by 1994 he no longer believed 'that Clause IV is an adequate definition of modern democratic socialism'.[81]

Tony Blair's election as party leader in July 1994 soon led to an acceleration of the pace of modernisation within the party which Kinnock had originally set. Together with his friend Gordon Brown, Blair had been among the most prominent of Labour's modernizers since the late 1980s, supporting Kinnock's policy changes and organisational reforms and, more lately, Smith's successful campaign for 'one member, one vote' in 1993.

In his own 'post-mortem' on Labour's 1992 election defeat, Blair had stressed the need for the party 'to continue and intensify the process of change...at the level of both ideas and organisation'.[82] In a series of speeches and articles written during the early 1990s, he therefore outlined the kind of ideological revision that he considered desirable for the party. This would involve an attempt, he wrote in 1991, 'to re-establish the agenda for public action without the old failings of collectivism' which included the 'limitations of public ownership through the State'.[83] In place of the inadequacies of state socialism, Blair wished to reaffirm the fundamental principles of early ethical socialism, particularly, its central emphasis on 'the need of society to act together to achieve what the individual cannot do alone' and its underlying notion, too, 'of a clearly identified community embodying the public interest or public good, standing up on behalf of individuals, against the vested interests that hold them back'.[84]

For Blair this restatement of the communitarian values of ethical socialism carried important policy and ideological implications. In the field of economic policy and strategy it underlay his view that:

the battle over theoretical forms of economic organisation is dead, or at least relegated to means, not ends. We need to develop instead a new economics of the public interest, which recognises that a thriving competitive market is essential for market choice.[85]

Within that 'new framework of public interest', he argued, in terms that would have been unfamiliar or perplexing to early socialist thinkers, it would be possible to appreciate the need both for the existence of the market and for government actions designed to facilitate its efficient operation, whilst at the same time subjecting it to social needs. For in Blair's view, modern socialism consisted not in a particular form of economic organisation but rather in a collection of values such as community and mutuality reinforced by the 'over-reaching concept of public interest'[86] invoked in support of the individual.

The main features, then, of this revised ethical socialism which Blair was commending as the 'governing philosophy of today's Labour Party'[87] thus seemed to include a strong emphasis on the idea of an inclusive community promoting the public interest, a rejection of the elevated status previously ascribed to public ownership; and an unequivocal defence of a competitive market economy, once regarded by socialists as incompatible with their communitarian ideals.

Blair developed these themes further in a 1994 Fabian pamphlet in which he maintained that his ethical conception of socialism, which he underlined with the hyphenated use of the term 'social-ism',[88] rested on the twin assumptions, first, 'that individuals are socially interdependent human beings [who]...owe a duty to one another and to a broader society', and, second, that 'it is only through recognising that interdependence and by acting upon it, the collective power of all used for the individual good of each, that the individual's interest can be advanced'.[89] For the purpose of Labour's ideological revision, this theoretical approach had the clear advantages, Blair believed, both of springing from deep historical roots and of avoiding the limitations of socialist doctrines that were either directed towards sectional interests or based upon 'particular economic prescriptions'.[90] The latter, of course, included the kind of ownership-based definition of socialism contained in Clause IV and favoured by Labour traditionalists.

There were, however, at least two major problems raised by Blair's ethical approach to socialism.. First, his emphasis on the ideal of community tended to obscure the abstract nature of that traditional socialist aspiration and hence the practical difficulty of translating it into concrete policy commitments. In the 1950s both Crosland and Gaitskell had been well aware of that problem, particularly in view of the individualistic attitudes fostered by a market economy.[91]

Secondly, by separating his socialist ideals from any particular form of economic organisation, and by strongly supporting, too, 'a thriving competitive market',[92] Blair was departing from the ethical socialist tradition of Tawney and others. This had always stressed the interdependence of ethical and economic concerns, of socialist ideals and their surrounding economic structures. The new Labour leader was thereby exposing himself to the traditional socialist charge that there was a basic contradiction between, on the one hand, his ideals of community and mutual responsibility and, on the other, the acquisitive and materialistic values of the market.

Nonetheless, it soon became clear, in 1994, that Blair was not concerned with developing his ideological position on a merely abstract level but rather as the theoretical basis of the first major initiative of his party leadership, his iconoclastic proposal, advanced at the end of his first conference speech as leader, to rewrite Clause IV of the party Constitution. Influenced by private poll findings which indicated that voters remained unconvinced that Labour had really changed its character,[93] Blair had already, in the summer of 1994, confided in his close associates Gordon Brown and Peter Mandelson about his desire to revise Clause IV. Shortly afterwards, he discussed his proposal with the party's deputy leader John Prescott, who was also the acknowledged but unofficial leader of Labour's traditionalist wing. In spite of initial doubts, Prescott consented to it on condition that trade union leaders could be assured that there would be no further modernising reforms before the next general election.[94]

Blair's controversial proposal eventually emerged in a brief passage towards the end of his conference speech in Blackpool on 4 October 1994. He told his audience that Labour required 'a modern constitution that says what we are in terms the public cannot misunderstand and the Tories cannot misrepresent'.[95] Without directly mentioning Clause IV, he therefore promised that he and Prescott would together shortly present 'a clear up to date statement of the objects and objectives of our party'.[96]

Unlike Gaitskell in 1959, Blair was also careful to invite a wide debate within the party on that statement. If, following the debate, the new Clause IV were to be accepted, then, he declared, 'let it become the objects of our party for the next election and take its place in our constitution for the next century'.[97] Justifying his initiative, he reminded the audience:

Parties that do not change die, and this party is a living movement not a historical monument. If the world changes and we don't, then we become of no use to the world. Our principles cease being principles and ossify its dogma.[98]

Blair had thus become the first Labour leader since Gaitskell to challenge Clause IV's entrenched status within the party's constitution as its statement of socialist purpose. Like Gaitskell, he considered that its revision was necessary not only in the light of major economic and social changes but also in order to dispel public misunderstanding and political misrepresentation. Like Gaitskell, too, he regarded this constitutional reform as an important symbol of Labour's modernisation.

In spite, however, of favourable media reaction to Blair's 'unexpected theatrical coup'[99] residual opposition within the party was underlined both by conference support only two days after Blair's speech for a motion in favour of the original Clause IV and by the launch in the following month of a Defend Clause IV Campaign, headed by Arthur Scargill and Alan Simpson and designed to mobilize support among trade unionists, party activists and MEPs.[100]

Nevertheless, Blair's undertaking gained momentum in December 1994 when Labour's National Executive Committee agreed a timetable for a special party conference to vote on the proposed constitutional change in April 1995. At the beginning of 1995 the NEC decided, too, to urge constituency parties to ballot their members on the proposal. In addition, Blair himself began a nationwide tour to argue the case for change, face-to-face with party members, in which he insisted that revising Clause IV was necessary because it was open to three important objections. First, it committed Labour to 'common ownership with no boundaries' and hence to 'common ownership of industry, retail and finance ' rather than to a mixed economy. Such a commitment made no sense on grounds of either socialist principle or economic reality. Second, Clause IV, by providing 'a statement of objectives which no government could or would implement', had helped to divide the party from its leaders'.[101] For as Blair later observed, 'the gap between our stated aims and policies in government fed the constant charge of betrayal, the view that...the leadership was too timid to tread the real path to true socialism'.[102] Third, public ownership, as enshrined in Clause IV, was not a value or principle but rather 'the means, in certain circumstances, of achieving our principles'. As a consequence, Clause IV did not, 'on its own, properly reflect our values or our total view of the economy'.[103]

The revised Clause IV, Labour's new statement of objects ought, therefore, Blair maintained, to embody certain enduring and distinctive socialist values, notably, social justice, a broad conception of freedom, equality of respect and status, democracy and social solidarity. By contrast, Sidney Webb's original Clause IV had focused on a specific means, the common ownership of the means of production, rather than on socialist ends. It appeared, moreover, in the 1990s, especially in the light of the fall of Communism, to constitute 'not merely an anachronism but a statement of our economic beliefs that carries no conviction inside our party whilst exposing us to maximum misrepresentation outside it.[104]

In seeking to replace that iconic document, that traditional article of faith, Blair still needed to overcome the intransigence of its defenders. As the political commentator Andrew Marr observed, Blair, who was 'not a traditional socialist nor a natural Labour man', would have to overcome the conservatism of those in his party who 'have not changed at all and are about as relevant to the Blair project as pre-Copernican scholars are to astrophysics, mentally inhabiting a world that is gone, one in which there is no global economy, no international mobility of labour or capital, in which strong states can deploy powerful and predictable levers, including the ownership of big corporations, for social ends'.[105]

By the beginning of 1995, however, the political circumstances surrounding Blair's revisionist project seemed far more favourable than those that had faced Gaitskell over 35 years earlier. He was unlikely, for instance, to face such fierce opposition as had been directed at Gaitskell in 1959–60. Blair was, after all, dealing with a trade union movement, which largely as a result of Labour's organisational reforms since 1987, did not exercise the same decisive political leverage with the party as in Gaitskell's day. Nor did Blair face the daunting prospect of confronting that formidable alliance of fundamentalists of the Labour left and pragmatists and loyalists of the party's centre which had been deployed against Gaitskell.

It was therefore against this political background that Blair proceeded to address about 30,000 party members at 35 meetings in his nationwide campaign between January and April 1995.

Meanwhile, in March of that year a new text of Clause IV was eventually published and approved by Labour's National Executive on 13 March. The main emphasis of its final draft, of which Blair was the principal author, assisted by contributions from Prescott and other senior colleagues, was upon the values of community, social justice and democracy rather than upon economic goals. Its Part One thus affirmed Labour's overriding belief in the principle of the community, declaring that:

The Labour Party is a democratic socialist party. It believes that by the strength of our common endeavour we achieve more than we achieve alone, so as to create for each of us the means to realise our true potential and for all of us a community in which power, wealth and opportunity are in the hands of the many not the few, where the rights we enjoy reflect the duties we owe, and where we live together, freely, in a spirit of solidarity, tolerance and respect.[106]

Part Two of the new Clause IV contained what remained for the left the most heretical aspect of Blair's project: a restatement of Labour's economic aims that embraced the notion of a competitive market economy. Labour, it stated, was now committed to the goal of: A dynamic economy, serving the public interest, in which the enterprise of the market and the rigour of competition are joined with the forces of partnership and co-operation, to produce the wealth the nation needs and the opportunity for all to work and prosper, with a thriving private sector and high quality public services, where those undertakings essential to the common good are either owned by the public or accountable for them.[107]

In justifying these commitments, Blair stressed their ethical socialist inspiration, stating that:

The central belief of the Labour Party is in social cohesion ... the basic principle is solidarity, that people can achieve much more by acting together than by acting alone. I think that all this is best represented by the idea of community, in which each person has the rights and duties which go with community.'[108]

Blair's left-wing critics, however, were quick to underline the tensions between Blair's ideal of community, forged by ties of 'common endeavour', and his celebration of the merits of a market economy. The MEP Ken Coates, for example, recalled how in 1917 Sidney Webb had drawn a stark contrast between the destructive 'competitive struggle for the means of life' and the productive process of 'conscious and deliberate co-operation' promoted within Labour's newly embraced socialist ideology.[109]

Nevertheless, in 1995 press reaction, at least, to Blair's new statement favourably emphasized the fact that it signified a major ideological revision. *The Independent* thus described the new text as 'the boldest attempt undertaken by the post war Labour Party to embrace a dynamic market economy', while *The Times* declared that its publication indicated that Labour had become 'a modern, progressive, left of centre party facing up to a new century with clarity and confidence'. *The Guardian*, too, regarded the new Clause IV as 'a defining document' that made crystal clear 'that Labour is no longer a party with a socialist project based on economic ownership but one with a socialist project based on community values'.[110]

Boosted by this support, Blair's revisionist undertaking reached its climax at the special party conference on 29 April 1995, held at the Methodist Central Hall, Westminster, London, where, ironically, the original Clause IV had been adopted in February 1918. There the party leader secured majority approval, by a 65 percent vote, of his new statement of aims and values. That support included the votes of 90 percent of constituency delegates and of 54.6 percent of trade union delegates in spite of the opposition of the two biggest unions, the Transport and General Workers' Union (TGWU) and Unison.

By endorsing, therefore, among other things, 'a dynamic economy', with 'a thriving private sector', strengthened by 'the enterprise of the market' and 'the rigour of competition', two thirds of conference delegates had thereby given their support 'to changes that marked a significant shift from almost eighty years of party history and doctrine'.[111] They had formally approved 'the sort of economy which since its foundation Labour had regarded with at least a profound mistrust'.[112]

Shortly before this vote of support, Roy Hattersley, Labour's former deputy leader and most prominent remaining advocate of Croslandite social democracy, predicted that 'in political folklore, April 29th 1995 will become the day when Labour turned itself into a social democratic party'.[113] For the special conference on Clause IV would be seen as 'a symbol of an evolution, which, although gradual and sometimes imperceptible, has been inevitable since 1979', taking place in the light of social and economic changes in Britain to which Labour had been forced to adapt.[114]

But this apparent watershed in Labour Party history, widely seen at the time as marking symbolically the ideological transition from traditional state socialism to a version of European social democracy, thereby involved, too, the formal abandonment of the party's socialist myth, of the visionary idea, that is, of economic and social transformation, of a future Socialist

Commonwealth built on the foundation of the public ownership of the means of production, the potent idea that had once been embodied in the original Clause IV.

Blair's 'decent burial of Clause IV, along with all its mythic force, had the effect, as Tim Bale has observed, 'of "historicising" the past he was prepared to honour', thereby enabling Labour 'to escape from a "living past", from being a party which lives on "cyclical" rather than "clock" time, a party which truncates time so that the heroes and deeds of old seem as relevant as the challenges of the present and the future'.[115] Blair had thus successfully confronted his party with the need to make this symbolic break with its past by renouncing the status of Clause IV as, in his own words, an 'icon' or a 'totem'.[116]

In doing this, Blair had demonstrated a lack of sentimentality and an 'unconcern about the inner workings of Labour's heart',[117] which no Labour leader since Gaitskell had dared to display. Yet in seeking to change Labour's political culture by removing the traditional symbolism represented by the old Clause IV, Blair had succeeded in this task both because he 'was telling people what they already knew, even if it took something to admit it, in a language they had come to understand' and because the sentiments of the old Clause IV 'had lost or at least changed their meaning in the contemporary lives of his members,'[118] lives affected by the major economic and political changes directly experienced in the recent past.

This point provides an important key to understanding why Blair triumphed in 1994–5 where Gaitskell had failed in 1959–60. For in radically changed circumstances the case for changing Clause IV had already been advanced after 1992, by Kinnock, Straw, Radice and the Fabian Society, before Blair launched his initiative in 1994. In this more receptive intellectual climate Blair, unlike Gaitskell in 1959, also carefully prepared the ground beforehand, consulting and gaining the support of prominent colleagues such as Brown, Mandelson and Prescott.

In addition, the terms of the entire debate on public ownership, within and outside the party, had been changed by the scale of privatisation of former renationalised utilities since the 1980s and by Labour's gradual abandonment of its nationalisation pledges after 1987. By the time, then, of the 1994–5 Clause IV debate, the political reality was that, as Riddell has recalled, 'no one at a senior level in the Labour Party or the trade unions was seriously advocating re-nationalisation of all privatised industries'.[119] As a consequence, an intellectually coherent, alternative case for either a large-scale restoration or a substantial extension of public ownership was not presented with any real conviction in the way that such a case had been made by Bevan, Castle, Foot and others in 1959. Indeed, by the mid 1990s that kind of deep-rooted, traditional socialist conviction had been eroded by economic and political developments, at home and abroad, over the previous 20 years.

Finally, unlike Gaitskell in 1959–60, Blair had invited and participated in an open debate on the whole issue within the party, and had eventually secured the support of individual party members, rather than merely party and union activists, with the aid of ballots and a grassroots campaign. In doing all this, he exploited his authority as the recently elected leader of a party that had suffered four successive election defeats, thereby contriving 'to make approval of change a key test of the party's electoral credibility'.[120]

In more favourable political circumstances, therefore, and with the exercise of greater tactical and strategic skills than Gaitskell had displayed, Blair had by 1995 achieved the revision of Clause IV which both he and his ill-fated predecessor considered an important symbol of Labour's modernisation and ideological adaptation. But in the changed world of the 1990s, an era of lost political and ideological certainties, in which not only traditional socialist beliefs but also central assumptions of Croslandite social democracy had been eroded or undermined, the future appeal and value, as opposed to the historic significance, of Labour's new Clause IV appeared untested and unclear.

Notes

1 Labour Party Annual Conference Report, January and February 1918 Appendix 1. Constitution of the Labour Party. Section 3 (d) (later known as Clause IV, Part Four, of the Party Objects).

2 GDH Cole, *A History of Socialist Thought*, Vol 4, London Macmillan, 1958, p422.

3 Ibid: See also Cole, *A History of the Labour Party from 1914*, London Routledge, 1948, p56.

4 SH Beer, *Modern British Politics*, London, Faber, 1982 pp. 125, 140.

5 *Ibid*; p126.

6 *Labour and the New Social Order*, London, Labour Party, 1918.

7 *Ibid*.

8 H Pelling, *A Short History of the Labour Party*, London, Macmillan, 10th edn, 1993, pp. 43–4.

9 See R McKibbin, *The Evolution of the Labour Party, 1910–1924*, Oxford, Oxford University Press, 1974, p96.

10   *Ibid.* See also J Winter, 'Arthur Henderson, The Russian Revolution and the Reconstruction of the Labour Party', *Historical Journal*,15, (1972)p772.

11   S Webb, 'New Constitution of the Labour Party', *The Observer* 21 October 1917.

12   K O Morgan, 'The Rise and Fall of Public Ownership in Britain', in JMW Bean (ed), *The Political Culture of Modern Britain*, London, Hamish Hamilton, 1987, p279.

13   *Ibid.*

14   'Basis' of the Fabian Programme, 1887, see E R Pease, *The History of the Fabian Society*, London, Frank Cass, 1918; 3rd edn, 1963, Appendix II.

15   S Webb, *Socialism: True and False* (Fabian Tract 51), London, Fabian Society, 1894.

16   Independent Labour Party Annual Conference Report, 1893.

17   For an examination of the Fabian socialists' view of public ownership, and of their underlying theoretical assumptions, see N Thomson, *Political Economy and the Labour Party*, London, UCL Press, 1996, Ch2.

18   GB Shaw 'The Economic Basis of Socialism' in Shaw (ed) *Essays in Fabian Socialism*, London, Constable, 1949 p52, quoted in Thomson 1996, pl9.

19   See E Hughes, *Keir Hardie*, London, Allen and Unwin, 1959, p37.

20   Beer, 1982, ppl23–5.

21   See McKibbin, 1974, pp96–7; Beer, 1982, pl45 S

22   See R Harrison, 'The War Emergency Workers' National Committee, 1914–1920', in A Briggs and J Saville (eds), *Essays in Labour History, 1886–1923*, London, Macmillan, 1971

23   J Winter, *Socialism and the Challenge of War*, London, Routledge and Kegan Paul, 1974, p272.

24   A Henderson, 'The Aims of Labour', Manchester, 1918; cited in Winter, 1972.

25   Winter, 1972, p771.

26   McKibbin, 1974, p92.

27   R Harrison, *New Labour as Past History*, Nottingham, Spokesman Press, 1996, p4.

28   Harrison,1971, p259.

29   See H Perkin, *The Rise of the Professional Society*, Routledge, 1989, p97.

30   McKibbin, 1974, p91.

31, *Ibid*, p.102

32   B Pimlott, 'The Labour Left' in C Cook and I Taylor (eds) *The Labour Party*, London, Longman, 1980, pl66.

33   *Ibid.*

34   McKibbin, pl974, pp. 96–7.

35   Harrison, 1971, p259.

36   Beer, 1982, pl49.

37   *Ibid.*, pl45.

38 Beer, 1982, pp. 125, 140.
39 *Ibid*. pl36.
40 See Winter, 1974, pp. 259–63; Harrison, 1971, pp. 211–59.
41 Winter, 1974, pp. 273–4.
42 *Ibid*. p274.
43 See H Gaitskell, 'Public Ownership and Equality', *Socialist Commentary*, June 1955. On Gaitskell's consistently favourable view of nationalisation as a means to socialist ends, see P Williams, *Hugh Gaitskell: a Political Iconography*, London, Cape, 1979, pp. 68–9, 449 n46, 890; B Brivati *Hugh Gaitskell*, London, Richard Cohen, 1996, pp83–4, 304.
44 Gaitskell, *Socialism and Nationalisation,* London, Fabian Society, 1956, p.34.
45 *Ibid*. p. 18.
46 See Williams, 1979, pp. 449, 659.
47 See T Jones, '"Taking Genesis out of the Bible:" Hugh Gaitskell, Clause IV and Labour's Socialist Myth', *Contemporary British History*, Vol II, No 2 (Summer 1997) p7.
48 Labour Party Annual Conference Report, 1959, p. lll.
49 *Ibid.*, pp. 111–112.
50 *Ibid.*, pll2.
51 For an expression of such views see Barbara Castle's earlier Chairman's address, LPACR, 1959, pp. 83–6.
52 Labour Party National Executive Committee minutes, 13 July 1960; quoted in D Howell, *British Social Democracy*, London, Croom Helm, 1976, p224.
53 Williams, 1979, p571.
54 See T Jones, *Remaking the Labour Party: from Gaitskell to Blair*, Routledge, 1996, pp. 58–64.
55 Williams, 1979, p570.
56 Harrison, 1971, p259.
57 CAR Crosland 'The Future of the Left', *Encounter*, March 1960.
58 For expressions of this viewpoint, see Howell, 1975, p222; Williams, 1979, p333; HM Drucker, *Doctrine and Ethos in the Labour Party*, London, Allen and Unwin, 1979, p38.
59 R Jenkins 'Hugh Gaitskell: a Political Memoir', *Encounter*, February 1964.
60 Williams, 1979, p570.
61 BBC Radio interview with Harold Wilson, February 1964; published in *The Listener*, 29 October 1964
62. On this point, see Williams, 1979, p549; Jones, 1996, pp. 63–4 See also Gaitskell's conversation with Labour's retiring deputy leader, Jim Griffiths, recorded in J Griffiths, *Pages from Memory*, London, Dent 1969, pl35 (also cited in Jones, 1996, p45).
63 D Marquand, *The Progressive Dilemma: from Lloyd George to Kinnock*, London, Heinemann, 1991, pl34.
64 For a discussion of the role of the idea of public ownership within Labour's socialist myth, see Jones, 1996, Chs 1 and 2

65   Labour's Programme 1982, London, Labour Party 1982.

66   See Jones, 1996, Ch 6.

67   See G Alexander, 'Managing the state and the state as manager' in B Brivati and T Bale (eds) *New Labour in Power: Precedents and Prospects*, Routledge, 1997, Ch 5.

68   See Thomson 1996, Ch 18.

69   G Foote, *The Labour Party's Political Thought: a History*, 3rd edn, London, Macmillan, 1997, p326.

70   P Seyd, 'Tony Blair and New Labour' in A King et al, *New Labour Triumphs: Britain at the Polls*, Chatham, New Jersey, Chatham House, 1998, p55.

71   J Straw, *Policy and Ideology*, Blackburn Labour Party, March 1993, pp. 2,4.

72   *Ibid.*, p.10.

73   *Ibid.*, p.12.

74   *Ibid.*

75   *Ibid.*, p.28.

76   See J Rentoul, *Tony Blair*, London, Little Brown and Co, 1996, pp. 408–9 See also Jones, 1996, p.180, n 18.

77   See Rentoul, 1996, pp. 408–9.

78   See G Radice, *Southern Discomfort*, London, Fabian Society, 1992, p.24; G Radice and S Pollard, *More Southern Discomfort*, London, Fabian Society, 1993, p.16.

79   The Archer Committee, *A New Constitution for the Labour Party*, Fabian Society, 1993.

80   N Kinnock, *Tomorrow's Socialism*, BBC2 Television, 5 February 1994.

81   *Ibid.*

82   *Fabian Review*, 9 May 1992.

83   A Blair, 'Forging a New Agenda,' Marxism Today, October 1991, p.32.

84   *Ibid.*

85   *Ibid.*

86   *Ibid.* p34.

87   *Ibid.*

88   Blair, *Socialism*, London, Fabian Society, 1994, p.4. On the influence upon Blair of the communitarian ideas of the Scottish philosopher John Macmurray, see Rentoul, 1996, pp. 42–5

89   Blair, 1994, p.4

90   *Ibid.*

91   See Crosland, *The Future of Socialism*, first published 1956, revised edn, London, Cape, 1964, pp. 67, 69–76; Gaitskell, 1956, pp. 5, 17–18; Jones, 1996, pp. 137–8

92   Blair, 1991, p.33

93   Blair in a note of a discussion with Peter Mandelson, quoted in J Sopel, *Tony Blair: The Moderniser*, London, Michael Joseph, 1995

94 See Rentoul, 1996, p.411; Sopel, 1995, pp. 273–4 See also P Riddell, 'The End of Clause IV, 1994–5,' *Contemporary British History*, Vol II, No 2 (Summer 1997), pp. 24–49.

95 LPACR, 1994.

96 *Ibid.*

97 *Ibid.*

98 *Ibid.*

99 P Riddell, 'Theatrical Blow Struck in Battle to Banish the Old Dogma', *The Times*, 5 October 1994.

100 See Riddell, 1997, pp. 34–5.

101 A Blair, 'Socialist Values in the Modern World', speech to Sedgefield Constituency Labour Party, 28 January 1995.

102 Blair, lecture at a commemoration organised by the Fabian Society to mark the fiftieth anniversary of the 1945 General Election, 5 July 1995.

103 *Ibid.*

104 Blair, 'Socialist Values in the Modern World', 1995

105 A Marr, 'He's Not One of Them and It Shows', *The Independent*, January 1995

106 Labour Party Constitution: 'Labour's Aims and Values,' London, Labour Party, 1995.

107 *Ibid.*

108 Blair, quoted in *The Guardian*, 13 March 1995.

109 S Webb, 1917.

110 *The Independent*, 13 March 1995; *The Times*, 14 March 1995; *The Guardian*, editorial, 14 March 1995.

111 Seyd, 1998, pp. 58–9.

112 Foote, 1997, p.3.

113 R Hattersley 'Tone of the Times', *The Guardian*, 27 April 1995.

114 *Ibid.*

115 T Bale '"The Death of the Past": Symbolic Politics and the Changing of Clause IV', in D Farrell, D Broughton, D Denver and J Fisher(eds), *British Elections and Parties Yearbook 1996*, London, Frank Cass, 1996. For a more extended discussion of these points, see Drucker, 1979, Ch 2; Jones 1996, Ch 1.

116 See Blair, 'Socialist Values in the Modern World', 1995; Fabian Society lecture, 5 July 1995.

117 Marr, 1995.

118 Bale, 1996, p.179.

119 Riddell, 1997, p. 40.

120 *Ibid.*, p.45.

A 'miracle of politics': the rise of Labour, 1900–1945

Andrew Chadwick

It is not without justification that we regard the Labour Party as the miracle of politics. Its progress in the relatively short period of thirty years is the outstanding romance of public affairs.[1]

Between 1900 and 1945, the Labour Party replaced the Liberal party as the main opposition to the Conservatives. Yet historians and political scientists have debated various explanations of the 'rise of Labour'; it is one of the most fertile topics of modern British history. This chapter therefore has two broad aims. First, it seeks to provide a clear and accessible introduction to the controversies generated by attempts to explain the 'rise of Labour'. Secondly, it seeks to provide a narrative of Labour's development which focuses on the broad themes covered by these various competing interpretations. In short, it tries to navigate a route through the complex, congested and contested terrain of Labour's rich historiography.

Labour, the 'progressive alliance' and the decline of the Liberal party, 1900–18

It is now well-established that the early Labour Party owed much to the ideological inheritance of nineteenth century radicalism. The precise meaning of the term 'radicalism' has differed according to historians' foci and assumptions. On the one hand, it can refer to a whole range of different ideas, campaigns, groups and demands, from movements for constitutional reform, to asserting the rights of religious nonconformists and campaigns for land nationalisation. It has also involved an emphasis on decentralisation and local politics, couched in terms of a general distrust of authority and a desire to place the political settlement on clear, regular and accountable lines as a means of avoiding arbitrary power and unconstitutionality. Alternatively, it is sometimes asserted that the radical tradition to which Labour belongs is altogether more revolutionary, and can be traced back to early quasi-socialist groups such as the Levellers of the 1640s, the Chartists of the 1830s and 40s, and the militant, direct democratic traditions of the Paris Commune of 1870–1. Both strands of radicalism had an influence on Labour's political ideas and political culture before 1945. As recent revisionist historians have demonstrated, it is important to place the established narrative of the various socialist and trade union influences on Labour's ideology alongside an equally important recognition that Labour emerged out of the peculiarly British context of a powerful reformist Liberalism which, for the latter part of the nineteenth century, had been led by the charismatic politicians such as William Gladstone and intellectuals such as John Stuart Mill. Labour's negotiation with the radical liberal tradition, and the implications of this negotiation for its political strategy, now provide the organising force for many accounts of the party between 1900 and the 1930s.[2]

Partly due to the weight of this radical tradition, the period between 1900 and 1918 saw Labour struggle to carve out a distinctive space in an essentially two party system. The immediate problem lay in challenging its immediate rivals, the Liberals, in order to gain a foothold in the electoral contest. A poor performance in the 1900 general election is easily explained: the party had been established only a few months earlier. But a similarly poor performance at the next election might have caused the disintegration of the Labour Representation Committee – the fragile alliance of trade unionists and socialists which became the Labour Party in 1906. By the turn of the century, the Conservative and Liberal parties had matured into relatively well co-ordinated, hierarchical, election-winning machines, with identifiable national leaderships, and activist grassroots memberships. The fundamental features of the modern British party system were laid down during the late Victorian period.[3] Before 1918, Labour had weakly developed versions of those structures which the two main parties took for granted, and, perhaps more importantly, these structures, and the operating assumptions upon which they rested, had been formed within the context of a simple majority electoral system, rather than some form of proportional representation (PR).

The Gladstone–MacDonald pact of 1903 represented, in part, an attempt to resolve such difficulties. The result of secret negotiations between Ramsay MacDonald and the Liberal chief whip, Herbert Gladstone, the pact established that at the next general election the Liberals would allow Labour a 'straight fight' with the Conservatives in a limited number of constituencies. The pact secretly cemented what quickly became one of the defining features of Edwardian politics: the 'progressive alliance' between Liberalism and Labour. The agreement lasted until the outbreak of war in 1914, and was largely responsible for Labour's modest electoral success in this period.

Yet the pact was only one solution to an obvious problem. Between 1900 and 1924, and to a lesser extent between 1924 and 1931, many Labourists and socialists considered PR the best solution to Labour's status as a minority party. Widespread support for reform could be found among the Independent Labour Party (ILP), the Social Democratic Federation (SDF) and trade unions such as the Amalgamated Society of Railway Servants. Prominent figures such as Philip Snowden and George Barnes supported reform, and pointed to foreign examples of socialist success in countries such as Germany and Sweden. The Proportional Representation Society, founded in 1885 and revived in 1904 under the leadership of the radical Liberal, Leonard Courtney, attracted many Labour members to its ranks. PR was advocated for various reasons. Some argued on purely instrumental grounds that, given a 'fair' electoral system, Labour's share of the popular vote would be more accurately translated into seats in the House of Commons; it would speed Labour's rise to major party status. But many invoked the language of radical constitutionalism, and drew upon intellectual heroes such as John Stuart Mill in order to assert the democratic and educative effect which it was thought PR would have on British political life. In this view, it would stimulate political participation, foster active citizenship, guarantee the rights of minorities, and provide, in a much-used slogan 'fairness and electoral justice'. Snowden and others argued that Labour should dispense with secret pacts and embrace the honest, 'purified' form of political life that would be guaranteed by a different electoral system.

Such reformist voices, were, however, opposed by a strong section of the Labour movement, led by figures such as MacDonald and leading Fabians such as Sidney Webb, Graham Wallas, Clifford Sharp and Henry Schloesser. MacDonald emerged as a particularly vociferous critic. Demonstrating foresight of the future development of the British party system, he argued that Labour could establish its electoral support by focusing on those key industrial constituencies containing large concentrations of working-class electors. He effectively prioritised what is now taken for granted by all party leaders in Britain, if not in principle then in practice: that given a concentration of support in certain constituencies, it is perfectly possible to win a general election on less than 40 per cent of the popular vote. Labour should build up its electoral base in working-class areas, claimed MacDonald, over a long period if necessary, rather than be misled by the false promise of a reformed electoral system. Alongside this, he questioned PR's contribution to democratic politics. This stemmed from what is best termed an organic approach to democracy, allied with a collectivist interpretation of state power. The supposed benefits of PR, he maintained, were likely to produce a fragmented, divisive and unstable political system, with segmented, multi-member constituencies creating pockets of Labour support from which the party would never be able to expand.[4]

This debate was crucial to Labour's long-term strategy. It reached its high point at the 1913 and 1914 annual conferences, and was to return to prominence immediately after the Great War. However, Labour's minority administration of 1924 effectively sealed the fate of the reformists, and, despite a brief resurgence of interest in the early 1930s, the issue of electoral reform was to lapse into a period of dormancy, from which it did not emerge until the late 1980s. MacDonald was to be proved right. Labour's electoral success, while not exclusively dependent upon working class votes in industrial areas, was certainly based on such 'core' support.

Despite the secrecy of the Gladstone–MacDonald pact, the progressive alliance was more than a marriage of convenience, more than simple electoral instrumentalism. For all but the most uncompromising, it was based upon well-established affinities between socialism, labourism and liberalism. Historians, led by Peter Clarke, have established the similarities between Labour's ideas and the progressive reformism of the 'new liberalism' in the writings of L. T. Hobhouse and J. A. Hobson, with its emphasis on state intervention in the economy, social equality and trade union participation.[5] Further, recent scholarship has suggested that the early Labour Party, along with socialist, radical and suffrage feminist groups also made use of an older, established discourse of 'radical constitutionalism'. With its themes of democratic constitutional reform (especially devolution; PR; women's and 'adult' suffrage, and reform of the House of Lords), this also contributed to the links between Liberalism, Labour and the diverse assortment of groups which made up the rich culture of oppositional politics during the period.[6]

Historians are divided on the overarching issue of the decline of the Liberal Party. The 'progressive alliance' thesis maintains that Liberalism was revitalised as an ideological and electoral force during the pre-1914 period, and that Labour benefited from the generally progressive climate of ideas. Liberalism managed to retain the support of the vast bulk of trade unionists, and maintained its hegemony over the left through the influential writings of the new liberals as well as the passionate style of David Lloyd George. For this group of historians, Liberal decline began during the traumatic experience of 'total war', which caused internal divisions from which it never fully recovered. The split in 1916 between the two outstanding figures of the Edwardian party – Asquith and Lloyd George – tore Liberalism apart, depriving it of the opportunity to mount a serious appeal to the newly-expanded electorate after 1918. Labour's place in this narrative is as the left-wing of the broader progressive movement, which, before the 1916 debacle, was dependent upon Liberal goodwill for many of its seats because it failed to attract sufficient trade union and working-class support. Both Liberalism and Labour benefited from the arrival of 'class politics' before 1914, but the Liberals were much better equipped to take advantage of it.

This explanation has been criticised by a number of historians. The original argument was put forward with literary panache by George Dangerfield, but recent scholarly research has been led by Ross McKibbin and Keith Laybourn.[7] In this interpretation, the Liberals, though performing well on the surface, were being steadily and fatally undermined by the rise of a new working-class political consciousness. This was not a 'socialist', but a 'labourist' vision: it stemmed from a gradual union recognition that working-class interests would be best served by the nascent Labour Party. They point to the increase in trade union membership which took place between 1910 and 1914, and which exploded during the first world war. They argue that Labour's growth was artificially stunted by the 'franchise factor' – the restrictive settlement of 1884; a problem rectified by the 'fourth' Reform Act of 1918, which enfranchised all adult men and the majority of women over the age of 30. Existing working-class male voters, it is argued, gradually switched their allegiance from the Liberals to Labour in sufficient numbers, but Labour and the Conservatives benefited from the new electors of the post-1918 settlement while the Liberals did not. Arguments over the contribution made by a restricted franchise have continued since Neil Blewett's pioneering work in the mid-1960s.[8] While advocates of the McKibbin thesis tend to argue that the pre-1918 franchise systematically discriminated against those groups who would have voted Labour if given the opportunity,[9] supporters of the 'progressivism' thesis point to new analyses of both local and national electorates which demonstrate that the effects of the franchise exhibit no particular pattern, but were random, and affected all parties.[10]

It is likely that the debate over the Liberals' decline will continue. It is difficult to deny McKibbin's argument that Labour's organisation steadily improved during the pre-war period. But it is equally difficult to deny the weight of evidence suggesting that the 'progressive alliance' was a vital force in Edwardian politics, operating at the level of ideas and electoral agreement. As for the debate over the 'franchise factor', the work has been dogged by the unavailability of hard evidence of the kind which post-war psephologists now take for granted.

The Impact of the First World War

Labour entered the first world war a struggling third party without a coherent platform and dependent upon Liberal charity for its tentative electoral advances. At its end, the party emerged with a new constitution and a coherent party programme. The wartime dissolution of the Gladstone–MacDonald pact, along with the split in the Liberal Party, signalled the decline of the progressive alliance.

Labour and the trade unions were divided over the war. A pacifist minority, led by ILPers such as MacDonald, Snowden and Fred Jowett, along with radical liberals like E. D. Morel and Norman Angell, founded the Union of Democratic Control, a small but important pressure group which campaigned for a more open system of international diplomacy and 'parliamentary control of foreign policy'. In many respects, this group was the last significant example of the type of temporary radical-socialist-labour alliance which characterised the high period of progressivism between 1904 and 1914. Although short-lived, it played a significant role in converting many progressive Liberals to the Labour and socialist cause after the war. Morel and J. A. Hobson were among the many 'recruits to Labour'.[11] But the majority of the party and the trade unions swung firmly behind the government's war policy, and it is significant that Labour's increased popularity in the 1918 general election, despite unfavourable circumstances, did not extend to MacDonald, Snowden and Jowett: all three lost their seats. Although unpalatable to the socialist-pacifists, who were mainly concentrated in the ILP, the fact that the majority of the party were supportive of the war and usually expressed that support in unreservedly patriotic language probably served Labour well in the 1918, 1922 and 1923 general elections.

The war assisted Labour's cause for various reasons, but historians are divided over their relative importance. First, it has been argued that Labour benefited from a sea change in working-class attitudes which occurred as a result of the extraordinary wartime conditions. According to this perspective, which largely draws upon the social historian Arthur Marwick, and the political sociologist Stanislav Andreski, the Great War increased living standards, social mobility and loosened the traditional ties of social hierarchy. The working classes became less deferential, joined trade unions in greater numbers, and this opened up the possibility of significant social and economic change.[12] A second explanation concerns the agency called upon to promote social and economic change: the state. It has been argued that increased state intervention in the wartime economy demonstrated the beneficial effects of production harnessed in the national interest. Ad hoc institutions, such as the War Emergency: National Workers' Committee, incorporated labour leaders in the process of national mobilisation, softened some of the more coercive elements of state direction, and demonstrated to the party the relative ease with which the state could be used to foster conciliation between the working, middle and upper classes. Such experiences are said to have had a significant effect upon debates leading up to the drafting of *Labour and the New Social Order* by Sidney Webb in 1918. This new programme, with its commitment to public ownership in the famous 'Clause Four', saw the rise to hegemonic status of Fabian, state-driven collectivism on the one hand, and a moderate, union-derived 'labourism' on the other. It was to prove the final nail in the coffin of both revolutionary and non-revolutionary libertarian alternatives such as syndicalism and guild socialism.[13] A third explanation is that the involvement of various Labour figures in the coalition governments demonstrated Labour's 'fitness to govern' in the minds of the wider electorate. It established the leadership's credibility as a respectable, moderate and competent team capable of disciplining the trade unions.[14] Finally, it has been argued that the war hastened the extension of the parliamentary franchise. But the extent to which this helped Labour depends upon one's view of the 'franchise factor'. These explanations, which are all dependent upon a view of the Great War as the locomotive of history, amount to a substantial and convincing set of arguments.

They have, however, been challenged by historians who are sceptical of the war's overall importance. There is some dispute over the nature of the working-class reaction to increased state activity. It has been argued that far from promoting a new receptiveness, increased state intervention was greeted with hostility by large sections of the working classes. Resentment at directed labour schemes – attacked using the slogan 'industrial conscription' – derived from deep-seated hostilities to state control which have always been an important strand of the unions' political culture. There is no obvious connection between a newly-interventionist state and a working-class demand for greater social equality.[15] A second criticism of the 'war' interpretation is that it is simply irrelevant. For McKibbin and others, the foundations of Labour's post-war success were laid in the pre-war period. They were largely to do with steady improvements in relations with the trade unions, party organisation and electioneering, especially at the local level. In this view, Labour was making slow but steady progress before 1914 and would have continued its development along the same lines even if war had been avoided.[16]

While McKibbin marshals convincing evidence of improvements in party machinery, the multi-dimensional character of the 'war' interpretation makes it an impressive body of research which cannot be easily dismissed. Even if Labour's electoral viability was steadily improving before 1914, this needs to be augmented by a recognition that the war represented the happy marriage of receptive social and political contexts with a pre-existing, powerful ideology of Fabian socialism. Alternatives were in existence; it was not until the early 1920s that guild socialism began its steep decline. But that alternative failed, not because it lacked coherence, but because it failed to connect with a social and political context which had been fundamentally re-shaped by the war. And although it is important to remember, as Martin Pugh has suggested, that war-time patriotism and xenophobia probably helped the Conservatives more than it did Labour, it must also be stated that the majority of senior Labour figures were eager participants in directing the war effort.

Expansion, office and disaster, 1918-1931

At its conference of February, 1918, Labour adopted a new party programme and a new constitution. Largely the product of Sidney Webb and Arthur Henderson, the constitution allowed the establishment of constituency Labour parties (CLPs) that would be free to recruit individual members, irrespective of union, ILP, or Fabian Society membership. The new party structure, with a powerful National Executive Committee (NEC), elected by Conference, was designed to cement the trade unions' hegemony over the party. But it was also designed with electoral success in mind. The new constitution signalled a shift from a loose, federal structure basically incapable of implementing a co-ordinated electoral strategy, towards a truly national organisation capable (in theory) of launching an appeal to all classes and regions at the grassroots. The NEC moved swiftly to create four new sub-committees: organisation and elections; policy and programme; literature, research and publicity; and finance and general purposes. The efficient and dynamic Egerton Wake was appointed as the new national agent. The party finally acquired its own national daily newspaper, when it took financial control of the *Daily Herald*. New women voters were targeted by Marion Phillips, who was appointed head of the Women's Section. CLPs increased in number from 400 to 527 in 1922, and by 1924 all but 19 constituencies had local parties. Although it would be many years before it would really reap the benefit, Labour became a national party in 1918.

In June that year, Labour adopted the programme that was in several respects to form the basis of its political strategy for the next thirty years. Excepting contemporary references to the immediate post-war tasks of foreign policy, much of *Labour and the New Social Order* can be traced down the years to 1945. The draft programme was written by Sidney Webb, and it showed. It called for full employment, fair wages, new state benefits for the unemployed, as well as housing, education and health reforms. The principle of public ownership appeared centre stage, with calls for the nationalisation of rail and canal transport, coal and electricity, and land. Webb also proposed a new 'capital levy' – a tax on the rich to pay off war debts and fund the programme of reconstruction.

Labour's new constitution and programme represented the fusion of trade unionist labourism and a moderate, respectable Fabian collectivism. The inclusion of Clause Four caused little debate at the time. Perhaps this is less surprising, however, if we consider Royden Harrison's argument that it was the vagueness of the idea which made it 'work' as a unifying force.[17] Socialists could look forward to the gradual extension of the state. Trade unionists could look forward to better pay and working conditions once exploitative and irresponsible private owners had been replaced. Even libertarian socialists such as Harold Laski and G. D. H. Cole agreed with public ownership as a first step, even if they did not share the Fabian emphasis on 'scientific' regulation by an enlightened bureaucracy working in consultation (and little more) with labour interests.

Armed with its new programme and constitution, and in the context of a newly expanded electorate, Labour was set to perform well at the 1918 'coupon' election. Yet unusual circumstances – an electoral agreement between Lloyd George Liberals and the Conservatives – resulted in a paltry 57 seats for Labour. The Liberals remained divided, with an opposition Asquithian section centred on the traditionally radical National Liberal Federation. However, the effects of Labour's new strategy soon began to emerge, and at the 1922 general election, caused by the Conservatives' withdrawal from the Lloyd George coalition, Labour secured a spectacular 29 per cent of the popular vote and 142 seats. MacDonald was elected official party leader soon after. Liberalism, still divided, secured a total of 115 seats; 62 for the Asquithians and 53 for supporters of Lloyd George. Only sixteen years earlier the Liberals had swept to victory with over 400 MPs. Now they were the third party in what had temporarily become a fully-fledged multi-party system.

Labour's campaigning machinery therefore made significant strides between 1918 and 1922. But these developments must be set alongside depictions of the reality of CLP activity during this period. Accurate reconstructions of local party life are difficult to obtain, but it has been argued that many struggled to maintain their membership, often failed to reach out to new women voters, and suffered from poor finances. The problem was especially acute in those rural constituencies which lacked the local political cultures of industrial trade unionism upon which Labour began to thrive, both politically and financially, elsewhere.[18] The narrative of inexorable expansion certainly needs to be moderated. At the same time, however, recent research by Pamela M. Graves on Labour's women members has dented some of this scholarly scepticism. By any standards, the numbers which joined the party in the 1920s is amazing. By 1922, 100,000 women were organised in 800 sections. In 1925 there were 200,000 in 1535 sections. By the end of the decade, women made up a quarter of a million of the party's members and were organised in 1867 sections. The majority were working-class, married and with families.[19] Of course, these figures reveal nothing of women's formal power in the party, which remained at low levels throughout the 1920s and 30s, and they need to be set alongside the party's poor record in selecting women candidates for parliamentary contests. But such factors appear to have made little difference to women's desire to join in order that they may fight for a cause in which they believed, regardless of whether they might achieve significant power in the party's internal machinery. Indeed, Graves's account is bolstered by oral testimony from other Labour activists, many of whom who joined the party in the 1920s and 30s.[20] Thus, although Labour's development in the 1920s was patchy, and limited by financial weakness, the characterisation of a struggling party appears broadly inaccurate.

The First Labour Government

The general election of 1923 gave Labour a total of 191 seats, a substantial increase on the 142 it managed to gain in 1922. Yet its share of the popular vote increased by only two per cent. MacDonald's prophecy of the future benefits of the British electoral system were beginning to materialise. This is not the place to discuss the detail of the minority Labour government of 1924.[21] Instead, I will focus on the implications of this short period in office for Labour's political strategy.

Several fundamental weaknesses affected the first Labour government, and many of these were to reverberate throughout the 1920s and early 1930s. First, MacDonald struggled to assemble a Cabinet team considered competent enough to demonstrate that Labour was a party 'fit to govern'. Despite a strong union presence in the cabinet (three mineworkers, and representatives of the textile, ironfounders, railwaymen and General and Municipal Workers), a total of seven cabinet members (five Liberals, two Conservatives) had not even been Labour politicians before 1914.

Second, the minority government was heavily dependent upon Liberal support in the Commons. This severely diluted the distinctiveness of its policies. It is generally agreed that the most successful example of innovation was John Wheatley's housing policy, which paved the way for the development of mass public housing. But despite the promise of *Labour and the New Social Order*, in most other areas Labour did little to distinguish itself from the Liberals. This is not surprising, given Snowden's role as Chancellor. Labour's first budget is good evidence of the influence of nineteenth-century radicalism on the early party; it paid homage to free trade and strict financial orthodoxy. But it must be stated that this was before the 'Keynesian revolution' in economic policy had truly gathered pace. Seen in the context of the early 1920s, and Labour's radical inheritance, Snowden's budget was not unusual. Criticism emerged from the new, younger generation of the Labour left, centred around prominent ILPers such as Fenner Brockway and 'red Clydesiders' such as Jimmy Maxton. Their view that Labour should deliberately provoke a Commons defeat and fight another general election on a full-blooded socialist programme, lacked credibility, not only because deliberately provoking instability would have alienated voters, but also because such views clashed with the fundamental absence of extreme socialist beliefs among the cabinet's most powerful members: MacDonald, Snowden, Arthur Henderson, and J. R. Clynes.

The government's third weakness (which has haunted the British left through much of the 20th century) stemmed from its genuinely internationalist attempts to establish good relations with Russia. Criticism of treaties, trade negotiations and loan agreements during the summer of 1924 were to rear their head in unfortunate circumstances during the autumn election campaign, when the now infamous 'Zinoviev letter' was published by the *Daily Mail*. In propaganda terms, it was a major weapon for the Conservatives, who presented themselves as the defenders of the British national interest in the face of the 'red menace'.

The Zinoviev letter was not the only cause of Labour's defeat at the 1924 general election. That is best explained by the inevitable structural weaknesses of a minority government, combined with poor ministerial performance, the reality of Labour's still-narrow electoral base, and the collapse of the Liberal vote, which largely benefited the Conservatives.[22] Labour was reduced to 151 MPs, while the Conservatives, with 412, secured a huge majority. The Liberal vote fell to just 18 per cent, and its Commons representation to just 40. Although it lost the election, defined in narrow electoral terms the 'rise of Labour' was seemingly complete. Despite criticism from the left that the Labour government had betrayed its followers and its principles, the party did not argue over the fundamentals of its future strategy. There were vague initiatives to have Ernest Bevin replace MacDonald as leader, but recognition of the decline of the Liberals contributed to Labour's forward momentum.

The party now entered what was to be a surprisingly short period of opposition. Of central importance between 1924 and 1929 were the General Strike, the gradual marginalisation of both the ILP, the Communist Party of Great Britain (CPGB) and the new Labour Party programme of 1928, *Labour and the Nation*. How did these impact upon Labour's political strategy?

The 1926 General Strike was a disastrous defeat for the trade unions, but its impact on Labour was ambiguous. The Trade Union Act of 1927 changed the basis upon which union members could contribute to party funds: 'contracting in' replaced 'contracting out'. The Act was designed to weaken Labour politically by damaging its financial base. As a result, trade union affiliated members fell by around one million within a year; a huge dent in Labour's resources. However, in the long term, as Ralph Miliband has argued, the strike helped establish Labour's credibility among the wider electorate by demonstrating the pitfalls of industrial militancy.[23] In addition, the 1927 Act made sympathetic strike action illegal. Union hostility to such measures was always likely to improve relations with Labour. The party thus emerged quite unscathed.

The discrediting of industrial action had knock-on effects in helping the leadership deflect the internal and external socialist challenges of the ILP and the CPGB. The ILP shifted direction during the mid-1920s and began to discard elements of the vague variety of ethical socialism which it had espoused since 1893. Previously content to remain within the broad alliance of labourists and socialists, a hardening of the ILP's position occurred under the leadership of Jimmy Maxton. A new set of concrete proposals in its new programme, *Socialism in Our Time* (1927), sharpened divisions with the unions and the Labour leadership. Although it was by no means outrageous, the ILP's new programme, containing demands such as a minimum wage to increase mass consumption, went against the grain of Labour's dominant stance on economic policy, the parameters of which were still being framed by Snowden. The programme was easily defeated at Labour's 1927 conference, and the ILP began to sever its long-standing ties. Similar factors led to the marginalisation of the CPGB. Indignant at Labour's 'betrayal' of the working-class during the General Strike, it shifted its strategy in 1928 towards one of antipathy to all 'capitalist' parties, Labour included. Many Communists undoubtedly remained as Labour members, but they had to forego open support for the CPGB. Between 1926 and 1928 Labour moved to purge Communists from CLPs. The grip on the party by moderates like MacDonald, Henderson and Snowden was duly strengthened by the marginalisation of these dissenting forces.

The leadership's hold was further tightened by the new party programme of 1928, *Labour and the Nation* – a curious combination of comprehensive, but vague, long-term socialist goals and short-term pragmatism. It reflected internal divisions between the moderate leadership and the ILP, and it also reflected the confusion of socialist intellectuals such as R. H. Tawney, its principal author, who had seen the heady optimism of *Labour and the New Social Order* dissolve, but who still wished to retain its core emphasis on state action to promote equality. Added to this was the uncertainty caused by the final extension of the franchise to all women over 21 in 1928. Labour now had to appeal to a wider number of voters, and the all-embracing nature of the programme was designed with this in mind.

The Second Labour Government

Labour therefore entered the 1929 general election with its party machinery in reasonable condition, a new party programme, and with a leadership with a tight hold on the levers of party power. But it had no reason to expect victory. Baldwin had proved adept as Conservative leader, and the radicalisation of the Liberals, under the Keynesian 'Yellow Book' proposals had allowed the government to establish a 'Safety First' platform which painted the dangers of Labour and Liberal 'socialism' in vivid colours. From Labour's viewpoint, the result was a genuine breakthrough, whose importance has long been overshadowed by the ensuing crisis of 1931. It emerged as the largest party, with 288 seats. The Conservatives fell to 260, while the Liberal revival in ideology and share of the vote (from 18 per cent in 1924 to 23 per cent) did not translate into seats in Parliament due to the vagaries of the electoral system: it won only 58 seats, and agreed to follow the pattern of 1924 and give its support to a Labour government.[24]

As prime minister for the second time, MacDonald faced the recurrent difficulty of choosing his cabinet. Snowden, Henderson, J. H. Thomas and J. R. Clynes all returned, along with seven other veterans of 1924. With the inclusion of the ageing socialist, George Lansbury – brought in at the expense of the other ILPers of 1924, Wheatley and Jowett – the cabinet had a rather elderly profile. Nevertheless, MacDonald was still forced to rely upon those whose political careers had been forged outside of the labour movement, as evidenced by his inclusion of William Wedgwood Benn, and he was again hindered by the necessity of maintaining Liberal support in the Commons.

But these factors pale into insignificance alongside what had become Labour's main weakness by the late 1920s: the inadequacy of its economic ideas. While the Liberals had adopted Keynesian demand management as part of their redefinition of party policy by this stage, Labour's economic policy continued to be dominated by Snowden's desire to 'balance the budget', to make capitalism more dynamic and prosperous in order to pave the way for socialism. The genuinely innovative Liberal 'Yellow Book', *Britain's Industrial Future* (1928), contained detailed economic analysis of the likely effects of deficit spending and public works programmes on unemployment. In contrast, Labour and the Nation was vague and imprecise. Despite MacDonald's partial recognition of the new mood among economists, exhibited in his establishment of the Economic Advisory Council in 1930, the conversion to Keynesianism came several years later. As Martin Pugh has argued, many followed Snowden's line out of deference.[25] But it must be added that when it came to the technical management of capitalism, Labour was still dependent upon its Gladstonian liberal inheritance. In this it was not alone, for large sections of the Liberal and Conservative parties shared a similar outlook.[26] It would be unwise to place too much emphasis on the element of choice involved in economic policy during this period.

The failure to come to terms with the implications of demand management meant Labour had little response to the intensifying economic crisis. Unemployment rose by 700,000 between November 1929 and July 1930, but the Treasury remained implacably opposed to government control of the Bank of England and public works. Failed attempts to introduce elements of the Liberals' programme into the government's orbit, by figures such as Oswald Mosley, fell on deaf ears.[27] When the fragility of the international banking regime was finally exposed in the summer of 1931, the government proceeded with budget-balancing measures designed to restore confidence in the hope of securing loans from New York and Paris financiers. This meant cuts rather than increases in public expenditure. Harshest of all was the ten per cent cut in unemployment benefit, pushed through cabinet by MacDonald and Snowden, but rejected by the TUC – a move which contributed to the downfall of the government, the defection of MacDonald, Snowden and Thomas, and the installation of the National government.

MacDonald's National Labour group consisted of just 13 MPs, and across the country there were very few defections. Yet, with the former foreign secretary, Henderson, as temporary leader, Labour staggered into the 1931 general election with its programme and strategy in ruins, tarnished by its failure to deal with the depression. In October, 1931, following the abandonment of the gold standard, MacDonald called a general election. The National government won over seventy per cent of the popular vote and a massive 556 seats, 470 of which went to the Conservatives. The scale of this defeat needs to be grasped. Labour lost two million votes, and was reduced to just 52 seats. It thus fell to its pre-1918 representation in the Commons. Labour also failed to benefit from the dramatic decline in the number of three-cornered fights. The Liberals' final retreat from a national electoral strategy, by reducing the number of split-vote constituencies, would have benefited Labour had it not been for the crisis. As Andrew Thorpe has written of this collapse: 'since the 1867 Reform Act it had been exceeded only by the Liberals, in 1918 and 1924 – hardly an encouraging precedent'.[28]

What were the effects of 1931 on Labour's future political strategy? First, Labour's leadership changed. MacDonald, Snowden and Thomas had embarked on their political careers at the turn of the century. Their age was beginning to show, and their grasp of the new style of politics, which increasingly came to be characterised by demanding technical debates on economic policy, was relatively weak when compared with new figures such as Hugh Dalton, Herbert Morrison, Arthur Greenwood and Stafford Cripps. The end of MacDonaldism ushered in a new era of TUC influence, as the National Joint Council was replaced with a new National Council of Labour, with increased TUC representation, often led by the General Secretary of the Transport and General Workers Union, Ernest Bevin. This was to assume a crucial role in broad policy decisions during the 1930s and 40s, while the NEC's role shifted to detailed planning.

Secondly, despite protestations from new left wing groups such as the Socialist League, the mainstream of the labour movement kept faith with its gradualist traditions. There were significant differences with the past, however, as the emphasis now shifted towards a more thorough concern with the details of economic policy. In effect, this led to the wholesale adoption of Keynesianism by the late 1930s. The move was headed by Bevin, who pointed to the success of Roosevelt's New Deal in producing immediate benefits. Keynesianism was a solution to the problem of finding a viable context for public ownership, as Labour focused its efforts on devising plans for a 'mixed' economy. This would involve the nationalisation of limited sectors: fuel and power, water, transport, agriculture, iron and steel, shipbuilding, engineering, textiles, banking and insurance.[29] The broader economic strategy allowed Labour's rising figures, particularly Herbert Morrison, to flesh out the future structures for public ownership. What became the 'Morrisonian model' of the public corporation received immediate criticism for its lack of workers' participation, but it undoubtedly served Labour well in the context of the 1930s and 40s by demonstrating quick solutions and efficient managerial competence in the Fabian tradition. In the form of the two major policy documents of the 1930s, *For Socialism and Peace* (1934) and *Labour's Immediate Programme* (1937), it was to provide the ideal bedrock for the Attlee-Bevin axis which was to dominate Labour politics between 1935 and 1951.

Thirdly, alongside this mainstream presence, there developed a new, more sophisticated socialist discourse in the labour movement. This was given shape by thinkers such as Cole, Laski and John Strachey, but also by the Socialist League, which, following the ILP's eventual disaffiliation in 1932, became the main left-wing presence. But the League differed from Maxton's ILP in its expressed loyalty to the leadership. This gave it greater legitimacy, and, consequently, greater influence. The League never challenged the hegemony of the Fabian-Keynesian nexus, and was ultimately marginalised. But it did provide a strident critique of capitalism alongside a genuinely new preoccupation with the problematic role of the state in a future socialist society.[31]

It would be unwise to argue that the 1931 crisis 'helped' Labour. However, its implications were not as severe as they might have been. By the mid-1930s, Labour had re-emerged with a strong and effective leadership, a solid financial base provided by the trade unions, a new public discourse on economic policy, and a level of intellectual creativity which had been lacking for several years. Of course, not all of these trends were compatible with a successful party strategy; tensions and conflict continued. But in the 1930s we can observe the essentially hybrid character of the party – its combination of socialist intellectuals and trade union leaders, its idealism and pragmatism, its doctrine and ethos, which became a taken for granted feature of its post-war years.

Labour recovered to win 154 seats at the 1935 general election. The underlying message was clear: in managing to secure a higher percentage of the vote than in 1929 (just over 37 per cent), Labour was not destined for electoral oblivion. The wounds of 1931 had begun to heal, and there was a possibility, if only a slight one, of a Labour victory at a 1940 general election. That election did not, of course, come until 1945.

Roads to 1945

Explanations of Labour's victory in 1945 have generated almost as much historiographical controversy as the debate over the decline of the Liberals. Two main avenues have been explored: the party's attitude to fascism, and the experience of the second world war.

By the mid-1930s, the principles underlying Labour's foreign policy had shifted. In 1914 the majority of the labour movement had been in favour of war, but by the 1920s the influence of the left had shifted policy towards a critique of militarism and its links with international capitalism. Slogans such as 'capitalist war' became commonplace, and often went alongside calls for international disarmament. Yet the resignation of the pacifist Lansbury in 1935 signalled the decline of what came to be viewed as 'impractical' idealism in foreign policy. His successor as party leader, Clement Attlee took a more pragmatic approach. The outbreak of civil war in Spain also helped shift left-wing figures such as Cripps towards support for intervention against fascism. At the 1937 party conference, support was finally given to British rearmament and the next two years saw Labour voice its criticism of Chamberlain's appeasement policy. When war was declared in September 1939, Labour was in full support. Such unity and clarity in the fight against fascism was to serve Labour well, both in its experience of government in the wartime coalition, and during the 1945 general election, when it rekindled its pre-war critique of the 'guilty men' of appeasement in the form of an attack on an old, discredited, political class.

Labour was invited to join the Churchill coalition government in May 1940. Attlee and Bevin proceeded to develop the central themes of what has been termed 'war socialism': public provision in the field of housing, health, education, food, the abolition of the widely-resented Means Test, and the state direction of production. Labour's presence on the Reconstruction Committee, formed in 1943, contributed to the 1944 education reforms and a White Paper outlining Keynesian policies for promoting full employment and a national health service.[32] As in the first world war, Labour's ministers demonstrated their 'fitness to govern' during a time of national crisis.[33]

Historians and political scientists have been in general agreement on the role played by the war in contributing to Labour's victory. The basis of this narrative was set down shortly after the war by Richard Titmuss. In *Problems of Social Policy* (1950) Titmuss argued that war generated a sense of community in British society which fostered support for Labour's egalitarian policies.[34] This interpretation was reinforced by Paul Addison's seminal work, *The Road to 1945*, which argued that the demands of total war led the government to adopt welfarist measures to maintain its legitimacy.[35] This meant handing over significant power to social liberals such as William Beveridge, who used his position to establish the foundations of the post-war consensus in the Report on Social Insurance and Allied Services of 1942. While the Conservatives equivocated, Labour was generally supportive of the Beveridge proposals.

Addison's interpretation has been supported by most historians, even neo-Marxist critics of the party such as Miliband.[35] However, a recent revisionist account has attempted a more precise interpretation of how Labour benefited from the shift in popular attitudes. Steven Fielding, Peter Thompson and Nick Tiratsoo have argued that popular radicalism and support for Labour's socialist policies were not one and the same. It was perfectly possible for Labour to be elected on the basis of a shift in attitudes, but that shift did not point in the direction of socialism, rather an inchoate set of sentiments about fairness that were further undermined by concrete divisions, between the middle and working classes, and, more importantly, within the working-class itself. They argue that Labour's victory can be explained by a combination of demands for limited reform and the superiority of the party's organisation in 1945.[36] With its innovative focus on the 'unofficial' sources of labour history, this view provides a useful corrective to some of the mythology that has built up around '1945', but it does not by itself demolish the established view that the war in some way assisted Labour. The limited extent to which the war fostered radical socialist ideas was always taken into account by Addison. It is arguable that a socialist class consciousness has never been integral to Labour's electoral success, and the war was no exception.

Indeed, the roots of Labour's victory can be found in its rapid recovery following the disastrous events of 1931. The emergence of a new leadership, together with the adoption of Keynesianism, meant that the experience of the wartime coalition was fruitful rather than frustrating. Without the seeds of recovery which had been planted in the 1930s, it would have been perfectly possible for Labour to reject Keynesian ideas as irrelevant when they finally arrived at the top of the political agenda during the war. Similarly, though it was undoubtedly flawed, the Morrisonian model of nationalisation did not go against the grain of the political context in the aftermath of increased bureaucratic regulation during the height of the war. The trade union influence on the party, which increased following the departure of MacDonald, had allowed Labour to continue to make financial demands in return. Despite the decline in membership of the early 1930s, Labour's financial bedrock among the unionised working classes remained strong. Even the newly resurgent left of the 1930s assisted Labour, as a new generation of gifted intellectuals popularised left-wing ideas in their role as journalists and authors. Figures such as George Orwell, John Strachey, Harold Laski and G. D. H. Cole, though often critical of the party leadership, nevertheless did much to ensure that Labour's ideas penetrated civil society to an extent that has been difficult to achieve since the 1940s.

Conclusion

Labour's development is best likened, not to a new, purpose-built house on an out-of-town development, complete with fixtures and fittings, but rather a roomy old town house whose owners gradually manage to decorate and furnish over a long period. The contingency of Labour's political development should not be underestimated, particularly with regard to the party's early years. The furniture was often rearranged, and sometimes thrown away. Much of the literature on the 'rise of Labour' exhibits a tendency to 'expect too much' from the new party. This is particularly true of the 'rise of class politics' interpretation associated with Ross McKibbin and others. It is still too often forgotten that the Liberal party was in the vanguard of reformist politics until at least 1918. In addition, as recent research has demonstrated, a crucial component of Labour and socialist ideas up until 1924 was to be found in a shared radical-liberal-socialist-feminist concern with democratic reform of the political structures of liberal democracy. This necessarily involved affinities with, rather than rejections of, pre-existing political ideas. It necessitated the forging of alliances, often temporary, but still important, with the myriad progressive groups which together composed early twentieth century oppositional politics.[37] It was not until 1918 that Labour possessed anything approaching a distinctive party platform, and even then its policies still had much in common with its main progressive rival. As we have seen, from the perspective of 1914, there was no inevitability about the replacement of the Liberals. Narratives of smooth and inexorable progress must always be questioned.

Yet while there were important similarities between the Liberals and Labour before the Great War, these gradually faded as the chief preoccupations of politics shifted away from those set down during the late nineteenth century, towards those we now recognise as forming the distinctive core of twentieth century politics: the relationship between the state, society and the economy, and the problems associated with finding an effective and popular mode of state intervention to promote social justice. Labour was initially ill-equipped to deal with the economic problems thrown up by free-market capitalism during the late-

1920s. It was not until the ascendancy of Keynesianism in Britain during the second world war that there was a solution. 1931 came too early, but 1945 did not, and Labour seized the initiative with great success.

One of the more outstanding, and constant features of Labour's early development was the support of the trade unions. Without this, in terms not only of financial resources, but also the penetration of Labour's ideas in civil society, the party would have struggled. Although the process was long and drawn out, the gradual shift of allegiance by the unions, from Liberalism to Labour, meant that by the early 1920s the Liberals' financial base and organisation among the working classes was eroding while Labour's was steadily improving. It is arguable that Labour's swift recovery from the debacle of 1931 was in large part the result of trade union strength. Yet this support, so crucial for electoral success, came at a price. The party's theoretical imagination has been limited due to the influence of labourist political culture. The marginalisation of the ILP and the Socialist League, as well as the inevitable compromises which intellectuals such as Cole and Tawney were forced to make, are testimony to the unions' hegemony over the party by the late 1930s. When combined with the leadership's selective reading of the British socialist tradition, which took Fabianism as the most important contribution, we have the bedrock, and the paradox, of Labour's high point – the Attlee–Bevin years.

It must be stated that the period between 1900 and 1945 was one of immense social change and upheaval. Of crucial importance here are the two world wars. Debate will continue over the extent to which the wars 'radicalised' the British people, but it is inescapable that Labour emerged from both in a better position, due mostly to the happy marriage of ideology and programme with the right political context. In both cases, the extension of the state conferred upon Labour's ideas a degree of legitimacy which they had previously lacked. The wartime coalitions also demonstrated Labour's 'respectable' moderation.

Generalisations from such a broad period are problematic, but it is arguable that the key to understanding the rise of Labour involves an awareness of the interconnectedness of ideology and context. We have been fortunate in the rich variety of work produced by historians and political scientists during Labour's first century; historiographical argument will undoubtedly continue into its second. Recent dramatic changes in the party's identity will only intensify the desire to fully understand its past.

Notes

1 Herbert Morrison speaking at Labour's Annual Conference, 1929. Labour Party, *Annual Conference Report*, Brighton, September-October, 1929, London, Labour Party, 1929, p. 150.

2 Duncan Tanner, *Political Change and the Labour Party 1900-1918*, Cambridge, Cambridge University Press, 1990. Patrick Joyce, *Visions of the People: Industrial England and the Question of Class 1848-1914*, Cambridge, Cambridge University Press, 1991. J. Shepherd, 'Labour and Parliament: the Lib-Labs as the First Working-Class MPs 1885-1906'; Pat Thane, 'Labour and Local Politics: Radicalism, Democracy and Social Reform 1880-1914'; Duncan Tanner, 'Ideological Debate in Edwardian Labour Politics: Radicalism, Revisionism and Socialism', all in Eugenio F. Biagini and Alistair J. Reid (eds.), *Currents of Radicalism: Popular Radicalism, Organised Labour and Party Politics in Britain 1850-1914*, Cambridge, Cambridge University Press, 1992. Jon Lawrence, 'Popular Radicalism and the Socialist Revival in Britain', *Journal of British Studies* Vol 31 1992. Eugenio F. Biagini (ed.), *Citizenship and Community: Liberals, Radicals and Collective Identities in the British Isles 1865-1931*, Cambridge, Cambridge University Press, 1996. Logie Barrow and Ian Bullock, *Democratic Ideas and the British Labour Movement 1880-1914*, Cambridge, Cambridge University Press, 1996. John Belchem, *Popular Radicalism in Nineteenth Century Britain*, Macmillan, London, 1996. Ian Christopher Fletcher, '"Prosecutions ... are Always Risky Business": Labour, Liberals, and the 1912 "Don't Shoot" Prosecutions', *Albion* Vol 28 1996.

3 For an excellent account, see Martin Pugh, *The Making of Modern British Politics 1867-1939*, London, Blackwell, second edition, 1993.

4 For a full account of the debate over PR see Andrew Chadwick, *Augmenting Democracy: Political Movements and Constitutional Reform During the Rise of Labour 1900-1924*, Aldershot, Ashgate, 1999. See also Vernon Bogdanor, *The People and the Party System: the Referendum and Electoral Reform in British Politics*, Cambridge, Cambridge University Press, 1981, and Logie Barrow and Ian Bullock, *Democratic Ideas and the British Labour Movement*, Cambridge, Cambridge University Press.

5 Peter Clarke, *Lancashire and the New Liberalism*, Cambridge, Cambridge University Press, 1971. H. V. Emy, *Liberals, Radicals and Social Politics 1892-1914*, Cambridge, Cambridge University Press, 1973. Peter Clarke, 'The Progressive Movement in England', *Transactions of the Royal Historical Society*, Vol 24 1974. Michael Freeden, *The New Liberalism: An Ideology of Social Reform*, Oxford, Clarendon, 1978. Peter Clarke, *Liberals and Social Democrats*, Cambridge, Cambridge University Press, 1978. Stefan Collini, *Liberalism and Sociology*: L. T. Hobhouse and ??? *Political Argument in England 1880-1914*, Cambridge, Cambridge University Press, 1979.

6 Chadwick, *Augmenting Democracy*. See also, Andrew Chadwick, 'Aristocracy or the People? Radical Constitutionalism and the

Progressive Alliance in Edwardian Britain', *Journal of Political Ideologies* Vol 4 1999.

7   George Dangerfield, *The Strange Death of Liberal England*, London, Paladin, 1970, (1935). Ross McKibbin, *The Evolution of the Labour Party 1910-1924*, Oxford, Clarendon, 1974. Keith Laybourn and Jack Reynolds, *Liberalism and the Rise of Labour 1900-1918*, London, Croom Helm, 1984.

8   Neil Blewett, 'The Franchise in the United Kingdom 1885-1918', *Past & Present*, Vol 32 1965.

9   Ross McKibbin, (written with Colin Matthew and John Kay), 'The Franchise Factor in the Rise of the Labour Party', *English Historical Review*, Vol 91 1976. M. G. Sheppard, 'The Effects of the Franchise Provisions on the Social and Sex Composition of the Municipal Electorate 1882-1914', *Bulletin of the Society for the Study of Labour History*, Autumn 1982.

10 Duncan Tanner, 'The Parliamentary Electoral System, the "Fourth" Reform Act and the Rise of Labour in England and Wales', *Bulletin of the Institute of Historical Research*, Vol 56 1983. John Davis, 'Slums and the Vote 1867-1890', *Historical Research*, Vol 64 1991.

11 Catherine A. Cline, *Recruits to Labour: the British Labour Party 1914-1931*, New York, Syracuse University Press, 1963. Marvin Swartz, *The Union of Democratic Control in British Politics During the First World War*, Oxford, Clarendon, 1971.

12 Arthur Marwick, *The Deluge: British Society and the First World War*, London, Penguin, 1967. Arthur Marwick, *Britain in the Century of Total War: War, Peace and Social Change 1900-1967*, London, Bodley Head, 1968. Stanislav Andreski, *Military Organisation and Society*, London, Routledge and Kegan Paul, second edition, 1968 (1954). J. M. Winter, *The Great War and the British People*, London, Macmillan, 1986.

13 Royden Harrison, 'The War Emergency: Workers' National Committee 1914-1920', in Asa Briggs and John Saville (eds.), *Essays in Labour History 1886-1923*, London, Macmillan, 1971. J. M. Winter, *Socialism and the Challenge of War: Ideas and Politics in Britain 1912-1918*, London, Routledge and Kegan Paul, 1974. Kathleen Burk (ed.), *War and the State: the Transformation of British Government 1914-1919*, London, Allen and Unwin, 1982. For guild socialism, see A. W. Wright, *G. D. H. Cole and Socialist Democracy*, Oxford, Clarendon, 1979.

14 Ralph Miliband, *Parliamentary Socialism: A Study in the Politics of Labour*, London, Merlin, second edition, 1973 (1961), p. 47.

15 Miliband, *Parliamentary Socialism*, pp. 47-52. See also James Hinton, *The First Shop Stewards' Movement*, London, Allen and Unwin, 1973.

16 McKibbin, *The Evolution of the Labour Party*.

17 Royden Harrison, 'The War Emergency: Workers' National Committee 1914-1920'.

18 See Christopher Howard, 'Expectations Born to Death: Local Labour Party Expansion in the 1920s', in J. Winter (ed.), *The Working Class in Modern British History*, London, Cambridge University Press, 1983.

19 Pamela M. Graves, *Labour Women: Women in British Working-Class Politics, 1918-1939*, Cambridge, Cambridge University Press, 1994, p. 1.

20 Daniel Weinbren (ed.), *Generating Socialism: Recollections of Life in the Labour Party*, Stroud, Sutton, 1997.

21 See Keith Laybourn's chapter in this collection.

22 For useful discussion of Labour in the 1920s, see Andrew Thorpe, *A History of the British Labour Party*, London, Macmillan, 1998, Chapter 3.

23 Miliband, *Parliamentary Socialism*, pp. 148-51.

24 Pugh, *The Making of Modern British Politics*, pp. 236-40.

25 *Ibid*, p. 266.

26 Robert Skidelsky, *Politicians and the Slump: the Labour Government of 1929-1931*, London, Macmillan, 1967.

27 Mosley's resignation and subsequent fascist trajectory should not mask the fact that his economic ideas, contained within a memorandum of 1930, were not radically different from those of leading Keynesian Liberals.

28 Thorpe, *A History of the British Labour Party*, p. 78. See also Andrew Thorpe, *The British General Election of 1931*, Oxford, Clarendon, 1991.

29 Pugh, *The Making of Modern British Politics*, p. 268.

30 For an account of the Socialist League see Ben Pimlott, *Labour and the Left in the 1930s*, Cambridge, Cambridge University Press, 1977.

31 Laybourn, *Rise of Labour*, pp. 102-3.

32 An overview of the wartime experience is Stephen Brooke, *Labour's War: The Labour Party During the Second World War*, Oxford, Oxford University Press, 1992.

33 Richard M. Titmuss, *Problems of Social Policy*, London, HMSO, Longmans, Green, 1950.

34 Paul Addison, *The Road to 1945: British Politics and the Second World War*, London, Pimlico, second edition, 1994 (1975).

35 See Miliband, *Parliamentary Socialism*, pp. 272-85, for the influence of 'popular radicalism' during the war.

36 '[P]olitical radicalisation, much commented on at the time and subsequently, has been greatly exaggerated ... [T]he experience of the Second World War – whether it was spent in the factory or at the Front – did not imbue most people with a new conception of public affairs.' Steven Fielding, Peter Thompson and Nick Tiratsoo, *England Arise! The Labour Party and Popular Politics in 1940s Britain*, Manchester, Manchester University Press, 1995, p. 212.

37 Chadwick, *Augmenting Democracy*, *op. cit.*.

'The future Labour offered': industrial modernisation projects in the British Labour Party from Gaitskell to Blair[1]

Brian Brivati

Introduction

In 1955, four years after the British Labour Party emerged from its most successful period of government, it selected a new leader, Hugh Gaitskell, who attempted to push through a programme of modernisation to shift the party away from an obsession with the ownership of capital, towards a new relationship to the economy based on the ideas of the revisionists.[2] In 1997, eighteen years after the last Labour government, a Labour Party led by a modernising tendency triumphed at the General Election.[3] Superficially, there was much in common between the Labour Party of Hugh Gaitskell and the New Labour Party of Tony Blair, in their attitudes to policy in general and to party reform in particular. Some readings of the history of the party over this period argue for a neat straight line to be drawn from the revisionists of the 1950s to the modernisers of the 1990s, implying that the historical dynamic for change was for a gradual shift towards free market economics in response to electoral 'reality'; that the Labour Party as a rational political party, would set out to modernise in order to win and that 'modernisation' meant a gradual shift away from the public ownership agenda of the Attlee years.[4] By definition, in other words, the social democratic right had represented the voice of modernity in the Labour Party debates since 1945 against the backward sounding voices of the left.[5] In turn, this gradual switch was a reflection of deeper forces, summed up in world history in Francis Fukyama's *End of History* thesis and in British history by the dominant picture of the passivity of British political culture in the face of relative economic decline. These 'common sense' ideas influenced perceptions of the modernising process and entailed a considerable rewriting of political history.

The story of Labour's ideology between the two poles of Gaitskell's Labour Party and Blair's New Labour Party is of a series of shifts in position as the party tried to find a policy mix that could compete with the electoral success of the British Conservatives. The sense of the modern was in the main not perceived to be synonymous with the market. Rather, at least on the surface of formal political presentation, what united Labour politicians before 1987 was their firm belief in the inferiority of the market over planning as the means of allocating resources. What they had in common with each other and did not share with the modernising leadership of the party after 1987 was any real faith in market economics. Their belief in the potential of state action reflects not passivity in the face of relative economic decline but dynamism in both an underlying sense of what could be done to avert decline and a faith in the electoral appeal of collectivism. This last faith is retained long after such a programme was a convincing vote winner. Arguably the last time collectivist policies decisively won a British general election was 1966, yet such ideas still formed the bedrock of the party's manifesto promises until the 1987 general election. Such confidence suggestions a very different notion of modernity and a very different structure of values. It might also question the notion of the dynamism of Labour's response to events in, for example, the 1970s. Clinging to ideas that had such a poor electoral record is a strange way of being politically dynamic. However this clinging to the wreckage of collectivism reflected a continuing belief that intervention was the best way of Britain responding to the global economic crisis and that nation states were not powerless in the face of the invisible hand: even if the electorate did not agree, giving up these ideas would mean and has meant, giving up the historical point of the Labour Party.[6] What is striking is the speed with which this world view was dismantled and the party's entire approach altered once the first changes in party structure and organisation are made by Neil Kinnock during the policy review.[7] There followed a set of events which suggest to me the trauma of death and the rebirth of something new, rather than a reconfiguration of the same historical entity.

Overall, the complicated and twisting story of policy invention and its varying success at the polls, shows that there was little continuity in the direction of the party but rather profound shifts of position and a constant battle to define the future Labour offered as a means of controlling the party, winning elections and, it seemed sometimes, reasserting faith. But there is little empirical evidence to support the notion that the party has steadily, or inevitably, shifted to the right over the period since the second world war in a gradual and rational pursuit of the middle political ground from which it could seek to win general elections. Rather it seems to have often moved because of its own internal political dynamic, in a series of zig-zag motions, until it came to rest, in the aftermath of the defeat of the 1987 general election, as an unelectable hulk. Thereafter, and particularly between the two elections of 1992 and 1997, as is clearly shown in a direct comparison of the two manifestos, there was a realisation that the historical journey that had started in Farringdon Road in 1900 was ended and that a new journey would need to begin. As with Disraeli and the Conservative Party between 1846 and 1867 and Gladstone and the Liberal Party from the late 1850s until the after the election of 1868, so the corpse of a political party has been revived by the injection of new sets of supports, new organisation and new ideology, until it requires a new name and is, in essence a new historical entity.

To explore these issues, this chapter will consider the Labour Party's General Election manifestos between 1945 and 1997. It will focus on what these documents had to say – and occasionally did not have to say – about industrial policy, trade union law and the private sector.

The use of manifestos

A number of methodological caveats need to be entered here. Firstly, election manifestos are very particular kinds of documents that are sometimes treated as meaningless as historical evidence or at least with a high degree of cynicism. There are a number of dimensions to this cynicism:

1) Manifestos are contingent documents whose purpose is to be an element in an election campaign and not part of a developing political identity

2) Manifestos are compromises that are relevant to internal party disputes and as the centralisation of campaigns developed over the postwar period become irrelevant to the campaign itself

3) Manifestos have increasingly become marketing devices that are used for presentational purposes rather than political development.[8]

4) Manifestos do not matter, what matters is what the government does once it is in power and the record of that government is what determines general elections

There are a number of responses to these somewhat contradictory critiques of manifestos. First, different political parties relate to their election manifestos differently at different elections. Second, the constitutional form – MPs present addresses to their constituents, political parties their manifestos to the electorate –

are actually an important element in judging change through time because they are recurrent processes which can be compared – the relative importance of the meaning and impact of them at different times and in different governments might hold significant clues as to the nature of the political party at any one time. Finally, there are no other comparable political opportunities in the British political system, aside perhaps from Queen's Speeches, for reflection about what politicians think they are in politics to do. They might not really be in politics to do these things, we might know their real purposes, but we can only guess these, we can judge what they said they were running on and we can compare what they have said with what they do in office.

Aside from the questions of the role of the manifesto itself, there are questions surrounding the form and function of different manifestos at different elections. Four manifestos were produced in a rather different form from usual. The October 1974 manifesto recapitulates and refers to its February predecessor. February 1974 and 1983 are essentially shortened versions of documents produced via the party's policy machinery, for instance *Labour's Programme* 1973 and refer the reader back to those documents. It is not accidental that they are the manifestos with the most wide ranging proposals on public ownership, because their preparation was under the least control from the parliamentary party and leadership. Perhaps most clearly, they demonstrate a leadership at the ebb tide of its strength in respect to the rest of the party, and in 1983 at least there was a feeling in some sections of the right that such a thorough left wing programme would be discredited by its inevitable defeat. It is notable that the 1979 manifesto does not refer back to *Labour's Programme 1976* in the area of industrial policy. In 1992 and 1997 the party leadership was in total control of the manifesto text; in the former because of the impact of the Policy Review and the presence of a supportive majority on the NEC, and in the latter because of a plebiscitary exercise on a draft version 'the road to the manifesto' in late 1996. The 1996–7 process was therefore constitutionally different from any of its predecessors: this will be the norm from now on.[9]

In addition to certain questions about the significance of manifestos, there have been two contrasting trends in the use of manifestos since 1945:

1) Lack of surprise. Publication of manifestos has made a diminishing impact over the years, being particularly low in 1992 (Shadow Budget, a separate exercise, excepted) and 1997 because the contents of each had been exhaustively discussed in the run up to the election and there was no suspense over

whether the party leader's preferences would prevail. Their importance as means of communicating with the public, and saying new things about the party's policy and philosophy, has diminished greatly since the 'declaration of Labour policy for the consideration of the nation' in 1945. Instead, effort has been concentrated on making its contents proof against misrepresentations (and legitimate attacks) from Labour's opponents.

2) This latter point has been particularly important since 1983, when Labour's plans were alarming to the electorate in general and gleefully pointed out by the Conservatives. 1983 was the apotheosis of the tendency in the 1960s and 1970s on the Labour left to regard the manifesto as a kind of charge sheet for the indictment of the record of Labour governments. The manifesto was a summation of the wishes of the party, and failure to carry it out amounted to betrayal by the leadership. Therefore, inclusion of a wide range of material, and maximalist demands, suited the purposes of a large section of the party: 1983 was not only the most radical but the most prolix Labour manifesto.

However, despite the sense of competing groups in the party fighting over the contents and the way in which the content of the manifesto reflects the balance of these forces at any one time, they are the only solid documents we have which are a photograph of belief. In a sense, these are the statements of the winners in the internal party battles and they must be taken, with all the above caveats and reflections, as representative of the place of the party in the political world at that moment.

Labour's Manifestos, 1945-1997

1945–59: Industry in the Service of the nation

The post war view of industrial policy can be summed up very simply: the main role of government policy towards industry is to ensure that the activities of industry serve the national interest (in 1955 this is elaborated as the expansion of the welfare state and overseas aid and the Conservatives are accused of wanting to 'return' to an economic free for all). The main method of achieving this is through public ownership of particular industries which have powerful effects on the nation in general. The precise industries affected change from election to election, with a particular emphasis on the evils of private sector monopoly in 1950. The alternative to public ownership, and a state run planning system, is seen as chaotic, unstable and likely to involve a return to mass unemployment and economic stagnation.

In 1945 there are several strongly pejorative references to 'Big Business' 'profiteering interests' and 'the privileged rich' which contrast their interests to those of the nation in general. In tone, the 1945 manifesto comes close to accepting the idea of an essential conflict between capital and labour. The 1950 manifesto makes a similar point, at somewhat shorter length, but starts to make a distinction between 'private enterprise' (good) and monopoly capitalism (bad), which is elaborated in later years. In 1951 and 1959 there are particular attacks on large firms and the power they wield over economic life. But a general hostile tone is found nowhere else in reference to private industry as a whole. By 1951 private industry (under planning) had proved itself capable of generating jobs and exports, in contrast to the evils of the interwar period at the forefront of the concerns of the 1945 manifesto. In 1945 and 1950 the virtues of small scale business are contrasted with the vices of big industry or monopolies, whose activities are as detrimental to small business as they are to the rest of the national interest.

Direction, planning and partnership of industry is a core feature of Labour doctrine appearing in each manifesto, but the emphasis shifts over time. In the early period a strong contrast is drawn between the picture of anarchy in the absence of controls and rational progress under planning and public ownership. Public ownership in 1945 and 1950 is clearly regarded as essential for planning the economy in general and achieving the objectives of full employment and export growth. But in 1955 a different emphasis creeps in to the stimulation of investment in industry: 'to use tax policy to help productive investment' which is therefore implicitly private productive investment. In 1959 there is a specific rejection of the 'obsolete and cruel' view that unemployment is a price worth paying to restrain inflation, which goes somewhat beyond Keynesian fine tuning into developing an argument for price controls, national wage agreements with the unions, and extension of the social wage via the welfare state.

In 1945 there are pledges to reverse Conservative laws on trade unions which are implemented. Traditionally, Labour has seen workplace conditions and rights as part of the trade union arm of the Labour movement rather than a subject for statutory action. The first breach in this was in 1955, when action to improve conditions in shops and offices was promised (note, not factories: like Wages Councils this applied to areas where union organisation was weak). In 1959 there was a 'Worker's Charter' which aimed at broadening non-wage benefits.

The idea that corporate governance should be reformed to include a voice for employees has a long history in British socialism – usually termed industrial democracy. In the post war period it crops up first in 1950 – although in 1945 it is referred to as desirable within the nationalised industries. But the detailed promises, for instance of disclosure of accounts to worker representatives, found in 1950 are not in the other manifestos of the period. The subject appears to be dropped, with only token references in 1951, 1955 and 1964. Though in 1970 industrial democracy recurs as an experiment worthy of support, and there are hints of possible 'stakeholder' reforms in corporate governance. In 1974 there is a more definite programme of extending joint control (management and workers) across the board, which is reflected in 1979 and 1983. There is a trend, which culminates in 1983, to equate industrial democracy with union control ('single channel' worker representation) rather than representative democracy via plant or company elections for specific posts. In 1987 industrial democracy is abruptly whittled down to a vague pledge, followed by a list of proposals that refer mainly to restoration of trade union rights.

1964–70: Modernisation through planning

In 1964–66 the public interest is identified with modernisation and an economic transformation based on scientific industries. The main instrument for achieving this goal shifts from public ownership to a plan for the entire economy, public and private, although there is an underlying presumption that this is 'an age when the economy is no longer self regulating and the role of government must inevitably increase' (1964). Public corporations are to be encouraged to diversify and compete. By 1970 there is an emphasis on partnership in industry between government, industry and trade unions, and the services government can provide private industry (research, aid for reorganisation), and a blurring of the boundary between private and public industry. The 1970 manifesto advocates public-private partnerships and co-operatives.

In 1966 incentives for private industry to invest are also stressed, within the context of government-set priorities and a national plan. Tax incentives to encourage investment remain a constant theme, until 1997. The most complete and startling assertion of socialist ideological self confidence is in the 1964 manifesto, where modernisation is synonymous with 'socialist planning' and the age is one where 'the role of government must inevitably increase'. Industrial conciliation first appears in 1966, and was worked up into detail in February 1974. ACAS was set up during the 1974 minority Labour government.

Equal pay reached the manifesto in 1950, in a watered down form, and until 1964 was seen as either advisory or as something to be introduced first through the public sector. Only in 1964 does it become a statutory right. It was implemented in 1970–75.

A right of recognition/representation for trade unions appears first in the 1964 manifesto and is explicitly stated in most subsequent manifestos, including 1997. It can be taken as implied by phrases such as 'new statutory support for collective bargaining' (1983), and its absence in 1979 is because the Labour government had managed to get some rather cumbersome machinery for recognition onto the statute book.

1974–87: The socialisation of industry

The influence of contemporary socialist economic theory is apparent in industrial policy (at least at the level of the manifesto) in this period. It also draws on strands apparent in both previous phases. Public ownership is perceived as a tool particularly appropriate in encouraging modern scientific and technological industries, and for the first time since 1950 there are significant and specific proposals for the extension of public ownership. But the blurring of the boundaries apparent in 1964–70 is taken further, with the policy of taking extensive holdings in private industry for the purpose of directing its operations (rather than recovering public funds as was the emphasis in 1964–70). This is alongside a more assertive version of partnership in industry through planning agreements with individual firms and a vigorous attack on the private sector. In 1987, though, there is a reversion to the less coercive approach of 1970 in which partnership and 'national economic assessment' is stressed. This period saw the peak of intra-party conflict over manifesto content, with the party leader having most control over the process in 1979 and 1987; in practice, the record of Labour government in the period was little different in approach to the previous period.

In 1970 the willingness of private business to co-operate with planning is contrasted with Tory dogma. The 1974 manifestos mark a return to the more coercive approach of government to industry, with public ownership again assuming pride of place as a method of controlling the economy to achieve much the same series of objectives as in 1945 and 1950. Along with public ownership came planning agreements and tripartism, with the emphasis shifting between each in the period to 1987. In 1974 and 1983, public ownership and a coercive form of planning agreement are the main tools, while tripartism is the main plank of industrial strategy in 1987. 1979 combines planning agreements and tripartism and, as in 1964, Callaghan's preface to 1979 contains a sharp attack on free market economics which are dismissed as an obsolete doctrine; the pernicious consequences that go with it are incidental; The Conservatives were again accused of wanting to 'return' to an economic free for all in 1970. which is not quite the same thing as saying that the free market is obsolete.

In February 1974 multinationals are 'irresponsible' and in October 1974 public ownership via the National Enterprise Board is an alternative to 'unacceptable' foreign control of British firms. Efforts on the part of large firms to stifle competition are condemned in 1950, 1951, 1955 and even in 1997.

In 1983 there is a minatory passage about financial institutions, and in several elections there are hostile references to particular aspects of the private sector, often land speculators and private medicine. But most of the time there is no attempt to criticise private firms directly, only to criticise the market mechanism as a whole as a bad way of allocating resources in the national interest (which includes indigenous firms). In the intervening period, particularly 1955–74, consumer protection legislation was a common pledge. In 1987 there is the first rejection of the view that everything could or should be done by government. It goes beyond the 1959 statement because the superiority of planning is not then stated.

On industrial relations pledges to repeal Tory laws were given and implemented in 1974 and again given in 1983. The 1987 proposals on industrial relations imply a reversal of much 1979–87 legislation except those parts of the 1984 Act which refer to the conduct of internal union elections and strike ballots; 1987 is also the most exhaustive attempt to spell out a framework of union legislation in the manifesto. From 1983 onwards there is emphasis on extending employment rights to part time and temporary workers. In 1992 restrictions on picketing were accepted, and in 1997 the 'key elements of the trade union legislation of the 1980s' on all sorts of industrial action would be kept. Charters also appear in 1964, 1970, 1992 and 1997 (the latter two through the Social Chapter of the Treaty on European Union). The Employment Protection Act 1975, as foreshadowed in brief in February and in detail in October 1974, was a charter of rights in all but name that was a considerable extension of rights and non-wage benefits.

1992–97: Enabling private industry

The 1992 manifesto marked an abrupt shift from 1987, in which Labour thought of government as the guiding strategic intelligence behind the development of industry. It was shorn of commitments to further planning or public ownership (other than the National Grid). Government activity should ensure economic stability, a trained workforce and modern infrastructure rather than directing or owning industry, and infrastructure investment should be via public private partnership. The 1992 manifesto is rather skeletal on the question of industry, perhaps reflecting a negative project of dispensing with previous policies, while 1997 is longer and contains more material praising the benefits of a market economy.

In 1992 the 1974–87 ideological schema disappears, with only a remnant of tripartite planning in the form of an annual national economic assessment (itself a 1987 introduction to replace a more elaborated form of planning) which appears to be advisory only. The 1987 emphasis on education and training as being one of government's main responsibilities to industry is deepened: 'the key to a successful modern economy is a well-educated and motivated workforce.' The development of the economy is left essentially to the market. The main thrust of government intervention is through tax incentives and a co-ordinating body to encourage high technology research and investment. In 1997, however, the main contribution government makes to increased investment is through macroeconomic stability (plus the constant feature of regional development agencies). In 1997 economic development is industry-led, with government equipping industry with a skilled workforce and a modern infrastructure.

Interestingly, there is some similarity between the thrust of 1951 and 1997 manifesto comments on anti-competitive monopoly, the only part of the 1997 manifesto that reads at all harshly about the activities of private business. Conservative links with big business are contrasted with Labour's wish to serve consumers. In 1950–51 the main remedy for monopolies and cartels was public ownership (sugar and cement) while in 1997 the creation of a competitive market serving small firms and citizens is implied but there is no framework laid out for how this might be achieved and the purpose of the state is clearly not to plan such a market.

Until 1992 the approving references to private industry tend to be rather back-handed. In 1979 praise of the financial sector is mixed with criticism. Only in 1992 is the state's role in industry conceptualised as enabling and providing a stable framework (through macroeconomic stability rather than planning) to a privately driven economy, and in 1997 there is the first tribute to the capitalist ethic of 'healthy profits as an essential motor of a dynamic market economy'.

It is in this area that 'New Labour' – or, more accurately, Labour since the 1987-89 Policy Review – is the biggest change from anything in the past. Two changes have been made. Firstly, the ideas of the Labour right as to the effectiveness and appropriateness of the tools of public ownership and planning have changed and in particular the idea that government direction of the most advanced sectors of the economy (the basis of Labour's appeal in 1964) is the way forward has been dismissed. Secondly, the left flank, which was never reconciled in its heart to the existence of significant private business, no longer has to be guarded. The need to avoid the charge of not being a proper socialist stopped the right or social democrats from voicing approval of the dynamism of private business (even if it was understood to be operating within an overall publicly controlled plan). In 1992 Labour recognises the market as the basis of the economy. In 1997 there is an inversion of the 1964 statement. State control of industry is dismissed as a demand of the 'old left' and therefore an obsolete aim, while an untrammelled free market is not called obsolete and implicitly recognised as within the terms of contemporary political discourse.

This policy minimum wage first appears explicitly in 1992, although in 1987 there is reference to extending the work of the Wages Councils and in October 1974 to ACAS having a role over low pay. It is the sole domestic survivor of the extensive list of rights of the 1992 manifesto (and the language of 1997 minimises the impact of those subsumed under the Social Chapter). Its failure to appear until this is partly explained by the operation of Wages Councils, and mostly with the presumption that an expansion of trade union activity was possible and desirable and sufficient to help low paid workers through collective bargaining.

In 1992 and 1997 employee participation is restored as a proposal, but in a very different form, as encouragement of employee share ownership and welcoming partnership in industry when it occurs. In 1992 socialisation of pension funds is proposed, but not in 1997. In the first part of the post 1945 period industrial democracy is seen as irrelevant to the main workplace role of trade unions. In the 1970s it is seen by the left as a device to extend worker control in the part of the economy that remains in the private sector and to restructure the management of the public sector, and by the right as a consensus producing device to reduce industrial conflict. In the 1980s this was expressed by Labour and the SDP–Liberal alliance advocating industrial democracy but meaning very different things. In the 1990s the influence of stakeholding ideas (and even Lawsonian popular capitalism) creeps in, as does the European social model through the Social Chapter.

The development of Labour's position on industry since 1945 evolves in the following stages:

Shopping lists: 1945, 1950, 1955, 1974 both, 1983.

These involve a substantial extension of the public sector into named industries currently run by private firms.

Planning the economy in the national interest: 1951, 1974 both, 1983

Raise the possibility of a substantial extension of the public sector according to a formula such as the 'national interest' or after some form of inquiry.

Accepting the balance between sectors but planning/ share holding rather than nationalising as the mechanism for extending the role of the state: 1959, 1964

These involve reversal of denationalising measures carried out by a Conservative government without extending the boundary of the public sector much beyond that under the previous Labour government, but using alternative means of intervention to extend the boundaries of the state.

Returning the boundary to its previous position but little clear indication of the basis on which future intervention would be managed: 1987

Renationalise the Conservative privatisations in the main, though not all are specified, and not extend the public sector beyond an investment bank.

Public enterprise: 1964, 1966, 1970, 1979

These do not involve large commitments to nationalising previously private industry, but stress the more gradual and flexible processes of stakeholding through enterprise boards, or diversification of existing public industry into new areas of operation.

Enterprise is public interest: 1992 and 1997

Superficially resemble 'status quo ante' but different in that the Status Quo Ante group presume a substantial public sector presence in industry and merely adjust the boundary. From 1992 the issue comes down to the possible renationalisation of industries that might be privatised on the future. Thus none of the existing privatisations are criticised – an inherent acceptance of their utility. There are no public sector institutions which can act as vehicles for expanding the state sector of the economy.

The categories are not watertight – the 1974 manifestos promised an extension of public ownership across the board and a shopping list. There is also the specific negative pledge not to nationalise which appears in 1959 but is immediately followed by what looks like a 'carte blanche' – it simply distinguishes 1959 from shopping lists such as 1950. Aside from the positive proportion of planning and intervention as being superior in form and efficacy to the market, there are periodically attacks on private industry. The lack of such attacks and the gradual acceptance and then keen embrace of the market as being superior to planning is another key dimension of change.

Conclusions

At the heart of the Gaitskellite programme was a notion of a mixed economy with a vibrant public sector and private sector that operated in a framework managed by the state. This was coupled with a commitment to full employment and a belief in the superiority of planning over the market as the mechanism for achieving economic growth from which would stem redistribution of wealth, but one which also accepted the existence of the private sector and wanted to promote opportunity: a vision of a society that was organised and based on an interventionist state with a forceful egalitarian ethos and an industrial policy which did not place ownership as the central determinant of economic intervention but elevated control to that level. Almost all the critical contemporary literature on this debate argued that this process of modernisation was designed to change the nature of the Labour Party and reposition it as a new political party.[11] The argument of this paper is that this was not the case.

There was actually little difference between the underlying ideological assumptions of the 'left' and 'right' of the Labour Party and the manifestos they dominated. There was indeed a worry on the left that these series of reforms would so alter the nature of the Labour Party as to make it something else: to make it a new political party, but in fact this was not the intention of the revisionist or modernising leadership, nor did it result from the changes that did take place. One part of the explanation of this is that the symbolic changes to, for example, clause four, failed to pass through the party conference which meant that the changes in policy that had taken place could be revoked at any time: the structure, constitution and ethos of the party had not been altered to marry the shift in selected means and therefore the Labour Party remained remarkably the same after the revisionist leadership of Hugh Gaitskell as it had been before. This was not only because the leadership was defeated on certain issues but because it was not the intention of the leadership to make such drastic changes. Moreover, this meant that the repositioning of the party in electoral terms had not been permanent and that large avenues of opportunity existed for the left of the party to pressurise it back towards older styles of intervention and forms of public ownership, trade union relations and so on. This the left of the party succeeded in doing in the early 1970s and again in the early 1980s. But in both cases the entire context of discussion was within the terms of reference of planning and intervention not debating whether not this should take place because the market could do the job better.

The New Labour government of Tony Blair talks a language of social and political modernisation. The vocabulary of the government was formed from an extended period of policy review with deep roots in the party's history and from borrowing from the experiences of other political parties as they adapted to the resurgence of economic liberalism in the 1980s and 1990s, most notably Bill Clinton's repositioning of the Democratic Party for the Presidential elections of 1992 and 1996.[12] The reformulation of British democratic socialism has taken place across virtually every area of policy and most significantly, from the time of Neil Kinnock onwards, it has concerned itself with symbolism, structure and ethos as much as policy. In relation to industrial policy there is now is an acceptance of the balance in the economy between public and private created by the privatisation programmes of the 1980s. This is matched by an employment programme which centres around welfare-to-work schemes designed to reduce the welfare budget, combat dependency and achieve a target of full 'employability' before the next general election. The changes in policy are fundamental and not presentational. The notions of planning, either through directive techniques of public ownership or through other means like select share purchase, has been superceded in the detail of the policy and in the structure, constitution, organisation and ethos of the party. Clause Four has been replaced which removes, permanently, the mechanism by which policy changes can be reversed because it removes the spring loaded appeal of collectivism. The structural changes of the party mean that the current modernising project is much more substantial, far reaching and permanent in its impacts that was the Gaitskell project. The political context means that is has also been much more successful. Most importantly, organisation as much as ideology, has been reformed in a concerted attempt to alter the nature of the party. In sum this means that the Labour Party of the 1990s is a different historical entity because the substance of its organisation, ethos and ideology, are different, than the party founded in 1900 or the that which last held power in 1979; this change took place between 1987 and 1992 when the market mechanism replaced intervention as the bedrock of Labour's approach for macro economic policy, this in turn removed the feature that united both left and right in previous generations and in essence stopped the Labour Party being what it was and made it into something else.

The industrial policy elements of this story, particularly the shifting role of nationalisation and state intervention through planning and demand management, reflect an almost complete reversal of positions from questions of ownership being central to Labour's ideology to these questions being peripheral, from state action being the default position of policy to partnership between public and private bodies predominating and from the state being primarily concerned with delivering services and managing industries, to the state being a hands-off regulator of the bulk of what was the public sector. This ideological flexibility forces a reexamination of the nature of the Labour Party itself and raises the question of whether, as under Robert Peel and the shift from Tories to Conservatives or William Gladstone and the shift from Whigs to Liberals, the contemporary New Labour Party is a new historical entity.

More broadly the story of Labour and modernisation suggests a dynamic political culture in which innovation, fundamental debate and reinvention are the norms rather than the exception. Such a conclusion questions the dominant view of a British political culture in this period which was generally stagnant or simply gradually declining and ossifying.

Labour and modernisation represents an extended case study of the response of the centre-left to the crisis of the social democratic state and economic policy in the 1970s through the resurgence of liberal economics under Thatcher. The length of the policy review process and the stubbornness with which certain, generally non-economic policies were held onto by the party, suggests some interesting interventions in the literature on vote maximising by democratic parties.

Notes

1 This paper was given at the American Social Science History Conference, Chicago, November 1998, I am grateful to Richard Toye and Dr Gerard Alexander for their discussion of the themes it raised.

2 See Brian Brivati, *Hugh Gaitskell*, London: Richard Cohen Books, 1996, pp 284-349.

3 See Brian Brivati and Tim Bale (eds) *New Labour in Power: Precedents and Prospects*, London: Routledge, 1997, and David Butler and Dennis Kavanagh, *The British General Election of 1997*, Basingstoke: Macmillan, 1997, amongst many other recent works on the New Labour programme.

4 See, Peter Mandelson and Roger Liddle, *The Blair Revolution: Can New Labour Deliver*, London: Faber, 1996, John Rentoul, *Tony Blair*, London: Warner 1996, and Jon Sopel, *Tony Blair: The Moderniser*, London: Bantam 1995.

5 This view is implicit in Tudor Jones's excellent study, *Remaking the Labour Party from Gaitskell to Blair*, London: Routledge, 1996 and is analysed in the consideration of Blair's political thinking in Andrew Vincent, 'New Ideologies for Old?', *Political Quarterly*, Volume 69, 1998, Michael Freeden, 'The Ideology of New Labour', *Political Quarterly*, Volume 70, 1999 and David Marquand, 'The Blair Paradox', *Prospect*, May 1998.

6 Many writers outside the Labour Party would argue that this occurred much earlier in the party's history, one of the most influential of such attacks was mounted by Paul Foot in his *The politics of Harold Wilson*, London: Penguin, 1968, see also David Coates, *The crisis of Labour*, Brighton: Spokesman, 1989, Ivor Crewe,, 'Why Labour has lost the British elections', *Public Opinion Quarterly*, July, 1983, Ivor Crewe, 'The decline of labour and the decline of Labour', *Essex Papers in Government and Politics*, No. 65, 1989, and Martin Jacques and Francis Mulhern, (eds) *The forward march of Labour halted?*, London: Polity, 1981.

7 See also Martin J.Smith, 'A return to Revisionism? The Labour Party's Policy Review', in Smith and Joanna Spear, (eds), *The Changing Labour Party*, London: Routledge 1992.

8 There are also influential policy documents produced during parliaments and governments such as Labour Party, *Industry and Society*, 1957, *Labour and the Common Market*, 1962, *Labour and the Scientific Revolution*, 1963, *Labour Believes in You*, 1949, *Policy for Peace*, 1961 and *Signposts for the Sixties*, 1962.

9 And might reflect a new kind of political party, see Patrick Seyd, 'New Parties/New Politics? A Case study of the British Labour Party', *Party Politics*, Vol 5, No.3, 1999, pp 383–405.

10 See David Butler and Dennis Kavannagh, *The British General Election of 1992*, London: Macmillan, 1992.

11 See for instance the first edition of *New Left Review*, Volume 1, Number 1, 1960.

12 For a discussion of Clinton's influence on a key area of policy see Desmond King and Mark Wickham-Jones, 'From Clinton to Blair: The Democratic (Party) Origins of Welfare to Work', *Political Quarterly*, Volume 70, Number 1, January-March 1999, pp 62-74, for the influence of the Clinton campaign on a key New Labour strategist see Philip Gould, *The Unfinished Revolution*, Little Brown, 1998, pp 164–71 and p 177.

Labour's International Policy:
A story of conflict and contention

Dan Keohane

This chapter argues that Labour's debate on international policy has been the most divisive issue within the party for much but not all of the century. For two reasons this is no surprise. First, in contrast with some European countries where the left was divided between Socialist and Communist parties, the British Labour Party encompassed the overwhelming proportion of the spectrum from the centre to the far left. This width was temporarily diminished, in small degree in 1932 with the departure of the Independent Labour Party, and to a greater extent in 1981 with the breakaway by the founders of the SDP and almost 30 Labour MPs. Second, international policy is not one discrete subject but a package of major inter-related issues concerning Britain's international role and status in a shifting international context. These include issues of how to respond to great military challenges in Europe and beyond, how to institutionalise the management of international conflicts, and how to devise procedures to facilitate trade, and other economic exchanges in the international arena.

Throughout the century, Labour's international policy manifests a keen and sometimes explosive tension between two approaches. One party tendency, which was in the ascendant for much of the interwar period, believed it should follow socialist principles to promote effective international co-operation and it should reject power-seeking by states. The other approach which dominated from the late 1930s, with a break during the 1980s, was more concerned to increase the party's chances to win and then retain power and to offer responses which melded socialist principles with pragmatic pressures to accommodate short-term international imperatives. Accordingly, the latter approach sometimes reluctantly accepted a policy involving maintaining a balance of power and establishing appropriate alliances. Both approaches included those who displayed a sense of moral responsibility for disadvantaged groups in other countries.

The examination of Labour's international policy over the century is arranged in six sections, reflecting major international events and relationships such as the world wars and the cold war. In each section the party's approach to international issues is considered by examining to what extent it adhered to the principles of internationalism, restricting force, and anti-capitalism.

Early Labour Foreign Policy Attitudes

From the start, the foreign policy of the Labour Representation Committee (LRC) and its successor, the Labour Party, was strongly influenced by the non-conformist background of many members who adhered to notions of the brotherhood of man, rejected authoritarian and military values and were keenly concerned about the morality of politics as expressed in the values of justice and dignity for oppressed groups and individuals. These values were supported by the trade unions, who dominated party decision-making and funding, the Independent Labour Party (ILP), the Fabian Society and writers such as John Hobson, Norman Angell and RH Tawney.[1]

Labour was strongly attracted by Angell's *The Great Illusion*[2] which focused on the irrationality of imperialism and Hobson's seminal study of *Imperialism*[3] which linked aggressive foreign policy to capitalists' search for profitable overseas investments resulting from under-consumption by and exploitation of workers domestically. Aggressive foreign policy was extremely detrimental to the recently enfranchised trade unions who gave the highest priority to favourable domestic economic conditions and radical social reform. It diverted the attention of government and shifted scarce resources away from vital domestic needs like health and housing while retarding mutually beneficial free trade. Even more important, aggressive wars denied the humanitarian values of the party in the most brutal fashion and had the potential to generate immense suffering and loss of life. Labour rejected traditional foreign policy whereby sovereign states competed aggressively to enhance their own national interest. Instead it advocated co-operation and the development of international institutions, such as the Hague Peace Conference of 1899 and its successor in 1907 in order to prevent, mitigate and resolve conflicts.[4] Labour's commitment to international working-class solidarity was expressed in its membership of the Second International from 1904, but participation in that body had little impact upon ordinary trade unions members.[5]

The intensifying political rivalry between Britain and Germany in the years before the First World War encouraged the LRC and the Labour Party to identify ways to prevent war. The party, including pacifist Quaker members, was deeply opposed to the use of or dependence on force, rejected reliance on a balance of power and opposed foreign intervention by capitalist governments. Accordingly, it also sought to oppose increased military spending, condemned arms manufacturers and those propagating their case while not always succeeding in these aspirations.[6]

Labour's international policy and the First World War

In the years leading up to July 1914, Labour was the fourth largest party in the House of Commons and principally concerned to secure domestic social reforms. It was also the uneasy junior partner of the Liberals, with no claim to be a nation-wide organisation.[7] The outbreak of war, faced Labour with a daunting challenge.

Leaders such as Henderson, MacDonald and Hardie sought to maintain the declared principles of anti-militarism, internationalism, anti-capitalism in an atmosphere of deep crises.[8] Initially Labour MPs voted that Great Britain should not partake in the war in alliance with the despised despotism of Tsarist Russia against a relatively progressive Germany. However, Germany's violation of Belgium's guaranteed neutrality shocked British opinion.

Accordingly, Labour, including most party MPs, succumbed to overwhelming sentiment among supporters in affiliated trade unions and nationally in favour of war, as did socialists in Germany and France. By contrast, the ILP and Ramsay MacDonald, chairman of the Labour Party, opposed the war and along with prominent middle-class radical Liberals like journalist E D Morel, MP Charles Trevelyan and intellectual J A Hobson formed the Union for Democratic Control (UDC) which came to exert much influence on Labour's policy from 1917. MacDonald resigned as Labour's chairman and was succeeded by Arthur Henderson, who supported the war and its related recruiting campaigns. Party divisions created by the war were tempered by the setting up of the Labour War Emergency Workers' National Committee (WEWNC), which included representatives from all sections of the movement and focused on the domestic economic and social effects of the conflict.[9]

Arthur Henderson joined Asquith's Liberal-led coalition Cabinet established in May 1915 in which Liberals, Conservatives and Labour were represented. Effectively he was an adviser on the vital issues of labour utilisation. Surprisingly, in December 1916, he joined the Cabinet of the Conservative-dominated coalition led by Lloyd George which replaced Asquith's coalition, despite that administration being much less sympathetic to Labour's unease about the war and turned its face against a negotiated end to the conflagration. Opponents of the war from Labour, ILP and other socialist groups suffered severe police harassment and campaigns depicting them as traitors.[10] Labour's participation in government did not prevent the introduction of conscription in 1916. Initially the party opposed this but it eventually acquiesced in compulsion which also led to the imprisonment of conscientious objectors.[11]

By late 1917 war-weariness and immense casualties influenced opinion in Britain and other belligerent countries. Henderson's visit to Russia after the first Russian Revolution, caused his ejection from Lloyd George's war Cabinet which was 'growing increasingly alarmed at the spectacle of a British minister [Henderson] consorting with notorious pacifists and pro-Germans'.[12] Labour, attracted by Russian proposals for a peace settlement with no annexations or reparations, and dissatisfied with the coalition government's disinterest in peace, withdrew its support for the administration in November 1917. Labour's Memorandum on War Aims issued in late December 1917, reflected the approach of the UDC. As a result, the party's international policy incorporated key UDC demands such as the democratisation of foreign policy, an end to secret diplomacy and to compulsory military service, establishing a League of Nations, rejection of force, setting up of an international court.[13] It also meant that the foreign policy ideas of the anti-war minority – deeply unpopular from 1914 to 1918 – were to dominate the post-war Labour Party.

During the war, despite the intense conflict between jingoistic pro-war trade unionists and vehemently anti-war members of the ILP, leaders like Henderson and MacDonald ensured the party remained together. Thus, by the end of the war, Labour emerged a national party with a comprehensive domestic programme, a new constitution, and strong trade union support. In the 1918 general election, which was an opportunistic referendum on Lloyd George's leadership in the war, Labour opposed the coalition government's policy to impose severe sanctions on Germany, which it predicted would generate intense resentment and hatred. The party's sharp increase in votes from 6.4 to 20.8 per cent of a much-enlarged electorate gave Labour 57 MPs,[14] compared to the 523 returned for the coalition – but Henderson, MacDonald and other leaders were defeated. However, with the collapse in the divided Liberal vote, Labour had now become the main opposition party and thus the alternative government.

Labour's international policy in the inter-war years

Labour's international policy, 1919–1923

The First World War persuaded millions – who previously took little interest in international affairs – that the security and prosperity of British people was indivisible from that of their fellows elsewhere. Thus, economic advance in Britain was impossible while Germans and others in Europe suffered intense dislocation, mass unemployment and high inflation. Similarly, so long as states felt menaced by external aggression, they would divert immense resources from national reconstruction and refuse to trust international institutions. Labour's approach was strongly influenced by prominent UDC figures like Morel, Trevelyan, and Ponsonby. Unlike other party members, they had a deep interest in and knowledge of international politics and in the 1920s and early 1930s, they served on Labour's Advisory Committee on International Questions.[15]

In the years immediately after the Great War, two inter-related issues dominated Labour's international policy, namely its approach to the Treaty of Versailles and the new League of Nations.[16] Labour had a vision of a league of peace-loving peoples, elected by the parliaments of member-states, responsible to their electorates, possessing supranational powers to settle disputes without force and pooling their security. It also wanted the League to promote free trade, and regulate production and distribution of food and raw materials. Not surprisingly, the party was deeply disappointed with the actual League.[17]

Labour vehemently opposed the Versailles Peace Treaty, which in the words of Charles Trevelyan meant 'the imperialist war had ended in the imperialist peace.'[18] Germany was humiliated and required to make unbearable reparations, disarm unilaterally, and lose territory and population. Likewise, the party was disillusioned with the Peace Settlement which guaranteed unjust territorial boundaries and it opposed the League provisions (Articles 11 and 16) which could require the use of force.

Labour's international policy 1924–31

The accession of Labour to office for eight and half months in 1924 dependent on Liberal support, gave the party a limited and brief opportunity to shape international conditions. The new government – with Ramsay MacDonald as Prime Minister and Foreign Secretary – was not interested in pursuing radical policies. Some Labour MPs, albeit a minority, were disappointed that their government acquiesced in the peace settlement, worked with the League of Nations and accepted agreements involving sanctions and a possible use of force.

Opposition from prominent MPs like E. D. Morel, a severe critic of the League, did not prevent the government from supporting the Dawes Plan which eased Germany's reparations and which promised to end the French military occupation of the Ruhr.[19] Despite opposition from pacifists like Lord Parmoor, the League of Nations Minister,[20] and from the armed services ministries, the government negotiated the Geneva Protocol on the Pacific Settlement of International Disputes which required League members and other states to submit their claims to arbitration. States refusing to accept arbitration would be subject to automatic and legally binding collective sanctions. The Protocol was to come into force only after a plan for international disarmament had been agreed.

Labour also established diplomatic relations with the Soviet Union, which were broken off by the Conservative government in 1927, and restored by Labour in 1929. Within a year of taking office, the government proposal to grant a loan to the Soviet Union led, along with other issues, to defeat by the combined votes of Liberals and Conservatives. In 1928, the party programme, *Labour and the Nation* maintained the approach enunciated at the end of the Great War, and adopted the 'six pillars of peace' including renouncing war, full-scale disarmament, international arbitration, international economic co-operation, open diplomacy and a strengthened League of Nations.[21] When it returned to office a year later, once again dependent on Liberal support, for what turned out to be a term of two years and two months, Labour's international policy included a commitment to conciliation and minimising the place of force in international affairs.

However, within months of taking office, the Achilles heel of Labour strategy, namely the absence of a strategy to reconcile its declared socialism with the dominant capitalist forces within and outside the UK, was exposed.[22] The Wall Street Crash of 1929 led to a sharp and sustained increase in British unemployment which was an immense failure for a Labour government pledged to achieving the opposite outcome. However, the very orthodox Chancellor of the Exchequer, Philip Snowden, had no coherent strategy on how to meet the increasing unemployment, and little interest or faith in alternatives proffered by figures like Keynes, a stance which was facilitated by the sense of resignation which gripped the Labour leadership.[23]

Despite the deep mistrust obtaining between Prime Minister MacDonald and Foreign Secretary Henderson,[24] the second Labour government had some limited achievements in foreign and defence policy. It helped to modify the reparation payments by Germany in the Young Plan and secured a restricted naval disarmament under the London Treaty of 1930. Despite opposition from the Admiralty and others, it adhered to the Optional Clause accepting compulsory arbitration for justiciable disputes by the Permanent Court of International Justice leading the Dominions and other states to follow suit, thereby greatly strengthening the procedures for peaceful settlement of disputes.[25] In increasingly unpromising international conditions, the government declared a high priority to achieving disarmament

Labour's international policy 1931–1939

The blizzard which swept over the world economies in the early 1930s produced dramatically higher unemployment, fostered economic nationalism and beggar-my-neighbour policies, which in turn stimulated extreme nationalism and aggressive foreign policies in European countries and beyond. Due to its failure to handle the acute financial crisis, the MacDonald government, unable to secure the acquiescence of the unions collapsed in August 1931 over proposals to reduce unemployment benefit in an atmosphere of crisis, uncertainty and economic distress.[26] This end of a Labour government inflicted enduring damage on Labour's reputation as a party of government, which was exacerbated by the defection of the leader, Prime Minister Ramsay MacDonald, Philip Snowden and others to the Conservative-dominated national coalition.

Following Labour's overwhelming electoral defeat in the 1931 General Election, the party chose the only undefeated member of the previous Cabinet, pacifist George Lansbury, as chairman (later as leader). In both domestic and international policy, Labour was controlled by the trade unions and in subsequent years of the 1930s it espoused more ideological policies. With Japan's invasion of Manchuria (1931), the Nazi seizure of power in Germany (1933), Italy's attack on Abyssinia (1934) and the fascist attack on the Spanish Republic (1936–8), the international environment became extremely hostile to Labour's gradualist approach to international policy. Labour continued to renounce war and argue for disarmament and arbitration along with the commitment of members of the League to resolve disputes by peaceful means.

By 1934, the party, strongly influenced by trade unions leaders in the National Council of Labour, 'the most authoritative body in the Labour movement in formulating policy, especially on foreign affairs'[27] accepted collective military sanctions, and put aside any residual reliance on strike action to prevent war (an approach discredited by the failure of the 1926 General Strike). The following year, after Hitler's introduction of conscription and rearmament and Mussolini's challenge to the authority of the League, the party was forced to adopt a more coherent policy. At the annual conference, the party rejected the left-wing contention that because capitalist governments could not be trusted to use military power, Labour should refuse support for collective military sanctions by the League of Nations. Labour's overwhelming support for collective security as advocated by General Secretary of the TGWU Ernest Bevin and Hugh Dalton led to the resignation of George Lansbury, the pacifist leader, within a few weeks.[28]

After 1935, despite the warnings of politicians like Hugh Dalton, a majority of the political wing of the Labour movement including its new leader, Clement Attlee, continued to oppose British rearmament. Many regarded the National Government as so hostile to Labour values and objectives and seemingly unconcerned about the destruction of democracy in Germany and Spain that it could not be trusted with stronger military forces. Others assumed that Germany's long-held grievances against the Peace Settlement explained Hitler's aggressive demands. However union leaders Ernest Bevin and Walter Citrine, the General Secretary of the TUC, reflecting practical working-class solidarity, demanded an urgent response to the disaster facing their comrades in Germany, Austria and elsewhere.

By 1937 the party acknowledged the ineffectiveness of the League of Nations and Labour MPs reluctantly ceased voting against government rearmament plans. These two major reversals of principle – on arms and the League – were fostered by the intervention of Italy and Germany in the Spanish Civil War, Italy's aggression in Abyssinia, and Germany's blatant violation of the Versailles Treaty by reoccupying the Rhineland. In 1938 Labour denounced the Munich Agreement, particularly the sacrifice of Czechoslovakia as 'one of the greatest diplomatic defeats that this country and France have ever sustained', contending that a declaration to defend Czechoslovakia involving Britain, France, the Soviet Union and others could have prevented Hitler's victory.[29] While the party's analysis was substantially correct, it shied away from an unambiguous and explicit advocacy of British rearmament, and it regarded the National Voluntary Service scheme as superior to conscription which it still opposed.[30]

Labour's International Policy and the Second World War

Unlike August 1914, Labour entered the Second World War relatively united, with only one eighth of Labour MPs, together with the ILP and the Communist Party of Great Britain opposed to what was generally regarded as a just war. The clear and pressing nature of the danger to Britain's security and interests placed immense responsibility on Labour and the trade unions to subordinate their concerns to the needs of national survival.

In May 1940, as 'disaster succeeded disaster '[31] in the war in Europe and the peril to France became acute, the new Prime Minister Winston Churchill brought Labour in from the wilderness. The appointment of Labour and trade union leaders, Attlee, Bevin[32] and Morrison, to the wartime Coalition gave the party a commanding influence on the vital domestic aspects of the war such as labour mobilisation and policies such as pricing and rationing of food. Concurrently, the war greatly enhanced the industrial wing of the Labour movement, the trade unions, by raising their membership, and developing their influence as partners with employers and government. The presence of Labour in government gave Attlee and Bevin a quite significant input into planning for international reconstruction in the post-war years.[33] But above all, Attlee and other Labour colleagues found their attitudes towards foreign and defence policy were profoundly influenced by their service in the wartime Coalition. Instead of adhering to the 'principles of a socialist foreign policy', their approach was shaped by their role in government with their 'minds focused on the national interest in a world dominated by power politics.'[34]

With regard to war aims, the single negative one of defeating the Axis powers, which predominated in the early years of the conflict, was later enlarged to include plans for a different international order of the post-war era. From 1942 to 1945, Britain relied increasingly on both the USA and USSR to shoulder the main burden of winning the war and found itself a relatively junior member of the Big Three powers. This emerging reality cast a strong shadow on plans for the postwar power configuration and Britain's place therein.

At the 1944 annual conference, while Labour's declared aspirations for the postwar era predominantly concerned domestic matters, the party did attend to international issues. The 1945 manifesto *Let Us Face the Future* promised to rebuild the labour movements in defeated countries and to establish a new world body to renounce war and 'settle all disputes by peaceful means', but it did not offer much specific guidance on the party's view.[35]

Labour's policy during the Cold War

The Labour government took office in 1945 with some major advantages. It had – for the first time – a decisive parliamentary majority, respected leaders who were experienced in the war-time national government and a strong mandate for change. On the debit side, a bankrupt Britain was desperate for adequate supplies of food and raw materials, owed heavy international debts, and faced a Europe devastated by war and controlled as far west as mid-Germany by Soviet forces. The British political elite, including the Labour leadership, still viewed Britain as a great power, one of the three participants at Yalta and Potsdam, head of an empire and leader of the sterling area. But the UK lacked the capacity to sustain that role while simultaneously constructing a welfare state domestically.

In the relatively fluid period from 1945 to 1947, the Labour administration had two possible options for international policy. Given that the USA was the only country with the resources to restore stability and security to Europe, Britain might well seek to extend the close war-time relationship with Washington. Another option was that Britain should lead a Socialist Third Force based on Europe and the Commonwealth. In the two years after the war, the first choice faced severe problems. These included the precipitate end of US Lend-Lease (1945), the imposition of multilateral free trade regime on the UK in return for the US loan (1946) and the abrupt cut-off of US co-operation on atomic weapons (1947). In the same period, the severe deterioration of Anglo-Soviet relations over Germany, Greece, Iran, Turkey, and especially over Moscow's destruction of socialist and other democratic parties in Eastern and Central Europe had a big impact on the Attlee government. That administration believed that Soviet preponderance of power and influence on the continent along with Moscow's intransigence on Berlin and Germany had to be contained and met by persuading the United States to help defend and restore Western Europe. For key members of the government, such as Foreign Secretary Bevin, an Atlantic alliance was the only viable course.[36] He harboured deep suspicions of communists, either in the British trade unions or in the leadership of the USSR and admired some aspects of US society.

On the other side, Labour's left-wing embraced both independent-minded MPs like Michael Foot and Richard Crossman associated with the 'Keep Left' group, and Communist fellow-travellers such as Konni Zillicus and William Warbey. The latter group judged that the main ideological struggle was between supporters and opponents of capitalism and thus felt socialists should avoid public criticism of the Soviet Union. The party's left-wing were uncomfortable with an international policy based on military power and on the search for an alliance with the leading capitalist power, the United States. Many regarded a balance of power approach as quite discordant with the party's values and, in the straitened economic circumstances of the late 1940s, viewed arms as 'imposing a crippling economic and financial burden on the nation' and a profound misuse of resources for 'the destructive purposes of modern war'.[37] In that perspective, it was deeply contradictory for a democratic socialist UK government to ally itself with the United States, a country whose capitalism 'is arrogant, self-confident, merciless and convinced of its capacity to dictate the destinies of the world.'[38] Instead, it perceived a affinities between a socialist Britain and the Soviet Union which espoused similar principles on key aspects of economic organisation.

Added to this, Labour MPs from both the left and right strongly disliked American foreign policy as fiercely anti-communist, anti-socialist and likely to generate avoidable tension and the risk of war. Much of the Labour left, agreed with the words of Michael Foot, uttered in August 1945, that Labour Britain 'at the summit of her power and glory ... could offer 'a commanding position of leadership if we choose to exercise it ...', a leadership based on a 'conception of political liberty which our friends in Russia unhappily have not been blessed with. We have at the same time a conception of economic democracy ... which is unhappily not yet shared by the people of the United States.'[39] They considered a Third Force socialist group of European countries would avoid the bleak alternatives 'of anti-Communism and Communism, [could] mediate between the USA and USSR and support anti-colonial movements and non-aligned countries'.[40] Cumulatively, however, the communist coup in Czechoslovakia in 1948, the Soviet refusal of Marshall Aid, and the Soviet blockade of Berlin in 1948–49 removed from the Third Force option whatever credibility it possessed. It also undermined the relatively small band of fellow-travelling Labour MPs who advocated co-operation between socialists and communists in Britain and in Europe.

From 1947 to 1949 the Attlee government succeeded in playing a vital part in establishing the Treaties of Dunkirk (1947) and Brussels (1948) to reinforce the Communist-threatened regimes in France and Italy. Likewise, it welcomed the establishment of West Germany in the western orbit in 1949, the advent of Marshall Aid and especially supported the formation of NATO. While the Attlee government was particularly successful in persuading the US to provide vital Marshall Aid to Europe and establish the Atlantic alliance, those achievements, particularly the latter, meant Britain had to support US leadership on key issues of military strategy and approach, which would be costly for both country and party.

In the four decades from the late 1940s until the end of the Cold War, Labour hosted a sometimes extremely divisive debate between the Atlanticist right and the left-wing of the party on security and defence issues. Many on the left and others not of that persuasion could see little difference between the foreign and defence policy of the Labour leadership and that espoused by the Conservatives, except that the former were more concerned about aid for developing countries and condemned oppressive regimes. The similarity of the two parties was underlined by bipartisan support for the key military-security aspects of the international policy of successive British governments, especially in the period when Ernest Bevin was Foreign Secretary, when his policies were criticised by Labour MPs and commended by Conservative MPs and journals.[41]

From Attlee to Callaghan, Labour followed an international policy which required the party to accept commitments which contravened the anti-capitalist and anti-militarist values of Labour adherents. Likewise, left-wingers were concerned by the introduction of conscription in 1947, the leadership backing for a Great Power role-manifest in the furtive decision to produce atomic weapons that same year and on maintaining an extensive military role East of Suez in the 1950s and 1960s. In early 1951, during the Korean war, the Labour government increased the defence budget by more than 50 per cent, raising it from about 6 to nearly 10 per cent of gross domestic product, with a pledge to increase it to about 14 per cent in subsequent years. This immense increase, 'imposed on Britain by the Truman administration',[42] conflicted sharply with the domestic priorities on health and public investment and also contradicted the party's anti-militarism and anti-capitalism.[43] The resulting resignation from the government of Aneurin Bevan, Harold Wilson and John Freeman, triggered by the imposition of prescription charges for National Health Services, generated a deep rift between the Bevanite left and the Atlanticist right which considered the socialist principles of internationalism had limited relevance in the cold war. For most of the Labour left, western estimates of Soviet military capability was greatly exaggerated and that Soviet advances would best be countered by a balanced programme to diminish poverty, improve democratic institutions and establish adequate military strength.

The deep contention over the level of British rearmament in the early 1950s continued with very strong and prolonged Labour opposition over German rearmament in the mid-1950s, on nuclear weapons in 1960–61, on the level of defence expenditure east of Suez in 1965–68 and 1976–9. Earlier, in 1965–68, the refusal of the second Wilson government to publicly condemn US military action in Vietnam in 1965–68 occasioned profound unease for many Labour MPs and party members.

Labour and the Use of Force in the Cold War Era

The distinctive attitude of the Labour Party towards the United Nations and the use of force post-1945 is well illustrated by four examples: Korea (1950), Suez (1956), the Falklands (1982) and the Gulf (1991). In all cases the stance adopted by the majority of the party, was clearly in line with that of the UN. On Korea, most Labour MPs and the party conference supported the dispatch of two infantry battalions and other British forces totalling some 12,000 personnel to join US and other countries' forces assisting South Korea. With the USSR absent, the UN Security Council demanded the withdrawal of North Korean forces from the South and supported the sending of multinational forces to assist South Korea. In 1956, the UN condemned the Anglo-French attack on Egypt as did the almost the entire party, with Labour using the world body's decision as one of the principal reasons for fiercely rejecting the action. In 1982, Labour reluctantly acquiesced in Prime Minister Thatcher's use of force in the daunting task of ejecting the Argentinian forces from the Falkland Islands following the humiliation of the initial Argentinian occupation. While a sizeable minority of the party, including prominent figures like Tony Benn, vehemently opposed the military action, UN Security Council Resolution 502 discouraged the party from opposing the action.

Eight years later in 1990–91, the majority of Labour MPs supported the international coalition's efforts to eject Iraqi forces from Kuwait. They were strongly influenced by the battery of UN Security Council Resolutions, which condemned Iraq and legitimised the coalition's use of force, and by the blatant nature of Iraqi aggression.

Labour's International Policy, 1980–89

At the turn of the 1980s, Labour replaced its strongly Atlanticist perspective on international policy with a security policy explicitly independent of NATO, while for reasons of party unity and electoral support insisting that it was still committed to NATO.[44] Thus, for the first time since the late 1940s, Labour rejected US strategic leadership of NATO and demanded the removal of US nuclear bases from Britain. Instead, Michael Foot, a keen advocate of a socialist Third Force in the 1940s, led the party in the early 1980s[45] to seek a transformation in East-West relations. This was to be achieved by a mix of confidence-building measures, removing all nuclear weapons from the UK, and increased trade and other contacts between East and West.

This shift, which the National Executive Committee espoused from the mid-1970s, derived from the bitter disillusion of activists and trade union leaders with the record of the Labour government of 1974–79, the passionate impact of the resurgent peace movement on the party and from widespread fears that strained superpower relations were seriously increasing the risks of nuclear war. While Labour effectively articulated British doubts about the siting of US cruise missiles in the UK, it did not secure broad support for its defence and foreign policy stance. This was especially true of unilaterally giving up British nuclear arms because UK opinion treated these weapons as key symbols of Britain's identity and international prestige. The failure to persuade British public opinion of the case for a full non-nuclear defence policy, together with the very public divisions within the party leadership in regard to the policy, contributed to Labour's worst general election result for decades in June 1983.[46] Labour's deeply insular mood in the early 1980s whereby it advocated ridding the UK of nuclear weapons whatever Britain's NATO allies decided, together with the party's pledge to take the UK out of the European Community, made it much more difficult for the party to secure at least understanding in Europe and North America.[47] Neither did Labour leader Neil Kinnock have any success in securing the understanding of US politicians and military figures for the non-nuclear strategy in 1983–87.

Accordingly, while the party maintained key elements of the non-nuclear policy until 1989, the decline of the peace movement and the advent of new thinking by the Gorbachev leadership in the Soviet Union saw the sense of urgency about implementing the unilateral denuclearisation of Britain declined in the second part of the decade. In this way, and as part of a wide-ranging policy review process which repositioned the party's stance in British politics in 1987–89, the leader Neil Kinnock played a decisive part in persuading Labour to renounce the advocacy of unilateral nuclear disarmament. Likewise, Labour accepted that US nuclear arms based in the UK should be dealt with in a multilateral framework.[48]

Labour's International Policy in the 1990s

In the decade following the end of the Cold War, some of the contradictions afflicting Labour's international policy declined; others were resolved while new issues emerged. First, with Russia no longer a communist country, the ideological rivalry between Labour and the Soviet Communist Party, which had fallen away by the 1960s, came to an end. Many in the Labour Party acknowledged that the collapse of the Soviet version of socialism strengthened the prestige of capitalist forces across the globe, and thereby weakened the capacity, not to mention the intentions of European democratic socialist parties to pursue egalitarian policies. Second, for the first time in decades, Britain faced no direct threat to its security, while NATO's agenda shifted quite sharply from potential conflicts between East and West to problems such as state collapse, often generating humanitarian disasters, proliferation of weapons of mass-destruction and international terrorism. NATO also sharply reduced its reliance on nuclear weapons, gave much greater prominence to issues of conflict prevention, and in 1999 welcomed into membership three former Communist countries, Poland, Hungary and the Czech Republic. For Labour, the shift in alliance strategy also made NATO a much more congenial coalition for the many MPs and members who were profoundly uncomfortable with its nuclear dependence in the late 1970s and early 1980s.[49]

From its election in 1997, the Blair government has depicted itself as less concerned with sovereignty and more internationalist and positive about human rights than previous Labour governments.[50] This approach was reflected in the Strategic Defence Review (1998) which gave a high priority to defence diplomacy involving 'arms control, non-proliferation, and confidence and security building measures.'[51] The Review promised to enhance UN capability in peace support and humanitarian operations, and it made the pledge that 'We do not want to stand idly by and watch humanitarian disasters or aggression of dictators go unchecked.'[52] Consonant with this pledge, the Labour administration played a leading and consistent part in two aspects of the NATO military intervention over Kosovo in March-June 1999. One dimension concerned the UK insistence on maintaining maximum military pressure on the Yugoslav authorities until they relented and accepted the terms for the return of the expelled Kosovar Albanian refugees enshrined in UN Security Council Resolution (1244) of June 1999. The other very notable perspective was to give a high priority to ensuring that Yugoslav politicians and security officials suspected of war crimes in Kosovo would be brought, sooner or later, before the International War Crimes Tribunal.[53] Labour's uncharacteristic clarity on the need to use force and its emphasis on sustaining that pressure was a product of the leadership's conviction in the Kosovo case that fundamental human values should not be compromised as happened in Bosnia earlier in the decade. Thus the Blair administration gave priority to human rights over deeply entrenched notions of state sovereignty. A likely consequence of the commitment to defend human rights, is that the heavy 1990s decline of British military spending-from 4.0 to about 2.6 per cent of GDP[54] might be halted and reversed.

Beyond Europe, in opposition and in government, Labour supported the US resort to force to maintain the effectiveness the UN Special Commission on Iraq in preventing or least delaying Iraq's acquisition or development mass destruction weapons. It did so without the explicit authorisation of the Security Council, but because of the close security relationship with the USA and the keen concern about proliferation.

Conclusion

In the early decades of the century, Labour's foreign and defence policy was marked by a commitment to internationalism, restricting and minimising force, and anti-capitalism. Labour's internationalism was characterised by three partly inter-related elements. First, there was a clear rejection of notions that the interests of the British people were necessarily or usually at odds with those of people elsewhere. This was and is coupled with great stress on the linkage between the welfare of Britain and the international community. Second, they included a vehement and exaggerated perception of the influence that Britain could exert in shaping international norms, attitudes and policies. Third, they embraced a strong sense of moral responsibility for oppressed peoples abroad and for those suffering intense poverty elsewhere.

All of these elements are prominent in Labour's international policy of the 1990s as they were in earlier decades.

Labour's approach to the threat and use of force has been marked by two strong influences. Over the century, the party's attitude to force responded to experience and particular configurations of international power. Until the mid-1930s, with the significant exception of the Great War, Labour had a highly negative perspective on Britain and other powers using force or strengthening their military capability. When the relatively peaceful international order of the 1920s gave way to aggressive international behaviour by Japan, Italy and Germany in the following decade, the party had to make an agonising re-appraisal of deeply held assumptions, values and policies. Thus the party's pacifist leader, George Lansbury, was forced to depart in 1935. Under the prodding of Ernest Bevin – leader of the Transport and General Workers Union – and others, Labour gradually and reluctantly came to accept that it was essential for Britain and other states to acquire adequate military capability and be willing to go to war.

Following the Second World War, Labour consistently rejected the use of force internationally by Britain unless it was legitimated – preferably in unambiguous terms – by the international community through the UN Security Council. Thus, consistent with UN decisions, it supported Britain's participation in the US-led coalition in Korea (1950–53) and the Gulf (1990–91), acquiesced in the Thatcher governments' recovery of the Falklands (1982) and fiercely condemned the Eden administration's use of force at Suez (1956). In 1999, the Kosovo conflict presented the Blair administration with a choice between its strong sense of internationalism and securing UN authorisation for NATO's resort to force. Britain and NATO's concern for human rights and the credibility of the alliance meant they acted without UN authorisation, thereby setting a risky precedent. But this disturbing example was mitigated when a large majority of the Security Council refused to condemn the military action and when NATO countries secured UN approval for the ending of the conflict.[55]

The anti-capitalist strand in Labour's international policy has shifted as its domestic attitude has altered. Labour's reservations and doubts about the impact of capitalism on its policies were deeply embedded before the Second World War. They gave way to a more nuanced revisionist approach articulated by figures like Crosland from the 1950s. In the late 1980s, Labour turned away from a big role for government and embraced market capitalism as the dynamic engine of wealth-creation in conditions of global competition and rapid technological advance.

At the end of the century, unlike the case for many previous decades, Labour's international policy is not a divisive topic within the party. This is the case largely because Britain does not face a direct military threat, the level of military spending is close to the lowest point for most of the 20th century, and many of the tasks undertaken by the UK armed forces are seen in a very positive perspective as contributing to sustaining international order, stability and human rights.

Notes

1   The relatively small Independent Labour Party (ILP) supplied many of the ideas, leaders and activists of the Party. The Fabian Society engaged in education and research and did not take collective decisions on policy matters. For indication of Tawney's influence on Hugh Gaitskell, see Brian Brivati, *Hugh Gaitskell*, Richard Cohen Books, 1996, p.291 and Philip M Williams, *Hugh Gaitskell*, Oxford UP, 1982, pp.22 & 48.

2   Norman Angell, *The Great Illusion*, first published 1910, William Heinemann, 1914.

3   J A Hobson, *Imperialism*, originally published in 1902, George Allen & Unwin, 1938.

4   See Douglas J Newton, *British Labour, European Socialism and the struggle for peace, 1889–1914*, Clarendon Press, 1985, pp.179–182.

5   As Newton, note 4 above observes, 'Without the active support of the trade unions ... the sentiment of socialist solidarity that was so often invoked was sentiment without power', p.34.

6   However only half of the Labour MPs opposed the naval estimates of March 1914. Source Newton, p.315.

7   See Duncan Tanner, *Political Change and the Labour Party: 1900–1918*, Cambridge University Press, 1990, ch.11.

8   Newton, pp.281–2.

9   G D H Cole, *A History of the Labour Party from 1914*, Routledge & Kegan Paul, 1948, p.19.

10 *Ibid.* pp.29–30 and David Marquand, *Ramsay McDonald*, Jonathan Cape, 1977, Ch.10.

11 Cole, *op. cit.*, pp.26–29 and Marquand, *op. cit.* pp.195–197.

12 Marquand, *op. cit.*, p.218.

13 Marquand, *op. cit.*, pp.221–22 and Mary Agnes Hamilton, *Arthur Henderson: a biography*, William Heinemann Ltd, 1938, pp.171–172.

14 F W S Craig, *British Electoral Facts, 1832–1987*, Dartmouth, Parliamentary Research Services, 1989, p.90.

15 William P Maddox, *Foreign Relations in British Labour Politics*, Cambridge, Mass. Harvard UP, 1934, p.100.

16 Winkler, *The League of Nations Movement in Great Britain 1914–1919*, Metuen, NJ, Scarecrow Reprint Corporation, 1967.

17 Henry R. Winkler, 'The Emergence of a Labour Foreign Policy in Great Britain, 1918–1929', *Journal of Modern History*, 28, 4, December 1956, p.247.

18 quoted in Catherine Ann Cline, *Recruits to Labour: The British Labour Party;1914–1931*, Syracuse UP, 1963, p.74.

19 Winkler, *The League of Nations,* pp257, 263.

20 The occupation had disastrous effects on Germany's economy and greatly exacerbated the peoples' feelings of humiliation and unfair treatment.

21 Marquand, *Ramsay MacDonald*, p.355.

21 See Labour Party Annual Report, 1928: Appendix X pp 349–350, which lists nine points. Three short-term points were not regarded as part of the six pillars.

22 Robert Skidelsky, *Politicians and the Slump: The Labour Government of 1929–1931*, Macmillan, 1967.

23 *Ibid.*, especially chs. 2–4 and 14.

24 Consult David Carlton, *MacDonald versus Henderson: the foreign policy of the Second Labour Government*, Macmillan, 1970.

25 See, Lorna Lloyd, *Peace Through Law: Britain and the International Court in the 1920s*, The Royal Historical Society, the Boydell Press, 1997.

26 Skidelsky, *op. cit.*, ch14.

27 Alan Bullock, *The Life and Times of Ernest Bevin: Volume One : Trade Union Leader 1881–1940*, William Heinemann, 1960, pp.211–228. For an account of Bevin's role at the 1935 conference, see pp561–574. In the Peace Ballot of June 1935, 6.8 million respondents of a total of 11.6 million ballots supported collective military measures against aggression, suggesting the pacifist sentiment was not in the ascendant. See John F Naylor, *Labour's International Policy: The Labour Party in the 1930s*, Weidenfeld and Nicolson, 1969, pp.65–67.

29 See statement by Clement Attlee, House of Commons, Official Report 3 October, 1938, Cols 50–66.

30 Labour's opposition to conscription in May 1939, owed much to the perception that in Great War, workers had been exploited by unscrupulous employers. See Alan Bullock, *The Life and Times of Ernest Bevin: Volume One*, pp636–8.

31 G D H Cole, p.381.

32 In May 1940, Bevin was neither an MP nor a member of Labour's National Executive Committee.

33 Alan Bullock, *Ernest Bevin: Foreign Secretary, 1945–1951*, Oxford University Press, 1985, pp.65–6.

34 *Ibid.*, p.66.

35 G D H Cole, *op. cit.*, pp.421–2.

36 Bullock, *Ernest Bevin: Foreign Secretary, 1945–1951*, Ch14.

37 Comment by Labour MP and pacifist Emrys Hughes in debate on Air Estimates, House of Commons: Official Report 4 March 1948, Col. 571.

38 Michael Foot's column in *Daily Herald*, 14 December, 1945.

39 House of Commons, Official Report 20 August 1945, Col. 340.

40 See Jonathan Schneer, 'Hopes Deferred or Shattered: The British Labour Left and the Third Force Movement, 1945–49', *Journal of Modern History*, 56, 2, 1984, pp.197–226.

41 'The constant applause for Bevin's policies from Churchill, Eden and right-wing journals in Fleet Street, was deeply disturbing for many in the Labour Party...', Kenneth O Morgan, *Labour in Power: 1945–1951*, Clarendon Press, 1984, p.239.

42 Kenneth O. Morgan, *Callaghan: A Life*, Oxford UP, 1997, p.95.

43 Brian Brivati, *Hugh Gaitskell*, Richard Cohen Books, 1996, pp.109–110.

44 See Dan Keohane, *Labour Party Defence Policy Since 1945*, Leicester University Press, 1993, p.68.

45 On Foot's leadership, see Mervyn Jones, Michael Foot Victor Gollancz, 1994, pp.448–56 and Ivor Crewe and Anthony King, *SDP: The Birth, Life and Death of the Social Democratic Party*, Oxford University Press, 1995, pp.72–78.

46 David Butler and Denis Kavanagh, *The British General Election of 1983*, Macmillan, 1983, pp.202–3, p.282.

47 Keohane, *Labour Party Defence Policy since 1945*, ch. 4.

48 *Ibid.*, pp.117–130.

49 *Ibid.* chs 2–4 and Frank Cook, MP, in debate on NATO enlargement, House of Commons, Official Report 17 July, 1998, Col. 719.

50 Denis McShane, MP, 'New Labour, New Foreign Policy? A Labour Perspective', *Oxford International Review*, Winter, 1998/99, pp.22–30.

51 *Strategic Defence Review*, Cm3999, Stationery Office, July 1998, Paragraph 49.

52 *Ibid.* Paragraph 19. With regard to enhancing UN capability, in June 1999 the UK pledged to place up to 8, 000 troops and equipment on permanent standby for UN peacekeeping. See Michael Binyon and Anna Blundy, 'UN chief hails Cook's standby force', *The Times*, 26 June 1999.

53 See Robin Cook in House of Commons, Official Report 19 April, 1999, Col. 573 and in House of Commons, Official Report 17 June, 1999, Cols. 584–5.

54 The *Strategic Defence Review* p 51 projects a fall in defence spending from 2.7 per cent in 1997/8 to 2.4 in 2001/2.

55 The UN Security Council voted by 12 to three against a Russian motion condemning NATO military action against Yugoslavia. No permanent member voted against Resolution 1244 of 10 June which authorised the establishment of an international security presence in Kosovo. In addition, in mid-April, the UN Commission on Human Rights voted by 44 to 1 in favour of a resolution condemning the atrocities in Kosovo and demanding the withdrawal of Yugoslav forces from the province. See Robin Cook, House of Commons, Official Report 19 April, 1999, Cols. 579–580.

Beyond Euro-Scepticism? Labour and the European Union since 1945

Richard Heffernan

Entering Europe could mean 'the end of Britain as an independent state ... It means the end of a thousand years of history. You may say 'Let it end', but my goodness, it is a decision that needs a little case and thought', Hugh Gaitskell, speech to the Labour Party conference, October 1962.

'We aim to develop a Europe which is democratic and socialist, and where the interests of the people are placed above the interests of national and multinational capitalist groups, but within which each country must be able to realise its own economic and social objectives, under the sovereignty of its own Parliament and people. A Labour Government will oppose any move towards turning the Community into a federation'. Labour manifesto, 1979.

'There are only three options for Britain in Europe. The first is to come out. The second is to stay in, but on the sidelines. The third is to stay in, but in a leading role ... The third is the path a new Labour government will take'. Labour manifesto, 1997.

Europe – or, more particularly, Britain's place within Europe – has bedevilled all British parties in the last third of Labour's first century, provoking sharp divisions, particularly in the case of Labour and the Conservatives. While eschewing a narrow, insular little-Englander opposition to things European, the Labour Party was clearly Euro-sceptic between the 1950s and the mid-1980s, although a great many vocal pro-Europeans always numbered among its ranks. When in government in 1967, Labour did apply to join the then EEC, but the party also opposed entry in 1962 and 1970–73 and declared in favour of withdrawal in 1983. Party divisions over Europe were all too apparent at the time of Edward Heath's application to enter, and during the 1975 referendum the Wilson government supported continuing membership of the EEC, while the Labour Party, in the form of a majority of MPs, the National Executive Committee and the party conference, favoured a no to Europe vote.[1] In rejecting entry into Europe Labour anti-Europeans held the whip hand within the party until the mid-1980s. Although the Wilson and Callaghan government's accepted Britain's place within Europe after 1974, the wider party opposed Europe as irredeemably pro-capitalist and certain to erode national sovereignty and autonomy. By favouring regional capital and finance, Europe would interfere with Labour's ability to manage the British economy, control and direct the domestic market, and pursue social and economic reform at home.

Yet, in spite of this record of hostility to Europe, Labour has presented itself since 1988 as an ever more firmer European, keen to pursue a constructive relationship with Britain's European partners. Declaring its 'vision of Europe is of an alliance of independent nations choosing to co-operate to achieve the goals they cannot achieve alone', the party's 1997 manifesto made clear Labour would provide leadership in Europe, without going down the road of a European federal superstate.[2] Identifying three options for Britain in Europe – 'The first is to come out. The second is to stay in, but on the sidelines. The third is to stay in, but in a leading role'[3] – Labour associates itself with the third, supporting closer co-operation among member states over economic policy, employment policy and defence, and more majority voting in European decision making. While retaining the right not to join should it be in Britain's interests to do so, Labour also cautiously supports a successful single currency. This rejection of outright Euro-scepticism is a product of Labour's most recent history; it reflects a recognition that out of a sense of self interest 'Britain has to be European; not on the margins but right at the centre of Europe ... co-operating, engaging and leading' in the European Union.[4]

Definitively Non-European, 1945–67

Labour's grudging willingness to move toward Europe results from a deepening European co-dependence in a world where national economic sovereignty is deemed to be restrained by global markets and the internationalisation of capital. European-isation is a complex process, embracing the transformation of the European Coal and Steel Community into the European Union via the European Economic Community and the European Community. Perceived economic necessity, strategic consid-erations and political pressures have all combined to structure the environment within which Labour has constructed its European policy. European integration is both political and economic in origin and a number of dynamic processes promote 'ever closer political union' between EU member states. Among these, national imperatives – in addition to deepening economic globalization; the specificity of Western Europe; functional integration arising from growing supra-national co-operation;

and Euro-federalist aspirations – help explain how the political and economic actors of nation states respond to Europe. Nation states choose how and when to respond to Europeanisation, but so too do political parties; neither simply react to demands but respond to internal and external pressures. Labour's past Euro-scepticism was a product of its historical identity, and its contemporary Europeanism is influenced by its present day political environment.

After 1945, Britain's political classes of all parties kept a distance from Europe.[5] Labour's formal and informal association with Europe was restricted to its support for the strictly inter-governmental discussion forum of the Council of Europe and, most significantly, its strong commitment to NATO. Labour and the British state were at one in supporting a concert of powers in Western Europe, part of a bipolar Europe under the military hegemony of the US and, it was initially hoped, the UK. Thus, Britain had little interest in the notion of an entangling, non-defence related alliance beyond the NATO alliance and the 'special relationship' with the United States. The Empire-Commonwealth aside, Britain saw itself as far more Atlanticist than it was European; and for its part Labour most certainly did as well. Both Britain and Labour reacted coolly to the Schuman Plan and rejected the idea of joining the ECSC in 1950–51, Labour taking particular exception to the sectors chosen for supranational co-ordination, coal and steel, with Herbert Morrison, Foreign Secretary in 1951, famously claiming: 'It's no good: the Durham miners would not wear it'.[6]

Of course, the Durham miners had nothing to do with the decision to stay out. Labour's decision was influenced by Britain's place in the world and Labour's intentions for government: a post-1945 Atlanticist outlook; an attachment to the Commonwealth and continuing links of Empire; support for parliamentary sovereignty; an objection to regional institutions advantaging capital; and the party's desire to pursue a notion of planned 'social democracy in one country' free from the interference of entangling, economic alliances beyond the financial system established at Bretton Woods. Labour prioritised national recovery and social reform at home with global responsibilities abroad, helping stabilise the emergent post-war bi-polar world. In 1945–51, Britain and Labour's geo-political world view was largely structured around the three interlocking circles of Atlanticism, Empire and Europe; with Europe being initially the least significant circle. From 1945 to the late 1950s, Labour-led or otherwise, the post-war Foreign Office looked to maintain

Britain's continuing world role through as close an international association with the United States as was possible and through the Empire reformed into the Commonwealth. Its world view fashioned by the emergent Cold War, Labour looked to the continent only to the promotion of West European stability and the resurgence of liberal democratic market economies. This may or may not have ben an 'illusion of grandeur', but it was British policy and something which owed a great deal to the attitude of the post-war Foreign Office and that of the 1945–51 Labour government.

If the refusal to join the ECSC in 1950–52 was a failure, it was a failure of national policy. While the Schuman Plan was rejected by a Labour government, it was a Conservative government which chose not to join the ECSC in 1951–52 or the EEC in 1955–58. As is so well attested, as the 1950s dragged on into the 1960s and Britain's economic limitations became apparent at the same time its independent influence in the world faltered, political opinion within the British state began to reconsider European economic co-operation. After 1959, Britain's rapprochement with Europe was prompted by a perception of European strength given the economic success of the ECSC/EEC six. When the Macmillan-led Conservatives led the first hesitant approach to Europe in 1961–63, Labour's caution was all too apparent. This application, merely a exploration of whether Britain should apply and the terms at which it might join, was brokered by the Conservatives, but Labour, although a parliamentary spectator unable to influence events, was obliged to take a position on the issue. Excepting the minority of committed, pro-European Labour MPs who enthusiastically welcomed Macmillan's application, the party's response was somewhat muted, its official stance hesitant until Hugh Gaitskell, party leader in 1955–63, declared against Europe at the 1962 Labour conference claiming entry would mean the 'end of a thousand years' of British history.[7] In the event, the issue was foreclosed by de Gaulle's first veto of British entry in 1963 and although the veto took much of the wind out of the European debate, Labour continued to hedge on the issue, consolidating a benign anti-Europeanism, but allowing its backbench pro and anti-Europeans to quietly pursue their own agenda.

For and Against Europe, 1967–83

Gaitskell's successor, Harold Wilson, inevitably trimmed with the wind on Europe, as on so much else. Although the party leader had been an anti-European in 1962, Labour under Wilson identified 'closer links with our European partners' as a priority in 1964 without yet endorsing EEC entry. However, in government in 1966, with official opinion – particularly within the Foreign Office – running strongly in support of entry, Labour accepted that 'Britain should be ready to enter the European Economic Community, provided essential British and Commonwealth interests are safeguarded'.[8] Fearful of the continuing threat posed by recurrent balance of payments problems and possible impending devaluation, the second Wilson government was persuaded that EEC entry could bring considerable benefits to Britain. In partisan terms, Labour thought Europe could shore-up the government's faltering modernisation efforts in the wake of the abortive failure at national planning, the radical deflationary measures of July 1966, and persistent economic under-performance in 1964–67. Brokering an application could also deny the Conservatives, now led by the pro-European, Edward Heath, an issue to use against Labour at the next election. In March 1967 the Cabinet determined unanimously, but with considerable misgivings on the part of a minority, to apply for entry. In the event, in spite of the House of Commons voting in favour of the application by 488 votes to 62 with 36 Labour MPs defying the party whip to vote against entry, Labour's application also foundered on the continuing intransigence on the part of de Gaulle, although Britain's application did remain on the table.

Wilson's application did little to address the European differences within the party, and Labour Euro-scepticism surfaced with a vengeance during the 1970 Parliament, this time encompassing substantial majorities within the Shadow Cabinet, the Parliamentary party and the party conference. Increasingly identifying EEC entry with support for the Heath government, Labour abruptly broke from the path it had previously – if cautiously – trod, opposing Heath's application by finding fault with the terms of entry his government secured. At the urging of Euro-sceptics such as Tony Benn, Michael Foot and Barbara Castle, and the growing scepticism of centre right figures like Denis Healey, Jim Callaghan, and, crucially, Harold Wilson himself, the Shadow Cabinet adopted an anti-European stance, one symbolised by the phrase rejecting entry 'on these terms, at this time'. This was not particularly new. In 1967, the Labour Cabinet had contained a number of EEC critics and had Labour's application progressed beyond de Gaulle's veto, political disagreements would have prompted divisions within the Parliamentary party and the government once the decision to join

– as opposed to apply – had actually to be taken. After 1970, the Labour left made a great deal of the anti-EEC running, but the bulk of the centre-right of the party also rallied around pragmatic objections covering Commonwealth relations, agricultural issues and food prices, the role of sterling, the size of the financial contribution that would be made to the Community, and, crucially, Britain's ability to plan and manage its own economy.

Labour's pro-Europeans held strongly out against this anti-Europe stance. Led by Roy Jenkins, deputy leader in 1970-72, they refused to compromise their pro-EEC credentials. Facing the prospect of considerable infighting on the European issue, Harold Wilson's objective was to maintain some degree of Labour unity and such was the balance of forces within the party he was obliged to oppose European entry in the short term, without foreclosing on entry or continued membership in the medium to long term. Of course, the fact that Wilson saw the pro-European Roy Jenkins, the only senior Labour figure to lead an organised faction within the Parliamentary party, as the immediate contender for the leadership reinforced his Euro-scepticism. Thus encouraged to oppose entry in the short term secure in the knowledge that this was what the manageable majority of the party wanted, Wilson was more content to be dependant on the support of non-Jenkins supporting Euro-sceptical MP's. Not for the last time – witness the problems of the Major-led Conservatives in 1992–97 – internal party considerations played a large part in determining where a party stood on Europe. Support for EEC entry among Labour pro-Europeans in 1970–72 was such an article of faith, critics alleged they were more pro-Europe than pro-Labour and when Heath called a free vote in October 1971 on the principle of entry, 69 Labour MPs voted against the three line whip opposing entry and another 20 abstained, providing the key to Heath's 112 vote majority. Given that 39 Conservative MPs voted against their party, the motion paving the way for British accession to the EEC in January 1973 only carried with Labour support.[9]

In April 1972, Labour declared it would hold a future referendum on continuing membership of the EEC, a device proposed by Tony Benn and described by Jim Callaghan as a 'little rubber dinghy' into which Labour could clamber to protect itself from continuing European in-fighting. In the event, the referendum on 'continuing membership' would become a means by which Wilson and other cautious Europeans could oppose Heath's application without foreclosing on a future Labour government staying in the EEC. This strategy went unrecognised by pro-Europeans bitterly opposed to the referendum, seeing in it an ploy to bring about future withdrawal, and in a spectacular tactical blunder, Jenkins, fed up fighting a European cause within an increasingly Euro-sceptical party, resigned from the deputy leadership in April 1972 and a majority of his supporters left the Labour front bench. Although Jenkins returned to front line Labour politics in the 1974–76 Wilson and Callaghan governments, he had vacated a position of party influence he was never again to enjoy. While Europe brought the former Chancellor of the Exchequer to unprecedented public notice, in Labour Party terms it proved his undoing. His association with a cause greater than party damned him in the eyes of much of the centre and centre-right of the Parliamentary party who were instinctively loyal to the party and its agreed line.

While Wilson's hedging in the face of Labour's anti-European majority did keep the party together in 1970-75, the Labour government – but not the Labour Party itself – swung back into its pre-1970 European mode on its return to office in February 1974. By 1975, in another Wilson-led volte face, the Labour leadership advocated continued EEC membership in the referendum it had promised. The 1974–75 re-negotiation of the terms of entry was a non-event, essentially a procedure in which leading members of the Labour government willing to stay in Europe were able to secure the agreement of a majority of their colleagues, and in March 1975 the Cabinet decided by 16 votes to seven to recommend a yes vote in the referendum to be held in June. With Cabinet antis including Tony Benn, Michael Foot, Barbara Castle, Willie Ross, Peter Shore, John Silkin, and Eric Varley, Wilson was obliged to suspend the doctrine of collective Cabinet responsibility to maintain the unity of the government. In the wake of the vote of Labour's National Executive Committee to commit the party to a no vote, a decision upheld by a two to one majority recorded in favour of withdrawal at a special Labour conference in April, this was a recognition of political realities. Indeed, in a free vote in the House of Commons the majority of Labour MPs voted against continuing membership as the Parliamentary party divided 145 against and 137 for with 33 abstentions, while the Commons voted in favour of continued membership by 396–172.

In Labour Party terms, it was the Prime Minister and the Cabinet in the minority on the issue, prompting 'the spectacle of a Labour government recommending to the people a line of action it was official Labour Party policy to oppose.'[10] Although the government officially campaigned for a yes vote, the Labour Party, having declared its difference of opinion, played no official part in the referendum. The campaign was fought out between two rival camps, the yes to Europe campaign organised by Britain in Europe, and the no to Europe effort run by the strangely named National Referendum Campaign, two organisation between which pro and anti Labour marketeers divided their allegiances on an individual basis. In the event, the Cabinet struck a victory over its own party as the pro-Europeans of all parties won the day and carried the referendum vote by a 67.2 to 32.8 majority in favour of staying in Europe.[11]

While Labour Euro-sceptics found little choice other than to accept the referendum outcome in the short term, opinions did not change and Labour Euro-scepticism resurfaced with a vengeance following the May 1979 defeat of the Callaghan government. In 1980, to the dismay of Labour Europeans, the Labour conference voted decisively by 5 million votes to 2 million in favour of withdrawal from Europe, a majority provided courtesy of the trade union block vote, but also one reflecting considerable Euro-scepticism on the part of constituency parties. Yet, the common assumption that after 1979 'Europe became part of the radical leftist catalogue that captured the party'[12] misreads the situation. Euro-scepticism was never confined to the Labour left. The 1980 vote was a logical continuation of Labour's approach to Europe since 1971. In 1975, only the Cabinet majority and some 50 per cent of the Parliamentary party had supported continuing membership; the party as a whole had been consistently Euro-sceptic by at least a two to one majority and feeling among Constituency Labour Parties had run as high as three to one against Europe.[13] As expressed in *Labour's Programme 1982* and the 1983 manifesto, *The New Hope for Britain*, opposition to Europe was then very much in the Labour mainstream, and was reflected by majority opinion within the Shadow Cabinet. Rather than having simply reverted 'with great speed to the anti-Europe stance that had been its instinct to adopt at almost all times when the party wasn't burdened with office',[14] Labour's anti-Europeanism had been softened in office in 1974-79 by the party's office holders, the leadership of the Parliamentary party ensconced in Cabinet, not by the party itself. The party's collective view as expressed in its federal decision making process between 1971 and 1983, was relatively constant in its Euro-scepticism, even if the degree of its hostility waxed and waned.

Despite the significance of the 1975 referendum vote for the European status quo, Labour had remained far from enthusiastic on Europe. Beset by economic difficulties and political weaknesses at home, Wilson and his successor, Jim Callaghan, had shown little interest in matters European, grudgingly supporting direct elections to the European Parliament but rejecting entry to the Exchange Rate Mechanism in 1979 because it was, in Callaghan's words, 'in the national interest to do so'.[15] Although withdrawal from the EEC did not feature in the the 1979 manifesto, which was essentially a right-wing document drafted by Callaghan in the face of left opposition, a latent Euro-scepticism was discernable in its call for 'a wider and looser grouping of European states' within which 'each country must be able to realize its own economic and social objectives, under the sovereignty of its own Parliament and people'.[16] Elements on the Labour right had long asserted that national governments should be free to pursue their own economic, regional and industrial objectives without European hindrance and, as Labour shifted leftward after 1979, Euro-scepticism was reinforced by the party's broad support for some form of national Keynesianism, and the belief that Europe would interfere with the collectivist, interventionist, protectionist and statist economic policy outlined in even the mildest form of the Alternative Economic Strategy.[17] Accordingly, the 1983 manifesto was unequivocal: Labour would withdraw from Europe because 'the rules of the Treaty of Rome are bound to conflict with our strategy for economic growth and full employment, our proposals on industrial policy and for regulating trade, and our need to restore exchange controls and to regulate direct overseas investment'.[18]

After 1979, the Labour mainstream rejected Europe in the belief that Britain, indeed any European nation-state, should be free to pursue its own economic and industrial policies. Far from being the product of Tony Benn's leftist ambitions, Euro-scepticism was rooted in the Parliamentary leadership and the Parliamentary party, two key elements within Labour's federal structure within which Benn enjoyed little support. Callaghan's successor as leader, Michael Foot, and his Shadow Chancellor, Peter Shore, were long-standing Euro-sceptics convinced membership was neither in Britain's interest, nor Labour's. Indeed, in the contest to succeed the retiring Callaghan in November 1980, three of the four candidates, Foot, Shore and John Silkin, were Euro-sceptics and the chief standard bearer of the Labour right, Denis Healey, had been a sceptic in 1972–74, a quiet 'yes' vote in 1975, and was by no shade of the imagination a vociferous Euro-enthusiast.[19] While pro-Europeans continued to be represented in the Parliamentary party, they were very much the minority in the wider party as Labour Europeanism was weakened as result of the 1981 exodus of key elements of the

Labour right to the fledging SDP.[20] In contrast to its anti-European stance, policies such as unilateral nuclear disarmament, to say nothing of the Labour left's constitutional campaign to capture the party, were the cause of significantly more disquiet in Labour's ranks.

Increasingly European, 1983 and After

In retrospect, Labour's 1983 election defeat drew a line under its Euro-scepticism. The party's preparedness to consider itself European was encouraged by repeated electoral setbacks and its slow but consistent march away from the left-wing economic policy agenda of the 1970s and early 1980s. Despite an established track record as an anti-marketeer, Neil Kinnock, Michael Foot's successor as leader, identified the qualification of Euro-scepticism as a symbol of the party's willingness to modernise its appeal. By 1984, the pledge to withdraw had ben replaced by a commitment to *consider* withdrawal should reform of the EEC prove impossible and exit be in Britain's interest. Yet, Kinnock's European policy reform was partial and hesitant. While a shift away from outright Euro-scepticism, his 1984 counsel that Britain should 'only realistically accept enduring membership if, at the very least, we suffer no significant material loss or disadvantage',[21] is not a ringing endorsement of Europe. Although Conservative Euro-sceptics damn the Thatcher government for acceding to the Single European Act of 1986, Labour voted against it in the House of Commons. While Thatcher's support for a liberalised single market blinded her to the integrationist measures of the Act, Labour supported neither liberalisation nor greater integration. Such was Labour's continuing Euro-scepticism, its 1987 manifesto made clear a determination to 'reject EEC interference with our policy for national recovery and renewal',[22] a position best described as 'only a conditional resumption of a hypothetically pro-Europe position ... a small fragment of British Europeanism ... minimalist, pragmatic, rather than in any way visionary'.[23] Labour under Kinnock in 1983–87 was far from being enthusiastic about Europe: the party may have accepted the inevitability of Community membership, but did not embrace the idea wholeheartedly. In no way did the party become pro-European overnight in 1983, and it was only renewed defeat at the 1987 general election that gave Europeanisation he chance to quicken its pace.[24]

This initial, half hearted abandonment of EEC withdrawal was gradually replaced by a willingness to work constructively within Europe. However, it was over five years into Kinnock's nine year term as Labour leader that the party began to embrace Europe with a degree of enthusiasm rather than reluctance; this change was however to prove 'significant. And it became decisive.'[25] Seeking solutions to the party's inter-related electoral and ideological crisis, Labour saw Europe less as a problem and more of a solution to the problems it would face should it ever return to government. After 1987, Labour Euro-scepticism was weakened by the party's abandonment of national Keynesianism and any form of collectivist or statist economic policy. This Europeanisation was the single element in the Kinnock and Blair-led reformation of the party to go relatively unchallenged. Few Euro-sceptical voices were raised in sustained anger, and only the most committed of Euro-sceptics raised any sort of challenge. Indeed, as the Labour right under Kinnock set about making Labour more Euro-friendly, the Labour left's position on Europe altered. Its support for radical social democracy in one country without hindrance from Brussels was supplanted by the idea of promoting social reform through European institutions. Many on the Labour left such as Ken Livingstone came to keenly favour European integration. Others, such as Tony Benn, remained sceptical on the whole question of Europe, a scepticism now often cast in terms of the democratic deficit agenda, rather than a matter of economic policy.

In a dramatic reversal of past form, Labour was clearly the most European of the two major parties in the election year of 1992. As the party moved toward Europe, the Conservatives moved significantly away from it; the more Europe became a Thatcherite bugbear, the more it became the Labour vogue. The year 1988–89 was pivotal. For the solid bulk of Labour's right, centre, realigning left, and elements of the less reconstructed left, it appeared there really was no alternative to a Britain's engagement in Europe. Moreover, support for withdrawal from Europe was seen by many as a symbol of 'how out of touch' Labour had been in 1983.[26] This shift was encouraged by a changed attitude toward Europe on the part of trade unions as the TUC became increasingly attracted to the idea of European co-operation. Where Thatcher denounced Europe in her September 1988 Bruges Speech for a creeping Euro-federalism, TUC pro-Europeanism deepened. Put at its crudest, denied influence on policy or access to government at home, trade unions were definitely 'pro-Jacques Delors', the proto-federalist Thatcherite bete-noire then President of the Commission, if he was in any way 'anti-Thatcher'. In September 1988, Delors' address to the TUC Congress symbolised the prospect of Europe rehabilitating trade unions in the political game at an international rather than national level.[27] Of course, it is simplistic to suggest Labour followed where the trade unions led – both the industrial and political wings of the changing Labour movement marched to the same destination by different directions, for different reasons. Yet, growing Europeanism was a marked feature of Labour politics 'not because it saw the light, but because it tired of the darkness. Largely, though not entirely, because Mrs Thatcher was anti-Europe ... Labour became pro-Europe. Because Thatcherism dominated the power structure of Britain, socialism, as it was still called, sought and found another outlet'.[28]

Yet, in response to continuing Euro-scepticism on the part of many voters, Labour did little to trumpet its new found Europeanism at the 1992 general election. Europe was not deemed a voter getter, and many thought it could prove a vote loser. Obliquely, its manifesto claimed that Labour would 'promote Britain out of the European second division into which our country has been relegated by the Tories', 'play an active part in negotiations on Economic and Monetary Union' (whatever that may have meant) and 'fight for Britain's interests'.[29] Of course, Europe as an issue featured little in the 1992 campaign and Labour's cautious but unmistakable Europeanism did nothing to forestall its unexpected defeat at the polls. Kinnock's immediate resignation as Labour leader in the wake of his second electoral loss paved the way for the brief leadership of John Smith, a consistent European who had voted in 1971 with Heath to join the then EEC (and, in due course, Kinnock was appointed a European Commissioner on the nomination of the British government).

While Labour undoubtedly became more Euro-friendly under Smith and his successor Tony Blair, its reaction to the 1992 Maastricht agreement was cautious; damning the government for its Euro-scepticism and rejection of the social chapter while accepting the opt out on monetary union. Labour had originally hoped to out-European the Conservatives in 1989–91 by supporting monetary union in principle, but instead shied away from the issue, declaring an 'interest in thinking about the issue' while favouring closer integration of European currencies in general without supporting a single currency. Thus, seeking a symbol of economic orthodoxy to copperfasten Labour's preference for market-based strategies prioritising low inflation even at the cost of high unemployment, Smith as Shadow Chancellor converted the party to ERM membership in 1989–90 and later welcomed the belated decision to join forced on Thatcher by her government in October 1990.[30] While Britain's ejection from the

ERM on 'Black Wednesday' did question the party's economic judgement, the calamity was ultimately to Labour's benefit by damaging a government which forfeited its record of economic competence. Nonetheless, the considerable political fall out experienced by the Major government led the party soberly to note the electoral impact European issues could have on domestic politics.

During the Major government's long Parliamentary struggle over Maastricht, Labour pledged not to block ratification; to do so, in John Smith's words, 'would be to undermine fatally the credibility of Labour's conversion to the European cause'.[31] Yet, seeking to exploit Conservative differences by making support for the Maastricht Bill conditional on the removal of the social chapter opt-out, Labour was concerned to harry, embarrass, and, if at all possible, defeat the government during its efforts to pass its legislation in the teeth of the opposition of some 25 to 35 hardline Euro-sceptic Tory MPs. Where Labour was probably more divided than the Conservatives (85 backbench MPs signed a hardline pro-Maastricht Early Day Motion in January 1993, and 66 MPs voted against the Bill at third reading), the party steered a careful path throughout the Commons skirmishing between the frontbench's private support for Maastricht, even without the Social Chapter, and its eagerness to encourage the government's difficulties without causing the loss of the Bill. Finally, in July 1993, the Major Cabinet was forced to enact the Bill by means of a vote of confidence, Conservatives having blocked its passage the previous day. Although Smith was charged by non-Labour pro-Europeans with running the risk of wrecking the Treaty, Labour's tactics were designed with the objective of allowing the party to demonstrate support for Maastricht minus the Social Chapter opt out, and oppose the government.[32] From Labour's vote-seeking, partisan perspective, the strategy worked like a dream.

Since 1994, Blair-led new Labour has made much of its willingness to participate effectively within the European Union while retaining a residual caution about Europe, one born of an awareness of a deep seated Euro-scepticism among the British electorate and the supra-national price ever closer political union will exert. Still, its commitment to 'co-operating in European institutions' (a phrase appearing in the new Clause IV of the party constitution proposed by Blair and adopted in April 1995) led the party to fight the 1997 election on a manifesto both 'patriotic' and 'pro-European'. This promised 'rapid completion of the single market' and 'proper enforcement of single market rules', 'enlargement of the European Union to include the countries of central and eastern Europe and Cyprus', support for 'institutional reforms necessary to make an enlarged Europe work more efficiently', while pledging a referendum on joining a single currency and promising to retain control over such areas as taxation, defence, security, and immigration.[33] In comparison with a Conservative predecessor hamstrung by divisions on Europe in general and the single currency in particular, the Labour government elected in May 1997 takes a more positive and constructive attitude to Europe, publicly championing pro-European credentials. Indeed, no overt Euro-sceptic is to be found on the Labour frontbench, and critics are confined to the backbenches, if not the very fringes of the Parliamentary party.[34]

In opposition before 1997, Labour's criticism of the Major government's isolation in Europe was a useful electoral stick to beat the floundering Tories. Its alternative of 'constructive engagement with our European partners' may be seen as a vote gathering ploy, but Labour's commitment to Europe is real despite objections to the idea of a European 'super-state'. Obviously, the most important European issue facing the Labour government is monetary union and Labour's manifesto commitment is that Britain would only join the single currency having overcome the 'triple veto' of Cabinet, Parliament and a referendum.[35] Having previously stated Britain was 'highly unlikely to join monetary union at its launch in 1999', the Blair government has formally adopted a 'wait and see' stance effectively ruling out entry under some time after the next general election. Privately, while prepared to wait until after the next election before advocating entry, Blair-led Labour is moving cautiously but inexorably to a position of joining 'when the time is right'; adopting a 'when, rather than if' attitude toward monetary union. Because electoral opinion is a most serious obstacle to joining the single currency, the government has moderated its support for the single currency for office-seeking reasons. In October 1997, February 1999 and May 1999, Labour declared in favour of entry provided certain economic tests were met and it was in Britain's national interest to join. Although suggestions that 'there is no over-riding constitutional bar to membership' are all too obvious when the British constitution can be reworked by a simple partisan Commons majority, entry is 'conditional', not yet 'inevitable',[36] and subject to economic and political conditions. Yet, while support for entry is subject to 'very real conditions', Labour's 'intention is real'[37] and preparing to enter *after* the next general election *should* economic conditions permit and political considerations allow' is the formal, if unstated, stance. In particular, with regard to the as of yet unstated political conditions, entry will be pressed only when it will not be to the political disadvantage of the Labour government to do so.

Definitively European, but 'British' First, 'European' Second

Britain's past Euro-scepticism reflects a European 'awkwardness' resulting from Britain's political culture, historical experience, established geo-political world view, and the specificity of its ancien political regime; factors which collectively shape the environment within which the European policy of Britain's political parties have been shaped. Labour's scepticism was reinforced by its sense of social democratic collectivism, its belief in the power of the British state to control the domestic economy, and its readiness to damn Europe for being pro-capitalist. Excepting the Conservative Party, Britain's parties are today more pro-European, either out of ingrained desire or perceived necessity and Labour's post-1988 Europeanism simultaneously reflects and encourages this. While Labour aspires to secure for Britain a position of European leadership unimagined since 1945–50, it does not do so out of any Euro-federalist aspiration. Deriving from a preparedness to benefit from a European enterprise protecting and enhancing British interests, its Europeanism is underpinned by a continuing inter-governmentalism which, continuing functional integration notwithstanding, may well help moderate a drift toward some form of European federation in the short and medium term.

Unsurprisingly, while supporting a stronger European defence capability as an adjunct to NATO, the Blair government rejects the idea of a European army. Here, its willingness to co-operate closely on matters of common concern is tempered by the firm belief that no nation should yield up its own sovereign right to determine the use of its own armed forces; an attitude born of an eagerness to preserve national autonomy and sovereignty wherever possible, and qualifying it only where it is in Britain's interest to do so. Indeed, because Labour continues to look toward Europe in terms of 'pooling' rather than 'surrendering' sovereignty, it is 'European' only in a 'national' sense, an attitude reflecting its well established fidelity to the ways and means of the British state. Its supports a non-federal Europe composed of co-operating nation states within an inter-governmental network benefiting each nation state. In echoing John Major's promise to put Britain at the 'heart of Europe', Prime Minister Blair is willing to promote European interests only when they coincide with those of Britain. He is not an out and out pro-European in the Ted Heath–Roy Jenkins mould. In his own words: Labour's European policy must 'resist things that are wrong and foolish and not in our country's interest'.[38] Thus, support 'in principle' for monetary union today does not necessarily include British entry tomorrow. As announced by Blair in February 1999, the government's position on the single currency is plain: 'And if joining a single currency is good for British jobs and British industry, if it enhances British power and British influence, I believe it is right for Britain to overcome these constitutional and political arguments and the fears behind them'.[39] Herein, lies the crux of Labour's contemporary Europeanism, one certainly fashioned by a belief that 'to be pro-British, you do not have to be anti-European',[40] but also influenced by national considerations and an awareness of public Euro-scepticism. Past Labour manifestos spoke of Britain being ready to enter or stay in Europe provided British interests are safeguarded. While membership is now guaranteed, the same premise continues to be applied with regard to determining Labour's attitude to developments in the widening and deepening union.

In the past, British governments of all parties and differing ideological persuasions have chosen to follow or object to European initiatives, rather than lead and suggest then. As a feature of an 'Old Britain' helping fashion 'Old Labour', time alone will tell if this is something that is dramatically changing in the 'New Britain' of 'New Labour'. Of course, while the strength of the European Union lies in the weakness of the nation state, the weakness of the European Union lies in the continuing political relevance of the nation state. Labour's stance on Europe still results from being a 'British' rather than a 'European' political party. Its Europeanism remains of a qualified inter-governmental character. Despite the internationalist perspective behind a great deal of its 'third way' rhetoric, the party continues to favour a Europe of nation states, but now accepts that the pursuit of national economic interests through Europe may ultimately exact a supra-national price in the form of 'ever closer political union'. Of course, the same could be said of all other EU member states, but this nonetheless suggests that Labour's contemporary 'Europeanism' should be placed squarely in the context of its continuing 'Britishness'.

Notes

1 Given the changing appellations applied to European institutions since 1952, for convenience sake the word Europe is applied throughout.

2   The Labour Party, *New Labour New Britain: Because Britain Deserves Better,* 1997 Labour manifesto, London, The Labour Party 1997.

3   *Ibid.*

4   The rhetoric is that of Gordon Brown (speech to TUC conference on Monetary Union, 13 May 1999, HM Treasury press release) but similar sentiments may be found in recent speeches by any number of Labour ministers.

5   Cf John W Young, *Britain and European Unity 1945–92,* London 1992; Sean Greenwood, *Britain and European Co-operation since 1945,* Oxford 1992; Sean Greenwood (ed.), *Britain and European Integration Since the Second World War,* Manchester 1996; Stephen George, *An Awkward Partner: Britain in the European Community,* Oxford, Oxford University Press 1994; Hugo Young, *This Blessed Plot: Britain and Europe from Churchill to Blair,* London, Macmillan 1998; Nigel Ashford, 'The Political Parties', in Stephen George (ed.), *Britain and the European Community,* Oxford, Oxford University Press, 1991.

6   Edmund Dell, *The Schuman Plan and the British Abdication of Leadership in Europe,* Ox ford, Oxford University Press 1995.

7   Cf Brian Brivati, *Hugh Gaitskell,* London, Richard Cohen Books 1996; Roy Jenkins, *Life at the Centre,* London, Macmillan 1991. To the dismay of pro-European Gaitskellites such as Roy Jenkins, Gaitskell's speech was well received at the conference, his rejection of entry welcomed by a Labour left usually more critical than supportive of a Gaitskell speech. Indeed, Gaitskell's wife, Dora, is said to have remarked of the standing ovation that 'all the wrong people are clapping'.

8   Labour Party, *Time For Decision,* 1966 Election manifesto, London, The Labour Party 1966.

9   Several biographies and memoirs deal with this period very usefully; Cf. Roy Jenkins, *A Life at the Centre, op. cit.*; Ben Pimlott, *Harold Wilson,* London, Harper Collins 1992; Tony Benn, *Office Without Power: Diaries, 1968–72,* London, Hutchinson 1988.

10 Stephen George, *An Awkward Partner: Britain in the European Community,* Oxford, Oxford University Press 1994, p.93.

11 David Butler and Uwe Kitzinger, *The 1975 Referendum,* London, Macmillan 2nd Edition 1996; Tony Benn, *Against the Tide: Diaries, 1973–76,* London, Hutchinson 1989.

12 Hugo Young, *This Blessed Plot, op. cit.* p 475.

13 Stephen George, *An Awkward Partner: Britain in the European Community, op. cit.*

14 Hugo Young, *This Blessed Plot, op. cit.,* p.474.

15 Philip Stephens, *Politics and the Pound: The Tories, The Economy and Europe,* London, Macmillan 1996. Callaghan had opposed entry in 1971. Indeed, in May 1971, dismissing the idea French become Europe's official language, he had bridled at the seeming threat posed to 'the language of Chaucer, Shakespeare and Milton', making

clear Britain's opposition in language the French would apparently understand: 'Non. Non merci beaucoup'. Cf. Kenneth O Morgan, *Callaghan: A Life*, Oxford, Oxford University Press 1997.

16 Labour Party, *The Labour Way Is The Better Way*, 1979 Election manifesto, London, The Labour Party 1979.

17 Cf. Noel Thompson, *Political Economy and the Labour Party*, London, UCL Press, 1996, ch.16,; Mark Wickham Jones, *Economic Strategy and the Labour Party*, London, Macmillan 1996; Eric Shaw, *Crisis and Transformation: The Labour Party Since 1979*, London, Routledge 1994.

18 The Labour Party, *The New Hope for Britain*, Labour's 1983 manifesto, London, The Labour Party 1983.

19 Today, in retirement, Healey opposes Britain joining the single currency.

20 On Europe and the SDP defection cf. Ivor Crewe and Anthony King, *SDP: The Birth, Life, and Death of the Social Democratic Party*, Oxford, Oxford University Press 1995. Of course, the rationale behind the SDP defection ranged wider than Europe; there is no direct association between pro-Europeanism and SDP defection. Roy Hattersley and John Smith are only two examples of 1971 pro-Europeans who never considered leaving Labour's ranks and saw their party careers prosper.

21 Neil Kinnock, 'A New Deal for Europe', in James Curran (ed.), *The Future of the Left*, Cambridge, Polity Press 1984.

22 Labour Party, *Britain Will Win With Labour*, 1987 Election manifesto, London, The Labour Party 1987.

23 Hugo Young, *This Blessed Plot*, op. cit. p.477.

24 After 1984, Labour prioritised European elections as contests in which it could aggressively compete against the incumbent Conservatives and assert its electoral credibility. Indeed, the party performed stronger at the European polls than in general elections, winning 45 out of the 81 European Parliamentary seats in 1989 and 62 seats out of 87 in 1994. After 1989, new Labour MEPs were invariably pro-European, and Labour naturally joined the Party of European Socialists in 1992 and since 1994 has supported moves toward promoting common policies for Europe by adopting a common manifesto for elections to the European Parliament.

25 Hugo Young, *This Blessed Plot*, op. cit. p.478.

26 Stephen George, *An Awkward Partner*, op. cit.; According to Seyd and Whiteley in 1989 89 per cent of party members supported continuing membership of the EC, with only 10 per cent opposed to further integration: Patrick Seyd and Paul Whiteley, *Labour's Grass Roots*, Oxford, Oxford University Press 1992.

27 Cf. Robert Taylor, *The Future of the Trade Unions*, London 1994; David Marsh, *The New Politics of British Trade Unionism: Union Power and the Thatcher Legacy*, London, Macmillan 1992; Also, Ben Rosamond, 'The Integration of Labour? British Trade Union Attitudes to European Integration', in David Baker and David

Seawright (eds), *Britain For and Against Europe*, Oxford, Oxford University Press 1998.

28 Hugo Young, *This Blessed Plot, op. cit.* pp.473-474.

29 Labour Party, *It's Time To get Britain Working Again,* 1992 Election manifesto, London, The Labour Party 1992.

30 Andrew Gamble, 'The Labour Party and Economic Management', in Martin J Smith and Joanna Spear (eds.), *The Changing Labour Party*, London, Routledge 1992; Noel Thompson, *Economic Strategy and the Labour Party*, London, UCL Press 1996; Philip Stephens, *Politics and the Pound, op. cit.*; Eric Shaw, *Crisis and Transformation, op. cit.* pp.96–99.

31 Hugo Young, *This Blessed Plot, op. cit.*

32 David Baker, Andrew Gamble and Steve Ludlam, 'The Parliamentary Siege of Maastricht 1993: Conservative Divisions and British Ratification', *Parliamentary Affairs* Vol 47 1994 pp.37–60.

33 The Labour Party, *New Labour New Britain: Because Britain Deserves Better,* 1997 Labour manifesto, London, The Labour Party 1997.

34 Cf. David Baker and David Seawright, 'A Rosy Map of Europe? Labour Parliamentarians and European Integration', in Baker and Seawright (eds.), *Britain For and Against Europe, op. cit.*; Philip Norton and Philip Cowley, *Blair's Bastards*, Hull, Centre for Legislative Studies 1998.

35 The Labour Party, *New Labour New Britain: Because Britain Deserves Better,* 1997 Labour manifesto, London, The Labour Party 1997.

36 Tony Blair, House of Commons Statement on European Monetary Union, February 23 1999, http://www.number-10.gov.uk/textsite/info/releases/speeches

37 Tony Blair, 'The New Challenge for Europe', speech in Achen, Germany, 14 May 1999, Http://www.number-10.gov.uk/textsite/info/releases/speeches

38 Tony Blair, transcript of remarks at press conference on Europe, 23 May 1997 http://www.number-10.gov.uk/textsite/info/releases/speeches

39 Tony Blair, House of Commons statement on European Monetary Union, February 23 1999, *op. cit.* Andrew Marr's comment is worth noting: '[U]nlike other eminent Europeans, Blair's aim is not simply to make Britain more continental; it is also to make the continent more British ... the Europe he wants is different from today's relatively rigid, social democratic union, bound together by integrationist treaties and run by the Commission', (*The Observer*, 16 May 1999). The idea that the Prime Minister favours 'a reformed, more democratic central structure, including a stronger European Council' (*ibid.*), may be another illustration that the pro-European Blair remains a British inter-governmentalist, one who supports British rapprochement with Europe for age old neo-realist reasons.

40 Tony Blair, 'The New Challenge for Europe', Achen speech, *op. cit.*

Questions of Gender: Labour and Women

Christine Collette

Labour historians have been accused of ignoring women and evading questions of gender. There is an element of truth in this; traditionalists who recount the story of Labour's élite miss women out by their choice of subject matter, as do others who concentrate on the analysis of a male social world.[1] The records of paid up, trades union or Labour Party members yield a preponderance of men, because men were more likely than women to have longer – term, full time employment and thus the opportunity and finance necessary for membership. As Brian Harrison justly wrote, there was a demographic reason for the greater numbers of Labour Party men, who outnumbered women in the coal and steel towns where Labour was strong. The problem of the missing women is magnified because leaders were drawn from the paid-up membership; when one recounts the history of leaders, one deals most often with men.[2]

Nonetheless, I argue that, at the end of Labour's first century sufficient literature exists to refute the 'missing women' argument. Reflecting their role in its development and activity, women have been included in Labour's history. Finding them has been an historical adventure, involving the use of oral history and less orthodox events such as 'history days'. For instance, Derby South constituency women discovered their history by displaying and discussing extant Women's Council minutes along with leaflets, banners, photographs and other memorabilia. Such events have their own history; in 1934 the pageant of labour at London's Crystal Palace included scenes from the Matchgirls' strike and the Rochdale Pioneers.[3] Labour Heritage was founded in 1981 to study and preserve Labour history and its women's research committee was set up in answer to the over-confident assertion of an Iron and Steel Trades' delegate that trades union men founded the Labour Party. Including women by such diverse means has lead to a broader and richer history that has taken account of membership groups and ad hoc activity.[4] This broader approach has meant writing outside the confines of the parliamentary party, or rather ignoring the artificial boundaries that traditionalist historians had imposed on the Labour Party structure.

This wider approach is doubly justified: first, to use an accurate, popular metaphor the Labour Party has been a 'broad church', including affiliated socialist societies and trades unions. Sarah Perrigo, referring to Labour's 'complex system of representation and delegation' has described its federal structure; labyrinth might be a better description. For Labour Party women federalism was institutionalised from 1916 to 1952 in the Standing Joint Committee of Industrial/Working Women's Organisations (SJC) which had Labour Party, trades union and Co-operative women under its wing.[5]. Second, Labour Party women have explicitly interrelated their political, industrial and consumer-oriented activity. For instance, life-long Labour activist Florence Davy wrote:

When I was eighteen I joined the Labour Party ... we were talking about setting up a League of Youth and I went along and came out secretary ... that was in 1931 and I have belonged to the Labour Party ever since. I joined the London Co-operative Society in 1937: in the League of Youth they argued for this, it was all part of 'three-winged approach'. I joined my trade union when I was sixteen ... the Union of Post Office Workers. Within two years I was its representative ... I was also an organiser for UPW. The unity of the Labour Party, the trade union movement and the Cooperative Movement is essential for success.[6]

Also a long-standing Labour Party member, Joan Davis was a minute secretary of Kensington Co-operative Party in the 1950s, and belonged to the Co-operative Trading District Committee; she also joined the League of Youth and was on the general committee of North Kensington Labour Party.

The current need is less to restore to Labour history the experience of such women (although complacency here is a danger) than to address the question of gender their history reveals. In addition, Labour's identity as a white, Anglo-Saxon party has been insufficiently appreciated. For instance, Ann Leff, a Jewish woman who joined the party after many years in the Communist Party, wrote of her entry into the latter.

For the first time in my life I felt confident with Gentiles, confident I would not hear anti-Semitic remarks. I never did, unlike the Labour party.[7]

More surprisingly, class issues *within* the Labour Party are undertheorised. These peculiarly British failings impact on the discussion of gender by obscuring difference between women. Abroad, links between gender and class activity, the impact of ethnicity and locality are more explored. Instances are the North American Labor history conferences, the Austrian-based Internationale Tagung der Historikerinnen und Historiker der

Arbeiterinnen- und Arbeiterbewegung and conferences and publications of the Netherlands International Institute of Social History.[8]

However, there is a fundamental problem specific to an engendered Labour history: that women sit uneasily in Labour's project to win full citizenship – social inclusion – for working people, through the achievement of political and industrial representation, because citizenship is itself a gendered concept. It derives from a Western male tradition of political philosophy that has justified male privilege by attributing to men the qualities necessary for political activity, while identifying women as subordinate homekeepers excluded from the political arena. Eleanor Barton, of the Women's Co-operative Guild, expressed this succinctly in 1934:

Years ago, when we were struggling in order that women should have the vote, we were told that women did not bear arms, and, consequently, should not have the vote, as she did nit fight for her country. We were told that woman's place was in the home; that she should remain there and not take an interest in things outside.[9]

Labour was liable to become infected with these patriarchal attitudes; its parliamentarianism was a lengthy project seeking gradual gains that did not include the feminist aim of challenging the established patriarchal hierarchy.[10] The application, to the non-revolutionary Labour Party, of once-fashionable assumptions that feminists and socialists were natural allies was misguided.[11] Women have been successful in many single-issue campaigns that have often been fought in the wider community, across and beyond party political lines, by loose alliances of women. In fact, the wonder is not that the Labour Party included women, but that women engaged in the Labour Party struggle.

There is a smaller but germane point: it has been recognised that women have been disabled from political practice by being deprived of political experience; Brian Harrison described 'women's sheer inexperience in public skills such as committee work, minute-taking and public speaking'. However, such a disability may be overcome, as Joan Davis shows;

At 22 I was the first women vice-chair of the North Kensington Labour Party and the youngest they ever had. At the first ... meeting I took the chair, some clever dick moved the 'previous question' ... [no one] knew what it meant but we quickly flicked through the Rule Book and fooled them with science.[12]

Formal meetings are but one way of communication. Both sexes have used entertainment, sport, music and art as political media, while women socialists have been renowned for their powers of rhetoric. The educative value of the formal meeting should not, however, be overlooked. Dorothy Rock joined the League of Youth before the war. In addition to its meetings:

We were attending classes and lectures, at the National Council of Labour Colleges, and the Workers' Education Association ... Co-operative Education classes, the Left Book Club Discussion Groups. Only later did I realise I had joined the best university in the country ... I had the chance to be the first emancipated woman of all my forebears throughout the generations.[13]

In order to appreciate the question of gender posed by including such women in Labour's history, and to understand why women participated in Labour's project, past incidences of women's political and industrial representation are investigated below. This examination will be completed by some comments on my own involvement as a Labour Party parliamentary candidate in 1987 and the questions of gender that were then being debated.

Political Representation

At the outset of Labour's century, the Women's Labour League posed a question which cut straight to the heart of the quest for citizenship: were women members wanted?[14] Founded in 1906 by Mary Fenton Macpherson on the model of the Railway Women's Guild she ran, the League eventually organised around 5,000 women. Its first leaders were married into Labour's élite: Margaret MacDonald to the party secretary (Ramsay MacDonald) and Lucy Middleton to the assistant secretary. The League nevertheless maintained a separate existence, served by devoted regional organisers such as Lisabeth Simm in the north-east. Application for Labour Party affiliation was won by persistence in the face of bureaucratic delays and the League dubbed the Labour Party 'the men's party'. The League networked with other co-operative, trades union and socialist women's organisations.

It has been argued that women engage with the Labour Party in order to achieve welfare measures[15] and, particularly in its early years, the League's activities and rhetoric justify such an assumption. Women were identified as practised carers and domestic managers whose input to social policy would be valuable. The League's single biggest campaign was for free school meals; however, the motivation was the recognition that mothers worked and the school meals campaign was fought not just in parliament, by Labour men, but in local councils by Labour women.[16] More attention was given to women's industrial representation from 1911, when both original leaders died at a tragically early age, and the League was taken over by professional women, Margaret Bondfield, followed by Marion Phillips.

The League was slow to back the campaign for women's enfranchisement; this is less surprising than may at first appear. Many members, such as Annot Robinson in Manchester, were already committed to suffrage organisations whose efforts there was no need for the League to duplicate. Moreover, the League successfully ensured the election of women to local bodies, where they have remained well represented. The League was not in the adult suffrage camp; Margaret Bondfield was, but received a sound reprimand for weakening a League suffrage resolution at the Labour Party conference. The League set up the Election Fighting Fund in 1911 to support parliamentary candidates who favoured women's enfranchisement and thereafter became more closely involved in suffrage campaigning.

When the 1918 constitution successfully recast the Labour Party in a new mould, which allowed for individual membership and made the constituency the heart of activities, the League disbanded. Its officers negotiated constituency women's sections, provision of a national women's officer and seats on the Labour Party executive. Women's separate representation was now in the hands of the SJC. This committee was founded in the First World War by League, trades union and Co-operative women. Eligible for SJC membership were representatives of industrial women's organisations which were national in character, consisted of women-only and had at least one thousand members. The SJC aimed to set policy guidelines for representatives of working women on national and local committees; at first it aimed at including and advising women on the wartime committee dealing with forces' pensions.[17]

At its outset, the SJC demanded; 'a franchise bill to give full suffrage rights to all men and women' in place of proposed electoral registration amendments aimed at restoring the forces' vote. Labour women proved fairly successful at lobbying Labour MPs, who, as Brian Harrison has written, had the best record of support for women's enfranchisement from 1906 to 1928, and in the event 1918 legislation enfranchised women from the age of 30. Emancipation demanded equal suffrage but was defeated by the introduction of the government's less advanced Sex Discrimination Act.[18] Until women were enfranchised from the age of 21, in 1928, the SJC continued to give qualified support to the suffrage campaign, occasionally attending National Union of Societies for Equal Citizenship (NUSEC) demonstrations; Marion Phillips lobbied Labour's national executive for a franchise bill.

After 1928 the SJC ceased activity on equal suffrage. At the same time, gender solidarity was demonstrated when women MPs who were not SJC members were invited to attend meetings as observers.[19]

Links between the SJC and the Labour Party were close: the Labour Party affiliated to the SJC in 1919, the SJC held its meetings at Labour Party headquarters and from 1920 the SJC secretary was the Labour Party Chief Women's Officer (Marion Phillips, followed by Mary Sutherland in 1932). The SJC advised the Labour Party on matters of interest to women and arranged the National Conference of Labour Women.[20] Identifying consciously and openly with 'industrial' women, the SJC acknowledged a class prejudice which middle-class feminists deplored and thus emphasised, for its newly enfranchised affiliates the importance of supporting the Labour Party. While it was important to get women into Parliament 'it is still more important that these women should have the aims of the working class movement at heart and properly represent the women they will serve'.[21] Nevertheless the SJC retained its independence, corresponding directly with external organisations such as government departments, the League of Nations and the Labour and Socialist International. The latter, the SJC declared: 'speaks for them as full citizens and members of a political body which has ... fully and without reserve accepted the economic, social and political partnership of men and women'.[22] By 1929 the SJC claimed to represent 'over a million women in the Labour Party, Trades Union and Cooperative Movements'.

Relations with affiliates were participative; SJC investigations into subjects such as maternity hospitals and housing design were models of feminist research. Exhaustive questionnaires contained plenty of space for comment; replies were debated at branch meetings and the SJC produced discussion memoranda:

We desire ... to emphasise the importance of 'collective' views expressed by groups of women after detailed discussion at meetings. It is through discussion ... that new ideas emerge and progress is made.[23]

The results were used to inform government. Pat Thane is of the opinion that, despite emphasising women's domestic role, SJC campaigns were perceived 'as a means to assault rather than to reinforce male power'.[24] The SJC's evidence on housing, requested by the Ministry of Health in 1942, was a case in point and demonstrated that Labour women did not assume the universality of the family unit:

we believe that the majority of women prefer a home ... for family life... some women with families (who) prefer a flat; and there many people who find a modern flat the most convenient type of home, e.g. childless couples, people who do not want a garden, single people.

Not only was this advice passed to the relevant government committee, but the SJC succeeded in placing its nominees thereon.[25]

Meanwhile, although they could not decide policy and had no direct representation on Labour's ruling executive, Women's Councils proved popular. Women provided half the party membership by 1939.[26] Labour women elected to parliament included Marion Phillips and Margaret Bondfield. When the latter became chair of the TUC in 1923 the SJC recorded:

This is not only a great personal honour and mark of recognition ... but an honour which raises the whole position of women in the Labour Movement and gives recognition to women's place in the Labour world.[27]

More controversial was Margaret Bondfield's record as Britain's first woman Cabinet Minister in the cost-cutting 1931 Labour government.[28] MP Ellen Wilkinson was less of a loyalist. Prominent in the struggle against fascism, Wilkinson was an exemplar of some Labour women's willingness to work outside the parameters laid down by leaders, willing to work with those in the Communist Party and in United Front (socialist and communist) groups. In a 1936 reorganisation that was, in part, intended to silence criticism of leadership opposition to the United Front, constituency parties were allowed to field their own candidates for the national executive, but male suffrage in the ballot for women national executive members remained unchallenged.[29]

On the campaign by Labour Party women for birth control, the SJC was largely silent. Pamela Graves gives a detailed history of the futile resolutions in favour taken by Labour women's conferences. Pat Thane writes that male support has been underestimated and that reluctance to act had much to do with fear of losing the Roman Catholic vote.[30] Facing the Labour Party up to dealing with women's sexuality was a challenge to its patriarchal attitudes. As the housing issue showed, Labour does have another, and still hidden history; that of women's partnership within the Labour world; we may too easily assume their heterosexuality.[31]

The Second World War made constituency organisation difficult. Irene Wagner, later Labour Party librarian, was of the opinion that the coalition government was 'a great hindrance' to the Labour Party politically:

So like many other socialists we were attracted to the Commonwealth Party ... here we could hear and say, and do, what the Labour party was officially not allowed to be concerned with.[32]

The SJC, however, operated extremely effectively during the war, for instance advising the ministry of health on evacuation. The 1941 name change to Standing Joint Committee of Working Women's Organisations appears to have carried no organisational significance. By the close of the war, the SJC claimed 2.5 million members. The war raised the profile of women MPs and Barbara Castle joined the short list of luminaries; however, the SJC noted in 1943 women's 'widespread desire ... to have more women candidates and more women members of Parliament'. Refuting a party myth that women attracted less electoral support, the SJC claimed that war was doing away with old prejudices and suggested a list of potential industrial and professional women candidates, the former to be included on both general (B) and trades union (A) listings. Calling for training and propaganda on the necessity for women candidates, the SJC recommended the use of women speakers in a national campaigns, plus the creation of a special fund earmarked for women candidates' expenses.[33]

However, the SJC became a victim of its own success; representation on the women's voluntary service national committee had led to complaints, from a Conservative committee member, of Labour Party privilege.[34] Mary Sutherland was forced on the defensive, denying that the SJC promoted party appointments, reiterating its main aim of representing working women and claiming that it advised the Labour Party solely at the latter's request. While broadly true, this belied the close links between the SJC and the Labour Party. Further, Mary Sutherland stated that the SJC had no authority to deal with women's organisation within the party. This fudge proved prophetic; the SJC constitution was reviewed in 1951 and a second name change in February 1953, to the National Council of Working Women's Organisations (NCW), was significant, spelling the end of 50 years of women's independent organisation in the Labour Party.[35]

Women within the party appeared to have grown in strength, the number of women's sections increasing to over 2,000 in 1951. The number of women's regional advisory councils also grew. The importance of women's election work was generally acknowledged.[36] The National Women's Advisory Council was formed in December 1951 and in addition to its eponymous role took over education and propaganda work for women and the chairing of the women's conference. It was also to give advice where necessary to the NCW. Party secretary Morgan Phillips was of the opinion that the Labour Party had been strengthened, but with hindsight, the benefits were a lot less obvious; independence had been exchanged for subordination.

Nevertheless, women's sections continued to attract members and a network of women's committees and federations at constituency level and regional women's conferences developed. To accommodate this growth of women's organisations and the expense incurred, the National Women's Advisory Council changed the Women's Conference to a biennial event and arranged that constituency women's sections elected the delegates thereto. This was promoted, with some justice, as a more democratic arrangement. In fact, it marked a decline, whereby Women's Conference became of little importance. Women lost both the direct representation that the SJC had afforded and a separate but equal voice in party counsels. Unsurprisingly, the 1950s and 1960s are generally recognised as the nadir of women's equal rights within the Labour Party. Nevertheless, women remained 42 per cent of Labour Party membership from 1951 to 1970 and women's sections and councils continued to attract members.[37]

Industrial Representation

The history of women's industrial representation followed the same pattern as their political history. Single sex groups, the Women's Trade Union League and the National Federation of Working Women (NFWW), merged with mixed groups, leaving the SJC as the focus of separatist organisation. In addition, a constant but neglected phenomenon, from the Railway Women's Guild to the recent Women Against Pit Closures, has been the formation of women's support groups, active at one remove from an industry. Again, there were problems specific to representation of women; as the existence of support groups indicated, it was not always easy to distinguish paid labour from domestic chores; moreover, women's work was often low-paid, part-time and casual. Emphatically believing in women's right to work, Labour women recognised these problems. Fabian women wrote: 'the "meantime" nature of many women's work makes it difficult ... for them to help themselves by organisation to the extent men do'.[38]

A good example was the difficulty of organising homeworkers who preponderated in the clothing, food and metal trades. Julia Varley, a formidable leading women's trades unionist, prepared a report for the International Federation of Women Workers on this subject in the 1920s. Isolated at home, distributing tasks amongst neighbours, these women worked at all levels, including the highly skilled. Varley wrote that by using homeworkers, for instance in the celluloid trade, employers were able to evade factory legislation and depress wages and conditions in an industry. It was difficult to convince homeworkers that 'their interests are the same as those of numerous workers whom they do not know and have never seen'.[39] Also blurring the distinction between domestic and wage labour, domestic service was poorly paid and resistant of organisation. The SJC after its usual detailed investigation, produced a Domestic Workers' Charter which, when the government promised a Domestic Service Commission in 1931, formed the basis for a deputation to the Ministry of Labour. As Marion Phillips pointed out, domestic workers formed a quarter to a third of female voters in constituencies such as Kensington and Westminster. It proved difficult, however, to interest the TUC, whose women's advisory committee despaired of effective union activity in this field.[40]

Such concerns make it easy to see why Labour women favoured protective legislation. Julia Varley was one of the chief campaigners for health and safety and statutory limitation of working hours. Feminist organisations such as NUSEC and the Open Door Council were strongly opposed, arguing that protection restricted women's working opportunities and pay. Joanna Alberti has rightly written that the protection debate illustrates the international affiliations of women between the wars.[41] Indeed, one of the reasons why few countries adopted the Hague and Montevideo conventions of the League of Nations, which would have given women equal citizenship right, was concern about gendered protective legislation.[42] In Britain, feminist organisations lobbied the Labour Home Secretary, Clynes, about repealing factory legislation. Clynes asked Labour women for a 'counter-blast'; the SJC already had this in hand and asked affiliates to send a representative to its deputation. The TUC refused an invitation to participate, but Clynes avowed: 'as far as he was concerned, he would not be a party to removing the protection which women enjoyed at present'.[43]

Due to widespread operation of a marriage bar, the female industrial labour force was characterised by its youth. The SJC and Labour women's conference repeatedly protested the divisive bar. Eleanor Barton attacked the exploitation of married women who were 'charitably' offered menial work while being expected to provide unpaid and undervalued labour in the home: 'why then expect every woman to be good at housework'. Further, Barton wrote that the bar took no account of widows and deserted wives and asked why women should 'stay at the level of his achievements?' An exhaustive inquiry into London County Council school cleaners was successful in winning their freedom from the bar, although SJC deputations failed to extend this exemption.[44]

Older and married women came into the workforce in the Second World War.[45] The post-war Labour governments sought to keep this reliable and experienced part-time workforce and removed the marriage bar for its own employees. In addition, the government asked for advice on reinforcing legislation on the closing hours of shops. The SJC 'three-winged approach' was particularly apt in this case, enquiries being made of consumer – Co-operative, shop worker – trades union, and Labour Party women, plus the Woman Public Health Officer's Association. Evidence was given to the relevant parliamentary committee, the SJC being able to refute authoritatively the need for late hours and to insist on Sunday closing.[46] The war also gave a boost to the equal pay campaign which the SJC had followed throughout the inter-war period; the SJC gave evidence to the 1944 Royal Commission on Equal Pay. Both the SJC and Labour Women's Conference persistently besought the postwar Labour governments to act but were reluctantly brought to accept pleas of economic difficulties. However, a major step towards equal pay was taken in 1951 when the TUC came out solidly for equal pay, despite the economy.[47]

The campaign for equal pay continued under Conservative governments and was finally won at the end of the 1970 Wilson government despite having been banned from discussion for the previous three years at the Labour Party conference (under the rule which forbade reintroduction of defeated policy resolutions).[48] The introduction of Employment Protection (1976) and Sex Discrimination (1975) legislation by the 1974–76 Labour government completed statutory protection for women. In my opinion, delay notwithstanding, the achievements of the Wilson governments have been very much underestimated in this respect. At first, when tribunals operated with minimal intervention by the legal profession and before case law accumulated at the Employment Appeals Tribunal, these acts were successful in challenging decades of discrimination. In addition, the Health and Safety at Work Act then introduced resolved the longstanding protection debate by making safety everyone's responsibility, that of employer, employee and the wider community. The provisions under these acts for time off for trades union and safety work opened up trades union organising positions for women.[49]

1987: Joining the Parliamentary Road

When I sought selection as a parliamentary candidate, I had just begun postgraduate research on international socialism and was teaching Modern History. Typically active at one remove in support of the Agricultural and Allied Workers trade group, I ran women's education weekends and participated in a loose grouping of women around the *Landworker* newspaper. I chaired my local Labour Party branch and was delegated to Labour Party conferences and Women's Conferences. I had helped found Labour Heritage and its Women's Research Committee, was engaged in women's oral history and writing about the Women's Labour League. As a working class, mature woman student at Oxford University I was conscious of class and gender tensions, but I was also aware of the disadvantages a woman faced in the male social world of trades unions, although this was being combated by women at both membership and officer level. The loss of male membership due to unemployment had not yet caused trades unions to define membership more creatively, but there was a willingness to ensure women's selection to steward and officer jobs. Women preponderated in rural constituency parties where they faced particular challenges, not of winning election to leading positions, but of getting the rural voice heard.[50]

Sarah Perrigo has written that, from 1983–87, the political priorities of women and the leadership were most at odds. The feminist agenda, in her opinion, had developed from 1979–83, when the Labour Party moved to the left and its weakened leadership was unable to enforce rules circumscribing links with other organisations: women (myself included) perceived a space to pursue feminist goals and were attracted into membership. Achievements included the adoption of equal opportunities' programmes by local councils, the prime example being the Greater London Council.[51] Women's sections and conferences were lively and the Women's Action Group (WAG) was formed. WAG campaigned for the election of the five women national executive council members by Women's Conference, that the latter should have the right to submit five resolutions to party conference, and for women-only parliamentary candidate shortlists.

While some feminists found WAG goals too limiting, in the more hostile climate from 1983 WAG had to contend not only with

Labour Party men, but with Labour Party women traditionalists who rejected positive discrimination. As Perrigo writes:

Women within the party were not a unified group ... older working class women ... often perceived the language and style of feminism to be patronising and offensive. Those who identified with the feminist agenda tended to be young, articulate and well-educated. They were often insensitive to the experience of other women in the party and lacked the political skills to appeal to wider constituency of women.[52]

Agricultural Workers' Group women, whom I persuaded into a WAG meeting, were impressed more by the clothes and jewellery than the political argument. Other women were active in Militant and prioritised class activity. The head-on conflicts between WAG and Militant women, and their joint impact on traditionalists, made Women's Conference an anarchic, exciting event. The notorious Isle of Bute conference in 1986 was the nadir, when punk hair clashed with power-dressing and the party secretary, Larry (now Lord) Whitty, was denied a hearing. However, from 1983, Labour was enriched by debate on domestic violence and sexual abuse, including harassment within trades unions. Ann Tobin writes, with some justice, that:

the new politics were forced on an often unwilling and certainly unenthusiastic Labour Party by socialists who were also feminists, by socialists who were also black, and by socialists who were also gay.[53]

A commitment to engage in the struggle for gay and lesbian rights was made by the Labour Party, although the campaign to create Black groups was avoided.

In this period, it seemed to me that I could focus my experience by offering myself as a parliamentary candidate. Despite nominations by my Transport and General Workers' union branch, I had, true to type, blotted my copybook by engaging with communist women in the miners' support group, but was selected by Whitney. I wanted to promote teamwork and to make space to debate socialist feminist issues, and had considerable support from my agent, Sue Stewart and the women's officer, Maggie Norris. Sue Stewart cogently expressed our feminist ideals of rejecting a solitary/heroine approach as 'not being men in suits'. I thus did not learn, at the 1986 Nottingham training session, how to apply my make-up, but I did learn how to change the fuses in my ancient and unreliable car. However, I found selection a silencing process; I lost my name and became 'The Candidate'; this typification limited my access to private debate while in public I had, necessarily to espouse Labour's policy uncritically. The final campaign fortnight, with headquarters donated by the Co-operative Party, occasional help from members of the Jay family, visits from descendants of Stafford Cripps and William Morris, letters from every conceivable pressure group, special branch airplanes guarding the sitting MP Douglas Hurd, was tremendously enjoyable but was marked by two instances which showed me how difficult it was to electioneer as a feminist. The first was when Sue and I, celebrating our birthdays at an eve-of-poll meeting, were handed bunches of red roses, like prima donnas taking a bow. The second was polling day, campaigning with a male colleague; exit pollsters assumed I was his wife and, indeed, the day felt like a marriage. We gained a three per cent swing against Douglas Hurd, no mean feat in 1987, but in terms of my personal goals the campaign was a failure.

It is generally accepted that the 1987 defeat convinced Labour, finally, to take the women's vote seriously and to pay attention to party women's views. Perrigo writes that a third phase then began, when goals of party modernisation and women's demands became 'increasingly congruent'.[54] Clare Short writes that since 1987, 'a quiet revolution has been taking place in the Labour Party'. The quota system recommended by Socialist International women was adopted and the shadow cabinet increased to accommodate women's places. The 1989 conference called for 40 per cent of women at all levels of the party. Short revealingly writes that: 'the senior committees around the leader's office were not similarly (affected) because appointments were more informal and party rules did not apply'.[55] Short was appointed by John Smith, whom she praises as very supportive, to chair the new Women's Committee of the national executive and was successful in pioneering the all-women shortlist, to apply in half the vacant parliamentary candidacies. Illustrating Perrigo's point, all-women shortlists were linked with reforms that ended union block voting for national executive seats. A Minister for Women with Cabinet status was proposed by John Smith; meanwhile, 'Emily's List' was formed by women to train prospective candidates in order to achieve 300 women MPs. An instance of local action was that of Sheffield and Nottingham women:

150 years of struggle and still underrepresented
WE WANT 50% OF WOMEN BY 2001...50% of all levels in the Labour Party ...filled by women. What the Suffragettes began, we must continue and succeed.[56]

Conclusion

Prophetically, Clare Short wrote that: 'Tony Blair was less firmly convinced of the (quota) policy than John Smith'.[57] As Labour completes its first century, women have yet to gain a half share of party positions of power and the Ministry of Women has dwindled into a web page. However, if Labour women's history has not been one of untrammeled progress, neither has it been one of stagnation. There were considerable successes. The Women's Labour League and the SJC were outstanding examples of single sex campaigning, of ensuring women's election and co-option onto policy-making local councils and government committees. The SJC pioneered what are now recognised as feminist methods of research. As is expected of feminist good practice today, both groups recognised differences between women, that they might be married but not necessarily domestic, single professional, industrial or service workers, schoolcleaners or sweated workers. While the League was strongly of the opinion that women had something special to offer in the field of social policy, neither the League nor the SJC assumed that this was all women's metier and both groups were interested in a range of women's activity. Never wholly, and rarely passionately committed to the women's suffrage campaign, Labour women made great practical strides towards women's enfranchisement.

There were less active periods, particularly the 30 years from the 1950s, when Labour women renounced separatism, to the efflorescence of the 'second wave' modern feminist movement. Nevertheless, the motives that drove women into a subordinate place within the Labour Party were understandable, springing from the class consciousness which caused Marion Phillips to define the Labour Party women's membership was, and remained buoyant. When, rarely, the Labour Party formed a government, Labour women did score some of their goals; the controversial one of protective legislation, married women's right to work, legislation towards equal pay. Success was inevitably limited because Labour has not been a revolutionary or even, even convincingly, a socialist party. It did/does not challenge patriarchy; the feminist revolution has not been part of its agenda. Given these limitations, the SJC experience was probably as good as women could get. The reinforcing of gender stereotypes which, contrary to popular opinion, is a natural corollary of waging war around national interests, may have contributed a great deal to women's low profile from the 1950s. The Labour Party federal structure, in addition, makes it difficult for groupings to find a voice; women did not necessarily organise within women's sections. They did join with Communist, United Front, Commonwealth Party, Co-operative, union support and other groups. The three-winged approach of which Florence Davy wrote seem to have a particular appeal for women.

Women's groups as diverse as the modern Women Against Pit Closures, or the 40-year-old SJC, have not received full acknowledgement from Labour historians, so that the lessons of their experience have yet to be understood. This is a function of traditional Labour historiography and its emphasis on male leaders and the male social – 'workerist' – world. There is no need for contemporary Labour and/or feminist historians to fall into the same trap. To borrow from feminist epistemology, the first stage of including women has been reached and this work should be acknowledged and built upon .[58] The second stage will be to take a feminist standpoint in our knowledge of Labour women; to write from their viewpoint, celebrate their gains, critique their progress. As Perrigo writes, many Labour women were confident of their value and fulfilled by their place in the Labour movement, resentful of intellectuals who wrote off their experience.[59] Women such as Florence Davy, Ann Leff, Irene Wagner, Dorothy Rock wrote their own Labour history with pride; it is no coincidence that their grounding in Labour politics took place before the 1950s nadir of women's activity. However, Joan Davis began her apprenticeship in the later time and overcame its difficulties. The third feminist stage is a postmodern approach; this may help us to address women's experience by weaning us from over-reliance on the metanarratives which cause many of our conceptual difficulties. Thus we will appreciate the differences between women that the SJC had little difficulty in acknowledging, and we will listen to their voices. We will understand that a lengthy project, such as Labour's, to infiltrate the élite and to extend privilege to the many will be a creature of imperfect and individual conception and we will start to address the special difficulties caused by a gendered idea of citizenship. Finally, we need to analyse how gender difference within the Labour world is eroticised, how sexuality impacts on Labour membership.[60] Again, abroad, for instance in American politics, there seems to be little difficulty in including sexual politics in party programmes. We may ask what a lesbian Labour history would look like and we may recognise that present Labour history is heterosexist. Labour ends its first century with many questions of gender still to be faced; but it is a hundred years of female and male activity which it celebrates.

Notes

1 June Hammond and Karen Hunt, Society for the Study of Labour History Conference, Nottingham University, 14 March 1998. See also: 'Is There a Future for Labour History?', *Labour History Review* 62 (3) 1997 pp. 253–57.

2 For operation of the labour market see Sylvia Walby, *Gender Transformations*, London: Routledge 1997, chapters 1–6. Brian Harrison, *Past and Present* 124 1989, p.12.

3 For instance, Christine Collette, *For Labour and for Women: the Women's Labour League 1906–1918*, Manchester: Manchester University Press 1989; Pamela Graves, *Labour Women,* Cambridge: Cambridge University Press 1994. 'Doing History', Labour Heritage Women's Research Committee (WORC) *Bulletin* 3 1990 pp. 5-6.

4 Cf. the chapter on gender in Martin Francis, *Ideas and Policies under Labour, 1945-51*, Manchester: Manchester University Press 1997.

5 Sarah Perrigo, 'Women, Change and the Labour Party', *Parliamentary Affairs*, 1996 p. 119; *Standing Joint Committee of Industrial Women's Organisations papers (SJC)*, Labour Party Archives, National Museum of Labour History, Manchester.

6 Florence Davy, 'From Zeppelins to Jets', *WORC Bulletin*, 2 1987 p. 10, p. 12. Joan Davis, 'A Life in the Labour Movement', *ibid* p. 12, p. 14. Many Labour Heritage women echoed these sentiments at conferences around Britain in the 1980s.

7 Ann Leff, 'My Brilliant Career in War Work', *WORC Bulletin* 5 1996 p. 16. Christine Collette and Stephen Bird (eds.), *Jews, Labour and the Left*, Ashgate, forthcoming; Kenneth Lunn, *Race and Labour in Britain*, Ashgate, forthcoming.

8 North American Labor history conference, Wayne State University; Internationale Tagung der Historikerinnen und Historiker der Arbeiterinnen-und Arbeiterbewegung, *Geschlect-Klasse-Ethnizitat*, Vienna 1993; *International Review of Social History 1999 supplement:* 'Complicating the Categories: Gender, Class, Race and Ethnicity in Western and Non – Western Societies', forthcoming; see also Archief en Museum van de Socialistische Arbeidersbewging, Belgium, International Colloquium Gender and Class in the Twentieth Century, Ghent April 1999.

9 Mrs. Barton, *Married Women and Paid Positions: A plea for solidarity amongst Women*, Co-operative Women's Guild 1934. The feminist argument about citizenship is most accessibly put in Jan Jindy Pettman, *Worlding Women: a Feminist International Politics*, London: Routledge 1996, *passim*.

10 Julia Kristeva, 'Women's Time', *Signs* 7 (1) Autumn 1981 discusses the problems of women's activity in a lengthy political project.

11 Harrison, *Class and Gender*, wrote to 'prise apart' socialism and feminism. Cf. *Feminist Review*, special issue 23 Summer 1986, 'Socialist-Feminism Out of the Blue'; Kristeva, 'Women's Time', *passim*.

12 Harrison, *Class and Gender*, p. 152; Joan Davis, 'A Life in the Labour Movement', p. 14.

13 Dorothy Rock, 'The Best University', *WORC Bulletin* 3 1990.

14 Collette, *For Labour and for Women, passim.*

15 Harrison, *Class and Gender,* p.153.

16 Collette, *For Labour and for Women,* p. 120.

17 SJC minutes 20 June 1916.

18 SJC minutes 20 June 1916, Women's Emancipation, a Bill, 9 & 10 Geo. 5. Harrison, *Class and Gender.*

19 SJC, General Purposes committee minutes, 12 February1925, 10 December 1925. SJC minutes 14 March 1929, 11 July 1929.

20 SJC, Mary Sutherland to Mr. Gaitskell, 12 January 1949.

21 SJC, Marion Phillips' circular, 7 June 1918, reissued June 1920. For middle class feminists attitudes see Johanna Alberti, *Beyond Suffrage: Feminism in War and Peace 1914 – 1928*, London: MacMillan 1985 p.95

22 *SJC*, SJC to League of Nations, Miss Gabrielle Radiziwell, 12 September 1932, 27 October 1932, Mary Hamilton, draft memorandum 9 May 1932.

23 *SJC3*, memorandum to Committee on Design of Dwellings, June 1943.

24 Pat Thane, 'Women of the British Labour Party and Feminism', in Harold J. Smith (ed.) *British Feminism in the Twentieth Century*, Aldershot: Elgar 1990 p.127

25 *SJC*, Housing Sub Committee minutes 6 August 1942, 29 October 1942.

26 Thane, *Women of the British Labour Party*, p.125.

27 *SJC*, report January to October 1923.

28 See Brian Harrison, *Prudent Revolutionaries*, Oxford: Oxford University Press 1987 p. 125 for praise of Margaret Bondfield; she is remembered with more ambivalence by her Wallsend constituency: Annie Lockwood, *A Celebration of Pioneering Labour Women*, North Tyneside Fabians 1995.

29 Johanna Alberti, 'British Feminists and Anti-Fascism', in Sybil Oldfield, *This Working Day World*, London: Taylor and Francis 1994; Christine Collette, *The International Faith*, Aldershot, Ashgate 1998 ch. 6.

30 Graves, *Labour Women,* ch.3. Thane, p.137; Harrison, *Class and Gender*, pp. 134-4; Harrison, *Prudent Revolutionaries,* p.147. The SJC formed a sub committee, SJC report January to October, 1923.

31 Collette, 'For Labour and For Women', p.132; Thane, p. 131-2; cf Harrison, *Prudent Revolutionaries*, pp. 130–1.

32 Irene Wagner, 'Socialist London at War', *WORC Bulletin 2* 1987; Christine Collette, 'Daughter of the Newer Eve' in Jim Fyrth, *Labour's Promised Land*, London: Lawrence and Wishart 1995 p.46.

33 SJC, report on evacuation problems October 1939. *SJC*, note February 1943.

34 SJC, Mary Sutherland to Mr Gaitskell 12 January 1949.

35 *Ibid.*; review of SJC, general purposes committee minutes 12 July 1951; National Labour Women's Advisory (NLWA) committee minutes February 1953.

36 SJC. NLWA minutes 6 December 1951; Collette, *Daughter of the Newer Eve*, p. 47.

37 SJC note headed National Conference of Labour Women February 1953.

38 *SJC Manchester Guardian*, 22 February 1930.

39 *International Federation of Trades Union papers*, International Institute of Social History, Amsterdam, International Committee of Trades Union Women, IFTU 128.

40 SJC, *What's Wrong with Domestic Service*, and *First Steps Towards a Domestic Workers' Charter*, June 1930; House of Commons (anon) to Dr. Phillips, 6 June 1931; deputation document 2 July 1931; TUC to SJC, 23 March 1932; Harrison, *Class and Gender*, p.120 claims that domestic service had a 'rightwards' political influence.

41 Alberti, *Beyond Suffrage*, p.205. Bob Reinada, *The International Transport Federation 1914-1945*, Amsterdam: IISH 1997 p.128 ff.

42 *International Federation of Trades Union papers*, IFTU 134.

43 SJC, Gertrude Tuckwell to Marion Phillips, 7 November 1929; Marion Phillips to Gertrude Tuckwell, 8 November 1929; Minutes 14 November 1929; Walter Citrine to Dr. Phillips, 3 December 1929; report on deputation; *Times* 5 November 1929, *Manchester Guardian* 22 February 1930.

44 SJC, deputation to London County Council, 1934; Eleanor Barton, *Married Women*; TUC and Labour Party, *Employment of Married Women*, n.d.

45 Collette, 'Daughter of the Newer Eve', p.44.

46 SJC, Home Office to SJC 27 February 1946, SJC questionnaire April 1946, Home Office May 1946, transcript of evidence.

47 Collette, 'Daughter of the Newer Eve', p.50.

48 Amy Black and Stephen Brooke, 'The Labour Party, Women and the Problem of Gener, 1951–66', *Journal of British Studies*, 36 October 1997.

49 I was a lay official for the National and Local Government Officers' Association at this time and found the legislation beneficial.

50 Christine Collette, 'Socialist Feminism in Oxfordshire', *Feminist Review*, 26, Summer 1987.

51 Perrigo, 'Women, Change and the Labour Party', *passim*. Sheila Rowbotham et al, Beyond the Fragments, London, Merlin 1979, wrote to map new territories for gender, ethnic and class politics.

52 Perrigo, p.123.

53 Ann Tobin, 'Lesbianism and the Labour Party, the GLC Experience', Feminist Review, 34, Spring 1990, p.58.

54 Perrigo, p.117.

55 Clare Short, 'Women and the Labour Party', *Parliamentary Affairs*, 49 (1), 1996, p.17.

56 Notice written by Sylvia Parry and Sylvia Parsons, in author's possession.

57 Short, 'Women and the Labour Party', p.21.

58 Sandra Harding, 'Feminist Epistemiology', in Mary Maynard and Jane Purvis (eds.), Researching Women's Lives from a Feminist Perspective, London, Taylor and Francis 1994.

59 Perrigo, p.123.

60 Ann Tobin, 'Lesbianism and the Labour Party', *passim*.

Labour and Welfare Politics

Nick Ellison

For the greater part of its century-long history the Labour Party has experienced considerable difficulty in realising its ambitions for social reform. This judgement may seem less than apt in view of the fact that Labour has been closely associated in the public mind with the creation of the welfare state in Britain and, until recently at least, with attempting to support and further develop collectivist forms of social provision. The point, however, is not that the party entirely failed to make progress with social reform per se, but that it rarely managed to do so on its own terms, or in a manner which successfully integrated progress towards the key objective of a greater equality of outcome in the social sphere with its 'socialist' ambitions for economic and industrial reconstruction.

Explanations for this lack of political autonomy and the effective failure of the socialist alternative have tended to concentrate on the party's colourful history of internal difficulties – commentators focusing in particular on leadership betrayal, organisational diversity and ideological incoherence.[1] However, this internalist perspective needs to be supplemented by the recognition that exogenous factors have significantly affected Labour's fortunes. For example, Labour administrations have consistently encountered problems in honouring their welfare commitments because their attempts to create a 'virtuous circle' of rising growth and higher social spending have fallen in the face of economic circumstances which conspire against policies designed to achieve this goal. When growth failed to materialise social reform faltered, which, in Labour's case, frequently led to disillusionment and an increase in intra-party strife.

In many ways Labour has never bettered the remarkable accomplishments of the Attlee years, a period in which the party's economic and social priorities found a brief synchronicity. But the rapid developments in welfare provision seen during these six years should be regarded as the exception rather than the norm. As this chapter demonstrates, while Labour developed an increasingly collectivist conception of welfare in the first half of the century – a conception embodied in the system of centralised state welfare created in the late 1940s – the party subsequently struggled either to update its thinking about welfare or build on its practical achievements.[2] In more recent times, of course,

Labour's understanding of the role of social policy has shifted substantially. Far-reaching changes in economy, society and polity have altered the collectivist social and political assumptions that governed the party's approach to welfare in the postwar period, substituting a range of new ideas around the notion of a 'third way'.[3] These ideas will be explored in the concluding sections of this chapter.

Before the Welfare State

The Labour Party in the Era of Liberal Progressivism, 1895–1918

The Labour Party, as is well known, did not set out as a party of welfare, but as an attempt to promote, shape and control the mass 'new unionism' of the 1890s.[4] With employer opposition to organised labour mounting throughout a twelve-year period, which began with a rash of strikes in 1889–90 and culminated in the infamous Taff Vale judgement of 1901,[5] different sections of the labour movement – the trade unions and socialist bodies like the Independent Labour Party (ILP), the Fabian Society and the Social Democratic Federation came to acknowledge the case for independent labour representation in Parliament. To this end, the emergence of the Labour Representation Committee (LRC) began a process of progressive independence from the existing 'Lib-Lab' electoral arrangements,[6] the Committee's developing importance being reflected in its increased capacity to field Parliamentary candidates without Liberal support. Trade union resources made the difference. With unions affiliating to the LRC in increasing numbers in the wake of the Taff Vale judgement, the Committee's funds rose to the point where it was able to field many more Parliamentary candidates. While the Liberal Party, used to the highly favourable terms of Lib-Labism, initially tried to obstruct LRC candidates,[7] by 1903, with LRC membership standing at 850,000, it was becoming clear that the Liberals would risk the loss of broad working class support if they were seen to be actively competing against the LRC. Accommodation was reached in September 1903 in the form of the 'Progressive Alliance'. The Liberal Party agreed not to run against LRC in designated constituencies, leaving the LRC to fight a two-way contest with the Conservatives while, in its turn, the Committee encouraged working class support for Liberals elsewhere.[8]

For present purposes, the Progressive Alliance was important because it resulted in a larger number of 'Labour' MPs entering Parliament. The 1906 general election saw 30 MPs elected, representation further increasing through three successful bye-elections between 1906 and 1909, and by a further twelve on the affiliation of the Miners' Federation to the LRC in 1908. Forty-five Members was a substantial improvement on the pre-1906 situation. With the party's influence further enhanced after 1910 during a period when its (at that time) 40 MPs, together with the Irish Nationalists, held the balance of power in the House of Commons, Labour had undoubtedly emerged as a substantial political force.

How was this new level of labour representation deployed in relation to social reform? Two factors are important here. First, the LRC was a fragmented entity – effectively a loose coalition of socialist organisations and trade unions, broadly sympathetic to the labour movement. In the absence of any definable programme and lacking any mass support for 'socialism', the best that early Labour leaders like Keir Hardie could achieve was a pragmatic alliance between socialist bodies such as the ILP and the (often Liberal-inclined) unions to represent working class interests. What these interests actually were was by no means clear. Second – and not surprisingly – ideas about social reform were not consistently held across the movement as a whole, divisions emerging within the socialist elements of the party as well as between these elements and the trade unions.

These divisions did not prevent a high degree of unanimity over certain reforms which the labour movement had traditionally supported: the provision of school meals, for example, or broad support for the Liberal government's amendments to the Workmens' Compensation Act in 1906. Again, Labour's desire for a more systematic approach to the problem of unemployment was illustrated by the 1907 Right to Work campaign, which united socialist groups and trade unions in the demand for state regulation of the national economy and a programme of public works for the unemployed. But outside these perennial and basic interests there was rather less unity. In particular, the early Labour Party displayed an ambiguous attitude to state-based social provision. ILP socialists like Ramsay MacDonald regarded the modern state as the cornerstone of the socialist commonwealth-in-waiting[9] and assumed that the state would increase its social and economic role as capitalism gradually gave way to socialism. Stripped of the ILP's ethical socialist rhetoric, this positive view of the state was partly shared by trade union leaders like George Barnes and J. R. Clynes. They advocated state support for unskilled, non-unionised workers because, in their opinion, public provision was a necessary alternative to self-help in circumstances where individuals lacked the resources required to sustain voluntary effort. However, the unions were chary of the state where it appeared to threaten the independence of unionised, skilled workers. Union priorities in the early 1900s were frequently conceived in terms of 'self-help' and mutual aid, state welfare support being regarded as dependency-inducing and a threat to working class self-reliance. The main goal of the unions in the Edwardian period was to win, once and for all, the right to free collective bargaining over wage levels and working conditions with employers, a goal regarded as far from secure. Free collective bargaining and the industrial weaponry which accompanied it symbolised independence. As Thane has written, 'for most trade unionists the capacity to strike or to threaten to do so was a more important guarantor of "welfare" for themselves and their families than social measures from the state'.[10]

Despite this ambivalence about state welfare, Labour in Parliament largely supported the Liberals' progressive social programme implemented between 1906 and 1914. There was a good deal of sympathy amongst Labour MPs for 'New Liberal' policies designed to reduce poverty and enhance individual liberty through the use of selected measures of state provision.[11] Liberal politicians like Lloyd George and Winston Churchill used the government's majority to introduce old age pensions and unemployment and sickness insurance in selected industries in addition to introducing employment exchanges and setting minimum wages for the 'sweated' trades. Of course, these measures, and the progressive 1909 'People's Budget' associated with them, were not intended to produce equality of outcome so much as to provide a rather more equitable 'starting gate' for the very poorest sections of the community. This quintessentially liberal social policy 'placed Labour in its customary dilemma of supporting "as a beginning" measures which it felt did not go far enough and of whose motives its left wing had acute and often justified suspicions'.[12] Many Labour MPs, as well as trade unionists, would like to have seen a more radically redistributive budget than that which Lloyd George actually produced and Labour was also disappointed with the stringent eligibility criteria written into the 1908 Old Age Pensions Act.

There was little choice other than to support the Liberal reforms, however. Although the ability to gain seats as an independent party in general elections was clearly a significant achievement, Labour's few MPs could not hope to pursue an independent social policy. Even after 1910, when the Liberal majority was wiped out, the Parliamentary Labour Party did not desert the Asquith government because the New Liberalism continued to offer a coherent social programme over which Labour – now holding the balance of power with the Irish home rulers – could hope to exercise at least a modicum of influence. Neither party nor trade union leaders wished to risk the consequences of a Conservative election victory and the possibility of a reversal of the trend to social reform should Asquith's administration fall. MacDonald, the party's most prominent politician, considered the electoral position to be uncertain and he, if not other leaders, was more than content to maintain the alliance with the Liberals even if this meant constraining Labour's social ambitions. As McKibbin has noted, MacDonald was 'impressed, above all, with the weakness of the Labour Party in the country'.[13] Although the party potentially could contest about 113 seats, the rise in the number of three-cornered contests which would inevitably follow the collapse of the Alliance, could reduce Labour's Parliamentary strength.[14]

Embracing State Collectivism

In the event, of course, calculations of this kind turned out to be irrelevant. The outbreak of the Great War in August 1914 created a natural hiatus and Labour was able to break from a weakening Liberalism during the four-year course of hostilities. If the war did not literally create the modern Labour Party it nevertheless exercised a powerful catalytic effect on the party's emergence as an independent political force. Not only did it see the beginning of the end of the Liberals as a party of government,[15] but the dramatic increase in state activity required by modern warfare went some way to resolving trade union doubts about state's potential as a vehicle for economic and social reform. Certain industries, such as mining and the railways, had effectively been nationalised for the duration of hostilities and workers in these occupations wanted these arrangements to continue. Again, full employment and rising wages provided a context for the extension of the state national insurance scheme,[16] while improvements in certain aspects of health care, particularly pre- and ante-natal care, together with the beneficial effects of food rationing demonstrated the benefits of a state-driven social policy.[17]

Organisationally, Labour emerged from the war considerably strengthened. In a development which pushed it beyond its trade union roots, the party was organised on a constituency basis and individual membership was permitted. In addition to a new constitution, a new programme, *Labour and the New Social Order*, was agreed in 1918. Despite a good deal of union opposition, *Labour and the New Social Order* embodied at least a rhetorical commitment to 'socialism' as the idea was construed through Clause Four – the pledge to 'secure for the producers by hand or by brain the full fruits of their industry, and the most equitable distribution thereof that may be possible upon the basis of the common ownership of the means of production'. The constitution on formed the basis of Labour's electoral programme for much of the interwar period. As Thorpe writes, this consisted of commitments to 'full employment at decent wages and, failing that, a comprehensive system of benefits; nationalisation of the railways, canals, coal and electricity; taxation based on ability to pay plus a capital levy to pay of the huge national debt ... and the use of the fruits of prosperity which would follow from all this for social reforms in housing, education, health and so on'.[18] Ambiguities remained, but, on paper at least, the programme's collectivist character marked an advance on party policy in the Edwardian era. Labour was moving towards a position in which the state, with the economy suitably reconstructed on socialist lines, was regarded as the best vehicle for achieving substantial measures of social reform. If the welfare measures proposed lack specificity and did not fundamentally differ from New Liberal social policies, it nevertheless seemed as if Labour intended to pursue such policies in a very different economic environment.

And yet throughout the interwar period the party made little practical headway with its social goals. There were high spots to be sure: the Wheatley Housing Act of 1924 built on earlier postwar measures to stimulate local authority house construction, with some success, and the short-lived 1924 Labour government also made efforts to maintain the value of benefits for the unemployed and improve security of tenure for those in private rented accommodation. MacDonald's second administration, which came to power in 1929, also set out with good intentions. Not unlike its earlier counterpart, the government made a promising start on housing issues, Walter Greenwood's Housing Act making progress on slum clearance and replacement housing, providing 'a direct assault on the housing problems of the very poorest'.[19] The Widows', Orphans' and Old Age Pensions Act of 1929 lowered the age at which widows could claim their husband's pension, removing a large number of women from the reach of the Poor Law, while the Unemployment Insurance Act not only extended arrangements for transitional benefits,[20] but made the eligibility criteria for unemployment benefit more generous by abolishing the 'genuinely seeking work' test. However, these initiatives have to be set against a distinct lack of progress elsewhere. Most importantly, Labour produced no answer to the problem of unemployment itself; continuing high levels effectively destroyed existing national insurance arrangements and, despite the measures detailed above, the piecemeal regime of transitional payments to the unemployed and the level of means testing that this involved were clearly provided no long-term solution. Elsewhere, Labour manifested little interest in health and did not pursue its stated policy of creating a free health service in the face of more pressing employment issues. In education, too, not only was the party internally divided about the best kind of school organisation,[21] but, the second MacDonald government retreated from its commitment to raise the school leaving age to 15 in the face of objections about the additional costs from the churches.

This is a mixed picture at best. The two Labour governments of the 1920s achieved no more, and possibly less, than their Conservative opponents, although it is important to understand that their difficulties cannot simply be ascribed to a failure of political will. It is obviously significant, for example, that both the 1924 and 1929–31 governments were minority administrations – the former being particularly constrained as Labour won only 191 seats and was therefore dependent on the 158 Liberal MPs for support. Moreover, as Coates has pointed out, Labour had to deal with financial institutions, like the Treasury and the Bank of England, which held tenaciously to accepted economic doctrines, specifically adherence to the gold standard and a preparedness to accept the high unemployment and associated social ills this could involve.[22] Britain also experienced a period of substantial industrial restructuring in the 1920s and, combined with the effects of world recession, unemployment mounted inexorably throughout the 1920s and early 1930s. In this difficult political and economic environment it is understandable that 'Labour's confidence was eroded by [these] harsh facts of post-war existence'.[23] After all, the policies contained in *Labour and the New Social Order* were not designed to address the problems posed by sustained recession – and in view of the rather different priorities of the party's trade union and socialist elements, Labour frankly lacked both the unity and intellectual sophistication needed to recast ideas and policy in the light of the deteriorating economic situation.

The absence of creative thinking was noticeable. MacDonald clearly had no answer to the problems facing his 1929–31 government, privately noting that 'the flood of unemployment flows and rises, and baffles everybody' and confessing that 'I am not happy about our work. It is too much of the onlooker oppressed by circumstances'.[24] This sense of passive bewilderment was not shared elsewhere. For example, discussions about solutions to unemployment which took place within the Liberal Party in the 1920s and early 1930s[25] found no consistent echo with Labour. With two exceptions – the ILP pamphlet *The Living Wage* and Oswald Mosley's *Memorandum* – which were dismissed by party and trade union leaderships,[26] Labour only seemed able to produce high-flown ideals of the variety contained in the 1928 election manifesto, *Labour and the Nation*, while simultaneously pursuing highly orthodox economic policies designed to thus appease the financial establishment by keeping Britain on the gold standard. The government was consequently in no position to combat the full force of the world slump when it hit Britain in 1931. With predictions of a budget deficit of £170 million and a run on sterling during August of that year the Cabinet was faced with having to respond to the crisis with the traditional recipe of tax increases and spending cuts. Although a majority of the Cabinet were in favour of retrenchment a significant minority, having initially agreed to a £56 million economy package, they found further demands for a 10 per cent cut in unemployment benefit too much to stomach. MacDonald was forced to tender the government's resignation before being asked to stay on as Prime Minister of a new National Government – his acceptance resulting in his expulsion from the Labour Party along with those like the Chancellor, Philip Snowden, who chose to accompany him.

Whatever the judgement on Labour's actions during those difficult August days, it is hard to resist the conclusion that, in terms of ideology, policy and practice, the party was adrift. Far from striving to advance towards more comprehensive forms of social equality in the context of socialist economic reconstruction, as promised in the 1918 constitution, Labour had proved unable to create the virtuous circle of economic growth and high public spending on which its social objectives depended. While the reasons for this lack of success are understandable, the consequence was that Labour had yet to move decisively beyond the legacy of piecemeal social reform bequeathed by the New Liberalism.

Towards the Welfare State

It is not clear that Labour ever really managed to distance itself from this legacy. While the party undoubtedly made efforts to produce a more coherent programme in the light of the electoral catastrophe of September 1931, which saw its representation reduced from 288 to 46 MPs, the clear approach to economic and social policy that emerged from this process was compromised by the different, and more urgent, demands arising from Britain's experience in the Second World War. The paradoxical result was that the price of Labour's success in creating the welfare state in the immediate postwar period was the abrogation of the programme agreed during the 1930s.

Labour's virtual eclipse as a Parliamentary force concentrated minds on how to integrate socialist principle and practice in a manner which provided the party with a clear sense of identity and direction.[27] Underpinning the plethora of ideas that emerged from a variety of internal sources was a continuing preference for state-based, collectivist solutions, the most tangible example of which came in the form of *Labour's Immediate Programme*, published in 1937. Described by Labour's leader, Clement Attlee as 'a table of priorities showing what will be done first',[28] the Programme set out what a Labour government would accomplish within a five-year Parliament. Significantly, 'measures of economic reconstruction took precedence over those of social amelioration'.[29] As Evan Durbin, one of Labour's most prominent thinkers, observed, the objective was to put 'the acquisition of power before the abolition of privilege, control before benefits, the pill before the jam, in social legislation'.[30] While this sequence echoed previous policy statements, the *Immediate Programme* provided a much clearer formulation of the attitude to welfare that a future Labour government would take. Social equality was regarded as the ultimate goal, but one which was contingent upon progress towards 'socialism', understood primarily as a combination of public ownership and economic planning.

The Second World War did not so much change these objectives as destroy the order of priority. Because the war saw a vast increase in state economic management and state intervention in key areas of social welfare, for example medical services, food rationing and child care, the state became increasingly identified with economic efficiency and with 'fair shares' – and Labour as the champion of state-based solutions became associated with both.[31] This association was such as to make it difficult for a Labour government to separate economic from social priorities. For one thing, the demand for a fairer society at the war's end was a hard one to resist. For much of the war's duration, civilians had been as much in the 'front line' as those in the armed services and this greater breadth of sacrifice arising from the blitz led to widespread expectations of immediate measures of social reform when victory was achieved, irrespective of policies for economic reconstruction.[32]

Importantly, too, it was Labour ministers who were associated with social reform. From the moment when Labour politicians entered the wartime coalition government in May 1940, they became directly implicated in drawing up plans for postwar reconstruction on both economic and social fronts. The party leader, Clement Attlee, 'bestrode the domestic scene between 1940 and 1945', while the 'Cabinet Reconstruction Committee ... was dominated by Attlee, Morrison and other Labour figures'.[33] These close connections with reconstruction meant that party leaders were intimately involved with social policy-making, and particularly in discussing plans for a national health service, an expanded secondary education system and a universal system of national insurance. In other areas like employment policy where social and economic objectives were intimately linked, Labour ministers like Hugh Dalton, a future Chancellor, contributed to the 1944 White Paper on Employment, which accepted for the first time that governments should actively 'manage' the economy to maintain full employment.

These factors allowed Labour to emerge from the war as a potential party of government. While the 'blueprints' developed between 1942 and 1945 were somewhat altered in the course of internal party debates,[34] *Let Us Face the Future*, Labour's 1945 election manifesto, offered the electorate a combination of moderate, if extensive, social reform, the details of which owed much to Labour's involvement in the Coalition's discussions about reconstruction, together with more radical economic reform, the ideas for which could be found in the *Immediate Programme*. As Brooke has written, the document's 'main strength lay in the balance found between a distinctive socialist alternative and a reasonable appeal to the middle ground in public opinion'.[35]

This sense of balance indicated a mixing of priorities which allowed Labour fully to exploit the singular economic and social circumstances which prevailed in the immediate aftermath of the war. Britain's economic condition was such as to permit no immediate return to a free market economy. Serious manpower shortages, low industrial output and the complexities of the transition to a peacetime economy necessitated continued state economic management. Despite the many economic difficulties encountered by the government during its period in office,[36] this effective absence of a free market alternative, combined with postwar enthusiasm for social reform and the financial resources supplied from the United States in the form of Marshall Aid ensured that collectivist economic and welfare policies would complement rather than undermine one another, establishing the 'virtuous circle' mentioned above.

Welfare Politics in Postwar Britain

Creating the Welfare State

The story of the welfare state's creation is well known.[37] The Attlee government introduced a system of social insurance reflecting the spirit, if not the letter, of the 1942 Beveridge Report which had promised to eliminate poverty and want by the introduction of a comprehensive, universal insurance system designed to protect individuals against the major 'risks' of unemployment, sickness and old age. In accordance with Beveridge's dictum that a comprehensive social insurance system would need to be supported by national systems of health care and education, Labour created a National Health Service designed to deliver medical care to all, free at the point of need and implemented the 1944 Butler Education Act which made secondary schooling compulsory until the age of 15. Crucially, too, the Government accepted the logic of the 1944 Employment White paper (and another of Beveridge's conditions for a successful national insurance system) that the state should manage the economy with the objective of maintaining full employment. If further pieces of social legislation such as the 1948 National Assistance Act are included, then it seems reasonable to suggest that 'Labour had ... set out the parameters for a welfare state more extensive than anything previously known in Britain'.[38]

There were drawbacks to be sure. Neither the Attlee government nor any of its postwar successors managed to make social insurance truly universal or sufficiently generous to create the framework of social protection that Beveridge had envisaged. Beveridge, of course, was a member of the Liberal Party and, staying close to his Liberal roots, remained sceptical about a distinctly redistributive social policy. His original scheme was certainly not egalitarian, only making provision for flat rate contributions in return for flat rate benefits, and the 1946 Social Insurance Act did not introduce a redistributive element. Labour, moreover, set benefit levels below the value required to meet normal financial needs with the result that many people were forced to rely on means-tested National Assistance to top up their incomes. As Glennerster notes, 'this muddling of the minimum with social insurance [damned] the future of social insurance in the UK. As a flat-rate scheme it never had a hope of securing the support of the middle class, as social security had done in the US'.[39] The scheme also excluded married women, making them dependent on their husbands' contribution record – a feature which contributed to the high incidence of female poverty, particularly in old age.

In other areas Labour either failed to overcome opposition to its plans or did not pursue reform with sufficient conviction. For example, the National Health Service, unquestionably the jewel in the Government's crown, was successfully created but only after its chief architect, Aneurin Bevan, had been forced to make substantial concessions to the doctors.[40] Again, success in introducing a system of compulsory secondary education and raising the school leaving age was marred by the Government's unwillingness to tamper with the tripartite system by which children were selected for different types of school according to their performance in the 11-plus exam – and this despite 20 years or so of demands within the party for 'multilateral' schooling.[41]

And yet these difficulties are scarcely to be wondered at. It is hard to imagine any legislative programme that would not produce problems of one kind or other and thus a legacy of criticism and debate with which future administrations would have to deal. For present purposes, however, the important issue does not concern the specific details of social reform as these developed during the Attlee years, but the impact that the welfare state's creation had on Labour's subsequent approach to welfare politics. This was by no means entirely positive. In short, having realised a good many of their welfare objectives, as these had been understood by 1945, Labour governments did not manage to build on these foundations in the second half of the century. Instead, in retrograde fashion, they defended their creation without seeking substantially to improve it and certainly without critically examining the collectivist nature of welfare provision itself. While, there were good reasons for this defensive posture, the result was that Labour did not fundamentally question the role or nature of the welfare state either in opposition or in government.

One reason for this defensiveness lies in Labour's dismal experience between 1951 and 1964 – during which time the party lost three successive general elections. When the short-lived second Attlee government fell in November 1951 it made way for a series of Conservative administrations which, though not inclined to dismantle the welfare state, were also ideologically indisposed to the collectivist trend in welfare Labour had initiated. Explicitly rejecting 'the use of the state as a tool to redistribute wealth or to maintain the egalitarian trends introduced during the war years',[42] Conservative governments advocated private as opposed to public provision where possible and selectivist or means-tested social protection where the state needed to intervene. This approach to social reform found favour with an electorate for whom the exigencies of wartime and the demand for 'fair shares' were becoming an increasingly distant memory. In fact, bolstered by the economic prosperity and unprecedented levels of 'affluence' which characterised the later 1950s, the Conservatives were – somewhat unfairly – able to contrast their period in office with the considerably more austere Attlee years. In the absence of any new ideas about how to regenerate enthusiasm for collectivist welfare solutions, Labour could do little other than defend its creation.[43]

There was a further reason why the social reforms of the 1940s were not questioned too deeply. The 'balance' between economic reconstruction and welfare reform struck in *Let Us Face the Future* did not last beyond 1950 when internal debates about the priority to be given to public ownership as opposed to further welfare state initiatives began to result in increasing factional strife.[44] These issues are examined elsewhere in this volume but it is important to note that the priorities initially agreed in *Labour's Immediate Programme* and obscured by wartime developments became the subjects of intense intra-party debate throughout the 1950s and beyond. In the main, left-wing arguments, though divided between Tribunite demands for public ownership and centre-left demands for 'planning', continued to perceive Labour's primary task as 'socialist' economic reconstruction, without which the ultimate goal of social equality could not be achieved. Revisionists like Labour's leader Hugh Gaitskell, on the other hand, believed that greater equality could be attained through a combination of Keynesian demand management techniques, redistributive taxation and the existing welfare state. In Tony Crosland's case, revisionism took the more egalitarian form of a concern with 'social envy' and the cultural effects of class divisions – but in general revisionist thinking assumed that equality could be achieved using existing economic and social policies, and so did not consider the further development of the welfare state per se in any detail.[45] The upshot of this factionalism was ideological stalemate, but a stalemate in which none of the protagonists was moved to give consideration to the role of welfare in a changing and increasingly prosperous society.

The Politics of Social Equality: 1964–75

Internal strife temporarily diminished in the early 1960s mainly because increasing Conservative difficulties lent hope to the prospect of a return to power.[46] The banner under which the party united, however, was essentially a technocratic one which preserved elements of 'socialist' economic management in the form of centre-left strategies of indicative planning, while making much of the view that Labour could use the state to harness the benefits of the emerging 'scientific revolution' in the public interest. First under Gaitskell, but with considerably more conviction under Harold Wilson, who became leader after Gaitskell's early death in 1963, Labour claimed to be the party of the new technological revolution with policies able to control irresponsible private economic power and promote an efficient, modern economy.[47] Although the welfare state was intended to be a significant beneficiary of this formula, no new thinking about welfare accompanied the enthusiasm for science and planning: indeed the party's concrete commitments were 'mostly extensions of the agenda the old 1945 government had left unfinished'.[48]

Had the Wilson governments of the 1960s – and for that matter the Wilson and Callaghan governments of the 1970s – been able to deliver on their economic policies it is possible that the complacent, collectivist version of welfare provision they were intended to support would have gone uncriticised. Higher economic growth could have been used to fund ever higher social spending and thus better and more extensive welfare services. But such was not the case, and the abiding image of Labour during these turbulent years is one of a party beset by criticism from within and without, in many ways doing its best to maintain the welfare state that it had created but, owing to constant economic difficulties, failing to live up to the egalitarian hopes of its supporters.

The economic story has been related elsewhere and does not need repeating.[49] It is sufficient to say that the failure of the much-heralded National Plan of 1965 left Labour vulnerable to constant speculation against sterling, successive currency crises causing the government to resort to an economic strategy dependent upon wage restraint and downward pressure on public spending. The union militancy that this provoked combined with increasing disillusionment amongst rank and file party supporters and a number of high-profile pressure groups, about Labour's apparent failure to protect the poorest and most vulnerable sections of society.[50] These difficulties were compounded during the 1970s when, in the aftermath of the 1973 oil price rises and the high inflation that ensued, first Conservative, then Labour administrations were forced to continue policies of wage restraint and progressively more stringent public spending cuts.[51] So far as Labour's internal politics were concerned, the fact that ministers were prepared to pursue such policies reawakened the factional strife of the 1950s in more virulent form, to the point where the party was severely undermined as an electoral force.[52]

In social policy terms, these problems were in many ways an updated version of the kind faced by the second MacDonald government. Hostaged to economic fortune, Labour (a minority administration in the late 1970s) could only make piecemeal attempts at social reform, leaving little sense of overall coherence, let alone a distinctive welfare strategy. However, this rather gloomy picture needs some balance. On the positive side, Labour governments undoubtedly carried out a number of incremental adjustments to the welfare state which were of benefit to the worst off. NHS prescription charges were abolished on the Wilson government taking office in 1964 and health spending increased by 3 per cent per year, on average, between 1964 and 1970. Even in the much colder economic climate of the 1970s, the party managed to ensure that spending on health increased as a proportion of GDP and that available resources were more equally distributed.[53] Pensions were increased in 1965 and short-term earnings related benefits were introduced for widows, the sick and the unemployed.[54] In fact social security spending in general rose from 7.2 per cent to 9.3 per cent of GDP between 1964 and 1970 and, in addition, institutional reforms to the social security infrastructure saw the replacement of the National Assistance Board with the new Supplementary Benefits Commission, the purpose being to remove the stigma from state support in an effort to improve take-up rates. In the 1970s, with unemployment rising beyond one million towards the end of the decade, the Callaghan government managed to protect the most vulnerable groups by ensuring that the value of benefits was maintained. As David Piachaud noted at the time, 'to have achieved a shift to social security at a time when real incomes were static or declining was a major achievement.'[55] Education offered rather less in the way of success, but even here Labour oversaw an expansion of higher education, including the creation of the polytechnics and the the Open University, as well as the development of educational priority areas in accordance with the recommendations of the Plowden Report, and, after 1965, an extensive assault on the selective principle through the introduction of comprehensive schooling.

These achievements appear to justify Thorpe's verdict, delivered on Labour's record in the 1960s, that 'given the constraints, we should perhaps be more surprised at what the government was able to do than condemnatory of what it failed to achieve in social policy'.[56] In the light of the history of welfare decline in the 1980s and 1990s, this judgement is a just one; Labour plainly tried to support the welfare state in the context of its continuing faith in welfare collectivism. However, for those contemporaries who had hoped that the party would achieve a much greater degree of social equality there was plenty of room for disappointment, most particularly in the 1964–70 period when Labour enjoyed a substantial Parliamentary majority. Budget cuts in the late 1960s saw the reintroduction of NHS prescription charges and thus breached the hallowed principle of free health care for all. Reductions in NHS spending after 1967 also gave the impression that the health service was not prospering under a Labour administration despite the fact that resources had increased on average. Pensions apart, the fact that Labour introduced a number of means-tested benefits during the 1960s – rent and rate rebates for example – drew criticism from welfare universalists, who argued that similar levels of benefit should be paid equally to all in any particular category of need. More significantly for a party which boasted that the welfare state had eliminated poverty, Labour was accused of allowing poverty, especially child poverty, to increase. Members of the Child Poverty Action Group, founded in 1965, believed that the government did not take their evidence about the increasing incidence of child poverty seriously and took their views to the point of initiating a campaign, 'The Poor get Poorer Under Labour', criticising the government's approach to child poverty in the run-up to the 1970 general election. When further criticisms are taken into account, particularly those which challenge the extent of the government's generosity to the rising numbers of unemployed,[57] we gain some insight not into the absence of any attempt to cater for the worst off, but into the lack of a coherent policy towards social protection.

This lack of coherence is amply displayed in Labour's approach to education. In many ways this area of social policy provided the best opportunity to move beyond the position reached in the 1940s. Conservative governments had done little to change the basis of state education during the 1950s and had of course done nothing to limit the private sector, which continued to flourish. Following some (unusually) constructive discussions in the 1950s, Labour came to power committed to a wide-ranging reorganisation of secondary schooling on comprehensive lines, raising the school leaving age to 16 and removing privilege in education by integrating the private schools into the state sector. Comprehensivisation went ahead but the manner of reform was heavily criticised mainly on the grounds that insufficient resources were devoted to the reorganisation and inadequate guidance given to local education authorities about the best form the move to comprehensive status should take. The result was that, in lieu of better buildings, new equipment and more teachers, LEAs were forced to adapt their existing provision to comprehensive ends as best they could.

Disappointment was not confined to the problems of comprehensivisation. If the lack of resources devoted to comprehensive reform, and indeed the similar absence of financial support for the newly created education priority areas, is contrasted with the relatively generous funding of the expansion of higher education from which the better-off differentially benefited,[58] it becomes difficult to sustain the view that Labour was unequivocally committed to greater social equality. The obvious reluctance to tackle the private sector,[59] combined with the failure to raise the school leaving age – an ambition which fell to the round of spending cuts agreed for the 1968 Budget – compounded disillusionment and provoked severe criticism from leftwingers in the aftermath of Labour's 1970 election defeat.[60]

The Decline of Welfare Collectivism

Much of the above has concentrated on Labour's social policy achievements, or the lack of them, in the 1960s – and for good reason. In spite of the growing climate of social and political change which characterised that decade, it was still just possible for Labour politicians to believe that the party continued to stand as a progressive force in social policy. Although by the late 1960s there were signs that Labour's faith in collectivist welfare solutions might be misplaced – student activism, the rising force of women's liberation, demands from trade union rank and file for greater measures of industrial democracy were indicative of a desire for a less 'universal', more 'plural', approach to social change – it was to be almost another decade before any serious doubts arose about the capacity of the state to generate social reform, let alone the kind of reform its increasingly heterogeneous citizenry actually desired.

These doubts were primarily born of the growing recognition that the belief in the state's ability to control the economy in the interests of growth and, ultimately, social equality had proved elusive if not downright chimerical. The very different responses to this crisis of faith in the state depended on existing beliefs about the nature of 'socialism' and how resolutely Labour had pursued the collectivist ideal. Put simply, those on the left believed that Labour governments had failed because they had not created a distinctly socialist economy; moderate elements, on the other hand, confronted by the apparent inability of governments to control wage levels, public spending or the exchange rate, lost faith in Keynesian techniques of demand management that had been a central aspect of their thinking since the 1950s. With the return of bitter factional strife went any semblance of a coherent welfare programme.

Leftwingers pushed various forms of an 'Alternative Economic Strategy', which sought to privilege socialist economic reconstruction over social welfare, while party moderates effectively had no ideas to offer. Crosland, for example, who had remained more optimistic than most about the continued impact of high public spending on social inequality, was forced to admit, in the wake of the 1976 IMF crisis, that 'the economic crisis inevitably imposes limits on how fast we can progress towards a more equal society'.[61] 'Progress' now had to be conceived in the limited terms of outlawing sexual and racial discrimination, and pursuing greater measures of industrial democracy, but these ideas could hardly be expected to produce the equality of outcome that Crosland desired. After his premature death in 1977 no further attempts were made to adapt Labour's collectivist social policy to changed times and, in defiance of leftwing demands, the Callaghan government began to cut public spending in line with what had become a deflationary, monetarist approach to social and economic policy.

The Changing Context of Welfare in the 1980s and 1990s

This approach was pursued with greater fervour by Conservative governments throughout the 1980s and much of the 1990s. As part of efforts to reform the supply side of the economy by reducing taxation and reshaping the labour market, Conservative administrations also attempted to limit welfare spending. Although they ultimately failed to achieve substantial spending cuts, the Conservatives were undoubtedly successful in reducing the role of the state in certain areas of social policy – housing being the most obvious – and changing the nature of delivery where the state continued to be involved in welfare provision.[62] For example, budgetary devolution within specific services such as education together with the introduction of internal markets in services like the NHS, mimicked free market provision and in so doing reduced the scope of the collectivist structures of provision on which the welfare state had been erected.[63] The Conservatives were also successful in their campaign to reallocate the burden of moral responsibility for individual welfare away from the state to individuals and their families. Here, ironically, the state's role was far from minimal. Cuts in the value of benefits, a sustained attack on 'welfare dependency' and the uncompromising view, during a period of historically high unemployment, that work could be found by those who were sufficiently motivated to find it, contrasted with traditional perceptions of the welfare state as a vehicle for social protection and replaced them with an approach to social policy that regarded its prime function as fostering economic competitiveness.[64]

This assault on postwar welfare collectivism took place in an environment of extensive economic and social change created by the increasingly rapid pace of 'globalisation'. Without addressing the issue of whether or not 'globalisation' is a new phenomenon,[65] there is a degree of agreement about the fact that its economic aspects entail rising competition amongst nation states for inward investment and a corresponding approach to production that looks not to goods designed for the domestic economy but for 'a world market, or at least several national markets.'[66] This shift of focus has changed the nature of production itself, particularly in countries like Britain where traditional, male employment in heavy industries like mining, shipbuilding and steel has given way to service sector employment and a higher incidence of part-time, casualised and poorly paid work often undertaken by women.

A rather different set of changes has also occurred as attitudes to politics and political engagement have shifted away from their typical postwar location within political parties. The period since 1980 has been marked by a greater readiness on the part of marginal or excluded sections of society to dispense with 'socialism' as a set of ideas thought capable of offering alternative forms of social, political and economic organisation to existing capitalist alternatives, and instead to adopt a variety of strategies which are concerned with the particular needs of specific communities. Although sections of the Labour left, in particular, attempted to harness a more diverse range of interests within their socialist paradigm in the early 1980s,[67] minority ethnic groups, women, disabled people and others have begun to form constituencies, and discover voices of their own, outside the parameters of traditional party politics. Groups of this nature want to make a claim for special needs on the basis of 'difference'[68] and, together with others with broader political agendas such as the Green movement, these interests frequently conceive welfare issues in a different manner to the traditional postwar welfare state.[69] There is no space here to go into the various arguments against welfare universalism (or, in some instances, in favour of new forms of 'differentiated univeralism'), coming from the women's movement and elsewhere,[70] but it is important to recognise the plurality of ideas that now exists about the nature of welfare and the possible role of the welfare state.

Labour at the Century's End: Third Way Welfare

This brief overview of the kind of changes that have affected Britain (and other countries) since the early 1980s forms the backdrop to the dramatic shift away from its welfare collectivist origins that Labour has taken over the past few years – a shift which has now been well documented.[71] The point here is that Labour's somewhat belated response to these changes has resulted, in the late 1990s, in a radically revised understanding of the role of welfare in contemporary British society. Viewed in historical perspective, the party has effectively abandoned its commitment to welfare collectivism. Beginning with the Policy Review in 1989, moving through the report of the Social Justice Commission in 1994 to present debates about Third Way welfare, Labour has progressively jettisoned not only the traditional leftwing priorities of state ownership and planning, but also its redistributive ambitions for social equality and social protection.[72] In the place of these key elements of 'old' Labour thinking, Tony Blair's New Labour Party now accepts the free market as the primary focus of wealth production, as well as recognising that labour flexibility is the core component of an economic strategy designed to maintain Britain's competitiveness in the global economy. In New Labour's view, welfare must be reorganised to reflect these competitive priorities, the key difference with previous Conservative administrations lying in the claim that the fragmenting effects of the marketplace and the needs of the most vulnerable members of society must be offset by policies designed to enhance 'social inclusion'.[73]

The nature of this reorganisation of welfare has much to do with new attitudes to employment. If the precise nature of the Third Way remains decidedly murky, it is nevertheless clear that a central aspect concerns the attempt to involve both the public and private sectors in the task of providing employment opportunities for individuals who would otherwise remain dependent on welfare benefits.[74] Work is regarded as a key – if not the key – to greater individual independence and responsibility, as well as to security and a sense of social inclusion. While this conviction may well prove to be over-optimistic, for much depends on the quality of the employment and training opportunities on offer,[75] there is little doubt that Labour places much faith in it. Gordon Brown, for example, has recently argued that the work ethic should be re–established 'at the centre of our welfare system', the tax and benefit systems being reformed 'to make work pay.[76]

This emphasis on employment means that 'welfare' is becoming increasingly linked to 'opportunity' – indeed some observers now argue that the focus of a welfare system should be on the redistribution of opportunities rather than income.[77] To pursue this very different vision, however, Labour is currently adopting a 'carrot and stick' approach to welfare recipients. To those willing to take up opportunities for employment, education and training, participation is held out as its own reward in the shape of the increased likelihood of access to better employment, further education or training, more generous pensions – and thus social inclusion. Conversely, those unwilling to participate in the new 'social investment state'[78] can have their benefits reduced or removed, the thrust towards the inclusive society becoming more coercive as not only individuals but entire communities experience a new welfare paternalism in the form of 'death by a thousand task groups' and compulsion 'to seek work, advice on training and how to manage money, testing for drugs and diversion schemes'.[79] Of course, 'reintegration' may be a valid goal – and those aspects of New Labour's approach which stress the importance of revitalising democracy and citizenship at regional and local levels need to be taken seriously – but the 'necessarily increased surveillance and increased challenges to [the] behaviour' of the 'poor and the deviant'[80] suggests a level of authoritarianism which rests uneasily with a commitment to human liberty, especially in circumstances where the opportunities to be 'redistributed' may not be particularly good.

Conclusion

From the viewpoint of welfare politics, Labour's century has been far from easy. While it is possible to point to clear successes accomplished under the ideological rubric of welfare collectivism, the greatest progress was made in those few years after the Second World War when popular demand for greater social equality briefly combined with a majority Labour government committed to economic and social reconstruction, and possessing the resources to act on its policy proposals. Looking either side of this period, it is hard to find evidence of sustained practical activity which matched this zenith in terms of the qualitative shift in the role and nature of welfare that it involved. For much of its history Labour has struggled to bridge the gap between vision and practical achievement.

As suggested at the beginning of this chapter, this seemingly harsh judgement has to be understood in the context of the economic difficulties that Labour governments consistently experienced. If sterling crises and a weakening economy, and frequent minority status are taken into account – not forgetting the corrosive effects of factional strife – it is possible to view Labour's record in kinder light. All Labour administrations attempted to undertake programmes of social legislation even where circumstances conspired to reduce pre-election egalitarian ambitions to the pragmatic business of piecemeal social reform. If a criticism remains, it is that, particularly in the postwar period, Labour failed to think creatively about how to develop the welfare collectivist legacy in ways that could move the party's approach to welfare politics beyond its narrow parameters.

It is doubtful, of course, whether any such rethinking could have survived the economic and political upheavals of the 1980s and to this extent Labour's eventual retreat from collectivism was inevitable. Looking to the future, whether or not New Labour's commitment to Third Way welfare politics will produce a distinctively different welfare state remains to be seen. Although it is tempting to suggest that Third Way perspectives could create a harsher, less protective welfare system similar to that which existed in the pre-1945 period,[81] such a view needs balance. Current concentration on the 'opportunity-income' axis of welfare ignores the fact that the overwhelming majority of the British population continues to depend on the state for its educational and health care needs. New Labour – indeed any government – will be obliged to ensure that these key public goods and services continue to be delivered, even if in certain instances by state-regulated private agencies rather than the state bureaucracies of the collectivist past. Nonetheless, to be worthy of the name, a welfare state must offer protection to society's vulnerable members and, in so far as the present government favours 'opportunity' over 'welfare', there must be some doubt about its commitment to those in most need. The real challenge for Third Way social policy is to demonstrate that, in perennially insecure economic circumstances, there remains a willingness to temper the drive for economic efficiency with the demands of equity; whether Labour's present conception of welfare is designed to strike this balance is far from clear.

Notes

1 See for example, R. Miliband, *Parliamentary Socialism: A Study in the Politics of Labour*, London, Merlin Press, 1972; J. Hinton, *Labour and Socialism: A History of the British Labour Movement. 1867–1974*, Brighton, Wheatsheaf Books, 1983; R. McKibbin, *The Evolution of the Labour Party. 1910–1924*, Oxford, Clarendon Press, 1974; H. Drucker, *Doctrine and Ethos in the Labour Party*, London, George Allen and Unwin, 1979; N. Ellison, *Egalitarian Thought and Labour Politics: Retreating Visions*, London, Routledge, 1994; T. Jones, *Remaking the Labour Party*, London, Routledge, 1996.
2 N. Ellison, 'From Welfare State to Post-Welfare Society? Labour's Social Policy in Historical and Contemporary Perspective', in B. Brivati and T. Bale (eds), *New Labour in Power*, London, Routledge, 1997.
3 A. Giddens, *The Third Way: the Renewal of Social Democracy*, Oxford, 1998.
4 R Aris, *Trade Unions and the Management of Industrial Conflict*, Basingstoke, Macmillan, 1998.
5 The decision removed the legal immunity of unions and made them legally liable for the actions of their officials which, as Hinton has written, 'virtually destroyed the right to strike.' See Hinton, *Labour and Socialism*. p68.
6 These arrangements enabled trade union nominees to stand for Parliament but, because the unions were reluctant to take full responsibility for fielding their own candidates, they normally only did so with the approval of local Liberal Patty associations – effectively allowing the Liberals to decide how many 'Labour' candidates should stand.
7 As they did in the Clitheroe by-election in July 1900. See G. L. Bernstein, *Liberalism and Liberal Politics in Edwardian England*, London, Allen and Unwin, 1986, pp.67–8.
8 G. L. Bernstein, *Liberalism and Liberal Politics,* pp.69–70.
9 J. R MacDonald, *Socialism in Society*, ILP Publications, 1905.
10 P. Thane, 'The Labour Party and State "Welfare"', in K D. Brown (ed), *The First Labour Party. 1906–14*, London, Croom Helm, 1985, pl85.
11 For discussions of New Liberalism see M. Freeden, *The New Liberalism: An Ideology of Social Reform*, Oxford, Clarendon Press, 1978.
12 P. Thane, 'The Labour Party and State "Welfare"', p.199.
13 R. McKibbin, *The Evolution of the Labour Party*, p.80.
14 M. Pugh, *The Making of Modern British Politics, 1867–1939*, Oxford, Blackwell,1982, p.154.

15 For example in the beginnings of a terminal split in the party when Lloyd George replaced Asquith as Prime Minister after the collapse of the wartime Coalition government in December 1916.

16 At the time of the Armistice about 4 million were insured, out of a total workforce of 14 million.

17 See J. M. Winter, *The Great War and the British People*, Basingstoke, Macmillan, 1986.

18 A. Thorpe, *A History of the British Labour Party*, Basingstoke, Macmillan, 1997, p.45.

19 P. Thane, *The Foundations of the Welfare State*, 2nd ed., London, Longman, 1996, p.196.

20 These benefits were paid to those whose entitlements to insurance-based benefits had elapsed – throughout the interwar years the 'price' of receiving transitional payments was an increasingly severe means-test on total household earnings.

21 See B. Simon, *The Politics of Educational Reform. 1920–1940*, Lawrence and Wishart, London, 1974.

22 D. Coates, *The Labour Party and the Struggle for Socialism*, Cambridge, Cambridge University Press. 1975, p.30.

23 R. Skidelsky, *Politicians and the Slump: The Labour Government of 1929–1931*, Basinstoke, Macmillan, p.37.

24 Quoted in D. Marquand, *The Progressive Dilemma From Lloyd George to Kinnock*, London, Heinemann, 1991, p.54.

25 See in particular, the Liberal Party's campaign document, *How to Conquer Unemployment*, London, Cassell, 1929.

26 See H. N. Brailsford, A. Creech Jones, E. F. Wise and J. A. *Hobson The Living Wage,* London, ILP, 1926. The pamphlet drew heavily upon Hobson's underconsumptionist position advocating a steep rise in family allowances and a generous minimum wage as means of raising demand.

27 See Ben Pimlott, *Labour and the Left in the 1930s*, Cambridge, Cambridge University Press, 1977; Elizabeth Durbin, *New Jerusalems: The Labour Party and the Economics of Democratic Socialism,* Routledge and Kegan Paul, 1985.

28 Labour Party Annual Conference Report, London, Labour Party, 1937, pp.182–83.

29 S. Brooke, *Labour's War: The Labour Party During the Second World War*, Oxford, Clarendon Press, 1992, p.30.

30 Evan Durbin, *The Politics of Democratic Socialism,* London, Routledge and Kegan Paul, 1940, p.306.

31 These observations need a little qualification. Fielding and others have cast doubt on the view that Labour was swept to power in July 1945 on the back of a homogeneous popular radicalism. It is likely that Labour emerged from the war as a party linked with social reconstruction in the 'public mind', but this association was prompted less by a desire for socialist equality than by an antipathy to Conservativism, born of pre-war experience, and the anticipation of greater 'fairness' understood in the mundane terms of a 'sure

steady job and a decent house at a rent we can afford to pay'. (Home Intelligence Weekly Report quoted by S. Brooke, 'The Labour Party and the 1945 General Election', *Contemporary Record*, 9 (1), 1995, p.11). See S. Fielding, 'What Did "The People" Want? The Meaning of the 1945 General Election', *Historical Journal,* 35, 1992.

32 See P. Addison, *The Road to 1945*, London, Quartet, 1975.

33 K. O. Morgan, *Labour People,* Oxford, Oxford University Press, 1987, pp.23–4.

34 See S. Brooke, *Labour's War,* Oxford, Clarendon Press, 1992.

35 S. Brooke, 'The Labour Party and the 1945 General Election', *Contemporary Record,* 9 (1), Summer, 1995, p.13.

36 K. O. Morgan, *Labour in Power, 1945–1951*, Oxford, Clarendon Press, 1984, Ch 8.

37 See H. Glennerster, *British Social Policy Since 1945*, Oxford, Blackwell, 1995, Chs 2–3; K. O. Morgan, *Labour in Power*, Ch 4; N. Timmins, *The Five Giants: A Biography of the Welfare State,* London, Fontana,1996, Part 2.

38 A. Thorpe, *A History of the British Labour Party*, p.124.

39. H. Glennerster, *British Social Policy Since 1945*, p.41.

40. R Lowe, *The Welfare State in Britain Since 1945,* Basingstoke, Macmillan, 1993, p.179.

41 See B. Simon, *Education and The Social Order, 1940–1990*, London, Lawrence and Wishart, 1991.

42 H. Jones, 'A Bloodless Counter-Revolution: The Conservative Party and the Defence of Inequality, 1945–51', in H. Jones and M. Kandiah (eds), *The Myth of Consensus: New Views on British History, 1945–64*, Basingstoke, Macmillan, 1996, p.13. See also N. Timmins, *The Five Giants*, p.178.

43 See N. Timmins, *The Five Giants*, p368.

44 An early example of what was to come can be seen in Cabinet disagreements about whether or not to nstionalise the iron and steel industry. See K. O. Morgan, *Labour in Power*, pp.110–121.

45 See N. Ellison, *Egalitarian Thought and Labour Politics,* Ch 4.

46 The apparently impregnable Macmillan government was rocked by a succession of sterling crises and subsequent Cabinet sackings in addition to a bad case of 'sleaze' in the shape of the Profumo affair. Macmillan resigned as Prime Minister in 1963, making was for a compromise candidate, Sir Alec Douglas Hume, whose aristocratic style contrasted sharply with the modernising image projected by Harold Wilson.

47 Labour's position is encapsulated in the party programme, *Signposts for the Sixties*, London, Labour Party, 1961.

48 H. Glennerster, *British Social Policy Since 1945*, p.95.

49 See, for example, K Middlemas, *Power, Competition and the State. Vol II, Threats to the Postwar Settlement. 1961–1974*, 1990; J. Tomlinson, *Public Policv and the Economv Since 1900*, Oxford, Clarendon Press, 1990; R. Opie, 'Economic Planning and Growth' in

W. Beckerman (ed), *The Labour Government's Economic Record. 1964–1970*, London, Duckworth, 1972.

50 For an account of Labour's relationship with the trade unions during this period see R Taylor, *The Trade Union Question in British Politics*, Oxford, Blackwell, 1993. M. McCarthy, *Campaigning for the Poor: CPAG and the Politics of Welfare,* London, Croom Helm, 1986, provides a good assessment of the origins and activities of the Child Poverty Action Group.

51 A. J. C. Britton, *Macroeconomic Policy in Britain 1974–1987*, Cambridge, Cambridge University Press, 1994.

52 See N. Ellison, *Egalitarian Thought and Labour Politics;* M. Hatfield, *The House the Left Built*, London, Gollancz, 1978; E. Shaw, *The Labour Party Since 1945*, Oxford, Blackwell, 1996.

53 R Lowe, *The Welfare State in Britain Since 1945*, p.341. See also N. Bosanquet, 'Health', in N. Bosanquet and P. Townsend (eds), *Labour and Equality: A Fabian Study of Labour in Power. 1974–79,* London Heinemann, 1980.

54 H. Glennerster, *British Social Policy Since 1945*, pp.109–10.

55 D. Piachaud, 'Social Security', in N. Bosanquet and P. Townsend (eds), *Labour and Equality,* p.173.

56 A. Thorpe, *A History of the British Labour Party,* p.167.

57 A. B. Atkinson, 'Inequality and Social Security', in P. Townsend and N. Bosanquet (eds), *Labour and Inequality,* London, Fabian Society, 1972.

58 H. Glennerster, 'Education and Inequality', in P. Townsend and N. Bosanquet (eds), *Labour and Inequality.*

59 The Public Schools Commission set up by the Wilson government to examine how the public schools might best be integrated into the state sector actually recommended that they should remain independent, but take half their numbers from non-fee-paying pupils. This idea was rejected by Labour's annual conference and no further progress was made on the issue.

60 See B. Jackson, *New Statesman*, 4 June 1971, pp.760–61.

61 C. A. R. Crosland, 'Equality in Hard Times', *Socialist Commentary.* October 1976, p3.

62 N. Ellison, 'The Changing Politics of Social Policy' in N. Ellison and C. Pierson (eds), *Developments in British Social Policy*, Basingstoke, Macmillan, 1998, pp.32–4.

63 See J. Le Grand and W. Bartlett (eds), *Quasi-Markets and Social Policy,* Basingstoke, Macmillan, 1993; N. Flynn, *Public Sector Management*, 3rd ed., Hemel Hempstead, Harvester Wheatsheaf, 1997.

64 See P. Cerny, *The Changing Architecture of Politics: Structure, Agency and the State*, London, Sage, 1990; B. Jessop, 'The Transition to Post-Fordism and the Schumpeterian Workfare State', in R Burrows and B. Loader (eds), *Towards a Post-Fordist Welfare State?*, London, Routledge, 1994.

65 See P. Hirst and G. Thompson, *Globalisation in Question*, Oxford, Polity, 1996, Ch l; D. Held, A. McGrew, D. Goldblatt and J. Perraton, *Global Transformations,* Oxford, Polity, 1999, pp.2–21.

66 S. Strange, *The Retreat of the State*, Cambridge, Cambridge University Press, 1996, p.44.

67 Tony Benn made great efforts to provide a more 'inclusive' version of socialist thought aimed at integrating the demands of various minority groups with the more traditional, trade union-oriented demands of the Labour left. See E. Hobsbawm, *The Forward March of Labour Halted?*, London, Verso, 1981, p89.

68 Iris Marion Young, *Justice and the Politics of Difference,* New Jersey, Princeton University Press, 1990.

69 J. Barry, 'Social Policy and Social Movements: Ecology and Social Policy', in N. Ellison and C. Pierson (eds), *Developments in British Social Policy.*

70 See R. Lister, *Citizenship: Feminist Perspectives*, Basingstoke, Macmillan, 1997; 'Citizenship and Difference', *European Journal of Social Theory,* 1 (1), 1998.

71 P. Alcock, 'The Labour Party and the Welfare State' in M. J. Smith and J. Spear (eds), *The Changing Labour Party*, London, Routledge, 1992; E. Shaw, *The Labour Party Since 1979: Crisis and Transformation*, London, Routledge.

72 See, for example, *Meet the Challenge, Make the Change,* London, Labour Party, 1989; *Social Justice: Strategies for Renewal,* The Report of the Commission for Social Justice, London, Vintage, 1994.

73 P. Mandelson and R Liddle, *The Blair Revolution: Can New Labour Deliver?*, London, Fontana, 1996, p22.

74 See M. Powell (ed), *New Labour. New Welfare State?*, Bristol, The Policy Press, 1999.

75 P. Stepney, R. Lynch and B. Jordan, 'Poverty, Exclusion and New Labour', *Critical Social Policy,* 57 (1), February, 1999.

76 G. Brown, 'Equality – Then and Now', in D. Leonard (ed), *Crosland and New Labour,* Basingstoke, Macmillan, 1999, p46.

77 M. Powell, *New Labour, New Welfare State?*, p.16.

78 A. Giddens, *The Third Way*, pp. 127–28.

79 S. MacGregor, 'Welfare, Neo-Liberalism and the New Paternalism: Three Ways for Social Policy in Late Capitalist Societies', *Capital and Class,* 67, Spring 1999, p.109.

80 S. MacGregor, 'Welfare, Neo-Liberalism and the New Paternalism', p.109.

81 M. Powell, *New Labour. New Welfare State?*, p.292.

Labour local government 1900–1999

Lewis Baston

This chapter is a brief history of the Labour Party *in* local government, rather than Labour Party policy *towards* local government.[1] At the start of the century, there was a flourishing system of largely independent local authorities, administering an extensive public sector, but very few Labour councillors; a kind of socialism without socialists. In the 1990s, the Labour Party had unprecedented success in local elections, although local government had little autonomy and had lost many of its powers.

The origins of municipal socialism 1870–1919

The first stirrings of labour participation in local government elections were in the 1870s, when elected school boards were established, in London and other large cities. Occasional working men and independent socialists stood as candidates. Local authorities were seen by late 19th century and early 20th century British socialist thinkers as extremely important, for both idealistic and practical reasons. The celebrated values of community were best reflected at local level and the Webbs, in their *Constitution for the Socialist Commonwealth of Great Britain*[2] saw a role for full time professional councils as representatives of citizens and consumers. In addition, 'socialism' already existed in the large cities in the form of municipal supply of utilities – gas, water and electricity – and transport services. Practically, control over national government seemed unimaginably distant to socialists and labourists, while control over working class boroughs seemed a highly feasible proposition.

Local councils in this period had different responsibilities from those they exercised by the end of the 20th century. The bulk of their spending was on 'housekeeping' services such as lighting, refuse, roads and public baths. They had some responsibility for public health. The history of municipal socialism is longer than the history of local Labour.[3] Council ownership of services such as gas and water had been introduced on a large scale by the Liberal boss of Birmingham, Joseph Chamberlain, from the 1870s. Chamberlain municipalised gas in 1875 and water in 1876. G.D.H. Cole admitted that ideas of municipal socialism were 'based more than most Fabians cared to acknowledge on Joseph

Chamberlain's.'[4] In the early years of the 20th century councils were also to start to employ builders and cleaners through 'direct labour' departments because many Liberal and Conservative councils felt that private contractors were delivering poor quality and high cost services. The issue of ownership was central to the concerns of early Labour and its predecessors, and these factors produced what was known as 'municipal socialism', the dominant Labour philosophy of local government in the early period.

The Local Government Act 1888 established a recognisable system of local government in smaller towns and rural areas for the first time, with a structure of county councils and boroughs; urban districts and rural districts were introduced in county areas in 1894.[5] Elections[6] for many of these bodies took place on a partisan basis from the start, although patterns of contesting seats were sometimes erratic and the extent to which party politics affected the actual administration of the council varied from place to place.[7] The first council to have substantial socialist influence was the London County Council, where a 'Progressive' party, a coalition of Liberals and Fabians, took control at the first elections in 1889. The first LCC embarked on a programme of municipalisation, public spending on services such as the fire brigade, and some of the first public housing in Britain.[8]

In other areas, socialists were operating outside a Liberal coalition. The Independent Labour Party was running candidates in its heartlands such as Bradford, and in 1898 briefly established control over West Ham borough, on the borders of Essex and London. It was the first Labour council.

The Progressive LCC frightened the Conservative government which took office in 1895, and its powers were reduced – some were given to a system of 28 'Metropolitan Boroughs' below the County Council. Exaggerated comparisons had been made between the LCC and the Paris Commune, although ironically the creation of the boroughs allowed Labour to gain a secure majority on a council, and exercise executive power, for the first time. In the impoverished East End, and the band of working class territory south of the river, there were several boroughs which were dominated by working class voters, such as Woolwich which had a Labour majority in 1903–06.

The establishment of the Labour Representation Committee as a national electoral force had relatively little immediate effect on local government, although local LRC organisations and municipal analogues such as the Bradford Workers' Muncipal Federation were founded in some areas.[9] Local election activity in many areas, though, was still largely left to the Independent

Labour Party and the developing system of Trades Councils, which generally worked on a municipal level uniting trade unions and all local socialist groups.[10]

Labour's municipal advance before 1914 was uneven.[11] Some illustrious figures were to serve on London councils, including Krishna Menon and George Bernard Shaw in St. Pancras, but only Woolwich was under majority Labour control. Elsewhere in the country, the pattern was extremely mixed. Labour gained footholds in some councils, and large groups in Bradford and Leeds, but control over very few. In York, for example, Labour was beaten back by a shift to the left among the Liberals after 1905 and recovered only uncertainly before 1914.[12] In contrast to the parliamentary alliance with the Liberals, relations between the two 'progressive' parties at municipal level were often poor, with Labour organisation chipping away at the basis of the Liberal Party and exposing the divisions between 'New Liberals' and supporters of old style retrenchment.

Poplarism and the rise of local Labour 1919–26

A party truce was declared for the local elections in 1914–18, but when contests were resumed in 1919 the results were dramatic – although turnout was low. Labour advanced, in one go, to take control over local authorities in significant areas of urban England, including 12 of the London metropolitan boroughs, three counties (Durham, Monmouthshire and Glamorgan) and the city of Bradford. In other cities, small pre-war Labour groups were transformed into serious contenders for power; in Sheffield Labour leapt from 2 councillors and about 15 per cent of the vote in 1913 to 12 and 45 per cent in 1919; in Liverpool from 17.5 per cent and 7 seats in 1913 to 40.1 per cent and 20 seats in 1919. Labour had arrived in the town halls.[13]

The surge of Labour support in 1919 had far reaching effects. The final collapse of the Liberal Party began in local government. In city after city, the Liberals fell into alliance with the Conservatives to keep rates low and serve local business interests. Local political parties, called 'Citizen', 'Moderate' or 'Progressive' were formed to oppose Labour in some areas such as Southampton, Bristol and Sheffield.[14] In others, such as Wolverhampton, Coventry and York, electoral pacts were arranged between the Liberals and the Conservatives. During the 1920s and 1930s councils that were technically 'hung' were usually run by the Conservatives with the aid of moribund Liberal groups, usually dependent on electoral pacts or the goodwill of the Tories in aldermanic elections.[15]

Anti-Labour pacts, plus a national swing towards the Conservatives, deprived Labour of control of many of the more marginal gains of 1919 over the succeeding years 1920–22, although Labour's share of the vote remained high. Local elections in 1919–22 were marked by hysterical 'red scare' campaigns.[16] A freak swing had given Labour the then middle-class borough of Hackney in 1919, but all Labour councillors lost their seats at the next election in 1922 – despite a cleverly opportunist budget which cut the rate demand to the lowest in London.[17]

The post-1919 Labour councils experimented in various ways with further municipal ownership.[18] In Fulham a municipal laundry service was set up. In Bermondsey, an extensive system of health centres and clinics was introduced by the Labour council under Dr Alfred Salter. A municipal savings bank was established by Walthamstow in 1932. In many authorities municipal provision of electricity was not only a demonstration of social ownership but a useful way of raising revenue without increasing rates.

The Fabian dream of gradually establishing an alternative economy, not based on the market, had some application to local government. Councils were capable of acting as model employers through wages, hours and union rights; their trading arms could often operate more cheaply than those of private contractors. Councils could also use the power of bulk purchases to affect the way businesses operated through 'contract compliance'.[19] The old councils in some London boroughs, or many smaller industrial towns, were very intimate institutions, covering – say – 20,000 to 50,000 people. Many of these areas were more or less single class, particularly in the mining districts. Councillors, officers and manual workers were drawn from the same streets and even families and the actions of some such councils reflected the wishes of the people of the area, regardless of what the law allowed them to do.

Many of the new councillors of 1919 felt that the boundaries of what a council could do for its people were unclear, or there to be tested. There was a difference in tactics and principle between the majority of Labour councillors, like Herbert Morrison in Hackney, who saw councils as a gradualist way of increasing the size of the public sector, providing a set of local services, and showing that Labour was fit to govern, with those who saw councils as a source of power for a confrontation with capitalism. The latter philosophy became known as Poplarism.[20]

Poplarism, named after the east London borough of Poplar, was more than a belief in the power of local government to go its own way. In the analysis of the rebel councillors it reflected the class struggle, and the council was one of several platforms for working class power to press for the transformation of society. When Labour won control of the Poor Law Guardians and Borough Council of Poplar in 1919, councillors used their position to present a series of challenges to the government on rates, the 1923 dock strike, the workings of the Poor Law, wages and sex equality.

Mass unemployment, consistently over a million every year between 1920 and 1940, wrecked the old system of public assistance, which had been designed for temporary and localised distressed areas. The rate burden on poor areas was extreme, and barely relieved by any 'equalisation' of resources from richer areas. The financial crisis was exacerbated in Poplar by the Labour councillors elected to the Poor Law Board of Guardians, who rejected the entire philosophy of the Poor Law. The assumptions of the 1834 Poor Law were still present, in its distinctions between 'deserving' and 'undeserving' poor, the means test and 'less eligibility' which insisted that relief rates were below the lowest local wage rates. George Lansbury, leader of Poplar, described their policy as 'decent treatment for the poor outside the workhouse, and hang the rates!'[21]

The borough council itself, which increased its own spending, decided in 1921 to default on payment of the rate precept[22] to London-wide bodies in protest at the unfair burden on poor ratepayers. The councillors were imprisoned, and the breakdown of local government, and possibly law and order, in parts of east London seemed possible. The government brokered a political deal to get the councillors out of prison and a measure of equalisation was introduced. The councillors' actions were vindicated by electoral success in 1922 and 1925 at a time when other Labour councils were losing ground. Poplar continued to pay generous poor relief, and got into further legal trouble by paying its staff above prevailing levels. The House of Lords ruled in 1925 that this violated the council's role as trustee for the ratepayers ('fiduciary duty') and was unlawful, describing the action as guided 'by some eccentric principles of socialistic philanthropy or by a feminist ambition to secure the equality of the sexes in the matter of wages.'[23] After Poplar, several sets of Labour Poor Law Guardians were removed from office by the Conservative government in 1926–29, including Bedwellty in south Wales,

West Ham and Chester-le-Street. The Poor Law system was collapsing.

Poplarism was a minority strand in Labour local government, and left-wingers increasingly concluded that a council could not do much to affect the big socialist issues of inequality and poverty, and that this sort of thing was better handled nationally. Nye Bevan recalling his father telling him that the council was a very important place, told the House of Commons that:

When I got older I said to myself, 'The place to get is the council. That's where the power is.' So I worked very hard, and, in association with my fellows, when I was about twenty years of age, I got onto the council. I discovered when I got there that the power had been there, but it had just gone. So I made some enquiries, being an earnest student of social affairs, and I learned that the power had slipped down to the county council. That was where it was and where it had gone to. So I worked very hard again and I got there and it had gone from there too.[24]

Labour thinking was increasingly emphasising the benefits of central planning, and technical developments – particularly in electricity – meant that national provision was more efficient than local. Labour government in 1924 – and the election victory of 1929 – proved that Labour was a national party of government, and there was a tendency to 'put away childish things' such as the infant party's dependence on local government and favour a strong central state. In the 1930s even Attlee feared obstructive local authorities and warned that a Labour government might have to send in commissioners to ensure that Whitehall's writ would run.[25]

The Labour Party's thought, as a national party, has neither been consistently localist or centralising, but instrumentalist. The division of power within government has traditionally been subordinate to the wider social aims of the party, and the desire to give the party the maximum say in the nation's affairs. This has meant upholding local autonomy in periods like the first quarter of the century, and the 1980s, when the party has faced a hostile national climate; and downplaying its role when the party has been in power during the 1940s and 1960s – and, so far, during the late 1990s.

However, local Labour has never been a straightforward expression of a national, uniform approach translated into each locality. Until the 1980s the role of local elections and local government was little addressed in academic work on the rise of the Labour Party. The rise of Labour was traditionally told as the emergence of national class interests and the decline of local particularism, but there has been an increasing realisation that it was, in form at least, the coalescence of forces working from the ground up. Granting the importance of national economic trends, it is still important to note the interaction of the rise of Labour with local units of government, economic conditions, social patterns and civic elites. Poplarism and the collapse of anti-socialist municipal forces in the 1920s were the product of the particular circumstances of East London at the time.[26] Municipal politics and the rise of Labour also subsumed, without replacing them with recognisable class politics, local social alignments. Nowhere was this more apparent than in Liverpool, where Labour became aligned with Catholicism because of the sectarianism of the local Conservative elite.[27]

Local Labour and Herbert Morrison 1926–45

The pace of Labour gains in working class areas accelerated during the late 1920s and was only briefly interrupted in 1931. Barnsley was gained in 1927; Rotherham followed in 1928. Labour gained Sheffield in 1926, and has lapsed from control of that city subsequently only in 1932–33, 1968–69 and since May 1999. It was the first of the great cities to enjoy sustained Labour control. The first Labour administration of Sheffield was a source of considerable pride in the party; until the London County Council was gained in 1934 it was Labour's municipal showcase. Labour Sheffield undertook a huge slum clearance programme, building 10,000 new houses and renovating some of the old slums, and invested in new schools and health centres. Sheffield Labour's cheap public transport policy[28] started, with a 25 per cent fares cut and free travel for the disabled on trams. It also undertook welfare provision, compensating workless households in full for the 1931 cut in unemployment benefit. Profits from municipal trams, electricity and other trading were used to improve services rather than reduce rates, as the previous anti-Labour administration had done at the cost of financial instability.[29]

The example of Sheffield was an instructive one; other Labour authorities pursued local priorities, such as the raising of the school leaving age in Barnsley and the massive investment in education in St. Helen's. Perhaps the most radical housing programme was that of Leeds, where Labour took control in November 1933. A new Housing Committee was set up under Charles Jenkinson, and work started almost immediately on the new plan which involved the clearance of 30,000 slums by 1940 and the construction of new estates.[30] The plan was not completed because of problems in the building industry, but the face of Leeds was being transformed well before the blitz and post-war planning policy took effect elsewhere.[31]

The slump of 1929–32 put a heavy burden on local government, because the public assistance system for the poor was administered by the counties and charged against local rates – the poorest areas ended up having to pay the most. It is a tribute to the solidarity of such areas that public assistance was not begrudged, and Labour administrations in Durham and Glamorgan which paid more than the minimum, and operated the means test more humanely than they were supposed to, were re-elected by the ratepayers. In the worst areas, the toll was shocking – Merthyr Tydfil had to charge 15s 6d in the £ (compared to 1s in prosperous areas) for its parsimonious programme, and was trapped in a vicious circle of high rates, declining rateable value and poverty. The burden was lifted somewhat by the government's creation of regional Unemployment Assistance Boards in 1934, which took over 95 per cent of the cost in stages between 1934 and 1937.

Defiance over the poor law was a particularly marked example of a general tendency of inter-war Labour authorities to humanise their services, reduce the harshness of the way welfare services operated, and allow working class people to experience the benefits of open space and culture. School architecture in Norwich was bright and modern. In Glasgow the Labour council ended the scarcely believable system whereby elderly couples claiming poor relief could be split up into separate hostel units; in many authorities such as West Ham and Norwich help was given to the disabled and poor mothers. 'Compassionate professionalism'[32] – humanised but efficient and honest welfare services – became the theme of Labour local government, and in some areas helped the party assemble a base of support reaching well beyond the trade union core.[33]

The hold of anti-Labour 'Independents' and local parties proved harder to break in the great Scottish cities. Despite the reputation of 'Red Clydeside' in the 1920s Labour did not run Glasgow until a minority Labour administration took over in 1933. It was faced with the appalling and overwhelming problems of poverty and bad housing – 19 per cent of the population on public assistance welfare (administered by the council) and 40,000 families living in one room accommodation. 60,000 houses had been built by Glasgow Corporation by 1947 by the Labour council and its predecessors, although the first large slum clearance took place in 1957.[34]

By the mid-1930s Labour had recovered the ground lost during 1930–32, and was in control of most of its old strongholds again. It slowly advanced into new territory such as the more working class cathedral cities of Norwich and Lincoln, which were captured in 1933, and Bristol (1937). But the biggest breakthrough was the capture of the most powerful and prestigious local authority in Britain, the London County Council, in 1934. It was a strong sign that Labour was on the way back from its 1931 disaster, and a chance to exercise executive power on a large scale. Like other Labour authorities of the 1930s, the LCC demonstrated 'responsible' government and avoided the confrontational politics of Poplarism. It was the making of Herbert Morrison, who had shuttled back and forth between parliament and London local government during the 1920s and early 1930s, serving as Minister of Transport in the 1929–31 government.

An indication of the assertiveness of Morrison's LCC was the demolition of the old Waterloo Bridge. An architecturally well regarded monument, it was however crumbling and incapable of carrying the volume of traffic expected of it. Discussions had meandered on for ten years between London councils and the government, but within ten weeks of taking over, Morrison ordered demolition work to start. The government, though furious, could do nothing because the LCC could pay for it out of current expenditure, which was not subject to government control, rather than having to borrow the money. The LCC also started an immense programme of slum clearance and construction of council houses. The LCC ran its own hospital service, which was by far the largest municipal health service in Britain. The LCC health service influenced Labour Party thinking through Somerville Hastings, a doctor who served on the LCC and later in parliament. Hastings chaired the national Labour Party's panel on post-war health policy and produced its influential report in 1943.

Morrison imposed a strict code of conduct on his LCC Labour group, banning councillors even from having dinner with officers or contractors. Morrison's drive for municipalisation was related to his ethical standards; the corruption, inefficiency and high costs of private contractors he had witnessed in London local government in the 1920s gave him a lifelong dislike of this kind of private enterprise. During his time in office the LCC became known as an honestly and efficiently run authority, and Labour was triumphantly re-elected in 1937, gaining six seats from the 'Municipal Reform' (Tory) party on a surge in turnout. Morrison had engaged the services of professional public relations advisers, the first time such techniques had been used in a local election.[35] Morrison joined the wartime Cabinet in 1940.

Morrison was one of relatively few Labour leaders to have emerged from local politics to national positions of leadership. Clement Attlee and George Lansbury had also served in London boroughs. It is perhaps a sign of the decline in the importance of local government, and Labour's increasing familiarity with Whitehall, that few among the two generations of Labour leaders to follow Morrison and Attlee had any local government experience. Attlee was the last Labour leader to have been a councillor, let alone a council leader. Since then, only David Blunkett has happily made the transition from local boss to national leader; Ted Short had briefly led Newcastle Labour Group before joining Wilson's Cabinet.

Labour councils in the welfare state 1945–75

In the round of local government elections held over from the war – for which the franchise was brought roughly into line with that for parliamentary elections[36] – the triumphs of the 1945 general election were repeated. Labour swept most of the provincial cities and large towns[37] for the first time and were to control most of them for most of the time until the late 1960s. The most working class areas, already overwhelmingly Labour in the 1930s, became even more solid after 1945. The parties battled it out in the large cities and mixed towns, such as York (also a parliamentary marginal) which changed hands in 1945, 1949, 1954, 1959, 1961, 1965, 1966, 1967 and 1973.[38] Moderate[39] Labour groups controlled working class councils, and moderate Tories controlled suburbs and seaside resorts. In rural areas, various shades of 'Independent', gradually being replaced by Conservatives coming out of the closet, were hardly challenged. Political control in local government had settled down into stability, even atrophy. The same individuals often held leadership positions for decades: Richard Crossman, minister for local government 1964–66, observed when visiting Southampton that the leader of the council was 74 and the chair of planning was 78: 'the usual age, I'm afraid, in Labour local authorities.'[40]

Local electoral behaviour was also becoming more sensitive to the ebb and flow of support for the national parties. In the late 1920s a Liberal revival on the national stage was not reflected in local elections, and in the 1930s London Labour were unable to translate their local dominance into strength in the 1935 general election – a pattern found also in provincial cities. But in 1945 the municipal campaign was fought as an extension of the general election, with electors from Essex to Leeds being urged to 'forge the link' between Labour Whitehall and town hall and ensure that the government's plans would not be obstructed.[41] The national parties became more interested in local elections during the post war period as an indicator of support and a means of keeping their electoral machines in working order.[42]

There was little traffic in the other direction. Labour local government was generally the province of the right of the party, which had become thoroughly integrated into local 'establishments' and generally avoided putting up the rates or making a fuss. Local authorities rarely impinged on national politics. There was a flurry of concern in the late 1950s, highlighted by Rab Butler in a Conservative broadcast, about 'authoritarian' tendencies in Labour local authorities such as Nottingham and Hugh Gaitskell was not the last Labour leader to be worried by the activities of local authorities. At the 1959 conference he criticised the 'apparently arbitrary and intolerant' conduct of some councils and in the post mortems of the 1959 election defeat the National Executive Committee (NEC) considered that some Labour Groups had 'detracted from the image of the party.'[43]

The Labour Party nationally had started to co-ordinate local government activities. In the inter-war period, Labour groups were left more or less to look after themselves; a Fabian newsletter for Labour councillors edited by William Robson[44] folded in 1931 and was not replaced, and the model standing orders for Labour groups were when first issued in 1930 not strictly enforced. In 1936 a local government department was established at Transport House, although the next moves were not until 1954, when a newsletter for groups was re-established, 1955 when an NEC subcommittee was set up, and 1956 when the annual local government conference was introduced.[45] The Conservatives made most of these moves in the 1940s.

Local government had, however, changed its role within the public sector. Ironically, 'Morrisonian' nationalisation removed many of the powers with which municipal socialism was mainly concerned. Gas and electricity were nationalised, and the National Health Service transferred most health provision to the national level. Although the socialists of boroughs such as Bermondsey supported the NHS, they ruefully realised that the standard of provision in their areas would be 'levelled down'.

Instead, local government after 1945 became the primary delivery system for several important nationally controlled welfare state functions – state education and public housing. In the 1960s and 1970s social services became increasingly important. Housekeeping functions such as street cleaning and lighting, refuse collection, environmental health, plus leisure and libraries remained, as did planning. In the decade after 1945 Labour councils were important players in post-war reconstruction of city centres.[46] Local authorities spent around one third of general government expenditure – 15 per cent of GDP by the 1970s – and ran many of the public sector operations most visible to the citizen.

However, these functions were grafted onto a tier of government which had traditionally been geared to 'housekeeping' functions. The patchwork structure of counties, county boroughs, municipal boroughs, urban districts and rural districts, funded by rates charged against an increasingly fictitious rateable value,[47] was an increasingly creaky machine for delivering important welfare services. Despite its importance in the welfare state, and the constant concern of national politicians with improving the capacity of local government, central-local relations and the internal politics of local authorities was rather a backwater of the political scene.

In practice, whatever the ideology of local councillors, there were quite strong constraints. Even if Conservative councillors wished to do so, the law prohibited local attempts to dismantle the welfare state, and central government gave financial incentives to spend. On the other hand, Labour councillors were hemmed in by the *ultra vires*[48] rule and fear of the electoral consequences of raising such a crude tax as the rates.[49] Amateur councillors were frequently content to follow the lead of professional officers. The existence or otherwise of something which could be called a post-war consensus is a matter of debate, but at municipal level there were wide areas in which there was little to choose between the parties.[50] In Leeds, political differences were apparent over private housebuilding and comprehensive education, but there was agreement on transport, social services, leisure, the environment and even on the desirability of housing clearance and low council rents.[51] Even so, recent work has tended to emphasise the intense political squalls that would flare up within this framework, such as the local furore over Nottingham's suspension of its Chief Constable in 1959.[52]

Council rents were a major political battleground in the post-war politics of local government. Labour councils often took the view that low rents for tenants of council houses was an important policy in support of working class interests. The Conservatives, by contrast, tended to favour raising council rents towards 'market' levels and compensating those on low incomes through a system of rebates. This philosophy was apparent in the period following the Rent Act 1957. Riots took place in Euston Road and on north London council estates when a Conservative controlled council in St. Pancras raised rents in 1960. A more serious confrontation took place in 1972 when the Heath government brought forward the Housing Finance Act, which required a series of rent increases. Many Labour authorities were extremely reluctant to implement it, and in the climate of the time several defied the Act but only one, the small Clay Cross Urban District in the Derbyshire coalfield, took defiance to the point of surcharge and disqualification.

Housebuilding was more consensual. Labour councils played an important part in the housing reconstruction that followed the war. Pre-war slums, and areas destroyed by bombing, had created a desperate need for new houses which was reflected by the 1945–51 government. The Conservatives shared the desire to build houses, and when they returned to power in 1951 the drive was accelerated. There were, however, two differences. One was that private housebuilding was to be more strongly encouraged; the other was that the standards were reduced. From the mid 1950s on, progressively larger areas were cleared and rebuilt, often using system building to put up large estates and tower blocks relatively quickly. Between 1955 and 1975 three million people were moved as a result of redevelopment.[53] The effect on individual cities could be massive; Richard Crossman visisted Manchester on 8 January 1965 to see the disastrous Hulme estate under construction:

They briefed me very well in the town hall and then took me to the top of a skyscraper to see the great area of slums they have cleared in the centre of the city ... It must be the largest hole ever created in a big city in the history of modern conurbations. I found myself impressed by the clearance but depressed by the standard of the houses with which they are filling it.[54]

The high rise boom was abruptly ended with the explosion at Ronan Point in Newham in 1968, but the problems it caused lingered on. Industrialised housing and town centre redevelopment, stagnant local leadership and the secrecy of local authority business combined to produce another blot on the record of post-war Labour local government: corruption.

T Dan Smith and Redcliffe-Maud 1955–75

The interface of government, particularly amateur government, and business always presents possibilities for corruption. The amount of money involved in the housing programme and town centre redevelopments was astronomical by the standards of many councillors,[55] and corrupt influence of councillors become systematised by John Poulson, an architect, and T Dan Smith, a senior Labour politician from Newcastle.[56]

Dan Smith was the most notable figure of Labour local government in the 1960s. Unlike many local government leaders, he had a clear vision of the future of his city and region. Under his leadership, Newcastle was 'modernised' in an accelerated way. New, innovative estates – such as the Byker 'wall' – replaced slum terraces, and there was an ambitious programme of public building and road construction. Much of the new Newcastle has worn far better than the 1960s changes to other cities, like Manchester and Birmingham, which were being undone by the 1990s. Smith also pressed the case for devolution, not just to Scotland but to the regions of England, and hoped that the Regional Economic Planning Councils set up by the Wilson government in 1964 would evolve into elected regional organs of government. He even made space for 124 elected members in the chamber and facilities of the new Newcastle civic centre, in the hope that it would one day become the seat of the North East regional government.[57]

Smith's admirable side was accompanied by corrupt activities on behalf of John Poulson, a mediocre architect (Smith kept his buildings out of the new Newcastle) in other areas. He recruited the formidable Andy Cunningham, boss of County Durham (and member of the National Executive Committee of the Labour Party), and leading figures in other Labour authorities such as Wandsworth, Mexborough and Pontefract to the Poulson network. Poulson went bankrupt in 1972, and his collapse implicated Smith and his allies. The Poulson affair cast a shadow over Labour local government (although Liberals and Conservatives were also involved), and exposed how the closed and secretive ways some councils did business could degenerate into crime. The NEC established a special committee to investigate Labour local government, which reported in July 1975. It recommended a series of measures aimed at opening up local leadership and preventing the same people serving too long as committee chairs or having a dual leadership role on the council and in the local party organisation.[58]

As well as the wave of arrests, resignations and quiet retirements that followed the Poulson bankruptcy, the world of local government in the early 1970s was disrupted by other factors. First was the result of the unpopularity of the Wilson government in 1967–69. More than ever, it was clear that national factors determined local election results. Labour lost nearly every single council in these years, including Glasgow, Sunderland and Sheffield and the London boroughs of Lambeth and Islington which were controlled by the Conservatives from 1968 to 1971. Only a few councils, in the mining heartlands of South Wales and the industrial north – plus odd scattered pockets like Bridgwater in Somerset – survived.

When Labour returned to local government power in the early 1970s, the scene was changed. Many of the councillors defeated in the late 1960s were too old to come back, and a newer – often more left wing – set of Labour councillors took over. The shock to the system provided by the freak Conservative victories also galvanised local Labour to perform better. In some authorities such as Lambeth, the Tories had been a high-spending, modernising force and done more to build houses and improve services than their Labour predecessors.[59]

These political currents were followed, and heightened, by reorganisation. The Labour government had appointed a Royal Commission, under Redcliffe-Maud – and with T Dan Smith as an member – to redraw the map of English local government and produce a more rational division of powers. It reported in 1969[60] in favour of large 'unitary' local authorities in most of England, plus a two tier system in the metropolitan areas. The incoming Conservative government of 1970 chose instead to have two tier counties and districts everywhere.[61]

However the boundaries were to be drawn, the national establishment was agreed that councils had to become larger and more professionally managed. There was much debate about the 'calibre' of councillors and what might be done to raise it. A certain amount of this, as critics pointed out, was the professional middle class complaining about working class people running things. Larger authorities would mean fewer elected councillors, hopefully of higher quality. It would also allow a reshaping of management according to modern corporate lines, and thereby make local government into a political and administrative system fit to run important parts of the welfare state.

The map of the counties was redrawn along what seemed more rational lines. Two sorts were created – six metropolitan counties around the large conurbations outside London, and 47 (8 Wales, 39 England) 'shire' counties covering the other areas. Below them was a uniform structure of district (and metro district) councils – old titles such as 'borough' persisted only in an honorific sense.[62] New counties were created at Avon and

Humberside, and local people found themselves ruled by authorities with strange names like 'Babergh' and 'Restormel'.

Elections for all these bodies took place in April and May 1973, a time when Labour was doing relatively well in the polls, but the period after reorganisation was not a happy one for Labour local government. In contrast to the good results was the first Labour collapse to take place against the tide – the sudden Liberal surge in Liverpool. Dan Smith's network was being picked apart in a series of journalistic investigations and well publicised trials. The costs were still being counted for the disastrous spread of system built housing during the 1960s. Many new local units had trouble establishing local loyalties, or – as London boroughs had in 1964 – had trouble reconciling the disparate smaller councils they absorbed. Some did not help themselves in the climate of concern over standards in public life by spending heavily on new town halls before local electorates noticed any improvement in services. In 1974–76 the system of local finance was coming under serious attack for the first time, as a revaluation and a series of massive rate rises caused by inflation and rising spending generated huge middle class dissatisfaction. This was reflected in the Conservative pledge to abolish rates in their October 1974 campaign, and in the Labour government's establishment of the Layfield committee to investigate local finance.[63]

In local authorities themselves, the traditional way of doing things was coming under challenge, particularly in the Labour Party.[64] The early concern of Labour councils with humanising the delivery of local services seemed to have been forgotten, as leadership groups stagnated into cliques and became part of a machine. Local residents, particularly working class people, were increasingly regarded as numbers: 'applicants' and 'cases'. People were moved across cities because of the dictates of comprehensive planning, and in many cases subject to bureaucratic restrictions such as control over the external appearance of their houses.[65]

In May 1975, as a national fiscal crisis loomed, Environment Secretary Tony Crosland coined a phrase at a local government dinner in Manchester which was to symbolise the end of more than the local government spending boom:

With its usual spirit of patriotism and its tradition of service to the community's needs, [local government] is coming to realise that, for the time being at least, the party is over.[66]

The left in local government in the 1980s

Some guests were unwilling to leave, and the party ended with a fight. Local government was the main political battleground of the

1980s. It was the scene of a clash of ideologies between some Labour controlled authorities and the Thatcher government; bitter divisions within the Labour Party; and a radical change in the relationship between central and local government.[67]

The politics of Labour party membership shifted decisively to the left in the early 1970s; but the left itself had changed since the 1950s, when it had emphasised national and international affairs which were not within local government's terms of reference. Dissatisfaction with the record of nationalised industries, and the failure of statist communism in eastern Europe, led to a growing interest in alternative economic models. Now, the emphasis on decentralisation, workers' control, participation and rights for women and minorities seemed to fit well with levels of government below the central state. The left also regarded local politics as an arena to prove that it could do better than centre-right Labour governments had done.[68] The disruption of local government in 1967–74 created an opportunity to translate these trends into action in some areas, and with left-wing organisation at its peak during the factional warfare of 1976–83 it was a relatively simple task to increase the left's strength on local councils.

With the election of the Thatcher government in 1979 the scene was set for confrontation. Local authorities were the front line of many of the welfare and public services the Conservatives now wished to cut.[69] The government did not have much power to force local authorities to do its bidding, and Labour local government was decreasingly willing to help voluntarily, as it had done in 1975 and on previous occasions. The left regarded councils as part of an extra-parliamentary mode of opposition, alongside trade unions and community groups; the moderate left David Blunkett called Labour town halls 'a rudimentary opposition movement against the ruling party in Westminster.'[70]

As in the 1920s the new left felt that the traditional boundaries of local government responsibilities should be pushed back, given the unsympathetic presence of a Conservative government. The new left took a broader view of the role of local authorities than provision of certain specified services and felt that a council had a local mandate which gave it a watching brief over the economy, society and culture in its area.[71] The national economic context also produced new responses from local authorities. Rising unemployment, as it had in the 1930s, led councils to examine what might be done and some, such as the GLC and the West Midlands County Council, set up local economic development policies.[72] The employment policies of the left councils aimed at promoting industrial democracy, co-operatives and trade unionism as well as providing jobs.

The most distinctive feature of the left-wing councils of the 1980s was not, however, their economic policies but the cultural change they were trying to bring to local government. Left town halls tried to be open to community groups outside the council and disrupt the traditional networks of power and secrecy. Their politics was based on a rejection of the paternalism of Morrisonian and post-war local government; the centralisation of post-war governments of both parties; and the economic conception of freedom stressed by Thatcherite Conservatism. They also had a view of society influenced by the women's movement, anti-racism and gay liberation rather than 'labourism' or a solidaristic 'local community', although they shared the traditional left concern with high spending and trade unionism. A political trend, known pejoratively as the 'loony left' or more neutrally as the 'new urban left' was established.[73] The number of councils applying the whole package was relatively small, and concentrated in London and a few other big cities such as Manchester. Some other councils took up parts of the agenda, such as Southampton, Basildon and Bristol and important Labour councils such as Birmingham and Newcastle remained under more traditional rule during the 1980s.[74]

The Greater London Council (GLC) from 1981 to 1986 was the best-publicised left-controlled council.[75] Its headquarters was just across the river from the Palace of Westminster and it was easy for the media to cover. Its leader, Ken Livingstone, was an unusually colourful and articulate local leader, whose opinions outraged the tabloid press while his presentational skills won him surprisingly broad support. The Conservative government was sufficiently worried and outraged by his challenge that the GLC and the metropolitan county councils were abolished in 1986. While the legislation went through in 1983–84, Livingstone ran a populist campaign against this removal of Londoners' democratic rights which was one of the few inspiring moments of opposition in the mid 1980s. Labour are to restore elected London-wide local government in 2000.

The GLC's handicap, which it turned into an advantage, was that it controlled relatively few services. The centrepiece of the 1981 London Labour manifesto was a 25 per cent cut in London Transport fares, a policy called 'Fares Fair'. Thanks to a rather eccentric House of Lords judgement this was ruled out, although a more subtle cheap fares policy replaced it before the government removed London Transport from GLC control in 1984. After the

Fares Fair defeat, the GLC looked around for ways to spend money. One result was the programme of grants to voluntary groups, which cost £47 million in 1984–85 (£100 million at 1999 prices), which included subventions to a range of minority groups. This priority was also apparent in the structure of the council, which was reshaped to produce new committees to cover various social groups.

The first women's committee was established by the GLC in 1981, and around one in ten local authorities established one at some stage in the next twelve years.[76] The GLC committee remained the best funded, spending £9 million in 1986. The main efforts of women's committees were put into changing employment policies and working conditions of local authorities, and distributing funds to voluntary groups.

The same was true of the 'minority' causes adopted by the new urban left councils. Most of them governed areas with a high proportion of ethnic minority residents who were poorly served by the traditional style of local government and Labour politics: in some areas councils pursued racially discriminatory housing policies and several Labour councils, particularly in the West Midlands, had pressed central government for immigration control in the early 1960s. A range of local government services and policies, such as housing criteria, recruitment for manual employment, fostering, training and policing, were, in effect, racist. The response was to set up race relations committees and units within the local authority, with wide powers to develop anti-racist policies. Anti-racist policies were introduced throughout personnel and education departments, and made the focus of several council-sponsored festivals.

There was minimal black representation on councils before the 1980s – and only 165 black councillors by 1986 – but London councils were becoming a route for black and Asian politicians to advance within the Labour power structure. Bernie Grant became leader of Haringey council in 1985 and MP for Tottenham in 1987; Paul Boateng moved from chairing the GLC's Police Committee to parliament, and thence to ministerial office in 1997.

At the time, the most controversial initiatives of the GLC, some London boroughs and Manchester concerned gay rights. As with women and race, employment policy and funding for voluntary groups followed, as did campaigns to present positive images of gay people and create a supportive environment in schools and society in general. In 1986–87 a ferocious press campaign was unleashed against councils such as Haringey and Ealing for clumsy gay rights initiatives, which contributed to

Labour's poor image in the run-up to the 1987 election. Patricia Hewitt, in a leaked memo to Neil Kinnock in early 1987, warned that the 'lesbian and gay rights issue is costing us dear, particularly among the pensioners' and Labour lost three seats against the trend in London. This was followed by government legislation – the notorious Clause 28 – to ban the 'promotion' of homosexuality by education authorities.[77] But in the longer term, the councils did contribute to the growth of homosexual equality. The demand for equal rights was quickly assimilated by the party leadership, and by providing a supportive climate councils encouraged increasingly confident gay communities to emerge in London and Manchester to the benefit of society and the local economy. They also contributed to the acceptance of gay people at all levels of politics, leading to the unremarkable presence of openly gay Cabinet ministers. Like the Poplar councillors, their aims had become assimilated into the mainstream.

By the 1990s, few in the Labour Party – and increasingly few in political life – would dissent from the aims of these policies, though there was considerable resistance at the time. Policies on equal employment opportunities, providing for working women, anti-racism, consultation, even support for local businesses, have been absorbed by the political mainstream. Many left-wing councils proved popular with local voters and had no trouble getting re-elected. The left greatly advanced the cause of women, blacks and gays within the political system; the story of the 1980s and 1990s would have been different had the councils not pursued these policies. The party leadership reluctantly came round to the view that all women shortlists were necessary in 1992–93, a step which would have been impossible had the local left not raised the profile of sex equality. The emphasis the left-wing councils placed on racial equality has contributed to a wider consciousness of the complexities of urban Britain's multiracial society. The 1999 Macpherson Report into the murder of Stephen Lawrence was an official recognition that a lot of what the left had been saying in the 1980s about institutional racism and police misconduct had been true.

However, the inexperience and zeal of the councillors in the 1980s sometimes led to blunders in implementing them. Questions over racist and sexist language, and personnel disputes over individual behaviour, could escalate into massive disputes and led to a 'climate of fear' among staff in some authorities such as Brent. Political life in some, such as Lambeth, became contaminated for years with sectarianism and there were ugly incidents of violence and intimidation, even within Labour groups. Despite the inaccuracy of tabloid scares about – fictitious – council bans on black bin liners and the like, there were genuine cases in which well intentioned policies proved divisive failures.

The aim of opening up council decision making also caused problems; community involvement would sometimes involve little more than co-option of activists who shared the political agenda, and often ward Labour Party membership, of councillors. This was hardly more democratic than the networks it replaced. There was an additional problem with industrial relations. Many new groups were committed never to implement job losses, and conditioned to accept every union demand as legitimate. Added to ideology, there was party structure. Council workers and their unions were often strong forces in local Labour Parties, and with the early 1980s emphasis on accountability to the party, councillors often found themselves accountable to the people they were supposed to negotiate with in the workplace. This problem was most intense where 'workerist' attitudes pervaded the local party, like Liverpool and Southwark. In Southwark and Hackney this led to appalling scandals involving abuse of old people and children; more usually, it resulted simply in weak management. Mistrust of officers also contributed in some councils to the virtual destruction of management systems;[78] in others, political criteria entered the professional bureaucracy. These pathologies of management were found in their most highly developed form in Liverpool.

Liverpool was a uniquely problematic part of the local left.[79] Liverpool's economy, in trouble in the 1970s, collapsed in the early 1980s; unemployment rose to 27 per cent in 1985. Parts of the city were drastically depopulated, and Toxteth burned in the 1981 riots. The city's housing stock had large quantities both of decaying old buildings and nightmarish new estates such as Netherley. Liberal minority administrations in 1973–83 had kept rates low, allowing services to deteriorate, and making life difficult when cuts were demanded.[80] Labour defeated the Liberals in the 1983 local elections and took control of the council. What followed was one of the strangest episodes in the history of local government.

Liverpool Labour politics had been influenced since the 1950s by the Trotskyite Militant organisation,[81] which became increasingly important in the early 1980s. Although never a majority on the council, Militant effectively controlled the Labour Group through strong organisation and alliance in caucuses with fellow travelling 'Broad Left' councillors and activists.[82] The public face of Liverpool was not its leader, but the flamboyant

Militant deputy leader, Derek 'Degsy' Hatton. Militant was helped by the extremely powerful position of the Liverpool District Labour Party (DLP), which was accustomed to choosing the council leader and committee chairs as well as pronouncing on policy. This was in blatant disregard of national policy. The post-Poulson special committee decided that:

Party branches must insist that Labour councillors shall report back and also hear the views of party members. Although this reporting back is essential, under no circumstances must there be any attempt to *instruct* councillors as to how they should vote, which has happened in some areas.[83]

This rule was broken in many areas because of the concern for 'accountability', but only in Liverpool was power so systematically transferred from the council Group to the party outside. A Labour Party inquiry into Liverpool in 1985–86 found that this shift was accompanied by a widespread culture of intimidation and threat.

Understandably, Marxist Liverpool was obsessed with housing and improving the quality of the inner city environment through the creation of new parks and sports centres, and the results were an improvement on previous councils run by all parties. But Militant also used the council, by far the largest employer in the city, as a source of jobs for its members, setting up new advisory departments and giving Militant shop stewards control over appointments in some sections. A Static Security Force, run by a neighbour of Derek Hatton's whose previous experience as a nightclub bouncer was his sole qualification for the job, started to appear at City Hall and DLP meetings.

The main priority of the council was propaganda ('raising consciousness') for class conflict. It added the slogan 'a socialist council' to Liverpool's official logo and presided over continual protests and 'days of action' in which council workers and even school pupils were officially encouraged to participate. The broad intention was spelled out in the 1982 city manifesto:

The entire strategy of the District Labour Party is based upon the premise that the Council position should be used as a political platform to expose the bankruptcy of capitalism, educate the working class and provide a political leadership on a local level to ensure a fight back against the Tory policy of cuts in public expenditure.

Liverpool leaders successfully confronted the government in 1984, but their triumphalism after managing this feat made the Tories determined to crack down on future rebellions – including the ratecapping revolt which took place in spring 1985.

The Conservative government used steadily more drastic tactics to press down on council spending; in 1984 it took the power to set maximum rate levels for named councils. With the Liverpool experience in mind, the affected councils agreed to avoid setting a rate until the government backed down. But the tactic failed, and the councils set rates one by one after warnings from the District Auditors that, pushed beyond a certain point, the tactic was illegal. Labour groups were bitterly divided by the collapse of the ratecapping revolt, and it was bitterly regretted by some of its leaders such as Margaret Hodge of Islington. Two councils, Liverpool and Lambeth, kept up the fight through summer 1985 and as a result their councillors were disqualified from office and surcharged. Even when Liverpool set a rate, it was insufficient to cover spending and Liverpool's finance officers warned that there would be no money to pay staff. Ninety-day redundancy notices were issued to Liverpool council employees. This shattered the support for Militant among town hall unions and outraged the leadership, who felt it was time to act. At the 1985 party conference, Neil Kinnock launched an attack on:

the grotesque chaos of a Labour council – a *Labour* council – hiring taxis to scuttle around a city handing out redundancy notices to its own workers ... you can't play politics with people's jobs.[85]

The Labour Party moved against Militant in Liverpool in 1985–86, expelling most of its leadership. The DLP remained under NEC tutelage for a considerable time. In more normal left-wing authorities, there was a retreat from confrontational tactics, and a greater stress on cultural politics. In some authorities spending levels were maintained despite ratecapping through 'creative accounting' and a hope that Labour would win the 1987 election and bail out councils in financial difficulties.

Even had Labour won, it is doubtful whether the cavalry would have arrived for the left-wing councils. The leadership had, by 1987, an exaggerated fear, even hatred, for the activities of the local left. This was a replay of the debates between Herbert Morrison and the supporters of Poplarism; Neil Kinnock feared that their antics would detract from Labour's statesmanlike image, and alienate traditional working class voters.

After the election, there was an outbreak of 'new realism' on the local left, in which Labour councillors had little choice but to stay in office and work within the system. The politics of Labour party membership was shifting away from the hard left. Some of the more left-wing councillors retired, disillusioned; others adapted to the new climate. Unity broke out in some perennially divided Labour groups, such as Manchester. Leaders such as Margaret Hodge (Islington) and Graham Stringer (Manchester) implemented packages of cuts with a surprising degree of party support: according to Stringer the 1988 council budget was 'the first time that the Labour group had voted all together since the cuts battles of the mid-seventies.'[86]

Local government after the left 1987–99

The 1980s, like the 1920s, were an exceptional period in Labour local government, but the collapse of the 'revolt' and the re-election of the Conservatives in 1987 brought the confrontational phase to an end. The politics of the Labour Party grass roots membership was changing, under the impact of successive election defeats and new political thinking – Neil Kinnock and Roy Hattersley won the 1988 leadership election in the CLPs by a comfortable margin. There was no appetite any more for experiment, and local Labour fell in behind the safety first strategy of the 1987–92 parliament.

Local authorities faced serious challenges from central government. Compulsory competitive tendering (CCT) was introduced in 1988, and control over education and housing was chipped away through 'opting out' and Housing Action Trusts (HATs). These changes proved less dramatic than local Labour feared, or the government hoped. In-house bids from council staff often proved competitive and able to win the CCT contracts, and relatively few schools chose to opt out. HATs were unpopular at the start, but as the 1990s progressed councils increasingly devolved control over their housing stocks to tenant management groups in order to gain access to increased central government money.[87] In some areas, economic development was handed over by the government to Urban Development Corporations, but except for the London Docklands Development Corporation (LDDC) these detracted surprisingly little from the role of local authorities.

Economic development policies were becoming increasingly traditional and market-oriented, with Labour councils vying to attract inward investment and build themselves up as retail and tourism centres. Southampton's relatively left-wing council was popular among property developers for its ambitious city centre plans, and Sheffield set up a partnership with business to redevelop a large part of the city abandoned by steel closures. Councils became more imaginative in the use of 'planning gain' to require developers to provide parks and facilities, and low cost housing, in exchange for permission to build. Small scale projects had a happier history than the prestige projects some authorities favoured as a method of improving the infrastructure and reviving the economy. Sheffield and Manchester bid successfully for sporting championships, but Sheffield was left severely out of pocket from hosting the World Student Games in 1991; the city's finances were disrupted for years. Birmingham had an ambitious scheme to build a virtually complete new city centre in the 'Heartlands' project, but could also boast a successful new International Convention Centre that hosted a European summit in 1992.

Local authorities were involved in developing alternative strategies of service provision, based more on the voluntary sector, and in assembling coalitions of local firms and community groups, than expanding direct municipal provision.[88] A few Labour councils such as Lewisham and York remedied the neglect of management and service delivery during the mid 1980s and introduced charters and guaranteed standards of service for local citizens before the Major government and its Citizen's Charter.

The biggest challenge came from the Community Charge, universally known as the poll tax, which was introduced in Scotland in 1989 and England and Wales in 1990. In introducing it, the government had intended to eliminate Labour local government by imposing severe costs on all local voters whenever a council spent more than the Department of the Environment considered a 'standard' level. The implementation of the tax was severely flawed, as local government politicians and professional associations had warned, and it proved nearly impossible to administer.[89]

Despite the inegalitarian basis of the tax, and its bungled implementation, the option of illegal resistance was by this time deeply unpopular with most Labour councillors, and only isolated individuals and Trotskyites supported it. Non-payment of the tax was a major issue leading to the breakaway of former Militant activists to form a separate party with appreciable support in Glasgow and Liverpool, but was rapidly dismissed as impractical by nearly every other strand of Labour local government. But many councillors were critical of the national party's failure to campaign sufficiently vigorously against it before it became law.

The poll tax briefly made local government and its financing the main subject of national debate, and caused a surge of interest in the May 1990 local elections. Labour won sweeping victories everywhere except a few parts of west London because of the hatred which had built up for the tax since bills had been sent out in April. It was an important reason for the unpopularity that toppled Margaret Thatcher in November 1990; the last round of that grudge match went to Labour councils. The scrapping of the tax was announced in March 1991; it was replaced by a 'council tax', based on property values, in 1993. But in contrast to the rates, which had raised half of local authority revenue, the council tax only produced about 15 per cent, and that was restricted by government-set maximums. Local fiscal autonomy was virtually destroyed by the poll tax.

A rather chaotic process of local government reorganisation also followed the poll tax. Many of the provincial cities, including Southampton and Bristol, regained county borough 'unitary' status, to the satisfaction of ruling Labour groups. Nationally, Labour reached record strength in local government in the 1990s, because of successive years of acute Conservative unpopularity. The peak year was 1995, when Labour won control of many small town and rural district councils, such as St. Edmundsbury (Suffolk) and East Northamptonshire. Many of these gains, such as suburban Castle Point (Essex) and seaside Thanet (Kent) foreshadowed gains at the 1997 general election.[90]

The Conservative government's unpopularity in 1985, and again in 1993, deprived the party of control over many of their traditional strongholds. In 1993 only Buckinghamshire withstood the advances of Labour and the Liberal Democrats; in 1985 councils such as East Sussex and Berkshire slipped beyond Tory control for the first time since their creation in 1888. In few of these councils could Labour mount a credible bid for an absolute majority, so the opportunity created by the hung councils was the greatest chance many county Labour groups had of exerting power. The national party's standing orders banned them from entering formal coalitions, but in many areas informal arrangements were made with the SDP-Liberal Alliance or the Liberal Democrats. In Oxfordshire and Berkshire, this spilled over into local electoral pacts in 1989, despite the disapproval of Walworth Road. After 1993, the ban was relaxed and a formal coalition was agreed in Berkshire. After 1997, this was taken a step further in Hertfordshire where a joint 'Administration Group' was formed including both Labour and Liberal Democrat councillors.

These revived progressive coalitions, and good relations between the Liberal Democrats and the Blair government at Westminster, contrasted strongly with confrontation in other areas. Years of unpopularity had removed the Conservatives from contention in most of the traditionally marginal cities, and the role of main opposition to Labour was ceded to the Liberal Democrats – even in cities such as Southampton and Birmingham, Tory controlled as late as 1984. The party system in local government was reminiscent of the 1920s in its range of different party systems in different areas. By the end of the century, Labour had been in power in its strongholds for nearly thirty years, and in most of the previously marginal cities for at least fourteen years. The party now faces the consequences of staleness, and occasionally corruption, that can develop with prolonged power.

Local government became an increasingly important training ground for national politicians during the 1980s and 1990s. Two thirds of the 183–strong 1997 intake of Labour MPs had previous experience as local councillors, 80 of those in the area they were subsequently elected MPs. A number of former council leaders won representation, including Alan Whitehead (Southampton City Council leader 1984–92), Bob Laxton (Derby council leader 1986–88, 1994–97), and Graham Stringer, long serving leader of Manchester City Council 1984–96. The new OMOV method of selection introduced in 1993 was felt to have favoured known local leaders because they tend to be better known to the mass local party membership.[91] But there is little sense that ex-councillors form a cohesive bloc pressing for local government. The New Labour constitutional agenda has concentrated on devolution, parliamentary reform and individual rights than restoring local authorities.

The Blair government's agenda for local government is modest.[92] Some of the more stringent restrictions on how councils can raise and spend money have been lifted, and the Department of the Environment is now encouraging another round of managerial reform, including the creation of an executive cabinet system and directly-elected executive mayoralties in the larger cities. There is also the possibility of proportional representation in local elections. Turnout in local elections has sunk to levels not seen since the inter-war period, with only 29 per cent voting in May 1999 (compared to over 40 per cent during the 1980s) and fewer than 10 per cent in some urban wards. Local government as currently constituted evidently fails to convince many electors that it is important. The 20th century of Labour local government ends placidly – complacently – with the dreams of the Fabians fading away.

Local government has often been an embarrassment to the Labour Party, its radical defiance in the 1920s and the 1980s conflicting with the national leadership's desire to prove to sceptical voters that the party was fit to govern. In the post war period it was noted more for misguided mass housing policies, paternalism and corruption than its achievements on behalf of local people. The record is far from wholly negative, however.

Local authorities have foreshadowed key elements of the party's shifting ideological appeal, including public ownership in the first years of the century and a humane and efficient welfare system in the 1920s and 1930s. The politics of social inclusion with which Labour successfully ends the century owes much to the initiatives that came through local government in the 1980s, and many Labour politicians had their first taste of office through local authorities. The party's interest in local government as a sphere of activity has been inversely related to its success as a party of government; the dream of 'municipal socialism' was abandoned in the 1920s when Labour first won power nationally. A similar process seems to have taken place in the 1990s.

Notes

1   For the policy context see Ken Young and Nirmala Rao, *Local Government since 1945*, Oxford: Blackwell, 1997; for a general history see Bryan Keith-Lucas and Peter Richards, *A History of Local Government in the Twentieth century*, London: Allen and Unwin, 1978.

2   London: Green and Co., 1920.

3   John Sheldrake, *Municipal Socialism*, Aldershot: Avebury, now Ashgate, 1989.

4   G.D.H. Cole, *History of the Labour Party from 1914*, London: Routledge and Kegan Paul, 1948, 1969, p451.

5   There were different systems of government in towns and country areas. The cities were ruled by County Boroughs which were responsible for all local services in their areas. There was a two tier system in the rest of the country, with a county council; below the county were district councils and boroughs with varying degrees of autonomy. Other institutions existed for education until 1902, 1929 in Scotland, and the Poor Law until 1929.

6   Though generally more restrictive than the parliamentary franchise after 1885, because only ratepayers could vote, the local government franchise allowed women property owners to vote and serve on school boards, and other councils from 1907. See Patricia Hollis, *Ladies Elect: Women in local government 1865–1914*, Oxford: Clarendon, 1987.

7   George Jones, *Borough Politics*, Basingstoke: Macmillan, 1969. The extent to which administration of the council was party political varied, even after 1945, between different cities. In some, such as London and Sheffield, the majority party would take all the committee chairs and run the city as the party of government; in others, such as Manchester, committee chairs would be shared roughly proportionally between the parties represented on the council. Jim Bulpitt, *Party Politics in English Local Government*, Harlow: Longman, 1965, describes the variety of local forms of party politics in greater Manchester, including power sharing. Very few

such arrangements survived the 1950s and 1960s in urban areas, and they are now found only in rural areas and where no party has an overall majority.

8   W. Eric Jackson, *Achievement: a short history of the LCC*, Harlow: Longman, 1965; Sidney Webb, *The Work of the London County Council*, London: London Reform Union, 1895. The LCC cleared the infamous Old Nichol slum in Shoreditch, the location of Arthur Morrison's 1896 novel *A Child of the Jago*, replacing it with perhaps the first public sector 'model' estate.

9   Cole p443; Keith Laybourn and Jack Reynolds, *Socialists, Liberals and Labour* 1890–1918, London: Croom Helm, 1984, p103–105.

10 The last such 'Trades and Labour Councils' with party as well as trade union functions were wound up in 1974.

11 The extent and significance of these advances have been the subject of decades of historical debate; it is an ancillary field to the key question of why – and when – Labour replaced the Liberal Party as the main anti-Conservative force in British politics. Historians emphasising the decay and conservatism of grass roots Liberalism before 1914, could argue that 'beneath.the compliant, contained Labour parliamentary campaigns in 1906 and 1910 lurked a municipal monster, whose tentacles reached out across the country … by 1914 the Liberal party was being strangled and devoured at the roots.' Evidence for this was the electoral weakness and lack of ideas of local Liberals, who lost council after council to the Tories and in some areas concluded limited anti-Labour pacts. Labour was slowly gaining in each round of municipal elections between 1909 and 1913, but by 1913 had only gained control of a few anomalous councils. See Duncan Tanner, *Political Change and the Labour Party 1900–1918*, Cambridge: Cambridge University Press, 1990.

12 Rodney Hills, 'The City Council and Electoral Politics 1901–71' in Charles Feinstein, ed, *York 1831–1981*, York: Sessions of York, 1981.

13 Tony Adams, 'Labour and the First World War: Economy, Politics and the Erosion of Local Peculiarity?' *The Journal of Regional and Local Studies* 1990 Vol 10.1 p23–47.

14 A rather tedious debate began with the rise of Labour about the acceptability of party politics in local government. Many of these municipal anti-Labour parties pretended somehow to be against party politics. The critique expanded after the war with Labour's successes in 1945 and 1946, although the Conservatives were quick and successful in responding in kind by 1949. Party politics had been intrinsic to local politics in many areas since the inception of local elections, and the general ideological issues between the parties about the appropriate balance between public and private provision were directly relevant to the activities of local authorities; see Bulpitt's *Party Politics in English Local Goverment* and many other works cited.

15 Except in Leeds in the late 1920s, where the local Conservatives grew tired of the situation and persuaded several Liberals to defect

directly to them. The move backfired as the city Liberals broke with the electoral pact, Labour made gains on a minority vote and took minority leadership of the council. See Michael Meadowcroft, 'The years of political transition' in Derek Fraser, ed, *A history of modern Leeds*, Manchester: Manchester University Press, 1980. In less politically charged authorities, such as Norwich, minority Labour groups were able to exercise considerable influence through all-party power sharing arrangements. 'Aldermen' were, until 1974, senior members elected by councillors rather than through local elections.

16 Ken Young, *Local politics and the rise of party*, Leicester: Leicester University Press, 1975, p120–122.

17 Bernard Donoughue and George Jones, *Herbert Morrison: Portrait of a Politician*, London: Weidenfeld and Nicolson, 1973, p58. Labour local politicians have only rarely been the subject of biographies, usually when like Morrison or Lansbury they have gone on to play a large role in national politics.

18 See, for example, Donoughue and Jones, and particularly Sue Goss, *Local Labour and Local Government*, Edinburgh: Edinburgh University Press, 1988, on municipal trading.

19 Contract compliance was also used by many authorities in the 1980s to ensure that contractors met their standards on equal opportunities and union rights. It was banned by the Conservative government in the Local Government Act 1988.

20 See Noreen Branson, *Poplarism* 1919–25, London: Lawrence & Wishart, 1979; Keith-Lucas p65–91.

21 P.A. Ryan 'Poplarism 1894–1930' in Pat Thane, ed, *The Origins of British Social Policy*, London: Croom Helm, 1978, p76; George Lansbury, *My Life*, London: Constable, 1928, p133 as cited by Keith-Lucas.

22 A precept is a rate levy collected by one council, in this case Poplar, on behalf of and at the rate set by another local authority covering the same area, in this case the London County Council and the Metropolitan Police.

23 Lord Atkinson, *Roberts v Hopwood*, 1925, as cited by Branson p217.

24 Hansard Vol 395, 15.12.43, as quoted by Michael Foot, *Aneurin Bevan* Vol 1, London: MacGibbon and Kee, 1962, p84.

25 As cited Gyford and James p49–50.

26 West Ham, the neighbouring borough outside the LCC area in which many of the same trends are apparent, is the subject of John Marriott, *The Culture of Labourism*, Edinburgh: Edinburgh University Press, 1991, which examines in detail the link between the local culture of 'labourism' and the Labour Party in the inter-war period.

27 On Liverpool's interwar politics see Philip Waller, *Democracy and Sectarianism*, Liverpool: Liverpool University Press, 1980.

28 After the creation of the South Yorkshire Metropolitan County centred around Sheffield in 1974, with control over passenger transport throughout the region, fares were frozen from 1975 to

1986, leading to conflict with Labour and Conservative central governments. See Gyford and James p138–147, David Blunkett and Keith Jackson, *Democracy in Crisis*, London: Hogarth Press, 1987, p70–82. On Sheffield 1926–32 see Blunkett and Jackson p59–63.

29 Henry Phillpott, *Where Labour Rules*, London: Methuen, 1934, p4–11. This fascinating book is by a *Daily Herald* journalist who visited many Labour-controlled boroughs and counties, none in London, in early 1934. It was clear that by the 1930s the local Labour agenda was an extremely ambitious programme of investment in health and education, new housing and help for the poor and disabled; municipal trading was still divisive between the parties locally but no longer the focus of Labour thinking.

30 Phillpott p30–36; Meadowcroft *op. cit.*

31 The small borough of Bermondsey had a revolutionary scheme to virtually demolish itself and rebuild on the model of the garden cities in the 1920s; only a small part of this was built before funding constraints prevailed. See Goss.

32 John Gyford and Mari James, *National Parties and Local Politics*, London: George Allen and Unwin, 1983, p47.

33 Mark Savage 'The Rise of the Labour Party in Local Perspective' *Journal of Regional and Local Studies* 1990 Vol10.1 p1–16.

34 Iain McLean, *The legend of Red Clydeside*, Edinburgh: John Donald, 1983, p229–230.

35 Donoughue and Jones; Young p141–143. W Eric Jackson, *Achievement: a history of the LCC*, Longman, 1965, describes the Morrisonian LCC in considerable detail.

36 Eight million parliamentary electors who were not ratepayers were enfranchised in 1945. Non-resident business ratepayers were, however, still allowed to vote in local elections until 1969. See Keith-Lucas p18–20.

37 The main prize from these elections was Birmingham, which Labour won in 1946. It had been run by a powerful Chamberlain machine since the 1870s. Liverpool did not fall until 1955, Cardiff until 1958. Edinburgh was the last big city in Britain never to have had a Labour council, until it went Labour in 1984.

38 Hills *op. cit.* Between the wars York had been continuously Conservative controlled, sometimes with the support of an ageing Liberal group.

39 Left-wing activity in local government between the 1920s and the 1970s was confined to a few colourful incidents, such as Coventry's defiance of civil defence regulations in 1954 and the 'Red Flag' at Marxist influenced St. Pancras in 1957.

40 Richard Crossman, *The Diaries of a Cabinet Minister* Volume 1, London: Hamish Hamilton and Jonathan Cape, 1975, p446. Crossman was given to making adverse comments on the age, stupidity and conservatism of Labour councillors he encountered and became enthusiastic about radical reorganisation.

41 Owen Hartley 'The post war years' in Derek Fraser *op. cit.* p438; Gyford and James p49.

42 A trend apparent in the interwar period; Labour's efficient London machine under Morrison had flourished on local elections, and as early as 1930 a Conservative agent wrote that 'if municipal elections were not available, it would be necessary to invent them in order to keep our organisations efficient.' Young p149.

43 National Museum of Labour History: NEC minutes October 1959.

44 Robson remained an advocate of local government and municipal socialism after the war. Robson was perhaps the first Labour scholar working on local government to form such a strong ideological attachment to localism, but he was far from unusual in this. During the 1980s in particular, academic writing on local government was often informed by a belief in the value of local institutions and a desire to defend them from the attack of the Thatcher government. Others combine research interests and their own political activity, including Sue Goss, Iain McLean and the prolific John Gyford, who has also led a successful Labour council in Braintree, Essex, since 1995.

45 Gyford and James pp52–67. Sporadic conferences had taken place in the inter-war period.

46 Nick Tiratsoo, *Reconstruction, Affluence and Labour Politics: Coventry 1945–60*, London: Routledge, 1990.

47 'Rates' were a property tax based on a rateable value, a rough estimate of its rental value. The proportion of privately rented housing in Britain fell over the 20th century from over 75 per cent to less than 10 per cent of the market.

48 Ultra vires, essentially, means that councils may only spend money when allowed to do so by Act of Parliament, and anything else is beyond its financial powers.

49 A painstaking study of the influence of party politics on local government, Jim Sharpe and Kenneth Newton's *Does Politics Matter?*, Oxford: Clarendon, 1984, concluded that party did make a difference to spending levels. Labour authorities tended to spend more on 'the ameliorative and redistributive services' than Tory ones, p214.

50 Local political decisions took place in a national context, and as well as little difference between the parties on a local authority the variations between different local authorities were of degree and emphasis rather than approach. The 'national local government system' worked through the political parties, but more importantly through the central government department, MHLG or DoE, and the professional networks of officers. See R.A.W. Rhodes *The National World of Local Government*. George Allen and Unwin, 1986. Patrick Dunleavy *The Politics of Mass Housing in Britain 1945–75* Clarendon 1981 shows these networks in action. Labour Secretaries of State had more influence on local government policies than the party's own local leaders; the classic case was Circular 10/65 from Crosland's

Department of Education and Science which spurred local authorities into comprehensive education.

51 Owen Hartley *op. cit.* p438–439.

52 Nick Hayes *Consensus and Controversy: City Politics in Nottingham 1945–66*, Liverpool: Liverpool University Press, 1996, deals with the issue of a local 'consensus'. George Jones's *Borough Politics* describes Wolverhampton, a council where there was a very sharp division between the parties on policy, and bitterness over the manipulation of the Aldermanic system for party purposes in 1961. Nick Tiratsoo *Reconstruction, Affluence and Labour Politics* links municipal politics to the debate on the effect of affluence on working class loyalty to Labour.

53 Dunleavy p1. Because Labour councils covered areas most affected by slum clearance, most of the new council house building was done locally by Labour. However, Conservative governments fostered the process and when the Conservatives won control of city councils they followed the same policies.

54 Crossman p124–125.

55 Before 1972 councillors were not compensated for the cost of their work, which encouraged poorer people serving on councils to regard gifts as legitimate. Pre-Labour councils had frequently been extremely corrupt, because slum landlords, contractors and publicans had the strongest incentive to serve as they were able thereby to further their business interests.

56 On the Poulson scandal, see Ray Fitzwalter and David Taylor, *Web of Corruption*, St. Albans: Granada, 1981; Michael Gillard and Martin Tomkinson, *Nothing to Declare*, London: John Calder, 1980, and Lewis Baston, *Sleaze*, London: Channel Four Books, 1999. A similar affair took place in Birmingham, centred around the Bryants building firm; see Dunleavy p292–295.

57 T Dan Smith *An Autobiography* Newcastle: Oriel Press, 1970; p87.

58 *Conduct of the Labour Party in Local Government* Report of Special Committee approved by NEC 23 July 1975.

59 John Major was Chairman of Housing in Lambeth in 1970–71.

60 Royal Commission on Local Government in England, Cmnd 4040, 1969.

61 Outside London. The Conservative government had reorganised London government in 1964, creating the Greater London Council, GLC, covering a much larger area than the old LCC, plus 32 London Boroughs, which were larger and had more powers than the old Metropolitan Boroughs under the LCC. The change was condemned by Herbert Morrison and was regarded as a fix to abolish the LCC and obtain a council dominated by the Tory suburbs. It backfired, producing Labour majorities in 1964, 1973 and 1981. On London reorganisation see G. Rhodes, *The Government of London: The struggle for reform*, London: Weidenfeld and Nicolson, 1972; Enid Wistrich, *Local Government Reorganisation: The first years of Camden*, London: London Borough of Camden, 1972.

62 The biggest losers from the changes were the non-metropolitan provincial cities such as Nottingham, Bristol and Southampton, whose powers were now the same as other district councils. City Labour Parties were particularly voluble in pressing for the return of their powers, and at the end of the Callaghan government Environment Secretary Peter Shore responded to this concern by the White Paper *Organic Change in Local Government*. Several of these cities recovered full powers in the reorganisation of the 1990s.

63 *Report of the Committee of Inquiry into Local Government Finance*, Cmnd 6453, 1976. The report favoured a local income tax but was not implemented. As well as facing discontent with the rates, the government was worried about the increasing cost of local government grants paid by central government, which accounted for 60 per cent of local spending by the 1970s.

64 The strength of this criticism was increased by several academic studies of old-style local government in operation. Perhaps most influential on the left was Cynthia Cockburn's *The Local State*, London: Pluto, 1977, although Patrick Dunleavy's *The Politics of Mass Housing* and Kenneth Newton's *Second City Politics*, Oxford: Oxford University Press, 1976, were if anything more damning – and much more plausible – indictments in detail. The fashion in the 1970s for using local authorities as case studies to examine the distribution and meaning of power, in a broad sense, has left several accounts of local politics, including Newton's, and works by John Dearlove and Peter Saunders on Conservative Kensington & Chelsea and Croydon respectively; see also David Green's *Power and Party in an English City*, London: Allen and Unwin, 1981, about the operation of the Newcastle City Council Labour Group.

65 Sue Goss, *Local Labour and Local Government*, Edinburgh: Edinburgh University Press, 1988, is a vivid account of the ossification of Labour councils in Southwark 1919–82.

66 As reported in David Butler and Gareth Butler, *British Political Facts 1900–94*, Basingstoke: Macmillan, 1995.

67 It was also a time of increasing sociological and politics science analysis of local government, some of which became extremely abstruse. The confrontation between local authorities and central government revealed patterns of power within the British state and relationships between economic and social change, state structures and political action. A recent review of these discourses is in Allan Cochrane, *Whatever Happened to Local Government?*, Milton Keynes: Open University Press, 1996. See also Jim Bulpitt, *Territory and Power in the United Kingdom*, Manchester: Manchester University Press, 1983; Ted Gurr and Desmond King, *The State and the City*, Basingstoke: Macmillan, 1987; John Gyford, Steve Leach and Chris Game, *The Changing Politics of Local Government*, London: Unwin Hyman, 1989; C. Pickvance and E. Preteceille, *State Restructuring and Local Power*, London: Pinter, 1991; R. Rhodes, *Beyond Westminster and Whitehall*, London: Unwin Hyman, 1988; J. Stewart

and G. Stoker, *The Future of Local Government*, Basingstoke: Macmillan, 1988, and G. Stoker *The Politics of Local Government*, Basingstoke: Macmillan, 1991.

68 In some local authorities the themes of 'betrayal' were played out locally as well as nationally. Like the Labour government of 1974, the Labour GLC elected in 1973 had a radical manifesto which proved impossible to implement in the straitened circumstances of the time, and which the leadership regarded with suspicion. The demands of the Campaign for Labour Party Democracy for intra-party accountability, mandatory reselection and a voice for the party structure in electing leaders were also made at local level.

69 They were unable to cut much from the central government budget because the slump of 1979–81 caused a large increase in social security spending. Health and defence were problematic for political reasons. Much of the large-scale government spending items were, by choice and default, in the local government sector.

70 David Blunkett and Paul Jackson, *Democracy in Crisis*, London: Hogarth Press, 1987; p3.

71 John Gyford, *The Politics of Local Socialism*, London: George Allen and Unwin, 1985, p52–54. Gyford points out that this wider role was approved by the official Bains Report in 1972. One might add that the active Corporations of the great Victorian cities felt a similar sense of wider responsibility.

72 There was no specific statutory authorisation for economic development activities by local councils until 1989, but many councils made creative use of planning and inner city redevelopment legislation to set up economic development agencies. Among the first was Wandsworth, under a moderate left leadership in the 1970s, and left-wing Hillingdon. See Cochrane 1996 p39–41; M. Campbell, ed, *Local Economic Policy*, London: Cassell, 1990.

73 On new urban left local government see John Gyford, *The Politics of Local Socialism*, London: Allen and Unwin, 1985; M. Boddy and C. Fudge, *Local Socialism*, Basingstoke: Macmillan, 1984; Blunkett and Jackson; S. Lansley, S. Goss and C. Wolmar, *Councils in Conflict*, Basingstoke: Macmillan, 1989. For a critical version, see David Walker, *Municipal Empire*, London: Maurice Temple Smith, 1983.

74 Lambeth was the first of the new left-wing councils, although it was more heavily influenced by traditional Marxism than most of the post-1982 councils thanks to its leader Ted Knight. The Knight administration ran into heavy trouble in 1980–81 because of a financial crisis.

75 On the GLC in particular, see John Carvel *Turn Again Livingstone* Profile, 1999, and the earlier version *Citizen Ken* Chatto and Windus, 1984, and Ken Livingstone *If voting changed anything they'd abolish it* Collins 1987.

76 Wendy Stokes *Not an Encounter Group: democracy and women's committees* PhD Thesis, London Guildhall University 1996.

77 Lansley, Goss and Wolmar p160–174; Baston.

78 The Thatcher government had hoped that the Widdicombe Report *The Conduct of Local Authority Business* 1986 would show a breakdown of the democratic process, but on the whole it did not; some councils were commended for opening out the power structure. The most damning report on management standards was Hackney's own Arden Report in 1987.

79 See Michael Crick, *The March of Militant*, London: Faber and Faber, 1986; Peter Taaffe and Tony Mulhearn, *Liverpool: a city that dared to fight*, London: Fortress Books, 1988; Derek Hatton, *Inside Left*, London: Bloomsbury, 1988; Michael Parkinson, *Liverpool on the brink*, Newbury: Policy Journals, 1985.

80 Parkinson p85–90.

81 Technically the Revolutionary Socialist League, at least in the early days. It was strong in the Walton constituency in the 1950s, but the rest of the city was run by the right wing Braddock machine. Like other traditionalist regimes, such as in Southwark, party membership was kept deliberately low to preserve the power of the ruling clique; once the machine had lost control it was relatively easy for Militant to take over. See Crick.

82 Crick p229–234.

83 Special committee report July 1975, para 11. Italics in original.

84 As cited Crick p224–225.

85 As cited Crick p277.

86 Quoted by Lansley et al p180.

87 There was a common thread of distrust of centralised municipal provision in both local leftism and Thatcherism. Some left-wing councils had attempted to devolve housing management to subsidiary units which would be more accountable to tenants; there was considerable similarity as it turned out between this idea and the transfer of housing to more flexible tenant management boards and Housing Associations as envisaged by the government.

88 See for example some of the contributions to John Stewart and Gerry Stoker, *Local Government in the 1990s*, Basingstoke: Macmillan, 1995. Some of the analysis of 'Post Fordist' local government has been overblown and relies on a misleading picture of the past, but it is correct to contrast the extension of direct provision in the 1920s and 1970s with the current indirect and plural arrangements.

89 David Butler, Andrew Adonis and Tony Travers, *Failure in British Government*, Oxford: Oxford University Press, 1994, is a history of the poll tax episode.

90 Little has been written about the experience of these Labour councils – or their mirror image, the Conservative controlled councils of 1968–71.

91 David Butler and Dennis Kavanagh, *The British General Election of 1997*, Basingstoke: Macmillan, 1997, p189.

92 See for example Ian Loveland 'Local authorities' in R. Blackburn and R. Plant, *Constitutional Reform*, Harlow: Longman, 1999, p307–326.

Labour's literary dominance

Brian Brivati

The chapters in this volume show that Labour has much to be proud in the last 100 years. There is also the stark reality that as an electoral force the Labour Party did not match its main opponent in terms of winning elections. Since 1900 the Conservative Party has been the natural party of government. However, at least since the 1930s, while the Conservatives have governed, Labour politicians have been publishing. Democratic socialists have written the best books about politics published in Britain in the last half century. This chapter is not concerned with the way in which this literary dominance might distort the historical record of our age; one sees it in the Tony Benn industry already, but with two other concerns. First, I need to prove my claim of Labour dominance. Second, I want to suggest some reasons for the unique generation of Labour writers – including Hugh Dalton,[1] Barbara Castle,[2] Richard Crossman,[3] Anthony Crosland,[4] Michael Foot,[5] Tom Driberg,[6] Tony Benn,[7] Denis Healey,[8] Roy Jenkins[9] and others – who produced the corpus of work that is the basis of Labour's literary dominance.

Politicians publish in different forms and in a variety of voices. In terms of volume the field is dominated by the personal memoir. This is the largest group of political books and contains the largest number of unread and unreadable volumes. At their best personal memoirs should give an insight into the relationship between the author and her or his times; an intimate and honest view of the politics of the age and some worthwhile reflection on the individuals contribution and failings. A range of good stories, a degree of insightful bitchiness about colleagues and opponents and some character portraits of the great and the good are also welcome. Memoirs like these speak with an intimate voice, they set out to reduce the distance between the 'record' and the real experience of politics.

There are surprisingly few classics in this genre, which is largely dominated by a glut of the second rate and the merely self-serving. All memoirs are by definition self-serving. The challenge is to transcend the form and feed the ego while also enlightening the reader. Increasingly, as we work our way through the Thatcher years, ego stroking reigns while enlightenment suffers. Depths have included most of the Tory memoirs of the 1950s, reaching bottom with Lord Kilmoir,[10] *NAB 1 portrait of a politician*[11] and Lord Young's *The Enterprise Years.*[12] The latter didn't really matter, but that such a pivotal figure as Willie Whitelaw[13] should have been so cautious in his memoirs leaves a huge gap in the contemporary record. We have been robbed of some interesting figures like Macleod by premature death and though Heath's were a pleasant surprise in many ways, there were not a contemporary classic.[14]

In contrast, Labour memoirs reveal a range of human experience and an attempt at reflecting on the processes of politics as they occurred. Two stand out for their contrasting evocation of the messiness of life: Tom Driberg's painfully honest *Ruling Passions*[15] and John Stonehouse's patently self-serving *Death of an Idealist.* Stonehouse's[16] book is a bizarre but essentially human attempt to explain his own dishonesty and the blatant mendacity of a former Czech agent gives it a compelling quality – compare it to the passages about Poulson in Maudling[17] for the difference in approach and temperament.

Ruling Passions consistently evokes the layers of hypocrisy through which Driberg navigated his life; his journalism is also worth revisiting. Driberg's volume is much more substantial a work than the only Tory equivalent I know of by Ian Harvey[18] – indeed Driberg's honesty and self-knowledge should be compared to Harvey's many layered repression. Harvey emerges as a figure to be pitied, Driberg almost as a source of inspiration.[19]

A different kind of inspiration can be derived from Denis Healey's memoirs *The Time of My Life.*[20] Healey's vanity is matched by his ability, a rarity among politicians and although there is an element of 'look at how clever I am' in Healey's view of himself, the compensations of the story of an intellectual in politics with more practical political ability than virtually any other postwar figure is sufficient. Roy Jenkins's (whom I will allow back into the Labour Party) memoirs *A Life at the Centre,* reflect his literary skill and a level of self-knowledge that I found surprising and engaging. Both these works are more conventional than Driberg but are perhaps the two finest postwar memoirs.

The Conservative Party, in comparison, has produced collections of inside accounts that barely deviate from the British Standard Version of political history, though with the occasional insight into motive and causality (Norman Tebbit's[21] acidic and in places moving volume and the elegance of Carrington's[22] diplomatic musings being examples). Churchill's Edwardian prose[23] does not count, because Churchill was never really a Conservative and he only ever really wrote the history of Churchill not of politics as conducted by mortals. Harold

Macmillan's[24] works read as a sustained sanitization of the politics of the 1950s. Despite the real quality of John Major's[25] memoirs and utter poisonousness of Norman Lamont,[26] Kenneth Clark is our last, best hope of getting a significant intimate first hand account of the Thatcher years. However, it is hard to imagine the former Chancellor staying up late into the night writing a diary when he could be in Ronnie Scott's. Thus Labour may not have had much of the power since 1945, but they win overwhelmingly as chroniclers of the period in personal memoirs that people read.

A subset of memoirs do not set out to give an intimate view of the process of politics but have a mission to explain and describe the public discourse of politics from the inside. These are the political textbook memoirs that try to understand and analyse the processes of politics: speaking with an authoritative voice from the inside to those on the outside. Among the political textbook memoirs, there is some heavy opposition from the Tories in the considerable bulk of Nigel Lawson's *The View from Number 11*[27] but this can be countered by the first of Harold Wilson's memoirs, *The Labour Government 1964-70*[28] which provides equal insight to Lawson and far surpasses the Thatcher volumes.[29] There are also the politician/academics, a breed that seemed, until the 1980s, to flourish more on the left than on the right. David Marquand's *Unprincipled Society*[30] and John Mackintosh's work[31] stand out in this field. Aside from Lawson – like many of the Labour writers a trained journalist – it is difficult to find impressive Tory books of either the memoir or the textbook kind. The key Tory intellectuals of the postwar period: Enoch Powell,[32] Rab Butler, Iain Macleod,[33] Keith Joseph,[34] Ian Gilmour and Chris Patten[35] have barely mustered a decent volume on politics between them, though *Inside Right* and *Dancing with Dogma* by Gilmour[36] and *The Art of the Possible* by Butler[37] both have interesting features – the later featuring Butler's words written up by a journalist. John Ramsden, the leading historian of the Conservative Party,[38] recently cited Lord Coleraine's *For Conservatives Only*,[39] but with such a title it has not achieved a wide recognition.

Politicians also write programmatic books, but the story of the interface between political action and political ideas is not dominated by practising politicians as much as by academics and internationally influential works. There have been many fewer influential political texts in the UK in the postwar period than in the US. Indeed, one of the striking features of Anthony Seldon and David Marquand's excellent collection, *The Ideas that Shaped Postwar Britain*,[40] is how few active politicians feature in the essays. The one exception is Anthony Crosland and *The Future of Socialism*, to whom there is an entire chapter devoted. No single book written by a politician has had the same impact as Crosland and it is hard to imagine, as David Marquand has pointed out, a contemporary politician being able to complete such a work – though it should be remembered that much of the work for it was done while Crosland was temporarily out of the House and was well funded by Jack Diamond. What else is there? Redwood on privatisation? Macmillan on the middle way? Blair on the Third Way?

The individual voice of the diary is the most compelling form of political publishing and a genre that has produced more than its share of classics. The political diarists who will last from our era – at least among those who have so far published – are the Labour diarists: Hugh Dalton, Barbara Castle, Richard Crossman and Tony Benn.[41] Hugh Dalton laid the foundations by the use he made of his diary in his memoirs but Castle and Crossman invented the form of the postwar political diary. They pushed against the restrictions of the Official Secrets Act and collective responsibility, and Tony Benn, after an initial rather dull volume, took the political diary to new heights. Even the lesser-known volume of Crossman's backbench diary is utterly compelling and captures the experience of opposition. It has many problems as a source and should not, of course, be treated uncritically, but in terms of getting inside the political process of Labour in opposition in the 1950s it has no equal. Gaitksell's[42] diary should be compared with Crossman: Gaitskell produces a political text book diary of events with some insightful comments but is very much a conventional view of politics: Crossman provides much more of the real feel of politics.

There are sections of each of these diaries which are dull and repetitive, and the individuals are astonishingly self-obsessed, but that simply adds to the roundness of the picture of politics they present: they have no real competitors from Tory writers. Besides Macmillan's diaries[43] – valuable as a source but hardly either honest or revealing – the interesting Tory diarists have not been politicians but observers, like Lord Moran[44] and John Colville,[45] and were, though fascinating, one step removed from the frontline of politics. The exception might have been Alan Clark.[46] His diaries opened windows into the psychology of the Thatcher governments like no other single work from the 1980s. But Clark is less interesting than his counterparts in the Labour Party because he was writing in the period of total disclosure: all politics is now in primary colours and because he offered very few real insights into politics, a process he little understood. What the diaries reveal of Clark's personality is interesting, what they have to say about the Thatcher revolution of minimal significance – this was a man who could back Tom King as a potential leader of the Conservative Party.

The most widespread form of non-fiction written by politicians, aside from their diaries and memoirs, are biographies. Robert Rhodes James[47] offers some spirited defence for the Tories, though his *Boothby* is unforgivably bad, and he is backed up by the military historians and spy writers amongst Tory backbenchers. But again the Labour Party wins out. Roy Jenkins is one of the finest biographers of the postwar era and then there is Michael Foot's biography of Nye Bevan. Roy Hattersley asked himself, in his own rather splendid, *Who goes home?*[48] 'Why should a first-rate Michael Foot want to be a second-rate Aneurin Bevan?': the two volumes of Foot's work are exquisite examples of the literary possibility of political biography and also monuments to the former Labour leader's obsession with Bevan. They are unsurpassed as partisan political biography and until or if Michael Foot writes his own memoirs, they stand as a monument to their subject and to the best writer of prose to sit in the House of Commons since World War Two: Michael Foot.

Below the level of biography we enter the collected zone. These range from the lowest form of political publishing, the 'collected speeches', through to expanded book reviews rushed out on the back of a more significant work, to collected book reviews that have been worked on and organised into a coherent and, occasionally, influential volume. Though a rather tired genre, there have been several gems: Michael Foot appears again with his collection of book reviews and portraits, *Loyalists and Loners*, Marquand with *The Progressive Dilemma* and Peter Shore with *Leading Labour*.[49] I am not aware of any significant collections by Conservative politicians. There are also books that are tied to a particular event or set of events, the Campaign Books. John Campbell's biography of Roy Jenkins – and indeed Jenkins himself on Attlee,[50] Kenneth Harris's conversations with David Owen[51] come to mind as passable versions of this genre: but is there anything else?

My categories of political writing are personal memoir, textbook memoir, diary, programmatic texts, biography, collected works and campaign books. Each of these categories, except perhaps the textbook memoir, has been dominated by Labour politicians. Why? There are broadly five kinds of reason:

1 Labour intellectuals were interested in the creation of a new society which could be described.
2 The war and postwar generation lived through a unique combination of events that marked them; it was, moreover, a literate age in which books and journals played a more significant role in political discourse than they do today.
3 The structure of the Labour Party enhanced argument on the meaning and expression of language.
4 Labour intellectuals have frequently had to earn their living as journalists.
5 Britain underwent a liberalising era and a profound shift in the balance between the public and the private and in the notion of a realm of public life and experience.

The golden age for Labour's political writing stretched from the mid-1950s to the mid-1980s; it was also a golden age for political journalism. This had its roots in the 1930s. A generation of well-educated, literate and committed people came to the forefront of the British left. Many of these having started their careers as political journalists in the ideological maelstrom of the 1930s and matured through six years of war.

There are exceptional people in every generation but there are not that many exceptional generations. The generation that came to prominence in the years between 1930 and 1964 was such a generation. This must be connected with war and the experience of war. It is not just the case that war but endless war still breed, it is more that war but endless words still breed: the debate on appeasement, the defence of democracy and the shape of the new Jerusalem produced a host of left wing literature. Beyond this there was a certain freeing up of class barriers, a decrease in deference, a new spirit. On the left, this was a political generation who believed they could make a difference to the basic structures of society in the name of equality. Not only did they have a concrete impact, which lasted until the mid-1980s, they also articulated their beliefs and argued them out with each other – and they wrote about their arguments in the press and later in diaries and memoirs. The long period of opposition in the 1950s helped because it forced many Labour politicians to earn extra money through journalism; that this was followed by two full periods of government, created a perfect mix of experience.

The fascination with the writing of this period is this mix of experience: born in the 1930s, it matured in the most successful period of Labour in power between 1945–51, and it reached its prime in the social revolution that occurred between 1955 and

1977. For a number of reasons these writers articulated the changes in British society as they occurred, reflecting on and reflecting social transformations. The way in which Labour writers struggled against the confines of what was supposed to be written about politics was part of a more general conflict between the traditional view of public life and the revolution in private experience that was occurring. There was a gradual liberalising process as affluence influenced the nature of British cultural and political life: the embryonic shifts in relations caused by the war began to take on a permanent nature. These changes expressed themselves in politics in lots of different ways. People suddenly changed. At one moment, there was a young technology obsessed MP called Anthony Wedgewood Benn, the next a firebrand socialist called Tony. At one moment a rather forbidding intellectual called C. A. R. Crosland was transformed into the *Match of the Day*-watching Tony and so on.

In terms of political discourse: something happened. The traditional way in which people had written about politics, a sort of standard Whig discourse of individuals and institutions, was gradually replaced by a more open and less reverential political discourse. Many things played a role, from Suez to TW3 to the impact of CND; it was Labour politicians who began to express these changes in political literature, personalising the voices of political memoir and opening the process of politics to greater scrutiny. This more accessible discourse ran alongside and did not replace the existing discourse of politics, traditional memoirs continued to be written and published but there was an increasing tension between the two. This conflict produced shafts of light into politics which continue to illuminate.

These sets of changes: war, reconstruction and affluence influenced people who believed in change. In *The Meaning of Contemporary Realism*,[52] George Lukacs concludes his comparison of the critical and socialist realist traditions in literature thus:

Great satirists, such as Swift, always saw character from the outside. Indeed, this refusal to enter into all the subjective complexities of the world they satirize is the presupposition of a good satirical typology ... [However] The "inside" method seeks to discover an Archimedian point in the midst of social contradictions, and then bases its typology on an analysis of these contradictions.

These 'inside' writers, Lukacs goes on, are socialists and concerned with the class struggle, therefore they must also be concerned with the future. They are writing from the inside of the characters they create not only about their pasts and their presents but by necessity about their futures: 'Socialist realism is able to portray from the inside human beings whose energies are devoted to the building of a different future, and whose psychological and moral make-up is determined by this.' This is a bold enough claim, but Lukacs goes on, 'Socialist realism is a possibility rather than an actuality; and the effective realization of the possibility is a complex affair.' Socialism is a possibility rather than an actuality – and possibility makes the best prose.

This element – the idea of a blueprint of a new society – was particularly significant in the period in which many of the Labour writers were educated. This was a unique generation of politicians on whom the great battle between democracy and fascism of the 1930s was a formative experience, for whom socialism was something they could write about from the inside and who believed, at some point in their career, in the possibility of the creation of a new society. These writers had been influenced in varying ways by Marxism – if only to reject it – and became active in politics. They earned their living as intellectuals either in universities or on newspapers and then went into parliament. Gradually, for many of them, the focus of their political lives shifted from the possible future that might be created if socialism was to triumph, to the actual experience of exercising power in a democracy with a majority Labour government. As their careers, and politics itself, frustrated them or fulfilled them, they focussed this powerful cocktail of belief and the ability to articulate it, onto the process of politics. This was a significant divergence. Crossman kicked against the limited scope of the postwar Labour government but Crosland saw it as completing the mission and creating new kinds of problems; Healey abandoned his pre-war Communism and was immersed in the problems of foreign policy while Benn devoted himself to party communications and moved in the opposite pattern from all the others: from moderate to radical.

The context of the interplay between broad social change, personal experience of Labour politics in peace and war and the possibility of describing the desired society, was one in which political writing was both in vogue and was largely an argument over collectivism. The arguments that Labour were having in these years were felt to be the arguments that mattered. Collectivism was the spirit of the age and the conversation about the meaning of collectivism seemed to be the conversation that would shape the future. Another important impact on the shift in these writings from socialism to process, was the slow realisation by most of these writers that the future did not belong to the kind of socialism that had informed their youth. This is most striking in comparing Crosland's the *Future of Socialism* with *The Conservative Enemy* and *Socialism Now* – nothing illustrates the impact of power better than the evolution in these programmatic texts; or compare the first volume of Tony Benn's diary with the last.

The individual experience and the wider context was complemented by the structure of the Labour Party itself: language matters in the way in which the Labour Party works. Look at the difference in the style and the content of the books about the parties. Contrast Lewis Minkin's volume on the Labour Party conference[53] with John Ramsden's volumes in the Longman history of the Conservative Party.[54] Ramsden is predominantly about people and Minkin is mainly about organisation and structure: the Tory Party seems to be run by individuals positioning themselves, the Labour Party by committees arguing over the compositing of resolutions. This is not so much a difference of writing as of institutional ethos. The writers I am talking about were mainly active in the golden age of democratic centralism. The National Executive Committee, its numerous sub-committees, the conference resolution committee, the Shadow Cabinet and the regular Party meetings are all dominated by an extended argument over wording. Controlling the language is as important in Labour politics as winning the votes. Factions and individuals matter in these battles but the weaponry is finding forms of words that will expose your opponents: it is a weekly training in the dialogue of politics. Moreover, socialism is about creating a new society. No matter how practical the Labour Party has often been or how anti-intellectual its collective instincts, it is a party whose purpose has been defined by ideas. The symbolic and political battles over Clause Four were not peripheral to Labour's power struggle but central. Nothing illustrated the victory of the modernisers better than Tony Blair's control of the language of Clause Four. However, although defined by ideas, the conversation about those ideas is open-ended and evolves through time in response to events: all of this produces fertile material for political authors.

The impact of the end of the Cold War and the arrival of Blair and New Labour is of course profound. All links – linguistic, ideological, organisational or connections with the ethos of the Empire built by committees – the USSR, have been cut. This in turn highlights how much of the aesthetic of the Labour movement, like the aesthetic of the eastern bloc, was set in the

1930s – frozen in a caricature of 1984 of smoke filled rooms, of standing order disputes and all the sterile futility of trade union-style branch politics – it is black and white and rather bleak!

The ending of the Cold War changed the nature of the Labour Party and meant that words, that winning an argument about the possible future, became not just symbolically but actually, less significant. In the long run this new-found freedom might help in the institutional structures and nature of the party, but there are countervailing forces that will offset these gains – at least as far as political writing is concerned.

We traditionally separate the Labour Party between left and right and think of the political world of the 40s, 50s and 60s in terms of this linear political spectrum. For much of the contemporary period it probably made some sense, given the cold war, to use this division between the political parties. However it has never seemed to me a very good way of understanding the nature of Labour politics in the 1950s – the Labour politics from which the bulk of the literature I have talked about emerged. I have suggested in other places that what united the factions in the Labour Party of the 1950s was much more important than what divided them. Broadly they shared a vision of collectivism's triumph but differed over the ability of capital to bite back, they shared a view of Britain's place in the world but differed over the role of the nuclear weapons within NATO as a way of maintaining that role and they were hopelessly split between and within factions over many specific issues and over Europe. As the 1950s progressed the actual issues often mattered less than the person arguing the position; the shared idealism from which the differing positions stemmed was increasingly obscured by wanting your team to win.

If we stop trying to fit the divisions of the left into a neat ideological structure we see more clearly the nature of the argument that inspired these books. The party was more significantly split between intellectuals and apparatchiks and in turn the intellectuals were divided between an overtly utopian group and a covertly utopian group but united in the notion that it was in some sense possible to articulate the kind of society that Labour wanted to create. Their followers attracted as much by personality and instinct as by the force of ideas battled on the ground for their team of intellectuals and politicians.

The poverty of theory in the Labour Party has been married to a lack of power to produce a fertile ground for reflection and long periods of opposition for argument. Lacking the ideological edge of the continental left, the British Labour Party both missed the opportunity of modernising early like the Germans, and thereby perhaps enjoying more power, or hanging on to their idealist/ utopian vision, like the Italians, but being kept out of power until the end of the cold war. The British party had some power but clung to ideology in ways that did not materially effect the way in which that power was exercised. It also suffered long periods of opposition in which it failed to modernise that ideology, but instead bickered over either inessentials or over policies that were designed to ensure electoral failure. Perhaps, in terms of a political party, Labour has enjoyed the worst of all worlds in the postwar period. But the layers of messiness go deeper because the staunchest defenders of the ideology that did exist were happy to ignore it in power – Tony Benn, Barbara Castle and the entire New Labour Cabinet on unilateralism, spring to mind. Perhaps a continental PR system designed to keep the extreme left out of power would have suited many of the ministerial wing of the party more because they would not have had to face the dichotomy between their ideological position as expressed and argued for in opposition and the policies they conducted once in power. Ideology would have had reduced significance earlier in the party's history. However, the winner takes all system ensured the periodic rejection of the Labour Party in power and the descent into internecine warfare that followed the great defeats of 1951 and 1979 produced both long periods of opposition and the renewed attempt to define the future or search for models of modernisation.

The upshot of all this compromise and argument between power and principle has not been the creation of a socialist realist literature that somehow describes the socialist future, but an obsessive concern with and analysis of the present: a focus on the process of politics itself as a substitute for the mapping out of the new society that seemed increasingly unlikely to be realised in practice. It is almost as if the energy of youth, formed in the period in which democracy was threatened and the basic tenets of democratic socialism had been worked out, was replaced by an almost obsessive concern with politics and how it worked: the political process became the excuse for the failure of the New Jerusalem and describing the process therapy necessary to help Labour politicians cope with failure. The Labour intellectuals gradually abandon what Radhika Desai in *Intellectuals and Socialism*,[55] calls the Revisionist struggle for hegemony, in favour of winning the battle of writing the past more vividly. Tony Benn ends his career with all his major political projects in tatters but as the central chronicler of the postwar era in terms of number of words published – almost an inverse relation between number of pages published and lasting legislative achievment. But the process started even earlier when Richard Crossman abandoned ministerial office in favour of the editorship of the *New Statesman*, a perfect example of a vain faith in words over actions, but Crossman had the last laugh because his diary defined our perception of the politics of the 1960s. And the two people who failed at the last hurdle to power, who charitably failed to stoop to conquer or who realistically lacked the final length of steel that makes a political winner, Roy Jenkins and Denis Healey, will be remembered long after the Torys with distinguished records, Maudling, Whitelaw, Butler, Barber, Heathcote Amory etc. have long since been forgotten.

If Labour has been so good, why has the Conservative Party been so poor? Emma Nicholson has said that writing a book was generally a bad idea in the Conservative Party. But that is not enough of an explanation, after all Conservative politicians were open to the same set of social and cultural changes as Labour politicians. I am not sure what the answer is. I begin with the premise that there is something different in the way in which the Labour Party and the Conservative Party relate to language and ideology.

This is about the history, structure and organisational ethos of the party and it is about the relationship of the party to a describable future. It is not strictly measured by the extent or lack of ideological commitment, the Conservative Party has gone through some significantly ideological phases, but it is about the extent to which that ideology has been intrinsic to the historical construction of the party. Competing strands of Socialism were intrinsic to the Labour Party from its inception; the ideology of the New Right should not be confused with the statecraft of the Conservative Party, as David Marquand has argued. Moreover the processes that the new right advocated do not necessitate a clear vision of the possible future, they rely only on a belief in the efficacy of market allocation.

Aside from the differing role of ideology in the two parties, I would suggest four broad reasons for the difference:

1   The connection with a perfectible world attracts literate people in a way that maintenance of the status quo or reforming to preserve – the position, broadly before the mid-1970s – does not.

2   There is something stubbornly pre-Freudian-pre-1960s about the ethos of the Conservative Party, which makes a positive

virtue of preserving the existing relation between the public and the private even if this is not sustainable.

3 Publishing is not seen as being a positive career move in the same way as it is in the Labour Party and less Conservative politicians have had to earn their living as journalists so less have learnt the craft.

4 There is a central underlying myth about the apolitical nature of the party which resisted for much of the postwar period series political writing.

5 Finally, the Conservatives have won so often that there have been fewer defeats to inspire an analysis of the party's position.

Thus the coincidence of a generation of Labour politicians dominated by intellectuals who made extra money through journalism and were being constantly trained in political communication because of the way the party was managed, resulted in a string of political classics. This combination of factors will not occur again. Collectivism is in terminal decline as a political force, the written word is no longer the dominant medium of political communication and fewer and fewer intellectuals are attracted to politics as a career: the dominance of television and the professionalisation of politics has undermined the conditions which were conducive to political literature.

During the collectivist age, Labour writers set out to show that politics was not like politicians' memoirs. Today we all recognise the difference between the official version of events and the reality, so, ironically, political memoirs have reverted, in the main, to the 'official' picture of politics. The old-fashioned reserve in many of the memoirs of the Thatcher era illustrates the extent to which banality has returned to political writing. If the age of political memoir as a revealing psychological and sociological document is really over, then one wonders how the politicians of the future will learn their craft. The great political novel is dead, there is no contemporary Trollope – unless one rates the 'sex on the dispatch box' style of Edwina Currie[56] or Susan Crosland[57] or the political thrillers of Dobbs,[58] Archer[59] and Hurd.[60] There is still quality political journalism but the books written by the political journalists today do not reflect on the art of politics but contain blueprints for improving political structures – Hutton,[61] Marr[62] and Jenkins.[63] Perhaps new generations of politicians will abandon books and sit next to their aspiring civil servants watching endless videos of *Yes Minister.*[64] This would be a shame because any page of Healey, Crossman, Castle, Benn or Foot, is worth a thousand hours of Jim Hacker.

The interwar and war experience of Labour politicians was enhanced by power and politics in a party in which control of language was a significant arena. This coincidence of a time in which first democracy itself needed to be argued for and then defended and then, in turn, the Labour Party achieved a majority status and implemented the bulk of an ambitious programme, would have been enough to produce an exceptional group of people: if it had not then these things would not have happened in the way that they did. That this then coincided with a broadly literate culture that was word orientated in comparison with the United States for example and a settlement in political economy that favoured collectivism but that had to be defended every step of the way: produced this extraordinary run of political writers. That they then failed to win power for 13 years gave them time to mature and practice their art in the internal battles of the Labour Opposition; that they then held two longish periods of power meant that the canvas on which the brush of the experience of power then painted was the richest and most expressive of the century. We will see different and possibly greater states people in the next century, who will deal with problems we can not imagine but they will communicate about them visually rather than in words and they will describe them in their multimedia memoirs rather than in hardbound volumes. I betray myself as a hopeless romantic victim of the 20th century when I concede to thinking that this will be a shame.

While it is certainly the case that Conservative historiography is now reaching more of a critical mass so the gap is perhaps less important than it would otherwise have been and that New Right politicians still active might have the books in them that the new right politicians in the first wave failed to produce. It is also true that the Blair generation of New Labour politicians will not produce the same kind of work, they are too professional, too connected to the project of winning power and will, perhaps, have too long in government. Old Labour's literary dominance, like old Labour's political relevance, did not survive its first century of life.

Notes

1   Hugh Dalton, *Call Back Yesterday, Memoirs, 1887-1931*, Volume 1, London, Frederick Muller, 1953, *The Faithful Years, Memoirs 1931-1945*, Volume 2, *High Tide and After, Memoirs 1945-1960*, Volume 3, London, Frederick Muller, 1962 and B Pimlott, editor, *The Political*

Diary of Hugh Dalton, London, Cape, 1986 and *The Wartime Diary of Hugh Dalton*, London, Cape, 1986.

2 Barbara Castle, *The Castle Diaries, 1964–1976*, London, Weidenfeld and Nicolson, 1980, see also Barbara Castle, *Fighting All the Way*, London, Macmillan, 1993.

3 Richard Crossman, *Plato Today*, London, Allen & Unwin, 1937, *The Charm of Politics*, London, Hamish Hamilton, 1958, *The Diaries of a Cabinet Minister, Volume 1, Minister of Housing, 1964–66, Volume II, Lord President of the Council and Leader of the House of Commons, 1966–68, Volume III, Secretary of State for Social Services, 1968–1970*, Hamish Hamilton and Jonathan Cape and Book Club Associates, 1975–76, Anthony Howard, editor, *The Crossman Diaries, Selections from the Diaries of a Cabinet Minister 1964–1970*, Book Club Associates, London 1979. Janet Morgan, editor, *The Backbench Diaries of Richard Crossman*, Hamish Hamilton and Cape, London, 1981.

4 *The Future of Socialism*, London, Cape 1956, *The Conservative Enemy*, London, Cape 1962 and *Socialism Now*, London, Cape 1975

5 Foot's work includes, *Guilty men 'Cato'*, London, Penguin New Edition 1998, *H.G. the history of Mr Wells*, London, Black Swan 1996, c1995, *Debts of Honour*, London, Poynter 1980, *Loyalists and Loners*, London, Collins 1987; *The Pen and the Sword: Jonathan Swift and the power of the press*, 3rd ed, London, Collins 1984, c1957; *Another Heart and Other Pulses: the alternative to the Thatcher society*, London, Collins 1984, *The politics of paradise: a vindication of Byron*, London, Collins 1988; *Aneurin Bevan, Volume 1, 1897–1945*, London, MacGibbon & Kee, 1962; *Aneurin Bevan, Volume 2 1945–1960*, London, Davis-Poynter, 1973; *Aneurin Bevan*, Single Volume Centenary London, Gollancz, 1997, *Dr Strangelove I presume*, London, Gollancz, 1998. His is the finest body of political writing produced by the Labour Party in its history.

6 Tom Driberg, *Ruling Passions*, London, Cape 1977. Some of his journalism is collected as *Colonnade 1937–47*, London, Pilot 1948 and *The best of both worlds, a personal diary*, London, Phoenix House, 1953.

7 Tony Benn, *Years of Hope 1940–62*, London, Hutchinson, 1994, *Out of the Wilderness, 1963–67*, London, Hutchinson 1987, *Office without Power*, London, Hutchinson, 1988, *Against the Tide, 1973–76*, London, Hutchinson, 1989, *Conflicts of interest, 1977–80*, London, Hutchinson 1990, *The end of an era, 1980–90*, London Hutchinson, 1992.

8 Denis Healey, *The Time of My Life*, London, Michael Joseph, 1989

9 Roy Jenkins, *Asquith*, London, Papermac 1994, *Sir Charles Dilke, a Victorian tragedy*, London, revised ed Collins 1965, *Baldwin*, corrected ed London, Papermac 1995, *The Chancellors*, London, Macmillan 1998, *Life at the Centre*, London, Papermac 1994, *Gladstone*, London, Macmillan 1995, *Truman*, London, Papermac

1995, *Portraits and Miniatures*, London, Macmillan 1993, *European Diary, 1977-1981*, London, Collins 1989, *Roy Jenkins' gallery of 20th century portraits and Oxford papers,* Newton Abbot, David & Charles 1988, *Mr Balfour's Poodle: an account of the struggle between the House of Lords and the government of Mr Asquith*, London, Collins 1989 – latest edition in each case.

10 Lord Kilmore: *Political Adventure*, London, Weidenfeld and Nicolson, 1964.

11 Gerald Nabarro, *NAB 1: Exploits of a Politician*, London, Barker 1973

12 Lord Young, *The Enterprise Years*, London, Headline, 1990.

13 William Whitelaw, *The Whitelaw Memoirs*, London, Aurum Press, 1989.

14 Edward Heath, *The Course of My Life*, London, Hodder and Stoughton, 1998

15 Tom Driberg, *Ruling Passions*, London, Cape 1977

16 John Stonehouse, *Death of an Idealist*, London, W.H.Allen, 1975

17 Reginald Maudling, *Memoirs*, London, Sidgwich and Jackson, 1978

18 Ian Harvey, *To Fall like Lucifer*, London, Sidgwich and Jackson, 1971

19 Though the Conservatives of the 1990s might have some interesting reflections to offer.

20 Healey, *Time of my Life.*

21 Norman Tebbitt, *Upwardly Mobile*, London, Weidenfeld and Nicoloson, 1988

22 Lord Carrington, *Reflect on things past*, London Collins, 1988

23 Winston Churchill: see Martin Gilbert, *Churchill: A life*, London, Heinemann 1991 for a full list.

24 Harold Macmillan, *Diaries in six volumes*, London Macmillan, 1966-73.

25 John Major, *The Autobiography*, London, Harper Collins, 1999.

26 Norman Lamont, *In Office*, London, Little Brown, 1999

27 Nigel Lawson, *The View from Number 11*, London, Bantam, 1992

28 Harold Wilson, *Memoirs: The making of a Prime Minister*, London, Weidenfeld and Nicoloson, 1996, *The Labour Government, 1964-70*, London, Weidenfeld and Nicolson, 1971, and *Final Term*, London, Weidenfeld and Nicolson, 1979.

29 Margaret Thatcher, *The Downing Street Years*, London, Harper Collins, 1993 and *The Path to Power*, Harper Collins, 1995.

30 David Marquand, *The Progressive Dilemma*, London, Heinemann, 1991 and
The New Reckoning, London, Polity 1997.

31 John Macintosh, *On Parliament and Social Democracy*, London, Longman, 1992.

32 Enoch Powell wrote no substanital work of political theory though he was perhaps the finest scholar, in other fields, that the postwar Conservative Party has produced.

33 Iain Mcleod, Neville Chamberlain, London, Muller 1961 is not worth revisiting.

34 Keith Joseph, *Reversing the trend: a critical reappraisal of Conservatism*, Chichester, Rose, 1975.

35 Chris Patten, *East and West*, London, Macmillan 1998.

36 Ian Gilmour, the finest writer the Conservative Party has produced since the war, many works include, *Dancing with Dogma*, London, Simon and Schuster, 1992 and *Whatever happened to the Tories*, London Fourth Estate, 1998.

37 R. A. Butler, *The Art of the Possible*, London, Hamilton, 1971

38 John Ramsden, 'The Age of Churchill and Eden, 1940-1957' and 'The Winds of Change: Macmillan to Heath', in *A History of the Conservative Party*, London, Longman 1995 and 1996

39 Lord Coleraine, *For Conservatives Only*.

40 David Marquand and Anthony Seldon, eds, *The Ideas that Shaped Postwar Britain*, London, Fontana, 1996

41 *Op. cit.*

42 Philip Williams, ed, *The Diary of Hugh Gaitskell*, London, Cape 1983.

43 Macmillan, *Diaries, 1966-73*.

44 Lord Moran, *Winston Churchill: The struggle for survival, 1940-65*, London, Constable 1966.

45 For example, John Colville, *The fringes of power*, London, Hodder and Stoughton, 1985.

46 Alan Clark, *Diaries*, London, Phoenix, 1994.

47 For example Robert Rhodes James, *Lord Rosebery*, London, Phoenix 1995.

48 Roy Hattersley, *Who goes home?*, London, Warner, 1996.

49 Peter Shore, *Leading the Left*, London, Weidenfeld and Nicolson, 1993.

50 John Campbell, *Roy Jenkins*, London, Weidenfeld and Nicolson, 1983.

51 David Owen, *Personally Speaking* to Kenneth Harris, London, Weidenfeld and Nicolson, 1987.

52 George Lukacs, *The meaning of contemporary realism*, London, Merlin 1963.

53 Lewis Minkin, *The Labour Party Conference*, London, Allen Lane, 1978.

54 Ramsden , *A history of the conservative party, op. cit.*

55 Radhika Deisa, *Intellectuals and Socialism*, London, Laurence and Wishart, 1995.

56 For example, Edwina Currie, *Parliamantary Affair*, Weidenfeld and Nicolson, 1989.

57 For example, Susan Crosland, *Ruling Passions*, London, Weidenfeld and Nicolson, 1989.

58 For example, Michael Dobbs, *House of Cards*, London, Harper Collins, 1990 and sequels.

59 For example, Jeffrey Archer, *First Among Equals*, London, Harper Collins, 1993.

60 For example, Douglas Hurd, *Vote to Kill*, London, Warner, 1999.

61 Will Hutton, *The State we're in*, London, Cape 1995.
62 Andrew Marr, *Ruling Britannia*, London, Penguin, 1996.
63 Simon Jenkins, *Accountable to None*, London, Penguin, 1996.
64 Jonathan Lynn and Anthony Jay, *The complete Yes Minister*, London, BBC, 1989.

Index

Abbott, Diane 284
Abyssinia 369–70
Adamson, Jennie 65
Addison, Paul 73–4, 339
Advisory, Conciliation and
    Arbitration Services 353, 356
Agricultural and Allied Workers'
    Group 413–14
Albania 378
Alberti, Joanna 411
Allen, Vic 191
Amalgamated Association of
    Operative Cotton Spinners 18
Amalgamated Engineering Union
    212, 223, 230, 237, 252
Amalgamated Society of
    Engineers 19, 21, 28
Amalgamated Society of Railway
    Servants
    18–20, 23, 27–8, 324, 332
Andreski, Stanislav 328
Angell, Norman 327, 364
Anglo–American Council on
    Productivity 195
Archer, Jeffrey 497
Archer of Sandwell, Lord 309
Argentina 375
Ashton, Thomas 18–19
Asquith, H H 34–35, 50, 52, 326
    331, 365, 426
Attlee, Clement 4, 68–75, 77–84
    158, 164, 187, 190–3, 205–6
    215, 250, 253, 260–1, 263
    272–4, 301, 337–9, 342, 370–1
    374, 422, 430–3, 454, 458
Austria 370

Bacon, Robert 92, 97
Baldwin, Stanley 69, 249, 335
Bale, Tim 316
Barge Builders' Union 19
Barker, Bernard 53
Barker, Sara 275, 278
Barnes, George 21, 324, 424
Barnett, Correlli 74, 78–80

Barton, Eleanor 404, 411
Basildon 466
Beckett, Margaret 130, 135
Beer, Max 36
Beer, Samuel 293, 299
Belgium 365
Bell, Richard 19, 27
Benn, Tony 89, 94–5, 101, 103–4
    114–15, 118, 122–3, 132, 164
    230, 233, 250, 256, 260–2
    281–3, 375, 387–9, 391, 393
    485, 488, 491–6, 498
Benn, William Wedgwood 335
Bentley, Michael 51
Bevan, Aneurin 71, 78, 81–3, 184
    205–6, 209, 252, 256, 258
    260–3, 272–6, 317, 375
    433, 454, 489
Beveridge, Sir William, report
    2, 73–4, 76, 78, 165, 258
    272, 339, 432
Bevin, Ernest 8, 44, 54, 57, 61, 63
    69, 75, 164, 187–91, 193
    216, 260, 271, 333, 337
    339, 342, 370–4, 379
Biagani, E 24
Biffen, John 170–1
Birmingham 462, 466, 473–4
birth control 56–7, 408
Black sections 414
Blair, Tony 1, 44, 112, 127–8
    132–3, 143–54, 156, 158–9
    163, 165, 166, 168–9, 174, 210
    220, 234–8, 246, 248, 254–5
    258, 260–1, 268, 287–9, 292
    306–17, 346, 359, 377–9
    394–8, 416, 441, 475, 488, 493
Blatchford, Robert 298
Blewett, Neil 32
Blunkett, David 120–1, 123, 128
    151, 282–3, 458, 465
Boateng, Paul 467
Boilermakers Society 25
Bondfield, Margaret 406, 408

Boot and Shoe Operatives Union 19
Bowerman, C W 19
Bradford Workers' Municipal
Federation 450
Brandt, Willy 167
Brent 468
Bristol 466, 474
Britain in Europe 390
Broadhurst, Henry 17
Brockway, Fenner 332
Brown, George 170, 261
Brown, Gordon 127, 130, 132
148–9, 157, 165, 261, 309
311, 316, 442
Brown, Michael Barratt 103
Brown, Nick 132
Brown, W J 55
Buckle, David 210
Bullock, Alan 188
Burgess, Joseph 20
Burt, Sir Thomas 17, 25
Butler, David 117
Butler, Rab 459, 487

Cairncross, Sir Alec 78, 203
Callaghan, James 80, 87, 90, 95
97–8, 100–1, 103–6, 112–13
147, 151, 220, 223, 226–7
229, 250, 254, 258, 260–1
280, 354, 374, 383
387–8, 390–91, 435–7
Campaign for a Labour Victory
261–2
Campaign for Democratic
Socialism 261–2
Campaign for Labour Party
Democracy 229–30, 279
Campaign for Nuclear
Disarmament 491
Campaign Group 259
Campbell, J R 58
Campbell, John 489
Canavan, Dennis 286
Carrington, Lord 486
Castle, Barbara 100, 171, 209
317, 387, 389, 409, 485
488, 494, 498

Chamberlain, Austin 249
Chamberlain, Joseph 22, 449–50
Chamberlain, Neville 70–2
249, 339
Chester, Norman 191
Child Poverty Action Group 437
Chisolm, Malcolm 286
Churchill, Lord Randolph 13
Churchill, Winston 24, 29, 71–5
77–8, 82, 84, 188, 207, 258
339, 371, 425, 486
Cigar Makers' Union 20
Citrine, Walter54, 55, 61, 191, 370
Clark, Alan 488–9
Clark, Kenneth 487
Clarke, P F 51
Clarke, Peter 325
Clause IV 5, 40, 146, 211, 235
287–8, 292–317, 328, 330
359–60, 395, 427, 493
Clegg, Hugh 35, 189
Clinton, Bill 359
Clynes, J R 58, 250, 333, 335
411, 424
Coates, David 10, 68, 428
Coates, Ken 87, 275, 287, 314
Cole, G D H 32, 64, 166, 293
330, 338, 341–2, 449
Coleraine, Lord 487
Colville, John 488
Commonwealth Party 409, 417
Commonwealth, the 372, 385–7
Communist Party 58, 189, 195–6
206, 270–2, 333–4, 371
403, 408, 417
Confederation of British Industry
236–7
Conservative Party, the 10, 13, 52
69–79, 82–3, 89–90, 92, 98–
101, 103–5, 116–17, 120–1
124, 133–4, 143, 145, 149
153–8, 167–8, 170–1, 174
176–7, 178, 180, 221–2, 229
239, 248, 251–2, 279, 281, 322
328, 330–2, 334, 337–8, 346
351, 355, 357, 360, 365, 368
374, 383, 386, 388, 392, 394

Conservative Party (cont'd)
  433–5, 437, 439–40, 450–4
  458–66, 470–4, 485–9, 496–7
Cook, Chris   50, 61
Cook, Robin   132, 174, 261
Cooper, Ben   20
Co–operative Movement
  20, 403, 406, 414, 417
Coopers' Union   31
Courtney, Leonard   324
Cousins, Frank   164, 170, 187
  189, 209–16, 222–3
Crewe, Ivor   117–18, 125
Cripps, Francis   87
Cripps, Stafford   63, 71, 77, 195
  198, 262, 272, 337, 339
Crosland, Anthony   90, 95, 166
  182, 184, 261, 277, 301–2, 311
  379, 434, 439, 464, 485, 488
  491–3
Crosland, Susan   497
Crossman, Richard   81, 209, 256
  260, 262, 276–7, 373, 458, 461
  485, 488, 492, 496, 498
Cunningham, Andy   462
Curran, Pete   18, 20, 31
Currie, Edwina   497
Curtice, John   134
Cyprus   396
Czech Republic   377
Czechoslovakia   370, 373

Dalton, Hugh   63–4, 70, 71
  75–7, 81–2, 198, 337
  370, 432, 485, 488
Dalyell, Tam   263
Dangerfield, George   326
Darwin Weavers' Association   31
Davidson, Ian   286
Davies, Liz   285
Davies, Ron   286
Davis, Joan   403–4, 417
Davis, William   20
Davy, Florence   402, 417
De Gaulle, Charles   386
Deakin, Arthur   187–209
  214–16, 274
Dell, Edmund   103

Delors, Jacques   393–4
Derby   475
Desai, Radhika   495
Dewar, Donald   165
Diamond, Jack   488
Dilke, Charles   12
Disraeli, Benjamin   13, 348
Dobbs, Michael   497
Dock, Wharf, Riverside and
  General Labourer's Union   18
Donelly, Desmond   278
Donovan Commission   99
Driberg, Tom   485–6
Durbin, Evan   430
Durham   456, 462

Eagle, Angela   183–5
Economic Planning Board   191
Eden, Anthony   82–3, 249, 379
education 5, 23, 35, 75, 81, 91, 147
  149, 151–2, 156, 293, 330, 339
  355, 427, 431, 433, 436–8, 442
  459–60
Edwards, Alfred   272
Edwards, Enoch   33
Edwards, W J   193
Eisenhower, President   164
Elliot, Gregory   87
Elliot, Larry   130
Eltis, Walter   92, 97
Emily's List   415
European Central Bank   150, 175
European Community/Union
  130–1, 133, 135, 148, 152
  155, 157–8, 165, 169, 175, 181
  212, 226, 235, 238, 249, 256
  258, 280, 287, 356–7, 376
  383–98, 494
European Convention on Human
  Rights   168
Evans, Moss   228

Fabian Society, the   8, 17, 19, 20
  30, 37, 54, 63–4, 177
  295–6, 298–9, 302, 309, 316
  328–30, 338, 342, 410, 423
  450, 452, 459
Falkland Islands   375, 379

Fenwick, Charles 17
Fielding, Steven 340
Fields, Terry 263
First World War 13–15, 26, 35–8
41, 43, 52, 60, 73
293, 406, 426, 451
Fisher, H A L 13
Flanders, Allan 214
Foot, Michael 3, 113–18, 122, 167
189, 230, 249, 258, 260–2
276, 280, 282, 317, 373, 376
387, 389, 391, 485, 489, 498
Foote, Geoffrey 307
Fox, Alan 26
France 365, 370–1, 374–5
Freeman, John 375
Fukyama, Francis 346
Fyrth, Jim 78

Gaitskell, Hugh 3, 78, 82–3, 146
164, 190, 206, 212–14, 250–1
253–4, 260–1, 274–5, 292
300–6, 311–13, 316–7
346, 358–9, 383, 386
434–5, 459, 488
Gamble, Andrew 89
Gasworkers and General
Labourers' Union 19
gay and lesbian rights 414, 466–8
General and Municipal Workers'
Union 228, 252, 332
George V 60–1, 72
Germany 365, 367, 369–70
372–4, 379, 494
Gilmour, Ian 487
Gladstone, Herbert 30, 323, 325
Gladstone, William 181, 323
348, 360
Glamorgan 456
Glasgow 456, 463, 473
Glasier, Bruce 30
Glennerster, Howard 432–3
Golding, John 117
Goldstein, Joseph 196
Goodman, Geoffrey 189, 209
Gorbachev, Mikhail 377
Gould, Bryan 129, 131, 134–5
Gould, Philip 87–8, 125–6

Graham, Tommy 285
Grant, Bernie 467
Graves, Pamela 331, 408
Greater London Council 413
465–7
Greece 372
Greenwood, Arthur 69, 71, 337
Greenwood, Tony 250
Gregory, Roy 33

Hackney 452, 469
Hardie, Keir 8, 14, 19, 20
27, 30, 31–32, 34, 163
251, 295–6, 365, 424
Harman, Harriet 256
Harris, Kenneth 489
Harrison, Brian 402, 404, 406
Harrison, Martin 10, 209
Harrison, Royden 298, 300, 330
Harvey, Ian 486
Hastings, Somerville 457
Hattersley, Roy 5–6, 118, 120, 122
127, 230–1, 307, 215, 472, 489
Hatton, Derek 167, 282, 469–70
Hay, Colin 153
Hayday 61
Hayek, Friedrich 4
Hayward, Ron 116, 278
Healey, Denis 95–6, 103, 113–15
163–5, 180, 222–3, 226–8, 239
261, 277, 282, 387, 391, 485–6
492, 496, 498
Heath, Anthony 134
Heath, Edward 87–90, 93, 100
103, 170, 223–4, 249, 256, 279
387, 394, 461, 486
Heffer, Eric 118, 132, 281, 283
Henderson, Arthur 31, 34–35
37–39, 40, 42, 44, 294, 297
329, 333–6, 365–6, 369
Hennessy, Peter 78, 80, 203
Hewitt, Patricia 145–6, 468
Higgins, Terence 171
Hinton, James 34, 68
Hitler, Adolf 369–70
Hobhouse, L T 325
Hobson, J A 325, 327, 364–5
Hodge, Margaret 471

Holmes, James 18
Houghton, Douglas 276
housing 58, 76, 81, 117, 293
330, 332, 339, 407–8, 427
455–7, 459–61, 472
Howard, Christopher 52, 56
Howard, Michael 154
Howe, Geoffrey 133, 171
Howell, David 74
Howell, George 17
Hughes, David 116
Hungary 377
Hurd, Douglas 415, 497
Hutton, Will 497

Incomes and Prices Board 155, 222
Independent Labour Party 8, 17
19, 20, 21, 30, 32, 39, 54, 59
62, 261, 271–2, 295, 298–9
324, 327, 329, 333–5, 342
363–6, 371, 423–4, 429, 450–1
Industrial Relations Corporation
171
International Federation of
Women Workers 410
International Monetary Fund
94–7, 150, 227–8, 264, 439
Iran 372
Ireland 22
Irish Nationalists 42, 424, 426
Iron and Steel Trades Union 402
Ironfounders; Union 31, 332
Isaacs, George 193
Islington 471
Italy 369–70, 374, 379, 494

Japan 369, 379
Jaures, Jean 11
Jay, Douglas 82, 301–2
Jay, Peter 104
Jenkins, Patrick 171
Jenkins, Peter 238–9
Jenkins, Roy 1, 114, 171, 258
261–2, 277, 280, 301, 305
388–9, 485–6, 489, 496
Jenkins, Simon 497
Jenkinson, Charles 455
Joint Consultative Committee 191

Jones, Jack 189, 213, 215–16
220, 223, 227
Joseph, Keith 487
Jowell, Roger 134
Jowett, Fred 327, 335

Kaufman, Gerald 122, 129
Kavanagh, Denis 117
Kelly, Pat 285
Kerr, Hugh 287
Keynes, John Maynard 2, 64, 89
95, 104, 129, 143, 179, 181
221, 337, 368, 434
Kilmoir, Lord 485
Kinnock, Neil 112, 115, 118–38
144, 146, 149, 151–3, 163–4
167, 230–3, 235, 249–50
260–1, 282–3, 306–8, 316
347, 359, 376–7, 392–4, 471–2
Knight, Robert 25
Knowles, K G J C 196
Korea 375, 379
Kosovo 378

Labour Heritage 402, 413
Labour International 407
Labour Representation
Committee 1, 3, 19–23, 28–31
33, 37, 44–5, 54, 423, 450
Labour Solidarity 261–2
Labour Women's Committee 415
Lambeth 468, 471
Lamont, Norman 487
Lancaster, Bill 51
Lansbury, George 3, 69, 249, 260
335, 339, 369–70, 379, 453, 458
Laski, Harold 330, 338, 341
Lawrence, Stephen 468
Lawson, Nigel 133, 487
Lawther, Will 190, 205
Laxton, Bob 475
Laybourn, Keith 326
League of Nations 366–70
407, 411
League of Youth 403
Leeds 460
Leff, Ann 403, 417
Left Book Club 405

lesbian and gay rights 415, 467–9
Lewisham 474
Leys, Colin 152
Liberal Democratic Party
  154, 167–9, 172, 174, 241, 475
Liberal Party 1–2, 3, 12–15, 17, 23
  24, 25, 31–32, 34, 42, 50–52
  55, 57–58, 90, 117, 125, 176
  178, 270, 298, 300–1, 323–8
  332–4, 336, 342–3, 349, 358
  361, 366–7, 369, 424–30
  434, 451–2, 459, 465
Liddle, Roger 150
Lincoln 458
Lipsey, David 151
Liverpool 122–3, 282–4
  452, 456, 465, 469–71, 473
Livingstone, Ken 287, 393, 466
Llewellyn Davies, Margaret 56
Lloyd George, David 24, 32, 34, 50
  52, 72, 293, 326, 331
  365–6, 425
Local government 412–13, 448–76
London County Council
  412, 450, 457
London Docklands Development
  Corporation 472
London Society of Compositors 19
London Transport 466–7
Lukacs, George 491–2

McAllion, John 286
MacDonald, Alexander 17
MacDonald, Calum 172–5
MacDonald, James Ramsay 14–15
  19, 21, 28, 30–2, 34–5, 39–40
  42, 44, 50–3, 57–61, 65
  69–70, 246, 250, 260, 269–70
  294, 297, 323–5, 327, 332–7
  365, 367–9, 424, 426, 428–9
MacDonald, Malcolm 60
MacDonald, Margaret 405
McKelvey, Jean 215
McKenzie, Robert 251, 253
McKibbin, Ross 10, 22, 51, 53
  297–9, 326–7, 329, 341, 426
Mackintosh, John 487
Maclennan, Robert 174

Macleod, Ian 486–7
Macmillan, Harold
  97, 249, 386, 488
MacNeill Weir, L 59–60
Macpherson Report 468
Macpherson, Mary Fenton 405
Major, John 5, 130, 133, 168, 235
  249, 388, 395, 397, 473, 487
Manchester 461–2, 466, 468
  471–3, 475
Manchuria 369
Mandelson, Peter 123–4, 127, 132
  150, 231, 311, 316
Manpower Services Commission
  155
Marquand, David 11, 22, 50, 60
  151, 305, 487–9, 496
Marr, Andrew 313, 497
Martin, Kingsley 68, 84
Marwick, Arthur 328
Matchgirls' strike 402
Maudling, Reginald
  90, 92, 170, 486
Maxton, Jimmy 332, 334
May, Sir George 59
Meacher, Michael 118, 123, 128
  132, 231, 283
Menon, Krishna 451
Merthyr Tydfil 456
Middleton, Lucy 405
Mikardo, Ian 262
Miliband, Ralph 10, 68, 334
Militant Tendency 116, 122–3, 167
  231, 263, 281–3, 414
  469–71, 473
Mill, John Stuart 323–4
miners' strike 101, 121–2
Miners' Federation 9, 19, 23, 33–7
  40, 59, 196, 304, 424
minimum wage 23, 157, 231–2
  238, 334, 356, 425
Minkin, Lewis 10, 63, 119, 231
  235–9, 493
Mitchell, Austin 178–82, 248
Mitterrand, Francois 307
Monckton, Sir Walter 207
Monetary Policy Committee 239
Monks, John 237–8

Moran, Lord 488
Morel, E D 327, 365, 367–8
Morgan, Kenneth 78, 97, 105
191, 203, 295
Morrell, Frances 87
Morris, William 166, 298
Morrison, Herbert 70, 71, 75–6
81–3, 192, 260–1, 274, 337
340, 385, 431, 452, 457–8, 471
Mosley, Oswald 262, 336, 429
Mundella, A J 12
Murray, Len 226, 228
Mussolini, Benito 369–70

Nairn, Tom 10
National Assistance Board 436
National Conference of Labour
Women 407, 412
National Council of Labour
Colleges 405
National Council of Working
Women's Organisations 409–10
National Economic Development
Council 155
National Government
9, 59–61, 429
National Health Service 133, 228
339, 431–3, 436–7, 459
National Joint Advisory Council
191
National Referendum Campaign
389
National Society of Amalgamated
Brassworkers 20
National Union of Dock Labourers
18
National Union of Gasworkers
and General Labourers 18
National Union of Mineworkers
101, 121–2, 224, 228
National Union of Public
Employees 228, 230, 252
National Union of Railwaymen 45
National Union of Societies for
Equal Citizenship 406, 411
National Women's Advisory
Council 409–10

nationalisation 293, 294, 298–9
301–5, 309, 316, 322, 330
337, 340, 358, 360
Nellist, Dave 263
Newcastle 458, 462, 466
Nicholas, H G 83
Nicholas, Harry 209
Nicholson, Emma 496
Norman, Montague 181
Norris, Maggie 414
North Atlantic Treaty
Organisation 148, 212, 376–9
385, 397, 494
Northern Ireland 90, 168
Norwich 456–7
Nossiter, Bernard 97
Nottingham 459–60

Open Door Council 411
Open University 436
Orwell, George 341
Owen, David 114, 166–9, 489
Owen, Robert 166

Pannitch, Leo 152
Parmoor, Lord 368
Patten, Chris 487
Pease, E R 19
Peel, Robert 360
Pelling, Henry 51, 78, 294
pensions 16, 134, 224, 228
425, 427, 436–7
Perrigo, Sarah 402, 413, 415, 417
Philips, Morgan 275, 302, 410
Phillips, Marion 56–57, 330
406–8, 411, 416
Piachaud, David 436
Pickard, Ben 17, 33
Pimlott, Ben 68, 299
Plaid Cymru 90
Platt–Mills, John 263, 272
Plowden, Lord 436–7
Poland 377
Policy Review 1989 125–31, 441
poll tax 133, 473–4
Poor Law 453
Poplarism 452–3, 455
Poulson, John 462, 486

Powell, Enoch   170, 487
Prentice, Reg   103, 279
Prescott, John   132, 135, 261
                       311, 314, 316
Priestley, J B   73
Pugh, Martin   61, 329, 336
Purdy, William   39

Quelch, Harry   19

racial discrimination   439, 466–8
Radice, Giles   308–9, 316
Railway Women's Guild   410
Ramsden, John   487, 493
Redcliffe–Maud Commission
                       463–4
Redwood, John   488
Reid, Alastair   24–25
Rhodes James, Robert   489
Riddell, Peter   316
Robertson, George   165
Robinson, Annot   406
Robson, William   459
Rochdale Pioneers   402
Rock, Dorothy   405, 417
Rodgers, Bill   114
Roman Catholics   57, 408, 455
Roosevelt, Theodore   164
Ross, Willie   389
Russell, Bertrand   275
Russia   366

Salter, Alfred   452
Sanders, William Stephen 9
Saville, John   10, 68, 78, 83
Sawyer, Tom   122–3, 132, 283
Scanlon, Hugh   223
Scargill, Arthur   121–2, 233
                       238, 312
Schloesser, Henry   324
Schmidt, Helmut   167
Schuman Plan   385–6
Scotland   26, 168, 238, 283
                       285–6, 462, 473
Scottish National Party 90, 286
Second World War, the   70–6
                       78–80, 412, 430, 443, 455
Seldon, Anthony   487

Sexton, Jimmy   18
Seyd, Patrick   307
Shackleton, David   29, 31–32
Sharp, Clifford   324
Shaw, Eric   275
Shaw, George Bernard   19, 296
                       298, 451
Shaw, Tom   38
Sheffield   455, 463, 472–3
Shinwell, Emanuel   76, 192, 276
Shipwrights' Union   39
Shore, Peter   113, 118
                       389, 391, 489
Short, Clare   176–7, 415–16
Short, Ted   458
Silkin, John   113, 115
                       276–7, 389, 391
Silverman, Sydney   263
Simm, Lisabeth   405
Simpson, Alan   284, 312
Skinner, Dennis   122, 285
Smith, Adam   4
Smith, F E   13
Smith, John   5, 120, 127, 129–30
          134–8, 146, 149, 151–2, 163–4
              166, 234–5, 250, 308–9
                       394–5, 415–16
Smith, Sir Ben   193
Smith, T Dan   88, 461–4
Snowden, Philip   14, 21, 27
              34–35, 42, 58–59, 61
                   324, 327, 332–9, 429
Social Democratic Federation
                       324, 423
Social Democratic Foundation
                       8, 17, 19, 20
Social Democratic Party 5–6, 114
               117, 125, 166–9, 230
               262, 357, 363, 392, 474
Social Justice Commission   441
Social Market Foundation   169
Socialist Campaign Group   261–2
Socialist International
                       166, 407, 415
Socialist Labour Party   238
Socialist League 271–2, 337–8, 342
Southampton 458, 466, 472, 474–5
Southwark   469

Soviet Union, the   369, 370–3
                    375, 377, 493
Spain   369–70
Standing Joint Committee (SJC)
  of Working Women's
  Organisations   403, 406–7
                    411–12, 416–17
Steadman, W C   19
Steadman–Jones, Gareth   21
Stevenson, John   50, 61
Stewart, Sue   414–5
Stonehouse, John   486
Strachey, John   338, 341
Strauss, George   262
Straw, Jack   308–9, 316
Stringer, Graham   471, 475
Suez   375, 379, 491
suffrage movement 22, 325, 405–6
Sunderland   463
Supplementary Benefits
  Commission   436
Sutherland, Mary   409
Swift, Jonathan   491

Tanner, Duncan   51
Taverne, Dick   279
Tawney, R H   63, 166, 311, 334
                    342, 364
taxation 5, 23, 91, 96, 98, 105, 124
       126–7, 130, 134, 144, 148–9
       156, 293, 330, 396, 427, 429
                    434, 439, 441–2
Taylor, R H   19
Taylor, Robert   238
Tebbit, Norman   486
Tewson, Vincent   191
Textile Workers' Union   40, 332
Thane, Pat   407–8
Thatcher, Margaret   88–9, 95–6
    105–6, 112, 116, 128, 130, 133
       143, 145, 153–4, 184, 231–2
             239, 249, 283, 375, 379
             391–3, 464–5, 472, 486
Thomas, J H   335–7
Thompson, Peter   340
Thorne, Will   19
Thorpe, Andrew   427, 437
Tiffin, Jock   209

Tillet, Ben   18, 20
Tiratsoo, Nick   340
Titmus, Richard   166, 339
Tobin, Ann   414
Trade Union Congress 1, 8, 9, 11
       16–18, 21–2, 27, 29–30, 32
       36, 54, 63, 101, 128, 187–8
       191–2, 194, 198–203, 207–8
             210–11, 213, 222–4
       226–8, 231–2, 236–7, 269
       296, 336, 370, 393, 408, 411
trade unions   1, 8–49, 54, 63
       98–102, 114, 119–22, 135–7
    152, 163, 170–1, 177, 187–245
       261, 270–2, 327, 334, 351–2
       356, 393–4, 410–14, 423–5
Trades Councils   451
Transport and General Workers'
  Union   8, 187–216, 223
             228, 231, 236, 252, 274
                  315, 337, 370, 414
transport   455, 466–7
Trevelyan, Charles 365, 367
Tribune Group   115, 131–2, 230
                    261–2, 277–8, 283
Turkey   372

unemployment 4, 9, 16, 23, 53, 55
       58–61, 63–4, 87, 90, 93–5, 97
       99, 112, 130, 221, 224, 227
       229, 231, 394, 425, 427–9
       431–2, 436, 440, 453, 455–6
unilateralism   124, 129–30
Union for Democratic Control
                    327, 365–7
Union of Post Office Workers 403
Union of Shop, Distributive and
  Allied Workers   212
Unison   315
United Front   408, 417
United Nations   375, 377–9
United States   359, 368, 371–3
                    376–8, 431–2

Varley, Eric   389
Varley, Julia   410–11
Victory for Socialism   275
Vietnam   375

Vorse, Mary Heaton   42

Wagner, Irene   408–9, 417
Wake, Egerton   53, 330
Wales 26, 168, 238, 283, 286, 463
Wallas, Graham   324
Walsh, Stephen   33
War Emergency Workers National
   Committee 35–6, 297, 328, 365
Warbey, William   373
Wardle, George   20
Webb, Beatrice   9, 32, 34, 36, 38
                39, 41, 62, 449
Webb, Sidney   36, 40, 62, 293–5
             297–8, 300, 313–14
             324, 328–30, 449
welfare state, the 5, 23, 75, 79, 91
             272, 422–44, 458–61
Wertheimer, Egon   8, 11
West Midlands County Council
                     465, 467
Wheatley, John   56, 58, 332
                     335, 427
Whitehead, Alan   475
Whitelaw, Willie   486
Whitty, Larry   228, 414
Wilkinson, Ellen   408
Williams, Len   278
Williams, Philip   190, 304
Williams, Shirley   114, 166

Williamson, Tom   190, 205
Wilson, Harold 9, 80, 81–2, 87–94
      97, 100, 103, 143, 151, 159
         170–1, 212, 215, 222–3
         249–50, 254, 256, 260–1
         273–4, 276–7, 280, 305
         375, 383, 386–91, 412
            435, 458, 461–2, 486
Winter, J   300
Women Against Pit Closures
                      410, 417
Women's Action Group   413–14
Women's Co–operative Guild
                      56, 404
Women's Labour League
          56, 405–6, 413, 416
Women's Sections   331–2
Women's Trade Union League 410
Woods, Sam   19, 21
Workers' Educational Association
                          405
World Trade Organisation   148

York   458, 473
Young, Lord   486
Yugoslavia, Federal Republic of
                          378

Ziegler, Philip   97
Zillicus, Konni   263, 373